REVELATION

THE ANCHOR BIBLE is a fresh approach to the world's greatest classic. Its object is to make the Bible accessible to the modern reader; its method is to arrive at the meaning of biblical literature through exact translation and extended exposition, and to reconstruct the ancient setting of the biblical story, as well as the circumstances of its transcription and the characteristics of its transcribers.

THE ANCHOR BIBLE is a project of international and interfaith scope: Protestant, Catholic, and Jewish scholars from many countries contribute individual volumes. The project is not sponsored by any ecclesiastical organization and is not intended to reflect any particular theological doctrine. Prepared under our joint supervision, THE ANCHOR BIBLE is an effort to make available all the significant historical and linguistic knowledge which bears on the interpretation of the biblical record.

THE ANCHOR BIBLE is aimed at the general reader with no special formal training in biblical studies; yet, it is written with the most exacting standards of scholarship, reflecting the highest technical accomplishment.

This project marks the beginning of a new era of co-operation among scholars in biblical research, thus forming a common body of knowledge to be shared by all.

William Foxwell Albright
David Noel Freedman
GENERAL EDITORS

Following the death of senior editor W. F. Albright, The Anchor Bible Editorial Board was established to advise and assist David Noel Freedman in his continuing capacity as general editor. The three members of the Editorial Board are among the contributors to The Anchor Bible. They have been associated with the series for a number of years and are familiar with its methods and objectives. Each is a distinguished authority in his area of specialization, and in concert with the others, will provide counsel and judgment as the series continues.

EDITORIAL BOARD

Frank M. Cross   Old Testament
Raymond E. Brown   New Testament
Jonas C. Greenfield   Apocrypha

THE ANCHOR BIBLE

REVELATION

Introduction, Translation
and Commentary by

J. MASSYNGBERDE FORD

1975

DOUBLEDAY & COMPANY, INC.

GARDEN CITY, NEW YORK

Library of Congress Cataloging in Publication Data

Bible. N.T. Revelation. English. Ford. 1975.
Revelation.

(The Anchor Bible; 38)
Includes bibliographies and index.
1. Bible. N.T. Revelation—Commentaries.
I. Ford, Josephine Massyngberde. II. Title. III. Series.
BS192.2.A1 1964.G3 vol. 38 [BS2823]   220.6'6s [228'.07'7]
ISBN 0-385-00895-3
Library of Congress Catalog Card Number 74–18796

The Scripture quotations from the Revised Standard Version Bible, copyright 1946, 1952 and © 1971, by the Division of Christian Education, National Council of the Churches of Christ in the U.S.A., and used by permission

Quotations from *New Testament Apocrypha*, Volume Two, edited by Edgar Hennecke and Wilhelm Schneemelcher. English translation edited by R. McL. Wilson. Published in the U.S.A. by The Westminster Press, 1966. Copyright © 1964, J. C. B. Mohr (Paul Siebeck), Tubingen. English translation © 1965, Lutterworth Press. Used by permission

Quotations from Martin McNamara, *The New Testament and the Palestinian Targum to the Pentateuch.* Copyright © 1966 by The Pontifical Biblical Institute, Rome. Reprinted by permission of The Pontifical Biblical Institute

Quotations from Josephus, *The Jewish War*, Bks. III, IV, V, VI and VII, tr. by H. St. J. Thackeray, Cambridge, Mass.: Harvard University Press, 1927 and 1928. Reprinted by permission of the publishers and The Loeb Classical Library

Quotations from *The Essene Writings from Qumran* by A. Dupont-Sommer, translated by G. Vermes. Copyright © 1962. Reprinted by arrangement with The New American Library, Inc., New York

Quotations from Louis Ginzberg, *The Legends of the Jews*, I–VIII. Copyright 1909, 1938, 1946, © 1961 by The Jewish Publication Society of America. Reprinted by permission of the Jewish Publication Society of America

Quotations from J. M. Allegro and A. A. Anderson, *Qumran Cave 4*, Discoveries in the Judaean Desert of Jordan, V, © 1968 Oxford University Press

Quotations from Austin Farrar, *The Revelation of St. John the Divine: Commentary on the English Text,* © 1964 Oxford University Press

Quotations from R. J. McKelvey, *The New Temple: The Church in the New Testament,* © 1968 Oxford University Press

Quotations from Yigael Yadin, ed., *The Scroll of the "War of the Sons of Light Against the Sons of Darkness,"* © 1962 Oxford University Press

Quotations from R. H. Charles, ed., *The Apocrypha and Pseudepigrapha of the Old Testament*, II

Quotations from J. F. Stenning, ed., *The Targum of Isaiah*
All reprinted by permission of The Clarendon Press, Oxford

Quotations from The Babylonian Talmud
Quotations from Midrash Rabbah
Both reprinted by permission of Soncino Press, Ltd., London

Illustrations redrawn by Leon Kortenkamp from photographs courtesy of: Hodder & Stoughton, Ltd., American Schools of Oriental Research, Weidenfeld & Nicholson, Ltd., Keter Publishing House, Ltd., Mrs. William F. Albright, Mr. Avram Biram, Iraq Museum, Oxford University Press, Inc., Jack Finegan, Princeton University Press, Hacker Art Books, Inc.

To the late Reverend Edward F. Siegman, c.pp.s.
and to the Reverend Francis B. Sullivan, c.pp.s.
true priests for God, true friends
for men and women

ACKNOWLEDGMENTS

It is my privilege to thank the following persons for their assistance which I have enjoyed over the past four and a half years. The Reverend Francis B. Sullivan, c.pp.s., graciously put forward my name for completing the work of our mutual friend and colleague, the Reverend Edward F. Siegman, c.pp.s. Although this work is distinctly different from the late Father Siegman's preliminary draft, I hope that it will be pleasing to the Congregation of the Precious Blood. It reflects my esteem for a scholar who suffered with poise and dignity so that Roman Catholics, like myself, should have the freedom to offer to the scholarly world new and provocative theses without incurring ecclesiastical disfavor. Without the religious devotion and scholarly courage of men of the caliber of Father Siegman (affectionately known as "Prince Edward") the present bold hypothesis would not have been advanced.

I am indebted to both David Noel Freedman and Doubleday for their patience and courtesy in waiting so long for the manuscript and their meticulous care when it arrived. I am especially grateful to Dr. Freedman for his perspicacious suggestions and timely emendations.

I thank the Reverend Harry Culkin for his enormous assistance in compiling the bibliographies for Revelation, and Mrs. Catherine McKinney and the other librarians of the University of Notre Dame for their ever ready help, especially in procuring books through the interlibrary loan system.

To Mrs. Alice Langel fell the task of typing a manuscript for which, indeed, she needed the "spirit of discernment"; the accuracy of her typing was remarkable. I also express my sincere appreciation to Mrs. Anne M. Jones and Mrs. Mary Lux for their careful and speedy proofreading and reference checking, and to Mr. James Reagan for his help in typing the preliminary draft of the bibliographies.

Finally, although I have taken a rather individual approach to Revelation, this does not mean a lack of interest in or appreciation of many secondary works which I neither cited nor quoted. I wished to keep Revelation reasonably uncomplicated for the educated nontheologian. I can only hope, not necessarily that my thesis will be accepted, but that it will stimulate discussion and further consideration both of Revelation and the other books in the New Testament.

University of Notre Dame   J. MASSYNGBERDE FORD

CONTENTS

INTRODUCTION

REVELATION

INDEXES

LIST OF ILLUSTRATIONS

Drawings
by Leon Kortenkamp

Following p. 168

Following p. 240

Plates

C. Monsters and the Lamb. Courtesy The Metropolitan Museum of Art, The Cloisters Collection, 1968

D. "Le sacerdos de la Vierge" (The Priest of the Virgin) painted by an unknown artist of School of Amiens, 1437. By permission of Phaidon Press, Ltd., London, from *A Century of French Painting, 1400–1500,* edited by Grete Ring. Copyright © 1949 by Phaidon Press, Ltd. All rights reserved

PRINCIPAL ABBREVIATIONS

Publications

Ant.	*Jewish Antiquities,* by Josephus
APCh	*Apocrypha and Pseudepigrapha of the Old Testament,* ed. R. H. Charles
BTS	Bible et Terre Sainte
CBQ	Catholic Biblical Quarterly
DJD	Discoveries in the Judaean Desert of Jordan
D-S	A Dupont-Sommer, tr., ed., *The Essene Writings from Qumran*
Epstein	I. Epstein, tr., ed., *The Babylonian Talmud*
Etheridge	J. W. Etheridge, tr., ed., *The Targums of Onkelos and Jonathan Ben Uzziel on the Pentateuch with the Fragments of the Jerusalem Targum*
ET	Expository Times
ICC	International Critical Commentary
JBL	Journal of Biblical Literature
NTS	New Testament Studies
RB	Revue Biblique
RevueSR	Revue des Sciences Religieuses
TS	Theological Studies
TWNT	*Theologisches Wörterbuch zum Neuen Testament,* ed. G. Kittel, tr. G. W. Bromiley
War	*The Jewish War,* by Josephus
ZNW	Zeitschrift für die neutestamentliche Wissenschaft und die Kunde

Versions

AB	Anchor Bible
KJ	King James Bible, The Authorized Version of 1611
RSV	Revised Standard Version
MT	Masoretic Text
LXX	The Septuagint

Dead Sea Scrolls

CDC	Cairo Genizah Document of the Damascus Covenanters
1QH	Psalms of Thanksgiving, from Qumran Cave 1

1QM   War of the Children of Light Against the Children of Darkness,
                from Qumran Cave 1
1QS   Rule of the Community, from Qumran Cave 1
1QpHab   Commentary on Habakkuk, from Qumran Cave 1; p. stands for
                Heb. *pesher,* "commentary"
4QpNah   Commentary on Nahum, from Qumran Cave 4

OTHER ABBREVIATIONS

Gr.   Greek
Heb.   Hebrew
R   Rabbinic Commentary, e.g. *Gen R* means rabbinic commentary on
                Genesis; R stands for Heb. *rabbah,* "great"
TI   Translator's interpolation
Lit.   Literally

NOTE TO THE READER

This translation is based on *Hē Kainē Diathēkē,* 2d ed., eds. Erwin Nestle and G. D. Kilpatrick, London: British & Foreign Bible Society, 1958.

The Apocrypha citations follow the order in APCh rather than the AB. In APCh, III Maccabees is included with the Apocrypha and what is II Esdras in the AB is included with the Pseudepigrapha as IV Ezra.

The General Selected Bibliography contains works most used in this volume. The reader may want to use it as a starting point for personal research. There are also bibliographies to the Introduction, to each of Sections I through XVI, and to Parts Three and Four. References are made by author's last name and page number. Titles and publication data missing in the sectional and part bibliographies may be found in the General Selected Bibliography.

REVELATION

Complete Translation in Traditional Order

1 1 A revelation concerning Jesus Christ, which God entrusted to him, to disclose to His servants the events which are destined to happen soon; indeed, by sending it through His angel He has given a sign of this beforehand to His servant John 2 who was borne witness to the Word of God, namely, the witness concerning Jesus Christ, all that he saw. 3 Blessed is he who reads and those who listen to the words of the prophecy and observe what is written in it; for the critical time is near.

4 John to the seven communities in Asia; grace to you and peace from He Who is and was and is to come and from the seven spirits which are before His throne 5 and from Jesus Christ, the faithful witness, the firstborn from the dead and the ruler of the kings of the earth. To him who loved us and freed us from our sins by his blood 6 and has established us as a priestly kingdom for God even his Father, to him be glory and power for ever and ever, Amen. 7 See, he comes with the clouds and every eye will see him, even those who killed him, and all the tribes of the earth will beat their breasts in mourning over him, yes, may that happen. 8 I am the Alpha and the Omega, proclaims the Lord God, who is and was and is to come, the Omnipotent.

9 I John, your brother and comrade in the tribulation and kingdom and patient endurance in Jesus, was on the island which is called Patmos on account of the Word of God and the testimony of Jesus. 10 I was in the Spirit on the Lord's Day, and I heard behind me a voice loud like a trumpet, 11 saying, "Write what you see in a book and send it to the seven communities, to Ephesus and to Smyrna and to Pergamum, and to Thyatira and to Sardis and to Philadelphia and to Laodicea." 12 And I turned to see the voice which spoke to me; and when I turned I saw seven golden lampstands, 13 and in the middle of the lampstands one like a son of man, clothed in an ankle-length garment tied above the waist with a golden girdle; 14 the hair of his head was snow-white, like white wool; his eyes were like flaming

fire; 15 his feet glowed like bronze that had been fired in an oven; and his voice sounded like the roar of rushing waters. 16 In his right hand he held seven stars and a sharp, two-edged sword issued from his mouth and his face shone like the sun in its strength.

17 At the sight of him I fell at his feet like one struck dead; and he touched me with his right hand, and said, "There is nothing to fear! I am the First and the Last, 18 the Living One; indeed I was dead, but, behold, I live for all eternity; yes, I hold the keys of death and of Sheol. 19 Now you are to write down whatever you see in vision, both present things and things that are to take place in the future. 20 The symbolism of the seven stars that you see in my right hand, and of the seven gold lampstands, is this: the seven stars represent the seven angels of the communities, while the lampstands represent the seven communities."

2 1 Write to the angel of the community in Ephesus: This is the prophecy of the one who governs the seven stars with his right hand, who walks among the seven golden candlesticks. 2 I discern your works and your toil and your steadfastness, also that you cannot tolerate evil people, indeed, you have tested those who called themselves apostles and who are not, and you have discovered that they are false; 3 certainly, you do possess steadfastness and you endure on account of my name and have not grown weary. 4 Yet I have this against you, that you have forsaken your first love. 5 Remember the height from which you have fallen and repent and perform what you did at first. If not I will come to you and snatch your lampstand from its position, if you do not repent. 6 But you have this to your credit, that you hate the works of the Nikolaitans which I also hate. 7 Let the one who has spiritual hearing heed what the Spirit says to the communities. To the one who prevails I will grant that he may partake of the tree of life, which is in the paradise of God.

8 Write to the angel of the community in Smyrna: This is the prophecy of the First and the Last, who was dead and became alive. 9 I discern your tribulation and your poverty, but you are rich and I perceive the blasphemy of those who call themselves Jews and are not but are of the assembly of Satan. 10 Do not fear the things which you are about to suffer. Behold, the accuser is about to throw some of you into prison that you may be tried, and you will have tribulation for ten days. Be faithful unto death and I will give you the crown of life. 11 Let the one who has spiritual hearing heed what the Spirit

says to the communities. The one who prevails will not be harmed by the second death.

12 Write to the angel of the community at Pergamum: This is the prophecy of the one who has the sharp two-edged sword. 13 I discern where you dwell; where is the throne of Satan. Indeed, you hold fast to my name, and you did not deny faith in me even in the days of Antipas, my faithful witness, who was killed among you where Satan dwells. 14 But I hold a few things against you, because you have there those who hold tenaciously to the teaching of Balaam, who taught Balak to throw a stumbling block before the children of Israel, by eating meats offered to idols and by fornication. 15 So, similarly, you have, too, those who cling to the teaching of the Nikolaitans, therefore, repent. 16 If you do not, I shall come quickly against you and shall wage war against them with the sword of my mouth. 17 Let the one who has spiritual understanding heed what the Spirit says to the communities. To the one who prevails, I will give him the hidden manna; also, I shall give him a white stone; and upon the stone is written a new name, which no one knows except the recipient.

18 Write to the angel of the community at Thyatira: This is the prophecy of the Son of God, whose eyes are like a flame of fire and whose feet are like fine bronze. 19 I discern your works and your love and your faith and your service and your patience, and your recent works are even better than the first ones. 20 But I hold this against you, that you tolerate the woman Jezebel, who calls herself a prophetess and teaches my servants to practice immorality and to eat things offered to idols. 21 I have given her time that she might repent but she does not wish to turn from her immorality. 22 Behold, I will throw her on a sickbed and those who commit adultery with her into great affliction if they do not repent of her works. 23 And her children I will slay by disease. All the communities will know that I am he who searches minds and hearts and I will give to each of you according to your works. 24 But to the rest of you in Thyatira, who do not follow this teaching, who do not know the deep things of Satan, as they call them, I place no further burden upon you. 25 Only what you do have cling to until I come. 26 And to the one who prevails and keeps my works to the end, I will give him authority over the nations, 27 and he will rule over them with an iron scepter, as the potter's earthenware is broken into pieces, 28 as even I have received from my Father; also I will give to him the morning star.

29 Let the one who has spiritual understanding heed what the Spirit says to the communities.

3 1 And write to the angel of the community at Sardis: This is the prophecy of the one who has the seven spirits of God and the seven stars. 2 I discern your works, that you have a reputation for being alive, but you are dead. Arouse yourself and strengthen what remains which is about to die. For I have not found your works perfect before my God. 3 Therefore remember what you received and heard, and keep it and repent. However, if you do not arouse yourself, I will come like a thief and you will not know the hour I will come upon you. 4 But you have a few people in Sardis who have not soiled their clothes, and they will walk with me clothed in white because they are worthy. 5 The one who prevails will be clothed thus in white vestments and I will not blot his name out of the book of life, and I will publicly acknowledge his name before my Father and in the presence of His angels. 6 Let the one who has spiritual understanding heed what the Spirit says to the churches.

7 And write to the angel of the community in Philadelphia: This is the prophecy of the Holy One, the True One, who has the key of David, the one who opens and no one shall close and who closes and no one opens. 8 I discern your works—see, I have placed before you an open door which no one is able to close—that you have little power and yet you have kept my word and you have not denied my name. 9 See, I will make those of the assembly of Satan, who call themselves Jews, and are not but are liars, behold, I will make them come and bow down before your feet and they will know that I have loved you. 10 Because you have kept the word of my endurance, I will keep you in the hour of trial which is to come upon the whole world to test the dwellers upon the earth. 11 I am coming soon. Hold what you have so that no one may seize your crown. 12 To the one who prevails, I will make him a pillar in the temple of my God, and he will not go out again, and I will write on him the name of my God and the name of the city of my God, the new Jerusalem which comes down from heaven from my God, and my new name. 13 Let the one who has spiritual understanding heed what the Spirit says to the churches.

14 Write to the angel of the community of Laodicea: This is the prophecy of the Amen, the faithful and true witness, the beginning of the creation of God. 15 I discern your deeds, that you are neither hot nor cold. I wish that you were hot or cold. 16 Thus, because you

are lukewarm, and neither hot nor cold, I will spit you out of my mouth. 17 Because you said: "I am rich and I have grown opulent and I am not in need"; indeed you do not realize that you are wretched, pitiful and poverty-stricken and blind and naked. 18 I counsel you to purchase from me gold refined by fire so that you may be rich, and white garments so that you may clothe yourself and not reveal the shame of your nakedness, and eye salve to anoint your eyes so that you may see. 19 Those whom I love I reprove and chasten, therefore stir up your energy and repent. 20 Behold, I stand before the door and knock. If anyone hears my voice and opens the door, I will come in to him and will dine with him and he with me. 21 To the one who prevails, I will grant that he may sit with me on my throne, as I have conquered and taken my seat with my Father on His throne. 22 He who has spiritual understanding let him heed what the Spirit says to the churches.

4   1 After these things I looked, and behold, an open door in the heaven, and the first voice like a trumpet which I heard spoke to me, saying, "Come up here, and I will show you what must happen after these things." 2 Immediately, I was in the Spirit; and behold, a throne was set in the heaven, and there was One seated on the throne, 3 and He who sat there was like the appearance of jasper and carnelian, and there was a bow around the throne which was like the appearance of emerald. 4 And around the throne there were twenty-four thrones and on the thrones sat twenty-four elders clothed in white garments, and on their heads crowns of gold. 5 And from the throne proceeded lightning and voices and peals of thunder; and there were seven torches of fire burning before the throne, which are the seven spirits of God, 6 and in front of the throne something like a glass sea like crystal.

And in the middle of the throne and around the throne were four living creatures full of eyes before them and behind them; 7 the first living creature was like a lion, and the second living creature like an ox, and the third living creature had the face as of a man, and the fourth living creature was like an eagle flying. 8 And the four living creatures, each of them had six wings, they were full of eyes around and within; and they did not cease day and night, saying,

"Holy, holy, holy,
Lord God almighty, who was and is and is to come."
9 And whenever the living creatures gave glory and honor and thanks to Him who sat upon the throne, to Him who lives forever and ever,

10 the twenty-four elders fell down before Him who sat upon the throne and worshiped Him who lives forever and ever, and they threw their crowns before the thrones, saying,

11 "Worthy are you, our Lord and God,
    to receive glory and honor and might,
    because you created all things,
    and through your will they were brought into existence and
    were created."

5 1 And I saw on the right of the occupant of the throne a document written on the obverse and the reverse sealed up with seven seals. 2 And I saw a mighty angel proclaiming with a loud voice, "Who is worthy to open the document and break its seals?" 3 And no one in the heaven, no one on the earth, no one under the earth, could open the document or read it. 4 And I mourned deeply but no one was found worthy to open the document or read it. 5 And one of the elders said to me, "Do not mourn; see, the Lion from the tribe of Judah, the Root of David, has prevailed, so that he may open the document and its seven seals."

6 And I saw between the throne and the four living creatures and among the elders a little Lamb standing as though it had been slain. It had seven horns and seven eyes, which are the seven spirits of God sent forth into all the earth. 7 And he went and took the scroll from the right hand of the occupant of the throne. 8 And when he received the scroll, the four living creatures and the twenty-four elders prostrated themselves before the Lamb, and each held a harp and golden shovels full of incense, which are the prayers of the holy ones. 9 And they chanted a new song, saying,

"You are worthy to receive the document
    and to open its seals,
    because you were slain and you purchased for God by your blood
    men from every tribe and tongue and people and nation
10 and you have made them a priestly kingdom for our God
    and they shall reign on the earth."

11 And I looked, and I heard around the throne and the living creatures and the elders the sound of many angels and their number was myriads of myriads and thousands of thousands, and 12 they said with a loud voice,

            "The Lamb who was slain is worthy to receive
            power and riches and wisdom and might
            and honor and glory and praise."

13 And I heard every creature in the heaven and on the earth and under the earth and on the sea and everything in them saying,

"To Him who is seated on the throne and to the Lamb,
praise and honor and glory and might
forever and ever."

14 And the four living creatures said, "Amen"; and the elders prostrated themselves and worshiped.

6 1 And I looked when the Lamb broke the first of the seven seals, and I heard one of the four living creatures give a command like a clap of thunder, "Come forth." 2 And I looked, and behold a white horse, and he who was seated upon it carried a bow, and a wreath was given to him, and he went out conquering that he might conquer.

3 And when he broke the second seal, I heard the second of the living creatures command, "Come forth." 4 And another horse came out, a fiery red one, and to him who was seated upon it was granted the power to take peace from the earth and that there should be internecine strife, and he was given a great sword.

5 And when he broke the third seal, I heard the third of the living creatures command, "Come forth." And I looked, and behold a black horse, and he who was seated on it carried a pair of scales in his hand. 6 And I heard, as it were, a voice in the midst of the four living creatures, calling, "A quart of wheat for a denarius, and three quarts of barley for a denarius; and do not injure the oil and the wine."

7 And when he broke the fourth seal, I heard the voice of the fourth of the living creatures command, "Come forth." 8 And I looked, and behold a yellowish-green horse, and the name of him who was seated upon it was Death, and Hades followed him; and authority was granted to them over a quarter of the earth, to kill with sword and famine and plague and by wild beasts of the earth.

9 And when he broke the fifth seal, I saw under the altar the souls of those slain for the Word of God and the testimony they bore. 10 And they cried out loudly, saying, "O Lord, holy and true, how long before you render judgment and deliver our lives from those who dwell upon the earth?" 11 And each of them was given a white robe, and they were told to rest a little longer until the number of their fellow servants and their brethren, who were about to be killed as they themselves, was completed.

12 And I looked when he broke the sixth seal, and there was a great earthquake, and the sun became dark like hairy sackcloth, and

the entire moon became like blood, 13 and the heavenly constellations fell to the earth, like a fig tree shedding its winter fruit when
shaken by a mighty wind, 14 and the heaven was wrenched apart like
a scroll that is rolled up and every mountain and island was shaken
from its place. 15 And the kings of the earth and the high officials and
the military tribunes and the rich and powerful and every slave and
freeman hid themselves in the caves and rocks of the mountains;
16 and they cried to the mountains and to the rocks, "Fall on us and
hide us from the face of Him who is enthroned and from the wrath
of the Lamb, 17 for the great day of their wrath has come, and who
can stand it?"

7 1 After this I saw four angels standing at the four corners of the
earth, controlling the four winds of the earth, so that the wind might
not blow upon the earth or upon the sea or upon any tree. 2 And I saw
another angel ascending from the east. He had the seal of the living
God and he called out loudly to the four angels to whom it was given
to injure the earth and the sea. 3 He said, "Do not injure the earth,
nor the sea, nor the woodland, until we seal the servants of our God
on their brows. 4 And I heard the number of those who were sealed,
one hundred and forty-four thousand, sealed from every tribe of the
sons of Israel.

> 5 From the tribe of Judah twelve thousand sealed,
>   from the tribe of Reuben twelve thousand,
>   from the tribe of Gad twelve thousand,
> 6 from the tribe of Asher twelve thousand,
>   from the tribe of Naphtali twelve thousand,
>   from the tribe of Manasseh twelve thousand,
> 7 from the tribe of Simeon twelve thousand,
>   from the tribe of Levi twelve thousand,
>   from the tribe of Issachar twelve thousand,
> 8 from the tribe of Zabulon twelve thousand,
>   from the tribe of Joseph twelve thousand,
>   from the tribe of Benjamin twelve thousand sealed.

9 After this I looked, and behold a great countless crowd, from
every nation and tribe and people and tongue, standing before the
throne and before the Lamb, clothed in white robes, and with palms
in their hands; 10 and they shouted loudly, saying,

"Salvation to our God Who is enthroned and to the Lamb."

11 And all the angels stood around the throne with the elders and

the four living creatures and prostrated themselves before the throne and worshiped God, 12 saying,

"Amen; praise and glory and wisdom and thanksgiving and honor and power and might to our God for ever and ever; Amen."

13 And one of the elders spoke to me, saying, "Who are these who are clothed in bright robes and from whence have they come?" 14 And I said to him, "My Lord, you know." And he said to me, "These are the people who have come from the great tribulation, and have bathed their robes and made them bright in the blood of the Lamb.

15 On this account they are before the throne of God,
    and they worship night and day in his sanctuary,
    and He who is enthroned will tabernacle over them.
16 They shall not hunger anymore or thirst anymore,
    neither shall the sun
    or any scorching heat fall upon them,
17 because the Lamb who is in the midst of the throne will shepherd them
    and guide them to springs of living water;
    and God will wipe away every tear from their eyes."

8 1 And when He broke the seventh seal, there was silence in heaven for half an hour. 2 And I saw the seven angels of the Presence, and they were given seven trumpets.

3 And another angel came and stood before the altar. He had a golden censer and he was given abundant incense to add to the prayers of all the holy ones on the golden altar before the throne. 4 And the smoke of the incense arose with the prayers of the holy ones from the hand of the Angel of the Presence. 5 And the angel took the censer, and filled it from the coals on the altar and hurled them onto the earth. And there were claps of thunder, and loud voices and streaks of lightning and an earthquake.

6 And the seven angels who had the seven trumpets prepared to blow them.

7 And the first one blew his trumpet; and there was hail and fire mingled with blood, and it was hurled to the earth. And a third of the trees were burnt up and all the green grass was burnt up.

8 And the second angel blew his trumpet; and something like a great mountain burning with fire was hurled into the sea. And a third of the sea became blood, 9 and a third of the living creatures in the sea died, and a third of the ships were destroyed.

10 And the third angel blew his trumpet; and a great star, burning like a torch, fell from heaven and it fell upon a third of the rivers and upon the springs of water. 11 And the star is called by the name, "The Wormwood." And a third of the waters became wormwood, and many men died from the waters, because they were made bitter.

12 And the fourth angel blew his trumpet; and a third part of the sun was stricken, and a third of the moon and a third of the stars, so that a third of them were darkened and a third of the day did not appear, and likewise the night.

13 And I looked, and I heard a solitary eagle flying in mid-heaven, shrieking loudly, "Woe, woe, woe, to those who dwell upon the earth because of the rest of the blasts of the trumpets of the three angels who are about to blow!"

9 1 And the fifth angel blew his trumpet; and I saw a star which had fallen from heaven to earth, and the key of the pit of the abyss was given to him. 2 And he opened the pit of the abyss; and from the pit arose smoke like the smoke of a great furnace, and the sun and the air were darkened because of the smoke of the pit. 3 And locusts came out of the smoke onto the earth, and power like that of earthly scorpions was given to them. 4 And they were told not to harm the grass of the earth or any plant or any tree but only the men who had not God's seal on their foreheads. 5 However, they were not allowed to kill them but only to torture them for five months; and the torture was like the torture of a scorpion, when it stings a man. 6 Now in those days men will search for death and they will not find it, and they will yearn to die and death will flee from them. 7 And the appearance of the locusts was like horses prepared for war, and on their heads they wore what looked like wreaths of gold, and their faces were like the countenances of men, 8 and they had hair like women's hair, and their teeth were like lions' teeth 9 and they had scales like iron breastplates, and the sound of their wings was like the sound of chariots with many horses rushing into battle. 10 Also they had tails and stingers like scorpions, and the power to harm men for five months abides in their tails. 11 Their king is the angel of the abyss, whose name in Hebrew is Abaddon and in Greek he is called Apollyon. 12 The first woe has passed; behold, two more woes come after these.

13 Then the sixth angel blew his trumpet; and I heard a solitary voice from the four horns of the golden altar before God, 14 saying to the sixth angel, who had the trumpet, "Unleash the four angels who are bound by the great river, Euphrates." 15 So the four angels,

who were prepared for the hour and day and month and year, to kill a third of mankind, were unleashed. 16 Now the number of the soldiers of the cavalry was twice ten thousand times ten thousand; I heard their number. 17 In my vision I saw the horses and those who sat upon them like this: they had breastplates of fire and sapphire and sulphur; and their heads were like lions' heads, and from their mouths came fire and smoke and sulphur. 18 A third of mankind was killed by these three plagues, from the fire and smoke and sulphur issuing from their mouths. 19 For the power of the horses was in their mouths and in their tails; for their tails are like serpents, they have heads, and by means of these they wound. 20 But the rest of mankind, who were not killed by these plagues, did not repent of the works of their hands by relinquishing the worship of demons and idols of gold and silver and bronze and stone and wood, which are unable to see or hear or walk, 21 and they did not repent of their murders or sorceries or unchastity or thefts.

10 1 And I saw another mighty angel descending from heaven, enveloped in a cloud with the rainbow around his head, and his countenance was like the sun and his feet were like pillars of fire, 2 and he held in his hand a little scroll which was open. And he planted his right foot on the sea, his left on the earth, 3 and he cried out in a loud voice like a lion roaring. When he cried out, the seven thunders spoke out. 4 I was about to write when the seven thunders spoke out but I heard a voice from heaven saying, "Seal up the words of the seven thunders, and do not write them down." 5 And the angel whom I saw standing on the sea and on the earth raised his right hand to the heaven, 6 and he swore by the One who lives for ever and ever, Who created the heaven and the things in it and the earth and the things in it and the sea and the things in it, that there would be no more delay 7 but in the days of the trumpet-blowing of the seventh angel, when he was about to blow, the mystery of God, which He announced to His servants, the prophets, would be fulfilled. 8 Then the heavenly voice spoke to me again saying, "Go, take the scroll which is open in the hand of the angel who stands on the sea and the earth." 9 And I went to the angel and asked him to give me the little scroll. And he said to me, "Take it and swallow it, it will be bitter to your stomach but it will be sweet as honey to your mouth." 10 And I took the little scroll from the hand of the angel and consumed it, and it was as sweet as honey to my mouth; but when I had eaten it, it

was bitter to my stomach. 11 And they say to me, "You must prophesy again to the peoples and nations and tongues and many kings."

11 1 And there was given to me a measuring reed like a staff; I was told, "Rise and measure the sanctuary of God and the altar and its worshipers. 2 But do not measure the outer court, exclude that, for it is given over to the Gentiles, and they will trample the holy city for forty-two months. 3 And I will allow my two witnesses, dressed in sackcloth, to prophesy for one thousand two hundred and sixty days." 4 These are the two olive trees and the two lampstands which stand before the Lord of the earth. 5 And if anyone would harm them, fire issues from their mouth and consumes their enemies; and if anyone wishes to harm them, he is destined to die in this way. 6 They have authority to lock the heaven so that no rain may fall during the days of their prophetic ministry, and they have authority over the waters to turn them into blood and to strike the earth with every plague as often as they wish. 7 And when they have finished their testimony, the wild beast which ascends from the abyss will fight against them and will win a victory over them and will kill them. 8 And their corpse will lie in the highway of the great city, which allegorically is called Sodom and Egypt, where also their Lord was crucified. 9 And peoples and tribes and tongues and nations will stare at their corpse for three and a half days, and will not permit their bodies to be placed in a tomb. 10 And the dwellers on the earth will rejoice over them and will make merry, and will send gifts to one another, because these two prophets tormented the dwellers on the earth.

11 And after the three and a half days a divine breath of life entered into them, and they stood upon their feet, and a great fear fell upon the spectators.

12 And they heard a loud voice from heaven saying to them, "Come up here"; and they ascended into the heaven in the cloud, and their enemies watched them.

13 And in that hour there was a great earthquake, and a tenth of the city fell, and seven thousand people were killed by the earthquake, and the survivors were terrified and they gave glory to the God of heaven.

14 The second woe has passed; behold the third woe is coming soon.

15 And the seventh angel sounded his trumpet; and there were loud voices in the heaven, saying,

"The kingdom of the world has become the kingdom of our God

and of His Anointed, and He will reign for ever and ever." 16 And the twenty-four elders, who sit upon their thrones in the presence of God, prostrated themselves and worshiped God, 17 saying,

"We thank You, Lord God, the Almighty, Who is and was, that You have taken Your great power and begun to reign; 18 and the nations raged, and Your wrath and the appointed time to judge the dead and to give recompense to Your servants the prophets and the holy ones and those who fear Your name, both small and great, and to destroy the destroyers of the earth has come." 19 And the sanctuary of God in heaven was opened, and the ark of His covenant was seen in His sanctuary, and there was lightning and voices and thunder and an earthquake and heavy hail.

12 1 And a great sign appeared in heaven, a woman clothed with the sun, and the moon under her feet, and on her head a crown of twelve stars, 2 and she is with child, and cries out in her pangs of birth, and is in anguish to bring forth. 3 And there appeared another sign in heaven, and behold a great red dragon having seven heads and ten horns and seven diadems on his heads, 4 and his tail sweeps down a third of the stars of heaven and he hurled them to the earth. And the dragon stood before the woman who was about to give birth, waiting to devour her baby when it was born. 5 And she gave birth to a son, a man, who is destined to rule all the nations with a rod of iron; and her child was caught up to God and his throne.

6 And the woman fled to the desert, for there she has a place prepared by God, that there she might be nourished for one thousand two hundred and sixty days. 7 And there was a war in heaven, (the) Michael and his angels fighting with the dragon. And the dragon and his angels fought, 8 and he did not prevail, neither was there found a place anymore for him in heaven. 9 And the great dragon, the ancient serpent, who is called Devil and Satan, was cast out, he who deceives the whole world, was cast out onto the earth, and his angels were cast out with him. 10 And I heard a loud voice in heaven, saying,

"Now is the salvation and the power and the kingship of our God and the authority of His Anointed, for the accuser of our brothers has been cast out, he who accused them day and night before our God. 11 And they overcame him through the blood of the Lamb and through the word of their testimony, and they loved not their life unto death. 12 On account of this rejoice, heavens and you who dwell there; woe to the earth and the sea, for the devil has descended to you with great fury, knowing that his time is short."

13 And when the dragon saw that he was cast down onto earth, he pursued the woman who had given birth to the man-child.

14 And the two wings of the great eagle were given to the woman, that she might fly to the desert to her place, where she might be supported for a time and times and half a time because of the serpent. 15 And the serpent spat water like a river from his mouth behind the woman, that she might be overwhelmed. 16 And the earth came to the assistance of the woman, and the earth opened its mouth and swallowed up the river which the dragon spat from his mouth. 17 And the dragon was furious with the woman, and he went off to fight against the rest of her children, who observe the commandments of God and have the testimony of Jesus. 18 And the dragon took up his stand on the sand of the sea.

13 1 And I saw a monster ascending from the sea; he had ten horns and seven heads, and ten diadems upon his heads, also blasphemous names upon his heads. 2 And the monster which I saw was like a leopard, and its feet like a bear, and its mouth like a lion's mouth. And the dragon gave to him his power and his throne and great authority. 3 And one of his heads seemed to have a lethal wound and the lethal wound was healed. And the whole world followed after the monster with admiration, 4 and they worshiped the dragon, because he gave authority to the monster; also they worshiped the monster, saying, "Who is like the monster?" and, "Who can fight against him?"

5 And the monster was given a mouth which spoke haughty and blasphemous words and authority was given to him to exercise for forty-two months. 6 And he opened his mouth to blaspheme against God, blaspheming His name and His dwelling, those who dwell in heaven. 7 And he was permitted to fight against the holy ones and to conquer them, and he was allowed to have authority over every tribe and people and tongue and nation. 8 And all the earth-dwellers will worship him, those whose name is not written in the book of life of the Lamb which was slain from the beginning of the world. 9 If anyone has an ear, let him hear.

10 If anyone goes to captivity, to captivity he goes; if anyone kills with the sword, he must be killed by the sword. Hence the endurance and faith of the holy ones.

11 And I saw another monster ascending from the land, and he had two horns like a lamb, and he spoke like a dragon. 12 And he exercises all the authority of the first monster on his behalf. And he

makes the earth and its inhabitants worship the first monster, whose lethal wound is healed. 13 And he performs great signs, so that he even makes fire from heaven fall on the earth in the sight of men. 14 And he deceives the earth-dwellers through the signs which he is allowed to perform in the presence of the monster; he tells the earth-dwellers to make an image for the monster, who was wounded by the sword and revived. 15 And he was allowed to put breath into the image of the monster, so that the image of the monster might even speak, and to cause those who would not worship the image of the monster to be killed. 16 And he made everyone, small and great, rich and poor, free and slave, be marked on their right hand or their forehead 17 so that no one could buy or sell if he did not have the mark, the name, of the beast or the number of its name. 18 This requires special insight. Let the person with understanding calculate the number of the beast; for it is the number of a human being. And its number is six hundred and sixty-six.

14 1 And I looked, and behold the Lamb standing on Mount Zion, and with him one hundred and forty-four thousand who had his name and the name of his Father written upon their foreheads. 2 And I heard a voice from heaven like the sound of many waters, like the sound of mighty thunder, and the voice which I heard was like the harpers playing on their lyres. 3 And they sang a new song before the throne and before the four living creatures and the elders; and no one could learn the song except the one hundred and forty-four thousand, who were redeemed from the earth. 4 These are they who have not defiled themselves with women; for they are virgins. These follow the Lamb wherever he goes. These were redeemed from men, the first fruit to God and to the Lamb, 5 and in their mouth was found no falsehood: they are unblemished.

6 And I saw another angel flying in mid-heaven, who had an eternal gospel to preach to those who are enthroned on the earth and to every nation and tribe and tongue and people. 7 He said in a loud voice, "Fear God and give Him glory, for the hour of his judgment has come, and worship the creator of heaven and earth and sea and the springs of water." 8 And another angel, a second one, followed saying, "Fallen, fallen is Babylon the great, who gave every nation to drink of the wine of the lust of her harlotry." 9 And another angel, a third one, followed them saying in a loud voice, "If anyone worships the monster and his image, and receives a mark on his forehead or on his hand, 10 that man will drink also of the wine of the wrath of

God poured undiluted into the cup of his anger, and he will be tormented with fire and brimstone in the presence of the holy angels and in the presence of the Lamb. 11 And the smoke of their torment will go up for ever and ever, and they will have no rest day and night, those who worship the monster and his image, and anyone who receives the mark of his name. 12 Hence the endurance of the saints, who keep the commandments of God and the faith of Jesus. 13 And I heard a voice from heaven saying, "Write: Blessed are the dead who die in the Lord from now on. Yes, says the Spirit, that they may rest from their labors; for their works follow them."

14 And I looked, and behold a white cloud, and on the cloud one like a son of man was enthroned; he had a golden crown on his head and in his hand a sharp sickle. 15 And another angel came out of the sanctuary, calling with a loud voice to the one who was enthroned upon the cloud, "Put in your sickle and reap, for the hour to reap has come, for the harvest of the earth is fully ready." 16 And the one who was enthroned upon the cloud cast his sickle upon the earth, and the earth was reaped. 17 And another angel came out of the sanctuary which is in heaven; he also had a sharp sickle. 18 And another angel came out of the altar; he had authority over fire, and cried with a loud voice to the one who had the sharp sickle, saying, "Put forth your sharp sickle, and gather the clusters of the vine of the earth, for its grapes are ripe." 19 And the angel swung his sickle onto the earth, and gathered the vine of the earth and threw it into the great winepress of the wrath of God. 20 And the winepress was trodden outside the city, and blood poured out of the winepress up to the horses' bridles for one thousand six hundred stadia.

15 1 And I saw another sign in heaven, great and wonderful, seven angels who had the seven last plagues, for in them is the wrath of God brought to completion. 2 And I saw, as it were, a crystal sea mingled with fire, and those who prevail over the beast and over his image and over the number of his name standing by the crystal sea; they held harps of God. 3 And they sang the song of Moses, the servant of God, and the song of the Lamb; they said:

"Great and marvelous are Your works,
   Lord God Almighty;
   just and true are your ways,
   King of Nations.
4 Who indeed will not fear You, Lord,
   and glorify Your name;

because You alone are holy,
because all the nations will come
and worship in Your presence,
because Your righteous acts have been revealed."

5 And after this I looked, and the sanctuary of the heavenly tent of witness was opened, 6 and the seven angels who had the seven plagues came out of the sanctuary; they were dressed in pure shining linen and wore golden girdles about their breasts. 7 And one of the four living creatures gave to the seven angels seven golden bowls filled with the wrath of God Who lives for ever and ever. 8 And the sanctuary was filled with the smoke of the glory of God and of His might, and no one was able to enter into the sanctuary until the seven plagues of the seven angels were completed.

16 1 And I heard a loud voice from the sanctuary saying to the seven angels, "Go and pour out the seven bowls of the wrath of God onto the earth." 2 And the first one went out and poured out his bowl upon the earth; and pernicious and evil sores came upon the men who had the mark of the beast and on those who worshiped his image. 3 And the second angel poured out his bowl upon the sea; and it became like the blood of a dead man, and every soul of life in the sea died. 4 And the third angel poured out his bowl upon the rivers and the springs of water; and it became blood. 5 And I heard the angel of the waters, saying, "You are just, You Who are and were, the Holy One, because You have made these judgments, 6 for they poured out the blood of the saints and prophets, and you have given them blood to drink. It is their desert." 7 And I heard a voice from the altar saying, "Yes, Lord God Almighty, Your judgments are true and just." 8 And the fourth angel poured out his bowl upon the sun; and it was allowed to scorch men with fire. 9 And men were scorched with a scorching heat, and they blasphemed the name of God who had power over these plagues, and they did not repent and give Him glory. 10 And the fifth angel poured out his bowl upon the throne of the beast; and his kingdom was plunged in darkness, and men gnawed their tongues in anguish, and 11 they blasphemed the God of heaven because of their anguish and sores, and they did not repent of their works. 12 And the sixth angel poured his bowl upon the great river, Euphrates; and its water was dried up, a road was prepared for the kings of the east. 13 And I saw from the mouth of the dragon and from the mouth of the beast and from the mouth of the false prophet three unclean spirits like frogs; 14 for they are the spirits of

demons who perform signs, who go out to the kings of the whole universe, to gather them for the battle of the great day of the Lord, the Almighty. 15 Behold, I come as a thief; blessed is he who maintains vigil and keeps his garments, so that he does not walk naked and they see his shame. 16 And they gathered them to the place which is called in Hebrew Armagedon. 17 And the seventh angel poured out his bowl upon the air; and a loud voice came out of the sanctuary from the throne, saying, "It is done." 18 And there were lightnings, and voices and thunders, and there was a great earthquake, such as had not been since man was on the earth, so great was the earthquake. 19 And the great city was split in three parts, and the cities of the nations fell. And Babylon the great was remembered before the Lord to receive the cup of the wine of the fury of his wrath. 20 And every island fled away, and no mountains were found. 21 And heavy hail like hundredweights fell from heaven upon men; and men blasphemed God because of the plague of hail, because that plague was very great.

17 1 And one of the seven angels who held the seven bowls came, and spoke with me, saying, "Come, I will reveal to you the verdict upon the great harlot who is established upon many waters, 2 with whom the kings of the earth have committed adultery, and the earth-dwellers have been intoxicated with the passion of her impurity." 3 And in spirit he carried me away into a wilderness: and I saw a woman enthroned on a scarlet monster, which was full of blasphemous names; it had seven heads and ten horns. 4 And the woman was clothed in purple and scarlet, and bedecked with gold and precious stones and pearls; she had in her hand a golden cup filled with abominations and the impurities of her adultery, 5 and on her forehead was written a mysterious name, Babylon the great, the mother of harlots and of the abominations of the land. 6 And I saw the woman drunk with the blood of the saints and with the blood of the martyrs of Jesus. And I wondered with great wonder when I saw her. 7 And the angel said to me, "Why do you wonder? I myself will tell you the mystery of the woman and of the beast who bears her, who has seven heads and ten horns. 8 The beast which you saw was and is not, and will rise from the abyss and goes his way to perdition; and the earth-dwellers, whose name is not written in the book of life from the foundation of the world, will marvel when they see the beast that was and is not and is to come. 9 Here one needs a mind with wisdom. The seven heads are seven mountains, upon which the

woman is established, and they are seven kings; 10 five have fallen, one is in existence, the other has yet to come and when he comes it is his destiny to remain for a short time. 11 And the beast which was and is not, indeed he is the eighth, and belongs to the seventh and goes to perdition. 12 And the ten horns which you see are ten kings, who have not yet received their sovereignty, but for one hour receive authority as kings with the beast. 13 These have one mind, and they give their power and authority to the beast. 14 These make war with the Lamb and the Lamb will conquer them, because he is Lord of Lords and King of Kings, and his companions are called and elect and faithful." 15 And he said to me, "The waters which you see, on which the woman is seated, they are people and multitudes and nations and tongues. 16 And the ten horns which you see and the beast, these will hate the harlot, and will make her desolate and naked and they will eat her flesh, and they will burn her with fire; 17 for God has put it into their minds to implement His decree and to be of one mind and to give over their royal power to the beast, until the words of God are fulfilled. 18 And the woman whom you saw is the great city who has dominion over the kings of the earth."

18 1 After this I saw another angel descending from heaven; he had great authority, and his glory filled the earth with light. 2 And he cried out with a powerful voice, saying,

"Fallen, fallen is Babylon the great,
 and she has become the dwelling of demons
 and the watchtower of every unclean spirit
 and the watchtower of every unclean and hateful bird,
3 because all the nations drank of the wine of the lust of her harlotry,
 and the kings of the earth have committed adultery with her,
 and the merchants of the earth have grown rich on the power of her
  lust."
4 And I heard a loud voice from heaven, saying,
  "My people, come out of her,
   so that you do not share in her sins,
   and so that you do not receive her misfortunes,
  5 because her sins have clung to the heaven,
   and God has remembered her unjust deeds,
  6 Render to her as she has rendered,
   and double the punishment for her double crimes;
   in the cup she mixed, mix a double draught.
  7 Just as she clothed herself in splendor and went awhoring,
   so in that measure give her torment and grief.

Because she says in her heart, 'I am established queen
and I am not a widow and I experience no grief at all,'
8 therefore, in one day her plagues will come upon her,
death and mourning and famine,
and she will be burned with fire;
for powerful is the Lord God Who judges."

9 And the kings of the earth, who committed fornication with her
and went awhoring, will wail and beat their breasts over her when
they see the smoke of her burning; 10 standing at a distance because
of her torment, they say,

"Woe, woe, great city,
powerful city, Babylon,
because in one hour your judgment has come."

11 And the merchants of the earth will wail and mourn over her,
because no one buys their cargo anymore, 12 cargo of gold and silver
and precious stone and pearls and linen and purple and silk and crimson and all kinds of scented wood and every type of vessel of ivory,
and every type of vessel of precious wood and of bronze and iron and
marble, 13 and cinnamon and spice and incense and myrrh and
frankincense and wine and oil and fine flour and wheat and cattle and
sheep, and horses and chariots and slaves, that is, human souls.

14 The fruit for which your soul longed has gone from you,
and all your luxuries and splendors have perished never to be
found again.

15 The merchants of these wares, who grew rich from her, will
stand at a distance for fear of her torment, weeping and mourning,
16 saying,

"Woe, woe, great city,
clothed in fine linen and purple and scarlet,
and ornate with gold and precious stones and pearls,
17 in one hour all your wealth is devastated."

All the shipmasters and seafarers and sailors and whosoever works
on the sea stood at a distance 18 and seeing the smoke of her burning
cried out, saying,

"Who is like the great city?"

19 And they threw dust upon their heads and cried out wailing and
mourning, saying,

"Woe, woe, great city,
by whom all those who had ships on the sea grew wealthy,
because in one hour there is devastation."

20 "Rejoice over her, heaven and saints and apostles and prophets,
   for God has pronounced judgment against her for you."
21 And one powerful angel lifted a stone like a great millstone, and
threw it into the sea, saying,
   "Thus will Babylon, the great city, be hurled down with violence,
   and will not be found anymore.
22 And the sound of harpers and musicians and flute players and
      trumpeters
   is not heard within you anymore,
   and no craftsman of any art
   is found in you anymore,
   and the sound of the mill
   is not heard in you anymore,
   and 23 no light of a lamp
   appears in you anymore,
   and the voice of the bridegroom and the bride
   is not heard in you anymore;
   for your merchants were the great men of the earth,
   for all the nations have been deceived by your sorcery
   and 24 in her was found the blood of prophets and of saints,
   and of all who have been slain on earth."

19 1 After this I heard, as it were, a loud sound of a great multitude
in heaven, saying,
"Alleluia; salvation and glory and power belong to our God,
2 for true and just are His judgments;
   for He has judged the great harlot who corrupted the earth by her
      adultery,
   and He has vindicated the blood of His servants shed by her hand."
   3 And a second voice said,
         "Alleluia; indeed her smoke goes up forever and ever."
   4 And the twenty-four elders and the four living creatures prostrated themselves and worshiped God Who sits upon the throne, saying, "Amen, Alleluia." 5 And
            "Praise our God, all His servants,
               those who fear Him, small and great."
   6 And I heard, as it were, the sound of a great crowd and, as it
were, a sound of many waters and, as it were, a sound of mighty
thunder, saying,
"Alleluia, the Lord our God, the Omnipotent, has taken sovereignty.

7 Let us rejoice and be glad and give glory to Him,
 because the marriage of the Lamb has come,
 and his wife has prepared herself,
8 and it is granted to her to be clothed in fine linen, bright and
 clean."

For fine linen is the just deeds of the saints. 9 And he said to me,
"Blessed are those who are called to the marriage feast of the Lamb.
And he said to me, 10 "These words of God are true." And I fell at
his feet to worship him. And he said to me, "Do not do that; I am a
fellow servant with you and your brothers who have the testimony
about Jesus; worship God. The testimony about Jesus is the spirit of
prophecy.

11 And I saw the heaven opened, and behold a white horse, and he
who rode upon it was called Faithful and True, and he judges with
justice and makes war. 12 His eyes are a flame of fire, and on his head
are many diadems; he has a name inscribed which no one knows except himself, 13 and he is clothed in a robe sprinkled with blood, and
his name is the Word of God. 14 And the armies of heaven, dressed in
clean white linen, follow him on white horses. 15 And from his mouth
proceeds a sharp sword, with which to smite the nations, and he himself rules them with a rod of iron, and he himself tramples the winepress of the wine of the wrath of God the Omnipotent. 16 And on
his cloak and on his thigh (or banner) he has a name written, "King
of Kings and Lord of Lords."

17 And I saw one angel standing in the sun, and he cried with a
loud voice, saying to all the birds which fly in the mid-heaven,
"Come gather for the great supper of God, 18 so that you may eat
flesh of kings and flesh of captains and flesh of mighty men and flesh
of horses and their riders, and flesh of all men slave and free and small
and great." 19 And I saw the beast and the kings of the earth and
their armies gathered to make war against the rider of the horse and
his army. 20 And the beast was captured and with him the false
prophet who performed signs before him, by which he deceived those
who received the mark of the beast and worshiped his image; the two
were hurled alive into the lake of fire which burns with sulphur.
21 And the rest were killed with the sword of the rider on the horse,
which proceeds from his mouth, and all the birds were gorged with
their flesh.

20 1 Then I saw an angel descending from heaven, holding in his
hand the key of the bottomless pit and a great chain. 2 And he

seized the dragon, the ancient serpent, who is the devil and the Satan, and bound him for a thousand years, 3 and threw him into the pit, and shut it and sealed it over him, that he should not deceive the nations anymore, till the thousand years were ended. After that he is destined to be loosed for a little while.

4 Then I saw thrones, and seated on them were those to whom judgment was given; also I saw the souls of those who had been beheaded for their testimony about Jesus and for the Word of God, and whosoever had not worshiped the beast nor its image and had not received its mark on their foreheads or on their hands; and they came to life, and reigned with the Anointed One for a thousand years. 5 The rest of the dead did not come to life until the thousand years were completed. This is the first resurrection. 6 Blessed and holy is he who shares in the first resurrection; over such the second death has no power, but they will be priests of God and of the Anointed One and they shall reign with him for the thousand years.

7 And when the thousand years are completed, Satan will be released from his prison, 8 and will come out to deceive the nations which are at the four corners of the earth, that is, Gog and Magog, to gather them for battle; and their number will be like the sand of the sea. 9 And they marched up over the broad earth and surrounded the camp of the saints and the beloved city; but fire came down from heaven and consumed them; 10 and the devil who had deceived them was thrown into the lake of fire and brimstone where the beast and the false prophet were, and they will be tormented day and night for ever and ever.

11 Then I saw a great white throne and Him Who sat upon it from Whose presence earth and sky fled away, and no place was found for them. 12 And I saw the dead, great and small, standing before the throne, and books were opened; also another book was opened, which is the book of life; and the dead were judged by what was written in the books according to their deeds. 13 And the sea gave up the dead in it, and Death and Hades gave up the dead in them, and all were judged according to their deeds. 14 And Death and Hades were thrown into the lake of fire. This is the second death, the lake of fire. 15 And if anyone's name was not found written in the book of life, he was thrown into the lake of fire.

21   1 And I saw a new heaven and a new earth; for the first heaven and the first earth had passed away, and the sea was no more. 2 And I saw the holy city, the new Jerusalem, descending out of heaven

from God, prepared as a bride adorned for her husband. 3 And I heard a great voice from the throne, saying, "Behold, the dwelling of God is with mankind. He will dwell with them, and they shall be His people, and God Himself will be with them, 4 and He will wipe away every tear from their eyes, and death shall be no more, neither mourning nor crying nor pain anymore. For the former things have passed away. 5 And He who sat upon the thone said, "Behold, I make all things new." Also He said, "Write this, for these words are trustworthy and true." 6 And He said to me, "It is done! I am the Alpha and the Omega, the Beginning and the End. To the thirsty I will give water without price from the fountain of the water of life.

7 He who conquered shall have this heritage, and I will be his God and he shall be My son.

8 But as for the cowardly, the faithless, the polluted, as for murderers, fornicators, sorcerers, idolaters, and all liars, their lot shall be in the lake that burns with fire and brimstone, which is the second death.

9 Then came one of the seven angels who had the seven bowls full of the seven last plagues, and spoke to me, saying, "Come, I will reveal to you the bride, the woman who is the wife of the Lamb."

10 And in spirit he carried me away to a great, high mountain, and revealed to me the holy city Jerusalem descending out of heaven from God, 11 possessing the glory of God, her radiance like a most rare jewel, like jasper, clear as crystal; 12 she had a great, high wall, with twelve gates, and at the gates twelve angels, and on the gates the names of the twelve tribes of the sons of Israel were inscribed, 13 on the east three gates, on the north three gates, on the south three gates, and on the west three gates. 14 And the wall of the city had twelve foundations, and on them the twelve names of the twelve apostles of the Lamb.

15 And he who spoke with me had a golden measuring rod to measure the city and her gates and wall. 16 And the city was foursquare, its length the same as its breadth; and he measured the city with his rod, twelve thousand stadia; her length and breadth and height were equal. 17 He also measured her wall, a hundred and forty-four cubits by man's measure, that is, an angel's.

18 And the structure of the wall was jasper, while the city was pure gold, clear as crystal. 19 The foundations of the wall of the city were adorned with every jewel; the first foundation was jasper, the second sapphire, the third agate, the fourth emerald, 20 the fifth onyx, the

sixth carnelian, the seventh chrysolite, the eighth beryl, the ninth topaz, the tenth chrysoprase, the eleventh jacinth, the twelfth amethyst. 21 And the twelve gates were twelve pearls, each of the gates made of a single pearl. And the highway of the city was pure gold, clear as crystal. 22 And I saw no temple in her; for its temple is the Lord God, the Omnipotent, and the Lamb.

23 And the city had no need of sun or moon to shine upon it, for the glory of God was its light, and its lamp was the Lamb. 24 By her light shall the nations walk; and the kings of the earth shall bring their magnificence into her; 25 and its gates shall never be shut by day; there shall be no night there; 26 they shall bring into her the glory and the honor of the nations. 27 But nothing unclean shall enter it, nor any who practice abomination or falsehood, but only those who are written in the Lamb's book of life.

22 1 Then he revealed to me the river of the water of life, clear as crystal, flowing from the throne of God and of the Lamb, 2 through the middle of the highway of the city; and on either side of the river, there was a tree of life with its twelve kinds of fruit, yielding its fruit each month; and the leaves of the tree were for the healing of the nations.

3 There shall no more be anything cursed. Indeed, the throne of God and of the Lamb will be in her, and His servants shall worship Him 4 and they will see His face, and His name shall be on their foreheads. 5 And night will be no more; and they need no light of lamp or light of sun, for the Lord God will shed His light upon them, and they will reign forever and ever. 6 And he said to me, "These words are trustworthy and true. And the Lord, the God of the spirits of the prophets, has sent His angel to show His servants what must soon take place. 7 And behold, I am coming soon." Blessed is he who keeps the words of the prophecy of this book. 8 I John am he who heard and saw these things. And when I heard and saw them, I fell down to worship at the feet of the angel who showed them to me; 9 but he said to me, "You must not do that! I am a fellow servant with you and your brethren the prophets, and with those who keep the words of this book. Worship God."

10 And he said to me, "Do not seal up the words of the prophecy of this book, for the critical time is near. 11 Let the evildoer still be evil, and the filthy still be filthy, and the righteous still do right, and the holy still be holy." 12 "Behold, I am coming soon, bringing My recom-

pense, to repay everyone according to his deeds. 13 I am the Alpha and the Omega, the First and the Last, the Beginning and the End."

14 Blessed are those who wash their robes, that they may have the privilege of the tree of life and that they may enter the city by the gates. 15 Outside are the dogs and sorcerers and fornicators and murderers and idolaters and all who delight in and practice false-hood. 16 "I, Jesus, have sent my angel to you with this testimony for the churches. I am the root and the offspring of David, the bright morning star." 17 The Spirit and the Bride say, "Come." And let him who hears say, "Come." Indeed, let him who is thirsty come, let him who desires take the water of life without price.

18 I warn everyone who hears the words of the prophecy of this book: if anyone adds to them, God will add to him the plagues de-scribed in this book; 19 and if anyone takes away from the words of the book of this prophecy, God will take away his share in the tree of life and in this holy city, which are described in this book.

20 He who testifies to these things says, "Yes, I am coming soon." Amen, come, Lord Jesus. 21 May the grace of the Lord Jesus be with everyone.

INTRODUCTION

HOW REVELATION BEGAN

Revelation, with regard to both content and construction,[1] is one of the most exquisite of all apocalypses both Jewish and Christian, and yet it was only with difficulty that it secured a place in the New Testament canon. It is with even greater difficulty that the meaning of this great work can be determined. Here a new approach is tried. Instead of the close analysis of texts exhibited in some other Anchor Bible volumes, such as those of Father Dahood and Father Brown,[2] the author presents to the general reader a broader interpretation of this unique text in the light of which they may approach a deeper understanding of other NT books and of the novelty that Christ brought.

The author concurs in principle with Boismard, Hopkins, and others[3] who find that this work falls into two distinct parts, chs. 4–11 and chs. 12–22. However, she suggests that:

1) 4–11 emanate from the circle of John the Baptist and reflect his own and his disciples' expectation of "He that cometh" before they could be enlightened by the life of Jesus Himself;

2) 12–22 are of later date but still originate from the disciples of the Baptist who may or may not have converted to Christianity. This section represents the view of those who predicted the Fall of Jerusalem under the Romans in A.D. 70 and ascribed this to the unorthodox behavior of their coreligionists. Such an attitude would be shared by such groups as the covenanters of Qumran and is intimated by the Baptist himself (Matt 3:7–10, cf. John 1:19–27) and perhaps the primitive Jerusalem church once led by James, the "brother" of the Lord.

3) 1–3 and 22:16a, 20b, 21, were added later by a Jewish Christian disciple, perhaps one who had come to know Jesus Christ more accurately, like the disciples of the Baptist at Ephesus in Acts 19:1–7 or the Scripture scholar Apollos in Acts 18:24–28. They still retained the fiery and somewhat pessimistic outlook of their former master. They looked forward to

---

[1] See Introduction, "The Structure of Revelation."

[2] Mitchell Dahood, S.J., *Psalms I, 1–50; Psalms II, 51–100; Psalms III, 101–150.* Raymond E. Brown, S.S., *The Gospel According to John, I–XII; The Gospel According to John, XIII–XXI.*

[3] See General Selected Bibliography.

the imminent second coming of Christ (contrast II Peter 3:1–18) and their addition to our text influenced others to relate this expectation to the rest of Revelation.

Originally, however, Rev 4–11 in its oral, not written, form would be assigned to the time of the Baptist and therefore to an era prior to Jesus' public ministry. Rev 12–22 would be dated in the mid-sixties as the Roman War gathered momentum. Part III appears to be later than this.

Thus, the original apocalypse, comprising 4–22, with some additions in the last chapter, was an almost entirely Jewish and/or Jewish Christian work. Revelation does not fit into the Christian apocalyptic genre. The fact that it received Christian additions was not unusual; the same destiny befell such works as the Testaments of the Twelve Patriarchs, I Enoch, II Enoch.

The suggestion that Revelation is not primarily a Christian work has been made by other scholars but further arguments may be supplied in favor of their hypotheses. This may be done especially by comparing and contrasting Revelation with other Christian apocalypses.

NEW TESTAMENT APOCALYPSES

I & II THESSALONIANS

The oldest apocalyptic text in the NT appears to be I Thess 4:16–18. It describes the coming, Gr. *parousia,* of Jesus succeeded by the resurrection and then the rapture of the saints. The text bears features characteristic of Jewish apocalyptic literature but clearly refers to Christ (vs. 16) and is preceded by a reference to his death and resurrection (vs. 14). Complementary to this text is the description of the parousia both of Christ and the Lawless One in II Thess 2:1–12. Here the scene reflects a Jewish judgment theophany.[4] But it is dominated by two new features, namely the central position of the Lord Jesus and his opponent, the Lawless One, who is distinct from Satan, although linked with him (vs. 9). II Thess 2:1–12 bears more similarity to Revelation than does I Thessalonians or, indeed, the synoptic apocalypse (Mark 13, Matt 24, Luke 21). It shares with Revelation the expectation of apostasy, the appearance of an impious character who parodies God Himself, the idea of the restraint of the evil one (cf. the chaining of Satan, Rev 20:1–3), the slaughter of the impi-

[4] M. Dibelius, *Handbuch zum Neue Testament,* cited in Hennecke, II, 611–12. See also C. H. Giblin, S.J., *The Threat to Faith.*

ous one with the breath from the mouth of the "Messiah," the activity of Satan, and the mimicking of signs and wonders together with deception. But its distinctive mark is the absolutely central position of the Lord Jesus and His parousia in vss. 1 and 8, (cf. I Thess 4:14, 16). It is Jesus who "by his appearing and his coming" slays the Lawless One. No such prominent position is given to Jesus in our apocalypse. Yet the affinity between the two texts might suggest a proximity in time (mid-first century A.D.). Incidentally, it is interesting to note that Paul's Christology becomes less and less apocalyptic as he matures in the Christian faith; this is evident if one reads his letters in the order in which they were written.

THE GOSPELS

There is, perhaps, one feature which is clear from the Gospels, namely, that Jesus is not represented as an apocalypticist, although in the past some scholars attempted to argue that he was. Neither is he primarily a visionary. Indeed, even taking the text literally, one can discover only four possible visions: Mark 9:3–13, Matt 17:1–13, Luke 9:28–36, his transfiguration; Luke 10:18, his having seen Satan fall like lightning from the heaven; Matt 4:1–11, his temptation by the devil; Luke 22:43, his being strengthened against temptation by an angel that appeared to him. His charismatic ministry (exorcism, healing, and such) was used late in his life and for the service of others. He eschewed the spectacular (Matt 4:1–11), avoided the honor of kingship (John 6:15), and does not seem to have indulged in asceticism (Matt 11:18–19). Although he gathered a group of intimate disciples his teaching was not esoteric in the same sense as was that of the Essenes. He did not use pseudonymity; indeed, he spoke clearly on behalf of his Father. He did not employ a literary form; rather his message, like the prophets', was oral. Although he was not sparing of metaphors and symbols in his teaching, these are markedly restrained when compared to such symbolic actions as those performed by Ezekiel or to the visions and mysterious language of the postexilic prophets and the author of Revelation. Jesus did not appear to take an interest in either cosmic history or division of history into epochs. Although he cured those afflicted with evil spirits his attitude cannot be said to be strongly dualistic or to offer a clear representation of the theory of the two ages. The only clearly apocalyptic, in distinction from eschatological, teaching which may have proceeded from the lips of Jesus appears in Mark 13 and its parallels in Matt 24, Luke 21:5–26, and in the passion narrative in Mark 14:62 and its parallels in Matt 26:24, Luke 22:69. Yet even here the teaching is extremely reserved when compared and contrasted with other apocalyptic works. Mark 13:24–27 speaks of cosmic disturbances and the arrival of the Son of Man with the clouds of heaven. As will be discussed below there is certainly a similarity between Rev 6 and Mark 13 but the differences are greater than the similarities. To quote Hennecke:

> Jesus' preaching of the Kingdom and his vocation presuppose the apocalyptic dualism in so far as he understands the coming of God's rule not as an event within the world, but as a divine miracle which puts a definitive end to this world and to time and brings in the eternal world of God. Nonetheless, the differences from Jewish Apocalyptic are unmistakable. They are already revealed in the choice of the central concept of the *sovereignty* of God, in terms of which Jesus replaces the popular apocalyptic notions of the eschatological salvation by the thought that God is king and assumes Lordship over all. The rigour and clarity of this concept puts an end to all descriptions of the *spectaculum mundi* and of the glory of the Beyond; only the image of the banquet as a symbol of community with God is retained. The imminent expectation also seems to link Jesus with Apocalyptic. But in addition to the statements concerning the nearness of the reign of God are those concerned with its contemporaneity, and its characteristic juxtaposition of future and present shatters the time-scheme of the Two-Ages doctrine. The question about the actual point in time then drops out, for the meaning of the expectation consists "in the qualifying of the human situation in view of the coming of the Kingdom. Now one can no longer watch and ask about the terminal event, but only prepare oneself immediately for the Kingdom, i.e. repent" (Conzelmann, RGG[3], II, col. 667).[5]

Thus Revelation differs radically from NT apocalyptic. Neither the word "parousia" nor the title, "The Son of The Man," in distinction from "one like a son of man" (Dan 7:13, Rev 1:13), occur. Indeed, save for the vision in Rev 1 (which is probably Christian) the figure of the Son of Man plays an extremely minor role. He appears only in Rev 14:14 and is probably to be identified as an angel. Further, he comes to wreak vengeance rather than "gather his elect from the four winds" (see Mark 13:27, RSV). In the Gospels (Mark 13:38, Luke 12:8) the Son of Man judges on the principle of the *lex talionis* but in our apocalypse judgment does not seem to be expected of him.

Other features in the synoptic apocalypse are missing from Revelation, namely, being delivered up to synagogues (Mark 13:9), preaching the Gospel to all nations (13:10); the Holy Spirit speaking in defense of the persecuted (13:11); domestic strife (13:12–13); false Christs (13:22) and the ignorance of the Son concerning the day and hour (13:32). Even though Mark 13 may include much Jewish apocalyptic material, the Christian elements within it distinguish it clearly from Revelation.

[5] Hennecke, II, 608–9.

JUDE AND II PETER

Jude and II Peter are also obviously Christian works.[6] Jude identifies himself as a "servant of Jesus Christ" (Jude 1)[7] whereas John (Rev 1:1) appears to be designated as a servant of God. Jude addresses those "called to be preserved by Jesus Christ." Moreover, in Jude 4 Jesus is called "only Ruler and Lord," and Jude's letter bears witness to the appearance of heresy which, in contrast to Rev 2–3, is the denial of specifically Christian belief (cf., however, Jude 11, Rev 2:14, II Peter 2:15). Further, both the predictions of the apostles of Jesus Christ (Jude 17) and prayer in the Holy Spirit (Jude 20) are mentioned. Finally, in this short epistle the title "Jesus Christ" occurs six times.[8] In II Peter the writer introduces himself as "servant and apostle of Jesus Christ" and refers to the recipients as people who are "of the righteousness of our God and Jesus Christ" (1:1). The name "Jesus" appears eight times.[9] There is a clear allusion to the transfiguration of Jesus and a reference to the commands of the Lord and Savior through "Your apostles" (3:2). II Peter predicts the conflagration of the world (3:7, 10, 12) and the creation of a new heaven and earth (3:13).

All the main apocalyptic passages in the NT except for Revelation are patently Christian. Revelation is the only one in which Jesus is not the central figure.

POST-NEW TESTAMENT CHRISTIAN APOCALYPSES

THE DIDACHE

At the end of the Didache, an early second-century manual on church discipline and worship, occurs a little apocalypse (Didache 16). While not quoting the NT directly, it has numerous allusions to it, especially to Matt 24, I and II Thess, and Rev 13.[10] Just as OT texts are woven in and

---

[6] Quotations are from Bo Reicke, *The Epistles of James, Peter, and Jude*, AB, vol. 37, 1964.

[7] References to The Letter of Jude are to verse numbers; Jude is only twenty-five verses long and is not divided into chapters.

[8] Jude 1 (*bis*), 4, 17, 21, 25.

[9] 1:1 (*bis*), 8, 11, 14, 16, 2:20, 3:18.

[10] For a complete list of texts see Hennecke, II, 627.

out of our apocalypse, so NT texts are woven in and out of Didache 16. This contrast is arresting. The text admonishes the reader to be watchful and to frequent the assembly, for the time of the Lord's coming is unknown. It warns against false prophets and corruptors. It predicts that lawlessness will increase, that there will be persecution and betrayal. Finally, "then the world deceiver shall appear as a son of God, and shall work signs and wonders, and the earth shall be delivered into his hands, and he shall commit crimes such as have never been seen since the world began." Those who pass through this time of testing will be saved and then the three signs of truth will appear: a rift in the heavens, the sound of a trumpet, and the resurrection of the dead. But this resurrection is not for all; it is for the saints. Then the Lord will come on the clouds. Hennecke quotes the Georgian translation of Didache 16:8 which appears to make the description of the coming of the Lord more complete:

> Then will the world see our Lord Jesus Christ, the Son of Man who (at the same time) is Son of God, coming on the clouds with power and great glory, and in his holy righteousness to requite every man according to his works before the whole of mankind and before the angels, Amen.[11]

The Didache apocalypse, therefore, differs from Revelation primarily in its use of NT texts and the stress on the second coming of Christ, as Son of God, who will be opposed by a deceiver who imitates Him as Son of God. The phrase "son of God" does not occur in the main corpus of Revelation.

THE SHEPHERD OF HERMAS

While some would not assign the Shepherd of Hermas to the apocalyptic genre, one cannot deny that it has apocalyptic features and that it seems to be a good example of the combination of prophecy and apocalyptic. In this work occur images of symbols similar to those found in Revelation but they are given a definite Christian interpretation. The good woman (cf. Rev 12) and the building of the tower represent the church (cf. the new Jerusalem, Rev 21:2); the false prophecy (cf. Rev 13:11–18) is specifically Christian prophecy, not Jewish or pagan. In addition, throughout the whole of the Shepherd of Hermas there occur Christian references to the church, to her leaders or officers, to baptism, to the Holy Spirit, to the kingdom of God, and, most important, to the Son of God. This is in complete contrast to Revelation. (The Shepherd of Hermas consists of three parts, Visions, Mandates, and Similitudes.)

[11] Hennecke, II, 628.

THE ASCENSION OF ISAIAH

This second-century A.D. apocalypse was probably written in two parts. Ascension of Isaiah 1–5 appears to be a Jewish document. The rest of the text, chs. 6–11, may be either Jewish with Christian interpolations or entirely Christian, but ch. 11 is Christian without a doubt. Of interest to us are the distinctly Christian references in 3:13–31, a revelation which, it was purported, Isaiah received. These are to the coming of the beloved from the seventh heaven, his being in the likeness of man, the persecution which he will suffer, the twelve disciples, the crucifixion, the resurrection, the disciples' mission to the nations, the Holy Spirit, faithlessness in the last times, false prophets, dissension between ministers in the church, among others. Ch. 4 is a prediction of Beliar's coming down to earth in the form of a man and deceiving people by speaking in the name of the beloved and performing signs and wonders. But the Lord will come with his angels and saints and drag Beliar into Gehenna. Then the Lord and the saints will be present in the world and resurrection and judgment will take place. In ch. 9 Isaiah is told about the Lord Christ who would be called Jesus on earth (cf. also 10:7). In 11 Isaiah is shown the family of David and a woman named Mary; the chapter also tells of the miraculous birth of the child of Mary. Isaiah in 11:41 witnesses Jesus' ministry in Israel, his crucifixion and resurrection:

> On account of these visions and prophecies Sammael Satan sawed asunder the prophet Isaiah the son of Amoz, by the hand of Manasses . . .[12]

Such clear references as these to the Christ events do not occur in Revelation.

THE APOCALYPSE OF PETER

This early second-century apocalypse purports to be teachings of Jesus to his disciples as He stood on the Mount of Olives. It concerns the parousia and the end of the world. In ch. 1 there are almost direct quotations from Matt 24:3–5, 26–27, Mark 13:26, Luke 9:26, cf. Matt 16:27, I Peter 4, II Tim 4:1. Thus, the Apocalypse of Peter at the very beginning is even more influenced by the NT than is Didache 16. The words "parousia," "gospel," and "church" are used, and the "sign of the son of man" (cf. Matt 24:30) is rendered "with my cross going before my face will

[12] Hennecke, II, 663.

I come in my glory, shining seven times as bright as the sun . . ." Ch. 2 of this apocalypse contains the parable of the fig tree and again there are almost direct quotations from Matt 13:28 f. and other NT texts.[13] There is a reference to "the first Christ whom they crucified . . ." In ch. 3 Jesus shows Peter the souls of all men. Ch. 4 contains a description of the judgment in the last days; here there is a clear allusion to Ezek 37:4 ff. and a more indirect one to I Cor 15:36 ff. Christ himself, coming upon a cloud with his angels to sit at the right hand of the Father, is introduced in ch. 6. In ch. 14 Christ gives the righteous the baptism and salvation which they desired; the recipients are probably the patriarchs. This chapter speaks of "my son who is without sin." Peter is told to proclaim the gospel throughout the world. Ch. 15 contains the phrase, "my lord, Jesus Christ, our king," and a description of how the disciples saw two men who possessed ineffable beauty. Three references to Jesus Christ, two of which allude to his divinity, occur in ch. 16. "God Jesus Christ" explains that these two handsome men are Moses and Elijah. Matt 17:5 and Matt 3:17 are quoted in ch. 17, which is a description of either the transfiguration or the triumphal ascension into heaven. This apocalypse, therefore, shows pronounced influence from the NT and begins a practice which will, unfortunately, be characteristic of some of these Christian apocalypses, namely the gruesome description of the punishment of the wicked. Save for some indirect quotations[14] it has no affinity with Revelation.

THE CHRISTIAN SIBYLLINES

The Jewish part of the Sibylline Oracles arose as propaganda, probably in the second century. In the same way, the Christian Sibyllines appear to have resulted from Christianity's fight against paganism. They give a clear indication of Christian doctrine. In 1:323 there is a reference to a maid who will give birth to the logos of God, 1:324 predicts the son of the Great God who shall come to men, and 1:331 mentions Christ, "the son of the immortal, most high God." These allusions are followed by indirect references, in the form of prophecies which clearly allude to events recorded in the Gospels but in an oblique way (i.e. no names are inserted) to the wise men offering gold and myrrh and frankincense, to the voice of the Baptist in the desert, to baptism, to Christ's miracles and exorcisms, to his walking on the water and multiplication of the loaves, to the abuse of the Son of God, to the descent into hell, and to the resurrection and the ascension. Book 1 ends with a reference to the fall of the temple in A.D. 70 and the dispersion of Israel.

[13] See Hennecke, II, 668–69.   [14] Rev 16:7, 17:8, 19:2, 20:13, 22:2.

Book 2 speaks of the triumphal entry into the heavenly city where Christ shall give rewards to the just and crown the victors, and makes special reference to the martyrs and the virgins. Then the end of the world is described. Elijah (the Tishbite) will come from heaven and show three signs. The world will be dissolved, especially by fire, and the universal judgment before the seat of God will take place. Uriel will open the gates of hell. Christ will come on a cloud with his angels, sit on the right hand of God, and judge the pious and the impious. Moses and some of the patriarchs and prophets will also be present. Book 2 lists some of the sins for which the wicked are punished and refers to the punishment of presbyters and deacons. It shows the influence of the OT, apocalyptic literature, the NT, and patristic works.

Book 4 is a hymn to Christ greeting him as the "Son of the Most High." It refers to his baptism, teachings, walking on the waves, healing, and raising of the dead. It mentions his passion and alludes to his second coming. Book 8 inveighs against Rome, probably because of persecution; Nero is called Antichrist. It ends with a description of the last judgment and the desolation of the world. Once again the sign and seal for all men is the cross, and at this point the work shows notable references to both the OT and the NT including Revelation.

SUMMARY OF CHRISTIAN APOCALYPSES

The major difference between NT and post-NT Christian apocalypses and Jewish apocalypses is that the former concentrate, for the most part, on the second coming of the Messiah, or Son of Man, and future bliss or punishment. In the Christian apocalypses the messianic woes which preceded the first coming of the Messiah are expected also before his second coming. These works pay little attention to cosmic surveys (journeys through the heavens) or historical surveys (journeys through Israel) or the two ages (of tribulation and of messianic bliss), for the writers believed that the world had already entered on the second age.

Pseudonymity and esoteric teaching characteristic of the OT were no longer always necessary, for the writer did not need to associate himself with an OT character. Rather he could announce plainly what Christ came to reveal. Symbolic language, for example animal symbolism, is largely discarded. Nevertheless, the apocalypses are attributed to apostles. Indeed, for Paul in the NT the mark of the Christian dispensation is that the secret or mystery which has been hidden for so long is now made manifest, Gr. *apokaluptō*. The Jewish fascination with numerology practically disappears because this is partly associated with calculating the time of the coming age. The Christian does not believe he can calculate the time of the parousia. Belief in the imminence of the parousia disappears quite early in Christian thought but recurs in revivalism.

Greek mythology affected the Christian apocalypses, whereas the Jewish apocalypses were influenced by such mythologies as the Babylonian and Persian. However, the major distinguishing features of the Christian apocalypses are the overt and the indirect quotations from the NT, and references to the events in the life of Christ as recorded in the NT.

THE CHARACTER OF REVELATION

Although chs. 1–3 are plainly Christian, compared with the above discussed apocalypses chs. 4–22 show little evidence of being a truly Christian work.

THE CHRISTOLOGY

Disproportionate occurrence of the phrases "Jesus Christ" and "Jesus" in chs. 1–3 suggests that these chapters are a later Christian addition. "Jesus Christ" occurs only in Rev 1:1, 2, 5, and nowhere else in the whole of the text. There are, however, some variants which read "Jesus Christ," e.g. Rev 1:9 which gives both the variants "Christ Jesus" and "Jesus Christ." Revelation presents only eight references to the name "Jesus," two of which occur in these chapters, one being a double reference in Rev 1:9: "I John, your brother and comrade . . . in Jesus . . . was on . . . Patmos on account of the word of God and the testimony of Jesus." Thus in this section "Jesus Christ" and "Jesus" are prominent; together they appear five times in chs. 1–3, compared with eight times in the whole of the rest of the text. Chs. 4–11 which probably comprised the first section of the original work, contain not one occurrence of either "Jesus Christ" or "Jesus." In chs. 12–22 the name "Jesus" appears in 12:17, 14:12, 17:6, 19:10 (*bis*), 20:4, 22:16, 20.

If chs. 4–11 originated with John the Baptist before God revealed to him that Jesus was "He that cometh," that explains why the name of Jesus does not occur in this section. If chs. 12–22 came from a follower of the Baptist who knew something (but not full details) about Jesus, that explains 12:17, 14:12, 17:6, 19:10, 20:4, which appear tautological and which could be removed from the text without destroying the sense. Perhaps the follower added these references to Jesus because the Lord had by then been identified as "Messiah"; cf. John 1:41. However, if he were thinking about Jerusalem rather than Rome when he wrote of the harlot (Rev 17; see COMMENT) he might have been making oblique references to the martyrdom of Stephen (Acts 6–7), the beheading (cf. Rev 20:4) of James and others (Acts 2:1–3), and the attempts to kill Peter (Acts 12:3–19). In this way he could assert that the city was drunk with the blood of the martyrs of Jesus (Rev 17:6) even before any persecution by the Romans began. Rev 19:10 might be seen in the context of the fulfillment of Joel 2:28–32 on the Feast of Pentecost, a prophecy attesting the Lordship of Jesus. Light may also be shed on this curious text in that in Acts 19:1–7 tongues and prophecy (vs. 6) are extraordinary gifts which help the disciples of the Baptist to distinguish between the water baptism of John and the Holy Spirit baptism of Jesus (vs. 6). One may compare also Rev 2–3, the prophecies to the churches.

Rev 22:16 and 20 appear to be later Christian additions comparable to Rev 1–3. Verse 16 is the only text in which Jesus speaks in the first person and is clearly linked to the prophecies to the churches by the references to "angel" and "churches." Verse 20 also concurs with the messages to the churches in the emphasis on the imminent (second) coming (cf. 2:5, 16, 25, 3:3, 11, 20). Verse 20c seems to be a liturgical addition equivalent to the Aramaic *Marana tha,* "Come, our Lord [Jesus]," in I Cor 16:22. Verse 20d appears to be an epistolary conclusion which completes the letters or prophecies to the churches.

The paucity of references to "Jesus Christ" or "Jesus" might not surprise us because of the literary genre of our work. However, a comparison with the Christian apocalypses shows that, although the name Jesus may not occur frequently, other titles of the second person of the trinity are used (see p. 12), e.g. while the Shepherd of Hermas does not use the name Jesus it makes frequent use of the title "Son of God" or "the Son," even though the Son of God is sometimes confused with the Spirit or with Michael.

MESSIANISM

In Revelation "anointed," Gr. *Christos,* is always definite, i.e. never without the definite article or the possessive pronoun. *Ho Christos,* "the Christ," occurs in 20:4 and 20:6.

"His Christ," Gr. *tou Christou autou,* appears in 11:15, 12:10.

Only one text, 20:4, associates *Christos* with the name Jesus and even here it is not a close association, for the "testimony of Jesus" is mentioned long before "the Christ." In the rest of the NT there are many references to *Christos* with the definite article, but the phrase *Christos autou,* "his Christ," does not occur. However, "his anointed" is standard usage in the OT, e.g. I Sam 2:10, 12:3, 5. Further, all four references in

Revelation refer either overtly or obliquely to kingdom, power, and reigning, the prerogatives which the earthly Jesus eschewed. In Revelation *ho Christos* might be translated "the Messiah" or "the Anointed" or "the Elect One" in a purely Jewish sense. The phrase resembles "the Lord of the spirits and His Anointed" found in I Enoch.

In I Enoch the Elect One, who may or may not be identified with the Son of Man, is found only in the parables (chs. 37–71). Some of the features of this personage are as follows: In I Enoch 40:5, Enoch hears one voice which blesses the Lord of spirits and a second which blesses the Elect One; cf. the praises of God and the Anointed One in Revelation, e.g. 11:15, 12:10. In 53:6 the Elect One causes the house of his congregation to appear. In 39:6 the Elect One of righteousness and faith dwells under the wings of the Lord of spirits, and righteousness prevails in his day. In 62:1 the kings, the mighty, and those who dwell on the earth are told to open their eyes so that they can recognize the Elect One; then the Lord of Spirits seats the Elect One on the throne of his glory, the spirit of righteousness is poured upon him, his word slays sinners. In 61:5, 8, 10, there is a reference to the day of the Elect One when none shall be destroyed before the Lord of spirits; the Elect One is placed on the throne of glory to judge the works of all and is to summon all the host of heaven and the powers of the earth. In 55:4 we are told that the Elect One will judge Azazel (Satan) and his associates, in 52:6, 9 that the mountains will dissolve before his presence. In 51:5 the Elect One speaks the secrets of wisdom and counsel. In 49:2, 4 there is a reference to his everlasting glory and, once again, to his wisdom; the text bears affinity to Isa 11.

Thus, the Anointed One in the parables is judge of the world, revealer of all things, champion and ruler of the righteous, and raiser of the dead. Many of these characteristics bear little affinity to those of Jesus in the Gospels, but they are consonant with the four texts cited above (20:4, 6, 21:15, 12:10) concerning the Anointed One in Revelation.

A more prominent figure than the Anointed One in our text is the Lamb. In apocalyptic literature animals usually represent human beings and men represent angels. This obtains in Revelation except for the living creatures. The author of Revelation probably used the figure of a lamb to emphasize the human, as well as the divine, aspect of his character.

The elders fall down before him (5:8) and he is given praise and honor (5:13, 7:10). He is associated with the throne of the deity (5:6, cf. 7:9, 17, 21:1, 3), and possesses the book of life (13:8, 21:27). On the one hand he is associated with the angels (14:10), but on the other he is associated with the world. He opens the seals (5:9, 6:1), suggesting that he has power to reveal secrets. He stands on Mount Zion and the righteous follow him (14:1–4). The wicked war against him and he conquers them (17:14). His relationship with the people is referred to metaphorically as a marriage, suggesting alliance or covenant (19:7–9, 21:9). When the new city appears he is its lamp (21:23). It is written that people washed their robes in his blood (7:14) and gained victory on account of it (12:11).

Some of these features approximate those of the Son of Man (perhaps the equivalent of the Elect One) both in Dan 7 and the parables in I Enoch. The Lamb is the antithesis of the beasts which are a parody of him in Rev 13, just as one like a son of man is the antithesis of the beasts in Dan 7. Both the Lamb and one like a son of man are in the presence of God.

In I Enoch 71:14–17 the Son of Man is said to be "born unto righteousness and to possess the righteousness of the head of days" (i.e. God). He will proclaim peace in the name of the world to come, and people will find their dwelling place and length of days with him. I Enoch 69:26–29 speaks of the revelation of the name of the Son of Man, his being seated on the throne of his glory and receiving the sum of judgment, his destruction of sinners and all evil. In 62:5–14 the Son of Man sits on his throne of glory while the kings, the mighty ones, and those who possess the earth bless and glorify him. The Son of Man is spoken of as hidden from the beginning, preserved in the presence of the Most High, and then revealed to the elect who worship him. Sinners are delivered to the angels of punishment and become a spectacle for the righteous; cf. Rev 14:10. The righteous will eat with the Son of Man; cf. Rev 19:9. In 48:2 Enoch sees the fountains of wisdom from which the thirsty drank and where the Son of Man was named in the presence of the Lord of spirits; cf. Rev 7:17. In 46:2–4 Enoch sees with the Ancient of Days the Son of Man, whose countenance is that of a man but is full of graciousness like that of the angels. Enoch is told that the Son of Man reveals "all the treasures of that which is hidden, because the lord of spirits has chosen him," his lot has preeminence before the Lord of Spirits in uprightness forever; cf. Rev 5.

It would seem, therefore, that the author(s) of Revelation has been influenced by the characteristics of the Elect One and the Son of Man from I Enoch. These were the materials which shaped his portrayal of the Anointed, the Lamb, and perhaps the rider on the white horse (ch. 19). It is not unlikely that the Baptist and his disciples knew the Enoch literature, for portions of it have been found at Qumran and are cited in the NT. Indeed, I and II Enoch have nearly secured a place in the NT canon, so popular was Enoch with the early Christians. However, the parables of I Enoch have not yet been found at Qumran and Dr. Milik and Dr. Cross have argued for a late date.[15]

---

[15] Frank Moore Cross, *The Ancient Library of Qumran,* rev. ed. (Garden City, N.Y.: Doubleday, Anchor, 1961), pp. 201–3, fns. 6, 7. Milik, *Ten Years of Discovery in the Wilderness of Judea.*

More important, however, is that the author has introduced a new and vital element into the concept of the Son of Man by employing the metaphor of the Lamb. This image suggests that as well as sharing in some of the divine attributes he is also expected to be a human leader, since animals in apocalyptic literature represent human beings. Similar imagery is used in I Enoch, especially in chs. 89–90. In 90:38 the Messiah is a lamb who became a large animal with great black horns on his head; the Lord of the Sheep rejoiced over it. The Lamb in Revelation is associated with the Davidic Messiah in 5:5 by the title "the lion of the tribe of Judah, the root of David." Thus the author through his symbolism has introduced what was probably a novel element into Jewish thought, namely a divine-human Messiah. The only possible instance of such a figure in available Jewish literature occurs in 1QS adjunct 2:11, if the reading "when God begets the Messiah" is correct; the text is difficult to read. There is no Jewish tradition of a divine-human Messiah or Anointed One.

THE SON OF MAN

In comparing Revelation to the Gospels, one notices immediately that they differ in their concept of the Son of Man. The Gospels appear to use "the son of the man" as a title, whereas Revelation speaks of "one like a son of man." Linguistically the phrase differs from that which we find in the Greek OT where both "man" and "son" are usually anarthrous, that is, they appear without the definite article. In I Enoch the demonstrative case is employed and this appears to be equivalent to the definite article. But in Revelation only the phrase from Daniel, "one like a son of man," is used.

Moreover, in the Gospels the concept of the Son of Man is very frequent, whereas in the main body of Revelation, chs. 4–22, "one like a son of man" appears only twice. In 14:14, as explained at the beginning of the COMMENT on Section XI, he is seen among angelic beings rather than human. There is only one other occurrence in Revelation and that is in the Christian prefix, chs. 1–3, specifically in the first vision which the seer receives, Rev 1:12–20. This vision is a prelude to the prophecies to the churches, but even here the author retains the Danielic phrase.

In the Gospel of John the Son of Man seems to be interchangeable with the Son of God.[16] One notes that in Revelation the title "the Son of God" in 2:18 is closely associated with the vision of "one like the son of man." In the light of Christ's life the Christians may have associated all three titles, the Lamb, one like a son of man, and the Son of God, with Jesus. It is interesting to note that John the Baptist does not refer to "the

---

[16] See Edwin D. Freed, "The Son of Man in the Fourth Gospel," JBL 86 (1967), 402–9; Ford, "The Son of Man—A Euphemism," JBL 87 (1968), 257–66.

son of man"; rather, the evangelist ascribes the use of the title "Son of God (John 1:34)[17] to him and this is associated with the Lamb in John 1:29–34. The title "Son of God" does not occur in the main body of Revelation. It may be significant that only in the later portion, chs. 1–3, is the one like a son of man identified with the Son of God (Rev 2:18).

THE LORDSHIP OF JESUS CHRIST

Perhaps one of the most convincing arguments that Revelation is a Jewish work is the absence of the proclamation, Gr. *kerygma,* of the Lordship of Jesus, a feature central to Christianity. "Lord" is used twenty-two times in Revelation. In sixteen cases it refers to God.[18] Once it is used as a courtesy title for one of the elders (7:14). Its use in 11:18, discussed in the COMMENT on Section VIII, is ambiguous. It occurs twice in the phrase "Lord of Lords," which is another name for the Lamb in Rev 17:14 and the written Word of God in 19:16. In 17:14 the phrase referring to the Lamb is "Lord of Lords and King of Kings." In 19:16 the phrase is reversed: "King of Kings and Lord of Lords." The title is obviously influenced by that which was applied to the Roman emperor, but cf. also Deut 10:14 and I Enoch 9:4. Only at the conclusion of Revelation, which may be a Christian addition to the text, do we find "Lord" linked directly with the name of Jesus: "Lord Jesus," 22:20, 21. This is another difference from Christian apocalypses, save for the gospel apocalypse where one would not expect to find the title "Lord," first because the evangelists place the apocalypse in the mouth of Jesus himself and second because the title "Lord" in its fullest sense is normally not used of Jesus before his resurrection.

The concept of the lordship of Jesus is found in Didache 16:7–8 and the title "Lord" is included in the Georgian translation. It appears in the Shepherd of Hermas (Similitudes 6.6.1). The Ascension of Isaiah speaks of "my lord Christ who shall be called Jesus" (10:7), and the Apocalypse of Peter refers to "my Lord Jesus Christ, our king" (15) and "my Lord and God Jesus Christ" (16). Although the phrase is not explicit it is implied in Christian Sibyllines 6:1–3, 8:245–50. The phrase "Lord Jesus Christ" occurs in Apocalypse of Paul 21.[19]

---

[17] Although Brown, AB, vol. 29, 55–57, prefers the alternative reading, "God's chosen one."

[18] 1:10, 18, 4:8, 11, 11:4, 17, 15:3, 4, 16:7, 14, 19, 18:8, 19:6, 21:22, 22:5, 6. In eight cases, 1:8, 4:8, 11:17, 15:3, 16:7, 18:8, 21:22, 22:5, the two words are linked directly in the phrase "Lord God." In three other cases the words are linked but not as directly: "Lord and God," 4:11; "Lord our God," 19:6; "Lord, the God," 22:6.

[19] Translations of verses in the Ascension of Isaiah, the Apocalypse of Peter, and the Apocalypse of Paul come from Hennecke, II.

SUMMARY OF THE CHRISTOLOGY

There are approximately fourteen references to "Jesus Christ" or "Jesus" in Revelation; the one in 11:8 is ambiguous. Considering the length of the work, this may be statistically important when contrasted with the rest of the NT. There are 152 such references in Matthew, 82 in Mark, 86 in Luke, 252 in John, 70 in Acts, 38 in Romans, 26 in I Corinthians, 19 in II Corinthians, 18 in Galatians, 20 in Ephesians, 22 in Philippians, 26 in Colossians, 15 in I Thessalonians, 13 in II Thessalonians, 15 in I Timothy, 14 in II Timothy, 4 in Titus, 6 in Philemon, 13 in Hebrews, 2 in James, 9 in I Peter, 9 in II Peter, 12 in I John, 2 in II John, 7 in Jude. Further, most of the references to Jesus in Revelation do not occur in the main body of the work but rather in the beginning and the end, which may be Christian additions. Five of the references to Jesus could be omitted without any violation to the sense of the sentence and two occur in sections which may be interpolations. Further, "Christ" is never anarthrous and could refer to any anointed one among the Jews, either priest, prophet, or king. However, both the concept of the Anointed One or Messiah, and of the Lamb, bear affinity to what we know about the characteristics of one like a son of man in Daniel and the Son of Man and the Elect One in I Enoch. Moreover, the Lamb symbolism is used instead of the Son of Man symbolism in order to convey the idea of humanity as well as divinity. Both the Son of Man in Daniel and I Enoch and the Lamb in Revelation obviously possess sovereignty or lordship, but in Revelation this lordship is associated only twice with the name of Jesus (22:20, 21).

THE HISTORICAL JESUS

We have said that the use of the Lamb metaphor would suggest that the figure about whom our author writes bears not only divine characteristics but also human, and we have referred to his family origin which is implied in Rev 5:5, namely, that he comes from the house of David. In the light of this, it is remarkable that there are practically no unambiguous references to the earthly life of Jesus. The principal chapters which are thought to refer to the historical Jesus are 5, 11, and 12; these will be discussed in COMMENTS. Here we wish to contrast them with Christian apocalypses.

The Ascension of Isaiah refers to the incarnation (8:8–10, 9:13, 11:1–15), the crucifixion (9:14), and the resurrection (9:16). The Apocalypse of Peter refers to the crucifixion (2) and to the transfiguration or the ascension (17). The Sibylline Oracles refer to the birth

(1:323), the miracles, exorcisms, etc. (1:350–59), and the passion, resurrection, and ascension (1:360–79). They also contain a long description of the birth from Mary (8:456–79). These and other references are unmistakable and when compared with Revelation indicate undeniably that what few Christological references Revelation contains are ambiguous at best.

The Pneumatology

Revelation exhibits an almost complete absence of Christian pneumatology in even its primitive development as found in the earliest epistles of Paul where the apostle vacillates between the "person" of Jesus and the "person" of the Spirit. The chief mentions of the Spirit in Revelation are the seven at the end of the exhortations to each of the seven churches, although compare 14:13, 22:17. They are all in the same words: "he who has an ear, let him hear what the Spirit says to the churches." But this sentence does not seem to be a reference to the Spirit as a distinct person. The noun is not qualified with the adjective "holy," Gr. *hagios,* and the Spirit is identified with the speaker of the exhortation, i.e. one like a son of man. Therefore, the Spirit spoken of in these chapters (2–3) is probably not the distinct entity known as the Holy Spirit.

If it is agreed that chs. 1–3 are a Christian addition, the only other possible reference to the Holy Spirit is that in Rev 22:17: "the Spirit and the Bride say 'Come.'" Further, the allusion to the seven spirits of God in Rev 4:5 is a concept which we should not expect to find in a Christian work unless "spirits" are to be identified with angels. The idea seems to be even more primitive than the concept of the spirit as an angel or the confusion between the Son and the Spirit which is found, e.g., in the Shepherd of Hermas, Similitudes 9.1.1. In fact, the seven spirits of God might be more readily associated with the idea of the Lord of the Spirits, i.e. God, found frequently in I Enoch; cf. also II Macc 3:24.

Yet, in contrast to Revelation, the Christian apocalypses do mention the Holy Spirit. The Markan apocalypse, Mark 13 and its parallels, Matt 24, Luke 21:5–36, in a section about Christian persecution (Mark 13:9–13, Matt 10:17–22), mentions that the Holy Spirit will inspire the confessor; cf. also Luke 12:8–12. In Revelation the Holy Spirit is not found in the context of the persecution of those who will not worship the beast. The Spirit appears in the Shepherd of Hermas.[20] The Ascension of Isaiah mentions "the angel of the Holy Spirit and Michael, the chief of

---

[20] Mandates 5.1.2–3, 2.5, 10.2.1–6, 3.2–3, 11.8.9. Similitudes 5.6.5–6, 7.2, 9.1.1–2, 25.2.

the holy angels" (3:16), people speaking in the power of the Holy Spirit (3:19), the departure of the Holy Spirit from many because of slandering and boasting before the parousia (3:26), the ascent of the righteous to the seventh heaven by the angel of the Holy Spirit (7:23). The Apocalypse of Paul mentions the Spirit of God resting over the tree (of life) (45).

Further, there is no clear reference to the trinity in Revelation (in 1:4 the seven spirits are mentioned before Jesus is and are therefore probably not to be placed on a level with him and God, meaning that the text is binitarian), while Christian apocalypses do bear witness to the doctrine of the trinity. It is present in the teaching of the Shepherd of Hermas, which contains explicit references to God, the Son, and the Spirit (*passim*). The Ascension of Isaiah mentions "the Most High and His Beloved . . . the angel of the Holy Spirit" (7:23) and "the primal Father and His Beloved, Christ, and the Holy Spirit" (8:18). The Christian Sibyllines mention the "logos with the Father and the Holy Spirit" (7:69; cf. Apocalypse of Paul 41). In contrast, therefore, to these writings, Revelation seems to be more primitive.

THE ECCLESIOLOGY

Revelation is also lacking in the sphere of ecclesiology. The word *ekklesia,* "church," occurs only in the seven exhortations in Rev 2–3 and in Rev 22:16 (all included in what have been established as Christian additions), but not in the main body of the text. One might argue that ecclesiology is not to be expected in an apocalyptic work, but the fact is that Christian apocalypses do contain references to the church. The Shepherd of Hermas has a rich ecclesiology; we are told specifically that the woman and the tower represent the church. No similar elucidation is given of the woman in Rev 12 or with reference to the new Jerusalem. In the Shepherd of Hermas, Sim. 9.1.1–2, the church is holy, created by God, and at one point identified with the Holy Spirit. Moreover, if, the date of Revelation were late, perhaps between A.D. 89 and 95, one may well ask why there is no trace of early Catholicism, no mention of bishops, deacons, or deaconesses. The Shepherd of Hermas mentions leaders and various officers within the church, e.g. apostles, teachers, bishops, elders, deacons, and those who preside. Further, there is a section on true and false Christian prophets (Mand. 11.1–21). The Apocalypse of Peter speaks about those "whom we install in Thy church" (ch. 1). The Christian Sibyllines mention presbyters and deacons (2:264). The Apocalypse of Paul gives gruesome details about the punishment of a degenerate presbyter (34), a bishop (35), a deacon and a lector (36).

BAPTISM AND THE EUCHARIST

Although scholars have seen a reference to baptism or even confirmation in the seal of Rev 7 and have detected traces of the Eucharist liturgy in parts of Revelation,[21] the present writer can see no explicit reference to either of the Christian sacraments. In contrast, the Shepherd of Hermas appears to refer to baptism when it mentions the seal and water.[22] In Apocalypse of Paul 22 there is a reference to Michael's baptising repentant sinners in Lake Acherusia, a fiery river in Hades, but whether this is first baptism or not is uncertain. There is also an allusion to the sacrifice at the altar (the Eucharist) in chs. 34, 36, and to the "bread of the Eucharist and the cup of blessing" as the body and blood of Christ in ch. 41.

THE HYMNS

Comparing the hymns in Revelation[23] with other hymns in the NT[24] reveals a vast difference between the two. The hymns in Revelation do not contain any Christology; most of them are composed of OT phrases and are closer to Jewish liturgical hymns or to the canticles in the Lucan infancy narratives than they are to other NT hymns. They are discussed in the COMMENTS.

THE JEWS

In Revelation the Jews do not appear to be opponents as they are in such Christian works as the Gospel of John or Acts. The only references to Ioudaioi, "Jews," are in 2:9 and 3:9, where the people in the community are criticized for not being true Jews. Such a criticism might come from either a Jew or a Jewish Christian, but here it is probably from a Jewish Christian who believed that the only true Jews are those who receive Christ. There is no harsh polemic against Jews as there is, for ex-

---

[21] E.g. Shepherd, Jr., p. 83. Prigent, pp. 46–76.

[22] Similitudes 9.16.3–5, 16.4, 31.1; Visions 3.3.5, 7.3; Mandates 4.3.1.

[23] Rev 4:8, 11, 5:9–10, 7:15–17, 11:17–18, 15:3–4, 16:5–7, 18:2–3, 4–8, 10, 14, 16–17, 19–20, 21–24, 19:1–3, 5b, 6–8.

[24] E.g. Phil 2:5–11, I Tim 3:16, Col 1:15–20, and the tiny fragment in Eph 5:14.

ample, in VI Ezra, e.g. 41–78, or in the Epistle of Barnabas, e.g. 2:6, the abolition of Jewish sacrifices, and 4:7, the claim that the covenant is Christian and not Jewish.

Moreover, the persecution motif in Revelation lacks some of the features found in Mark 13, Matt 24, Luke 21, e.g. the flogging in the synagogues and bearing testimony before "them" and the Gentiles; cf. Mark 13:9, Luke 21:12–13. In the Shepherd of Hermas, although the word "martyr" is not used, the persecution is specifically said to be for the name (of Jesus); Visions 2.3.4, 3.2.1. The Leviathan that appears is symbolic of Christian persecution (Visions 4.1.1–10). The Apocalypse of Peter speaks about those who deny "him to whom our fathers gave praise (?), the first Christ whom they crucified and thereby sinned exceedingly . . ." (2). VI Ezra also mentions the persecution (chs. 41–78), and the elect referred to appear to be Christians.[25] The idea of persecution in Revelation has the atmosphere more of Maccabees or Zealots than of Christian affliction, e.g. the warlike heavenly apparitions in II Macc 2:21, 3:25–26, 30, 5:1–4, 11:8.

JEWISH APOCALYPSES WITH CHRISTIAN ADDITIONS

Revelation might be a Jewish apocalypse redacted by Christians who altered the text, as in ch. 22. Many Jewish apocalyptic works contained Christian interpolation. Here are some examples.

Commenting on the Books of Adam and Eve 29:7–10, Charles[26] declares that the verses are certainly Christian in origin; however, it is possible that certain Christian phrases were interpolated, e.g. in 29:7, 10, ". . . God will dwell with men on earth [in visible form] . . . And in that time, shall men be purified by water from their sins. But those who are unwilling to be purified by water shall be condemned." In the Books of Adam and Eve 42:2–5 there is a very clear Christian interpolation from the gospel of Nicodemus. This is much more Christian than any part of Revelation:

> When five thousand five hundred years have been fulfilled, then will come upon earth the most beloved king Christ, the son (sic) of God, to revive the body of Adam and with him to revive the bodies of the dead. He Himself, the Son of God, when He comes will be baptized in the

[25] See Hennecke, II, 689–90.
[26] APCh, II, 140. The bracketed words are the Christian interpolations.

River of Jordan, and when he hath come out of the water of Jordan, then He will anoint from the oil of mercy all that believe in Him. And the oil of mercy shall be for generation to generation for those who are ready to be born again of water and the Holy Spirit to life eternal. Then the most beloved Son of God, Christ, descending on earth shall lead thy father Adam to paradise to the tree of mercy.[27]

In the Martyrdom of Isaiah[28] Charles contends that Christian additions have been made, e.g. in 1:7 a reference to the Lord is expanded into a trinitarian concept by the addition of an allusion to "the Beloved of my Lord", cf. also 1:13.

The last verse of I Enoch (105:2) is an obvious Christian addition[29]:

For I and My Son will be united with them for ever in the paths of uprightness in their lives; and ye shall have peace: rejoice, ye children of uprightness. Amen.

The Testaments of the Twelve Patriarchs[30] show considerable Christian interpolation, to such an extent that de Jonge[31] formerly argued that the whole was Christian; he has now modified his thesis. The Testament of Simeon 6:5 reads:

Then the Mighty One of Israel shall glorify Shem,
For the Lord God shall appear on earth,
And Himself save men. [Restored Text]
Then shall Shem (mss. "Seth") be glorified,
For the Lord our God shall appear on earth as man
And Himself saves again. [Armenian, 3 mss.]

Testament of Simeon 6:7 reads:
Then shall I arise in joy,
And will bless the Most High because of His marvelous works,
[Because God hath taken a body and eaten with men and saved men].

The bracketed line is undeniably a Christian interpolation; cf. Testament of Asher 7:3; Testament of Dan 5:13, 6:9.

There are several Christian interpolations in the Testament of Levi, such as 2:11, "And by thee and Judah shall the Lord appear among men, saving every race of men," and 4:4, "And there shall be given to thee a blessing, and to all thy seed, Until the Lord shall visit all the Gentiles in His tender mercies forever." One Armenian and one Slavonic manuscript and two others read, "in His Son's tender mercies." One Armenian manuscript reads, "And it shall come to pass in the last days

---

[27] APCh, II, 144.   [28] APCh, II, 155–62.
[29] APCh, II, 277.   [30] APCh, II, 282–367.
[31] M. de Jonge, *The Testaments of the Twelve Patriarchs: A Study of Their Text, Composition and Origin,* Assen, 1953.

that God shall send [His Son] to save the created things [and thy sons shall lay hands on and crucify Him]."[32]

Another clear Christian interpolation (in brackets) appears in 10:2:

And behold I am clear from your ungodliness and transgression, which ye shall commit in the end of ages [against the Saviour of the world, Christ, acting godlessly] . . .

Still another appears in 14:2:

For our father Israel is pure from the transgression of the chief priests [who shall lay their hands upon the Saviour of the world].

There may be another addition in 16:3:

[And a man who reneweth the law and the power of the Most High, ye shall call a deceiver; and at last ye shall rush (upon him) to slay him, not knowing his dignity, taking innocent blood through wickedness upon your heads.]

However, this may refer to an Onias (cf. Josephus *Antiquities* [*Ant.*] 14.22, Dan 9:26, 11:22, II Macc 4:33–36), a righteous man who was stoned to death because he would not do evil. A further Christian section is found at the end of Testament of Levi 16:5:

And ye shall have no place that is clean; but ye shall be among the Gentiles a curse and a dispersion until He shall again visit you, and in pity shall receive you [through faith and water].

Finally, there is a resemblance between the baptismal scene in Matt 3:16–17 and Testament of Levi 18:6–7

The heavens shall be opened,
And from the temple of glory shall come upon him sanctification,
With the Father's voice as from Abraham to Isaac.
And the glory of the Most High shall be uttered over him,
And the spirit of understanding and sanctification shall rest upon him [in the water].

Charles,[33] however, suggests that it may refer to Hyrcanus who received a *Bath Qol,* a Hebrew phrase inferring a voice from God, cf. *Ant.* 13.282–83, and meaning literally "daughter of a voice."

The Testament of Naphtali 8:3 also shows what might be Christian influence:

For through their tribes shall God appear [dwelling among men] on earth, To save the race of Israel . . .

A notable Christian adaptation or perhaps complete interpolation is found in Testament of Joseph 19:8: "And I saw that [from Judah was born] a virgin [wearing a linen garment, and from her] was born a lamb,

[32] APCh, II, 307.   [33] APCh, II, 314.

[without spot] . . ." (Slavonic). "And I saw in the midst of the horns a virgin [wearing a many-coloured garment, and from her] went forth a lamb . . ." (Armenian). As Charles states,[34] the virgin does clash with the animal symbolism found in this chapter, and "a bull-calf became a lamb" would be a more plausible rendering.

An even clearer interpolation is found in the same chapter, vs. 11b. The Slavonic text reads, ". . . honour Levi and Judah; for from them shall arise unto you [the Lamb of God, who taketh away the sin of the world] one who saveth all the Gentiles and Israel.

In two Slavonic manuscripts of Testament of Benjamin 3:8 a similar interpolation occurs:

> In thee shall be fulfilled the prophecy of heaven [concerning the Lamb of God and Saviour of the world], and that a blameless one shall be delivered up for lawless men, and a sinless one shall die for ungodly men [in the blood of the covenant, for the salvation of the Gentiles and of Israel, and shall destroy Beliar and his servants].

In Testament of Benjamin 9:2 (cf. Luke 9:12, 18:32) there is another Christian addition:

> Nevertheless the temple of God shall be in your portion, and the last (temple) shall be more glorious than the first. And the twelve tribes shall be gathered together there, and all the Gentiles, until the Most High shall send forth His salvation in the visitation of the only-begotten prophet (some mss. have "His only betotten Son") [and He shall enter into the (first) temple, and there shall the Lord be treated with outrage, and He shall be lifted up upon a tree. And the veil of the temple shall be rent, and the Spirit of God shall pass onto the Gentiles as fire poured forth. And He shall ascend from Hades and shall pass from earth into heaven. And I know how lowly he shall be upon earth, and how glorious in heaven.] (Two Slavonic mss.)
>
> But in your portion shall be His inheritance. And on account of the temple of the Lord, Jacob exalted me that I should be glorified through it. And the twelve tribes shall be gathered there and all the Gentiles. [And the Lord shall be treated with outrage and set at nought. And He will depart from earth to heaven: for I knew you how he is on earth and how in heaven, or what is His measure and place and way.] (Armenian)

A further interpolation occurs in Testament of Benjamin 10:7-9:

> Then shall we also rise, each one over our tribe, worshipping the King of heaven, [who appeared upon earth in the form of a man in humility. And as many as believe on (*sic*) Him on the earth shall rejoice with Him.] Then also all men shall rise, and some unto glory and some unto shame.
>
> And the Lord shall judge Israel first, for their unrighteousness; [for

---

[34] APCh, II, 353.

when He appeared as God in the flesh to deliver them they believed Him not]. And then shall He judge all the Gentiles, [as many as believed Him not when He appeared upon earth]. (Two Slavonic mss.)

Then shall we also rise, each over our own tribe, and we shall worhsip the heavenly King.

Then shall we all be changed, some into glory and some into shame; for the Lord judges Israel first for the unrighteousness which they have committed.

And then so (shall He judge) all the Gentiles. (Armenian)

For many of these texts, there is another version which omits the interpolation.

Christian interpolations are also found in the Jewish Sibyllines 5:256–59, III Baruch 12–17, Psalms of Solomon, esp. 17–18.[35]

It has been submitted above that Revelation is not a typically Christian apocalypse. When compared with the Christian interpolations into Jewish texts quoted above, the ones in the body (chs. 4–22) of Revelation, e.g. 5, 11:8, 12, are not so patently Christian. It can therefore be said that the body of Revelation fits neither into the category of Christian apocalypse nor into that of Jewish apocalypse with Christian additions.

THE UNIQUENESS OF REVELATION

One may compare the Revelation of John with Jewish apocalypses and find many similarities, e.g. animal symbolism, numerology, throne scenes, sealing, tribes, the new Jerusalem (an idea found among the Montanists, who expected the new Jerusalem to descend at Pepuza, but not stressed in primitive Christianity), two resurrections, the idea of the Messiah, the millennium. The harlot, as will be seen, is also a Jewish OT theme depicting Jerusalem. Further, ch. 11 is concerned with the temple and the ark of the covenant, both themes of interest to Jews, especially the Maccabees (II Macc 2:1–8), but superseded in the Christian dispensation.

Ch. 12 appears to be directed toward the first coming of the "Messiah;" although the woman's child is not explicitly said to be the Messiah. The beasts of ch. 13 stand in the same relationship to the Lamb as the beasts in Daniel to one like the son of man and the Ancient of Days (God). Ch. 14 refers to Mount Zion rather than the Mount of Olives which is mentioned in two Christian apocalypses, that of Peter, ch. 1, and that of Paul, ch. 51. Rev 15 refers to the temple and the tent of witness; these allusions do not occur in Christian apocalypses. In ch. 16 the seven angels come out of

[35] APCh, II, 402, 540–41, 625–52, esp. 647–52.

the temple. Ch. 17 appears to refer to the faithless Jerusalem and there is no clear indication that Babylon is Rome as in the Christian Sibyllines. The rider on the white horse in ch. 19 is called the Word of God; he is not identified with the Son of God or with Jesus but is far closer to the Word of God in the Exodus Midrash in Wisd Sol 18.

Further, one finds, in contrast to the Christian apocalypses, a predominance of allusions to the OT. According to Krister Stendahl:

> We have already established that texts of apocalyptic nature seldom contain quotations in the strict sense, while at the same time, it is just these texts which are abounding in allusions which with supreme freedom and skill have been woven into the context. Revelation is itself a striking example of this. Without a single true quotation, it is nevertheless interwoven with O.T. material to a greater extent than any other writing in the N.T. In the apocalypses of the gospels, as in their sayings of apocalyptic nature, we have the same phenomenon. Consequently, there is no attempt to quote exactly in this form, and the citing is certainly freely given from memory. The prophetic spirit creates, it does not quote in order to teach or argue.[36]

Revelation 4–22 has over four hundred allusions to the OT in contrast to significantly fewer ones to the NT (see below, p. 42). Moreover, it shows a heavy influence from Jewish apocalyptic works but very little from the Christian apocalypses. Clearly, Revelation is more akin to Jewish apocalyptic literature than to Christian.

An analogy might be made with an early interpretation of the Qumran scrolls. Some years ago Abbé Carmignac replied to Professor Dupont-Sommer's extravagant claims that the Dead Sea scrolls contained a pre-Christian Christianity.[37] He showed the paucity of unequivocal references to the Teacher of Righteousness and demonstrated that the scrolls must be examined objectively, not with a Christian bias. One wonders whether a similar fate befell Revelation. Indeed, if one placed this apocalypse in the hands of a non-Christian reader what would he or she learn about the Christian *kerygma*, "proclamation," or *didache*, "teachings"? Have Christian scholars presupposed a Christological interpretation and performed an isogesis such as would not be acceptable for other biblical texts either in the OT or the NT? This question applies especially to Rev 5, 11, 12. Can we fail to take into consideration the fact that practically all the apocalyptic works of the first century and earlier are Jewish, most of them with Christian adaptation?

We have seen that Revelation is unlike Jewish apocalypses adapted to Christianity because there are no clear Christian interpolations woven into the text; rather, a block of Christian material (chs. 1–3) has been

---

[36] Stendahl, *The School of St. Matthew*, pp. 158–59.
[37] Carmignac et al., *Textes de Qumrân.*

grafted onto the beginning and four Christian verses (22:16–17a, 20–21) have been grafted onto the end. Neither shows the NT Christ. Revelation is therefore unique.

THE AUTHORSHIP OF REVELATION

Who, then, was the author of this apocalypse? The writer gives his name as John in four places: Rev 1:1, 4, 9, 22:8. Nowhere does he claim to be one of the twelve apostles. The fact that he refers to himself as "John" in contrast to the description "the disciple whom Jesus loved" in John 19:26 arouses doubt that he was the evangelist, although early Church tradition supported this.

One point is clear; in Revelation "John" is presented as prophet (1:3, 22:19). The book is prophetic. The author not only speaks the language of the prophets of Israel but also assumes one of the missions of the prophets, namely, an insistence on monotheism. Further, he incorporates one of the characteristics of later prophecy, namely, the reinterpretation of the classical prophets, in the same way as, e.g. Daniel (cf. 9:1–27) or the Teacher of Righteousness at Qumran whom God enables to explain "all the words of his servants the prophets" (1QpHab 7:4–5). The author's work reveals an allusive theology similar to that which one finds in the infancy narratives of Luke. It is, as it were, a contemplation on some of the most arresting OT citations which he weaves into a new pattern to herald the dawn of a new age. When considering, then, who the author or originator of Revelation might have been, one needs to look for a Jew who was firmly grounded in the prophetical tradition of Israel, one who believed in the imminence of the Kingdom which would usher in "He that cometh" and the "Day of the Lord"; cf. Matt 3:2–3. The candidate who seems most suitable is John the Baptist.

John the Baptist, without doubt, was regarded as a prophet *par excellence* (cf. Matt 11:9) and some, indeed, wondered whether he was the Messiah (Luke 3:15). In John 1:19–23 the Baptist denies that he is the Messiah, Elijah, or the prophet, and answers in the words of Isaiah that he is "a voice in the desert crying out . . ." (vs. 23, AB). Either the evangelists or John the Baptist himself reinterpret Isa 40:3–5 and apply the text to the contemporary situation Mark 1:1–5, Matt 3:1–6, Luke 3:1–6), indicating that John is associated with prophecy in the form of reinterpretation of Scripture.

In the view of many Jews prophecy had ceased after the Persian period but in the intertestamental period there was an expectation of one prophet who would come with the arrival of the new age; cf. I Macc 4:45–46, Testament of Benjamin 9:2. Some identified this prophet with Elijah or Moses. The identification with Elijah is found in Mal 3:23–24 (4:5–6) which speak of Elijah coming before the Day of the Lord. Mal 3:1–4 may refer to the same person, namely, the "messenger of the covenant." He will purify the temple and its cult before the Lord comes in judgment. Sir 48:9–10 (RSV) elaborates this expectation:

> You who were taken up by a whirlwind of fire,
> in a chariot of horses of fire;
> you who are ready at the appointed time, it is written,
> to calm the wrath of God before it breaks out in fury,
> to turn the heart of the father to the son,
> and to restore the tribes of Jacob.

Some identified Jesus with Elijah (Mark 6:15, 8:28, Matt 16:14, Luke 9:8, 19) but Jesus Himself pronounced him to be the Baptist (Matt 11:13–15, AB):

> For all the prophets, and the Law up to John, prophesied. If you wish to accept it, he is the expected Elijah. Let him who has understanding listen.

(Compare Matt 11:15 with the endings of the prophecies to the seven churches[38]). Similar sentiments identifying the Baptist with Elijah are expressed in Mark 9:11, Matt 17:10–13. C. H. H. Scobie[39] may be right when he says:

> Prophecy was dead; its rebirth will be a sign of the new age. It is quite wrong therefore to speak of someone claiming to be 'merely a prophet' in contrast to someone claiming to be 'a Messianic figure'. Anyone who claimed to be *a* prophet was automatically claiming to be *the* prophet. Anyone claiming to be a prophet was claiming to be the Messianic figure, not in the sense that he was the Messiah himself, but in the sense that he was preparing for the ushering in of the new age.

Jesus, therefore, in making this assertion about his kinsman (cf. the infancy narratives of Luke 1–2, esp. 2:76–79) was claiming nothing insignificant for him. The evangelists regard John as the eschatological prophet, Mark 1:2–8 associating him with Mal 3:1 and Isa 40:3. That the people themselves so regarded John is seen from the statement of Matt 14:5, AB, "But although he [Herod] wanted to put him [John] to death, he was afraid of the common people, who regarded him as a prophet"; cf. also Mark 11:27–33, Matt 21:23–27, Luke 20:1–8.

Although John himself does not explicitly state that he is a prophet, the circumstances of his ministry suggest this. It takes place in the wilderness, which has eschatological associations. His dress is the traditional garment of a prophet, the hair mantle identical to that of Elijah which was inherited by Elisha; see I Kings 19:19, II Kings 2:13–14, cf. Zech 13:4. The import of John's message was prophetic; he called people to repentance, warned of impending judgment, and spoke of preparing the way before the Lord. Indeed, he amply fulfilled the prediction of his father Zechariah (Luke 1:76–79, RSV):

And you, child, will be called the prophet of the Most High;
for you will go before the Lord to prepare his ways,
to give knowledge of salvation to his people
in the forgiveness of their sins,
through the tender mercy of our God,
when the day shall dawn upon us from on high
to give light to those who sit in darkness and in the shadow of death,
to guide our feet into the way of peace.

Cumulative evidence indicates that the Baptist's prophetic calling was recognized, respected, and feared. It would therefore be surprising if some disciple or disciples had not troubled to record and preserve his message. It is our contention that this is the origin of Revelation. Not only does the Baptist's teaching not conflict with the message of our apocalypse, but it has certain themes in common.

REVELATION AND TRADITIONS ABOUT THE BAPTIST

THE LAMB

The image of the Lamb of God, applied to Jesus, is found only in the Gospel sections which are associated with John the Baptist. In John 1:29, 36, John the Baptist uses the title "the Lamb of God" directly with reference to Christ, but he does not explicitly associate Christ with the suffering servant of Isaiah (Isa 42:1–9, 49:1–13, 50:4–11, 52:13–53:12) or, indeed, with suffering at all. In other words, there is no indication that the Baptist knew that the one who came after him would suffer and die. Although the Lamb in Revelation is seen as though slain (5:6) and the effect of his blood is to cleanse (7:14) we are not given any details about his death. This forms a contrast to the lamb image in Acts 8:32 and perhaps I Peter 1:19, although in these texts the actual title "Lamb of God" is not used. In the Greek I Cor 5:7 the word "lamb" does not occur. The Lamb in John 1:29, 36, might point to the paschal lamb but the most likely interpretation is that John used the phrase with reference to the apocalyptic Lamb.[40]

Jewish apocalyptic works predict a conquering lamb who will appear in the days of the final judgment and will destroy evil. Testament of Joseph

[40] See C. H. Dodd, pp. 230–38.

19:8 shows the lamb conquering the beasts; in I Enoch 90:38 the horned bull changes into a lamb with black horns and the Lord of the sheep rejoices over it. In Revelation 6:16 there is a reference to the wrath of the Lamb. The Lamb is represented as shepherd and leader in 7:17, stands on Mount Zion in 14:1, and overcomes his enemies in 17:14. He is associated with God and His throne in 5:6, 7:9–10, 21:22, 22:1–3.

The idea of the apocalyptic, victorious, and destroying lamb is consonant with the fierce preaching of John the Baptist. The concept of the Lamb of God taking away sin is also consistent with the thought of Revelation. As Brown[41] suggests, the reference may be to the destruction of the world's sin or the devil's works; cf. I John 3:8. Brown concludes "thus, we suggest that John the Baptist hailed Jesus as the lamb of Jewish apocalyptic expectation who was raised up by God to destroy evil in the world, a picture not too far from that of Rev 17:14."[42]

"HE THAT COMETH"

Save for the quotation from Ps 118 in Matt 21:9, 23:39, Luke 19:38, John 12:13 (Blessed is the King of Israel that cometh, KJ), the phrase "He that cometh" as a title occurs only in the sections of the NT, primarily in the Gospels, which are related to the Baptist,[43] and in Revelation. John proclaims the Coming One will be the judge holding the winnowing fork in his hand and separating the wheat from the chaff (Matt 3:12, Luke 3:17). A similar picture occurs in Rev 14:14–16, which depicts one like a son of man holding a sickle who reaps the earth.

The Synoptic Gospels describe "He That Cometh" as "mightier than I"; see fn. 43. Walter Grundmann[44] interprets this phrase in the light of the only other NT text where the epithet "mightier," Gr. ischuroteros, occurs, namely, Luke 11:20–22. Here the Mightier One would seem to be the Messiah who overcomes the strong man, that is, Satan. Whereas Grundmann suggests that the phrase "divides his spoil" (Luke 11:22, RSV) is based on Isa 53:12, one might observe that the phrases used with reference to arms, assailing, attacking, and spoil suggest a fighting figure such as we find both in the Lamb (Rev 17:14) and the rider on the white horse (Rev 19:11–16). As Scobie[45] observes there is no evidence that the title "mightier one" was messianic. However, the word "mighty" can be applied to a person given special powers by God, e.g.

---

[41] R. Brown, The Gospel According to John, I-XII, pp. 59–60.

[42] Ibid., p. 60. Cf. also Dodd, pp. 230–38.

[43] Mark 1:7; Matt 3:11; Luke 3:16, 7:19–20; cf. also John 6:14, 11:27; Acts 19:4; Heb 10:37. Acts 19:14 is associated with the Baptist's disciple but Heb 10:37 is a citation from Hab 2:3–4.

[44] Cited by Scobie, p. 64.

[45] Scobie, p. 64 ff.

Isa 9:6 and Psalms of Solomon 17:43–44, both of which refer to a messianic figure. This unique title, therefore, may express a peculiar Baptist concept of the messianic figure. "Coming" may bear an eschatological sense of coming to make a visitation. In the Baptist's mind "He that cometh" is an awe-inspiring figure whose sandals one is not worthy to touch or before whom one may not wear sandals.[46]

BAPTISM BY FIRE

Another theme seldom found in the NT except in the passages about John the Baptist in the Gospel of John and in Revelation is the concept of baptism by fire. In Matthew and Luke, but not in Mark, the Baptist predicts "He that cometh" will baptize with the Holy Spirit and with fire (Matt 3:11, Luke 3:16; cf. Mark 1:8). Significantly, however, the concept of baptism "with fire" is omitted in Acts (1:5, 11:16) when the saying about baptism with the Holy Spirit is attributed to the risen Christ, not to John. It is also omitted from John 1:33, which was written later than Acts 1:5, 11:16. The baptism with fire, therefore, may have been a peculiarly Baptist teaching but not perpetrated by Jesus, although it is true that Jesus does refer to eschatological fire, e.g. in his parables as recorded in Matt 13:40, 42, 50, cf. Matt 5:22, 7:19, 18:8, 9, 25:41, Luke 12:49.

Biblical references to fire occur for the most part in OT and seldom in the NT. Of those in the NT, the majority (twenty-five) are found in Revelation; cf. the use of fire images in the vision of "one like a son of man" in Rev 1:12–16. In the OT, baptism by fire is a judgment. In the NT, baptism with fire is a purification, e.g. the "tongues as of fire" at Pentecost in Acts 2:3. Unlike the rest of the NT, with the possible exception of the Gospel of John, a major theme of Revelation is not purification but judgment; therefore, in this apocalypse it is probable that baptism by fire is a baptism of judgment.

Perhaps the Baptist imagined the character of "He that cometh" as akin to that of Elijah who called down fire upon the Samaritans (II Kings 1:10–14; cf. Luke 9:51–56). Further, John's reference to baptism by fire may be related to his other allusions to fire, e.g. the trees thrown onto the fire (Matt 3:10, Luke 3:9), the chaff burnt with unquenchable fire (Matt 3:12, Luke 3:17), the vipers escaping from a desert fire (Matt 3:7, Luke 3:7). John is well within the OT tradition, especially the apocalyptic (cf. Amos 7:4, Ezek 38:22, Mal 4:1, Isa 31:9, Sir 7:17, 16:6, 21:9. The same concept occurs in the apocalyptic and Qumran literature, e.g. I Enoch 90:24–26, Psalms of Solomon 15:6, 1QS 2:8, 1QH 3:27–32. Scobie[47] also draws attention to the river of fire "from before" God in

---

[46] P. G. Bretscher, JBL 86 (1967), 81–87.
[47] *John the Baptist,* pp. 68 f.

Dan 7:9, 10, and the fiery stream which destroys the enemies of "one like a son of man" in IV Ezra 13:10.

Kraeling[48] thinks there is an influence from Persian eschatology in which "the mountains which are made of metal melt at the end of the world, and the molten metal pours over the earth like a river. All men pass into this river of molten metal and in doing so are either purified or destroyed." However, there seems to be no reference to the good passing through fire in the NT; they endure fiery ordeals but fire seems to be associated with Gehenna. Revelation portrays the closest parallel in the idea of fire descending upon all men to test and purify them (Rev 8:5, 7, 8, 9:17, 18, 14:18, 16:8; cf. II Peter 3:7, 10).

THE BRIDEGROOM

Revelation, although it does not explicitly call the Lamb bridegroom, does speak of his nuptial relations; 19:9, 21:9–14. The Greek word *numphē*, "bride," occurs four times in this apocalypse. In the rest of the NT it occurs only in the Q source[49] concerning domestic disturbance (Matt 10:35, Luke 12:53) and in the parable of the ten virgins (Matt 25:1, cf. 22:1). Gr. *numphios*, "Bridegroom," occurs only in Matt 9:15, Mark 2:19–20, Luke 5:34–35, John 3:29. The synoptic texts use the word *numphios* in the context of a question raised about the disciples of John the Baptist, not Jesus' disciples. The Johannine Gospel yields a direct identification of Jesus as bridegroom pronounced by the Baptist himself. The only other occurrences of "bridegroom" are in the parable of the ten virgins in Matthew and in the story of the marriage feast at Cana, John 2:9. Therefore, as an image applied to Jesus the bridegroom occurs only in the sources related to the Baptist. In John 3:29 the Baptist is clearly referred to as the "best man" (AB) and Jesus is bridegroom at his first coming, the incarnation, not the parousia. It is interesting to observe that the theme of Christ as bridegroom is elaborated in an epistle probably written to Ephesus (Eph 5), a city where there were disciples of John (Acts 19).

MINOR BAPTIST AFFINITIES

One may find smaller affinities between the traditions about John the Baptist and Revelation. His message is radically different from that of Jesus; John's is one of wrath and doom rather than salvation. The Baptist speaks about the wrath, Gr. *orgē*, to come (Matt 3:7, Luke 3:3) and, if John 3:36 is attributed to the Baptist, he refers also to the "wrath of

---

[48] Carl H. Kraeling, *John the Baptist* (New York: Scribner's, 1951), p. 117.
[49] That is, the Quelle source, the material common to Matthew and Luke but not found in Mark.

God." Otherwise, *orgē* does not occur in the Gospels save in Luke 21:23, which may be part of a Jewish apocalypse. The word does not appear in the teaching of Jesus. It is a theme, however, of great importance in Revelation, which contains both words for "wrath," *orgē* and *thumos*. A special references to the wrath of the Lamb occurs in Rev 6:16–17.[50]

Revelation contains both the Baptist's unconcealed hostility towards the priests and others from Jerusalem and his description of the contemporary generation as "adulterous." These attitudes are consistent with the Jerusalem-harlot theme in the apocalypse. Indeed, the cleansing of the adulterous Jerusalem by punishment and the rise of a purified city would fulfill the vision in Mal 3:1–4 of the messenger of the covenant purifying the temple and its cult. If the Baptist, like Jesus, anticipated the fall of Jerusalem (cf. Luke 20:41–44, 21:27–31), then Rev 12–22 expresses this prediction; the purification would be the fulfillment of the prophetic word.

John uses the symbolism of "tree," probably as a metaphor for the leaders of the people; Matt 3:10, Luke 3:9; cf. Matt 7:16–20, 12:33–35. Trees, oaks, and cedars, were used as metaphors for leaders of the people. In Isa 61:3 "oaks of righteousness" (AB) is interpreted as "princes of righteousness" in the Targum. Isa 2:13, "And upon all the cedars of Lebanon" (KJ), appears as "upon all the strong and mighty kings of the nations, and upon all the princes . . ."; cf. 1QH 8, Psalms of Solomon 14:3–4. In 1QH 8 "trees by the waters" could have been taken from Ezek 31:14 to represent the proud and the wicked who will be condemned—they will sink like lead into the mighty waters and shall be a prey to fire and be dried up. The tree as a symbol of men is used in the Baptist's preaching and in Q but does not occur elsewhere in the Gospels. However, it does occur in Jude 12 and Rev 7:1, 3, 8:7, 9:4; see COMMENTS.

Because Revelation reflects intimate knowledge of the liturgy and the temple, its author was probably a priest as well as a prophet. John the Baptist came from a priestly family. The prophet was expected to be a forerunner, not only of the Messiah, but of God Himself. Revelation portrays the action of God more vividly than it does the Messiah or even the Lamb.

Of the nine elements common to both the Gospel tradition concerning John and Revelation, five can be found elsewhere, primarily in the OT, in which John the Baptist was well versed. These are divine wrath, adultery, corrupt Jerusalem, trees as metaphors for leaders, and priestly knowledge. The other four the Lamb, "He that cometh," baptism by fire, the bridegroom—could have been adapted from OT tradition, but they

---

[50] For a full discussion of wrath see Bishop Anthony Hanson, *The Wrath of the Lamb*, London: SPCK, 1957.

appear exclusively in the Gospel material concerning John and in Revelation. This evidence indicates that the author of Revelation in all probability was John the Baptist. No doubt the apocalypse was expanded, and perhaps even first written down, by his disciples. Probably they all shared his explosive temperament, as did the two sons of Zebedee, John and James, who were nicknamed the *Boanerges,* a Greek word meaning "sons of thunder or rage" (Mark 3:7; cf. Mark 10:35–40, Luke 9:54).

The Baptist had previously taught about "He that cometh." In John 1:30 he says: "It is he about whom I said, 'After me is to come a man (Gr. *anēr*) who ranks ahead of me, for he existed before me'" (AB). He has an exalted idea about the one whom he heralds, and perhaps even intimates his preexistence; cf. John 1:1–5, 8:58, 17:5. Even if John did not reach this point of sophistication theologically, he could, as J. A. T. Robinson argues,[51] be thinking of Elijah with whom he may have identified Jesus; in this case Elijah would have been before John in time. "The one to come" might have been a designation for Elijah based on Mal 3:1, ". . . behold he is coming . . ." (RSV); cf. Mal 3:2, 4:1; Sir 48:1. If, however, the substance of John 3:31–36 is to be attributed to the Baptist, he would, as he does, express belief in the heavenly origin of "He that cometh" and his sonship to the Father. The former would not conflict with the characteristics of the Lamb and the rider on the white horse. The latter would conform to Rev 2:18.

In John 1:20–27 the Baptist averred the Messiah was already in the world. But not until the Spirit descended upon Jesus was John able to recognize him and testify, "this is God's son" (John 1:33–34). (Some authorities support the reading "the chosen one."[52]) Here God's testimony is not given to Jesus (cf. Matt 3:16) but to the Baptist (cf. John 5:33–35, AB):

> You have sent to John,
> and he has testified to the truth.
> (Not that I myself accept such human testimony—
> I simply mention these things for your salvation.)
> He was the lamp, set aflame and burning bright,
> and for a while you yourselves willingly exulted in his light.

Brown[53] observes that in the reference to the lamp there may be an echo of the picture of Elijah found in Sir 48:1, RSV "Then the prophet Elijah arose like a fire, and his word burned like a torch." Brown also considers the lampstands in Rev 11:4 to be imagery clearly drawn from Elijah's

[51] John A. T. Robinson, *Twelve New Testament Studies* (Naperville, Ill.: Allenson, 1962), pp. 28–52.
[52] P⁵ᵛⁱᵈ ℵ* itᵇ,ᵉ,ff2* Syrᶜ, ˢ Ambrose.
[53] AB, vol. 29, p. 224.

career. He draws attention to Josephus, *Ant.* 18.116–18, who confirms the enthusiasm with which the Baptist was received by the people.

Therefore, Revelation must have grown out of the type of apocalyptic expectation entertained by the Baptist and his disciples and some other Jews. As with all prophecies the danger is not so much in pronouncement as in misinterpretation. John may have been a prophet like Ezekiel or Daniel. However, the subject of his predictions was obscure to him and his disciples. Although John predicted "He that cometh" was greater than he and existed before him, when Jesus did appear John was amazed at his conduct. Hence, when John was imprisoned by Herod, he sent his disciples to Jesus with the question: "Are you the Coming One, or are we to look for someone else?" (Matt 11:3, AB).

John probably anticipated a figure like Elijah, a man of fire, power, and perhaps vengeance in the OT style. When Jesus appeared bearing a different mien, John was surprised perhaps in the same way as those who rejected the Lord at Nazareth because of his clemency, especially towards the Gentiles.

As Jeremias has shown, Jesus removed the idea of vengeance from the eschatological expectation and promised the Gentiles (e.g. Matt 11:4–6), even the Ninevites, those of Tyre and Sidon, and those of Sodom and Gomorrah, a share in salvation. When Jesus answered the Baptist's question about his identity as the "Coming One" (Matt 11:5–6) he omitted the day of vengeance, as he did at Nazareth (Luke 4:16–19). Jesus had a theology of, not a mission towards, the Gentiles, but of this both the Baptist's preaching and this apocalypse are innocent. It is significant that Jesus in his reply to John cites a beatitude, "Fortunate is the man who does not find me a stumbling block" (Matt 11:6, AB), meaning that "the Messianic age wears a different aspect from what he had expected."[54] This beatitude is in contrast to the beatitudes in Rev 1:3, 14:13, 16:15, 19:9, 20:6, 22:7, 22:14.

In Matthew it is after this beatitude that Jesus utters his eulogy of John (11:7–15) as a man of strength and austerity who is considered more than a prophet (11:9), the messenger in fulfillment of Mal 3:1, etc. Yet Jesus tempers this praise by saying that the least in the kingdom is greater than the Baptist (vs. 11), by speaking of "violence" and the kingdom at the time of John (vs. 12). Finally, Jesus pronounces John to be Elijah, and concludes with the phrase, "Let him who has understanding (literally, an ear to hear) listen" (vs. 15, AB). This formula occurs throughout Rev 2–3. Matthew completes the whole pericope with the Song of Jubilation, Matt 11:25–27, in which Jesus praises God for having hidden the mysteries of the Kingdom from the wise and revealed them to babes. Thus these passages, while commending the Baptist, also present

---

[54] Jeremias, *Jesus' Promise to the Nations,* pp. 40–54.

a marked difference between him and Jesus, his concepts and those of the Lord.

John was the forerunner and Jesus "He that cometh." Thus some, perhaps many, of the Baptist's disciples left him to follow Jesus (John 1:35-51) and these disciples are called followers of the Lamb (John 1:35-37, cf. Rev 14:4b-5; see COMMENT). When the Gospel of John describes the gathering of Jesus' first disciples, Philip says to Nathanael, "We have found the very one described, in the Mosaic Law and the prophets—Jesus, son of Joseph, from Nazareth" (John 1:45, AB).

Indeed, it has been computed[55] that in the 404 verses of Revelation, 518 OT citations and allusions are found, 88 of which are from Daniel and 278 from reminiscences of Scripture, especially (besides Daniel) Isaiah, Jeremiah, Ezekiel, Zechariah, Psalms, and Exodus. Revelation is, accordingly, a rereading of the OT, perhaps a reflection not wholly different from the study of Scripture at Qumran; 1QS 6:6-8. If this is the work of John and his disciples, OT references would not have been considered sufficient. The apocalypse needed further elucidation by the events of the life, death, resurrection, and exaltation of Christ.

To recapitulate, we propose, therefore, that Revelation emanates from the circle of the Baptist and his disciples. Chs. 4–11 originated with the revelations given to the Baptist before and during the time he recognized Jesus as "He that cometh." Because chs. 12–22 actually contain the name of Jesus (14:12, 17:6, 19:10 (bis), 20:4, 22:16), they were probably written by a disciple who knew more than John. His knowledge perhaps amounted to the same as the disciples at Ephesus (Acts 19) or that of Apollos, the Scripture scholar (Acts 18). He knew about the Jewish War but he could have done so even if he wrote from Ephesus. He foresaw, like many previous prophets, the fall of Jerusalem and entertained the hope of a new city which was realized in the Christian Church. The Church could not become the central focus of Christian thought until Jerusalem had fallen. Jesus also foretold the fall of Jerusalem and bade her daughters to weep for themselves.

Thus chs. 4–11 and 12–22 should be placed earlier than the Gospels, perhaps earlier than most of the NT. They form a prophetic link between the Old and the New Covenants and prepare the way for the Gospels. The three parts of Revelation conform to the three periods postulated by Conzelmann: that of Israel, including the Baptist (chs. 4–11), that of Jesus (chs. 12–22), and that of the Church (chs. 1–3).[56]

---

[55] A. Vanhoye, Biblica 43 (1962), 436–76.

[56] Hans Conzelmann, The Theology of St. Luke. In a later work I shall show the affinity between Revelation and the Lucan infancy narratives and perhaps the influence of Revelation on both the Gospel of Luke and that of John. The comparison might help to explain the prominence of the Baptist in Luke and the anti-Baptist polemic in John.

THE LAST TWO CHAPTERS

Within those chapters of Revelation that were probably written later by a disciple of John (Rev 12–22), there are two that pose special problems because of both their content and their structure. These are the last two chapters of the book.

Rev 20–22 contain several distinctive features that set them apart from the rest of the apocalypse. First, they expound ideas which do not occur in the rest of the text, e.g. the millennium (20:3, 4, 7); Gog and Magog (20:8); the camp of the saints (20:9); the first resurrection (20:5, 6); "the souls who had been beheaded" for not renouncing their faith (20:4); the white throne (20:11); "books," in the plural (20:12).

Second, in various places the text seems to fit badly. The future tense occurs in 20:7, 8—"Satan will be released"—but then two verses later (20:9) the past tense occurs—Gog and Magog and their forces "marched" and "surrounded." In 20:12a "books were opened," but in vs. 12b suddenly "another book was opened, which is of life," Gr. *allo biblion . . . ho estin tēs zōēs.* Previous references were merely to "the book of life," Gr. *biblion tēs zōēs;* cf. 13:8, 17:8. Further, 20:13 states that the sea and Death and Hades gave up their dead, yet the previous verse states that all the dead were already standing before the throne and waiting to be judged.

These discrepancies indicate that the text of ch. 20 is suspect. However, those in chs. 21–22 are even greater. The major one is that the two descriptions of the new Jerusalem, in 21:1–4c and 21:9 – 22:2, conflict with each other.

P. Gaechter[57] concludes that there are two new Jerusalems, one which coexists with the present world (21:9 – 22:2) and one which is eternal (21:1–4c, 22:3–5). The former will last until the disappearance of this heaven and this earth, and will then be replaced by the latter. The eternal city is the same as the temporal but it is transformed. According to Gaechter, the two descriptions follow one another in the wrong order. The description of the city which is of this earth should come before that of the eternal city: 21:9 – 22:2 and then 21:1–4c with 22:3–5. Gaechter also believes that the duration of the city on earth corresponds to the thousand years and the period of the chaining and imprisonment of Satan. When Satan is chained the way is opened for the conversion of the nations which the millennial Jerusalem presupposes; 20:3, cf. 21:4.

[57] Gaechter, TS 10 (1949), 485–521.

Gaechter suggests a triplet: 20:1–3, the chaining of Satan "for a thousand years"; 21:1–22:2, the millennial Jerusalem; 20:4–6, Christ and his saints reigning "for a thousand years." He brings chs. 20–22 into close relationship to Rev 12. The millennial Jerusalem is the woman who is protected from Satan by his imprisonment. After the millennium there is another triplet of scenes: 20:7–10, Satan's release, last onslaught, and final ruin; 20:11–15, the last judgment and the condemnation of the wicked; 21:1–4c, 22:3–5, the eternal Jerusalem.

The book ends with the conclusion of the visions (22:7b, 10–13, 16b–17b, 20) of the epistle (22:21) and of the prophecy itself (22:18–19). The present writer believes that 22:16a, 20b, 21, are Christian interpolations akin to chs. 1–3; see Part Five.

The translation in traditional order has been placed before this Introduction for easy reference. The commentary, however, has been arranged according to the sequence of Gaechter save for the Christian additions. The following table is taken from Gaechter and includes Charles's order for comparison.[58]

Charles	CONTENT	Gaechter
20:1–3	Satan's chaining	20:1–3
21:9 – 22:2, 14–15, 17	Millennial Jerusalem	21:9 – 22:2
		22:14–15 *clausulae*
20:4–6	Millennial Kingdom	20:4–6
20:7–10	Satan Unchained	20:7–10
20:11–15	Last Judgment	20:11–15
21:5a, 4d, 5b, 1–4c	Eternal Jerusalem	21:1–4c, 22:3–5, 21:5ab, 4d, 5c–6
22:3–5		7, *clausulae*
Epilogue		Conclusion of the visions
21:5c, 6b–8		22:10–13, 7b, 16b–17b, 20
(God's testimony)		
22:6–7, 18a, 16, 13, 12, 10,		Conclusion of epistle
(Christ's testimony)		22:21
22:8–9, 20, 21		Conclusion of book
(John's testimony)		22:18–19.

THE CHRISTIAN PREFIX

Along with the Christian concluding verses, 22:16a, 20b, 21, chs. 1–3 had to have been written by someone even better informed than the disciple of John who wrote chs. 12–22, for the first three are the ones that

[58] Gaechter, TS 10 (1949), 485–521; APCh, II, 140–226.

deal most extensively with Jesus Christ. Indeed, the prophecies to the
seven churches are said to have come directly from Christ to God's
"servant John" (1:1). This indicates that chs. 1–3 and the three verses in
ch. 22 were probably written by a Baptist disciple who became a follower
of Jesus like those described in Acts 19:1–7, the former as an introduction,
the latter as a conclusion, which would place this essentially Jewish
apocalypse securely within a Christian context.

CHRISTOLOGICAL FEATURES

Chs. 1–3 differ considerably from the rest of Revelation in literary form,
style, purpose, and, as shown in the linguistic survey below, in "Linguistic
Features." They may be the work of a Baptist disciple (or disciples)
converted to Christ. He or they incorporated clear Christological characteristics into this part of the work. These Christological features are not
found anywhere else in this apocalypse. Among them are the title "Jesus
Christ" and three features characteristic of the Gospel of John: the concept of witness with regard to Jesus, his resurrection from the dead, and
his universal kingship; Rev 1:5. Whereas chs. 4–22 speak only about the
cleansing and victorious power of the blood of the Lamb, chs. 1–3 speak
more specifically about the love of Christ, the freedom from sin given
through his blood, and believers' elevation to the status of kingship and
priesthood; cf. I Peter 2:9–10, Rev 5:10, 20:6, where the same idea is
found without any specific reference to Jesus.

In 1:12–16 the portrait of one like a son of man appears in much
greater detail than it does anywhere else in the text, even in 14:14. Unlike 14:14, 1:12–16 is strongly influenced by Daniel and Ezekiel—
more, indeed, than the apocalyptic texts concerning the Son of Man found
in the Gospels; see COMMENT on Section XXVI. Following the vision of
1:12–16 there appears in vs. 18 what may be construed as a direct allusion to the resurrection. Nowhere else in the body of the work is such a
statement made. Moreover, the details of the description of one like the
son of man, who is most probably to be indentified with Christ because of
the reference to the resurrection in vs. 18, point to a Christology which
is much more advanced than that found in chs. 4–22. Vs. 20 states that
the figure holding in his right hand the seven stars, which are identified
with the seven angels of the churches, walks in the midst of the lampstands,
which symbolize the ecclesial communities themselves. This passage illustrates the authority of one like a son of man over the churches and their
ministers. The warning to Ephesus in 2:5 that he will shake the lampstand
out of its place if the church does not repent suggests his power to judge or
to punish, perhaps to excommunicate. The promise of rewards to "the one

who prevails" at the end of each prophecy indicates authority over the just as well as the wicked; cf. Matt 25:34. The whole vision is the epitome of the light-darkness motif in the Johannine corpus—the figure walks amidst seven-fold light and is itself composed of light of dazzling brilliance.

The titles of the speaker to each church or community present a high Christology, that is, they stress the divine aspect of Christ. In 2:8 the title "the First and the Last" places the one "who was dead and became alive" on a level with God, for this title was taken from Isaiah (cf. Isa 44:6, 48:12), where Yahweh uses it as an epithet for Himself. The Lamb is never clearly placed on such a level. Moreover, in the message to Thyatira one like a son of man is clearly designated "the Son of God" (18:1). This title does not occur anywhere in Rev 4–22, where the messianic figure is the Lamb. In the message to Sardis the speaker is said to possess "the seven spirits of God and the seven stars" (3:1). This is not written of the Lamb. Although the image of the book of life (3:5), over which this figure has authority, occurs in the body of Revelation as the book of life of the Lamb, nowhere is it stated that the Lamb will confess the victor's name before his Father and before God's angels or that the one who occupies the throne is the Father of the Lamb. In the prophecy to Laodicea the speaker is designated "the beginning of the creation of God" 3:14. There is no similar statement with reference to the Lamb, the Messiah, or the messianic figure of the rider on the white horse in chs. 4–22. At the end of the prophecy to Laodicea Christ speaks about sitting with his Father on His throne. In Rev 4–22 the Lamb is near the throne of God but it is not explicitly said that he shares it. In 22:1, 3, the expression "the throne of God and of the Lamb" is doubtful; it is even omitted in one variant.

The Christology of chs. 1–3 is much more advanced than that in the rest of Revelation. It must therefore have been written later by someone who had knowledge of and perhaps contact with Jesus Christ or Jesus' followers.

ECCLESIOLOGICAL FEATURES

These opening chapters are not directed to the Church in general, but to specific local churches. These are not all Pauline churches i.e. founded by Paul. Indeed, they may be Baptist Christian churches. Two appear to be Jewish Christian in that they complain about those who falsely claim to be Jews (2:9, 3:9). The direction against fornication and eating food sacrificed to idols might even suggest a violation of the apostolic decree (Acts 15:19–20). The "angel of the community" might be equivalent to "bishop," which would indicate a formed ministry. However, it is unlikely that Gr. *diakonia,* "service" or "ministry" (2:19) is used in the technical sense, which would signify an official position. The writer seems to be fully acquainted with the situation obtaining in the churches. They have been long enough in existence to be troubled by false apostles and false prophecy, and to have developed heterodoxical teaching which is associated with specific people, the Nikolaitans and Balaam and Jezebel. Persecution is arising but we are not told from whom this comes. There is no indication that it is persecution from the secular state. It must remain an open question whether this is Jewish or Roman hostility. The words "parousia" and "antichristos" are not used but there is expectation of an imminent second coming of Christ. This coming is expressed in a warlike and retributive manner. The description is not unlike II Thess 1:5 – 2:8, but the man of lawlessness is not mentioned. In contrast to Rev 4–22, these chapters concentrate on the eschatological picture of Christ and omit any description of his opponents or of the functions of the angels. Indeed, Christ seems to have taken the place of the angels (e.g. his having the keys "of death and of Sheol," 1:18), and there is no suggestion of the necessity to overcome Satan.

The first three chapters show thirty-eight allusions to the NT, nine in ch. 1, eight in ch. 2, and twenty-one in ch. 3. Nine of these are from John and Johannine texts. The only other chapters in the entire text that come close to this number are 20–22, which contain thirty: thirteen in ch. 20, eight in ch. 21, and nine in ch. 22.[59] The following table shows the number of NT allusions and where they occur in all the rest of Revelation.

Chapter	NT Allusions
4	0
5	3
6	5
7	3
8	2
9	2
10	0
11	2
12	2

[59] *Ch. 1:* Col 1:18; I Peter 2:5, 9; Matt 24:30; Mark 13:26; Luke 21:27; I Thess 4:17; John 19:34; Matt 24:30. *Ch. 2:* I John 4:1; James 2:5; II Cor 11:14, 15; James 1:2; Heb 4:12; Rom 2:6; II Tim 4:14. *Ch. 3:* Matt 24:43–44; Luke 12:39–40; I Thess 5:2, 4; II Peter 3:10; Philip 4:3; Matt 10:32; Luke 12:8; I Cor 16:9; II Cor 11:14, 15; Luke 21:19; II Tim 2:12; Heb 10:36; John 1:3; Col 1:15; I Cor 11:32; Heb 12:6; John 14:23. *Ch. 20:* II Peter 2:4; Jude 6; Luke 22:30; I Cor 6:2; I Peter 2:5, 9; Matt 25:31–46; Philip 4:3; Rom 2:6; I Cor 3:8; II Cor 11:15; II Tim 4:14; I Peter 1:17; I Cor 15:26, 55; Matt 25:41; Philip 4:3. *Ch. 21:* II Peter 3:13; Heb 11: 10, 16; II Cor 6:16, 5:17; John 7:37; Matt 25:41; I Cor 6:9–10; II Peter 3:13; Philip 4:3. *Ch. 22:* Matt 5:8; Acts 10:15–26; Rom 2:6; I Cor 3:8; II Cor 11:15; II Tim 4:14; I Peter 1:17; I Cor 6:9–10; Rom 1:3; John 7:37.

Chapter	NT Allusions
13	5
14	2
15	0
16	4
17	1
18	2
19	3
	36

LINGUISTIC FEATURES

There is a significant linguistic difference between Rev 1–3 and the three Christian verses of ch. 22, and chs. 4–22. A study of the words used in the former contrasted with the latter and compared with the rest of the NT, especially the Gospel of John, yields the following approximate results.[60] Citations from Scripture are not included in the calculations.

CHARACTERISTIC WORDS OF THE CHRISTIAN ADDITIONS TO REVELATION

Greek	English	No. in Rev 1–3, 22:16b, 20, 21	No. and locus in Rest of Rev	No. in Rest of the NT	No. in John
apocalupsis	apocalypse	1		17	0
Jesu Christo	Jesus Christ	3		ca. 5	ca. 3
sēmainō	foretell	1		2	3
apostellō	send	1	1 (22:6) 1 (5:7)	129	27
martureō	to bear witness	2	1 (22:16a) 1 (22:18)	69	31
John	John	3	1 (22:8)	30	0
anaginōskō	read	1		29	1
ekklēsia	church	18	1 (22:16a)	92	0
charis	grace	2		149	3
eirēnē	peace	1	1 (6:4)	84	6
martus	martyr(s)	(3)	1 (11:3) 1 (17:6)	30	0
prōtotokos	firstborn	1		7	0
archōn	ruler	1		35	7
patēr	father	4	1 (14:1)	ca. 391	129
Alpha kai Omega	Alpha and Omega	1	1 (21:6) 1 (22:13)	0	0

60 These statistics are described as "approximate" because of the variants. After checking with J. B. Smith, *Greek-English Concordance*, Scottdale, Pa., 1955, I find that our results do not always concur. His analysis is based on the KJ but my *intrumentum studiorum* was W. F. Moulton and A. S. Geden, *Concordance to the Greek Testament*, Edinburgh: Clark, latest reprint 1957.

Greek	English	No. in Rev 1–3, 22:16b, 20, 21	No. and locus in Rest of Rev	No. in Rest of the NT	No. in John
sunkoinōnos	one who shares	1		3	0
thlipsis	tribulation	4	1 (7:14)	39	2
kuriakos	belonging to the Lord	1		1	0
epistrephō	turn around	2		34	1
luchnia	lampstand	6	1 (11:4)	6	0
luchnos	lamp	0	1 (18:23) 1 (21:23) 1 (22:5)	11	1
mastos[61]	breast	1		2	0
zōnē[61]	girdle	1	1 (15:6)	6	0
phlox	flame	2	1 (19:12)	4	0
puroomai	make red hot	2		4	0
distomos	two-edged	2		1	0
opsis	face	1		0	2
ho prōtos kai ho eschatos	the first and the last	2	1 (22:13)	0	30
tade legei	thus sayest	7		1	0
peirazō	test	3		33	1 or 2
pseudus	false	1	1 (21:8)	1	0
pseudos	falsehood	0	1 (14:5) 1 (21:27) 1 (22:15)	7	1
kopiaō	grow weary	1		21	3
agapē	love	2		115	7
paradeisos	paradise	1		2	0
ptōcheia	poverty	1		2	0
'ioudaios	Jew	2		189	26
sunagōgē	synagogue	2		54	2
paschō	suffer	1		41	0
thronos tou Satana[62]	throne of Satan	1		0	0
krateō	hold fast	6	1 (7:1) 1 (20:2)	38	1
'arneomai[63]	deny	2		30	4
didachē	teaching	3		26	3
didaskō	teach	2		92	9 or 10
skandalon	stumbling block	1		14	0

[61] In Rev 15:6 the same phrase, "girded with golden girdles," is used of the angels, but mastos is not used; rather, stethos, "breast," is used. Stethos occurs four times in the rest of the NT, including twice in the Gospel of John (13:25, 21:20).

[62] Although the word "throne" occurs in nearly every chapter of Revelation, the "throne of Satan" appears only in Rev 2:13.

[63] The rest of Revelation does not describe apostasy by the phrase "deny my faith" or "deny my name" but rather speaks about the worship, etc., given to the beast.

Greek	English	No. in Rev 1–3, 22:16b, 20, 21	No. and locus in Rest of Rev	No. in Rest of the NT	No. in John
eidōlothutos	eating idol meat	2		7	0
manna	manna	1		3	2
psēphos	small pebble	2		1	0
huios theou	son of God	1		78	ca. 4
chalkolibanon	bronze	2		0	0
diakonia	service	1		32	0
prophētis	prophetess	1		1 (Luke 2:36)	0
klinē	bed	1		8	0
moicheuo	commit impurity	1		12	1 (8:4)
eraunaō	search	1		5	2
nephros	reins	1		0	0
bathus	in pl., deep things	1		3	1
baros	burden	1		5	0
prōinos	morning	2		0	0
gregoreuō	keep awake	2	1 (17:16)	20	0
stērizō	establish	1		13	0
plēroō	fulfill or perfect	1	1 (6:11)	85	15
kleptēs	thief	1	1 (17:15)	14	4
homologeō	confess	1		25 (n.b. Matt 20:32)	3 (esp. 1:20)
thura	door	3	1 (4:1)	34	7
pseudomai	be false	1		11	0
peirasmos	trial	1		20	0
peirazō	try	3		33	1 or 2
stulos	pillar	1	1 (10:1)	2	0
ktisis	creation	1		18	0
psuckros	cold	3		1	0
zestos	hot	3		0	0
chliaros	lukewarm	1		0	0
emeō	spit	1		0	0
talaipōros	poor	1		1	0
eleeinos	wretched	1		1	0
tuphlos	blind	1		46	16
gumnos	naked	1	1 (16:15) 1 (17:16)	12	1
sumbouleuō	council	1		3	1
aischunē	shame	1		5	0
gumnotēs	nakedness	1		2	0
kollourion	eye salve	1		0	0
egchriō	anoint	1		0	0
paideuō	educate	1		12	0
zeleuō	be in earnest	1		0	0
krouō	knock	1		3	0
deipneō	dine	1		3	0

Rev 1–3, 22:16b, 20, 21 are so different in character from the rest of the text that they have been placed at the end. In this way the reader may experience the Baptist's inaugural vision and the earlier parts of the book before proceeding to the Christian additions.

THE STRUCTURE OF REVELATION

The construction of this apocalypse is unique; in fact, it is the most exquisitely and artistically constructed of all the apocalypses. So masterfully is the text arranged that one cannot doubt the work of an editor. Here is a scheme subscribed to by scholars who have perceived a series of seven sevens in Revelation.[64]

SEVEN SERIES OF SEVEN

THE FIRST SEPTET

After a preliminary section to the whole apocalypse (1:1–8) and an introduction to the first septet (1:9–20) there are seven prophecies to the seven churches:

1) Ephesus, 2:1–7
2) Smyrna, 2:8–11
3) Pergamum, 2:12–17
4) Thyatira, 2:18–29
5) Sardis, 3:1–6
6) Philadelphia, 3:7–13
7) Laodicea, 3:14–22

THE SECOND SEPTET

After chapters 4–5, which are introductory to the second septet, come the seven seals:

1) The white horse, 6:1–2
2) The red horse, 6:3–4
3) The black horse, 6:5–6
4) The yellowish-green horse, 6:7–8
5) The souls under the altar, 6:9–11

[64] Adapted from R. J. Loenertzop, *The Apocalypse of St. John*, tr. H. J. Carpenter, London: Sheed & Ward, 1947.

6) The earthquake (6:12–17)

7) The seventh seal seems to comprise all of the third septet.

THE THIRD SEPTET

After a preparatory vision (8:1–6) the seven trumpets are sounded:

1) The earth is set on fire, 8:7
2) The sea is turned to blood, 8:8–9
3) The rivers and springs become bitter, 8:10–11
4) The heavenly bodies are dimmed, 8:12–13
5) The locusts, 9:1–12
6) The horsemen, 9:13 – 11:14
7) The seventh trumpet seems to comprise all the fourth septet.

THE FOURTH SEPTET

After an introductory section (11:6–19) seven signs appear:

1) The woman with child, 12:1–2
2) The dragon, 12:3–6
3) The beast rising out of the sea, 13:1–10
4) The beast rising out of the earth, 13:11–18
5) The Lamb and the virgins, 14:1–5
6) The seven angels, counting one like a son of man, 14:6–20
7) The seventh sign seems to comprise all the fifth septet.

THE FIFTH SEPTET

After an introductory section in 15:1 – 16:1, seven bowls of wrath are poured out:

1) On the earth, 16:2
2) On the sea, 16:3
3) On the waters, 16:4–7
4) On the sun, 16:8–9
5) On the throne of the beast, 16:10–11
6) On the Euphrates, 16:12–16
7) The seventh bowl seems to comprise all the sixth septet.

THE SIXTH SEPTET

After an introductory section (16:17–21) there are seven stages in the fall of Babylon:

1) The description of Babylon, 17:1–6
2) The explanation of Babylon, 17:7–18
3) The fall of Babylon, 18:1–8
4) The mourning for Babylon, 18:9–20
5) The final ruin of Babylon, 18:21–24

6) The song of praise at her fall, 19:1–5
7) The seventh stage seems to comprise all the seventh septet.

THE SEVENTH SEPTET

After an introductory portion (19:6–10) there occur the following scenes:

1) The rider on the white horse, 19:11–16
2) The supper of God, 19:17–18
3) The capture of the two beasts, 19:19–21
4) The angel of the abyss, 20:1–3
5) The first resurrection, 20:4–10
6) The judgment scene, 20:11–15
7) The new Jerusalem, 21:1 – 22:5

Rev 22:6–21 is a recapitulation and finale but does contain Christian additions and doublets.

SIX SERIES OF SIX

Certainly this type of arrangement is attractive. However, there is an even stronger possibility that originally the formation was six series of six, that is, a symbol of incompleteness congruous with the 666, the number of the beast, expressing a lack of fulfillment felt by the Baptist and his followers before the coming of Christ (13:18). This formation would avoid "inventing" the seventh part of the second, third, fourth, and sixth septets. The Christian editor, seeing the fulfillment in Christ, added the first septet (chs. 1–3), perhaps, and some of the last, i.e. the Christian additions in ch. 22. In this way he balanced the six sextets in the center by making the fourth one a septet. That way he could throw into higher relief the importance of the Christological features in Rev 1–3, 22, since the number of Christ and the numerical value of the Aramaic word *Skehan,* "Lord of Lords and King of Kings," being 777; see COMMENT on Section XVI.

The series might have been set out as follows:

SERIES ONE: A SEXTET

1) The white horse 6:1–2
2) The red horse 6:3–4
3) The black horse 6:5–6
4) The yellowish-green horse 6:7–8
5) The souls under the altar 6:9–11
6) The earthquake 6:12–17

SERIES TWO: A SEXTET

1) The earth is set on fire 8:7
2) The sea is turned to blood 8:8–9
3) The rivers and springs become bitter 8:10–11
4) The heavenly bodies are dimmed 8:12–13
5) The locusts 9:1–12
6) The horsemen 9:13–11:14

SERIES THREE: A SEXTET

1) The woman with child 12:1–2
2) The dragon 12:3–6
3) The beast rising from the sea 13:11–18
4) The beast rising from the earth 13:11–18
5) The Lamb and the virgins 14:1–5
6) The seven angels, counting one like a son of man 14:6–20

SERIES FOUR: A SEPTET

1) The bowl on the earth 16:2
2) The bowl on the sea 16:3
3) The bowl on the waters 16:4–7
4) The bowl on the sun 16:8–9
5) The bowl on the throne of the beast 16:10–11
6) The bowl on the Euphrates 16:12–16
7) The bowl on the air 16:17–21

SERIES FIVE: A SEXTET

1) The description of Babylon 17:1–6
2) The explanation of Babylon 17:7–18
3) The fall of Babylon 18:1–8
4) The mourning for Babylon 18:9–20
5) The final ruin of Babylon 18:21–24
6) The song of praise at her fall and the marriage of the Lamb 19:1–10

SERIES SIX: A SEXTET

1) The rider on the white horse 19:11–16
2) The supper of God 19:17–18
3) The capture of the two beasts 19:19–21
4) The angel of the abyss 20:1–3
5) The first resurrection 20:4–10
6) The judgment scene 20:11–15

These six series, the fourth of which is a septet, would remind the reader

of the sevenfold threat in Lev 26:18, 21, 28; see COMMENTS on Sections
XIV–XVI.

The new Jerusalem description is so long that it appears to be a
separate section, an epilogue, parallel to chs. 4–5, the prologue. The
heavenly throne seen in chs. 4–5 reappears in the epilogue, in 21:5.

SUMMARY OF THE ARGUMENT

Revelation falls into three or four distinct parts: chs. 1–3, the letters or
prophecies to the churches; chs. 4–11, the visions especially concerned
with the Lamb; chs. 12–22, which may be broken down into chs. 12–19
containing the well known picture of the harlot and chs. 20–22 which
seem to show several marks of redaction and interpolation.

THE BAPTIST'S REVELATION

Chs. 4–11 contain the revelation given not to John the evangelist after
the death, resurrection, and ascension of Jesus, but to John the Baptist,
the forerunner of Jesus before his public ministry. The Gospel of John
1:15–34 states that the Baptist received a revelation from God about
"He that cometh," whom we traditionally call the Messiah. God told
John, "When you see the Spirit descend and rest on someone, he is the
one who is to baptize with a holy Spirit"; John 1:33, AB. There are four
themes which in all the NT are unique to Revelation and to the sections of
the Gospels which concern John the Baptist: the Lamb (of God), the
title "He that cometh," the concept of baptism by fire, and the direct
application of the figure of the bridegroom to Jesus. Other Baptist affinities
with Revelation are: the wrath of God, tree as a metaphor for leaders
of the people, the interest in the liturgy (the Baptist's father was a priest
and the Baptist's vision occurred in the sanctuary), and the idea of the
adulterous generation. All these themes are amplified in Revelation.
Further, it must be remembered that Jesus spoke very highly of the
prophetical office of John the Baptist (Matt 11). Could it be that this
part of Revelation contains what was then revealed to John committed
to writing by a disciple?

In Rev 4 John receives an inaugural vision of the throne of God
surrounded by twenty-four elders and the four living creatures. This vision is similar to those received by Micaiah (II Kings 22) and Isaiah
(ch. 6) but especially to Ezekiel (ch. 1) and Daniel (ch. 7). It is the

great prophets who receive the throne vision which was regarded as the climax of Jewish mystical experience, rather akin to the experience of the Blessed Trinity in Christian mysticism. We do not find throne visions in Christian literature. John the Baptist, therefore, receives a glimpse of heaven as did the prophets of old.

In the next chapter (5) one finds an element in the vision which is only barely hinted at in the visions of the Old Testament prophets. This is the Lamb on the right hand of the throne. Ezekiel thought that he saw one who had "the appearance of a man," (Ezek 1:26, KJ; cf. 10:2-3). Daniel had seen "one like a son of man" (Dan 7:13, RSV) coming to the throne of God and receiving power, honor, and dominion. John, instead of a similar apparition, sees a Lamb. In Jewish mystical and apocalyptic literature animals represent men, men represent angels, and often precious stones or light or fire indicate the presence of God. This gives one a clue to the identity of the Lamb. He must be human.

Looking back into Jewish literature written just before the Christian era, one discovers that lambs, rams, and lions, represent warlike leaders of the Jewish people who will be victorious over Israel's enemies. John the Baptist probably saw his Lamb in this way. He is "as though slain" but one does not know whether this refers to martyrdom or to being killed in a battle. He is also worthy to open a seven-sealed scroll describing the disasters to befall either the world or Palestine or both. These disasters are: domestic warfare, famine, death or pestilence, martyrdom, and earthquake (ch. 6). Such calamities did befall Palestine in the first century A.D., covering the period of the Baptist and afterward. This could be the "divorce scroll" of the Lamb, warnings designed to bring the wife Israel to repentance; see Section VII.

Although the Lamb is human the fact that he is near the throne of God and that he has seven eyes which "are the [seven] spirits of God" (5:6) suggests that he also has a divine nature. In this capacity he may stand as mediator between Yahweh and his people as regards the covenant.

The horsemen are manifestations of Yahweh reflecting his character or actions; cf. II Macc 10:29. The first horseman, on the white horse, represents the conquering power of Yahweh; he is distinguished by a bow and wreath and he goes forth "a victor and to repeat his victory" (6:2). He is probably the Angel of the Lord about whom we read in the OT, e.g. in II Sam 24:16, Zech 1:11-14. The second horseman, on the red horse, represents civil war ("take peace from the earth . . . internecine strife," 6:4), such as that which broke out in the Roman provinces from A.D. 41-54 and, more important, those in the year 69 which saw the rise and fall of three Roman emperors and finally the establishment of Vespasian on the throne. The third horseman, on the black horse, represents famine ("A quart of wheat for a denarius . . ." 6:6); food shortage was reported in Judea in 45–46. The fourth horseman, on the yellowish-green horse, represents disease or death which would naturally follow war and famine ("to kill with sword and famine and plague and by wild beasts of the earth," 6:8).

In ch. 7 John receives a vision of the sealing or securing of all the twelve tribes of Israel (7:1–8) and another vision that could be interpreted either as the return of the exiles from the Jewish Dispersion or the inclusion of the Gentiles in salvation (7:9–17). These people are said to be washed in the blood of the Lamb, 7:14. In other words, John sees a redemptive aspect in the character of the Lamb who stands by the throne of God.

Breaking the seven seals in ch. 6 is paralleled by sounding the seven trumpets in ch. 8. Chapter 8 is also influenced by Ezekiel. In Ezek 10:2 an angel, described as "a man clothed in linen," RSV, takes burning coals from under the throne of God. In Rev 8:5 an angel throws coals on the earth; this action is followed by thunder, lightning, and an earthquake, phenomena associated with theophany. Indeed, it is this chapter that begins the phase of the holy war in which God Himself, rather than angels, uses His weapons against the faithless.

The concept of the Divine Warrior is well known if not congenial to contemporary thought. In Num 21:14 there is a reference to "the Book of the Wars of the Lord," RSV. God appears as "a man of war" in Exod 15:3, RSV (cf. Isa 42:13, 59:17, Pss 24:8, 25:1, 68:4, Hab 3:9, Zeph 3:17, Wisd Sol 5:17–23). He leads the armies of the heavenly hosts (hence his epithet "Yahweh of Hosts") and the armies of Israel. His weapons are the forces of nature. In Rev 8 the disasters are what we would call "acts of God," that is, they are not due to conditions subject to human control. The ancients saw such phenomena as direct punishment or ill omen from God indicating that mankind had better amend their lives. In ch. 8 they are hail, pollution of the waters, a comet or shooting star; eclipse of the sun, moon and stars. It ends with the reference to the eagle which may represent the invading Roman army about to swoop down on Jerusalem.

In Rev 9 at the sound of the fifth trumpet God permits the appearance first of a demonic infantry in the form of grotesque locusts with features of scorpion, man, and lion, and then of a demonic cavalry in the form of horses with features of lion and snake; see illustrations 6 and 7. The composite animal was a sign of evil in the ancient world; see illustration 9. God permits these armies, which may be described as the forces of darkness, to try the faithful on the earth. Among the Dead Sea scrolls found at Qumran about 1947 was discovered a document called "War of the Children of Light against the Children of Darkness" (1QM). Rev 9 depicts the "children of darkness" but in a far more terrible way than 1QM. In that document, both men and angels fight in the holy war.

Rev 10 opens with a vision of a mighty angel perhaps to be identified with such a personage as the Prince of Lights mentioned in 1QM. This chapter too is influenced by Ezekiel. In Ezek 3 the prophet is told to eat a scroll before he predicts the siege of Jerusalem. The scroll tastes "sweet as honey" (Ezek 3:3, RSV) but ends in bitterness (3:14). In the same way the seer in Revelation consumes a scroll which is "as sweet as honey to my mouth; but . . . bitter to my stomach" (10:10).

Here the prophet personifies either Israel or, more specifically, Jerusalem, which will be depicted later as a harlot. The eating of the small scroll symbolizes the trial by bitter water undergone by a woman accused of adultery (Num 5:11–28; see COMMENT on Section VII). In the next part of his vision (ch. 11) the prophet is told to "measure," that is test, God's temple, presumably the one in Jerusalem. One recalls that John the Baptist was far from complimentary towards the priests and people who came from Jerusalem. He addressed the Pharisees and the Sadducees as "You brood of vipers" (Matt 3:7; cf. 12:34, 23:33, Luke 3:7) and he asked them who told them to flee from the wrath to come. In the last verse of ch. 11 the war palladium of the Divine Warrior, the ark, is revealed. In Num 10:35 Yahweh goes before the ark of the covenant as general in chief of the army and the cry arises from Moses (RSV):

Arise, O Lord, and let thy enemies be scattered, and let them that hate thee flee before thee.

Ch. 11 ends the first part of Revelation. In summary: The Baptist catches a glimpse of the Lamb who will have both a human and divine nature, who will in some way redeem the people. He learns that there is a period of disaster coming for the people of Israel who do not repent. However, many will be saved. The temple of Jerusalem will be tested. The city will not listen to the two prophets (ch. 11) whom I suggest symbolize the house of Aaron (the priests) and the house of Israel (the laity), such as we find at Qumran; see COMMENT on Section VIII. There they are witnesses to the truth. However, it is one gift to receive a genuine prophecy; it is another gift to understand the full implications of that prophecy. The Baptist rightly identified the Messiah but he does not seem to have divined accurately his character. Indeed, Matt 11:2, which records that John sent his disciples to Jesus to ask, "Are you the Coming One, or are we to look for someone else?" (AB), indicates John's doubt that Jesus was the Messiah (and the Lamb). John was looking for a warrior leader, not a gentle teacher with charismatic powers to heal body and soul. It was only the life of Jesus which could interpret the details of the revelation to John.

THE DISCIPLE'S INTERPRETATION

Chs. 12–22, with the exception of a few verses from ch. 22, come from a disciple of John the Baptist, one who knew about Jesus but who may not have known all the facts about his character, life, death, resurrection, and ascension. Such disciples were at Ephesus in the time of Paul, as in Acts 19:1–7. This part of Revelation may have been written between A.D. 60 and 70 when the war between the Romans and the Jews in Palestine was gathering momentum. Naturally many fled for safety into the Judean desert, a site which is known to have been occupied at various periods by those who wished to escape the ravages of war or to practice their religion in peace.

This may be the key to interpreting Rev 12. A woman clothed with the sun escapes a dragon (that is, Satan) who seeks to devour her, so God prepares a place for her in the desert. The woman represents the faithful —perhaps both Christians or Jews (not distinguished at this early date) —who fled the threat of apostasy that hung over the heads of the Jewish people at least from the forties A.D. when the mad Roman emperor Gaius commanded that his own statue be placed in the temple at Jerusalem. This catastrophe was averted but it must have left a deep, fearful impression upon the Jews. Jewish literature from the first century B.C. to the first century A.D. shows that some Jews were faithless and fell in with the Roman customs. They defiled the sanctuary, made a mockery of their religion, amassed unlawful wealth and fell prey to blasphemy and idolatry.

The threat of idolatry is reflected in the vision of the two beasts. In Rev 13:1 the beast from the sea is the Roman empire. In 13:11 the beast from the earth is the local priesthood and leaders who apostasize. They, together with Satan form the Satanic trinity. The monster symbolism is taken from the OT and nonbiblical literature. It recaptures the "divine warrior" theme of the earlier chapters, in Scripture Yahweh is the victorious smiter of the mythical monsters of chaos (Pss 74:13–14, 89:10–11; Isa 51:9). There is nothing here to suggest specific Christian persecution.

Rev 14 shows those who resisted the temptations to idolatry and blasphemy. They are the companions of the Lamb, the one hundred and forty-four thousand "virgins," that is, those who have not adulterated their religion. That they are "before the throne" and "redeemed from the earth" (vs. 3) indicates they are in heaven; perhaps they are martyrs, or those who died in the war. The seer then receives a warning from an angel that Babylon has fallen. The past tense is used although the event has not yet occurred; cf. Amos 5:2. "Babylon" is the adulterous generation in

Jerusalem against whom both John the Baptist and Jesus spoke; in the OT only twice is a non-Israelite nation called a harlot.

Before "Babylon" actually falls seven more plagues take place (Rev 15–16: the seven bowls, probably of coals with incense, poured over the earth), reflecting the plagues which the Egyptians suffered when they would not let Israel go free. Now not a foreign country, but Israel herself, suffers the plagues. This had been foretold in Deut 28:60: if the Israelites disobeyed God they would suffer the same plagues as Egypt. In Rev 9:5, 10, the stinging locusts and horses' tails like scorpions' are reminiscent of the "fiery serpents" (probably "serpent-demons") of Num 21. See illustrations 6, 7, and 13.

Rev 17–18 introduces the great harlot, Jerusalem. Her fall is the "death of the firstborn" equivalent to that of the Egyptian firstborn. She may represent the high priesthood especially, as she wears "a name of mystery" on her head; cf. Sir 45:12, RSV, which says of Aaron, the father of the priesthood

> with a gold crown upon his turban,
> inscribed like a signet with "Holiness,"
> a distinction to be prized, the work of an expert,
> the delight of the eyes, richly adorned.

As a harlot, she is punished not only as a woman accused of adultery (cf. Num 5) but as a priest's daughter (Lev 21:9). Her death is by fire, by having molten lead poured down her throat; hence the reference to the cup in Rev 16:19. After her fall the rider on the white horse, who is called the Word of God, destroys the heathen nations. Like Yahweh he is a divine warrior. He does not reflect the Gospel image of Jesus. Yet with him the conflict between the kingdom of God and Satan is resolved. The theocracy is triumphant.

Rev 20–22 reveal the thousand-year reign of the Messiah with his saints and the new Jerusalem. This was fulfilled in the new type of orthodox Judaism which flourished at Jamnia after the fall of Jerusalem to the Romans in A.D. 70, which still inspires Jews today. It is a religion of the Word rather than of animal sacrifice. However, it is also fulfilled in the Church, which Jesus founded and which was free to mature independently after the fall of the holy city to become a universal religion. It, too, has no temple or sacrifice. Chs. 20–22 were probably composed in the late sixties A.D.

THE CHRISTIAN'S REDACTION

Rev 1–3 was added by a later writer who knew more details about Jesus Christ. It is difficult to assign a date to this portion. However, because it shows seven fully formed Christian churches in Asia Minor to which the "one like a son of man" in Rev 1:13 (probably a picture of the Resurrected Christ), sends messages, it could not have been composed before A.D. 60. These messages are prophecies which stress his imminent second coming, a belief which was held among the very early Christians but which was moderated as the Church grew and matured. They display a higher Christology than chs. 4–22 and promise unheard of rewards to those who are faithful to Christ—even a place with him beside his Father (3:21).

Therefore, Revelation is a composite work from the "Baptist School" who represented a primitive form of Christianity and inherited the Baptist's prophetic, apocalyptic and "fiery" (boanergic) tendencies. As Käsemann[65] observes "the Gospels themselves presuppose the existence of a Baptist community in competition with the young Church." It fell, I believe, to the task of Luke and John, the evangelist, to modify this theology and to place it in a secondary position in comparison with the theology of the "Gospel Christ." It is for this reason that I suggest Revelation may be assigned to a period prior to the writing of the first Gospel.

[65] *Essays on New Testament Themes*, p. 142.

BIBLIOGRAPHY

Black, M. *Apocalypsis Henochi Graece.*

Bretscher, P. G. " 'Whose Sandals'? (Matt 3:11)," JBL 86 (1967), 81–87.

Brown, R. E. *The Gospel According to John, I–XII.*

———. *The Gospel According to John, XIII–XXI.*

Charles, R. H. *Apocrypha and Pseudepigrapha of the Old Testament* (APCh), I, II.

Cross, Frank Moore. "The Divine Warrior," in *Biblical Motifs,* ed. Alexander Altmann (Harvard University Press, 1966), pp. 11–30.

Denis, A. M. *Introduction aux Pseudepigraphes Grecs d'Ancien Testament.*

Dodd, Charles H. *The Interpretation of the Fourth Gospel.* Cambridge University Press, 1955.

Ford, J. Massyngberde, "Orthodox Judaism and the Heavenly Jerusalem" (forthcoming).

Gaechter, P. "The Origin Sequence of Apocalypse 20–22," TS 10 (1949), 485–521.

Giblin, C. H. *The Threat to Faith: An Exegetical and Theological Re-examination of 2 Thessalonians 2.* Analecta Biblica, 31. Rome: Biblical Institute, 1967.

Hennecke, Edgar. *New Testament Apocrypha,* I, II. London: Lutterworth, 1963, 1965.

Jeremias, J. *Jesus' Promise to the Nations.* London: Mackay, 1970.

Käsemann, E. "The Disciples of John the Baptist in Ephesus," in *Essays on New Testament Themes*. London: SCM, 1964.

Miller, Patrick D. "God the Warrior," *Interpretation* 19 (1965), 39–46.

Russell, David S. *Between the Testaments*. Philadelphia: Fortress, 1964.

———. *The Method and Message of Jewish Apocalyptic*. Philadelphia: Westminster, 1964.

Scobie, C. H. H. *John the Baptist*. Philadelphia; Fortress, 1964.

Stendahl, Krister. *The School of St. Matthew and Its Use of the Old Testament* (Lund, 1954). Philadelphia: Fortress, 1968.

Wink, W. *John the Baptist in the Gospel Tradition*. Cambridge University Press, 1968.

GENERAL SELECTED BIBLIOGRAPHY

REFERENCES

The Ante-Nicene Christian Library, vols. 1–12, eds. A. Roberts and J. Donaldson. Edinburgh, 1867–72.

The Apocrypha and Pseudepigrapha of the Old Testament, I, II, ed. Robert H. Charles. Oxford University, Clarendon, 1913, 1969. *Cited as* APCh.

The Babylonian Talmud, tr., ed. I. Epstein. London: Soncino: 1935, 1961. *Cited as* Epstein.

The Dead Sea Scrolls, ed. Miller Burrows. New York: Viking, 1955.

Discoveries in the Judaean Desert of Jordan. Oxford University Press. *Cited as* DJD.

    I. *Qumran Cave 1*, tr., ed. Jean-Dominique Barthélemy and J. T. Milik. 1955.

    II. *Les Grottes de Murabba'at*, tr., ed. Pierre Benoit, J. T. Milik, and Roland de Vaux. 1961.

    III. *Les "Petites Grottes" de Qumran*, tr., ed. J. T. Milik and Roland de Vaux. 1962.

    IV. *The Psalms Scroll of Qumran Cave 11*, tr., ed. J. A. Sanders. 1965.

    V. *Qumran Cave 4*, tr., ed. John Marco Allegro, with Arnold A. Anderson. 1968.

Encyclopedia Judaica, vols. 1–16. Jerusalem: Keter, 1972.

Encyclopedic Dictionary of the Bible, by A. van den Born, tr., ed. Louis F. Hartman. New York: McGraw-Hill, 1963.

The Essene Writings from Qumran, tr., ed. A. Dupont-Sommer, Eng. tr. Geza Vermès. New York: Meridian, 1962. *Cited as* D-S.

Interpreter's Dictionary of the Bible, vols. 1–4. New York and Nashville: Abingdon, 1962.

Jewish Encyclopedia, vols. 1–12, ed. Isidore Singer. New York and London, 1901.

Josephus. *Jewish Antiquities*, Books 1–4, tr. Henry St. John Thackeray. Loeb Classical Library. Harvard University Press and London: Heinemann, 1926, 1966. *Cited as* Ant.

———. *Ant.* 5–8, trs. Henry St. John Thackeray and Ralph Marcus. Loeb. 1934, 1958.

———. *Ant.* 9–11, tr. Ralph Marcus. Loeb. 1937, 1958.

———. *Ant.* 12–14, tr. Ralph Marcus. Loeb. 1943, 1961.

———. *Ant.* 15–17, trs. Ralph Marcus and Allen Wikgren. Loeb. 1963.

———. *Ant.* 18–20, tr. L. H. Feldman. Loeb. 1965, 1969.

——. *The Jewish War*, Books 1–3, tr. Henry St. John Thackeray. Loeb. 1927, 1967. *Cited as War*.

——. *War* 4–7, tr. Henry St. John Thackeray. Loeb. 1928, 1968.

——. *The Life* and *Against Apion*, tr. Henry St. John Thackeray. Loeb. 1926, 1966.

The Manual of Discipline, tr., ed. Preben Wernberg-Møller. Leiden: Brill, 1957.

Mekilta de Rabbi Ishmael, tr., ed. Jacob Z. Lauterbach. 3 vols. Philadelphia: Jewish Publication Society of America, 1933–35.

Midrash Rabbah, vols. 1–9, trs., eds. H. Freedman and M. Simon. London: Soncino, 1949.

The Mishnah, vols. 1–7, ed. P. Blackman. New York: Judaica, 1963.

Philo Judaeus. Philosophical Works, ten volumes tr. from the Greek by F. H. Colson et al. and two supplementary volumes from the Armenian by Ralph Marcus. Loeb Classical Library. Harvard University Press and London: Heinemann.

Talmud Yerushalmi, Le Talmud de Jerusalem, tr., ed. M. Schwab. Paris, 1871–90.

Targum of Isaiah, tr., ed. J. F. Stenning. Oxford University, Clarendon, 1949. *Cited as* Stenning.

The Targums of Onkelos and Jonathan ben Uzziel on the Pentateuch with the Fragments of the Jerusalem Targum, tr., ed. J. W. Etheridge. New York: Ktav, reprint 1968. *Cited as* Etheridge.

The Text of Habakkuk in the Ancient Commentary from Qumran, tr., ed. William H. Brownlee. JBL Monograph XI. Philadelphia: Society of Biblical Literature, 1959. *Cited as* 1QpHab.

Theologisches Wörterbuch zum Neuen Testament, I–IX, eds. G. Kittel and G. Friedrich. Stuttgart: Kohlhammer, 1933–73. Tr. G. W. Bromiley. Grand Rapids: Eerdmans, 1964–74. *Cited as* TWNT.

BOOKS

Allo, E. B. *Saint Jean, L'Apocalypse*. 3d ed. Etudes Bibliques. Paris: Gabalda, 1933.

Allegro, J. M. *The Treasure of the Copper Scroll*. Garden City, N.Y.: Doubleday, Anchor, 1964.

Barclay, W. *Letters to the Seven Churches: A Study of the Second and Third Chapters of the Book of Revelation*. The Living Church Books. London: SCM, 1964.

Barrett, C. K. *The Gospel According to St. John*. London: SPCK, 1962.

Barth, Karl. *Hommage et Reconnaissance*. Neuchatel, Switzerland: Delachaux & Niestle, 1964.

Beasley-Murray, George R. *Jesus and the Future*. London: Macmillan, 1954. New York: St. Martin's, 1954.

Betz, Otto. *What Do We Know About Jesus?* Philadelphia: Westminster, 1958.

Black, Matthew, ed. *Apocalypsis Henochi Graece and Fragmenta Pseudepigraphorum Quae Supersunt Graeca*. Leiden: Brill, 1970.

————. *The Dead Sea Scrolls and Christian Origins*. London: Athlone, 1966.

Boismard, M. E. *L'Apocalypse*. La Sainte Bible. Paris: Du Cerf, 1959.

Bonsirven, P. J. *L'Apocalypse de Saint Jean: Traduction et Commentaire*. Verbum Salutis 16. Paris: Beauchesne, 1951.

Bousset, Wilhelm. *Die Offenbarung Johannis*. Meyer 16. Gottingen: Vanderhoeck & Ruprecht, 1906, 1966.

Bowman, John W. *The Revelation to John: Its Dramatic Structure and Message*. (Philadelphia: Westminster, 1955), pp. 436–53.

Braun, Herbert. *Qumran und das Neue Testament, II*. Tübingen: Mohr, 1966.

Brown, Raymond E. *The Gospel According to John, I–XII*. AB, vol 29. *The Gospel According to John, XIII–XXI*. AB, vol. 29A. Garden City, N.Y.: Doubleday, 1966, 1970.

Brownlee, William H. *The Meaning of the Qumran Scrolls for the Bible*. Oxford University Press, 1964.

Brox, Norbert. *Zeuge und Märtyrer*. Munich: Kosel, 1961.

Bruce, Frederick F. *Second Thoughts on the Dead Sea Scrolls*. Grand Rapids, Michigan: Eerdmans, 1961.

Brütsch, Charles. *La Clarté de l'Apocalypse*. 5th ed. Geneva: Labor & Fides, 1966.

Caird, George B. *The Revelation of St. John the Divine*. New Testament Commentaries. London: Black, 1966. New York: Harper, 1966.

Campbell, Jr., Edward F., and Freedman, David Noel, eds. *The Biblical Archaeologist Reader, 3*. Garden City, N.Y.: Doubleday, Anchor, 1970.

Carmignac, P., Cothenet, E., and Lignée, H., trs., eds. *Les Textes de Qumrân, Traduits et Annotés*. Paris: Letouzey & Ane, 1963.

Carrington, Philip. *The Meaning of Revelation*. London: SPCK, 1931.

Cerfaux, L., and Cambier, J. *L'Apocalypse de Saint Jean lue aux Chretiens*. Lectio Divina 17. Paris, 1964.

Charles, Robert H. *A Critical and Exegetical Commentary on the Revelation of St. John*. ICC, I, II. Edinburgh: Clark, 1920, 1956. *Cited as Revelation*.

————. *Lectures on the Apocalypse*. The Schweich Lectures, 1919. Oxford University Press, 1923.

Comblin, J. *Le Christ dans l'Apocalypse*. Paris: Desclée, 1965.

Conzelmann, Hans. *The Theology of St. Luke*. New York: Harper, 1960.

Dahood, Mitchell. *Psalms I, 1–50*. AB, vol. 16. *Psalms II, 51–100*. AB, vol. 17. *Psalms III, 101–150*. AB, vol. 17A. Garden City, N.Y.: Doubleday, 1966, 1968, 1970.

Daniélou, Jean, S.J. *The Work of John the Baptist*. Baltimore: Helicon, 1966.

Daube, David. *The New Testament and Rabbinic Judaism*. London: Athlone, 1956.

Davies, W. D., and Daube, David. *The Background of the New Testament and Its Eschatology*. Cambridge University Press, 1964.

Le Déaut, R. *La Nuit Pascale*. Rome: Institut Biblique Pontifical, 1963.

Denis, Albert Marie. *Introduction aux Pseudepigraphes Grecs d'Ancien Testament*. Leiden: Brill, 1970.

Derrett, J. Duncan M. *Law in the New Testament*. London: Darton, Longman & Todd, 1970.

D'Souza, John, D.D. *The Lamb of God in the Johannine Writings*. Allahabad: St. Paul's Society, 1966.

Epstein, Louis M. *Sex Laws and Customs in Judaism*. New York: Ktav, 1967.

Farbridge, Maurice H. *Studies in Biblical and Semitic Symbolism*. New York: Ktav, 1970.

Farrer, Austin. *A Rebirth of Images: The Making of St. John's Apocalypse*. London: Westminster, Dacre, 1949. Boston: Beacon, 1949.

————. *The Revelation of St. John the Divine*. Oxford: Clarendon Press, 1964.

Feuillet, A. *L'Apocalypse, État de la Question*. (S.N. s. 3). Paris and Bruges, 1963.

————. *The Apocalypse*. Staten Island, N.Y.: St. Paul, 1964.

————. *Johannine Studies*, tr. Thomas E. Crane. New York: Alba House, 1965.

Finkelstein, Louis, ed. *The Jews, Their History*. New York: Schocken, 1970.

Fiorenza, Elisabeth Schussler. *Priester für Gott*. Munster: Aschendorff, 1972.

Ford, J. Massingberd, and Keifer, Ralph A. *We Are Easter People*. New York: Herder & Herder, 1970.

Frend, W. H. C. *Martyrdom and Persecution in the Early Church: A Study in a Conflict from the Maccabees to Donatus*. New York University Press, 1967.

Freedman, David Noel, and Campbell, Jr., Edward F., eds. *The Biblical Archaeologist Reader*, 2. Garden City, N.Y.: Doubleday, Anchor, 1964.

Le Frois, Bernard J. *The Woman Clothed with the Sun: Apoc. 12*. Rome: Herder & Herder, 1953.

Gaster, Moses. *The Samaritans, Their History, Doctrines and Literature*. The Schweich Lectures, 1923. Oxford University Press, 1925.

Gerhardsson, Birger. *Memory and Manuscript*. Copenhagen: Willadsen og Christensen, 1964.

Giet, Stanislaus. *L'Apocalypse et l'Histoire: Étude historique sur l'Apocalypse Johannique*. University of Paris, 1957.

Ginzberg, Louis. *The Legends of the Jews*, I–VIII. (Philadelphia: Jewish Publication Society of America, 1946–61), 5716–21.

Glasson, Thomas F. *The Revelation of John*. Cambridge University Press, 1965.

Glatzer, Nahum N. *The Jewish People in the Time of Jesus*. New York: Schocken, 1967.

Goldin, Judah. *The Song at the Sea*. Yale University Press, 1971.

Goodenough, E. R. *Jewish Symbols in the Greco-Roman Period*, vols. 1–12. New York: Pantheon, 1953.

Goulder, M. D. *Type and History in Acts*. London: SPCK, 1964.

Gry, Leon. *Le Millénarisme dans ses Origines et son Développement*. Paris, 1904.

Hadorn, W. *Die Offenbarung des Johannes*. Theologische Handbuch zum Neue Testament, 18. Leipzig, 1928.

Harrington, Wilfrid J. *Understanding the Apocalypse*. Washington and Cleveland: Corpus, 1969.

Hartman, Lars. *Prophecy Interpreted*. Uppsala, 1966.

Hastings, Adrian. *Prophet and Witness in Jerusalem*. Baltimore: Helicon, 1958.

Hatch, E., and Redpath, H. A. *A Concordance to the Septuagint and Other Greek Versions of the Old Testament Including the Apocryphal Books*. Oxford University Press, 1897–1907.

Hilgert, Earle. *The Ship and Related Symbols in the New Testament*. Assen, The Netherlands: Royal Vangcorum, 1962.

Holtz, T. *Die Christologie der Apokalypse des Johannes*. Berlin, 1962.

Isaakson, Abel. *Marriage and Ministry in the New Temple*. Lund, 1965.

James, Montague Rhodes. *The Apocryphal New Testament*. Oxford University, Clarendon, 1963.

Jeremias, Joachim. *Jerusalem in the Time of Jesus,* trs. F. H. and C. H. Cave. Philadelphia: Fortress, 1967. London: SCM, 1969.

Kadushin, Max. *The Rabbinic Mind*. New York: Blaisdell, 1965.

Kiddle, M., and Ross, M. K. *The Revelation of St. John*. Moffatt New Testament Commentary. New York: Harper, 1941.

Kummel, W. G. *Promise and Fulfillment*. Studies in Biblical Theology, 23. 2d ed. London: SCM, 1961.

Lampe, G. W. H. *The Seal of the Spirit*. London: SPCK, 1967.

Laurentin, Rene. *Structure et Théologie de Luc,* I–II. Paris: Gabalda, 1964.

Leaney, A. R. C. *The Gospel According to St. Luke*. London: Black, 1966.

———. *The Rule of Qumran and Its Meaning*. London: SCM, 1966.

Leon, Harry J. *The Jews of Ancient Rome*. Philadelphia: Jewish Publication Society of America, 1960.

Lindblom, J. *Prophecy in Ancient Israel*. Philadelphia: Muhlenberg, 1962.

Loisy, Alfred. *L'Apocalypse de Jean*. Paris, 1923.

MacDonald, John. *The Theology of the Samaritans*. London: SCM, 1964.

Mansoor, Menahem. *The Thanksgiving Hymns*. Leiden: Brill, 1961.

McKelvey, R. J. *The New Temple: The Church in the New Testament*. Oxford University Press, 1968.

McNamara, Martin, M.S.C. *The New Testament and the Palestinian Targum to the Pentateuch*. Rome: Pontifical Biblical Institute, 1966.

Meeks, Wayne A. *The Prophet-King*. Leiden: Brill, 1967.

Michl, J. *Die 24 Altesten in der Apokalypse des hl. Johannes*. Munich, 1938.

Milik, Jozef T. *Ten Years of Discovery in the Wilderness of Judea*. London: SCM, 1959.

Minear, Paul S. *I Saw a New Earth: An Introduction to the Visions of the Apocalypse*. Washington: Corpus, 1968.

Montgomery, James Alan. *The Samaritans: The Earliest Jewish Sect*. New York: Ktav, 1968.

Moore, A. L. *The Parousia in the New Testament*. Leiden: Brill, 1966.

Moore, George Foot. *Judaism in the First Centuries of the Christian Era,* vols. 1–3. New York: Schocken, 1971.

Moulton, J. H., and Milligan, G. *The Vocabulary of the Greek Testament*. London, 1914–29.

Mowry, Lucetta. *The Dead Sea Scrolls and the Early Church*. University of Notre Dame Press, 1966.

Munck, Johannes. *Petrus und Paulus in der Offenbarung Johannis: Ein*

Beitrag zur Auslegung der Apokalypse. Theologiske Skifter, 1. Kobenhaven, 1950.

Nineham, D. E. *Studies in the Gospels.* Oxford: Blackwell, 1957.

van der Ploeg, Jean. *Le Rouleau de la Guerre.* Leiden: Brill, 1959.

Poirier, L. *Les Sept Eglises ou le Premier Septénaire Prophétique de l'Apocalypse.* NT Series 78. Washington: Catholic University of America, 1943.

Pope, Marvin H. *Job.* AB, vol. 15. Garden City, N.Y.: Doubleday, 1965. 3d ed., 1973.

Prigent, Pierre. *Apocalypse et Liturgie.* Cahier Theologiques, 52. Paris: Delachaux & Niestle, 1964.

Ralt, Edmund, and Laud, Willibald. *Die Heilige Schrift.* Freiberg: Herder & Herder, 1942.

Ramsay, W. M. *The Letters to the Seven Churches of Asia.* London: Hodder & Stoughton, 1904.

Reisner, Erwin. *Das Buch mit den Sieben Siegeln.* Göttingen: Bandenhoed & Ruprecht, 1949.

Rigaux, Beda. *Saint Paul—Les Épitres aux Thessaloniciens.* Paris: Gabalda, 1956.

Rohr, Ignaz. *Der Hebraerbrief und die Geheime Offenbarung des Heiligen Johannes.* Bonn, 1932.

Satake, Akira. *Die Gemeindeordnung in der Johannesapokalypse.* Norway, 1966.

Schick, Eduard. *Die Apokalypse.* Würzburg: Echter, 1952.

Scholem, Gershom G. *Kabbalah and Its Symbolism.* New York: Schocken, 1965.

———. *Major Trends in Jewish Mysticism.* New York: Schocken, 1965.

Schürer, Emil. *The Jewish People in the Time of Jesus.* New York: Schocken, 1967.

Selwyn, E. *The Christian Prophets and the Prophetic Apocalypse.* London, 1900.

Shepherd, M. H., Jr. *The Paschal Liturgy and the Apocalypse.* Ecumenical Studies, I, Worship 6. Richmond: John Knox Press, 1960.

Sickenberger, Joseph. *Erklarung der Johannesapokalypse.* Bonn: Hanstein, 1942.

Smith, J. B. *A Revelation of Jesus Christ.* Scottdale, Pa.: Herald, 1961.

Speiser, Ephraim A. *Genesis,* AB, vol. 1. Garden City, N.Y.: Doubleday, 1964.

Spitta, F. *Die Offenbarung des Johannes.* Halle, 1889.

von Speyr, Adrienne. *Apokalypse,* vols. 1–2. Vienna, 1950.

Stauffer, Ethelbert. *Christ and the Caesars.* London: SCM, 1965.

Steinmann, Jean. *Saint John the Baptist and the Desert Tradition.* New York: Harper, 1958.

Stendahl, Krister. *The Scrolls and the New Testament.* London: SCM, 1958.

Strack, Hermann, and Billerbeck, P. *Kommentar zum Neuen Testament aus Talmud und Midrasch,* I–VI, Munich: Beck, 1922–61.

Sukenik, Eleazar L. *Ancient Synagogues in Palestine and Greece.* Oxford University Press, 1934.

Swete, Henry Barclay. *The Apocalypse of St. John.* Grand Rapids, Michigan: Eerdmans, 1909. London: Macmillan, 1909.

――――. *The Septuagint.* Cambridge University Press, 1891, 1894. Stuttgart, Rahlfs, 3d ed., 1948.

Teeple, Howard M. *The Mosaic Eschatological Prophet.* JBL Monograph X. Philadelphia: Society of Biblical Literature, 1967.

Thackeray, Henry St. John. *Josephus, The Man and the Historian.* New York: Ktav, 1967.

――――. *The Septuagint and Jewish Worship.* Oxford University Press, 1931.

Torrey, Charles C. *The Apocalypse of John.* Yale University Press, 1958.

de Vaux, Roland. *Ancient Israel, Its Life and Institutions,* tr. John McHugh. London: Darton, Longman & Todd, 1961.

Vermès, Geza. *Scripture and Tradition in Judaism.* Leiden: Brill, 1961.

Volz, Paul. *Die Eschatologie der Jüdischen Gemeinde.* Hildesheim: Tübingen, 1966.

Vos, L. A. *The Synoptic Traditions in the Apocalypse.* Amsterdam: Kampen, 1965.

Wikenhauser, Wilfred. *Offenbarung des Johannes.* Regensburg: Pustat, 1947.

Winstanley, Edward William. *Jesus and the Future.* Edinburgh: Clark, 1913.

Wright, G. Ernest, and Freedman, David Noel, eds. *The Biblical Archaeologist Reader,* 1. Garden City, N.Y.: Doubleday, Anchor, 1961.

Yadin, Yigael. *The Art of Warfare in Biblical Lands,* I, II. New York: McGraw-Hill, 1963.

――――. *The Excavation of Masada.* Jerusalem: Israel Exploration Society, 1965. New York: Masada, 1966.

――――, ed. *The Scroll of the War of the Sons of Light Against the Sons of Darkness.* Oxford University Press, 1962.

Zahn, Theodor. *Die Offenbarung des Johannes,* I, II. Leipzig: Deichert, 1924–26.

ARTICLES

Bailey, J. W. "The Temporary Messianic Reign in the Literature of Early Judaism," JBL 53 (1934), 170–87.

Baillet, Maurice. "Description de la Jérusalem Nouvelle," RB 62 (1955).

Boismard, M. E. "L'Apocalypse ou les Apocalypses de St. Jean," RB 56 (1949), 507–41.

――――. "Notes sur l'Apocalypse," RB 59 (1952), 161–81.

Bornkamm, G. "Die Komposition der apokalyptischen Visionen in der Offenbarung Johannis," in *Studien zu Antike und Christentum, Gessammelte Aufsatze,* II. Beiträge zur evangelischen Theologie, 28 (Munich: Kaiser, 1959), 204–22.

Boyd, W. J. P. "I Am Alpha and Omega: Rev 1:8; 21:6; 22:13," *Studia Evangelica* 2 (1964), 526–31.

Brewer, R. R. "The Influence of Greek Drama on the Apocalypse of John," *Anglican Theological Review* 18 (1936), 74–92.

Brown, S. "The Hour of Trial: Rev 3, 10," JBL 85 (1966), 308–14.

Brownlee, William H. "The Priestly Character of the Church in the Apocalypse," NTS 5 (1958/59), 224–25.

———. "Priestly Christ of Revelation and Priestly Messiah of Essenes," NTS 3 (1956), 207 ff.

Considine, J. S. "The Rider on the White Horse, Apoc 6:1–8," CBQ 6 (1944), 406–22

———. "The Two Witnesses, Apoc 11: 3–31," CBQ 8 (1946), 377–92.

Devine, R. "The Virgin Followers of the Lamb," *Scripture* 16 (1964), 1–5.

Feuillet, André. "Le Cantique des Cantiques et l'Apocalypse: Etude de Deux Réminiscences du Cantique dans l'Apocalypse Johannique," *Recherches des Sciences Religeuses* 49 (1961), 321–53.

———. "Le Chapitre X de l'Apocalypse, son Apport dans la Solution du Problème Eschatologique," *Sacra Pagina* XII–XIII (1959), 414–29.

———. "Essai d'Interpretation du Chapitre XI de l'Apocalypse," NTS 4 (1957/58), 183–200.

———. "Le Messie et sa Mère d'apres le Chapitre XII de l'Apocalypse," RB 66 (1959), 55–86.

———. "Les 144.000 Israelites Marques d'un Sceau," *Novum Testamentum* 9 (1967), 191–224.

———. "Le Premier Cavalier de l'Apocalypse," ZNW 57 (1966), 229–59.

———. "Les Vingt-quatre Vieillards de l'Apocalypse," RB 65 (1958), 5–32.

Fiorenza, Elisabeth Schussler. "The Eschatology and Composition of the Apocalypse," CBQ 30 (1968), 537–69.

Fitzmyer, Joseph A., S.J. "Further Light on Melchizedek from Qumran Cave 11," JBL 86 (1967), 25–41.

Gaechter, P. "The Original Sequence of Apocalypse 20–22," TS 10 (1949), 485–521.

———. "Semitic Literary Forms in the Apocalypse and Their Import," TS 8 (1947), 547–73.

Gazov-Ginzberg, A. M. "Double Meaning in a Qumran Work, 'The Wiles of the Wicked Woman,'" *Revue de Qumrân* 22 (1967), 279–85.

Giet, Stanislaus. "À-propos d'un Ouvrage Recent sur l'Apocalypse," RevueSR 38 (1964), 71–92.

———. "Les Episodes de la Guerre Juive et l'Apocalypse," RevueSR 26 (1952), 1–29.

———. "Retour sur l'Apocalypse," RevueSR 38 (1964), 225–64.

Goguel, M. "Les Nicolaites," *Revue de l'Histoire des Religions* 115 (1937), 5–36.

Gry, Leon. "Les Chapitres XI et XII de l'Apocalypse," RB 31 (1922), 203–14.

Hadorn, W. "Die Zahl 666, ein Hinweis auf Trajan," ZNW 19 (1919/20), 11–28.

Hillers, Delbert R. "Revelation 13:18 and a Scroll from Murabba'at," *Bulletin of the American Schools of Oriental Research* 170 (1963), 65.

Hopkins, M. "The Historical Perspectives of Apoc 1–11," CBQ 27 (1965), 42–47.

Jeremias, Joachim. "Har Magedon, Apoc 16:16," ZNW 31 (1932), 73–77.

Johnson, S. E. "Laodicea and Its Neighbors," *Biblical Archaeologist* 13 (1950), 1–18.

Kallas, J. "The Apocalypse—an Apocalyptic Book?" JBL 86 (1967), 69–80.

Klassen, W. "Vengeance in the Apocalypse of John," CBQ 28 (1966), 300–11.

Minear, Paul S. "The Wounded Beast," JBL 72 (1953), 93–101.

Mowry, Lucetta. "Revelation 4–5 and Early Christian Liturgical Usage," JBL 71 (1952), 75–84.

Mussies, G. "YO in Apocalypse IX:12 and 16," *Novum Testamentum* 9 (1967), 151–54.

Newman, B. M. "The Fallacy of the Domitian Hypothesis," NTS 10 (1963/64), 133–39.

Power, Edmund. "A Pretended Interpolation in the Apocalypse (14:4e, 5ab)," *Biblica* 4 (1923), 108–12.

Rissi, M. "The Rider on the White Horse: A Study of Revelation 6, 1–8," *Interpretation* 18 (1964), 407–18.

Schlatter, Adolf. "Das Alte Testament in der Johanneischen Apokalypse," *Beiträge zur Förderung Christlicher Theologie* XVI/6 (Gutersloh, 1912).

Schweizer, E. "Die sieben Geister in der Apokalypse," *Evangelische Theologie* 11 (1951/52), 502–12.

Silberman, L. H. "Farewell to O AMHN. A Note on Rev 3, 14," JBL 82 (1963), 212–15.

Skehan, Patrick W. "King of Kings, Lord of Lords (Apoc 19, 16)," CBQ 10 (1948), 398.

Stott, W. "A Note on the Word KYPIAKH in Rev. I. 10," NTS 12 (1965/66), 70–75.

Strand, K. A. "Another Look at Lord's Day in the Early Church and in Rev. I. 10," NTS 13 (1966/67), 174–81.

Vanhoye, A. "L'utilisation du livre d'Ezéchiel dans l'Apocalypse," *Biblica* 43 (1962), 436–76.

Vischer, E. "Die Offenbarung Johannis, eine Jüdische Apokalypse in Christlicher Uberarbeitung," *Texte und Untersuchungen* II/3 (1886).

REVELATION

Part One: Revelation to the Baptist

I. THE PROPHET'S INAUGURAL VISION
(4:1–11)

4 ¹ After these things I looked, and behold, an open door in the heaven, and the first voice like a trumpet which I heard spoke to me, saying, "Come up here, and I will show you what must happen after these things." ² Immediately, I was in the Spirit; and behold, a throne was set in the heaven, and there was One seated on the throne, ³ and He who sat there was like the appearance of jasper and carnelian, and there was a bow around the throne which was like the appearance of emerald. ⁴ And around the throne there were twenty-four thrones and on the thrones sat twenty-four elders clothed in white garments, and on their heads were crowns of gold. ⁵ And from the throne proceeded lightning and voices and peals of thunder; and there were seven torches of fire burning before the throne, which are the seven spirits of God, ⁶ and in front of the throne something like a glass sea like crystal.

And in the middle of the throne and around the throne were four living creatures full of eyes before them; ⁷ the first living creature was like a lion, and the second living creature like an ox, and the third living creature had the face as of a man, and the fourth living creature was like an eagle flying. ⁸ And the four living creatures, each of them had six wings, they were full of eyes around and within; and they did not cease day and night, saying,

"Holy, holy, holy,
Lord God almighty, who was and is and is to come."

⁹ And whenever the living creatures gave glory and honor and thanks to Him who sat upon the throne, to Him who lives forever and ever, ¹⁰ the twenty-four elders fell down before Him who sat upon the throne and worshiped Him who lives forever and ever, and they threw their crowns before the throne, saying,

¹¹ "Worthy are you, our Lord and God,
to receive glory and honor and might,
because you created all things,
and through your will they were brought into existence and were created."

NOTES

4:1. *After these things I looked.* This type of phrase usually introduces a new vision; cf. 7:1, 9, 15:5, 18:1. "After these things" was probably added by the editor.

door. The Hebrews conceived of a solid firmament (cf. Gen 1:7–8) which divided heaven and earth; therefore, some aperture was necessary in order to communicate between the two dimensions. In Ezek 1:1 and II Baruch 22:1 the heavens open but there is no mention of a door. In Testament of Levi 5 an angel opens the "gates of heaven" and the visionary sees the holy temple and the Most High upon a throne of glory. However, a text closer to ours is I Enoch 14:15, in which Enoch is led through various doors to a greater house where God's presence is manifested. This concept of many apartments in heaven with doors leading to the holier parts was reflected in the architectural structure of the earthly temple. Here there were different divisions according to the grades of holiness. The Gentiles and the women were not allowed beyond a certain barrier, whereas the Jewish men, thought to be levitically purer, were permitted to enter further into the interior. Only the high priests could enter the holiest section, the holy of holies.

first voice. This seems to be the voice mentioned in 1:10–12. In this case the editor links the present vision with that of one like a son of man. Voices associated with the sound of trumpets occur elsewhere in the NT; cf. I Cor 14:8, I Thess 4:16, Heb 12:19. The phenomenon is also a Sinai motif, as in Exod 19:16, 19, 20:18.

Come up. The command is reminiscent of that which was given to Moses when he was bidden to ascend Mount Sinai, Exod 19:24. It is also an invitation addressed to mystics approaching a higher stage.

2. *in the Spirit.* The definite article does not appear in the Greek; the writer may not refer to the Holy Spirit. This phrase could indicate that the seer entered a new supernatural experience. It may be a rapture such as intimated in II Cor 12:1–4. The phrase does not necessarily imply a bodily translation as e.g. in I Kings 18:12, II Kings 2:16, but the writer may have in mind Ezek 8:1–4, and 11:1–2, where the prophet is lifted up by the Spirit and taken to Jerusalem. Our writer is much influenced by Ezekiel. Cf. the temptation of Jesus in Matt 4:5, 8, Luke 4:5, 9.

throne. Originally the term could be used for an oracular seat, a teacher's chair, a judge's bench, even a favorable combination of planetary positions. Later, however, the concept of "throne," Gr. *thronos*, was reserved for kings and gods and often was used with a genitive, such as "throne of glory." In the Orient, the absolute ruler sat on an ornate throne. Archaeological discoveries show such thrones with a high back, a base decorated with pictures of conquered peoples and several steps leading up to it; cf. Ps 110:1. There was an Asiatic custom of representing the throne of the invisible deity without an image; cf. the mercy seat with the cherubim but no image in the tabernacle and temple in Exod 25. But the throne, in such texts as Rev 4, is not an actual chair or seat, but is meant to represent the monarch's estate, dignity, or presence. Indeed, "throne" may well be a synonym for the deity as "heaven" is in the phrase "kingdom of heaven." Synonyms were used extensively in the times contemporary with our apocalypse and are consonant with the general character of apocalyptic literature. Hellenistic Judaism showed little interest in the eschatological throne of divine judgment, but it was a subject of concern to Palestinian and rabbinic Judaism and became an important feature in Jewish mysticism, especially the *Kabbalah*. It was thought to have been made before the creation of the world (*Pesachim* 54a). The importance given to the throne in Revelation would not suggest Hellenistic influence. In Christianity the throne is replaced by the Lordship of Christ.

3. *bow*. The Greek word, *iris*, may mean "rainbow," "halo," or "radiance." However, *iris* is not used for rainbow in Greek versions of Gen 9:13 or Ezek 1:28; the word used is *toxon*. In the Genesis narrative the rainbow appears to be Yahweh's war-bow just as flashes of lightning are seen as His arrows; cf. Ps 7:13, Hab 3:11. The covenant with Noah in Genesis means that Yahweh sets aside His bow and hangs it up in the clouds as a sign that His anger has subsided. When men gaze upon this rainbow, they feel assured that the storm has passed and no flood will come again; cf. Sir 43:11, 50:7.

Rabbinic thought elaborated on this concept of the rainbow. It was said to be one of the ten things created on the eve of the sabbath at twilight, *Pesachim* 54a; that it was a revelation of God's glory on earth, cf. *Gen R* 35:3; and that, just as one should not look upon a high official, one should not gaze upon the rainbow, *Hagigah* 16a. Rabbi Joshua ben Levi even thought that one should fall upon one's face at the sight of a rainbow as Ezekiel did when he saw the appearance of the "bow that is in the cloud" (Ezek 1:28, RSV). However, others disapproved of this practice and said that one should recite "Praised be the Lord our God, the king of the universe, who remembers the covenant and is faithful in his covenant and maintaineth his word" (*Berakoth* 59a, Epstein). On the other hand, some saw the rainbow as a sign of judgment. In *Gen R* 35:2 it is said that the generation of Rabbi Hezekiah and the men of the Great Synagogue founded by Ezra to act as the official guardians of the Law did not need the sign of the rainbow because they were completely righteous. However, to others the rainbow was given as a sign of censure and reminded one of the wickedness of the earth; cf. *Ketuboth* 77b. Thus the rainbow had theological significance for Judaism.

jasper and carnelian . . . emerald. These are referred to in Exod 28:17–21, where they explicitly represent three of the twelve tribes of Israel. The passage describes the high priest's breastplate on which are arranged four rows of three stones, each stone representing one of the tribes. The first row contains sardius (carnelian), topaz, and carbuncle; the second, emerald, sapphire, and diamond; the third, jacinth, agate, and amethyst; the fourth, beryl, onyx, and jasper. Note that jasper and carnelian are the last and first stones i.e. Benjamin the youngest and Reuben the eldest, and that the emerald, the fourth stone, represents Judah. Cf. also Ezek 28:13, where the carnelian, jasper, and emerald are among the stones of paradise.

4. *there were*. TI.

elders. Gr. *presbuteroi.* This word occurs twelve times in Revelation: 4:4, 10, 5:5, 6, 7, 11, 14, 7:11, 13, 11:16, 14:3, 9:4. There is a difference of opinion regarding the identity of the twenty-four *presbuteroi.* The opinions fall under the following headings: angels, men, prophets or wisemen, or tribal heads. The most comprehensive article on the subject is by Feuillet, in RB 65.

Allo sees in the elders angels who have charge of the world committed to them. He bases his view partly on astronomical considerations, e.g. allusions to the twelve signs of the zodiac. These were known to the Hebrews as early as the seventh century B.C. See illustration 11. For the ancient Semite the transition from star to angel was perfectly natural. Yahweh created astral as well as terrestrial beings. The astral ones were called the "host of heaven" or "sons of God"; cf. Gen 6:1, 4. For a clear association between stars and angels, see Job 38:7. For further details, see Albright, *From the Stone Age to Christianity,* pp. 295–98. Charles, APCh, I, 129, regards the elders as the angelic or heavenly representatives of the whole body of the faithful in their two-fold aspects of priests and kings.

Feuillet believes the elders are men, i.e. the saints of the OT (some scholars would include NT saints). He has devoted a careful study to this point, "The Twenty-Four Elders of the Apocalypse," in *Johannine Studies,* pp. 183–214, and comes to the same conclusion as Michl and many others. He gives four reasons why the elders cannot be angels: 1) Angels are never said to occupy thrones; they stand in God's service. 2) Nor are crowns ever ascribed to them. 3) The designation "elders" is likewise unparalleled for angels. 4) In 19:4 they cannot be angels but must be men, especially if they are redeemed. Feuillet supports his thesis with Ascension of Isaiah 9:6–12, which assigns thrones, crowns, and robes, to the just men of the OT. He points out that the elders are dressed in white robes like Jewish priests and that the number twenty-four may recall the twenty-four classes of priests mentioned in Chronicles. However, neither white robes nor the number twenty-four are exclusively priestly. Feuillet quotes the 1QM 12:1–8, which refers to the saints in heaven. A strong argument for Feuillet's view is the analogy with Heb 11–12, where there are examples of saintly men, chiefly known from the OT, designated as *presbuteroi* in 11:2. Feuillet has made a strong case for the view that the elders are glorified saints in distinction from angels. They may be prophets and/or wisemen. The elders bear no distinctly Christian features.

twenty-four. Twenty-four, a multiple of the sacred number twelve, was regarded as a round number and probably perfect; see Ginzberg, I, 173; II, 41; III, 164, 287; IV, 159; V, 113, 431; VI, 391, 407, 474. Of these references perhaps the most interesting are the twenty-four oxen for a peace offering as atonement for the twenty-four thousand men who owing to their worship of Peor (Num 24:3, 31:16; Deut 4:3; Josh 22:17) died of the plague (Ginzberg, III, 208); the twenty-four gifts due the priests (Ginzberg, I, 363); the twenty-four books of the Bible (Ginzberg, III, 208; IV, 357–358); and the twenty-four divisions of priests and Levites (Ginzberg, III, 208, 228). There had to be about twenty priests and an as yet unknown number of Levites in attendance at the temple at all times. They made up an officiating unit known as a course. The purpose of appointing twenty-four courses was to enable the men to rotate periods of service. Each course would serve at the temple for one week beginning on the sabbath; by the end of the year each course would have served two weeks. In addition, all of the courses would officiate together at the annual festivals. For the rest of the year the priests and Levites participated in secular community life. Zechariah, the father of the Baptist, is shown performing his duties in Luke 1:8–23.

If there were twenty-four divisions of priests and Levites one might expect a corresponding number for the laymen. D. N. Freedman remarks (personal correspondence) that the number twenty-four is more closely connected with the tribes than with the divisions of the priests and that the elders might be associated with the tribal chiefs. The double number may reflect the reunion of the northern and southern kingdoms about which Ezekiel was most concerned; cf. Ezek 37:15–23. There is evidence that both north and south were divided into twelve administrative districts, twenty-four in all. In view of the emphasis on the twelve tribes, which is also true of Ezekiel, one may suppose that two representatives from each tribe comprised the elders. Dr. Freedman's interpretation would associate the elders more closely with the Lamb who is described as the "Lion of the tribe of Judah, the Root of David" (cf. Ezek 37: 24 which refers to David as king) and with the twelve tribes in Rev 7:5–8 where Judah appears first. In Ezek 37:16 Joseph is called the "stick of Ephraim."

were. TI.

5. *lightning and voices and peals of thunder.* This recalls the Sinai motif. The voice may refer to the voice of God which was said to be heard in several different languages; cf. *Shabbath* 88b. However, these phenomena are traditional accompaniments to theophany.

there were. TI.

torches. These occur in Ezekiel's vision, but there they flash to and fro. We must note, however, that the Greek word is *lampades,* not *luchniai* as in Rev 1:12, which might denote a different writer.

the seven spirits. The manuscripts **046** 82, 1006, 2028 al do not contain the definite article here.

6. *like.* Omitted in 1, 2059al, sa Prim, TR.

glass sea. The motif of the sea is a very old one in Canaanite and Near Eastern religion, and Yamm, the Canaanite sea god (now Heb. *yām,* "sea"), plays an important role in the epic poetry of Ugarit. However, the symbolism used here may be associated with the Bronze Sea in Solomon's temple; I Kings 7:23–26. Albright, in *Archaeology and the Religion of Israel,* pp. 148–50, has shown that it had cosmic significance. The word *yām* is similar to the Mesopotamian word *apsû* which refers to both the fresh water ocean "from which all life and all fertility were derived" and to a basin of holy water in the temple. The author of this part of Revelation, because of his interest in liturgy, may have been thinking not only of Solomon's temple but also of the significance of blue in the priestly vestments. In *Hullin* 89a (Epstein),

R. Meir says, Why is blue singled out from all the varieties of the colours? Because blue resembles the colour of the sea, and the sea resembles the colour of sky and sky resembles the colour of a sapphire, and a sapphire resembles the colour of the Throne of Glory, as it is said, *And they saw the God of Israel and there was under His feet as it were a paved work of sapphire stone*; and as it was also written, *The likeness of a throne as the appearance of a sapphire stone*."

But cf. *Num R* 17:5 which omits the reference to the sea. These passages and their parallels invite redaction criticism. However, here the sea may be a crystal firmament (cf. Exod 24:10; Ezek 1:22, 26) for it is described as glass, Gr. *hualinē*. He may be influenced by these biblical texts and the concept of the "waters above" and the "waters below" (Gen 1:7). A celestial sea is mentioned in I Enoch 14:9 and Testament of Levi 2; this appears to be suspended between the first and the second heavens.

in the middle . . . and around the throne. This phrase is explained best by Brewer. He comments on Goodspeed's translation "standing in the centre of the throne and the four animals and of the elders a Lamb" and Moffatt's "in the midst of the throne and the four living creatures and the presbyters" and the RSV "between the throne and the four living creatures and among the elders." He thinks that the explanation may be found in the arrangement of the Greek amphitheater. There was an orchestral circular area of ground containing a speaking place of the gods on the perimeter of the orchestra and a semicircular row on the perimeter of carved stone seats, "thrones," for high priests and dignitaries. Twelve such marble thrones have been found in the theater of Ephesus, which the editor of Revelation may well have seen. Within the orchestra stood an altar. The chorus taking part in the play consisted of twenty-four members. Brewer, therefore, thinks that the throne of God may correspond to the theologium of the Greek theater. The glass sea may represent the paved orchestra and the living creatures, the massed chorus.

living creatures. (Gr. *zōon hayyōt*). Most probably they originated from the cherubim which formed part of the throne in the tabernacle, both over the ark of the covenant in the tabernacle (Exod 20:19) and in the temple of Solomon (I Kings 6:25 ff.; Pss 80:1, 89:2; Isa 37:16). There were two representations of the cherubim. Albright, in *The Biblical Archaeologist Reader*, 1, 95–96, identifies them with the winged sphinxes or winged lions having human heads. In Babylonia and Assyria one finds the winged bull with human head, and in Syria and Palestine the winged sphinx. Representations of kings sitting on thrones supported by cherubim have been found at Byblus, Hamath, and Megiddo; they date between 1200 and 800 B.C. For Yahweh riding upon a cherub see II Sam 12:11; Ps 18:10. In Ezek 9:3, 10:2ff., the *hayyōt* are identified with the cherubim. See illustration 1.

In this verse the living creatures are a class of *merkabah* (Heb., chariot serving as a throne) angels, ranked with the cherubim in the seventh heaven. They are sometimes portrayed as angels of fire who support the throne. In III Enoch they have four faces, four wings and two thousand thrones and they are placed next to the wheels of the *merkabah*. In the *Zohar* there are thirty-six living creatures (cf. II Enoch 3). They constitute what is called the camp of the *Shekinah* (Heb., symbol of the divine presence) and according to the *Zohar* they support the universe.

The impressive thing is that the author has eliminated all technical names for these creatures, such as cherubim, seraphim, watchers. He does not even call them angels, so that he only presents to us spirits and living forces. This is why *zōa* is here translated as the plural of *zōon hayyōt*, which merely means living things rather than beasts or angels. In Christian thought, as opposed to Ezekiel, the work of the *hayyōt* is assumed by the cosmic Christ and the Holy Spirit.

7–8. *the first . . . a lion . . . an ox . . . the face . . . of a man, and the fourth . . . an eagle . . . each of them . . . six wings.* Allusions to Ezek 1:5–14, esp. vss. 10–11.

7. *lion . . . ox . . . man . . . eagle.* Some scholars believe the four living creatures represent four constellations of the zodiac marking the four quarters of the sky: the lion, the bull, the water-carrier, and the scorpion. See illustration 11. However, one needs great ingenuity to find this in the text. Rather, these creatures symbolize a power which is world-wide and manifold in its operation and which holds up and pervades the entire universe, even transcending it. The living creatures are symbolic of creation and the divine immanence. They are what is noblest (lion), strongest (ox), wisest (man), and swiftness (eagle).

the face as of a man. In 046 82 al this phrase reads "the face of a man"; in P 1, 2059s pm sy^h TR, "as it were like a man"; in A pc R, "as it were of a man."

was. TI.

8. *six wings.* They signify the velocity of nature. Cf. Isa 6:2.

full of eyes. They are probably not only for the purpose of sight, but for sparkling, as in Ezek 1:18. They represent the sleepless vigilance and secret energies. John notes that the living creatures do not pause; contrast Exod 16:23, the holy rest of the sabbath. This indicates that the divine activity in nature never rests. The essence of their ceaseless activity is to praise God; cf. I Enoch 39:12, 40:2, 71:7; II Baruch 51:11.

Holy, holy, holy. "Holy" is repeated twice in 181, thrice in AP 1, 104 al, six times in 2020 pc, seven times in 1678, eight times in ℵ* 385, 2021, nine times in 046 82, 2073 pm.

Walker shows that fifteen out of sixteen assertions of Divine Holiness in the MT have only one acclamation of "holy." The exception is Isa 6:3, but in exemplar a of Isaiah in Qumran Cave 1 there is a double form, as also in the miniscules 18 and 181 of Rev 4:8. In the LXX by the fourth century there is a triple form and this became acceptable to Christians because of their trinitarian beliefs. In Rev 4:8 the acclamation is increased three-fold even to nine, as above.

11. *our Lord and God.* 046 82, 1006 al sy^h add "the holy."

to receive. Gr. *labein.* This verb is probably used in the sense of "reserve to Himself."

through your will. I.e. in the world of thought.

they were brought into existence and were created. I.e. by one definite act. The imperfect "were," Gr. *ēsan,* may be equivalent to the present, and "were created" may have been added to distinguish creation from God, who is Uncreated Being. The construction is admittedly strange. One would expect the verbs to be inverted: "because of thy will they were created and, therefore, they exist." Bonsirven (see General Selected Bibliography) suggests that rhythmic considerations may account for the inversion, or perhaps John wished to state the important fact, i.e. existence, first, and then go back to the cause. Boismard hesitantly adopts the reading of some manuscripts which have a negative with "were," so that the sentence would be rendered: "because of thy will what was not was created." This would then be a parallel to Rom 4:17: ". . . calls into existence the things that do not exist," RSV.

were created. In **046** 2020 pc "not" is inserted before "were."

COMMENT

The inaugural vision places the seer in the heart of the Jewish prophetical and apocalyptic tradition. It indicates that he is one of the privileged few who experienced the vision of the throne or chariot, Heb. *merkabah,* an experience which was regarded as the climax of mystical progress. Indeed, it cannot be a coincidence that the word "throne" appears in every chapter of Revelation except 9, 10, 15, 17, 18. Twice it is used with reference to "Satan's" throne: Rev 2:13, 16:10 (the beast's throne). This suggests that the main theme of the work is theocracy versus dominion of Satan.

The language in this chapter is unpolished and reads almost as if a disciple had "taken dictation" while the seer was in his trance; see p. 79. The evolution of the throne vision may be traced back to Exod 24:9–11, which describes Moses, Aaron, Nadab, Abihu, and the seventy elders of Israel, going up the mountain and "seeing" God. Although in Exod 24:9–11 no throne is mentioned, under the feet of the deity is "as it were a pavement of sapphire stone, like the very heaven for clearness," 24:10, RSV. Noth assigns the text to the Elohistic redactors. For our purpose it is interesting to note the presence of the "elders" and their designation with the four named characters as "chief men of the people of Israel." The Targum of Onkelos removes the reference to "feet" and renders "under the throne of His glory." The Palestinian Targum mentions the "footstool of His feet" beneath His throne. The "vision" is important because of its association with the establishment of the theocracy through the Sinai covenant.

Another early "throne vision" is found in I Kings 22:19–23, where Micaiah, the true prophet, in opposition to the band of false prophets led by Zedekiah ben Chenaanah, reports that he "saw the Lord sitting on his throne, and all the host of heaven standing beside him on his right hand and on his left . . ." 22:19, RSV. The burden of the message of Micaiah is that the lying spirit in the mouth of the false prophets will bring about the downfall of the king of Israel. There are three themes in this throne vision: Yahweh's court, the host of heaven; the political context in which the vision occurs; and the false prophets as opposed to the true prophet. It appears that this vision was given to Micaiah in close association with his prophetic mission to support the genuine word of Yahweh.

The next "throne vision" in the OT is Isa 6. Here the description appears much more elaborate than in I Kings 22. The text mentions the throne "high and lifted up" (6:1, RSV), the seraphim, the trisagion (i.e. "holy, holy, holy"), the shaking of the thresholds of the house, and the profusion of smoke (6:2–4). The vision culminates in the cleansing of Isaiah's lips and his being sent forth on a mission to Israel (6:7–13). He is told that some will be impervious to his message and that there will be destruction of the land, but a remnant will remain and this will be the holy seed. Once again, the vision is closely associated with the prophetic work which Isaiah undertakes. This particular throne vision elaborates the idea of the throne, the attendant host of heaven, the song sung by the holy ones, and the awesome aspect of the voice of the angels. The Lord is seen but He is not described. Some scholars think that this vision constituted the call of Isaiah and in time preceded what we now find in chs. 1 to 5.

In these three throne visions in Revelation, II Kings, and Isaiah, the seers have caught a glimpse of the presence of the deity in the throne room. This throne room is essentially a royal court where God is Judge, King, Magistrate, and Executive. Although Micaiah's vision might suggest Yahweh's interest in war, it is only with the throne visions in Ezek 1,10, that a feature is introduced which suggests the divine figure in his character as warrior; wheels are added to the description of the throne and it becomes a war chariot. This is not a new concept. Yahweh rides on the cherubim or fiery cloud birds in Pss 18:10, 68:5, Deut 33:26, Isa 19:1. He has a war chariot in Isa 66:15 and Hab 3:8. For the warrior god, who drives his chariot across the heavens, the throne room is the point from which he departs for war and to which he returns from war. The chariot shows him as commanding general at the head of his host and as victorious warrior; see COMMENT on Section III.

The blending of kingship and military chief was almost inevitable when the roles were so compatible in the ancient world. They were combined in earthly kings, whose prowess in war was often a prerequisite to assuming the other responsibilities. In early Israel the kings were closely associated with the cult and their palace with the temple. See illustration 11. The cherubim are naturally associated with the chariot, since they pull it across the sky. The cherubim throne, however, is an adaptation of this motif to the palace. The king sits on a throne which, with its cherubim arms, reflects the chariot. Even though this order is the reverse of that in the OT, the basic theme is that of the chariot from which the throne is derived, at least the throne in the tabernacle and temple with its cherubim. In other words, the chariot has been converted into a throne, not the other way around and in Ezekiel "throne," Heb. *ks'*, is used, not "chariot," Heb. *merkabah*. The throne reflects the basis for the dominion of the king, namely his victories in the field. In Revelation Yahweh Himself stays in the throne room, from which He directs operations first through the command of the living creatures and the ministry of angels (e.g. Rev 6), and second (implicitly) through the Lamb (Rev 17:14) and the Logos, Faithful and True, the rider on the white horse (Rev 19).

The descriptions of the throne-chariot in Ezek 1, 10, are extremely complex; 1:4–28 describes it as being like the glory of the Lord. The predominant features are: fire and brightness; the strange living creatures which have the form of men but also possess animal features and whose main characteristics are speed, agility, and brightness; the emphasis on the wheels of the throne, which gleam like a chrysolite and are full of eyes (probably stars) and are intimately associated with, perhaps attached to, the living creatures; the firmament shining like crystal and above the firmament a throne like sapphire. But the most surprising detail is the hesitating, yet daring, description of the occupant of the throne as "a likeness as it were of a human form" (1:26, RSV). Feuillet, RB 60, would describe this as a kind of incarnation of the glory of the Lord.

It is important, however, to notice once again the context in which this vision occurs. After describing the vision of glory, a voice comes to the prophet Ezekiel bidding him to go to Israel, which is rebellious, impudent and stubborn, telling him not to be afraid for they will know that he is a prophet. Then Ezekiel is given a written scroll to consume; Ezek 3:1–3, see COMMENT on Section VII. On this scroll are written words of "lamentation and mourning and woe" (2:10, RSV). The Book of Ezekiel predicts the siege (ch. 5) and disaster (chs. 7–8) of Jerusalem. Once again, therefore, we see that the throne vision is placed in the context of a prophetic mission. As in Micaiah and Isaiah, the mission will not be wholly successful.

Differing from Ezekiel's vision, yet falling into the same category, is the throne vision recorded in Dan 7:9–28. Here one is introduced to the court or judgment room, but the throne again possesses wheels. Two figures, the Ancient of Days and one like a son of man, predominate, but the court is thronged with attendants. The court sits in judgment upon the earthly kingdoms and dominion is given to the saints of the Most High. The Daniel vision is even more politically orientated than that of Ezekiel.

In the same genre of throne visions is I Enoch 14:15–25. The visionary sees a lofty throne as of crystal: the wheels of this throne are like the shining sun. He sees also the cherubim and streams of fire beneath the throne. He can describe the great glory and the occupant of the throne as clothed in raiment more bright than the sun, whiter than the snow; not even the angels, still less men, can behold his face because of its glory. Ten thousand angels stand before him, yet he needs no counsellor.

A fragment of a text from Qumran (4QSerek 40, 24, D-S, pp. 333–34) approximates more closely the text of Ezekiel than that of I Enoch or Revelation. The beginning of the fragment is missing, but the remainder describes the ministers of a glorious face in the abode of the God of knowledge. These ministers fall down before the cherubim and utter blessings. The fragment makes a specific reference to "the likeness of the throne of the chariot" and "the majesty of the firmament of the light beneath the throne of his glory." Reference is made to the wheels, the angels of holiness, and "visions of streams of fire similar to scarlet." A new feature appears in the "[sh]ining creatures clothed in glorious brocades, many coloured marvelous garments, more (brilliant) than pure salt, spirits of the living [G]od, unceasingly accompany the glory [of] the marvelous Chariot (or chariots)" (D-S; brackets signify conjectured text, parentheses signify TI). The fragment, as preserved, breaks off on the customary note of joyous shouting and endless praise to the deity.

Later Jewish mystical tradition influenced by Ezek 1 made its highest theme the throne mysticism, the perception of the glory of God on his throne. Scholem, e.g., in *Gnosticism*, refers to ch. 18 of the greater *Hekhaloth* which presents Rabbi Mehuniah seated in the temple of Jerusalem. He is in ecstasy and his pupils record his words, which describe the secret chambers of the *merkabah*. Only four rabbis are said to have entered the garden, i.e. paradise, namely, Ben Azzai, Ben Zoma, Aher, and Akiba. The first died, the second became insane, the third apostasized, and the fourth survived (*Hagigah* 14b). This mysticism may have been practiced in esoteric circles in the time of the second temple, probably during the first centuries B.C. and A.D. Later there gradually developed the doctrine of the *Shiur Qoma*, that is, the body of the deity described in detail. He is of colossal height, sometimes with his arms folded upon his shoulders. Maimonides and other later rabbis reacted sharply against such tendencies.

Seen against this background, Rev 4 presents a vision based on theocracy, the heavenly court, the function of the host of heaven, and the idea of prophetic mission closely modelled on that of Ezekiel. The throne room will be the place from which the commander directs his operations towards and on the earth. He will be assisted by his angels who will seek to reestablish the theocracy in the face of opposing satanic powers. There does not appear to be any specifically Christian element in this chapter and the present writer has not been able to find a throne or *merkabah* vision in Christian literature. The "throne" in Christianity recedes to give place to the contemplation of the Lordship of Christ; cf. Acts. 7:56. Paul does not boast of his ascent to the third heaven but of the power of Christ tabernacling over him in his weakness; II Cor 12:9.

In Revelation the scene is predominantly one of color, brilliant light, and sound. The center of attention is the form of the occupant of the throne, who is said to be like jasper, a translucent green stone, and carnelian (sardius), a blood red stone. The description reminds one of the "angel" in Dan 10:6 whose body was like beryl and whose arms and legs were like burnished bronze. Around the throne there is a halo or rainbow of emerald green. Charles, *Revelation*, I, comments that in "combining the sard, a reddish-tinted gem, with the jasper, the Seer seems to indicate a transparent crystal, suffused with warm red light such as the rising sun displays in the firmament. . . . The throne was encircled by an emerald or green-coloured rainbow; which would rest the eye, dazzled by the vision of the throne." The description may well be derived from the idea of the sun chariot in non-Jewish religions; cf. Ps 19; Ezek 28:13 ff. Two more colors are added by the elders, who are dressed in white and have golden crowns. The torches contribute the color of fire and the sea that of crystal. It is reminiscent of the "great Sea, greater than the earthly seas" which Enoch saw before he came before the elders and the rulers of the stellar orders; II Enoch 3:1–3, 4:1–2. The eyes of the *hayyōt* (living creatures) sparkle like stars adding yet another "celestial" color.

There is a continual sound of heavenly singing both from the living creatures and the elders, whose prostrations also indicate liturgical movement. Some light may be shed on the hymns by a comparison with the songs in the *Hekhaloth* literature, although these are later. The hymns in ch. 4 are the songs of praise sung by the living creatures; they correspond to the hymns which the mystics must recite before and during their ascent. Scholem, in *Jewish Gnosticism*, p. 21, describes them as "outstanding paradigms of what Rudolf Otto has called Numinous Hymns. They are full of majesty and solemnity and all end with the trisagion" (p. 21). However, the hymns in Revelation are simpler and shorter than those in the *Hekhaloth* literature. The living creatures unite in themselves the highest powers of nature and life: "physical force as patient and tenacious in the bull; as impetuous and violent in the lion; as lightning-like swiftness and power in the eagle; intelligence and reason in man" (notes from the late E. F. Seigman) and their song expresses praise to the creator of these powers.

Just as the creatures represent the universe, so do the elders represent Israel. They are associated with the kingship or the ruling power over the state. According to Sir 44–49, there are twenty-four fathers of Israel, "our fathers in their generations," "leaders of the people," who stood valiantly for Yahweh and did not submit to pagan rulers; cf. Sir 48:12b. They are listed as follows: Enoch, Noah, Abraham, Isaac, Jacob, Moses, Aaron, Phinehas, Joshua, Samuel, Nathan, David, Solomon, Hezekiah, Josiah, Jeremiah, Ezekiel, Zerubbabel, Jeshua, Nehemiah, Joseph, Shem, Seth, Adam. Simon ben Onias (Sir 50) seems to begin a new section although it is puzzling why the author returns to earlier individuals at the end of his list.

If this list, or a similar one, were in the mind of the author of chs. 4–11, the elders would form a contrast to the kings of the earth who appear frequently in Revelation (and will be discussed later). The later Wisdom literature has a motif similar to that of Revelation, namely speaking against idolatrous submission to foreign rulers and in favor of living a life of faithfulness to the covenant of Yahweh. The word for kings, Heb. $m^e l\bar{a}k\bar{\imath}m$, appears nine times in Sir 14–51 and nineteen times in this apocalypse. The crowns which the elders wear need not mean that they are actually kings, for the rabbis spoke of the crown of the priesthood, the crown of the kingship, and the crown of scholarship. One may compare, too, the twelve apostles on thrones judging the twelve tribes (Luke 22:30), which appears to be a later development of the idea of the elders on the throne. The Qumran community had a "hierarchy" of twelve men including, or in addition to, three priests; 1QS 8:1.

Therefore, in distinction from the living creatures, who signify creation, and the angels, who signify the celestial host, the elders represent those leaders of the people of Israel who have kept the covenant and acknowledged the theocracy of Israel. However, the word *presbyteroi* is not used in Sir 44:1, the word "fathers," Gr. *pateras,* is used. This vision of all creation and the elders of Israel praising God and completely in harmony is a necessary prelude and sharp contrast to the disharmony of nature revealed in the cosmic catastrophes which Revelation predicts and which are due to the disobedience of the earthly rulers, the kings of the earth. It is in this context that the prophet proclaims his message.

The liturgical aspect of this chapter remains to be explored. In the ancient world, the kingship of God and his earthly representative, the political regime and the liturgical life, were not distinguished as sharply as in our own day; in fact originally "liturgy" was a secular word meaning "service." The heavenly vision is supposed to be the model for the earthly exercise of kingship and priesthood. The throne room takes the place of the sanctuary. The living creatures correspond to the cherubim placed over the mercy seat and the ark of the covenant. The seven lamps perhaps signify the *menorah*, the seven-armed candelabrum. See illustration 19. The twenty-four elders, according to Johannine usage, may have a double meaning and represent both the fathers of Israel and the twenty-four courses of priests and Levites. The glass sea may represent the laver of the temple. Later there is presented more liturgical equipment: the altar of holocausts, 6:9, 8:3–5; a sanctuary with an altar of incense, 8:3–4; an ark of the covenant, 11:19; see illustration 10. The last liturgical characteristic is the two hymns. The trisagion, that is, the "Holy, holy, holy," according to Isa 6:3, was originally sung by the seraphim. This song begins the great liturgical service in heaven in honor of God the Creator and Ruler of the Universe; to this is joined the elders' song. Ch. 4, therefore, presents the perfect picture of kingship and the perfect liturgical worship.

Pesachim 54a enumerates the seven things which were created before the world: the Torah, repentance, the Garden of Eden, Gehenna, the Throne of Glory, the temple, and the name of the Messiah. All these elements appear in our apocalypse. Ch. 4 contains the Throne of Glory and implicitly the heavenly temple. That these seven things were created before the world indicates that they are prerequisites for the orderly progress of mankind upon the earth. "The Torah, the supreme source of instruction; the concept of repentance, in recognition that 'to err is human,' and hence, if man falls, the opportunity to rise again; the Garden of Eden and the Gehenna, symbolizing reward and punishment; the Throne of Glory and the temple, indicated that the goal of Creation is that the Kingdom of God (represented by the temple) shall be established on earth, as it is in heaven: and finally, the name of the Messiah, i.e. the assurance that God's purpose will ultimately be achieved" (*Pesachim* 54a, Epstein, p. 265, n. 11). This epitomizes the message of Revelation.

BIBLIOGRAPHY

Albright, W. F. *Archaeology and the Religion of Israel.* 2d ed. Johns Hopkins University Press, 1946.

——. *From the Stone Age to Christianity.* 2d ed. Garden City, N.Y.: Doubleday, Anchor, 1957.

——. "What Were the Cherubim?" in *The Biblical Archaeologist Reader,* 1, eds. G. E. Wright and D. N. Freedman, 95–96.

Allo, E. B. *Saint Jean, L'Apocalypse.*

Brewer, R. R. "Revelation 4, 6 and the Translations Thereof," JBL 71 (1952), 227–31.

Feuillet, A. "Le fils de l'Homme de Daniel et la Tradition Biblique," RB 60 (1953), 170–202, 321–46.

——. RB 65 (1958), 5–32.

Ford, J. Massingberd. " 'The Son of Man'—A Euphemism," JBL 87 (1968), 257–67.

Ginzberg, L. *The Legends of the Jews,* I–VIII.

Leiser, B. M. "The Trisagion of Isaiah's Vision," NTS 6 (1960), 251–53.

Moffatt, J. *The Revelation of St. John the Divine.* London, 1910.

Mowry, L. JBL 71 (1952), 75–84.

Noth, Martin. *Exodus, A Commentary.* London: SCM, 1959.

Otto, R. *Idea of the Holy.* 2d ed. Tr. J. W. Harvey. Oxford University Press, 1950.

Scholem, G. G. *Jewish Gnosticism, Merkabah Mysticism, and Talmudic Tradition.* 2d ed. New York, 1965.

——. *Major Trends in Jewish Mysticism.*

Swete, H. B. *The Apocalypse of St. John.*

Walker, Norman. "The Origin of the Thrice Holy, Apoc. 4, 8," NTS 5 (1958/59), 132–33.

II. A TIME FOR OPENING SEALS
(5:1–14)

5 1 And I saw on the right of the occupant of the throne a document written on the obverse and the reverse sealed up with seven seals. 2 And I saw a mighty angel proclaiming with a loud voice, "Who is worthy to open the document and break its seals?" 3 And no one in the heaven, no one on the earth, no one under the earth, could open the document or read it. 4 And I mourned deeply but no one was found worthy to open the document or read it. 5 And one of the elders said to me, "Do not mourn; see, the Lion from the tribe of Judah, the Root of David, has prevailed, so that he may open the document and its seven seals."

6 And I saw between the throne and the four living creatures and among the elders a little lamb standing as though it had been slain. It had seven horns and seven eyes, which are the seven spirits of God sent forth into all the earth. 7 And he went and took the scroll from the right hand of the occupant of the throne. 8 And when he received the scroll, the four living creatures and the twenty-four elders prostrated themselves before the Lamb, and each held a harp and golden shovels full of incense, which are the prayers of the holy ones. 9 And they chanted a new song, saying,

"You are worthy to receive the document
　and to open its seals,
　because you were slain and you purchased for God by your blood
　men from every tribe and tongue and people and nation
10 and you have made them a priestly kingdom for our God
　and they shall reign on the earth."

11 And I looked, and I heard around the throne and the living creatures and the elders the sound of many angels and their number was myriads of myriads and thousands of thousands and 12 they said with a loud voice,

"The Lamb who was slain is worthy to receive
　power and riches and wisdom and might
　and honor and glory and praise."

13 And I heard every creature in the heaven and on the earth and under the earth and on the sea and everything in them saying,

"To Him who is seated on the throne and to the Lamb,
praise and honor and glory and might
forever and ever."

14 And the four living creatures said, "Amen"; and the elders prostrated themselves and worshiped.

NOTES

5:1. *document.* Gr. *biblion.* This is a term used for writing material of papyrus, leather, skin, or parchment. It also denotes a book, letter, record, or statute. In Tobit 7:14, it refers to the record of a marriage. In Deut 24:1, 3, Mark 10:4, Math 19:7, with a qualitive genitive, it is used for a bill of divorce.

Biblion is a diminutive of *biblos,* but is usually used without reference to the size of the document. There is some dispute about the form of the word. Grotius, Zahn, and Nestle think that this is not a roll or scroll but a codex; see APCh, I, 136. Spitta believes that it is a book composed of parchment sheets, each pair of sheets fixed together with a seal. But most scholars (see bibliography to this Section) would take this to be a scroll as in Ezek 3:1, Ezra 6:2. In Revelation *biblion* occurs twenty-three times, in several different senses: 1) The *biblion* sent to the communities in Asia; 1:11. It contains words of prophecy and is not said to be sealed. 2) The *biblion* which is sealed (with the seven seals); 5:1, 2, 3, 4, 5, 8, 9. that is, withdrawn from human knowledge. When it is opened, it implements the will of the testator. 3) The book of life; 13:8, 17:8, 20:12, 21:27. The same image occurs in Luke 10:20, Phil 4:3, Heb 12:23. 4) *Ta biblia* (plural), that is, the books of judgment, distinguished in 20:12 from the book of life; cf. Dan 7:10, Isa 65:6, Mal 3:16, Esther 6:1. It is said that Michael, Elijah, and Enoch were the scribes who recorded deeds in these books of judgment. To these four categories may be added *biblaridion,* which the prophet swallows in 10:8–10. Note that Revelation itself is called *biblion* in 22:7, 9, 10, 18 (*bis*), 19.

obverse. ℵ sa read "in front."

sealed. Gr. *katesphragismenon.*

seven. This is a sacred number. For the Jews it was sacred because of the Sabbath (the seventh day), the seven days of creation, the seventh year which was the year of release, and in the temple the seven altars, seven lamps, and the sprinkling of sacrificial blood seven times.

seals. Gr. *sphragisin.* Seals were used as a stamping device in place of signatures to make a document valid. The impression was normally made on clay, wax, or some other soft material; cf. I Kings 21:8, Isa 8:16, 29:11, Jer 32:10. Seals were ordinarily the personal property of the owner and sometimes were decorated with special symbols. Some were made with gems or semiprecious stones; cf. Sir 32:5–6, where there is "a seal of carnelian in a setting of gold" and "a gold mounting around an emerald seal," and Exod 28:17–21, 36, where the priest's breastplate was ordered to contain twelve gemstones, each engraved with one of the names of the twelve tribes "like a seal" (RSV). Some seals bore only the name rather than a decoration. In keeping with the imagery in Revelation it is interesting to note that seals from the first millennium B.C. were decorated with such symbols as winged griffins, cherubim, or winged sphinxes. See illustration 4.

2. *mighty angel.* Gr. *aggelon ischuron.* The Greek may merely mean a mighty or powerful angel, but it might also refer to the angel Gabriel, Hebrew for "God is my strength." Gabriel is the only angel, apart from Michael, mentioned in the protocanonical books of the OT. In Tobit, Raphael also appears. In Dan 8 the prophet prostrates himself before Gabriel, who teaches him the meaning of the vision which he received. In this vision a ram having two horns stood on the bank of a river. It encountered a he-goat, who had one great horn between its eyes but later received four horns, and a little horn grew from one of them. In Daniel's vision, the ram with the two horns signified the kings of Media and Persia, and the he-goat, the king of Greece. The great horn was the first king, Alexander the Great.

4. *mourned.* Gr. *klaiō,* lit. "wailing." This word is frequently used to mean professional mourning. In the NT it occurs only in this connection. In John 11:35 the weeping of Jesus, Gr. *dakruō,* stands in sharp contrast to the wailing, *klaiō,* of those who mourn over the dead Lazarus (John 11:33). In the non-western world, this wailing is an exceedingly loud crying.

In the OT grief was proclaimed by such ejaculations as "Alas, my brother" (I Kings 13:30); "Alas, my sister" (Jer 22:18). Dirges were also sung. They were usually written in the *qinah* (Hebrew for "lamentation") meter, the first half of the verse having three accents, and the second half, two. It is interesting to observe that in Rev 5:3 there is a triad,

> no one . . . in the heaven,
> no one on the earth,
> no one under the earth.

which may suggest a dirge; cf. Exod 20:4, Deut 5:8.

5. *Lion.* The lion is the most frequently mentioned animal in the Bible. Sometimes there were so many lions in Palestine as to constitute a plague. They also had their home among the people of Asia Minor. The lion was an emblem of strength, majesty, courage, and menace; cf. Prov 22:13, 26:13, 30:30. It also was symbolic of intellectual excellence; in this regard it was contrasted with the fox; *Sanhedrin* 37a, *Aboth* 4:15, *Baba Kamma* 117a. Judah (Gen 49:9), Gad (Deut 33:20), Dan (Deut 33:23), Saul and Jonathan (II Sam 1:23), and Israel (Num 23:24, 24:9), are compared to lions. God Himself is so described, as in Isa 31:4, Hosea 5:14, 11:10. In the OT lions were depicted on the throne of Solomon (I Kings 10:19–20, II Chron 9:18–19). Well into the Christian period lions remained a very frequent decorative symbol on glasses and graves and in synagogues.

the Lion from the tribe of Judah. This epithet is based on Gen 49:9, a passage which later Judaism applied to the Messiah (see Strack and Biller-beck III, 801). The Palestinian Targum (Etheridge, pp. 330–31) reads:

> I will liken thee, my son Jehuda, to a whelp, the young of a lion; for from the killing of Joseph my son thou didst uplift thy soul, and from the judg-ment of Tamar thou wast free. He dwelleth quietly and in strength, as a lion; and as an old lion when he reposeth, who may stir him up? Kings shall not cease, nor rulers, from the house of Jehuda, nor *sapherim* teach-ing the law from his seed, till the time that the King, the *Meshiha*, shall come, the youngest of his sons; and on account of him shall the peoples flow together . . ."

The Targum then refers to the Messiah's prowess in war: "The mountains become red with the blood of the slain; his garments, dipped in blood, are like the outpressed juice of grapes" (ibid., p. 331). In Isa 29:1, Jerusalem is ad-dressed as Ariel, "lion of God."

Root of David. This epithet is based on Isa 11:1, 10, which refers to the descendant of Jesse who will be an ensign to the people, whom the nations shall seek. Instead of "root of Jesse" the targum reads: "And a king shall come forth from the sons of Jesse, and an Anointed One (or, Messiah) from his sons' sons shall grow up. And there shall rest upon him a spirit from before the Lord, the spirit of wisdom . . ."

and its seven seals. ℵ 2067 pc vg[s,cl] arm, read "and to loose its seven seals." For the significance of the number seven, see third NOTE on 5:1.

6. *lamb.* Gr. *arnion.* There is dispute about whether this word is "lamb" or "ram." The Greek word used here is a diminutive. It occurs four times in the LXX: Jer 11:19, 27(50):45; Ps 93(94):4, 6; Isa 40:11 (Aquila), in each case denoting "lamb." It also means "lamb" in Psalms of Solomon 8:28 and *Ant.* 3.221, 251. "Ram" is usually translated in Greek as *krios* from the Hebrew *'ayil.* In the NT Heb. *'it,* Gr. *arnion,* "little lamb," occurs only in John 21:15, where Jesus asks Peter to feed his lambs. The lambs depict the community as the object of the loving care of Peter and Jesus. However, the word appears twenty-nine times in Revelation, twenty-eight times referring to "the Christ" and once (13:11) to the second beast who is compared to a little lamb.

There are four bases on which to argue that *arnion* should be translated as "ram": 1) the reference to wrath, 2) the horns, 3) the sign of the ram in the zodiac, 4) the similarity to Dan 8:3 and I Enoch 90:9, 37. Linguistically the only possible translations are "little lamb" or "lamb" (cf. II Clement 5:2–4) but the character of the animal does suggest a ram. One may compare this verse from exemplar a of Psalms, Qumran Cave 11: "A halleluia of David, the son of Jesse" (DJD, IV, 55, vs. 1): "Smaller was I than my brothers and the youngest of the sons of my father, so he made me shepherd of his flock and ruler over his kids." The idea of David's being small and yet a ruler is compa-rable to the Messiah's being a lamb and a lion at the same time.

seven horns. The horn is proverbially a symbol of courage, strength, and might in both gods and men, although it can be a symbol of arrogance (Job 16:15). In II Enoch 90:9, the growing horns on the lambs denote their in-creasing power. In Luke 1:69 refers to a horn of our salvation (cf. II Sam

22:3, Ps 18:2) in the house of David. Some, e.g. Farrer, *Revelation*, pp. 94–95 and Caird, *The Revelation of St. John the Divine*, p. 75, suggest that the seven horns on the lamb express the divine plenitude of power (see last NOTE on 11:2), but the horn is not necessarily associated with divinity. A wrong interpretation of Exod 34:29, 35, gave rise to the idea that Moses had two horns on his face; the word "to shine," Heb. *qāran*, was confused with "horn," Heb. *qeren*. Does the close association here between horns and eyes in the lamb suggest a similar confusion; could the horns really be rays of light emanating from the face of the lamb? Cf. Hab 3:4.

seven spirits. The word "seven" is disputed.

7. *took the scroll*. On the authority of **046,** 104, 1006, 2031, pc g sy co TR "the scroll" is added.

8. *harp*. Gr., *kithara*. This is a general term for a kind of harp or lyre. Cf. I Cor 14:7; Rev 14:2, 15:2.

shovels full of incense. See illustration 5. Incense (resinous materials) to produce fragrant perfumes was used both in secular life and liturgical life. Incense was one of the luxuries imported from abroad; cf. Rev 18:13. Garments (Pss 45:9), beds (Prov 7:17), the groom (Song of Songs 3:6), and guests of honor (Luke 7:46; cf. *Berakoth* 6:6) were all perfumed with incense as a sign of honor and dedication. Some suggest that it was also used to dispel demons; cf. Tobit 6:1–7, smoke from the heart and liver of a fish. In Israelite worship, it usually accompanied sacrifices. Later custom regarded the offering of incense as the prerogative of the priest (cf. Num 16:6–7, II Chron 26:16–18). The offering was usually made in a pan containing the coals; the incense was in a spoon and the smoke arising from the burning coals blended with the incense was taken to symbolize prayer; cf. Ps 141:2. Josephus, *War* 5.217 says that in the incense there were thirteen ingredients gathered from the sea, the desert, and the fertile country to signify that all things belong to God and are intended to serve him. Philo speaks of four ingredients, probably representing the four terrestrial elements, air, earth, water, and fire.

9. *for God by*. In ℵ P **046** 82, 2059s 2329 pm TR "us" is added after "God."

10. *them*. In 792 it vg[s], cl, sa Prim TR, the word is "us."

kingdom. P **046** 1, 82, 2059s pl TR read "kings".

they shall reign. A **046** 2060, 232g al read the present tense. In vg[s], [cl], arm[pt] Prim TR the phrase reads "we will reign."

14. *worshiped*. The verse is continued in 2045* vg[s,cl] Prim TR by the addition of "to him who lives for ever and ever."

COMMENT

Rev 5 is a transitional scene linking the throne vision, symbolic of divine sovereignty, with the Lion of Judah who will reign on earth (5:10b), symbolic of earthly sovereignty. It provides the contrast between the harmony which is found in heaven, as represented by the worship of the living creatures, elders, angels, and creation, and the earthly disharmony and cosmic catastrophes which will be revealed in the rest of the apocalypse. It also introduces the

Messiah, called the Lamb, and the Torah, if as is most likely that is what the scroll represents.

In ch. 4 the prophet was influenced chiefly by his predecessor, Ezekiel. Here, however, the influence of Daniel and Enoch prevails, especially in the introduction of a secondary figure who is both "lion" and "lamb" who stands in a position analogous to that of one like a son of man. The Lamb is to the one seated on the throne as the one like a son of man is to the ancient of days in Daniel 7:13 and I Enoch, e.g. 48:2 (see Introduction, "The Son of Man").

Nevertheless, the Lamb has several features which are different from those of the Son of Man. Although the Lamb stands on the right hand of the occupant of the throne, signifying that he has a privileged place beside the deity, unlike the Son of Man, the Lamb has human attributes; he comes from the tribe of Judah, and his nature contains the characteristics of both the lion and the lamb. The apocalyptists use animal figures of all kinds to represent human beings and nations but never angels or God. This symbolism is prominent in Daniel and I Enoch. For example, Daniel uses a ram with two horns to signify the kings of Media and Persia and a he-goat for the king of Greece. In I Enoch the bull is symbolic of the patriarchs from Adam to Isaac (I Enoch 85–86); Moses and Aaron appear as sheep or lambs (I Enoch 86:16, 18; cf. APCh, II, 252); David and Solomon are sheep before their accession to the throne and rams when they are enthroned (I Enoch 89:45, 48). In the Testament of Joseph the twelve tribes of Israel are first symbolized as twelve harts (19:2), then twelve sheep (19:1–4), then twelve bulls (19:5–7). The Gentile nations appear as such wild beasts and birds of prey, as lions, wolves, hyenas, vultures, and ravens; cf. I Enoch 90:2–13. The author of Revelation is not, therefore, introducing the reader to new symbolism in the lion and the lamb. His readers would naturally think about Jewish leaders.

The lion was a frequently recurring symbol in the Greco-Roman world. Goodenough, I, 36–37, suggests that it represented the sun deity which rules the world, destroys evil, and takes the dead to security in the next world. However, to the Jew, the lion also represented the power of God and the power of the Torah. In works of art lions are portrayed flanking a tree, perhaps the tree of life or the Torah. In six cases they flank a central vase and guard the Torah; this may convey the idea that the Torah has leonine power, or that it must be preserved with leonine strength and diligence, or that it confers leonine power on all who adhere to it. The lion also represented both the destructive power of Israel against her enemies and the wrath of God which was both destructive and saving. Sometimes the lion is represented with a victim under its paws, but frequently this is missing from the archaeological remains. On tombs, the lion sometimes expresses hope for personal immortality. In this text the Lion is associated with conquest; vs. 5. He may open the scroll; vs. 5. He (identified with the lamb) was slain but lives; vs. 12.

Readers would not have been unfamiliar with the comparison of Judas Maccabeus to a lion in I Macc 3:3–4, RSV (cf. II Macc 11:11):

> He extended the glory of his people.
> Like a giant he put on his breastplate;
> he girded on his armor of war and waged battles,

protecting the host by his sword.
He was like a lion in his deeds,
like a lion's cub roaring for prey.

Moreover, in IV Ezra 10:60–12:35, the Messiah is represented by a lion whom God has chosen and reserved for the end days to destroy the eagle, which represents the Roman power. Other references to lions in Revelation are in keeping with the concept of conquering; they allude to the fierce and destructive power of the lion (Rev 9:8, 17, 10:3, 13:2). In the symbol of the lion, therefore, our author wishes us to see the warlike Messiah such as is portrayed in the Palestinian Targum; see second NOTE on 5:5.

Just as in Testament of Joseph 19 (which mentions both lion and lamb) the tribes of Israel are portrayed first as harts, next as sheep, and finally as bulls, so the image of a lion in Rev 5:5 changes to that of a lamb in Rev 5:6. Although instead of *arnos*, Greek for "lamb," the diminutive form *arnion*, "little lamb" is used, the strength and maturity of the animal is suggested by its possession of seven horns, the plenitude of strength, and seven eyes, the plenitude of discernment. These features and a study of the background of the image indicate that the character of the Lamb is not sharply contrasted with that of the Lion. Taking into consideration all the information concerning the Lamb which our apocalypse offers, it cannot be doubted that the Lamb is the apocalyptic ram, a synonym for the Messiah, a traditional symbol in such literature and quite consonant with the eschatological, fierce preaching of the Baptist. The diminutive is traditionally used as a sign of affection, so the transition from lion in vs. 5 to little lamb in vs. 6 may simply mean that the Messiah is loved as well as feared.

The Lamb stands near the throne (vs. 7); receives adoration (vs. 8); is the savior, leader, and shepherd of others (7:10, 17); stands on Mt. Zion (14:1–5); engages in war and is victorious (17:14). Kings hide from his wrath (6:16); he is judge (13:8, 14:10, 21:27); he shares the throne with God (22:1, 3). As Dodd avers, at first sight the juxtaposition of violence and power in the figure of the Lamb appears paradoxical, but the explanation is found in Jewish apocalyptic.

In I Enoch 89–90 the leaders of Israel are depicted as sheep, rams, or bell-wethers. David is a lamb who becomes a ram, leader of the sheep. In I Enoch 90:6–19, still using the animal symbolism, the author describes a great conflict, which Charles, APCh, II, 257, identifies with the Maccabean revolt. Some identify the great horned sheep in those verses with Judas Maccabeus, others with the Messiah. Dodd thinks that here we have "a prototype of the militant seven-horned Lamb" of Rev 5. He compares a similar passage in Testament of Joseph 19:8 where there is a lamb who overcame beasts and reptiles. Dodd sees John 1:29, 36, in the light of these texts, and suggests that "Lamb of God" is a messianic title "virtually equivalent" to "King of Israel"; cf. John 1:49. Barrett, p. 213, asserts that it "would be entirely consistent with John the Baptist's message in its original form that he should have described the Messiah as the Lamb of God in the apocalyptic sense." The apocalyptic aspect receded as the early Church fused the Lamb with the idea of the Passover, the Suffering Servant, and the Eucharist.

There is one more aspect of the Lamb to discuss, namely, his association with redemption and sin. In accordance with Dodd, he "who takes away the sin of the world" can be seen as the Messiah who abolishes sin without any association with redemptive death. As proof he cites Testament of Levi 18:9, a passage dealing with the priestly Messiah.

> In his priesthood shall sin come to an end,
> And the lawless shall cease to do evil.

He also cites Psalms of Solomon 17:29(27), dealing with the Davidic Messiah:

> And he shall not suffer unrighteousness
> to lodge any more in their midst,
> Nor shall there dwell with them
> any man that knoweth wickedness.

He then compares the Apocalypse of Baruch 73:1–4. However, the Lamb in our apocalypse is seen "as though slain" (5:6); to have been slain (5:9, 12; 13:8); to have bought people by his blood (5:9) and to have made them into a kingdom and priests (5:10). People washed their robes in his blood (7:14) and conquered through it (12:11); the Lamb is also a temple (21:22). This adds more to the Messiah than the Jewish expectation described above.

The lamb was said to have been slain. Although "slay," Gr. *sphazō*, may be used in the sense of an animal sacrifice ritual, the more usual meaning is "to kill a person with violence"; cf. II Kings 10:7; Jer 52:10 (LXX); Josephus *Against Apion* 1.76. In the NT it is never used in the sacrificial sense and only occurs in Revelation and I John. It refers to fratricide (I John 3:12), slaughtering (Rev 6:4, 13:3), and "martyrdom" (Rev 6:9, 18:24). It is not, therefore, obvious that the lamb is sacrificially slain. Indeed, as Dodd remarks on p. 233, it is the blood of bulls and goats, not lambs, that takes away sin, Lev 16. Therefore, the slaughter of the lamb and the function of his blood must be seen against the background of battle and/or martyrdom. Either he is slain in battle or martyred but the text does not tell us. On the whole, martyrdom (by this era seen as sacrifice) seems to be the most likely interpretation; it would class the slaughtered lamb with the souls under the altar (6:9) and the saints, and other slain prophets, (18:24). Martyrdom was thought to bring atonement (Frend, pp. 46 f.).

The prototype of the martyr in rabbinic thought is the figure of Isaac. The theology of the binding of Isaac is known in Hebrew as the *akedah*. Rabbinic tradition elaborates the theology of Gen 22 so that the emphasis is not so much on the faith and obedience of Abraham as on the voluntary, even joyous, self-sacrifice of Isaac. In reward for the obedience of Abraham and the generosity of Isaac, God promised to remember Israel on their account. The *akedah* theology associated Isaac with the Suffering Servant. Isaac was called the lamb of God; see Vermès. Note that Yahweh provided a ram to be sacrificed in Isaac's place; see Vermès, also Ford, *Wellsprings of Scripture* (London: Sheed & Ward, 1968), pp. 25–30.

Sacrificing lambs in the Temple was seen as a memorial of the sacrifice of Isaac. It was said that through the merits of Isaac God would raise the dead.

Indeed, some Jewish writers saw Isaac as the prototype of the risen man. In the words of Vermès, p. 208:

> In short, the binding of Isaac was thought to have played a unique role in the economy of the salvation of Israel, and to have a permanent redemptive effect on behalf of its people. The merits of his sacrifice were experienced by the chosen people in the past (especially in their redemption from Egypt) invoked in the present, and hoped for at the end of time.

It seems, therefore, that the *akedah* may well cast light upon the theology of the lamb. In IV Macc 13:12, the martyrs are bidden to remember Isaac, who yielded himself as a sacrifice; cf. 16:20, 18:11, also *Ant.* 1.222–236. Both Vermès and Schoeps assign the *akedah* theology to a pre-Christian date.

However, the lamb in Revelation is a far greater figure than Isaac. The fact that the lamb of this apocalypse receives adoration along with the occupant of the throne suggests a certain equality, although the divinity of the Lamb is not yet established at this stage; cf. 5:13. The facts known so far indicate that he is eschatological and apocalyptic in nature, he will die a violent death, and after death he will receive power, riches, wisdom, strength, honor, glory, and praise. Except that he will die, his position is similar to that of the Son of Man in Daniel and Enoch.

In the light of the life, death, and resurrection of Jesus, the author of John, and/or the Baptist's disciples, may have seen the Lord as the martyred prophet *par excellence* replacing Isaac. They refined the Baptist's concept. It was later Christian authors who made the association with the Suffering Servant (Acts 8:32, citing Isa 53:7; cf. I Peter 2:21–25) and with sacrificial animals (I Peter 1:18–19), thereby developing the concept of the bearing or removal of sin. Revelation does not use the word "sin," Gr. *hamartia*, in relation to the Lamb; cf. 1:5, 18:4–5, the only places in Revelation where *hamartia* occurs. Neither is "to bear or lift," Gr. *airō*, applied to lifting of sin; cf. 10:5, 18:21. Rev 1:5 speaks about Christ loving us, Gr. *agapaō*, and either freeing or washing us, Gr. *louō*, but neither *agapao* nor *louō* are activities of the Lamb; robes are "bathed," Gr. *eleukanan*, not washed, *louō*, in his blood. The Lamb may, therefore, be seen as a martyr but cannot, as yet, be regarded as a sacrificial offering per se. It remained for John the evangelist in John 12–21 to reveal this in the light of Christ's teaching and death.

The covenanters of Qumran expected two messiahs, the Davidic or kingly and the Aaronic or priestly. There is no trace of such an expectation in this apocalypse. The Lion/Lamb is identified in 5:5 with house of David and called the Root of David. The root or branch of David, in distinction to the root or branch of Jesse (Isa 11:1, 10) occurs in some of the exegetical writings from Qumran. In a commentary on II Samuel, D-S, p. 313 (italics denote quotation from Scripture) one reads:

> . . . *And I will raise up thy seed after thee, and I will establish his royal throne (11)* [*for ev*]*er I wi*[*ll be*] *a father to him and he shall be my son* (2 Samuel vii 11c, 12b–c, 13, 14a). This is the branch of David who will arise with the Seeker of the Law and who will sit on the throne of Zion at the end of days . . .

Here, the seeker of the Law may be the Teacher of Righteousness; cf. CDC 6:7, 7:18. That he is the branch or root of David means that he is the kingly, not the priestly, Messiah. He appears again in the Patriarchal Blessings which relate to Gen 49. The fragment is a commentary on Gen 49:10 from D-S, p. 315 (49:9 refers to Judah as "a lion's whelp," AB):

. . . a monarch will [not] be wanting to the tribe of Judah when Israel rules, (2) [and] a (descendant) seated on the throne will [not] be wanting to David. For *the (commander's) staff* is the Covenant of kingship, (3) [and] the *feet* are [the Thou]sands of Israel. *Until* the Messiah of righteousness comes, the branch (4) of David; for to him and to his seed has been given the covenant of the kingship of his people for everlasting generations, because (5) he has kept [. . .] the law with the members of the community . . .

These texts appear to have been influenced by Jer 23:5, 33:15, which say that a righteous man who is a branch of David will reign as king and implement law and justice on earth. Further, Deut 17:18–20 speaks of the king reading the law each day and keeping all its words and statutes. Revelation might therefore be presenting that righteous descendant of David, who because he has kept the law is worthy to open the scroll.

The scroll is sealed with seven seals. Yigael Yadin found such a scroll in the Judaean desert with seven threads, each one attached to the name of a witness. All the seals are on the outside; see illustration 2. The scroll is a deed dating from the end of the first century A.D. or the beginning of the second, so it is roughly contemporary with Revelation and shows that contracts or legal documents with seven witnesses were known and in use at that time. Such documents, however, could not be opened until all seven seals were broken.

It is certainly possible that the scroll in Revelation is similar to the one Professor Yadin found. However, there is an alternative. Commentators have remarked that the seals are broken one by one but the contents of the scroll appear to be proclaimed as each seal is broken. The reader is not obliged to wait until the last or seventh seal is opened in order to learn the message. Can all the seals, therefore, be on the outside?

The scroll has three distinctive features. It is written on both the obverse and the reverse; cf. Exod 32:15, Ezek 2:10. It has more than the two witnesses required to make an ordinary document legal, if the number of seals indicates the number of witnesses. The contents are revealed as each seal is broken rather than when the last is removed, although what follows the breaking of seals may be accompanying action rather than discovery of the contents.

The Hebrew document which resembles the apocalyptic scroll most closely is the *get m⁽e⁾quššar*, the tied (folded and sealed) deed. This was one which each witness folded, signed on the back, then folded and signed again; cf. Jer 32:9–25. Although the interpreters of the *Mishnah* do not appear to know exactly what it was, or exactly what it looked like, the deed appears to have required more than two witnesses, at least three, although there is dispute concerning the actual number. There is a description of such folded deeds in *Baba Bathra* 10:1–2 (Epstein):

A plain document has [the signatures of] the witnesses inside, and a *folded* [*document*] has [the signatures of] the witnesses on the back. . . . a *plain document* requires [at least] two witnesses, and a *folded* [*document* must be signed by no less than] three /witnesses/. If a *plain* [*document*] were signed by but one witness or if a *folded* [*document*] were signed by only two witnesses, they are both invalid.

Another such occurs in *Gittin* 8:9–10; cf. 81b. The document was apparently knotted or stitched and written on every other line. Thus, the blank lines and written lines alternated and the written one was folded over the blank one. Each fold bore the signature of a different witness, probably on the external upper side, that is, the witnesses probably wrote on the reverse, the contents of the document being written on the obverse. Where a signature was missing, this was known as a bald *get; Gittin* 81b. Apparently, the more folds, the more witnesses had signed. The document in Revelation must have had seven folds.

The Talmud adds three further points of interest. The description of the document as sealed is understood by some, but not all, rabbis to refer to the folded *get; Baba Bathra* 160b. The purpose of increasing the number of witnesses is to give the document greater publicity or importance; *Baba Bathra* 161a, note 18, p. 703. It is said that the folded *get* originated with priests who wished to divorce their wives, as in *Baba Bathra* 160b (Epstein):

What is the reason why the Rabbis instituted a folded (deed]?—They were [in] a place [inhabited] by priests, who were very hot-tempered and they divorced their wives (for the slightest provocation). Consequently the Rabbis made [this] provision, so that in the meantime they might cool down.

Compare the note by the editor, on *Gittin* 81b, note 7 (Epstein):

If the husband did not wish to act too impetuously, he could get the *Get* written in folds, the scribe folding the paper over after every two or three lines and the witness signing on the back. If any fold was left without a signature, the *Get* was called 'bald' and not valid. . . .

While this explanation of the origin of the folded *get* may be questioned, the fact that it was used in divorce cases is interesting. This type of document was supposed to protract the proceedings in order to give the husband time to change his mind. It was especially desirable in the case of priests, who could not take back their divorced wives. Could the Lamb's *biblion* have been a *get* m*e*quššār? If so, was it a nuptial document, either the marriage contract (Heb., *ketubah*) or a bill of divorce? The bride and adulteress motifs in Revelation point to such a scroll. It might easily be a bill of divorce; the Lamb divorces the unfaithful Jerusalem and marries the new Jerusalem.

Biblion is used for a bill of divorce in LXX Deut 24:1, 3, Isa 50:1, Jer 3:8, Mark 10:4, Matt 19:7, although it is always followed by the genitive of *apostasion*, "divorce." *Apostasion* without *biblion* is used in Matt 5:31. Although the

Greek *biblion* is usually qualified by *apostasion,* the Semitic word *get* is often used without qualification when it means "bill of divorce." Further, the references from Isaiah and Jeremiah pertain to the relationship between Yahweh and His people. Jer 3:8 actually interprets the text of Deut 24:1–4 as a rule for divorce between Yahweh and Israel. If the sealed scroll is the Lamb's bill of divorce, the seals and the trumpets, in contrast to the vials, reveal disciplinary punishment or warnings to give the wife time to repent.

However, there are many other interpretations. The scroll may contain the Torah, the understanding of which is hidden from the sons of darkness but revealed to the Teacher of Righteousness and the sons of light. Or it may contain the words of the prophets; the Lion/Lamb, like the Teacher of Righteousness, has a special office of interpreting aright the words of the prophets; cf. 1Qp Hab 2:8–9, 7:4–5, and John 1:18 where the Son "exegetes" the Father. Or, the scroll may contain something similar to the curses and the blessings for the breaking or keeping of the commandments, respectively, in Deut 27, 28. Indeed, there is an echo of Exod 20:4 and Deut 5:8 in the reference to the three categories "heaven," "earth," and "under the earth" (Rev 5:3). But it is not so likely that these blessings and curses would be sealed.

Another explanation of this scroll might be to identify it with the heavenly tablets, such as were shown to Enoch. These contained the deeds of all mankind, I Enoch 81:1–4. The scroll in Revelation is not identified with the book of life (3:5, 13:8, 17:8, 20:15, 21:27) and the books mentioned in 20:12. On the whole, it is feasible to identify the contents of the scroll either with a covenant or "marriage" deed, or an understanding of OT prophecies.

In this case, the Lamb is similar in character to Moses and the expected prophet like Moses (Deut 18:15–22), to the Teacher of Righteousness and to the Samaritan *Taheb,* "Messiah" (see MacDonald), who was expected to be a second Moses. The Lamb's function is to reveal the meaning of the Torah, especially the prophets, just as Revelation itself is a reapplication of OT prophecy. The Lamb stands as a contrast to the false prophets (as represented by the second beast, 13:11–18), just as the Teacher of Righteousness is antithetical to the Man of the Lie in the Qumran documents.

Three hymns are sung as the Lamb takes the scroll. The first 5:9–10, is by the living creatures and the elders. It echoes Exod 19:6, in which Yahweh declares to Moses that Israel "shall be to me a kingdom of priests and a holy nation," RSV. The term in vs. 9 translated by "purchased" is the ordinary Greek word for "buying," *agorazein,* but is used with reference to redemption; cf. I Cor 6:20. The OT speaks of "buying" effected by Yahweh; through the mediation of the Sinai Covenant the people of Israel became the property or special possession of Yahweh, "the people that Yahweh acquired for Himself," or more exactly, "a most precious thing," Heb., *segullah.* Dr. Freedman has reminded me that *segullah* was the privy purse of the king; Israel was therefore Yahweh's private possession, whereas the other nations were in the public domain. The basic text is precisely the one to which the author alludes in vs. 10, namely, Exod 19:5–6; cf. Deut 7:6, 14:2, 26:18, Pss 74:2, 78:55, 135:4, Isa 43:21, Mal 3:17 of the future acquisition in Messianic times.

In vs. 9 the purchase price was the blood of the Lamb. In the OT the reference to blood is to the blood that seals or reaffirms the covenant. In Exod 12:3–13, 21–27, the blood of the paschal lamb aids in Israel's liberation from Egypt; sprinkled on the doorposts it warns the destroying angel that the residents are Yahweh's people. The blood sprinkled on the altar representing Yahweh (cf. Exod 24:6–8) and on the people signified a blood relationship, a community of life between the two, since "the blood is (or is the bearer of) life" (Gen. 9:4).

This first hymn might (but it is not clear) suggest the redemption of the Gentiles. On the other hand, it might refer to gathering together the diaspora Jews "from every tribe and tongue and people and nation." The second hymn (vs. 12) is sung by the angels. It enumerates seven desirable attributes, perhaps to signify the completeness of the praise or veneration given to the lamb. In the third hymn, vss. 13–14, the great chorus is joined by all creation. This doxology has four terms, "heaven," "earth," "under the earth," "sea," indicating that all nature—heaven, hell (Heb. *sheol*), earth, and the sea; or the four points of the compass; or the four elements, air, fire, water and earth—join in the praise. Note the crescendo in the three songs of praise. In vss. 8–10 it is the four living creatures and the elders who sing. They are joined by the myriads of angels for the second hymn, vss. 11–12. Then all creation joins in the final hymn, vss. 13–14.

The vision in this chapter is proleptic; it predicts what will happen in the future. It is not, however, necessary to argue that the seer understood its full import. Later Christians could see it fulfilled in a richer sense through the life, death, and resurrection of Jesus, but there is no intimation that the seer realizes this. He adds no explanation to the vision. He may be in the position of the disciples of the Baptist whom Paul met at Ephesus (Acts 19:1–7) or of Apollos who needed to hear more accurately concerning the way (Acts 18:24–28). It is possible that these people knew of the apocalyptic preaching of the Baptist and certain aspects of the earthly life of Jesus but did not know of his death, resurrection, and the sending of the Spirit.

BIBLIOGRAPHY

Barrett, C. K. "The Lamb of God," NTS 1 (1954/55), 210–18.

Burrows, M. *The Dead Sea Scrolls.*

Dodd, Charles H. *The Interpretation of the Fourth Gospel.* Cambridge University Press, 1953.

MacDonald, J. *The Theology of the Samaritans.*

Schoeps, Hans Joachim. *Paul.* Tr. Harold Knight. Philadelphia: Westminster, 1961.

Spitta, F. *Die Offenbarung des Johannes.*

Vermès, G. *Scripture and Tradition in Judaism.*

Walker, N. "The Origin of the Thrice Holy, Apoc. 4, 8," NTS 5 (1958/59), 132–33

Zahn, T. *Die Offenbarung des Johannes,* I, II.

III. THE ANGELIC ARMY
(6:1–17)

6 ¹ And I looked when the Lamb broke the first of the seven seals, and I heard one of the four living creatures give a command like a clap of thunder, "Come forth." ² And I looked, and behold a white horse, and he who was seated upon it carried a bow, and a wreath was given to him, and he went out conquering that he might conquer.

³ And when he broke the second seal, I heard the second of the living creatures command, "Come forth." ⁴ And another horse came out, a fiery red one, and to him who was seated upon it was granted the power to take peace from the earth and that there should be internecine strife, and he was given a great sword.

⁵ And when he broke the third seal, I heard the third of the living creatures command, "Come forth." And I looked, and behold a black horse, and he who was seated on it carried a pair of scales in his hand. ⁶ And I heard, as it were, a voice in the midst of the four living creatures, calling, "A quart of wheat for a denarius, and three quarts of barley for a denarius; and do not injure the oil and the wine."

⁷ And when he broke the fourth seal, I heard the voice of the fourth of the living creatures command, "Come forth." ⁸ And I looked, and behold a yellowish-green horse, and the name of him who was seated upon it was Death, and Hades followed him; and authority was granted to them over a quarter of the earth, to kill with sword and famine and plague and by wild beasts of the earth.

⁹ And when he broke the fifth seal, I saw under the altar the souls of those slain for the Word of God and the testimony they bore. ¹⁰ And they cried out loudly, saying, "O Lord, holy and true, how long before you render judgment and deliver our lives from those who dwell upon the earth?" ¹¹ And each of them was given a white robe, and they were told to rest a little longer until the number of their fellow servants and their brethren, who were about to be killed as they themselves, was completed.

¹² And I looked when he broke the sixth seal, and there was a great earthquake, and the sun became dark like hairy sackcloth, and the entire moon became like blood, ¹³ and the heavenly constella-

tions fell to the earth, like a fig tree shedding its winter fruit when shaken by a mighty wind, 14 and the heaven was wrenched apart like a scroll that is rolled up and every mountain and island was shaken from its place. 15 And the kings of the earth and the high officials and the military tribunes and the rich and powerful and every slave and freeman hid themselves in the caves and rocks of the mountains; 16 and they cried to the mountains and to the rocks, "Fall on us and hide us from the face of Him who is enthroned and from the wrath of the Lamb, 17 for the great day of their wrath has come, and who can stand it?"

NOTES

6:1. *And I looked when the Lamb.* **046** 82, 2026 al vg arm^pt read "that" in place of "when."

command like a clap of thunder. In apocalyptic works, sounds, size, and color are often grossly exaggerated. In the case of voices they are often said to travel an incredible distance. The reference to thunder here may indicate that a theophany, i.e. a manifestation of God, is to take place. Thunder accompanied the theophany and the giving of the Torah on Mount Sinai, Exod 20:18. Ps 29 describes the power, majesty, and effect of the voice of Yahweh.

"Come forth." Gr. *erchou.* The Greek word frequently denotes making a public appearance and is used with special reference to a divine epiphany, such as the coming of God to bring judgment or salvation. In Revelation it refers to the coming of God or the Christ (1:4, 7, 8, 2:5, 16, 3:11, 4:8, 6:17, 22:7, 12, 14, 20). Here it is associated with the manifestation of the wrath of God; cf. vs. 16, also 22:17, 20, for a more benign use (of the Spirit and the Bride).

א **046** 82, 2028, 2329 al g vg^s,cl read "Come forth and see." So also for vss. 3, 5, 7.

2. *And I looked.* Omitted in **046** 82, 2028, 2329.

white. Gr. *leukos.* This word was obliged to serve for many shades of white from the whiteness of hair or goatskin to the bright or radiant light of, e.g. Jesus' raiment in the account of the transfiguration. It is also used for reddish white, pink, dull white, and gray, e.g. the whiteness of leprosy, Lev 13:13–43. It may also mean gray horses, as in Zech 1:8, 6:3, 6. The Hebrew *laban* may mean either white or gray. The variety of meanings may explain why the word is frequently qualified, e.g. white as snow or white as salt. Because the adjective is not qualified in this verse one does not know whether the horse is gray or white. White is usually symbolic of purity and joy; cf. Isa 1:18, Ps 51:7.

horse. The horse was not indigenous to Palestine. Although after the exile horses were more popular in Israel, in the OT the horse is primarily a war animal, usually the war steed of the enemy. *Sanhedrin* 93a distinguishes red, yellow, and white horses, and says that the appearance of a white horse is a favorable sign. In the later rabbinic writings the coming of the Messiah was associated with the sight of a horse, e.g., "If you see a Persian horse tethered in Eretz Israel look for the feet of the Messiah"; *Lam R* 1; 13:41. Cf. *Song of Songs R* 8; 9:3, which adds that the horse will be tethered to a grave, and *Berakoth* 56b, which says that a man who sees an ass in a dream should look for the signs of redemption; see also *Pirke of Rabbi Eliezer,* 31. Perhaps war horses were associated with the messianic woes, i.e. the sufferings which would precede the advent of the Messiah.

bow. Gr. *toxon.* Scripture speaks of the bow of Yahweh; Gen 9:13; Ps 7:13; Lam 2:4, 3:12; esp. Hab 3:8–9, LXX.

wreath. Gr. *stephanos.* This refers to a laurel crown won at athletic competitions rather than a diadem or permanent crown; contrast the diadems in 19:12, and see second NOTE on 19:11.

was given. Gr. *edothē.* See COMMENT.

3. *he.* The Lamb.

Come forth. See third NOTE on 6:1.

4. *another horse came out.* In ℵ pc, "another" is preceded by "I looked and behold" as in vss. 2, 5, 8, but the formula is altered here.

red. Gr. *purros.* Cf. Zech 1:8, 6:2, for this color applied to horses. *Purros* means literally red as fire; *pur* means "fire," cf. II Kings 3:22, LXX. It is the color of the dragon (Rev 12:3) and represents bloodshed and sin; cf. also I Clem 8:3.

the power. TI.

from the earth. Gr. *ek.* A 2059 al omit *ek.*

great sword. Gr. *machaira.* In distinction from *rhomphaia,* which is used in vs. 8 (see NOTE on 6:8, "sword"), *machaira* is symbolic of violent death (cf. Rom 8:35), war (cf. Gen 31:26), and the power of the authorities to punish evil-doers (cf. Rom 13:4).

5. *"Come forth."* See third NOTE on 6:1.

And I looked. Omitted in 046 82, 2028, 2329 al g vg[s,cl].

black. This color is symbolic of mourning or affliction.

6. *quart.* Gr. *choinix.* A *choinix* was a dry measure of about a quart, i.e. approximately 1.92 pints. One *choinix* was the daily ration of grain for one man.

denarius. A denarius was a Roman silver coin equivalent to one day's wages. It amounted to about twenty cents. Thus enough wheat to feed one man for one day cost a full day's wages. The cost of wheat here is five to twelve times its normal price. Famine is indicated.

barley. This grain was used in the preparation of cheaper kinds of bread.

the oil and the wine. The still unpublished Temple Scroll, rescued during the Six Day War in Israel, mentions two Jewish feasts of which scholars had no knowledge before, a Feast of Oil and a Feast of New Wine. These products were sacrificial elements in the temple especially for the daily burnt offerings. J. Duncan Derrett, pp. 220 ff., draws attention to some interesting points about them. They were stored in a special place and handled only by the priests. Josephus, *War* 5.565, describes with horror the sacrilegious plundering of the temple by one John in the time of Titus:

He accordingly drew every drop of the sacred wine and of the oil, which the priests kept for pouring upon burnt-offerings and which stood in the inner temple (cf. Mishna, *Middoth* 2:6), and distributed these to his horde, who without horror anointed themselves and drank therefrom.

In Josephus' opinion this sacrilege warranted the destruction of Jerusalem.

8. *And I looked.* Omitted in 046 82, 2028, 2329 al vg[s,cl] sa.

green. Gr. *chloros.* This word means a yellowish-green and would denote anything from the light green of plants to the color of a person in sickness.

Death. Gr. *thanatos.* The definite article is omitted from ℵ C 1006, 1611, 2031, 2031 al. *Thanatos* may be translated as either "death" or "plague."

Hades. In this verse there are two figures, Death and Hades, but only one horse. Many scholars have suggested that the phrase concerning Hades was interpolated into the text by a scribe who was familiar with the combination of death and Hades; cf. 1:18, 20:13, 14.

followed. 1 al Or TR have "follows."

Sword. Gr. *rhomphaia.* This is a large and broad sword used by barbarian people. In Philo *rhomphaia* is always used for the angel's flaming sword, as in Gen 3:24; cf. Rev 2:16, 19:15 and NOTES. Elsewhere in the NT it is used only in Luke 2:35 of the sword which will pierce Mary's soul. It indicates pain and anguish. It may be the prophetic word which pierces like a sword; cf. Heb 4:12. It is referred to in the Jewish Sibyllines 3.316; cf. Ezek 14:17.

wild beasts of the earth. These are probably to be contrasted with the hellish animals, which occur in Rev 9.

9. *the altar.* Gr. *tou thusiastēriou.* An altar is not mentioned in ch. 4, where the heavenly stage is set, the presence of the definite article, *tou,* here indicates there was a heavenly altar in the throne room; indeed, one would be needed for burning the incense. This altar is the prototype of the earthly altar; cf. Heb 8:5. It is present also in Rev 8:3, 5, 9:13, 11:1, 14:18, 16:7. It is not known whether this heavenly altar was the altar of incense or the altar of burnt offering or, indeed, a combination of both, but the belief in it seems to have been very early, possibly as early as Isa 6:1–3. The idea was, at least, current in the second century B.C.

the testimony they bore. 046 82, 205, 2028 al sy[h] read, "the testimony of the Lamb they bore."

10. *cried.* Gr. *ekrazan.* This word is used for the crying of the prophet Isaiah in Rom 9:27, for the fervent prayer of the Spirit in the hearts of men in Gal 4:6, and for the urgent speech of a prophet in *Ant.* 10.117.

Lord, holy and true. "Lord" in Greek is *despotēs.* This could refer either to God or the Christ but the former is more likely. In the LXX *kurios* is the commoner appellation for God but *despotēs* is employed twenty-five times. A reference from Josephus may cast light on its use here. He relates, in *War* 7.418–19, that the Jewish rebels (Zealots) endured torture and death rather than acknowledge the Roman emperor as *despotēs.* In Rev 6:10 the martyrs use the title to acknowledge that God is the authentic sovereign.

deliver. Gr. *ekdikeō*. D. N. Freedman, in private communication, drew my attention to the fact that, according to Mendenhall, "The 'Vengeance' of Yahweh," in *The Tenth Generation* (Johns Hopkins University Press, 1973), pp. 69–104, the original meaning of the Hebrew equivalent *nqm*, still attested in the Amarna letters and in numerous passages in the OT, is "to deliver, save," and is regularly followed by the preposition *min*, "from." Hence, God delivers a man from his enemies; that is the basic idea behind all the subsequent uses and nuances. Retribution in the sense of punishing the wicked does enter into the picture but the idea of vengeance in the sense of personal satisfaction does not. Here the martyrs refer to the final judgment and vindication of the righteous with eternal life. It might be added that the development of the doctrine of the resurrection of the dead is closely associated with martyrdom and is seen as one aspect of vindication by a just and righteous God. He rewards the innocent who suffer on the earth. Perhaps it is not only eternal life but resurrection of the body for which the martyrs pray here; cf. the magnificent words of the mother of the seven Maccabean martyrs in II Macc 7:20–23.

those who dwell upon the earth. Minear, pp. 261–69, draws attention to the fact that this phrase is used eleven times in four separate visions. He feels that "the dwellers on the earth" are probably to be identified with the "beast worshippers." The phrase describes those who are opposed to the faithful and the word "earth" itself is symbolic of the "antichristic" forces. Minear cites 1QH 8:19–36, where the "dwellers on earth" are opposed to the army of the holy ones; p. 262, citing Burrows, *Dead Sea Scrolls*, pp. 404 f. "Earth" is a term which is the "common denominator for all antichristic forces," although it has four distinctive uses in this apocalypse: 1) It is used with heaven to denote the range of God's creation. 2) It signifies the sphere where God is making a new creation. 3) Most frequently it is used for that which has been corrupted and destroyed by those opposed to God. 4) It is the area in which God inflicts His punishments (p. 264).

11. *was completed*. ℵ P **046** 1, 82, 2031 pl; R^m read, "they may have completed"; 2029 pc TR read "will complete."

12. This verse opens like vs. 1 with the phrase "And I looked when"; perhaps it is meant as an inclusio.

and there was. A c vg (6) Prim TR read, "and behold there was."

sackcloth. This was made of the hair of black goats and was a fabric dark in color; cf. *War* 2.237, *Ant.* 5.37, I Clement 8:3.

the entire moon. P 1, 2059s, 2329 pm sa Prim TR omit "entire."

14. *rolled up*. Gr. *elissō*, lit. "to split, separate, or rend," but it may also be used to describe the rolling up of a cloak (cf. Isa 34:4, Heb 1:12) or scroll or even an inscribed lead tablet. The ancient Hebrews thought the firmament of heaven (Gen 1:7) was composed of solid material. Thus, heaven's having been "wrenched apart like a scroll that is rolled up" leads to an image not of a papyrus or leather roll but rather a scroll like the two copper ones found in Qumran. The idea of noise is conveyed more dramatically if the reader is meant to picture a metal scroll suddenly snapping shut.

Here the neuter nominative singular of *elissō* was used. ℵ 82, 205, 1854 al use the masculine nominative singular.

15. *military tribunes.* Gr. *chiliarchoi,* lit. "leaders of a thousand soldiers." However, the term was commonly used of the military tribune no matter how many he commanded.

16. *and they cried to the mountains and to the rocks, "Fall on us . . . hide us . . ."* Allusion to Hosea 10:8b.

face. Gr. *prosōpon.* This word means either "face" or "presence." The ancients spoke about the awe-inspiring glamor of kingship which blinds and terrifies people. In the words of Ahiqar, ". . . a hard look [on the f]ace of a k[ing] (means) 'Delay not!' " (*Ancient Near Eastern Texts Relating to the Old Testament,* 2d ed. [Princeton University Press, 1955], p. 246).

17. *great day of their wrath.* A P **046** 1, 82, 2059s pl sa[pl] bo[pt] Prim TR read "his" instead of "their."

COMMENT

THE HOLY WAR BEGINS

The six seals lie between the victory of the Lamb predicted in ch. 5 and of the saints in ch. 7. Ch. 4 celebrates God as Creator and ch. 5 adds that the Lamb, as well as Yahweh, is worthy to be worshiped. As Minear avers, "Chapters 6 and 7 answer the corollary 'who is worthy to join in that worship?' " (p. 266). It is the martyrs and the sealed. The first four seals form a unit which can be differentiated from the last three. At the breaking of each of the first four seals, one of the living creatures commands, "Come forth," and a horse and rider appear. Each of the four is allotted two verses. The fifth seal takes three verses and the sixth seal takes six. Neither has anything to do with living creatures or horses. The seventh seal is not mentioned until ch. 8.

Ch. 6 may comprise the beginning of a holy, or rather eschatological, war, for it introduces the struggle between the two sovereignties, earth, i.e. the ungodly, and heaven, i.e. the godly; see vss. 14–15. Operations seem to be directed from the throne room itself. This is suggested 1) by the four commands, "Come forth," from the living creatures who are associated with the movements of the throne-chariot; vss. 1, 3, 5, 7; 2) by the four repetitions of *edothē,* "it was granted" or "given," the impersonal passive frequently used euphemistically when God is the agent; vss. 2, 4, 8, 11; 3) by the phrase *ho kathēmenos,* "he who was seated upon it (the horse)," rather than the usual Greek word for cavalier or rider, *hippeus.* This may have been done deliberately to associate the riders on the horses with "he who sat upon" the throne. The same Greek participle with the definite article, *ho kathēmenos,* is used. The catastrophes affect the political and social order and cause a partial destruction of all parts of the cosmos; they are of such magnitude that they could not have been caused purely by human agency, and indeed are clearly eschatological. In the last phase of the battle the Word of God Himself fights (Rev 19), but here the action is performed by angel-horsemen.

The chapter is heavily influenced by OT texts, especially Ezekiel. In Ezek 5: 12–17 Yahweh predicts that his anger will fall in chastisement on Jerusalem and his own people and that a third of the people will die of pestilence and famine, a third will die by the sword, and a third will be scattered to the winds. The LXX has a different textual tradition from the MT and approximates our apocalypse more closely; a fourth will perish by death and a fourth by famine, a fourth will be scattered to the winds and a fourth will fall by the sword. This theme is resumed in Ezek 14:21 where Yahweh threatens to send upon Jerusalem "my four sore acts of judgment, sword, famine, evil beasts, and pestilence, to cut off from it man and beast!" RSV. The Dead Sea scrolls also anticipate these acts of judgment, in a *pesher* on Ps 37:1, Qumran Cave 4 (D-S; brackets indicate conjectured text, and parentheses indicate TI):

> [*Fret not yourself because of him who succeeds in his undertakings,* (*because*) *of the man who carries out evil designs*] . . . (they) will perish by the sword and by famine and by plague . . .

But a text which may have been paramount in the mind of the writer is Hab 3:4–15. This was a text read for the Feast of Weeks, telling of the theophany of God from Mount Paran, on the north side of the Sinai peninsula. Yahweh appears in dazzling brightness. Before him went pestilence, and plague followed close behind, Hab 3:4–5, RSV; cf. Rev 6:8. He is said to ride on horses (Hab 3:8; cf. Rev 6:2, 4, 5, 8) and his chariot of victory. He strips the sheath from his bow (Hab 3:9; cf. Rev 6:2) and puts arrows into the string. He cleaves the earth (Hab 3:9; cf. Rev 6:12) and rivers, shakes the mountains and the deep (Hab 3:10; cf. Rev 6:14) and affects the sun and the moon (Hab 3:11; cf. Rev 6:12) when he strides upon the earth in his fury, trampling down the nations (Hab 3:12; cf. Rev 6:15).

Yahweh, or the angel of the Lord, is represented as a horseman or warrior in several other texts. A most notable one is Exod 15:3, "the Lord is a man of war; the Lord is his name" (RSV); cf. Isa 42:13. The verse from Exodus is elaborated in the *Mekilta de Rabbi Ishmael,* tr. Lauterbach, I, 30 ff.:

> the Lord is a man of war, *the Lord is his name.* . . . it tells that He appeared to them with all the implements of war. He appeared to them like a mighty warrior girded with a sword . . . He appeared to them like a horseman . . . at the sea He appeared to them as a mighty hero doing battle . . . at Sinai He appeared to them as an old man full of mercy . . .

In 1QM 12:7–12 (D-S, p. 187) Yahweh is also presented as a man of war:

> And Thou art a ter[rible] God in Thy kingly glory and the congregation of Thy saints is in the midst of us (for) fina[l] succour. [Among] us (is) contempt for kings, disdain and mockery for the brave! For Adonai is

holy and the King of Glory is with us accompanied by the saints. The pow[ers] of the host of angels are among our numbered men and the Valiant of Battle is in our congregation and the host of his spirits accompany our steps. And o[ur] horsemen are [like] the clouds and like the mists of dew which cover the earth and like the shower of rain which waters in the desired way all its fruits.

Arise, O Valiant One!
Lead away Thy captives, O glorious Man! Do Thy plundering, O Valorous One! Set Thy hand upon the neck of Thine enemies and Thy foot upon the heap of the slain!
Strike the nations Thy enemies and let Thy sword devour guilty flesh!
Fill Thy land with glory and Thine inheritance with blessing!

The author of II Maccabees records a similar apparition, which occurred while the Jewish priests and people were making earnest supplication to Yahweh (II Macc 3:24–25, RSV):

the Sovereign of spirits and of all authority caused so great a manifestation that all who had been so bold as to accompany him (Heliodorus) were astounded by the power of God, and became faint with terror. For there appeared to them a magnificently caparisoned horse, with a rider of frightening mien, and it rushed furiously at Heliodorus and struck at him with its front hoofs. Its rider was seen to have armor and weapons of gold.

The same author also reports that while Judas Maccabeus was fighting, "five resplendent men on horses with golden bridles" appeared from heaven (II Macc 10:29). They protected the Jews but wounded their enemies.

The four horsemen, therefore, are manifestations of Yahweh or angels reflecting his character or actions. Angels' names are theophorous, e.g. Gabriel, strength of God; Uriel, fire of God. To them the duty of retribution or implementation of justice is given. Thus Sir 39:28–31, RSV, reads:

There are winds (the Greek can also be translated as "spirits") that have been
    created for vengeance,
    and in their anger they scourge heavily;
in the time of consummation they will pour out their strength
    and calm the anger of their Maker.
Fire and hail and famine and pestilence,
    all these have been created for vengeance;
the teeth of wild beasts, and scorpions and vipers,
    and the sword that punishes the ungodly with destruction;
they will rejoice in his commands,
    and be made ready on earth for their service,
    and when their times come they will not transgress his word.

Winds or spirits created for vengeance may here denote angels of vengeance.

Another text even more pertinent to Rev 6 is Zech 6:1–8. The prophet sees four chariots in a vision. The first has red horses, the second black, the third white, and the fourth dappled gray. An angel explains to Zechariah that they are going to the four winds of heaven but must first present themselves before the Lord of the whole earth. Then the black will go to the north, the white to the west, and the dappled gray to the south; the red horse and the east are omitted (Zech 6:5).

Still another passage in Zechariah is reflected in Rev 6. Zech 1:8–10 is the prophet's record of a similar vision. A man was riding on a red horse, and behind him were red, sorrel, and white horses. Like the horses in Zech 6:7, these were also sent to patrol the earth.

As Z. C. Hodges avers, horsemen are symbols of divine agencies. Indeed, in Zechariah's first vision the man on the red horse turned out to be none other than the angel of the Lord, who interceded on behalf of Jerusalem (Zech 1:11–12). Hodges cites Ps 45, where the king is exhorted to "ride triumphantly" (vs. 5, AB; vs. 4, RSV); cf. Rev 6:2. (He also remarks the arrows mentioned in Ps 45:5 and the bow in Rev 6:2.) The four horsemen in Rev 6 are therefore angels, obviously of retribution for they send disciplinary suffering on Jerusalem.

Rev 6 bears some affinity to Mark 13 and its parallels listed below in a table adapted from Charles, p. 158. Both are heavily influenced by Jewish apocalyptic thought. But the Little Apocalypse in the Synoptic Gospels has no angelic horsemen.

Matt 24:6, 7, 9a, 29	Mark 13:7–9a, 24–25
1) wars;	1) wars;
2) international strife;	2) international strife;
3) famines;	3) earthquakes;
4) earthquakes;	4) famines;
5) persecutions;	5) persecutions;
6) eclipses . . .	6) as in Matt . . .

Luke 21:9–12a, 25–26	Rev 6:2–17, 7:1–3
1) wars;	1) war;
2) international strife;	2) international strife;
3) earthquakes;	3) famine;
4) famines;	4) pestilence;
5) pestilence;	5) persecutions;
6) signs in sun . . .	6) 6:12 – 7:3, earthquakes, etc.

The four horsemen of Revelation present the retributive aspect of the character of "the One seated on the throne" (4:2). The symbolism is probably derived from the ancient Exodus imagery of Yahweh as a warrior hero. The aspect of Yahweh's character which they reveal is mainly one of judgment, but this statement must be qualified with respect to the first horse.

THE FIRST SEAL

At the breaking of the first seal, one of the four living creatures calls forth the first horseman. He rides a white horse, carries a bow, and is given a wreath. To him is attributed multiple victory. His identity, however, is much disputed. Is he on the side of God or Satan?

Rissi thinks that this rider, in keeping with the others, must be demonic in character, and that the OT source may be Gog as portrayed in Ezek 38–39. Gog does appear by name in Rev 20:7. The apocalyptic last enemy of the people of God, Gog carries bows and arrows; Ezek 39:3; cf. Jer 4:29, 6:23. The rider on the white horse carries a bow. Rissi sees in him the Antichrist, who is depicted in various guises in Revelation (e.g. as a beast in Rev 11:7, 13:17) and seen in action during the entire eschatological time. He believes the color white is eschatological and signifies that the satanic powers are perverted imitations of God and Christ; he cites the satanic trinity, the red dragon, the monster from the sea, and the monster from the land, in Rev 12–13. He draws attention to the fact that crowns are placed on the followers of both God and the satanic powers, e.g. Rev 12:1, 2, and that victory is a mark of both Christ and the Antichrist, e.g. Rev 11:7, 13:7. Thus Rissi suggests, on pp. 417–18, that "as a terrible imitation of Christ, as a Christ of hell, this rider moves through history to meet his anti-type, the rider on the white horse who is in reality the ruler and the almighty judge who will appear at the very end of history," and that "the motive of the seductive power of the antichrist, who appears in the shape of Christ and yet carries the bow of the enemy, is connected with the warnings in the message to the seven churches, who have to fight against the false doctrines, false apostles, indifference and relaxation of faith and love. This effort to mislead through miracles and fire from heaven reveals the essence of the antichrist, who is acting through the pseudo-prophet (Rev 13:14)."

Hodges, on the other hand, identifies the rider on the white horse with the Messiah and the rider in Rev 19 who also rode a white horse and who "was called Faithful and True" (vs. 11). He sees the first horseman as coming forth at the beginning of the divine judgments on the earth and the last horseman as revealed at the consummation of these judgments. In Rev 6 the victory is predicted, in ch. 19 it is realized. It is possible to contradict Hodges by proving that the only feature common to both riders is the color of the horse. They differ in the weapons they carry (bow in 6:2, sword in 19:15), in the crowns they wear (wreath, Gr. *stephanos,* in 6:2, and diadems, Gr. *diadēma,* in 19:12), and in many other details. However, many interpreters have taken a position similar to Hodges'. Some of the church fathers, such as Irenaeus in *Adversus Haereses* 4:21, 3, Victorinus of Pettau, and Bede, as well as some modern scholars, such as Allo and Giet, do identify this first horse with Christ and the victory of the Gospel, which must be preached first before the judgments are given on the earth; cf. Mark 13:10; Matt 10:23.

A third interpretation, cf. Charles, p. 163–64, identifies the first horseman with some form of war or domination, and cites the historical events of the first century A.D. The most popular identification is with the Parthians, especially because the rider carries a bow, a weapon widely used by the Parthians. During the last decades of the first century these people were a constant threat to the Roman empire. They were always ready to cross the Euphrates, and indeed in A.D. 62 their military leader, Vologesus, did overcome some Roman legions. Charles, p. 163, finds the idea of a Parthian victory implied in Rev 17:16. Further, Seleucus, the Parthian king, who founded

Seleucia on the Tigris, was named Nikator, "the victor." The Parthian soldiers, according to Wetstein (cited by Charles, p. 163), rode white horses into battle.

Four other questions must be taken into consideration in deciding what the first horseman represented. Would the living creatures have commanded a satanic force to come forth? Remember that they could just as easily, if not with greater ease, initiate judgment by angels. Could "conquering" not be understood in the sense of winning souls to righteousness or overcoming evil? Remember also that the first horseman is not said to cause affliction as the others do. Although, as Rissi shows, satanic forces are said to conquer, does the double use of the verb imply that the victory is more than a temporary evil one? The phrase *nikōn kai hina nikēsē*, "conquering that he might conquer," is similar to the Hebrew construction of absolute infinitive accompanied by a derivative finite verb for emphasis. If the infinitive preceded the finite, the phrase could be rendered "he will surely conquer" but the *hina* clause seems to be equivalent to the infinitive and thus, with the infinitive second, the idea of continuance would be suggested and the meaning be "he came out conquering continually." Last, consider Zech 1:8–12, which describes the man on the red horse as in front of red, white, and sorrel horses, identifies him as the angel of the Lord and specifies that the other horses patrol the earth.

In the light of this passage and the acknowledged OT influence on Revelation, might not the first rider be the angel of the Lord and the other riders lesser angels who affect the earth? Consider further that the function of the angel of the Lord in the OT is to protect the people of God. Only once does he come to punish (II Sam 24:16; cf. I Chron 21:16); he is to implement God's wrath against Jerusalem. Yet even that unique mission was countermanded by Yahweh. According to Jacob, pp. 75–77, the angel of the Lord functions solely by divine will. In Zech 1:12 he asks how long Yahweh will delay before showing mercy to Jerusalem, and the Lord answers in vs. 13 with comforting words. There is some similarity to the sixth seal in that the martyrs are consoled.

THE SECOND SEAL

When the second seal is broken, the second horseman comes forth on a horse which is red, denoting bloodshed; cf. II Kings 3:22. This horseman is given a great sword and power to take peace from the earth. The phrase *allēlous sphazousin*, "to kill one another" indicates civil strife. This would not have been hard to predict. Wars broke out in Britain, Germany, Armenia, and Parthia under Claudius between A.D. 41 and 54. In the year 66 the Jewish War occurred. The period following Nero's death, A.D. 69 saw three emperors, Otho, Galba, and Vitellius, quickly succeeding each other and civil upheavals shaking the empire to its foundations. However, the great sword suggests a catastrophe which is more than human. In Num 22:23 (LXX) the angel of the Lord appears with sword, Gr. *rhomphaia*, in hand before Balaam and the ass; in Ezek 21 the sword (*rhomphaia*) is wielded by Yahweh Himself against Jerusalem. The prophet is told to say (Ezek 21:9–10, RSV):

A sword, a sword is sharpened
and also polished,
sharpened for slaughter,
polished to flash like lightning!

The actual words "a large sword," Gr. *machaira*, are found in II Enoch 90:19, where a great sword is given to the sheep, i.e. Israel, and they proceed against the beasts of the field, i.e. infidels, to slay them; cf. also 10:9–10, 88:2). 1QM 11:11–12 mentions "blows of a sword which shall not be that of a man, and a sword which shall not be human shall devour him" (D-S, p. 186). The second rider, therefore, must be an angel of Yahweh who implements His (disciplinary) punishment by permitting civil strife (of which the sword is a symbol). The Qumran commentary on Ps 37:1 predicts that people "will perish by the sword and by famine and by plague," which is the order demonstrated in the second, third, and fourth seals. 1QpHab 6:10 commenting on ". . . *he drew his sword unceasingly* . . ." says, ". . . this concerns the Kittim who slay many people by the sword, youths, grown men, the aged, women and children, and have no pity (even) on the fruit of the womb" (D-S; italics indicate quotation from Scripture).

Although *machaira* is used in Rev 6:4, *rhomphaia* is employed in 6:8. The word *rhomphaia* is more frequently used for the sword of God.

THE THIRD SEAL

The third seal is broken, and the third horseman appears on a black horse, denoting death or mourning. Its rider carries a pair of scales in his hand. The balance does not in this context represent justice, as in Prov 16:11 and Ezek 45:10. Rather, it represents famine, reflecting the sentiment of Ezek 4:16: "Son of man, behold, I will break the staff of bread in Jerusalem; they shall eat bread by weight and with fearfulness; and they shall drink water by measure and in dismay," RSV. The black horse follows the red, as famine follows war. Indeed, it would have been logical for the author of these verses to envision war and famine. During Claudius' reign famine occurred in Rome in A.D. 42, and food shortage was reported in Judea in 45–46, in Greece in 49, and in Rome in 51.

A mysterious voice, which remains unidentified, commands that the wine and the oil should not be injured. This may be an allusion to Titus' order during the siege of Jerusalem (A.D. 66–70) that olive groves and vineyards were not to be ravaged. Or it might refer to the edict of Domitian in A.D. 92 which forbade the planting of any more vineyards in Italy and ordered that the vineyards in the provinces be reduced by half. This measure was to counteract the tendency to restrict land used for grain cultivation because of the policy of importing grain, especially from Africa. The edict caused a tremendous uproar in the Asiatic cities. Those who neglected their vineyards were punished. Later the emperor was obliged to rescind the edict; see Suetonius *Domitian* 7. However, this edict seems to be in opposition to the command of the voice from the living creatures. The words might also indicate a merciful tempering of the famine for the sake of the elect; cf. Matt 24:22. Or perhaps they refer to the scarcity of bread and the abundance of vintage in the times which herald the coming (that is, the first coming) of the Messiah; cf. *Sotah* 49b. However, the sentence in Mishna *Sotah* 9:15 which mentions "dearth" is in Aramaic and in *Sotah* 49b "and dearth reach its height" is omitted and the *gemara*, "commentary," ends before this sentence is discussed.

More pertinent is the observation of Bonsirven and others who refer to the view of some Christian fathers that the order not to injure the wine and oil is given because of their importance in the liturgy. However, the reference is more likely to be to the Jewish, not the Christian, liturgy; see fourth NOTE on 6:6. The voice from the midst of the living creatures thus orders the avoidance of sacrilege, such as mentioned by Josephus, with respect to sacred oil and wine. This indicates that the third seal refers to the temple area rather than to the whole country: the preservation of these commodities might be associated with the Feasts of Oil and Wine mentioned in the Temple Scroll.

THE FOURTH SEAL

In due course the Lamb breaks the fourth seal and the last of the four living creatures summons the fourth horseman. His horse is yellow-green, pallid, corpse-like, or ashen. This color sometimes characterized a corpse in advanced state of corruption. In the Greek OT *thanatos*, "death," translates Heb. *deber*, "pestilence," e.g. in Amos 4:10, Jer 14:12, 24:10, Ezek 5:12, 17, 6:11, 12. The fact that death or plague is followed by Hades may simply indicate lethal plague. "Hades" was originally the name of the god of the nether world and then began to signify the abode of the deceased. Even then "Hades," like death, could be personified; cf. I Cor 15:55. However, death (in distinction from plague) and hell are associated in Rev 1:18, 20:13, 14; vs. 8 could be similarly interpreted. In this case Hades or second death (cf. 20:6) follows physical death.

In vs. 8, in the clause "authority was granted to them," "them," Gr. *autois*, refers to death and Hades. The restriction of their influence to one-fourth of the earth may be symbolic of God's mercy but it may indicate that the catastrophes only affect the temple area and its neighborhood. Jeremias, pp. 120 ff., points out that as Jerusalem lay in an unfavorable position as regards trade and commerce, she suffered more acutely than other cities in times of emergency. He mentions shortage of food and clothing, drought, hurricane, earthquake (cf. 6:12), epidemics, and conflicts within the city.

Vs. 9, with its reference to the altar (unless this is the heavenly altar), draws our attention to Jerusalem. Power over a fourth part of the land (vs. 8) might refer to power over a quarter of the population; contrast the rest of mankind in 19:20. Counting the pilgrims coming to Jerusalem, the population of that city could have been close to a quarter of that of the nation; see Jeremias, pp. 77–84. Further, the disasters accompanying the seals are more specific than those released by the trumpets and bowls.

Jeremias, pp. 140–44, lists the disasters occurring in Jerusalem from 169 B.C. (capture of Jerusalem by Antiochus Epiphanes) until A.D. 70. Of interest for ch. 6 (in addition to those mentioned above) are the following historical incidents.

A hurricane destroyed the crops of the whole country in 64 B.C. (*Ant.* 14.28; cf. the falling of the stars "as a fig tree sheds its winter fruit when shaken by a gale," Rev 6:13). Josephus sees this disaster as a punishment from God for the killing of Onias, the circle-drawer, who refused to place a curse on Aristobulus and his fellow rebels. The people had to pay eleven drachmas for a *modius* (about one-quarter of a bushel) of wheat. Jeremias, p. 123, calculates that eleven drachmas were paid for 8.752 liters (just under 1½ gallons). Normally, one drachma would purchase 13 liters (three gallons).

Famine occurred in 38–37 B.C. during the sabbatical year (*Ant.* 14.7; cf. 14.471 and *War* 1.347; also Rev 6:6). This was the time when Herod besieged Jerusalem. Josephus reports that the "feebler folk, congregating round the Temple, indulged in transports of frenzy and fabricated numerous oracular utterances to fit the crisis" (*War* 1.347).

There was an epidemic in 29 B.C. after the execution of Queen Mariamme (*Ant.* 15.243). Josephus describes the remorse of Herod in detail and in conclusion says, "While he was in this state there arose a pestilential disease which destroyed the greater part of the people and also the most honoured of his friends, and this caused all to suspect that their misfortune had been brought upon them by God in His anger at what had lawlessly been done to Mariamme."

A famine in 25–24 B.C. was accompanied by drought and plague (*Ant.* 15. 299–300). Josephus writes that the plague was intensified by change of diet due to scarcity of cereals and by lack of medical care.

In 31 B.C. an earthquake occurred (*War* 1.370; cf. Rev 6:12). Josephus says it destroyed "cattle innumerable and thirty thousand souls."

These disasters are listed according to the order of their occurrence in Revelation, not chronologically. The author may not be referring directly to them, but the visions received by even authentic mystics are normally colored by phenomena occurring in their epoch and by cultural, political, and even economic conditions as well as religious. The mystic would be influenced by what he himself had witnessed or learned from his parents or teachers. Influence of this kind does not undermine the mystical experience. By understanding the past and present, the mystic is better able to foretell the future. The events recorded by Josephus bring a greater sense of reality to catastrophes foretold by the author of Revelation and show that contemporaries did view them as punishments from God.

THE FIFTH SEAL

The fifth seal may appear to strike a discordant note. The breaking is discussed in three verses instead of two. Living creatures and horsemen play no part. Instead, the action centers on an unspecified number of martyrs. Yet there is continuity, if all the seals originate in the heavenly throne room which is intimately associated with the earthly temple, and if the second, third, and fourth seals are especially focused on Jerusalem and the temple area. The first four seals show the commands of Yahweh executed towards the earth;

the fifth seal shows the faithful appealing to heaven for justice. They appear to appeal from the earthly altar.

The fifth seal may be seen as the key to the whole chapter for it looks backward to the concept of the "martyr" Lamb in ch. 5 and forward to the number of those sealed and the configuration of angels in ch. 7. It confirms that all the seals are in the context of the just judgment of God. It properly stands after the political, economic, and social upheavals because it is within these that martyrdom occurs. However, the martyrs need not have been contemporary; the author may have had in mind something akin to the Jewish theology of the merits of the fathers. It was the teaching of the scribes that one could merit benefit not only for oneself but for posterity, not only during this life but in the next world.

The idea of souls under the altar is also a Jewish, not a Christian, concept. Rabbi Akiba is reputed to have said that whoever was buried in the land of Israel was considered as if he were buried under the altar, and "whoever was buried under the altar was just as if he were buried under the throne of glory" (*Aboth, Rabbi Nathan,* 26). *Shabbath* 152b refers to the souls of the righteous preserved under the throne of glory. *Deut Rabbah* 11:10 reports that God told Moses He would bring him to the highest heaven and cause him to dwell under the throne of glory amid the cherubim and the seraphim and the heavenly host. In *Gittin* 57b the mother of the seven Maccabean martyrs says that she has built seven altars, a metaphor for her dead sons. The idea may have been derived from the fact that the blood of a sacrifice, which was considered the life of the victim, ran down to the base of the altar; thus the life would literally be under the altar. Spitta (quoted by Charles, p. 174, note 1) thinks that this passage refers only to persecutions of Jews.

The importance attached to martyrdom is discussed by W. H. C. Frend, pp. 22–57. The martyr was seen as representative of the people of Israel, "an example of nobility and a memorial of courage, not only to the young but also to the great body of his nation" (II Macc 6:31, with reference to Eleazar). More than this, his death was a vicarious sacrifice for his people (II Macc 7:37), which might restrain the wrath of the Almighty (II Macc 7:35) and bring about reconciliation between God and His people through the "hastening of God's mercy." However, the wrath of God would fall upon the one who caused the martyrdom and he would not rise to life (II Macc 7:14). The wrath of God and the Lamb is mentioned at the end of ch. 6. Finally, the martyr was regarded as "the agent for the preparation of the age to come." Thus, the martyrs in 6:9–11 are revealed just before the breaking of the sixth seal, which portrays the violent collapse of the old creation. Such destruction precedes the new creation.

The cry of the martyrs in vs. 10 for the Lord to render judgment reflects the appeal of Abel's blood recorded in Gen 4:10, and their manner of addressing God, as "true," "master," etc., recalls the words of Eleazar, the zealot commander of the Jewish forces in Masada (A.D. 70–73): "We have resolved for a long time to be subject neither to the Romans nor to anyone else, but to God alone, *for he alone is the true and just master of men*" (*War* 7.323; cf. 7.10, 1, quoted by Frend, p. 43). In the Ascension of Isaiah 9:6–7, Abel appears with Enoch and others who are clothed in the seventh heaven; his appeal has been recognized by a just God.

The response to their prayer is phrased in impersonal passives, i.e. *edothē*, "there was given," and *errethē*, "it was said." Since this mode of expression is used euphemistically when God is agent, it follows that their prayer is answered directly by God. Perhaps the robe signifies the spiritual body or the resurrection from the dead, but vss. 9–11 do not contain enough data to confirm this interpretation. Further, such an interpretation conflicts with 20: 4–6, where the martyrs rise and reign with the Messiah. In vss. 9–11 there is no mention of the millennium or the Messiah. The idea of waiting a little is found in IV Ezra 4:33–37, where the souls of the righteous ask how long they are to remain in their chambers. The archangel Jeremiel replies (vss. 36–37) that it will be until the number of those like themselves is fulfilled (APCh, II, 567; cf. I Enoch 22:5, 7; 48:1–4):

> For he (God) has weighed the age in the balance,
> And with measure has measured the times,
> And by number has numbered the seasons:
> Neither will he move nor stir things,
> till the measure appointed be fulfilled.

The author of Revelation is expounding current Jewish thought. In the Christian apocalypses it is not the completion of the martyrs' role but the coming of Christ which brings the righteous their full reward. Gradually there developed the concept of Christ's descent into hell or limbo, the place where pre-Christian people waited for the message of the Gospel. The doctrine first appears in the Christian creeds of the fourth century. The martyrs in Rev 6 may be only Jewish, not Christian.

THE SIXTH SEAL

When the Lamb breaks the sixth seal, natural disasters occur which come from the direct intervention of God. They could not have been effected through social conditions. In ancient Jewish thought the obedience of the cosmic order was to be copied by the obedience of the faithful to the commands of God; cf. Ps 19. If the commandments were broken, the constellations would forsake their order and creation would begin to disintegrate. Thus, Testament of Naphtali 3:2–5 (APCh, II, 337) reads:

> Sun and moon and stars change not their order; so do ye also change not the law of God in the disorderliness of your doings. The Gentiles went astray, and forsook the Lord, and changed their order, and obeyed stocks and stones, spirits of deceit. But ye shall not be so, my children, recognizing in the firmament, in the earth, and in the sea, and in all created things, the Lord who made all things, that ye become not as Sodom, which changed the order of nature.

In apocalyptic thought cosmic catastrophe is a consequence of sin; apocalyptic literature employs expressions similar to those found in the present passage. The Assumption of Moses 10:3–10 depicts God going from his royal throne with indignation and wrath, the earth trembling, the confines of the earth shaken, the high mountains brought low and the hills falling, the horns or rays of the sun broken, and the moon not giving its light but turning into blood, the circle of the stars disturbed, the sea receding into the abyss, and the waters failing.

In Rev 6:12–15 seven phenomena are listed: 1) the earthquake (cf. 8:5, 11: 13, 16:18); 2) darkening of the sun, perhaps suggesting an eclipse (cf. Joel 2:31); 3) the moon becoming like blood (cf. Joel 2:31); 4) the stars falling; 5) rolling up of the heavens (cf. Isa 34:4); 6) the mountains and islands moved out of their place; 7) mankind's universal consternation. In this last phenomenon, seven social classes are mentioned. The number seven indicates completeness. Therefore the author's meaning is that no enemy of God, no matter what his position in society, will escape the terrors. Amos 2:14–16 lists seven classes of soldiers in his description of the great battle in which Israel will be defeated. The high officials, Gr. *megistanes,* literally "great men" in Rev 6:15 may denote the Parthian princes: the word *megistanes* is used six times in Theodotion's translation of Daniel to describe the order of nobles and court officials under Belshazzar and Darius.

That the wrath of the Lord and the Lamb will be unendurable is typical of predictions about the great and terrible day of Yahweh; cf. Joel 2:11, 31; Nahum 1:6; Zeph 1:14; Mal 3:2. Isa 2:19 predicts that men shall enter into the rocks of the caves in the face of the terror and glory of God. Investigations in the Judaean Desert have produced evidence of the occupation of caves when the Jewish people scattered during the revolts from the second century B.C. to the first century A.D. The order in which the universe is destroyed follows approximately the order of creation in Genesis: 1) the earth; 2) the sun; 3) the moon; 4) the stars; 5) the sky or firmament; 6) the mountains and islands, that is, the land revealed by the separation of the waters; 7) man, made in the image and likeness of God. In vss. 16–17 men hide themselves from the presence of God as Adam and Eve did after their sin (Gen 3:8).

Vischer, Spitta, Weyland, Völter, and Weiss (see Charles, pp. 182–83) argue that "the wrath of the Lamb" (vs. 16) is an interpolation. There is, however, a strong argument for its retention despite the alternative reading "his wrath" instead of "their wrath" in vs. 17; see NOTE. Wrath is characteristic of the conquering apocalyptic Lamb. Further, the chapter ends with the significant question: Who is able to stand? This is taken from Nahum 1:6 and Mal 3:2. It is probably meant to be associated with the Lamb, who is depicted in ch. 5 as standing, and with the redeemed, who are portrayed in 7:9–10 as standing. The last word of this chapter leads directly into ch. 7, which opens with a vision of four angels standing.

BIBLIOGRAPHY

Bonsirven, P. J. *L'Apocalypse de Saint Jean.*
Charles, R. H. *Revelation.* ICC, I.
Derrett, J. D. M. *Law in the New Testament.*
Frend, W. H. C. *Martyrdom and Persecution in the Early Church.*

Hodges, Z. C. "The First Horseman of the Apocalypse," *Bibliotheca Sacra* 119 (1962), 324–34.

Jacob, Edmond. *Theology of the Old Testament.* Trs. A. W. Heathcote and P. J. Allcock. London: Hodder & Stoughton, 1958.

Jeremias, J. *Jerusalem in the Time of Jesus.*

Minear, P. S. *I Saw a New Earth.*

Pritchard, James B. *Ancient Near Eastern Texts Relating to the Old Testament.* 2d ed. Princeton University Press, 1955.

Rissi, M. *Interpretation* 18 (1964), 407–18.

Yadin, Y. "The Temple Scroll," *Biblical Archaeologist* 30 (1967), 135–39.

IV. GOD KEEPS HIS PROMISE TO SECURE
A REMNANT
(7:1–17)

7 1 After this I saw four angels standing at the four corners of the earth, controlling the four winds of the earth, so that the wind might not blow upon the earth or upon the sea or upon any tree. 2 And I saw another angel ascending from the east. He had the seal of the living God and he called out loudly to the four angels to whom it was given to injure the earth and the sea. 3 He said, "Do not injure the earth, nor the sea, nor the woodland, until we seal the servants of our God on their brows. 4 And I heard the number of those who were sealed, one hundred and forty-four thousand, sealed from every tribe of the sons of Israel.

> 5 From the tribe of Judah twelve thousand sealed,
>   from the tribe of Reuben twelve thousand,
>   from the tribe of Gad twelve thousand,
> 6 from the tribe of Asher twelve thousand,
>   from the tribe of Naphtali twelve thousand,
>   from the tribe of Manasseh twelve thousand,
> 7 from the tribe of Simeon twelve thousand,
>   from the tribe of Levi twelve thousand,
>   from the tribe of Issachar twelve thousand,
> 8 from the tribe of Zabulon twelve thousand,
>   from the tribe of Joseph twelve thousand,
>   from the tribe of Benjamin twelve thousand sealed.

9 After this I looked, and behold a great countless crowd, from every nation and tribe and people and tongue, standing before the throne and before the Lamb, clothed in white robes, and with palms in their hands; 10 and they shouted loudly saying,

"Salvation to our God who is enthroned and to the Lamb."

11 And all the angels stood around the throne with the elders and the four living creatures and prostrated themselves before the throne and worshiped God, 12 saying,

"Amen; praise and glory and wisdom and thanksgiving and honor and power and might to our God for ever and ever; Amen."

13 And one of the elders spoke to me, saying, "Who are these who

are clothed in bright robes and from whence have they come?"
14 And I said to him, "My Lord, you know." And he said to me,
"These are the people who have come from the great tribulation, and
have bathed their robes and have made them bright in the blood of
the Lamb.
15 On this account they are before the throne of God,
and they worship night and day in his sanctuary,
and He who is enthroned will tabernacle over them.
16 They shall not hunger anymore or thirst anymore,
neither shall the sun
or any scorching heat fall upon them,
17 because the Lamb who is in the midst of the throne will shepherd
them
and guide them to springs of living water;
and God will wipe away every tear from their eyes."

NOTES

7:1. *four corners*. The phrase "four corners of the earth" reflects the ancient
cosmology which conceived of the earth as a square. Cf. Rev 20:8, where
the nations are gathered by Satan from the four corners of the earth to attack
the Holy City, which was thought to be the center of the earth (Ezek 5:5;
I Enoch 26:1, APCh, II, 205; cf. Ezek 38:12, *War* 3.52). Isa 11:11–12 speaks
of God recovering His people "from the four corners of the earth," RSV.

four winds. I Enoch 76:1–4 refers to the twelve portals which open to the
four quarters of the heaven from which proceed the winds. There are four
winds of blessing and eight hurtful winds. *Jubilees* 2:2 and other texts mention angels who are in charge of these winds.

upon the earth or upon the sea or upon any tree. "Tree" is in the accusative but "earth" and "sea" are in the genitive. The change of case suggests
that the word "tree" is an addition to the text. Support for this is found in
I Enoch 76:4 which mentions only the land and the water and those who dwell
thereon; cf. Dan 7:2 where the four winds of heaven stir up the great sea.
However, "tree" might be used here in the metaphorical sense and therefore
be equivalent to Enoch's phrase "those who dwell thereon." Trees, oaks,
cedars, etc. were used as symbols for leaders of the people. Isa 2:13 reads
"And upon all the cedars of Lebanon" (KJ) but the Targum renders the
phrase "and upon all the strong and mighty kings of the nations, and upon
all the princes, or, tyrants of the provinces . . ." Isa 14:8 reads "the cypresses
rejoice at you, (and) the cedars . . ." The Targum renders it " . . . the rulers
rejoice . . . those who are rich in possessions say . . ." In Isa 61:3 the
Masoretic Text refers to "trees of righteousness," but the Targum reads
"princes of righteousness."

Arboreal symbolism also occurs in the Dead Sea scrolls, e.g. in 1QH 8:5–6 (D-S):

> [Thou hast plant]ed unto Thy glory a planting of cypress and elm mingled with box. Trees of life are hidden among all the trees by the waters in a mysterious realm, and they shall send out a Shoot for the everlasting planting.

The phrase "trees by the waters" shows influence from Ezek 31:14 where trees represent the proud or the wicked who will be condemned. Dupont-Sommer, p. 226, notes 1, 2, 3, comments:

> In the "divine planting," the saints are "hidden" among the wicked (like the good grain among the weeds). But this mingling of the two is providential; at the end of time, as is explained further on (lines 19–20: "And the tr[ees by the waters shall sink like] lead into the might[y] waters, [and shall be] [prey] to fire and be dried up.") the saints "that were hidden in secret" will destroy the bad trees and nothing but the "fruitful planting" will remain.

The trees of life, according to Dupont-Sommer, represent the holy ones, the elect in the Ps Sol 14:2(5): "The pious of the Lord shall live by it (the Law) for ever; The Paradise of the Lord, the *trees of life*, these are His pious ones . . ." The metaphor is continued into Christian writings. In the Shepherd of Hermas (Similitudes 4.5.2) the trees represent the just who dwell in the world to come.

2. *another angel.* The Greek, *allon aggelon*, may mean either "another, an angel" or "another angel." He comes from the rising of the sun, i.e. the east. The east was traditionally the place whence the divine manifestation came, e.g. Isa 41:2, "Who stirred up one from the east whom victory meets at every step" (RSV). Mal 4:1–2 says "the Sun of Righteousness shall rise, with healing in its wings" (RSV) for those who fear the Lord. But the text which is most pertinent is Ezek 43:2–3, where the prophet sees the glory of the Lord coming from the east and shining on the whole earth. This vision is like the one which he received before the destruction of the city.

the seal of the living God. Some scholars, e.g. Shepherd, *The Paschal Liturgy and the Apocalypse,* p. 83, also Lampe, *The Seal of the Spirit,* pp. 7–18, see in this seal the Sacraments of Baptism and/or "Confirmation"; they cite II Cor 1:21–22; Eph 1:13–4, 4:30. However, all these texts pertain to anointing, Gr. *chrisas* (II Cor 1:21–22), and the Holy Spirit, both of which are absent from Rev 4–21. To the prophet's contemporaries "seal" would have connoted:

1) the branding of cattle and the tattooing of slaves and soldiers, especially those in the service of the emperor who could be recognized by this mark if they deserted. However, this custom is post-Pauline (Lampe, p. 9). One interesting example is found in Jewish documents from the Elephantine Colony in Egypt. Here one reads of a slave "having a *yod* marked on the arm at the right of a marking in the Aramaic language," quoted by Lampe, p. 9. For the branding of people see Ps Sol 2:6 (although the text is uncertain) and Tertul-

lian *De Praescriptione Haereticorum* 40, in which the author complains that the pagan rites imitate the Christian.

2) the marking of a soldier or a member of a guild on the hand, brow or neck to seal him as a religious devotee, i.e. a member of a sacred militia. The soldier or guild member stood as a slave before the god; the mark on his body was a sign of consecration to the deity. This practice was common in the pagan cults, especially in the Oriental or the semi-Oriental ones. Herodotus (ii 113) states that in Egypt a fugitive could take sanctuary in a temple, where he would receive a physical mark and be stamped as God's property, "inviolable and sacrosanct," Lampe, p. 12. Lucian describes a similar practice in the cult of the Syrian goddess (*De Syria Dea* 59). These pagan customs may account for the prohibition against marking the dead, found in Lev 19:28; cf. Lev 21:5, Deut 14:1. Philo, speaking about bondage to God and bondage to idols, inveighs against those who acknowledge idolatrous slavery "by indentures not written on pieces of parchment, but, as is the custom of slaves, branded on their bodies with a red-hot iron." The marks remain "indelibly, for no lapse of time can make them fade" (*De Specialibus Legibus* i 58).

3) the mark prophets might have worn on their foreheads, either incised or tattooed. This is inferred from I Kings 20:41, Zech 13:6 (on the back), inferred from I Kings 20:41, Zech 13:6, Isa 44:5 (on the hand).

4) the phylactery, in later times, worn on the forehead and hand. It became the sign or "seal" of devotion to Yahweh; Deut 6:8, 11:18; cf. Exod 13:9. The high priest wore a mitre with "holy to the Lord" engraved on the petalon; Exod 28:36–38.

5) circumcision, seen as a "seal for a day of redemption"; cf. Jubilees 15:26, Lampe, p. 15. Circumcision became a matter of great importance in the Maccabean and post-Maccabean era; cf. I Macc 1:15, 48, 60, Assumption of Moses 8:1, *Ant.* 12.241. The Greek term *asēmos,* "without a mark or token" was a title for the uncircumcised. The Jews were branded by Ptolemy Philopator when they refused to apostasize; III Macc 3:39.

6) the man formed after the image of God, described by Philo as "an idea or type or seal (Gk., *sphragis*) . . . incorporeal . . . incorruptible" (*De Opificio Mundi* 134). The Logos himself is "the archetypal seal" (*Gk. archetupos sphragis,* ibid. 25) and is impressed upon the universe: "the Word of Him who makes it is Himself the seal, by which each thing that exists has received its shape" (*De Fuga et Inventione* 12). It is also stamped upon the human soul (*De Plantatione* 5, 18). This idea is associated with the Spirit in *De Plantatione* 11, 14. In Philo, however, there is no eschatological dimension with regard to sealing.

four angels to whom it was given. Note, again, the impersonal passive implying that the authority is given by God; see second paragraph of COM- MENT on ch. 6. The angels doubtless are those mentioned in vs. 1. They are agents of divine retribution. A clear association between winds and angels is to be found in 1QH 1:8–15, which refers to God's creation of the mighty winds and the laws which govern them "before they became [Thine] angels of hol[iness]"; cf. Ps 104:4. For the destructive power of the wind cf. Isa 11:15–16, which speaks of the scorching wind which will dry up the water in Egypt.

3. *nor the sea.* A pc c vg^{s,cl} read, "and the sea."

seal the servants of our God. In Ps Sol 15:8(6) the "mark of God is upon the righteous that they may be saved" but the "mark of destruction" is upon the forehead of the wicked, 15:10, APCh, II, 646. IV Ezra 6:5 mentions the sealing of the "gatherers of the treasures of faith," APCh, II, 574.

4. *the number of those who were sealed, one hundred and forty-four thousand.* The number represents a perfect square. It recurs in Rev 14:1. Twelve contingents of one thousand were sealed from each of the twelve tribes. The underlying idea appears to be the census of the chosen people, i.e. the ideal Israel coming from the ancestors of the twelve tribes. In 1QM 2:1–4 the priests and Levites who serve in the liturgy are twelve in number and correspond to the tribal system (Yadin, *The Scroll of the War,* p. 204).

were sealed. The Greek for "sealed" here is normally *esphagismenoi,* the masculine nominative plural, but in **046** 82, 104, 2036 al it is rendered *esphagismenōn,* the genitive plural.

5–8. Traditionally the "house of Israel" or "the sons of Israel" comprised twelve tribes. When the tribe of Levi was absorbed into the priesthood and lost its ancestral lands, the number twelve was restored by making Joseph into two tribes, Ephraim and Manasseh. Eventually the tribes lost their political importance and merged into two groups, the tribe of Judah and the tribe of Ephraim (called "Israel"). This list of tribes is peculiar because it omits Dan and includes both Joseph and Manasseh. Perhaps Dan should replace Manasseh. Perhaps Dan is omitted because of the tradition that the Antichrist would come from this tribe, as suggested in Irenaeus and Hippolytus. Both quote Jer 8:16 (cf also vs. 17), and Hippolytus cites Deut 33:22 and Gen 49:17. It is true that in Gen 49:17 Dan is "A horned snake . . . , that bites the horse's heel," AB, and that in Testament of Dan 5:6 it is written that the prince of the tribe of Dan is Satan. Nevertheless, the reason for omission from our list may be simply the idolatry of Dan as recorded in Judg 18:30 and I Kings 12:29. Revelation is directed against idolatry. The list starts with the tribe of Judah, from which the Messiah is born.

5. *Gad.* "Dan" appears here in 42, 1854 pc.

6. *Manasseh.* "Dan" appears here in Bo.

9. *After this I looked.* This indicates the introduction of either another vision or a new theme.

standing. The Greek is *hestōtes,* the nominative, but in **046** 82, 1611, 2036, 2329 al it is rendered *hestōtas,* the accusative plural.

palms. Here too the Greek is in the nominative, *phoinikes,* but in ℵ* **046** 82, 2036 pm it is rendered in the accusative plural, *phoinikas.*

11. *around the throne with the elders.* The Greek text is perplexing. Literally it reads, "And all the angels stood around (*kuklō,* 'in a circle') the throne (genitive singular) and the elders (genitive plural) and the four living creatures (genitive plural)." But "elders" and "living creatures" seem to hang loosely in the sentence. Perhaps the angels encircle the throne, the elders, and

the creatures, but this seems unlikely. I have taken the liberty of adding "with" to the text to keep the ambiguity.

12. There are seven attributes of praise to God: in 4QS 1:37–40, of the "Chief of Princes" poem found in cave 4 at Qumran, the chief princes (angels) bless God with seven words: "of majesty," "of righteousness," of [His] sublime truth," "of His marvellous Powers," "of [His] marvellous holiness," and "with seven marvellous words" (D-S, pp. 330–32). This liturgy records the words of the fourth, fifth, sixth, and seventh angels, but the rest is missing. Perhaps it is not a coincidence that seven attributes are mentioned in our text. Seven signifies completeness.

14–17. These verses comprise a conventional dialogue between the seer and one of the elders. This is one of the few places where an explanation of a vision is given. But an "angel" interpreter is common in other apocalyptic texts, e.g. Dan 9:20–21.

14. *My.* This word is omitted from A 1, pc g vg (2) sa bo (1) arm^pt Prim TR.

bathed their robes. Instead of "bathed," Gr. *eplunan,* (1) 82, 1854, 2329 al read *eplatunan,* "enlarged," or "made broad." "Bathed" may be used either in sense of washing one's clothes, sometimes in preparation for a ritual act, or of sanctifying or purifying one's conscience. Cf. Exod 19:10; part of Moses' ritual preparation of the Israelites to receive the covenant consisted of having them wash their garments. In the Greek OT the same verb is used. Cf. 22:14, NOTE and COMMENT.

and make them bright. Gr. *leukainō.* This verb may mean "to make white," "to clarify (as oil)," or "to cause to appear white (as the effect of dawn or lamplight)." It is hard to see how blood could dye clothes "white" but it could make them "bright." The juxtaposition of "bathed" makes it clear that the robes are not stained or dirty.

This is a startling figure of speech. Although it might refer to baptism there is no sure indication that it does so. It could represent martyrdom or participation in the holy war or acceptance of the covenant of Yahweh; cf. the practice of sprinkling sacrificial blood on the altar and the people, Exod 24:8. Note that *leukainō* is in the aorist tense, indicating completed action in the past.

15. *tabernacle over them.* Notice the Exodus motif. In the NT the verb is found only in John 1:14, see Brown, AB, vol. 29, third NOTE ad loc. This text differs from John 1:14, which has "in" or "among" (Gr. *en*), rather than "over." Here, "tabernacle over" connotes a sense of power or protection; cf. II Cor 12:9. The author may also have been influenced by Isa 4:2–6, which mentions the cleansing of the daughters of Zion: "for over all the glory there will be a canopy and a pavilion. It will be for a shade by day from the heat, and for refuge and a shelter from the storm and rain" (vss. 5–6, RSV). The Targum (Stenning), reads:

At that time shall the anointed one (or, Messiah) of the Lord be for a joy and for a glory . . . And the Lord shall create over the whole sanctuary of Mount Zion, and over the place of the house of the Shekinah (holy presence), a cloud of glory: it shall be a covering over it by day, and thick darkness, and brightness like flaming fire by night: for with greater glory than that which he promised to bring upon it shall the Shekinah be protecting it as with a canopy. And over Jerusalem shall be the covering of my cloud to cover it in the daytime from the heat, and for a shelter and for protection from storm and from rain.

16. *hunger anymore or thirst anymore.* The first "anymore" is omitted in ‭א‬ pc vg sy 6. The second is omitted in P 052 1, 1006, 2059s al g sy[ph].

scorching. The scorching of blasphemers in 16:8 forms a contrast with this text.

17. *springs of living water.* In 1, 2028, 2329 al TR this phrase is replaced with "living springs."

COMMENT

Rev 7 is an intermission scene between the breaking of the sixth and seventh seals. There are similar pauses before the deluge (Gen 6–7), before the building of the ark (in I Enoch 66:1–2, 67), and before the destruction of the temple (in II Baruch 6:4–7:1). The purpose of the interlude before breaking the seventh seal is to secure God's people who will receive the seal of the living God (or perhaps more literally, the God who gives life); the Lamb is not mentioned. Ch. 7 must be seen in relation to ch. 16 where the bowls of wrath are poured out (see Introduction, p. XXXIX), because what our author presents here is a theology of the remnant, i.e. those who are saved. This is an important part of most of the prophetic proclamation in the OT but, although Paul deals with it in Rom 9–11, it is not a prominent theme in NT theology. The concept of the remnant has three facets: destruction, salvation, and an opportunity for the sinners to repent. The prophet has predicted destruction in the second, third, fourth, and sixth seals, where there is no mention of the role of repentance. In ch. 7 he deals with salvation, a theme which will be continued in chs. 12, 14, the end of 19, and 21. In ch. 9 (the trumpets) and ch. 16 (the bowls of wrath) the writer(s) turns to disciplinary punishment which is designed to bring about repentance; indeed, 9:20–21 and 16:9, 11, contain the only references to repentance in the whole of this apocalypse save for the Christian addition of chs. 1–3. The bowls of wrath in ch. 16 are the corollary to the sealing in our present chapter and take up the theme of wrath with which ch. 6 ends. There is a subtle play on "sealed" and unsealed. To the question in 6:17, "who can stand?" comes the answer in 7:3: only the sealed servants of God. The wrath theme reaches its climax in the destruction of the harlot.

The Hebrew word for "remnant," *š'erit,* expresses the idea of those "left," "delivered," or "escaped." Although the survivors can refer to an historical entity who are preserved from disaster, the notion of "remnant" is often used in an eschatological context, which involves salvation and judgment; those who belong to the remnant escape the judgment. The Baptist preached a type of remnant theology when he sought to give people the means to repent and thus escape the wrath to come. However, the securing of a remnant depends on the saving power of God, not the merits of men. Thus, the chapter begins with the command to the angels of the winds to postpone their destructive tasks in order to show that operations are under the control of God and his angels.

Anemos (wind) is used for a storm wind in Matt 14:30, 32, Mark 6:51, John 6:18, and for a hurricane-like wind in Acts 27:14. The noxious winds in I Enoch 76 bring desolation, drought, heat, destruction, and cold (from the east winds); heat, locusts, and desolation (from the south winds); locusts and desolation (from the north winds); drought and desolation, burning and destruction (from the west winds). Some of these disasters occur in the rest of Revelation. Enoch is shown the secrets of the winds, "their laws," "their plagues" and all "their benefits" (I Enoch 76). However, the author of Revelation had in mind especially the sirocco, Gr. *kauma*, "hot wind," or "scorching heat," in 7:16; by the phrase "any scorching heat" the verse indicates more than one hot wind. The sirocco is the scorching wind, which would burn up vegetation. But it could be used as a metaphor for the destruction of the wicked, as in Hosea 3:15, RSV (cf. Rev 7:16–17):

> Though he may flourish as the reed plant,
>> the east wind, the wind of the Lord, shall come,
>> rising from the wilderness;
> and his fountain shall dry up,
>> his spring shall be parched;
> it shall strip his treasury
>> of every precious thing.

Eschatologically this wind was seen as the manifestation of divine wrath; cf. 16:9. The scorching wind, however, might well bring to mind fire as well as heat; cf. the fire and burning in ch. 8. The ancients would have known well the horrors of a rural fire. This is the picture the Baptist presents when he speaks of the vipers fleeing; they flee from a blazing desert fire; Matt 3:7, 12. It is from the scorching heat and its consequent destruction that the sealed are delivered. Charles (*Revelation*, I, 191) argued that these opening verses (vss. 1–3) were originally a separate, older fragment. However, they harmonize well with vss. 15–16. The noxious winds are the very catastrophe from which the elect are sealed or preserved. On the other hand, this same disaster befalls the enemies of God as illustrated by the Targum of Isa 41:16 (Stenning): "Thou shalt fan them and the wind shall carry them away, and my (text, 'his') Memra (Word) shall scatter them as a whirlwind the stubble; but thou shalt exult in the Memra of the Lord, *and* glory in the Holy One of Israel." Cf. the winnowing fork in Matt 3:12.

The remnant are delivered through the intervention of an angel carrying the seal of God. He commands the angels who hold the winds to abstain from harming the earth and sea until the servants of God are sealed on their foreheads. The seal may go back to the protective mark which God placed on Cain (Gen 4:15). The biblical text is elaborated in the Palestinian Targum to Gen 4:15 (Etheridge, pp. 171–72): "And the Lord sealed upon the face of Kain the mark of the Name great and honourable, that any one who might find him should not kill him when he saw it upon him."

R. Eisler (cited by Lampe, p. 14) suggested that the wandering nomads associated with Cain wore an "X" incised on their foreheads. Lampe, p. 14, observes that, whether or not this association is admissible, the "X" sign did play an important role in the history of religious sealing. It was in this form that the sign of the bond service to God took on an eschatological significance as a seal marking off the elect and saving them from the divine wrath. The Palestinian Targum, however, adds the important fact that it is the name of Yahweh which protects the people. The concept of "name," either the saving name of God or the Lamb or the name honored by the beast-worshipers, is prominent in Revelation both in the main text and in chs. 1–3. In OT thought "name" is practically synonymous with "character."

There may also be a connection between the idea of sealing and the blood which was placed on the doors of the Israelite homes in Egypt to protect them against the angel who destroyed the Egyptians (Exod 12:23). The text in the Palestinian Targum appears as follows (Etheridge):

> And the blood of the paschal oblation, (like) the matter of circumcision, shall be bail for you, to become a sign upon the houses where you dwell; and I will look upon the worth of the blood, and will spare you; and the angel of death, to whom is given the power to destroy, shall have no dominion over you in the slaughter of the Mizraee (Egypt). (N.b. the phrase "to whom is given power to destroy").

However, the most influential source for ch. 7 is Ezek 9:4, 6 (RSV):

> And the Lord said to him, (the man in linen), "Go through the city, through Jerusalem, and put a mark (Hebrew, *taw*) upon the foreheads of the men who sigh and groan over all the abominations that are committed in it . . . slay old men outright, young men and maidens, little children and women, but touch no one upon whom is the mark. And begin at my sanctuary." So they began with the elders who were before the house.

It is important to notice the context of this command. It concerns people within the city of Jerusalem; the angel is to begin with the sanctuary (cf. Rev 11:1) and with the elders. It occurs in association with a vision of the slaughter of the guilty before the glory of the Lord leaves the temple. The man clothed in linen (in later rabbinic texts designated Gabriel) places the *taw* on those who are distressed about the breaking of the covenant with Yahweh. He is followed by six other men, making a total of seven whose function is to execute judgment. The slaughter is to be wholesale. In ch. 6 the locale is most likely Jerusalem; see COMMENT, Section III. In the COMMENTS on chs. 17–19 (Sections XIV–XVI) is proposed the identification of the harlot with Jerusalem. Here the prophet models his text on Ezekiel probably so that his readers will think of Jerusalem.

It might be possible to connect the *taw* of salvation or preservation with the judicial proceedings involving the *Urim* and the *Thummin,* the objects, probably sacred lots, by which the priest gave an oracular decision in the name of Yahweh. These were set into the breastplate of the high priest (Exod 39:8–21) but originally were small stones of the same size or shape but with different marks on them, such as *aleph* and *taw,* respectively the first and last letters of the Hebrew alphabet. In judicial proceedings the decision *aleph* would mean guilty ('*rr,* "to curse") and *taw* innocent (*tmm,* "to be blameless"). If the author of Revelation is influenced by this knowledge, the mark for the beast-worshipers would be *aleph.*

The quotation from Ezek 9:4, 6, occurs in CDC 19:12 in a passage concerning the unfaithful covenanters. Zech 13:7, concerning the striking of the shepherd, is cited. The poor of the flock are identified as those who obey the covenant (CDC 19:12, ms. B, D-S):

> But the others will be delivered up to the sword
> when the Anointed of Aaron and Israel comes,
> as came to pass at the time of the first Visitation;
> as He said by the hand of Ezekiel,
> *A mark shall be put on the forehead of those who sigh and groan;*
> but the others will be delivered up to the avenging sword, the avenger of the
>   Covenant.
> And such will be the lot of all who enter His Covenant,
> but hold not firm to these precepts,
> when He visits them for destruction by the hand of Belial.

The covenanters of Qumran were convinced that they were a remnant called by God from a corrupt Israel (CDC 1:4–5, 2:11–12). The rewards and punishments of those who follow the Spirit of Truth and Spirit of Perversity are described repectively in 1QS 4:2–8, 4:11–14. Once a year they renewed their covenant with Yahweh and underwent purificatory baths, clothed themselves in white garments, and offered praise to Yahweh; cf. Rev 7:13–15. The annual renewal of the covenant may have taken place on the Jewish Feast of Weeks, or, Pentecost.

Rabbinic texts show a diversity of interpretation with regard to Ezek 9:4–6. *Shabbath* 55a reports that God ordered Gabriel to place a *taw* of ink on the forehead of the faithful to protect them from the destroying angel and a *taw* of blood upon the foreheads of the wicked. Rabbi Joseph read "sanctified ones" for "sanctuary," i.e. those who fulfilled the Torah from *aleph* to *taw.* Rabbi Hisda identified the six men in the Ezekiel text with Indignation, Anger, Wrath, Destroyer, Breaker, and Annihilator. Rab said the *taw* stood for the Hebrew words *tihyeh,* "thou shalt live," and *tamuth,* "thou shalt die," but Samuel said it denoted that the "merit of the Patriarchs is exhausted (Heb. *tamah*)," i.e. it no longer shielded the wicked. Rabbi Johanan suggested, "The merit of the Patriarchs will confer grace (Heb. *tahon*)." Resh Lakish said, "*Taw* is the end of the seal of the Holy One . . ." and Rabbi Hanina pronounced this to be truth (Heb., *emeth*). Finally, Rabbi Samuel ben Nahmani said, "It denotes the people who fulfilled the Torah from *alef* to *taw.*"

In *Lam R* 2:1, paragraph 3, Rabbi Eleazar's explanation of Ezek 9:5–6 was as follows (*Midrash Rabbah,* trs. Freedman and Simon):

> At that time the prosecution sprang before the Throne of Glory and spake before Him: "Lord of the universe, which of them was slain for

Thy name? Which of them gave his life for Thy name? . . . God replied, 'There is not in them [such wickedness] as to merit a document [of extermination].'" Rabbi Aibu declared: "The Holy One, . . . replied to him, 'Let the Temple be destroyed, but let not a hand touch the righteous.'" R. Judah b. R. Simon said: "[God said:] 'Both the sanctuary and the people have merited a document [of extermination].'"

The passages *Shabbath* 55a and *Lam R* 2:1 show the variety of explanations given to Ezek 9:6 and suggest that one cannot be dogmatic about the meaning of Rev 7. *Taw* also was written on the jars for the *teruma* (that which was lifted or separated) which was the offering given from the yearly harvest. Metaphorically the sealed could be seen as the holy offering to Yahweh.

If this chapter depicts the preservation of the remnant, it might be asked what comprised this remnant. Vss. 4b–8 suggest the tribes of Israel. However, vss. 9–17, beginning with the phrase "After this I looked, and behold," which usually indicates a new vision, suggest that more than Israel will be saved; these verses reflect universalism rather than particularism. The disparity between the two halves of this chapter—vss. 1–8 stating Israel was to be saved, vss. 9–17 indicating universal salvation—has led scholars to question its integrity, despite the consistency of diction and idiom.

Charles in *Revelation*, I, suggests that vss. 4–8 are an independent Jewish source which has been recast, that the one hundred and forty-four thousand are Jews or Jewish-Christians and that particularism is a central idea of this first half. It reflects Exod 7:7, 13, 23. The inclusion of Levi as the eighth tribe is interesting because after the Maccabees the tribe of Levi acquired a greater importance, and even predominated over Judah. He identifies the great crowd in vss. 9–17 with the one hundred and forty-four thousand in vss. 4–8, but postulates that vss. 4–8 refer to a spiritual Israel comprising contemporary Christians, the faithful still living, whereas vss. 9–17 and Rev 19:1–5 are proleptic and refer to the martyrs. Neither of the visions, however, is incompatible with Jewish theology and neither shows unambiguous Christian traits in spite of the reference to the blood of the Lamb in vs. 14. They accord with the remnant theology as it developed in the prophetic literature.

At first the remnant was conceived of as Israel or part of Israel. This aspect is portrayed in vss. 5–8. The order and composition of the tribes need not exercise the reader. In the OT the tribes are arranged in twenty different orders, only one of which recurs, i.e. in Num 2:7, 10:14–29. The arrangements are normally based either on their geographical position in Palestine or according to the mothers of the patriarchs. The arrangement in Ezek 48 reflects a prophetic ideal; it is discussed below. A list of the tribes does not appear in the Dead Sea scrolls but 1QM 3:13–14, 5:1, says that the names of Israel and Aaron and the names of the twelve tribes of Israel, according to their genealogy, are written on the great standard which is at the head of all the people and on the staff of the prince of all the congregation (respectively). In 1QM the tribes are mentioned in a military context.

Austin Farrer thinks that the census is the background to this chapter. He compares II Sam 24:8–10 where David regrets that he has numbered the people. The census in ch. 7, however, is conducted by Yahweh. Farrer also suggests that the tribes are arranged according to the matriarchs, six sons of Leah, two of Rachel, two sons of Rachel's handmaid, two of Leah's (see diagram). The emphasis on the maternal origin is consonant with the symbolism of woman in Revelation; cf. 12, 17, possibly 2:20. The tribes in 21:9–14 are intimately associated with the figure of the bride; Jerusalem is said to have twelve foundations, each made of one of the twelve stones representing the twelve tribes in the high priest's breastplate. Thus, the twelve tribes reveal an "Israel-remnant" theology.

The prophet will develop his theme in a way which corresponds to the distinctive development in Ezek 14:21–23; namely, when Jerusalem is destroyed, there will be a remnant who will be consoled for the evil which Yahweh has wrought on Jerusalem. This section of Ezekiel follows the prediction of

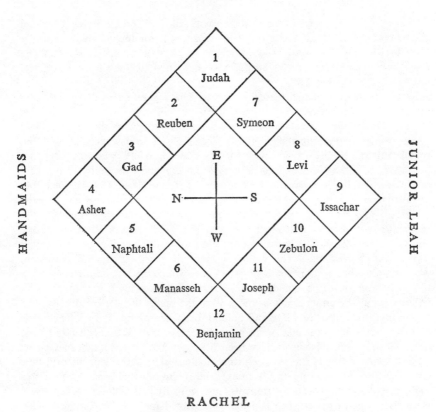

sword, famine, evil beasts, and pestilence, just as Rev 7 follows the six seals which when broken reveal similar disasters.

The second vision need not be disconsonant with an Israel remnant. It may refer to the gathering of the diaspora from every nation. The chapter is undoubtedly influenced by Isa 49, which concerns the redemption of "Jacob" from Babylon; the people Yahweh addresses are "peoples from afar" (Isa 49:1, RSV). Yahweh is to restore the "tribes of Jacob" and "the preserved of Israel" and to let his salvation (cf. Rev 7:9–10) reach the "end of the earth" (Isa 49:6, RSV). The Targum on Isa 49:6 refers to the exiles, as does the Targum on Isa 49:18 (Stenning) which reads:

> Lift up thine eyes round about, O Jerusalem, and see all the children of the people of thy exiles, which gather themselves together and come into thy midst. As I live, saith the Lord, all of them *shall be* to thee as a glorious garment, and their works within thee as an ornament of a bride. (Cf. Rev 19:18.)

The Targum also refers to exiles in Isa 49:20–21. The gathering of Israel and its completion by the inclusion of the diaspora is the theme which naturally precedes the nuptial motif in Revelation; cf. Rev 21:2–4, Isa 49:18. The Epistle of Baruch (II Baruch) purports to be written to the nine and one-half lost tribes.

However, the idea that the great crowd in Rev 7:9 refers to the ingathering of the exiles does not necessarily preclude universalism. Proselytes may well be included in the final salvation of Israel, for the theology of the remnant had room for the "remnant of the Gentiles" (Zech 9:7). This passage deals with the remnant of the Philistines and their incorporation into the messianic kingdom. Isaiah refers to the Gentiles in general (45:20–25) and exhorts Israel to bring brothers from all the nations into the service of Yahweh (66:19–24). Zech 14: 16 also mentions the nations but alludes specifically to those who attacked Jerusalem and who will go year by year to worship Yahweh. Further, the remnant is not necessarily a small number. Micah 4:7 describes it as a "strong people"; cf. Jer 23:3. The "great countless crowd" in 7:9 should be understood in the light of these texts. This would be in keeping with the call of Abraham, who was told that all the families of the earth would bless themselves by or in him. This multitude is countless, just as God promised Abraham that his children would be innumerable as the sand of the sea or the stars of the sky.

The multitude, clad in white and holding branches, stands before the throne and the Lamb. The branches might refer to the Feast of Tabernacles, but need not. Indeed, the prophet may have been influenced by the Maccabean victory. I Macc 13:51 refers to the Jews returning to Jerusalem after their victory; they are described as entering "with praise and palm-branches, and with harps and cymbals and stringed instruments, and with hymns and songs, because a great enemy had been crushed and removed from Israel," RSV. Simon decreed that this day should be celebrated each year, i.e. on the Feast of Dedication. A similar reference occurs in II Macc 10:7, where again beautiful branches, palms, hymns, and thanksgiving are mentioned.

The cry in 7:10 "Salvation to our God who is enthroned and to the Lamb," is a cry of victory. However, Brownlee observes that "my salvation" is a designation for the servant in Isa 49:6. He shows how closely the functions of Yahweh and the servant are linked in 1QIsa. In a similar way in Rev 7:10 God and the Lamb receive praise together. "Salvation" as a messianic title is found in Luke 2:30.

The dialogue in vss. 13–14 is a literary device; cf. Zech 4:4–13, 6:4–5. The "great tribulation" in vs. 14 may point to the destruction of Jerusalem or the trials that precede the end of the world or both. If the scene is influenced by Ezekiel it would refer to Jerusalem but the actual Greek phrase *thlipsis megale*, "great tribulation," can be used in other contexts. In I Macc 9:27, RSV, it refers to the lawless and troubled condition of Israel in the aftermath of Judas' death: "Thus there was great distress in Israel, such as had not been since the time that prophets ceased to appear among them." A similar sentiment occurs in 1QM 1:11 (D-S): "And it shall be a time of distress fo[r al]l the people redeemed by God, and among all their afflictions there will be nothing to equal it from the beginning until its end (in) final redemption."

Thus, that those who came "from the great tribulation" washed their garments in the blood of the Lamb may mean they either entered into battle alongside him as the warrior Lamb or Messiah (cf. Isa 63:1–6) or died a martyr's death in union with him. However, *Gen R* 98:9 suggests another interpretation (*Midrash Rabbah,* trs. Freedman and Simon):

> HE WASHETH HIS GARMENTS IN WINE, intimates that he [the Messiah] will compose for them words of Torah (i.e., propound new meanings and interpretations of the Torah, note 6); AND HIS VESTURE IN THE BLOOD OF THE GRAPES—that he will restore to them their errors (i.e., he will point out where they have misunderstood the Torah). R. Hanin said: Israel will not require the teaching of the royal Messiah in the future, for it says, *unto him shall* the nations *seek* (Isa xi 10), but not Israel (i.e., Israel will receive its teaching direct from God). If so, for what purpose will the royal Messiah come, and what will he do? He will come to assemble the exiles of Israel and to give them [the Gentiles] thirty precepts . . .

This interpretation gives another sense to washing one's robes and includes not only the exiles but also the Gentiles. The reference, however, is to wine, not blood. If this explanation is taken, washing or bathing the robes (robe is probably a metaphor for personality) might be akin to Jesus' words in John 15:3, "You are clean already, thanks to the word I have spoken to you," AB. Brown, AB, vol. 29A, 676–77, expounding on this *mashal* (proverb) refers to Borig's interpretation of "clean" as "fruit-bearing." This "cleansing" will come with a clearer understanding of Jesus' message and a closer union with his life.

In Rev 7 there is probably a similar notion. The people unite themselves to the Lamb and their lives become ones of ceaseless praise. Perhaps the Qumran community attempted to anticipate the perpetual adoration of the holy ones in requiring continuous study of the Torah, e.g. in 1QS 6:6–8 (D-S):

And in the place where the ten are, let there not lack a man who studies the Law night and day, continually, concerning the duties of each towards the other. And let the Many watch in common for a third of all the nights of the year, to read the Book and study the law and bless in common.

The deity responds by tabernacling over them (vs. 15). The use of "tabernacle" continues the Exodus motif which runs through Revelation, e.g. in the sealing and in the washing of robes. Redemption, as Deutero-Isaiah shows, will be like a second Exodus when God will dwell with His people. The Greek verb *skēnōsei*, "tabernacle," suggests the *Shekinah*, the rabbinic term for divine presence or residence. In the Targum the cloud of the "Glory of the Majesty of the Lord" is often referred to as the *Shekinah*.

The promise in vs. 16 that there will be no hunger or thirst continues the prophecy in Isa 49:10, but also reflects the Exodus motif and Yahweh's care for Israel in giving manna, quails, and water. The Lamb imitates the shepherd functions of Yahweh as portrayed in Ezek 34 and of the king-shepherd as in Ps 23. There is a similarity, too, between Rev 7:16 and psalm 151a of the Syriac Apocryphal Psalms, edited by Sanders (DJD, IV, 55), where David is described as the shepherd of the flock and the ruler over his kids, leader of his people and ruler over the sons of the covenant.

While Rev 7:17 draws on the prophecy of Isa 49:10, the author has made some changes. Compare the following verses (MT translation from RSV, LXX translation from *The Septuagint*, London: Bagster, n.d.):

Isa 49:10, MT	*Isa 49:10, LXX*	*Rev 7:17*
. . . they shall not hunger or thirst, neither scorching wind nor sun shall smite them, for he who has pity on them will lead them, and by springs of water will guide them.	They shall not hunger, neither shall they thirst; neither shall the heat nor any sun smite them; but he that has mercy on them shall comfort them, and by fountains of waters shall he lead them.	Because the Lamb who is in the midst of the throne will shepherd them and guide them to springs of living water; and God will wipe away every tear from their eyes.

BIBLIOGRAPHY

Brown, R. E. *The Gospel According to John, I–XII.*
———. *The Gospel According to John, XIII–XXI.*
Brownlee, W. H. *The Meaning of the Qumran Scrolls for the Bible.*
Farrer, A. *The Revelation of St. John the Divine.*
Lampe, G. W. H. *The Seal of the Spirit.*
Philo Judaeus. Philosophical Works, Loeb Classical Library.

V. THE DIVINE WARRIOR ENTERS THE SECOND PHASE OF THE WAR
(8:1–13)

8 ¹ And when He broke the seventh seal, there was silence in heaven for half an hour. ² And I saw the seven angels of the Presence, and they were given seven trumpets.

³ And another angel came and stood before the altar. He had a golden censer and he was given abundant incense to add to the prayers of all the holy ones on the golden altar before the throne. ⁴ And the smoke of the incense arose with the prayers of the holy ones from the hand of the Angel of the Presence. ⁵ And the angel took the censer, and filled it from the coals on the altar and hurled them onto the earth. And there were claps of thunder, and loud voices and streaks of lightning and an earthquake.

⁶ And the seven angels who had the seven trumpets prepared to blow them.

⁷ And the first one blew his trumpet; and there was hail and fire mingled with blood, and it was hurled to the earth. And a third of the trees were burnt up and all the green grass was burnt up.

⁸ And the second angel blew his trumpet; and something like a great mountain burning with fire was hurled into the sea. And a third of the sea became blood, ⁹ and a third of the living creatures in the sea died, and a third of the ships were destroyed.

¹⁰ And the third angel blew his trumpet; and a great star, burning like a torch, fell from heaven and it fell upon a third of the rivers and upon the springs of water. ¹¹ And the star is called by the name, "The Wormwood." And a third of the waters became wormwood, and many men died from the waters, because they were made bitter.

¹² And the fourth angel blew his trumpet; and a third part of the sun was stricken, and a third of the moon and a third of the stars, so that a third of them were darkened and a third of the day did not appear, and likewise the night.

¹³ And I looked, and I heard a solitary eagle flying in mid-heaven, shrieking loudly, "Woe, woe, woe to those who dwell upon the earth because of the rest of the blasts of the trumpets of the three angels who are about to blow!"

NOTES

8:1. *silence.* Charles, p. 221, compares, *Hagigah* 12b, where the angels are silent during the day because of the glory of Israel, and suggests that here the praises are hushed so that the prayers of all the suffering saints may be heard before the throne. *Eccles R* 3:7, commenting on the phrase "a time to keep silence," observes that at a time of mourning it is even inopportune to expound the Torah.

half an hour. Brütsch suggests that this is not half an eschatological hour but rather a symbol of threat, a symptom of crisis.

2. *the seven angels of the Presence.* (See NOTE on 4:5.) They are Uriel, "fire of God"; Raphael, "God has healed"; Raguel, "friend of God"; Michael, "who is like God"; Sariel, "prince of God"; Gabriel, "God is my strength"; Remiel, perhaps as Roberta C. Chesnut (private conversation) suggests, "thunder of God" or "height of God," from the root *r'm.* Yadin, p. 237, quotes 1QM 12:7–8 (D-S):

> And Thou art a ter[rible] God in Thy kingly glory and the congregation of Thy saints is in the midst of us (for) fina[l] succour. [Among] us (is) contempt for kings, disdain and mockery for the brave! For Adonai is holy and the King of Glory is with us accompanied by the saints. The pow[ers] of the host of angels are among our numbered men.

Yadin observes that these lines express the covenanters' belief that Israel will overcome her enemies because God and his angels will fight with them. This concept arises from a number of biblical passages, e.g. Exod 23:20, where the angel leads the people; Exod 33:2, where he drives out the Canaanites; II Kings 19:35, II Chron 32:21, when the angel destroys Sennacherib's camp. The Maccabees, too, invoked the help of angels in their wars, e.g. I Macc 7:41, II Macc 15:23. In II Macc 10:29 angels appear to help Judas; cf. II Macc 11:6. In IV Macc 4:10, ". . . when Apollonius with his armed host marched in to seize the moneys (of the Holy Place), there appeared from heaven angels, riding upon horses, with lightning flashing from their arms . . ." (APCh, II, 670). The date of this work is between 63 B.C. and A.D. 38. Cf. Matt 26:53, Jesus' ability to call twelve legions of angels.

In 1QM 9:14–16 (D-S) the shields of the four towers bear the names of four angels:

> On all the shields of the towers, they shall write, on the first, Mi[chae]l; [on the second Gabriel, on the third] Sariel, on the fourth, Raphael. Michael and Gabriel shall be to [the right (?) and Sariel and Raphael to the left (?)]."

The names were inscribed thus to express the belief that the four angels personally led the four units (Yadin, *The Scroll of the War,* p. 240). Yadin compares *Pirke,* Rabbi Eliezer, 4:

Four companies of serving angels give praise before God. The first company under Michael at His right, the second company under Gabriel at His left, the third company under Uriel before Him, the fourth company under Raphael behind Him and the Divine Presence in the middle.

Thus it is perhaps not without reason that the author has divided his septet into units of four and then three angels. The first four trumpets could have been blown by the angels mentioned above, Michael, Gabriel, Uriel, and Raphael.

3. *the altar.* For a discussion concerning the number of altars in heaven, see Charles, pp. 227–28.

censer. Gk. *libanōtos.* Usually this word means incense but here it appears to signify censer.

incense to add to the prayers. The image conjured up here likens "the prayers" to the live coals in a smoking censer. The angel combines incense with "the prayers" to denote divine acceptance. In vs. 8 the prayers are identified with the incense. See illustration 5.

5. The angel appears to have placed the censer aside to take it up again here. Now it is used for judgment, not intercession. The prayers of the saints return to the earth in wrath.

hurled them onto the earth. This is reminiscent of the brimstone and fire which the Lord rained upon Sodom and Gomorrah (Gen 19:24).

voices. Gr. *phonai.* Cf. Pss 18:13, 29:3, where thunder is Yahweh's voice.

6. *seven trumpets.* The trumpets are midway in the crescendo of divine judgment. When the horsemen appeared a quarter of the earth was affected, when the trumpets are blown a third of the earth is affected, when the bowls are poured on the earth there is total destruction. Charles has tried to alter the order of the trumpets and to omit the first four, but there seems little reason to do this. He thinks the original order was 8:1, 3–5, 2 (restored), 6 (restored), 13, and then ch. 9. He finds the four trumpets a colorless repetition of what has gone before.

The command to make trumpets and the instructions for their use were given to Moses by God, Num 10:1–10; cf. II Chron 13:12–14. They were employed in summoning the congregation, breaking camp, sounding alarm in time of war, and celebrating festivals. The trumpet is used in an eschatological setting in Zeph 1:16, Zech 9:14, Psalms of Solomon 11:1 where it heralds the return of the people from the diaspora. In the pseudo-Apocalypse of John 9, it announces the final judgment; cf. I Thess 4:16. Yadin, *The Scroll of the War,* pp. 87–113, gives a detailed description of the war trumpets mentioned in 1QM. The inscriptions on the "battle" trumpets or trumpets of pursuit are revealing, e.g.

God's mighty deeds to scatter the enemy and to put to flight all opponents of justice and disgraceful retribution to the opponents of God.

Arrays of God's battalions for His wrathful vengeance upon all Sons of Darkness.

Vengeful remembrance at the appointed time of God.

The hand of God's might in battle to strike down all sinful slain.

Mysteries of God for the perdition of the wicked.

God hath smitten all Sons of Darkness, His wrath shall not cease until they are annihilated.

On the trumpets of withdrawal are inscribed: "God has gathered." "Rejoicings of God in peaceful return."

The inscriptions on the trumpets of pursuit are influenced by Jer 23:20. Their main emphasis lies in the insistence on pursuit and annihilation. All the inscriptions contain the word "God." Josephus gives a description of the trumpet in *Ant.* 3.291. He says it was a narrow tube about a cubit in length, "slightly thicker than a flute, with a mouthpiece wide enough to admit the breath and a bell-shaped extremity such as trumpets (Gr. *salpigx*) have." He distinguishes between clarion, Gr. *bukanē,* and trumpet, Gr. *salpigx.* A trumpet is depicted on the Arch of Titus and a Bar Kochba coin. Originally the trumpet was not so much a musical instrument as an alarm. It was sounded to gather the people together, to signal, to indicate the breaking of camp, and such. Later is became a priestly instrument sounded during the liturgy.

7. *the first one.* **052** 1, 2020, 2329 pm g vg co arm[pt] TR read "the first angel."

mingled with blood. Gr. *memigmena en haimati.* The usual construction is with *meta,* "with" or the simple dative rather than *en,* "in." Perhaps the hail and fire are thought to be mixed with blood because in a semitropical thunderstorm the red sand blows up and gives the appearance of red rain.

a third. The result of this catastrophe is only partial destruction, one-third of the trees and all the green grass.

all the green grass was burnt. Charles believes this phrase to be inconsistent with Rev 9:4, where the locusts are said to destroy the grass. One cannot, however, require such exact logicality in an apocalyptic work. Further, 9:4 is influenced by Ezek 9:4. Charles cites *Baba Metzia* 59b, which reports events following the excommunication of Rabbi Eliezer. When the news was brought to him ". . . The world was then smitten: a third of the olive crop, a third of the wheat and a third of the barley crop. Some say, the dough in women's hands swelled up" (Epstein).

Predictions that fractions of the land would be affected were not unknown among the prophets and the idea is closely associated with the remnant theology; the part unaffected is the remnant. Thus when Ezekiel is told to perform a prophetic *'ot,* that is, dramatic symbol, to predict the siege of Jerusalem, it takes this form: he must shave his head and beard, burn one-third of the hair in the fire in the midst of the city, strike one-third with a sword around the city, and scatter one-third to the wind; Ezek 5:1–5. The LXX reading is that the hair is divided into quarters, not thirds. The first two quarters the prophet burns; he kindles, Gr. *anakaiō,* the first quarter, and burns completely, *katakaiō,* the second. The prophetic sign in Revelation is also directed against Jerusalem and occurs before the angel marks the *taw* on the foreheads of the faithful; 9:4.

Fractions are employed again in Ezek 5:12 in parceling out those who will die by plague, famine and sword and those who will be dispersed. Zech 13:8–9 foretells that two-thirds in the whole land shall be cut off and one-third shall be left alive, and this last third will be put into the fire and refined.

8. *a great mountain burning.* In Jer 51:24–25 Yahweh describes Babylon as a mountain which destroys the whole earth and says that he will stretch out his hand against her and roll her down the crags, making her into a burnt mountain. In I Enoch 18:13–16, 21:3, the seer notes seven stars like burning mountains imprisoned in "the end of heaven and earth" (18:14, APCh, II, 200) and is informed that they are stars that violated the commandments of God by not rising at their appointed time. Consequently, they were bound for ten thousand years.

with fire. This phrase is omitted by **046** 82, 104 al.

9. *a third.* 1611 pc latt arm read " a third part."

living creatures in the sea. Cf. Zeph 1:3. The author does not use *ichthus*, "fish," but a phrase which is closer, although not identical, to Gen 1:20–21. The phrase "in the sea" is omitted by 1, 2059 pc.

ships were destroyed. Palestine was not a sea fishing country. Fish was imported by ship from Phoenicia and sold by Tyrians in Jerusalem; see Neh 13:16. Fish eating became popular in Hellenistic times. For the merchants, cf. Rev 18:17–19.

10–11. The fresh water being smitten with wormwood is suggestive of Isa 14:12–14, which is a taunt against the king of Babylon, mockingly addressed as Lucifer, the day star, the offspring of dawn, who has fought to ascend to the heaven above the stars of God and to rule there. Now he is brought down to Sheol and the pit. There may be an allusion to the myth of Hēlēl, the morning star (Venus), who climbed the walls of the northern city to make himself king of heaven and was driven away by the rising sun. In this legend there is a link with Canaanite mythology since the father of this god Šahar, "Dawn," is well known in the Ugaritic tablets.

Ugarit was the chief city on the Phoenician coast in the second millennium B.C. Its site was discovered in 1928. Among other documents, tablets written in the indigenous language, Ugaritic, were discovered. Many of these are mythological in character and include the Baal Epic, the King Keret Legend, and the Story of Aqhat, son of Dan-el. "Wormwood," Gk. *apsinthos,* is used in Prov 5:4 (Aquila), to describe the speech of a loose woman who is destined for Sheol. In Jer 9:15(14) (Aquila) Yahweh threatens to feed his people with wormwood because they followed idols. In Jer 23:15 (Aquila) tht same punishment is predicted to befall the false prophets of Jerusalem. The Hebrew word for "wormwood," *la'ănāh,* denotes perversion of justice (Amos 6:12), the bitter fruits of idolatry (Deut 29:17–18), divine chastisement (Jer 9:14–15). Caird, p. 115, gives a similar interpretation to Rev 8:10–11:

We are justified therefore in supposing that *Wormwood* is the *star* of the new Babylon, which has *poisoned* by its idolatry the *springs* of its own life. When Babylon's star drops from the zenith, Babylon's ruin is at hand.

This is the reversal of Exod 15:22–25, where Moses threw a tree into bitter water and made it sweet.

11. *"The Wormwood."* Gk. *Ho apsinthos. Ho* is omitted by א 1, 2329 al TR. Many manuscripts have a different spelling for *apsinthos*.

12. *sun . . . moon . . . stars.* Cf. the disturbance of the cosmic bodies in Amos 8:9, Joel 3:15. The catastrophe forms a contrast to the ideal state of the righteous predicted in Isa 30:26, where it is said that the light of the moon will be like the light of the sun and the light of the sun will shine with seven-fold strength; cf. Rev 21:23.

likewise the night. This phrase must mean a third of the night also was without light, i.e. the moon and stars were dimmed to one-third their brightness.

13. *eagle.* P 1, 2059s al TR read "angel." 42 Prim reads "angel like an eagle."

in mid-heaven. Gr. *en mesouranēmati,* lit. "in the meridian" or "at the zenith." See COMMENT.

shrieking loudly. 104, 2037 al read "shrieking loudly three times."

Woe, woe, woe. Worse disasters are to follow. One may compare the significant verse in Hosea 8:1, RSV:

> Set the trumpet to your lips,
>> for a vulture is over the house of the Lord,
> because they have broken my covenant,
> and transgressed my law.

COMMENT

The chapter begins with an ominous silence. This has an important dramatic effect as well as theological relevance, by providing a sharp contrast to the loud and ceaseless songs of praise sung in ch. 7 by the angels, elders, and living creatures in heaven. The silent pause is calculated to fill the reader with expectation.

The theological import is seen by comparison with three OT texts. A reference to silence occurs in Hab 2:20: "But the Lord is in his holy temple; let all the earth keep silence before Him" (RSV). This verse is followed (Hab 3:3) by an awe-inspiring description of the coming of Yahweh "from Teman . . . from Mount Paran," i.e. from the direction of Sinai. 1QpHab 13:2–4 interprets Hab 2:20 as referring to the "Day of Judgment" when "God will destroy all those who serve idols, together with the wicked, from the earth" (D-S), but unfortunately it breaks off at this point. Zech 2:13 bids all flesh be silent before God when he arouses himself from his holy dwelling. Zeph 1:7–8 commands silence before God, "For the day of the Lord is at hand; the Lord has prepared a sacrifice and consecrated his guests" (RSV), and predicts punishment for those who have sinned. Zeph 1 ends with a horrendous description of the day of wrath (Zeph 1:14–16, RSV):

> The great day of the Lord is near,
>> near and hastening fast;
> the sound of the day of the Lord is bitter,

the mighty man cries aloud there.
A day of wrath is that day,
a day of distress and anguish,
a day of ruin and devastation,
a day of darkness and gloom,
a day of clouds and thick darkness,
a day of trumpet blast and battle cry
against the fortified cities
and against the lofty battlements.

In these three texts silence heralds theophany and probably indicates a short period of mourning before the Day of Wrath.

On a less exalted level there is also a "military silence". In 1QM 9:1 the troops are ordered to cease the fanfare (the Hebrew can mean "to be silent"; Yadin, *The Scroll of the War*, p. 298), while the trumpets of the slain are blown by the priests (cf. I Macc 5:31–34; for a full description of the sounds and signals of the trumpets see Yadin, pp. 99–104).

Silence is also associated with creation. IV Esdras 6:39 observes that, when heaven and earth were created, there was darkness and silence everywhere and no sound of man's voice. IV Esdras 7:30–31 predicts that the world will return to its primeval silence for seven days when the four hundred year period is ended and a new creation begins, but this passage may be a Christian addition. Silence, therefore, could herald theophany, a new phase in battle, or creation, or, as in Hab 2:20, Zeph 1:7, Zech 2:13, it could be a liturgical rubric. In Rev 8 all four meanings of silence may be important.

A theophany, through the mediation of angels, is indicated by several features of ch. 8. One notes again the emphatic use of the impersonal passives: "was given," *edothē*, vs. 3; "was hurled," *eblēthē*, vs. 7; "was burnt up," *katekaē*, vs. 7; "was hurled," *eblēthē*, vs. 8; "is called," *legetai*, vs. 11; "was stricken," *eplēgē*, vs. 12; and "were darkened," *skotisthē*, vs. 12. See second paragraph of COMMENT on ch. 6 and third NOTE on 7:2. The angel sounds the trumpet but the agent of the disaster is not named; the audience is meant to assume that it is God. The seven angels are expressly said to "stand before God" (vs. 2), i.e. they are the angels nearest the throne, angels of the Presence, one might say "angels of the theophany." The angel with the censer hurls the coals from the altar onto the earth. The Jewish reader would think immediately of Ezek 10:2 where the man (an angel) clothed in linen is told "go in among the whirling wheels underneath the cherubim; fill your hands with burning coals from between the cherubim, and scatter them over the city" (RSV).

Four astonishing reversals occur. 1) From the throne and altar, whence one might expect mercy and atonement, comes wrath. 2) Incense, which originally meant "fragrant smoke," Heb. *qetōret* (cf. Pss 65:15, 141:2, Isa 1:13), and was used with burnt offerings to be "a sweet savor to the Lord," a phrase repeated often in Leviticus, e.g. 1:13, 17, becomes an instrument of punishment both in this chapter and in ch. 16 (in ch. 16 the seven angels are not those of the Presence). The hurling of the coals is in rude opposition to the gentle rise of the cloud of incense, symbolizing prayer penetrating heaven and calling down God's mercy. 3) The trumpets, in association with the altar and throne, should suggest the instrument which was played during the pauses in the psalms, when the people prostrated themselves and worshiped, and on special occasions, e.g. in Sir 1:16, where Simon offers a sacrifice on the Day of Atonement; I Macc 4:40, before the Maccabean cleansing of the temple; *Sukkah* 51b, at the joyous Feast of Tabernacles. Now the same instrument calls "Woe" and disaster, seemingly upon the faithless Jews. More startling still is the fact that Neh 12:41, I Chron 15:24, infer that there were *seven* trumpets in the temple orchestra. 4) Liturgy, conducted from heaven, brings destruction, not life.

One can recapture the scene of the daily sacrifice of incense offered in the temple; cf. Exod 30:34–36. This took place in the morning after the lamb had been immolated but before it was placed on the altar of holocausts. The incense offering was repeated in the evening after the lamb was placed on the altar but before the libation. Accompanied by two other priests, the sacrificing priest, chosen by lot, entered the holy place. One of the assisting priests carried in a brazier burning coals which he had taken from the altar of holocausts with silver pincers. He placed the coals on the altar of incense, prostrated himself in adoration, and then retired. The celebrant took the incense from its container, which he handed to the second assisting priest, and poured the incense upon the coals. Then having inclined profoundly toward the holy of holies, he departed slowly, walking backwards in order to avoid turning his back on the altar. Finally, while the incense was burning, the priests prayed, and the sound of trumpets, interrupting the chanting of Ps 150 by the Levites, announced to the people that they should join in adoration with the sacred ministers. In the context of Rev 8 the offering is made in heaven, not on earth, and it is an angel who offers the incense sacrifice rather than a human priest.

However, even though the scene depicted in ch. 8 appears to be an imitation of the temple services, there is another liturgical context which should be considered, namely, the prayers offered at the appointed time on the day of battle. These are discussed by Yadin, in *The Scroll of the War*, pp. 210–16. In 1QM prayers, thanksgiving, and exhortations are offered in this order: before arraying the formations; after the arraying but before the battle; after the defeat of the Sons of Light; after the beginning of defeat of the Sons of Darkness; and after their defeat, in association with the slain, on return to camp, on the day after the victory, and perhaps on the return to Jerusalem.

Yadin draws attention to the battle prayers of the Maccabees; I Macc 4:8–9; II Macc 12:15, 15:22–23. It is not, therefore, surprising to find in Revelation liturgy associated with "divine warfare" and hymns and canticles amidst cosmic catastrophe; see 11:15–19 and COMMENT. The prayer in 1QM 10:8–14 speaks of the election of Israel and makes special reference to God as creator and controller of the elements, the angels (spirits), and mankind; cf. the first four trumpets in Rev 8. It recalls past victories, such as that of David of the kings of Israel, of Israel over the drowning Egyptians and over Sennacherib. Allusion is made to these particular historical events because they were victories won directly by the miraculous help of Yahweh. The testimonium in Num 24:17 concerning a star that will arise from Jacob is interpreted eschatologically in 1QM 11:6 and reference is made in 11:8–9 to prophetic testimonia which have announced:

. . . the times of the battles of Thy hands
in which Thou wilt be glorified in our enemies;
in which Thou wilt bring down the bands of Belial, the seven nations of vanity
into the hand of the Poor whom Thou hast redeemed
[by the migh]t and fullness of marvelous Power.

This background is a precedent for the direct intervention of Yahweh in Rev 8:6–12.

In Rev 6 the horsemen of the seals embodied four manifestations of Yahweh in the guise of angels. This theophany, heralded by "battle prayer" in heaven, is more directly the epiphany of Yahweh in his capacity as Divine Warrior. The three OT texts concerning silence have already provided precedent for this, but the clearest is Hab 3.

In Hab 3:8 the Divine Warrior rides upon his horses, upon the chariot of victory; in vs. 9 he strips the sheath from his bow and puts the arrows to the string (cf. the first horseman). As he comes cosmic disturbances occur which affect the mountains, vss. 6, 10; the rivers, vs. 8; the sea, vss. 8, 10; the sun and moon, vs. 11. The cause is the light of His arrows, the flash of His glittering spear, vs. 11. The nations and people are also stricken. This canticle of Habakkuk studiedly reflects God's powerful coming at Sinai, vss. 2–3.

Not unlike the Phoenician storm-god who holds a thunderbolt in his hand (J. B. Pritchard, *Ancient Near Eastern Texts Relating to the Old Testament,* 2d ed. [Princeton University Press, 1955], p. 140), Yahweh's approach is like a violent thunderstorm. The theophany in Hab 3 and other texts, such as Ps 18, bear affinity to Rev 8. Its portrayal is more arresting because Rev 8–9 reflects the Sinai tradition in both the Yahwist and Elohist strands. At Sinai the people feared lest they should die when God manifested himself; Exod 19:12, 21; cf. Judg 5:4–5; Pss 77:15–21, 94:3–7). The blast of the trumpet plays an important part in the appearance at Sinai; Exod 19:13, 16, 19. In Rev 8 the weapons of Yahweh are activated by the trumpets; the angels who blow them are comparable to the trumpeters in the Israelite army who signaled for different tactics to commence.

The thunder, lightning, and earthquake in vs. 5 are reminiscent of the Elohist Sinai tradition, which describes the theophany in terms of a thunderstorm. At the blast of the first trumpet these are followed by hail and fire. The phenomena have a parallel in Pss 18:13, 29:3, where thunder is a metaphor for the voice of Yahweh (n.b. *phonai,* "voices" in Rev 8:5) and leads to such disasters as "hailstones and coals of fire" in 18:13, RSV, and the seven catastrophes in 29:4–10. Note also the seven-fold repetition of "voice" in Ps 29. Streaks of lightning were deemed Yahweh's arrows; Pss 18:12–14, cf. 29:7, 77:18).

Hail, frozen rain falling in pellets of various shapes and sizes, might remind the reader of the stones shot from a sling or by hand. Thus Josh 10:11 reports that in the battle of the Amorites against Gibeon and Joshua, God "threw down great stones from heaven . . . and they (the enemy) died; there were more who died because of the hailstones than the men of Israel killed with the sword," RSV, cf. Isa 30:30. Job 38:22–23, AB, speaks of the storehouses of snow and hail reserved for the day of battle and war:

> Have you entered the snow stores,
> Or seen the hoards of hail
> Which I reserve for troublous times,
> For the day of attack and war?

Sir 46:5–6, RSV, reads as follows:

> He [Joshua] called upon the Most High, the Mighty One,
>   when enemies pressed him on every side,
> and the great Lord answered him
>   with hailstones of mighty power.
> He hurled down war upon that nation,
>   and at the descent of Beth-horon he destroyed those who resisted,
> so that the nations might know his armament,
>   that he was fighting in the sight of the Lord;
> for he wholly followed the Mighty One.

Yadin, in *Art of Warfare*, II, 296–97, refers to various reliefs showing ancient slingmen; they operated in pairs and kept close to them sacks of "ammunition"—stones. Yadin reports that the slingmen "could direct high-angled fire up steep slopes," p. 297. Cf. "fire" in Rev 8:7 and see the photograph of the accumulation of *ballistae*, "stones," discovered at Masada, in Yadin, *Masada*, plate 15b. Yahweh's weapons harm the vegetation just as winter storms in Palestine, often accompanied by hail, damage crops.

At the blast of the second trumpet, vs. 8, "something like a great mountain burning with fire" appears. This image reflects the Yahwist tradition of the Sinai theophany in Exod 19:16–20, where the language suggests a volcano; see Noth, pp. 156, 159. "Something like a great mountain burning" is probably also a volcano. The effect of its being "hurled into the sea" is that a third of the water "became blood." The color of molten lava reflected on the water, and the pollution caused by ash or debris falling into water after volcanic eruption, lead easily to the image of water turned to blood. Consequently the creatures in the water would die. That "a third of the ships were destroyed," vs. 9, further suggests a volcano. Such a disaster is illustrated by the eruption of Vesuvius which desolated the Bay of Naples in A.D. 79. There was also a volcanic island in the Aegean; cf. Strabo *Geography* I iii 16. However, the author may be referring not to a specific incident, but rather to an eschatological event.

When the third angel sounds his trumpet a star burning like a torch falls upon the fresh waters. The Divine Warrior now brings into play angelic hosts, "a great star," rather than such physical "weapons" as hail, fire, and volcanoes. The ancients regarded the stars as living creatures. Judg 5:20 portrays the stars as fighting "From their courses . . . against Sisera," AB. Here the poet is probably thinking of falling stars and seeing them as warriors swooping down. In later times, the stars were called the hosts of heaven. The Assyrians conceived of the stars as soldiers serving Anu, the god of heaven. In I Kings 22:19 and II Chron 18:18, the hosts stand in God's presence on his right and left. In Neh 9:6 and Ps 103:21, 23, the hosts serve and praise Him.

Stars can also be the object of God's judgment and may be removed to the nether world; cf. Isa 29:21. In I Enoch 18:13 – 19:3 the seer is told that the "seven stars like great burning mountains" have been placed in prison because they have transgressed the commandment of God by not coming forth at their appointed times; cf. I Enoch 21:1–6, where Enoch sees "seven stars bound together . . . like great mountains and burning with fire," APCh, II, 199–201. Rev 8:10–11, however, refers to a falling star rather than ordinary ones. Shooting stars or meteors were deemed bad omens in the ancient world and the darkening of the stars was thought to manifest the wrath of God; cf. Isa 13:10 concerning the fall of Babylon; Ezek 32:7, lamentation over Pharaoh; Joel 2:10, 3:14–15, with reference to the Day of the Lord.

The name of the star in Rev 8:11 is "The Wormwood." Wormwood is a plant of the genus Artemisia; it has a bitter taste. In Deut 29:17–18 it is used in reference to one who spreads idolatry. Amos 6:12 speaks about turning "the fruit of righteousness into wormwood," RSV. In Jer 9:14 God says that he will feed his idolatrous people "with wormwood, give them poison to drink!", AB. The same punishment is predicted for false prophets in Jer 23:15. In times of war supplies of fresh water were of first importance; cf. Yadin, *Art of Warfare*, II, 320–22). Poisoning the water, therefore, is not without "military" importance.

When the fourth trumpet sounds, the sun, moon, and stars are dimmed, probably because of the brightness of the theophany. The canticle of Habakkuk, Hab 3:11, RSV: reports

> The sun and moon stood still in their habitation
>   at the light of thine arrows as they sped,
>   at the flash of thy glittering spear.

Yahweh's armor obscures the light of the sun, moon, and stars. One recalls also the blinding effect of metal shields with the sun shining on them; they glittered "like a face mirror" (Yadin, *The Scroll of the War*, pp. 117–22). The ornamentation with jewels and such would increase this effect. Darkness and light thus were important in the art of warfare. In Rev 8:12 Yahweh restricts the light. He reverses the favor he showed to Joshua (Josh 10:12–14; cf. Sir 46:4) and Hezekiah (II Kings 20:8–11) for whom he had extended the period of daylight. An eclipse of the sun or moon was regarded as an evil sign. Further, because the liturgical feasts had to be celebrated at precisely the right time, according to the movements of the sun and moon, and kept from sunset to sunset, the disturbance of the two "great lights" (Gen 1:16, AB) would jeopardize meticulous observance.

Thus Rev 8 shows Yahweh beginning to bring his weapons and troops into action, to war against his people in order that they may repent, Rev 9:20. As in Isa 42:13, Yahweh is portrayed as a furious man of war.

In vs. 13 the seer relates his vision of a solitary eagle or vulture projected against the sky, either "in the meridian" or "at the zenith," where the sun is at noon; cf. 14:6, 19:17. The course of the eagle can be seen by all. The cry of the eagle is three repetitions of "woe," signifying the last three plagues to be announced by the trumpets. One should bear in mind the piercing screech of an eagle. The three remaining woes, unlike those heralded by the first four trumpets, which appear to strike directly at inanimate nature, are aimed at mankind, "those who dwell upon the earth."

It is difficult to decipher the symbolism of the eagle. However, if this verse, like the preceding ones, is influenced by Hab 3 and Ps 18, the image is probably that of Yahweh, pictured in Hab 3:3–4 as interpreted by Dahood in *Psalms I*, third NOTE on 18:11, "as an eagle . . . whose extended wings fill the heavens: 'His Majesty covered the heavens, and his brilliance filled the earth. His shining was like the sun, two wings were at his sides.' " Dahood points out that the motif of the divine bird with great wing span is documented in Canaanite and biblical literature. Baal is the "glorious phoenix, phoenix wide of wings" and Yahweh is an eagle in Exod 19:4 and Deut 32:11. Wings are mentioned in both cases; cf. Pss 17:8, 36:7(8), 57:1(2), 61:5, 91:4, in Dahood, *Psalms I, Psalms II:* verse numbers in parentheses are Dahood's where he differs from RSV.

In Exod 19:4 Yahweh tells the Israelites that he has borne them on eagle's wings and brought them to Himself. This Exodus motif fits admirably into chs. 8–9, but in 8:13 it is turned sharply around; Yahweh proclaims "Woe," not safety. The vision stands as an antithesis, too, to the symbolism in II Baruch 77:19–26, where the prophet sends a letter to the nine and a half tribes by means of an eagle, which he commands to fly directly and tarry in no place till he has crossed the width of the river Euphrates and gone to the people on the other side. In the letter he reminds the nine and a half tribes of the bond with which they are united to the rest of the tribes. He bids them be comforted and tells them that if they accept their suffering they will be rewarded at the end of times. He informs them of the fall of Jerusalem to the Babylonians, but says that God has revealed to him that vengeance will come to Israel's enemies and mercy to His people.

In Rev 8 there is no such comfort. While the eagle may symbolize Yahweh, it may also carry a secondary meaning. In Ezek 1:10, 10:14, the eagle is mentioned in association with the throne of God, but ordinarily the eagle ranked as an unclean bird; *Hullin* 61a. Further, in English the word vulture renders several different Hebrew terms in the OT, all of which refer to unclean birds, birds of prey. The vulture is used as an image of an invading army in Deut 28:49, Jer 48:40, Hosea 7:1, Hab 1:8. In Rev 8:13 the eagle or vulture may also represent the invading Roman army, used as an instrument of Yahweh as He had used political forces in the past to discipline His people. The eagle is ready to swoop down on its prey.

BIBLIOGRAPHY

Brütsch, C. *La Clarté de l'Apocalypse.*
Caird, G. B. *The Revelation of St. John the Divine.*
Charles, R. H. *Revelation.* ICC, I.

Dahood, *Psalms I, 1–50.*

———. *Psalms II, 51–100.*

———. *Psalms III, 101–150.*

Noth, M. *Exodus, a Commentary.* London: SCM, 1959.

Yadin, Y. *The Art of Warfare in Biblical Lands,* II.

———. *The Excavation of Masada.*

———. *The Scroll of the War of the Sons of Light Against the Sons of Darkness.*

VI. THE INFERNAL ARMIES
(9:1–21)

9 1 And the fifth angel blew his trumpet; and I saw a star which had fallen from heaven to earth, and the key of the pit of the abyss was given to him. 2 And he opened the pit of the abyss; and from the pit arose smoke like the smoke of a great furnace, and the sun and the air were darkened because of the smoke of the pit. 3 And locusts came out of the smoke onto the earth, and power like that of earthly scorpions was given to them. 4 And they were told not to harm the grass of the earth or any plant or any tree but only the men who had not God's seal on their foreheads. 5 However, they were not allowed to kill them but only to torture them for five months; and the torture was like the torture of a scorpion, when it stings a man. 6 Now in those days men will search for death and they will not find it, and they will yearn to die and death will flee from them. 7 And the appearance of the locusts was like horses prepared for war, and on their heads they wore what looked like wreaths of gold, and their faces were like the countenances of men, 8 and they had hair like women's hair, and their teeth were like lions' teeth 9 and they had scales like iron breastplates, and the sound of their wings was like the sound of chariots with many horses rushing into battle. 10 Also they had tails and stingers like scorpions, and the power to harm men for five months abides in their tails. 11 Their king is the angel of the abyss, whose name in Hebrew is Abaddon and in Greek he is called Apollyon. 12 The first woe has passed; behold, two more woes come after these.

13 Then the sixth angel blew his trumpet; and I heard a solitary voice from the four horns of the golden altar before God, 14 saying to the sixth angel, who had the trumpet, "Unleash the four angels who are bound by the great river, Euphrates." 15 So the four angels, who were prepared for the hour and day and month and year, to kill a third of mankind, were unleashed. 16 Now the number of the soldiers of the cavalry was twice ten thousand times ten thousand; I heard their number. 17 In my vision I saw the horses and those who sat upon them like this: they had breastplates of fire and sapphire and

sulphur; and their heads were like lions' heads, and from their mouths came fire and smoke and sulphur. 18 A third of mankind was killed by these three plagues, from the fire and smoke and sulphur issuing from their mouths. 19 For the power of the horses was in their mouths and in their tails; for their tails are like serpents, they have heads, and by means of these they wound. 20 But the rest of mankind, who were not killed by these plagues, did not repent of the works of their hands by relinquishing the worship of demons and idols of gold and silver and bronze and stone and wood, which are unable to see or hear or walk, 21 and they did not repent of their murders or sorceries or unchastity or thefts.

Notes

9:1. *a star which had fallen from heaven.* One notes the past perfect tense, contrasted with the simple past of vss. 2–5, 7–21. The seer did not see a star falling from heaven to earth but a star which had already fallen. The author probably identified the star with an angel (cf. II Enoch 30:14), but stars may also represent men, as in CDC 7:18, where "the Star" appears to mean the Teacher of Righteousness.

pit. The Greek word, *phrear,* can mean well, pit, or shaft. In the Qumran scrolls Heb., *šht,* "pit," from the root *šht,* meaning "go to ruin," is used a number of times and may be equivalent to *phrear* here. In 1QS 4:12 ocurs the phrase, "everlasting pit"; Dupont-Sommer, p. 80, note 2, compares *War* 2.155, where the Essenes relegate evil spirits to a dark pit. "The men (or sons) of the Pit" are mentioned in 1QS 9:16, 22, 10:19, CDC 6:15, 13:14. "The Pit" is an important feature in 1QH 3.

abyss. Gr. *abussou,* lit. "unfathomably deep"; see Jeremias. It is a place of imprisonment for disobedient spirits and/or the sphere of the dead. In later Judaism it signified the original flood and the interior of the earth where evil spirits are confined. Descent into the pit stands in sharp contrast to ascension into heaven; see Jeremias. In the NT it occurs only in Luke 8:31, which reports Jesus' sending the demons into the abyss; in Rom 10:7, "'Who will descend into the abyss?'" RSV, and seven times in Revelation, 9:1, 2, 11, 11:7, 17:8, 20:1, 3.

was given to him. Note again the impersonal passive implying that the agent is God.

2. *And he opened the pit of the abyss.* This clause is omitted in ℵ **046** 82, 205, 1611, 2053 al vg^pc sy^ph sa (2) bo.

smoke. Cf. Ps 68:2, AB, Dahood's vs. 3:

> Like drifting smoke they [God's enemies] are driven,
>> like melting wax before the fire;
> At the sight of God the wicked disappear.

great furnace. In **046** 82, 104 pm "burning" is substituted for "great." 1778 pc g sy[ph] read "great furnace burning."

because of the smoke of the pit. This phrase is omitted in ℵ* pc Prim.

3. *And.* Omitted in ℵ* pc Prim.

them. Because this pronoun refers to "locusts," the Greek is usually masculine, but in AP 0207 1, 1611, 2059[s] pl TR, "them" is feminine.

4. *they were told.* Gr. *edothē autois,* lit. "it was said to them." See COMMENT.

grass. Gr. *chortos,* lit. "grass" or "hay." In the NT *chortos* usually refers to "green grass" in a meadow or "wild grass," in distinction from cultivated plants.

plant. Gr. *chlōros,* lit. "yellowish green." This word describes plants, green branches, sticks, and vegetation generally. For the figurative use of *chlōros,* cf. Isa 40:6–7:

MT (AB)	Targum (Stenning)
. . . All flesh is grass,	. . . All the wicked are grass,
and its constancy like	and all their strength as
the blossom of the field.	the flower of the field.
The grass withers,	The grass withereth,
the blossom fades,	its flower fadeth;
when the wind of Yahweh	for the wind from before the Lord
blows on them.	hath blown upon it;
Surely the people is grass.	therefore the wicked among the people
	are counted as grass.
The grass withers,	The wicked dieth,
the blossom fades;	his thoughts (or, *plans*) perish;
but the word of our God	but the word of our God
shall endure forever.	abides for ever.

only the men. The word "only" appears in 2053 pc vg arm TR.

God's seal. In 1, 2059s pm "God's" is omitted.

5. *they were not allowed to kill.* Gr. *edothē autois hina mē apokteinōsin,* lit. "it was granted to them not to kill." See COMMENT.

kill them. Even though the pronoun refers to "the men" in vs. 4, its gender in P **046 0207** 82, 1006, 2036, 2329 pm TR is feminine.

torture them. The pronoun here is TI.

five months. Prim reads "six months."

stings. The sting of a scorpion, such as these locusts were supposed to give, was well known to the ancients. There is a pass in the Negeb called the Acrabbim Pass; it means "the ascent of the scorpions." This pass lies southwest of the Dead Sea; cf. Num 34:3, Josh 15:3, Judg 1:36. It is probably on account of the pain of a scorpion bite that the type of whip referred to in I Kings 12:11 was called a scorpion. Flogging with a scorpion whip was practiced in the Maccabean times; cf. II Macc 6:30, 7:1. Therefore the sting of a scorpion probably had a double meaning to the readers of Revelation, particularly if they were descendants of the Maccabees and/or their followers.

6. Note the four verbs in the future tense.

death. Cf. the personification of death in the fourth seal, Rev. 6:8.

7. *locusts . . . like horses.* in P **046 0247** 1, 82, 2059s, 2329 pl TR the gender of "like" is neuter rather than masculine.

horses. The author may have been influenced by the concept of centaurs, a tribe of mythical monsters who appeared as human beings in the upper part of their bodies and as horses in their lower parts. They were reputed to live in woods or mountains in Greece. Myths concerning these creatures occur in Homer. They symbolize wildlife, barbarism, and animal desires, and are characterized as licentious and given to much wine. Stories are told of individual centaurs, e.g. the one killed by Heracles which is often depicted on vase paintings. Other centaurs appear as types of medicine men.

they wore. TI.

9. *chariots with many horses rushing.* In 325, 2031 pc "horses" is omitted; thus the reference in these manuscripts is to "many chariots."

11. *Abaddon.* The name is derived from Heb. *'ābad,* "to perish," and is employed as a poetic synonym for the abode of the dead. Abaddon is personified in Job 28:22. In Jewish literature Abaddon is used as the name of the lowest part of Gehenna.

P[47] reads *Battōn* for "Abaddon," and bo reads *Makedōn.*

12. *woe.* Swete remarks the feminine "woe" and suggests that this may be used in the light of the female figures in Greek mythology, the erinyes and the eumenides, who were spirits of punishment for avenging wrongs done to relatives, especially when there was murder within the family or clan; cf. the Oresteia. Originally, they seem to have been either the ghosts of the slain persons or personified curses, since a curse was not merely a matter of words, but a potent stirring up of mysterious powers which caused vengeance to take place. They were associated with the earth rather than heaven. If Swete's suggestion is correct, one could relate the spirits to the souls under the altar in 6:9–11.

13. *four horns.* P[47] א* A 0207 1611, 2060 al g vg^w co, R omit "four."

The horn represents strength. The horns on the altar (see illustration 15) were the symbol of God's power. They were required to be of one piece with the altar and, if one were broken off, the altar was considered desecrated. They were sprinkled with blood on the Day of Atonement and they also served as an asylum for criminals, e.g. I Kings 2:28–35, where Joab, fearing death at the hands of Solomon, caught hold of the horns of the altar. In this verse the voice releasing hostile forces comes from the very place where one would look for reconciliation and asylum. The horns were also used in connection with swearing oaths.

14. *saying.* This word is a masculine participle, but P[47] 0207 1 pm TR render it as feminine. In 046 82, 1006, 2329 al the genitive is employed instead of the accusative.

sixth. Omitted in A 0207 pc.

trumpet. See NOTE on 8:6. Yadin, pp. 110–13, discusses the use of trumpets in the Maccabean and Roman period. They were employed when the Judean army was pursuing the remnant of the army of Nicanor (I Macc 7:45) and in the battle against Gorgias (I Macc 4:13). Josephus in *War* 3.89–92, refers to the trumpet signals used in the Roman army for striking camp, to prepare for the march, and as a signal to depart, but also to direct the throwing of missiles when Vespasian besieged Jotapata, A.D. 67, *War* 3.266. If, as Giet suggests,

Rev is linked with the Roman wars of the 60's, then this reference to Vespasian adds a note of reality to the introduction of the trumpets. Yadin, pp. 111–13, concludes his discussion of trumpets in the Roman army as follows: "It must be noted that the number of trumpets and horns at the disposal of the "central command" of the legion did not exceed seven of each type."

four angels. The word "four" is omitted in P⁴⁷.

Euphrates. The Euphrates is the longest river in western Asia: seventeen hundred miles long. David's power is reputed to have extended as far as the Euphrates (II Sam 8:3, I Chron 18:3) and, hence, this river was regarded as the ideal extent of the land promised by God to Israel (Gen 15:18; Deut 1:7, 11:24; Josh 1:4). Between 53 B.C. and A.D. 63, and again after the withdrawal of Trajan, the river Euphrates separated Rome from Parthia. The forts situated on the west bank guarded the boundaries of the empire against the Sassanids. In Jer 51:59–64, Seraiah is commanded to throw Jeremiah's book into the Euphrates and to say, "Just so shall Babylon sink to rise no more, because of the evil that I am going to bring upon it," AB. The mention of the river Euphrates may, therefore, prepare us for the oracle on Babylon in 16.

17. *sapphire*. Gr. *huakathinous*. The Greek word means hyacinth-colored cloth in the LXX, Philo, and Josephus in *Ant*. 3.164. The stone of this color was made into gems; cf. Pliny *Natural History* 37.9.41–42.

18. *these*. Omitted by P⁴⁷.

plagues. Gr. *plēgē*. In the LXX this word is used for the plagues in Egypt. See COMMENT.

20. *idols of gold*. Only here is gold associated with a nonheavenly object. See first NOTE on 17:4.

21. *sorceries*. Gr. *pharmakeia,* lit. "sorcery" or "magic arts." The cognates of this word may also be used for poison, potions, and charms. It might also have referred to contraceptive potions; see Noonan, pp. 44–45, and the references there given.

unchastity. This word is replaced by "wickedness" in ℵ* A pc.

COMMENT

The first four trumpets, in ch. 8, introduced "acts of God," i.e. cosmic disturbances uncontrollable by man. Here in ch. 9 the fifth and sixth trumpets are blown, introducing hostile powers from the nether world and from the earth. Yet everything is still under the authority of God. This is indicated by the bestowal of the key of the abyss in vs. 1, the voice from the altar in vss. 13–14, and the use of impersonal passives, e.g. "was given," vss. 1, 3; "were told," vs. 4, see first NOTE on 9:4; "were not allowed," vs. 5, see first NOTE on 9:5.

This and chs. 10–20 present a concept similar to that in the Qumran scrolls and elsewhere in first-century B.C. and A.D. literature: God, his angels, and the "sons of light" fighting against Satan, or the "Prince of Darkness," his angels, and the "sons of darkness." The hostile forces are associated in Revelation, as in the scrolls, with the Pit; see second NOTE on 9:1. There are several features in ch. 9 that reflect this theme of supernatural conflict.

First, the prophet records having seen a fallen star, probably an angel who has transgressed the commandments of God and whose realm is now not heaven but earth. The idea of the fallen angels, based on Gen 6 which relates how the sons of God came down on earth and seduced women, was a very popular "original sin" story among the Jews. Indeed, before the first century A.D. it was given more prominence than the sin of Adam. The fallen angels, together with the fall of the king of Babylon, mockingly referred to as Lucifer intimated in Isa 14:12, gave rise to the belief in fallen angels as progenitors of hosts of evil spirits who enticed men and women into sin. I Enoch 6–15 relates the fall of angels, the demoralization of mankind, and the doom upon the angels. Such references also occur in the Qumran scrolls, e.g. in CDC 2:18–19 (D-S):

The [Watchers] of Heaven fell because of this (stubbornness of heart) they were taken because they had not kept the commandments of God.
And their sons as tall as cedar trees whose bodies were like mountains fell [because of this].

CF. I Enoch 14. The angels are given the title "Watchers" also in Daniel, Jubilees, Enoch, and the Testaments of the Twelve Patriarchs.

Second, for the first time in Revelation the idea of the pit of the abyss occurs. This is the antithesis of the heavenly court. In the LXX *abussos*, in English "abyss," is used to render the Hebrew word *tehom* about thirty times. *Tehom* has four meanings. It can signify the ocean which once spread over the earth but is now restricted to a subterranean abyss which is closed and sealed and accessible only through a shaft; cf. Ps 33:7, Prayer of Manasseh 3. It can also mean the deep abode of Yahweh's enemy, the sea dragon; cf. Isa 51:9, Ps 74:13. A third meaning for *tehom* is earth, a pit which is a place of intermediate punishment; cf. Isa 24:21–22. Finally, in I Enoch 18:12–16, 19:1–2 (cf. 21:1–6), *tehom* signified the temporary residence of fallen angels; it was a waterless, birdless, fiery place beyond the confines of earth and heaven, where the angels are in utter darkness and covered by rocks (I Enoch 10:5–12). In Rev 9 "the pit of the abyss" may connote an especially deep part of the abyss, the shaft or the well. The fifth angel is given the key of the pit of the abyss. He need not be a good angel, as witness the description of those who hold the keys and guard the gates of hell in II Enoch 42:1, APCh, II, 456: "I saw the key-holders and guards of the gates of hell standing, like great serpents, and their faces like extinguished lamps, and their eyes of fire, their sharp teeth . . ." Cf. the serpents in this passage with locusts and scorpions in Rev 9:3, 6, 10, extinguished lamps and eyes of fire with the smoke and fire in vss. 2, 3, 17, 18, and teeth with lions' teeth in vs. 8.

Third, the idea of smoke and darkness enters the scene with greater force than in 8:12; it is a sharp contrast to the colors of jewels, the radiance, and the white robes in heaven. In the Qumran scrolls Belial or Satan is the evil spirit or the angel of darkness, the commander of the army of evil, e.g. 1QS 3:13–

4:26. The visitation upon those who follow him is described in 1QS 4:12–14
(D-S) thus:

. . . it consists of an abundance of blows administered by all the Angels of
    destruction,
in the everlasting Pit by the furious wrath of the God of vengeance,
of unending dread and shame without end,
and of the disgrace of destruction by the fire of the regions of darkness.
And all their times from age to age
are in most sorrowful chagrin and bitterest misfortune,
in calamities of darkness till they are destroyed
with none of them surviving or escaping.

One notes the stress on darkness. The wicked are referred to as the "sons of
the Pit" in 1QS 9:16, 22, 10:19.

Once this stage is set in vss. 1–2, we are introduced to the infernal army. It
is awful to behold. It emerges out of the smoke from the pit of the abyss,
which is compared to a great furnace, and is depicted as a swarm of locusts.
The locust is the most frequently mentioned insect in the OT and has nine
different names in Hebrew. Figuratively, locusts are used to represent swarming hordes or mighty hosts. Many biblical texts might spring to the reader's
mind, e.g. Judg 6:5, where "locusts" is a simile for the numerous hosts of the
Midianites; Judg 7:12, a simile for the combined forces of the Midianites and
the Amalekites and all the people of the east; Joel 2:4, where the simile is
reversed and locusts are compared to prancing horses; Job 39:20, where the
simile is restored and the horse is compared to the locust, stressing fearlessness;
Isa 33:4, in which man is made as despicable as possible by likening him to the
locust; Amos 7:1, which illustrates the locust's appetite; Nahum 3:17 where
the suddenness of their appearance and disappearance becomes a disdainful
simile for the habits of scribes.

So serious were the consequences of an insect invasion that even on the
Sabbath it was permitted to blow the *shophar* (trumpet) as a sound of alarm
in the event of visitations from locusts, flies, hornets, gnats, snakes, scorpions,
and such; *Ta'anit* 14a, 19b. A plague of locusts was looked upon as a chastisement for sin; Deut 28:38, 42, I Kings 8:37. The association of the locusts
with darkness is not accidental. Often observers described them coming in a
cloud so compact that the light of the sun was actually obscured. Thus the
whole image in ch. 9 conveys the idea of the sudden appearance of swarming,
swift hordes prancing like horses, greedy for prey, causing darkness.

However, the insects which appeared to the author were no ordinary locusts.
They are distinguished by the possession of a venomous sting which makes
them like scorpions. Unlike locusts they do not destroy vegetation but instead
strike at man directly; vs. 4. In Palestine scorpions are four to five inches long
and distinguished from certain spiders by a long, flexible, segmented tail. They
sting by injecting poison from the sharp end of this tail the way a snake injects
venom through its fangs. Although it is rarely fatal (cf. vs. 6) the sting of a
scorpion causes extraordinary pain.

The implications of the vision of the locusts which bear the characteristics of
scorpions may be understood a little better if one has knowledge of CDC

8:9–12, where the unfaithful sectaries and the Chief of the kings of the Yāwān are described as follows (D-S):

Their wine is the poison of serpents and the head of asps is cruel. The serpents are the kings of the peoples and their wine is their ways; and the head of asps is the Chief of the kings of the Yāwān who came to wreak vengeance upon them.

Cf. CDC 5:13–15. The enemies, therefore, of the sons of light were thought of as serpents and asps. The scorpion imagery in 9:5, 10, is similarly used. One may compare the Baptist's reference to "vipers" in Matt 3:7.

The locusts do not kill men, but torment them for five months; vs. 5. The five-month period may be interpreted literally as indicating no more than the ancients' fear of locust invasions, which occurred during the last five months of the Jewish year. Cerfaux and Cambier have arrived at a less literal interpretation. They think that because five months is less than half the total twelve months of the year, the author wishes to indicate that the punishment is only partial. However, a more interesting interpretation is Giet's. He believes that the breaking of the first four seals points to the context of the troubles which preceded the Jewish War, i.e. those under the reigns of Claudius and Nero. When the monstrous locusts strike the earth, they torment man for five months. Giet suggests that this period reflects the five months during which the troops of Gessius Florus cast terror over Palestine. This interpretation is consonant with the eagle symbolism (suggesting the Roman army) and with the image of locusts as invading hordes. It also prepares one for the metaphor of the harlot for the faithless Jerusalem; see Sections XIV and XV.

In vs. 6 the writer combines the role of seer and prophet. The verse expresses the same sentiment as Job 3:20–21, AB:

> Why gives he light to the wretched,
> Life to the bitter of soul,
> Who yearn in vain for death,
> Seek it like a treasure-trove . . .

Cf. Jer 3:3, Eccles 4:2–3, where the writer avers that the dead are more fortunate than the living, but even better off is the one who is unborn. Cf. also II Baruch 10:6, the lamentation over the desolation of Zion.

The situation of men predicted in vs. 6 is different from that of the first-born of the Egyptians who died under the last plague before the Exodus. It is written in 9:6 that men will seek death but death (personified) will flee from them; contrast 6:8. In Exod 12:33 the Egyptians urge the Israelites on their way saying "We are all dead men." The role of death is even more dramatic in the Midrash on Exodus in Wisd Sol 18:12, 15–16, RSV:

> and they all together, by the one form of death,
> had corpses too many to count.
> For the living were not sufficient even to bury them,
> since in one instant their most valued children had been destroyed.
> . . .
> thy all-powerful word . . .
> . . . stood and filled all things with death . . .

The same theme is related in graphic detail by Melito of Sardis in *Homily on the Passover*, written about A.D. 160

The author has drawn upon Joel 2:4–11 for his comparison of locusts to war horses and chariots. There is probably a play on the Hebrew word *hargol*, "locust," and the Arabic word *harjal*, "troops." Joel's description in 2:4–11, RSV, is as follows:

> Their appearance is like the appearance of horses,
> and like war horses they run.
> As with the rumbling of chariots,
>   they leap on the tops of the mountains,
> like the crackling of a flame of fire
>   devouring the stubble,
> like a powerful army
> drawn up for battle.
> Before them peoples are in anguish,
>   all faces grow pale.
> Like warriors they charge,
>   like soldiers they scale the wall.
> They march each on his way,
>   they do not swerve from their paths.
> They do not jostle one another,
>   each marches in his path;
> they burst through the weapons
>   and are not halted.
> They leap upon the city,
>   they run upon the walls;
> they climb up into the houses,
>   they enter through the windows like a thief.
> The earth quakes before them,
>   the heavens tremble.
> The sun and moon are darkened,
>   and the stars withdraw their shining.
> The Lord utters his voice
>   before his army,
> for his host is exceedingly great;
>   he that executes his word is powerful.
> For the day of the Lord is great and very terrible;
>   who can endure it?

Joel's description identified the invasion with the Day and Army of the Lord. A curious feature of the vision in Rev 9 is first the omission of reference to and then the description of the riders on the steeds. Although the Hebrew *rekeb* may mean either "horses" or "horses with their riders," and *pārāš* means unequivocally "a horse with its rider" (cf. II Sam 8:4, Isa 36:8–9, Josh 11:9, Yadin, p. 179, note 2), and the Greek *hippos* also may mean either "horse" or "cavalry," and may thus be used to translate both *rekeb* and *pārāš*, the reader is left uncertain whether the locusts are compared with horses or horsemen. If horses rather than horsemen are described, they might still be wearing armor; cf. Yadin, p. 122, note 3, in reference to the excellent treatment of horse armor in *Dura-Europos*, VI, pp. 144 f. and plates 21–23.

The arresting feature is the absence of the expression *ho kathēmenos*, "he that sat upon," a phrase that would have been reminiscent of "he who sitteth upon the throne" in the preceding chapters and used of the riders in ch. 6. This might suggest that here there is no epiphany of God but that these horses belong entirely to the infernal realm. They stand in stark contrast to the horses of the seals which are described with simplicity and dignity.

These locust-horses wear crowns or wreaths like gold upon their heads. This trait may be borrowed from the bronze helmets of the Roman legionnaires which were burnished with gold. Yadin, pp. 123–124, refers to the headguard or helmet mentioned in 1QM but does not describe it. The horsemen in 1QM wear helmets, greaves, and cuirasses and carry round shield, spear, bow, arrows, and javelin; 1QM 6:15–16.

The physical build of the horses would class them as monstrosities; it runs counter to Gen 1:20–22, where God created plants, animals, and men, each "according to their kinds," vs. 21, RSV, the one carefully distinct from the other. The demonic character of the locusts is brought out by mixing both species and sexes. The faces are human, but not necessarily male; the word is *anthrōpos*, not *anēr*. The hair, however, is like women's hair, and the teeth are animals' teeth, like those of lions. See illustrations 9 and 13.

It is possible to compare the long hair of these locusts to antennae, but it may also have represented the long hair worn by the Parthians. Long hair is not necessarily a sign of femininity, but rather of vitality and strength. Samson wore his long hair in seven braids (Judg 16:13, 19) and it was said to have been the source of his strength. In rabbinic tradition, elaborating this, it is reported that his hair made a noise like bells, which could be heard from Zotah to Eshtaol; Jerusalem Talmud, *Sotah* 17b. Absalom, also a warrior, wore his hair long; II Sam 14:25–26. The Nazirites, formerly chaplains in the army for the holy war, did not cut their hair. Hair, therefore, like teeth, is a symbol of strength.

This idea is continued in the author's description of the breastplates; vs. 9. Although this may be influenced by the scaly backs and flanks of the insects it is also reminiscent of Goliath, who wore a coat of mail, the weight of which was five thousand shekels of bronze. The armor contemporary with the author of Revelation was like fish scales, with the plates overlapping each other and allowing free movement. A cuirass was made of metal plates, with long flexible bands of steel over the shoulders. On the other hand, the armor might consist of a shirt, possibly made of leather and covered with metal scales. In Israel, the breastplate was probably used only by the military leaders to begin with, but later worn by the ordinary soldiers. However, more pertinent to the understanding of the horses' armor is the fact that in I Macc 6:43 the war elephants wear coats of mail and these were probably made of iron links. Such armor, itself, would raise a fearful clangor as the animals rushed into battle. The author intimates this dreadful din in vs. 9.

Vs. 10 adds that the sting of scorpions rests in the tails of the horses and has the power to hurt men for five months. This may be a reference to the

Parthians who shot poisoned arrows over their shoulders as they retreated. Martindale, however, collects some interesting facts from ancient lore that give a hint as to the pictures in our author's mind:

Men-scorpions and men-horses . . . were common in Babylonian imagery, and these centaurs have scorpions' tails. In the Hellenistic Roman period, this composite figure had also passed to Egypt, and stood as a symbol for the zodiacal sign Sagittarius, or the archer . . . It further appears that in Hellenistic calendars locusts appear in the zodiacal sign of the scorpion, and since from then to the end of the year there are five months, it may be that St. John's "five months", a reckoning found only here in the Apocalypse, may imply that this "plague" is to last to the end of the symbolic year of the world's endurance. I add that Sagittarius was known as "diadem-wearer", and represented very often with long hair, and so in an ancient treatise are centaurs described.

Does the author suggest the release of a whole army of centaurs? Although Prov 30:27 says . . . "the locusts have no king, yet all of them march in rank" . . . the author of ch. 9 tells us that these locusts do have a king over them, the angel of the abyss, whose name in Hebrew is Abaddon. Abaddon means destroyer or perdition. Hell is sometimes personified under this name in the OT, in the Talmud and in 1QH 3:16. His Greek name is Apollyon, which might possibly link him with the god Apollo (*Apollōn*) although the spelling here is *Apolluōn*. The grasshopper or locust was one of the emblems of this archer god who poisoned his victims. This name may be introduced into our text with deliberate intent to identify one of the principal pagan gods with hell and destruction.

Delphi was Apollo's chief oracular shrine and, as H. J. Rose avers, "became the nearest approach to a Vatican which Greece possessed . . . Delphi propaganda may be traced in the tendency to introduce Apollo as adviser, inspirer, etc. into any and every myth which contains a prophet or a prediction. Delphi claimed to be the centre of the world . . ." (*Oxford Classical Dictionary*, eds. M. Cary et al., Oxford: Clarendon Press, 1957, under *Apollo*). The emperor Augustus was devoted to Apollo, especially as the battle of Actium was won near one of his temples. He built a temple to him on the Palatine.

The role of the angel of the abyss may also be compared to that of Belial in the Qumran scrolls where he is mentioned some thirty-three times. He is the military leader of the forces of darkness, who is allowed to be "unleashed against" Israel; note the word "unleashed," cf. Rev 9:15, CDC 4:12–13. During the time of his dominion he spreads terror but does not prevail against the sons of the covenant; cf 1QM 14:9–10. On the appointed day Yahweh, with the assistance of his angels, will destroy Israel's enemies, which are led by Belial. Belial himself and all his hosts will come to an end, as predicted in 1QM 18:1 (D-S) ". . . when the great Hand of God is raised over Belial and over all the [lo]t of his empire to strike a final blow . . ." Cf. Belial bound in fetters in Testament of Levi 18:12, and cast into the fire in Testament of Judah 25:3.

At this point, however, the reader is only introduced to the armies of Belial, probably to be identified with the angel of the abyss, under the guise of stinging animals. In 1QH 3:18 these subordinate spirits are called *rûhê,* "spirits of vipers (or the Asp)," or possibly "spirits of nothingness," *'ep'eh,* Ringgren, p. 91. The Asp or the Viper occurs four times in the scrolls (1QH 2:28, 3:12, 17, 18) although some take the meaning to be "nought" rather than "viper"; Mansoor, p. 114, note 7.

The sixth trumpet shows the earthly allies of the infernal host. The seer hears a solitary voice coming from the horns of the golden altar which stands in the presence of God. This is the heavenly altar, a counterpart of the earthly one; Exod 27:1–2, 30:1–2. It was this golden altar which Antiochus Epiphanes took away from the temple in Jerusalem (I Macc 1:21) and which Judas Maccabeus replaced (I Macc 4:44–49).

From the heavenly altar comes the command to release the angels bound on the Euphrates. The Euphrates is mentioned as the fourth river which flows through paradise. See fifth NOTE on 9:14. In ancient times it was an important commercial highway and of political significance. To the eighth-century prophets it was the symbol of the great Assyrian world empire (Isa 7:20, 8:7; cf. Jer 2:18) and during the ascendency of the Babylonians it was the scene of the decisive battle between the Egyptian king Necho and Nebuchadnezzar (II Kings 23:29). In the Roman period the Parthians were expected to break loose on the east side of the Euphrates, to cross the river and invade the empire. This fear began in 53 B.C. with the defeat of Crassus at Carrhae and the loss of the eagle standards of his legions. It was renewed by the capitulation to Vologeses in A.D. 62 and was only ended much later when Trajan earned the title of Parthicus by his victories in A.D. 114–16. It could, therefore, be expected to be the scene of another decisive and possibly eschatological battle. This is suggested in apocalyptic literature.

In I Enoch 56:5, APCh, II, 222, it is said that after the judgment of Azazel (Satan), the watchers, and their children:

. . . in those days the angels shall return
And hurl themselves to the east upon the Parthians and Medes:
They shall stir up the kings, so that a spirit of unrest shall come upon them,
And they shall rouse them from their thrones,
That they may break forth as lions from their lairs,
And as hungry wolves among their flocks.

Is the author of Revelation thinking on an historical or eschatological level? Vs. 15 indicates a particular moment in time, a precise hour and day and month and year. One notes that all these four points of time are placed under one definite article. Compare the detailed chronology of the war anticipated by 1QM. Yadin, p. 36, gives a table indicating the various phases in the war, which was expected to last for forty years plus seven sabbatical years. This particular number was derived from the forty years of wandering in the wilderness after the Exodus, which served as the model for various calculations attached to expectations concerning the Messiah; *Sanhedrin* 99a, cf. N. Wieder, *Journal of Jewish Studies* 4 (1953), 172, notes 6–7. It would seem, however, that we must not take our author too literally. The main point of his statement is to ensure that his audience will know each moment is under the control of the deity.

The release of these hostile forces will kill only a third of mankind. It is not the final catastrophe.

Charles sees vss. 16b–17a as a gloss. Indeed, the mention of the number of the cavalry does appear to be rather sudden, giving an impression of an intrusion, but the author might have done that intentionally in order to form a further contrast with the hosts of Yahweh Sabaoth; cf. Rev 5:11; Deut 33:2; Ps 68:17. No calculation is made of God's army; the multitude seen in 7:9–17 is countless. In contrast, the enemy's army, even though large, is not innumerable.

This time, in vs. 17, the riders are again described periphrastically as "those who sat upon them" as were the four angelic manifestations of Yahweh in ch. 6. Their breastplates, in contrast to the iron ones worn by the forces from the abyss, are made of fire, sapphire, and sulphur. Swete compares the phrase "fire and flame" in Ps 104:4, and suggests that the Greek word *huakinthinous,* which can mean either "sapphire" or "hyacinth," could be a translation of the Hebrew word *tikelet,* signifying the color of the famous Tyrian dye. Probably it is meant to describe the blue smoke of the sulphurous flame. It is also the color of the dark blue flowering iris whose pale yellow pollen may suggest brimstone; cf. I Macc 6:2, which refers to golden shields, breastplates, and weapons left in a temple in Persia. It may be that the author's description of the riders' breastplates was influenced by the armor worn by the common troops of the Parthians. It was made of steel, which quickly rusted and turned fiery red.

It is more likely, however, that the materials of the armor where chosen to reflect details of vs. 17. The heads of the horses are like lions'; and fire, smoke, and brimstone issue from their mouths. These are the characteristics of the infernal pit and it associates the riders of the horses or the horses themselves with the demonic. Fire-breathing monsters are frequently mentioned in the works of the classical authors. A third of mankind die from the fire, smoke, and brimstone breathed by these creatures. Their tails, which are like serpents, also harm mankind.

Giet compares this infernal force, the four angels bound on the Euphrates, to the four sections of the army of the legate Cestius, which was particularly strong in cavalry and did come from regions near the Euphrates to invade Palestine. This may, indeed, be the historical matter underlying the vision. Those who did not die from the plagues did not repent of the work of their hands but continued to worship demons and idols. They did not cease from murder, sorcery, unchastity, and theft. It is these verses, 17–21, which show the purpose of the trumpets, namely, to try to bring men back to covenant commitment and to prepare the reader for the struggle with the worshipers of the beast. There are, however, other interesting aspects of chs. 8–9 to consider.

Just as the Exodus theme was recalled at the end of ch. 7 in the vision of the "redeemed," so chs. 8–9 reflect the same theme, but with a startling difference. The plagues of Egypt are repeated but this time against God's own people. The first trumpet recalls the seventh Egyptian plague when God sent thunder, hail, and fire upon the earth; Exod 9:23–26. The second has some analogy with the first Egyptian plague when the Nile turned to blood and all the fish died; Exod

7:20–21. The third portrays a reverse of the miracle of the sweetening of water which occurred at Marah; Exod 15:22–25. Marah means bitterness; cf. the Wormwood in Rev 8. The fourth resembles the ninth plague when there was thick darkness over Egypt for three days; Exod 10:21–23. Wisd Sol 17:1 – 18:4 gives a long description of the plague of darkness, with its attendant fear and the complete failure of the magic of the Egyptians to help in this catastrophe. Ch. 17 ends (vss. 20–21, RSV) with the graphic words:

> For the whole world was illumined with brilliant light,
> and was engaged in unhindered work
> while over those men alone heavy night was spread,
> an image of the darkness that was destined to receive them;
> but still heavier than darkness were they to themselves.

The eagle in Rev 8:13, as was observed in Section V, COMMENT, recalls the same image used for Yahweh; Exod 19:4, but cf. also IQpHab 3:7–11. The fifth trumpet is an elaborated form of the eighth plague in Egypt when locusts covered the face of the land; Exod 10:4–20. The sixth might implicitly reflect a situation which is the reverse of that which occurred at the Red Sea. There the waters returned to their place and drowned all the hostile forces, chariots and horsemen; Exod 14:26–29, cf. 15:4. Here in vss. 14–19 the enemy is released at the river and a third of mankind die.

The Midrash on the Exodus in Wisd Sol 11:5 – 19:22 shows how the Israelites received benefit from the very things which punished the Egyptians according to the principle expressed in 16:24, RSV:

> For the creation, serving thee who hast made it,
> exerts itself to punish the unrighteous,
> and in kindness relaxes on behalf of those who trust in thee.

Wisd Sol 11:6–14 shows how God gave water to his children (cf. Exod 17:5–7, Num 20:8–11) but polluted the Nile because of infanticide (cf. Exod 7:17–24; Rev 8:9, 9:21). Wisd Sol 11:15–16 explains that plagues of animals were sent upon the Egyptians, frogs, gnats, flies, and locusts (cf. Exod 8:1–24, 10:3–15) because they worshiped animals (cf. Rev 9, locusts and fire breathing horses). The same theme is taken up in 12:8–9, 23, which mentions wasps or hornets as forerunners of Yahweh's army to destroy the enemy little by little; cf. Rev 9. Fire, wind, swift air, the stars, the water, and the luminaries of heaven revered as gods are mentioned in 18:2. The plague of storms is contrasted with the "rain" of manna in 16:16–29. The ungodly are discouraged by the strength of Yahweh's arm, for they are pursued by unusual rains, hail, and storms, and are utterly consumed by fire. In 17:1 – 18:4 the pillar of fire is interpreted as the antithesis to the plague of darkness. In 18:5 – 19:22 the tenth plague is seen as the reversal of the saving and glorification of Israel. In other words, the author adopts the principle of exact retribution, legal, theological, and literary. Everything reaches a just balance.

The author of Revelation uses a similar approach. After recounting the plagues he refers to the refusal to relinquish idolatry and other sins. In the Midrash on the Exodus in Wisd Sol, "the word *metanoia* (repent 9:23; repentance

12:10, 19), in its only occurrences in the book, marks the beginning of each of the three subsections," Wright, p. 564. Throughout Rev 4–22 repentance is mentioned only in 9:20, 21, 16:9, 11. The plagues are a challenge to "unharden" the heart. The next chapters of Revelation suggest that the author has not only pagans in mind. The four classes of violation listed in 9:21 have some affinity to the three nets of Belial mentioned in CDC 4:12–18; lust, riches, and defilement of the sanctuary. 1QpHab 9:4–5 refers to "the last Priests of Jerusalem who heap up riches and gain by plundering the peoples" (D-S). At the end of days they are destined to fall into the hands of the Kittim (probably the Romans).

BIBLIOGRAPHY

Cerfaux, L., and Cambier, J. *L'Apocalypse de Saint Jean lue aux Chretiens.*

Charles, R. H. *Revelation.* ICC, I.

Giet, S. RevueSR 38 (1964), 71–92, 255–64.

Jeremias, J. "Abussos," in TWNT.

Mansoor, M. *The Thanksgiving Hymns.*

"Melito of Sardis, 'Homily on the Passion,'" tr. Campbell Bonner, in *Studies and Documents,* eds. K. Lake and S. Lake. University of Pennsylvania Press, 1940.

Noonan, J. T. *Contraception.* Harvard University Press, 1965.

Ringgren, H. *The Faith of Qumran.* Philadelphia: Fortress, 1961.

Swete, H. B. *The Apocalypse of St. John.*

Targum of Isaiah. Tr., ed. J. F. Stenning.

Wright, A. G. "Wisdom," in *The Jerome Biblical Commentary,* eds. R. E. Brown et al. Englewood Cliffs, N.J.: Prentice-Hall, 1968.

Yadin, Y. *The Scroll of the War of the Sons of Light Against the Sons of Darkness.*

VII. THE ANGEL OF LIGHTS
(10:1–11)

10 1 And I saw another mighty angel descending from heaven, enveloped in a cloud with the rainbow around his head, and his countenance was like the sun and his feet were like pillars of fire, 2 and he held in his hand a little scroll which was open. And he planted his right foot on the sea, his left on the earth, 3 and he cried out in a loud voice like a lion roaring. When he cried out, the seven thunders spoke out. 4 I was about to write when the seven thunders spoke out but I heard a voice from heaven saying, "Seal up the words of the seven thunders, and do not write them down." 5 And the angel whom I saw standing on the sea and on the earth raised his right hand to the heaven, 6 and he swore by the One who lives for ever and ever, Who created the heaven and the things in it and the earth and the things in it and the sea and the things in it, that there would be no more delay 7 but in the days of the trumpet-blowing of the seventh angel, when he was about to blow, the mystery of God, which He announced to His servants, the prophets, would be fulfilled. 8 Then the heavenly voice spoke to me again saying, "Go, take the scroll which is open in the hand of the angel who stands on the sea and the earth." 9 And I went to the angel and asked him to give me the little scroll. And he said to me, "Take it and swallow it, it will be bitter to your stomach but it will be sweet as honey to your mouth." 10 And I took the little scroll from the hand of the angel and consumed it, and it was as sweet as honey to my mouth; but when I had eaten it, it was bitter to my stomach. 11 And they say to me, "You must prophesy again to the peoples and nations and tongues and many kings."

NOTES

10:1. *another mighty angel.* "Another" is omitted in P **046** 1, 82, 2036, 2053 pm.

enveloped. Gr. *periballō,* lit. "to throw or put around." This word is used of encircling or throwing an embankment around a city (Luke 19:43), clothing someone (Ezek 18:7, 16), or plunging oneself into torture or misfortune (III

Macc 6:26, *Ant.* 2.276). Cf. also Pss 109:19, 147:8; Wisd Sol 19:17: being surrounded by "yawning darkness," RSV. In the context of vs. 1 *periballō* indicates that the angel is encircled by a cloud.

the rainbow. Cf. "bow" in Rev 4:3 and NOTE. The definite article is omitted in P 1, 2059s pm TR.

sun. Cf. Sir 50:7, where Simon, the high priest, the son of Onias, is compared to the sun and the rainbow. Comparison to the sun is not applied to the deity only. The missing fragment of the Genesis Apocryphon of Qumran Cave 1 (col. 1) must have described the child born to Lamech and Bath Enosh in terms similar to the way he is described in the Fragment of the Book of Noah in I Enoch 106–107, particularly 106:2–5, APCh, II, 278.

> And his body was white as snow and red as the blooming of a rose, and the hair of his head and his long locks were white as wool, and his eyes beautiful. And when he opened his eyes, he lighted up the whole house like the sun, and the whole house was very bright . . . And . . . Lamech . . . said . . . "I have begotten a strange son, diverse from and unlike man, and resembling the sons of the God of heaven . . . and his eyes are as the rays of the sun, and his countenance is glorious.

There is a tradition that in the future life the faces of the righteous will shine like bright lights; I Enoch 38:4, cf. Dan 12:3; I Enoch 39:7, 104:2; Matt 13:43. In Rev 1:16 the visage (*opsis,* not *prosōpon*) of one like a son of man appeared like the sun in its strength (cf. Dan 8:18, 10:15–19) but the wording of the description differs considerably from that of 10:1. In the account of Jesus' transfiguration Matthew says that his face shone like the sun, Matt 17: 2, but the other evangelists do not make this comparison.

feet . . . like pillars of fire. Contrast Rev 1:15. Rabbinic tradition refers to the "feet of the Shekinah" (*Kiddushin* 31a). However, there was also a pagan belief that the foot or imprint of a person or god can bring about miraculous cures. Both Tacitus (*Histories* 4.81) and Suetonius (*Caesar* 7.2) speak of this in relationship to Vespasian and Sarapis. A statue of Sarapis is set on a colossal foot as a sign of conferring life. Caligula gave his left foot to a criminal to kiss (Seneca *Beneficiis* 2.12).

The size of this angel is not unique. In rabbinic thought the stature of angels is enormous; one is said to extend from heaven to earth, and the angel Sandelfon, according to *Hagigah* 13b is supposed to be taller than his fellows by the length of a journey of five hundred years. "According to one tradition, each angel was one-third of a world; according to another, two thousand parasangs (a parasang equals 3.88 miles), his hand reaching from heaven to earth," Bacher, "*Ag.Pal.Amor.*" III 371, 547, cited from *The Jewish Encyclopedia,* "Angelology."

2. *a little scroll.* Gr. *biblaridion,* lit. "a very small book." Charles sees the contents of the little scroll as a proleptic vision of the reign of the Antichrist and argues that, if the seven-sealed scroll embraces chs. 6–9, the small scroll embraces very much less: the contents may perhaps be limited to 11:1–13.

right . . . left. Right denotes the auspicious side, left the ominous side.

3. *like a lion roaring.* Gr. *mukâtai,* "roar," occurs only here in the Bible.

It means a low sound, like the lowing of an ox (cf. Symmachus, Job 6:5; Aquila, I Kings 6:12) or a growl of thunder. It describes a voice which is not only loud in volume but extremely deep and not necessarily conveying actual words.

the seven thunders. The definite article is omitted in ℵ* 1, 1611, 1876, 2059 al, and "seven" is omitted in P⁴⁷ 1876 pc.

The word "thunder" is often rendered in the Bible by the simple Hebrew word *qol,* "voice," frequently followed by *Yahweh* or by the plural *elohim,* "angels" or "gods." Cf. John 12:28–29, where a voice from heaven spoke to Jesus and the crowd said that it had thundered, although some thought that an angel had spoken to him. This passage is followed by a reference to the judgment of the world and the expulsion of its ruler. In III Enoch 176, Ramiel is called the angel of thunder. The mysterious nature of thunder is suggested in the following quotation from *Gen R* 12:1 (*Midrash Rabbah,* trs. Freedman and Simon):

> *But the thunder of His mighty deeds who can understand,* R. Huna said: When thunder goes forth in its full force, no creature can understand it. It it not written, none understands, but *who can understand?* (which implies that some may understand). The intelligent know His hints and His thoughts. Said R. Huna: If you cannot comprehend the essential nature of thunder, can you comprehend the essence of the world! If a man tells you, "I can comprehend the essential character of the universe," say to him, *"For what is the man that cometh after the king?"* Eccl. ii 12) i.e. after the King of the Universe, the supreme King of Kings, the holy one, blessed be He!

Speaking of the proclamation of the Law on Sinai, Philo observes that the sound of the Law was produced with flames and did not grow less distinct because of distances, as a human voice would (*De Decalogo* 33–35). In *De Specialibus Legibus* 2.189, he refers again to the fact that the voice reached the extremities of the earth and speaks about the general laws which came from the mouth of God, "not like the particular laws, through an interpreter? This is a significance peculiar to the nation. What follows is common to all mankind." Whatever the correct tradition is, the symbolism is evident; the idea which the Jewish teachers wished to convey was that the law or revelation from Sinai was universal, but only Israel accepted it. The other nations rejected it; Ginzberg, III, 80–82.

4. *write.* The seer is taking notes.

when. ℵ 2036 pc g Tyc read "what."

Seal up. Swete observes that this phrase is from Dan 12:4, "But the application of the metaphor to unwritten utterances is a bold innovation." He adds that there is a sharp contrast with Rev 1:19. The sealing of the message means that it is not permitted to be revealed to anyone.

5. *raised his right hand.* In Hebrew this is often a synonym for swearing (cf. Gen 14:22, Exod 6:8, Num 14:30, Ezek 20:15, 28; especially Dan 12:7) but the diction is neither that of the LXX nor of Theodotion. A 2060 al vg TR omit "right."

6. *swore*. The oath of the angel in vss. 6–7 suggests that he is not wholly identified with Yahweh, for he swears by God. However, it was not unprecedented for Yahweh to swear by himself; e.g. Deut 32:39–41.

heaven . . . earth . . . sea . . . it. There is an echo of the commandments; Exod 20:11, cf. also Gen 14:22; Deut 32:40; Neh 9:6. Charles remarks that references to the creative activity of God are very frequent in later Judaism but rare in the NT save for Revelation.

The phrase "the earth and the things in it" is omitted in A 1, 2059s al, and the phrase "and the sea and the things in it" is omitted in ℵ* A 205 (1611) al g syph Tyc Rm.

no more delay. Swete compares Hab 2:3, Heb 10:37, and contrasts Rev 6:11. Some scholars have referred to the early Christian belief in the imminent parousia. Swete, for example, comments: "But how necessary so solemn an assurance became towards the end of the apostolic age, when the early hopes of an immediate parousia had been dispersed, is clear from such a passage as II Peter iii 3 ff." Compare Luke 12:45.

7. *mystery of God*. Bousset would see this as the overthrow of Satan, Rev 12:8–9. Vischer (cited by Charles) and other scholars point to the birth of the Messiah. Charles views it as the whole purpose of God with reference to the world. It has both a joyful and a sorrowful aspect. He avers that the content of the divine purpose may be inferred from the thanksgiving of the twenty-four elders after the seventh trumpet, when the kingdom of God is established; Rev 11:17.

which He announced. The rare active Gr. *euaggelizein* occurs also in I Sam 31:9, II Sam 18:19, Rev 14:6. The verb in the passive is frequent in Luke-Acts.

His servants, the prophets. P47 2329 sa read "his servants, and the prophets."

fulfilled. Cf. IV Esdras 14:5; II Baruch 85:10.

The latter (APCh, II, 525) which expresses the thought exquisitely:

> For the youth of the world is past,
> And the strength of the creation already exhausted,
> And the advent of the times is very short,
> Yea, they have passed by;
> And the pitcher is near to the cistern,
> And the ship to the port,
> And the course of the journey to the city,
> And life to (its) consummation.

9. *stomach*. Gr. *koilia*. This generally means the inferior sphere of corporeal life in constrast to *kardia*, "heart," which is the central organ of the spiritual life. However, compare John 7:38 where *koilia* probably corresponds to *kardia*.

10. *sweet . . . mouth . . . bitter . . . stomach*. Note the change of order from the angel's statement in vs. 9. There is a remarkable variant, ℵ 1854, 2321 arm (vt co d) Primas, which reads *egemisthē*, "filled," for *epikranthe*, "made bitter."

11. *they say*. Both the plural "they" and the present tense are difficult. Charles suggests that it might be a voice from heaven (cf. vss. 4, 8) or that of an angel or the thunders; probably it is a plural of indefinite statement as in 13:16, an idiom sometimes found in Hebrew and frequent in biblical Aramaic.

prophesy to the peoples and nations and tongues and many kings. Charles, p. 269, observes:

It is interesting that this enumeration, which occurs seven times in the Apocalypse . . . is here given a different form, and *basileusin* (kings) is put in the place of *phulais* (tribes). The "kings" are especially those mentioned in xvii 10, 12. The Seer is recasting this characteristic phrase with a view to the contents of his later visions.

The commission to prophesy recalls the mission of the Israelite prophets, especially that of Jeremiah and Ezekiel. The second prophecy will begin after the seventh trumpet (11:15) and then the destinies of nations and rulers will be more fully revealed. Swete observed that the seer is not to prophesy in their presence (*epi* with the genitive) or against them (*epi* with the accusative), but with a view to their cases, and that *pollois,* "many," refers to the vastness of the mission field, applying to not one empire alone, but to a multitude of races and kingdoms and crowned heads.

COMMENT

The angel of ch. 10 appears in sharp antithesis to the fallen star of 9:1 and the hostile forces in 9:3–19. The cosmic phenomena—cloud, rainbow, and sun —associated with him are in contrast to the disarray of those forces in ch. 8. The star of 9:1 "fell," Gr. *peptōkota,* to earth. This angel descends, Gr. *katabainonta,* from heaven—with the implicit inference that he acts on his own volition; no impersonal passives are used with reference to him. The star is connected with the abyss and smoke, which obscures the light of the sun, but this angel is "enveloped in a cloud" (probably the reader is meant to think of a white cloud), and has attributes of the rainbow (suggesting the whole spectrum of colors), the sun, and fire. He could be seen as the Prince of Lights contrasted with the Prince of Darkness. In 1QS 3:20 it is said, "Dominion over all the sons of righteousness is in the hand of the Prince of light(s); they walk in the ways of light."

Leaney, pp. 148–49, commenting on this text observes that the phrase "prince of lights" is found only here and in CDC 5:18. This being is equivalent to an angel (as in Rev 10:1) and belongs to a special order of creation. Leaney refers to Guilbert's suggestion (cited in Leaney, pp. 145–49) that this angel is called Prince of Lights (plural) in the scrolls because he controls the stars whose behavior affects the calendar by which the righteous in heaven and on earth regulated their liturgy. Leaney also compares James 1:17, which refers to God as the Father of lights, meaning of celestial bodies, and concludes that in his nature—"in contrast to that of the entities which he controls—there is no *parallagē* (variation of position due to parallax) nor obscuration (*aposkiasma*) caused by variability . . . ," p. 149.

The angel of ch. 10 stands in opposition to the beings who cause cosmic disturbances. The rainbow and the cloud suggest the Noachic covenant whereby

God promised not to send storms and floods upon the earth to destroy all flesh; Gen 9:8–17, contrast Rev 8.

The angel is more than a sign of Noachic covenant; his features bear traces also of the Sinai covenant. The words *katabainō*, "descend," *nephelē*, "a cloud," *stuloi puros*, "pillars of fire," recall the following texts: Exod 33:9, where the pillar (*stulos*) of the cloud (*nephelē*) descended (*katabainō*) and stood at the door of the tabernacle; Exod 34:5, Num 11:25, where the Lord came down (*katabainō*) in a cloud (*nephelē*); Num 12:5, where He came down in a pillar of cloud; Num 14:10, which mentions the glory of the Lord in the cloud on the tabernacle of witness (cf. Rev 11:19); Deut 31:15, where the Lord came down in a pillar of cloud which then stood before the tent of witness. Cf. Rev 11:19.

The cloud indicating the presence of God is also mentioned in association with the temple; I Kings 8:11, II Chron 5:13–14. In the Palestinian Targum the cloud is identified with the Shekinah, the glory of the Lord, and his Word. In the Jerusalem Targum on Exod 13:21 it is said that the glory of the Shekinah of the Lord went before the Israelites in the column of the cloud. But in the same Targum on Exod 14:19 it is the angel of the Lord who leads the way. Thus there is an oscillation between angel and Shekinah. In Rev 10 the description is one of an angel but there are also hints at a theophany. The cloud not only symbolizes the Divine Presence but is also Yahweh's chariot; Isa 19:1, Ps 104:3.

The rainbow, *iris*, is a feature of the throne visions in Ezek 1:28, Rev 4:3. *Prosōpon*, "countenance," can be used in the sense of "person" or "presence" (cf. II Sam 17:11, of Absalom) but in many passages it denotes God's face. In the Aaronic blessings, Num 6:22–27, prayer is offered that His face will shine upon the Israelites. The Palestinian Targum adds to this a petition for protection against night, noon, and morning demons, and malignant spirits and phantoms. In Rev 8, 9, God's face has been against the people to smite them with his wrathful glance; cf. Ps 33:17; Lev 17:10; Ezek 14:8, 15:7. Here the angel's face is like the sun, as if to symbolize bestowal of favor and blessing; cf. Ps 84:11, where God is compared to sun and shield).

The angel's feet which are like pillars of fire are reminiscent of the pillar of fire in the Exodus narrative. "Foot" represents the power possessed by a person; that which is under his foot is subordinated to him. This is why Joshua's officers, for example, place their feet on the necks of five defeated kings of the Amorites; Josh 10:24. The ark of the covenant is called a resting place for the feet of God; cf. e.g. Ezek 43:7, Pss 99:5, 132:7. Hab 3:6 speaks of Yahweh standing and measuring the earth and Zech 14:4 says that Yahweh's feet shall stand on the Mount of Olives. Thus, when the angel places one foot on the sea and the other on the earth, vs. 2, it indicates that all things are subjugated to him, "sea and land" being an OT formula denoting the totality of terrestrial things; cf. Mark 6:48, Matt 14:28–36.

The voice of the angel is that of the deity; it sounds like the roaring of a lion and is associated with the seven thunders in vss. 3–4. In Amos 1:2 the Lord "roars from Zion"; in 3:7–8 the prophet compares the Lord's revelation to a lion's roar. Cf. Amos 3:4, Joel 3:16, Hosea 11:10, Jer 25:30. Rev

10:7 echoes Amos 3:7–8, and the chapter concludes, vs. 11, with a command to prophesy.

Yahweh's voice is also compared to thunder. The best example is Ps 29 which describes the power of the seven aspects of Yahweh's voice. However, the seven-fold thunder-voice of Yahweh is also associated with the Sinai tradition. The pertinent references are found in Ginzberg, VI, 39. He reports that all these sources refer to the "seven voices," that is, sounds or tunes, which were heard on Sinai, although *Berakoth* 6b and *Beth Ha Midrash* v 33 mention only five voices and vi 41 only four. The seven sounds of the trumpet at the resurrection referred to in *Beth Ha Midrash* vi 58 are modeled on the seven sounds of Sinai (see Ginzberg). Another tradition speaks of the voice of Yahweh dividing into the seventy languages of the world so that all might understand it.

Through the cloud, the rainbow, his countenance like the sun, his feet, and his voice like thunder, the angel reflects the character of God. He is probably the Angel of the Covenant sometimes identified with Yahweh. He may also be the Prince of Lights.

Yet he might be identified with Gabriel, who reveals the meaning of the vision of the ram and he-goat to Daniel; Dan 8:16–26, cf. 9:21–27. The oath sworn in Rev 10:6–7 reflects Dan 12:7–9 where the angel clothed in linen swears with his right and left hands towards heaven that there will be "a time, two times, and half a time" before the end of the wonders; Dan 12:7, RSV. Rev 10:6 states there will be no delay. The mystery of God will be completed as God told "his servants, the prophets," vs. 7. This phrase also occurs in 1QpHab 7:1–5, where it is said that although God did not give the full revelation to Habakkuk he did reveal all the mysteries of the words of his servants, the prophets, to the Teacher of Righteousness. For the members of the Qumran community, however, God appeared to have delayed this final period beyond the prophetic expectation. Revelation goes a stage further and tells us that there is no delay, God's secret plan is now completed. The Hebrew word *raz*, "mystery," is frequent in Daniel and the Qumran scrolls and refers primarily to the secret of the times, the sequence of events and the consummation. Our prophet stands in a position analogous to the Teacher of Righteousness.

Vss. 8–11 contain a prophetic *'ot*, i.e. a dramatic, dynamic, prophetic symbol in keeping with the OT tradition, in this case the eating of the scroll. In I Kings 22:11–12 Zedekiah made horns of iron as an *'ot* to dramatize the defeat of the Syrians by the King of Israel. In Jer 13 the prophet hid a linen waistcloth in the cleft of a rock near the Euphrates; when he went to recover it, it was spoiled and good for nothing. He employed this sign to show that Yahweh would spoil the pride of Judah and Jerusalem. In a similar way, Jeremiah is bidden to abstain from marriage (Jer 16) to represent the idea of mourning or the separation of Yahweh from Israel; cf. the allegory of the potter in Jer 18 and the broken flask in Jer 19.

The prophet who employs the *'ot* most frequently is Ezekiel. We have already referred to the burning of his hair; Ezek 5. Another example would be the symbol of baggage for exile; Ezek 12. But more pertinent to Rev 10:9–11 is

Ezek 2:8 – 3:3, where the prophet is bidden to eat a scroll filled with words of lamentation and mourning written both on the front and on the back. He is told that the house of Israel will not listen to him. The scroll of lamentation may be connected with another prophetic *'ot* in Ezek 4, which predicts the siege of Jerusalem, and with still another in Ezek 16, where the prophet graphically describes the city as a harlot.

When the prophet of Rev 10:9–11 ate the scroll, it tasted sweet, but caused bitterness in his stomach. For Israel sins would be "sweet" in the act of commitment but the consequence would be bitter. Sweetness of sin and bitterness of consequences is a concept found in Prov 20:17, RSV, "Bread gained by deceit is sweet to a man, but afterward his mouth will be full of gravel," and Job 20:12–14, AB:

> Though evil is sweet in his mouth,
> And he hide it under his tongue,
> He relishes it, will not let it go,
> Retains it under his palate,
> The food in his bowels is changed
> To viper's venom within him.

But the text which may have influenced the author of Revelation more directly is Prov 9:17–18, AB:

> "Stolen water tastes sweet,
> Food eaten secretly is delightful";
> But he does not perceive that ghosts will be there,
> That her guests are in the hollows of Sheol.

This passage occurs in the context of admonitions against adultery (Prov 6:20 – 7:27) and the contrast between Lady Wisdom and Harlot Folly, who advocates sin as sweet.

This writer suggests that perhaps the key to the interpretation of both Ezekiel's scroll and the one in Rev 10 may be found in Num 5:12–31 and *Sotah,* the tractate on the suspected adulteress. If a husband were suspicious of his wife's behavior, he delivered a command of jealousy bidding the wife to abstain from meetings with the suspected correspondent; this command was known in Hebrew as *kinnui.* The *kinnui* had to be delivered by the husband to the wife in the presence of two witnesses, and the correspondent had to be named. If the wife met secretly with the correspondent after being given this command, the meetings were technically designed as *setirah.* Violation of the command of jealousy (*kinnui*) was proven also by two witnesses but this did not establish the evidence of adultery. Adultery could be tested by the ordeal of bitter water.

The procedure of the ordeal by bitter water was as follows. The woman was subjected to a preliminary examination by the local court and to a second by the Sanhedrin. It was hoped that she would confess. If she did not, she was conducted to the East Gate of the temple in front of the Nicanor Gate and a priest performed the ceremony described in Num 5. He tore her dress and loosened her hair, removed all ornaments, clothed her in black, and placed a rope around her neck. All except her servants were permitted to gaze upon her. The humble jealousy offering of barley, the food of beasts, was placed in her hands. Then the priest took dust from the temple floor and mixed it in a vessel of water taken from the laver in the temple together with wormwood and bitter herbs; cf. *Sotah* 2:2, 20a. After this the priest charged her with the solemn oath of purgation; Num 5:19–22. He wrote the curse on the scroll and soaked it in the bitter water until all the writing, including the name of God, was blotted out. The woman drank the water. This was supposed to make her abdomen swell and her thigh fall away, if she were guilty, but to increase her beauty and fertility if she were innocent. Rev 10 and the preceding chapters show various points which are not disconsonant with this ceremony.

The seven-sealed scroll (5:1) may be the marriage or divorce document of the Lamb. It is a "mighty angel" who asks who is worthy to unloose the scroll (5:2). In Rev 10 it is a "mighty angel" who holds the small scroll (10:1–2), which is open and is not said to be either signed or sealed. One might conjecture that this scroll represents the parchment on which the priest wrote the curse for the woman accused of adultery. This was required to be a scroll like a Torah, but no signing or sealing appears to have been necessary.

In 10:6–9 the angel swears a solemn oath (two oaths were sworn in the Ordeal) and then delivers the scroll to the seer. Our author adds an important factor, namely, that the scroll will be "bitter to the stomach." He expressly mentions this twice, vss. 9, 10, using an impressive chiastic structure for emphasis:

> A . . . swallow it, it will be bitter to your stomach
> B   but it will be sweet as honey to your mouth
>   . . .
> B   it was sweet as honey to my mouth;
> A   but . . . bitter to my stomach.

It was the abdomen which the bitter water was supposed to affect. One notes that Ezekiel eats the scroll before his denunciations of Jerusalem, the most potent of which is in ch. 16 concerning her adultery. Num 5, Ezek 3, and Rev 10 are the only biblical texts which refer to the words of a scroll being consumed.

Other symbols relevant to the theme of a suspected adulteress will be noted in chs. 11, 12, 14, 17, 18. This interpretation would mean that the symbolism of the little scroll is related to the scroll held by the Lamb. Both symbols stand within the Sinai-Exodus motif, which runs throughout this apocalypse. The beginning of the covenant on Mount Sinai was known as the Day of Espousals between Yahweh and Israel, and the descent of the cloud on the tent of meeting was regarded as a consummation of the union. In *Num R* 9:49, the law of jealousies in Num 5 is accommodated to this relationship between Yahweh and his people:

THIS IS THE LAW OF JEALOUSIES (v, 29). Thus said the Holy One . . . 'The law of jealousy against idolatry shall remain in force for ever'; so that, in the same way as the Holy One . . . had exacted punishment from the worshippers of the Calf in His jealousy, so He would exact punishment in the future generations . . . '*Her belly shall swell*' . . . 'swollen with

famine' . . . OR WHEN THE SPIRIT OF JEALOUSY COMETH UPON A MAN
(v, 30). Moses prophesied that the Holy One . . . would at some future
time be jealous against them . . . *And the spirit of jealousy* has passed
over him (*ib.* 14), for He speaks in allusion to the jealousy aroused by
the Calf . . .

The seals of the "bill of divorce" may correspond to the curses consequent
on infidelity listed in Deut 27, 28. *Num R* 9:48 also accommodates these to
the ordeal by bitter water:

AND THE PRIEST (v, 23), namely, Moses, SHALL WRITE THESE CURSES (*ib.*).
IN A SCROLL (*ib.*) alludes to the Table on which was written, *Visiting the
iniquity of the fathers,* etc. . . . AND HE SHALL BLOT THEM OUT INTO THE
WATER OF BITTERNESS; for, on account of Israel's iniquity, he broke the
Tables . . . and for that obliteration of the writing Israel drank the
water of their punishment. AND HE SHALL MAKE THE WOMAN DRINK (v, 24)
alludes to what you read, *And made the children of Israel to drink*
(Ex xxxii, 20); he tested them like suspected wives . . .

The punishment of drinking water containing the dust of the Golden Calf
was brought into association with the ordeal in *Num R* 9:47:

THIS WATER alludes to the water of the brook into which Moses cast the
dust of the gold of the Calf . . . AND THE WOMAN SHALL SAY: AMEN,
AMEN (v, 22): THE WOMAN alludes to Israel who answer *'Amen'* after the
curse against idolatry . . .

Thus, the symbolism of both scrolls comes predominantly from the Exodus
motif of spiritual adultery, a motif which recurs frequently in the prophetical
literature. Ch. 10 also extends the Exodus theme of the plagues in Rev 8–9.
The angel reminds the reader of the Sinai covenant and the little scroll reminds
him of the spiritual law of jealousies. The plagues constitute the warning
prior to the ordeal by bitter water and anticipate the punishment of the
harlot in Rev 17.

BIBLIOGRAPHY

Beth Ha Midrash. Ed. Adolph Jellinek. Leipzig, 1853–77.
Bousset, W. *Die Offenbarung Johannis,* pp. 307–15.
Charles, R. H. *Revelation.* ICC, I, 256–69.
Ginzberg, L. *The Legends of the Jews,* I–VIII.
Leaney, A. R. L. *The Rule of Qumran and Its Meaning.*
Swete, H. B. *The Apocalypse of St. John,* pp. 126–31.

VIII. THE JUDGMENT BEGINS
(11:1–19)

11 1 And there was given to me a measuring reed like a staff; I was told, "Rise and measure the sanctuary of God and the altar and its worshipers. 2 But do not measure the outer court, exclude that, for it is given over to the Gentiles, and they will trample the holy city for forty-two months. 3 And I will allow my two witnesses, dressed in sackcloth, to prophesy for one thousand two hundred and sixty days." 4 These are the two olive trees and the two lampstands which stand before the Lord of the earth. 5 And if anyone would harm them, fire issues from their mouth and consumes their enemies; and if anyone wishes to harm them, he is destined to die in this way. 6 They have authority to lock the heaven so that no rain may fall during the days of their prophetic ministry, and they have authority over the waters to turn them into blood and to strike the earth with every plague as often as they wish. 7 And when they have finished their testimony, the wild beast which ascends from the abyss will fight against them and will win a victory over them and will kill them. 8 And their corpse will lie in the highway of the great city, which allegorically is called Sodom and Egypt, where also their Lord was crucified. 9 And peoples and tribes and tongues and nations will stare at their corpse for three and a half days, and will not permit their bodies to be placed in a tomb. 10 And the dwellers on the earth will rejoice over them and will make merry, and will send gifts to one another, because these two prophets tormented the dwellers on the earth.

11 And after the three and a half days a divine breath of life entered into them, and they stood upon their feet, and a great fear fell upon the spectators.

12 And they heard a loud voice from heaven saying to them, "Come up here"; and they ascended into the heaven in the cloud, and their enemies watched them.

13 And in that hour there was a great earthquake, and a tenth of the city fell, and seven thousand people were killed by the earthquake,

and the survivors were terrified and they gave glory to the God of heaven.

14 The second woe has passed; behold the third woe is coming soon.

15 And the seventh angel sounded his trumpet; and there were loud voices in the heaven, saying,

"The kingdom of the world has become the kingdom of our God and His Anointed, and He will reign for ever and ever." 16 And the twenty-four elders, who sit upon their thrones in the presence of God, prostrated themselves and worshiped God, 17 saying,

"We thank You, Lord God, the Almighty, Who is and was, that You have taken Your great power and begun to reign; 18 and the nations raged, and Your wrath and the appointed time to judge the dead and to give recompense to Your servants the prophets and the holy ones and those who fear Your name, both small and great, and to destroy the destroyers of the earth has come." 19 And the sanctuary of God in heaven was opened, and the ark of His covenant was seen in His sanctuary, and there was lightning and voices and thunder and an earthquake and heavy hail.

NOTES

11:1. *there was given.* Once again the impersonal passive is used.

reed. This served for a surveyor's rule. It might have been the cane of the *arundo donax* which grows along the Jordan Valley, also known as the "giant reed" of Mediterranean lands. It grows in swampy areas and sometimes forms jungles, the habitats of wild animals. It may reach to the height of twelve or even fifteen or twenty feet. Although it can be beaten down by a strong wind (cf. I Kings 14:15, Matt 11:7), it is also sturdy enough for a walking staff (cf. Ezek 29:6, Mark 6:8). It appears as a measuring rod in Ezek 40:3, 5, 41:8, 42:16–19. Ezekiel's reed appears to have been six cubits or nine feet in length.

I was told. Gr. *edothē moi . . . legōn,* lit. "there was given to me . . . saying . . ." The Greek construction is strange, for the position of the present participle makes it appear to modify the noun before it, which would mean that the staff was performing the action of "saying," when clearly the speaker is the celestial power that has been speaking all along. Proper construction calls for the impersonal passive. Throughout this chapter the tenses oscillate between present, future, and past. This may indicate the composite nature of the chapter.

The phrase, "and the angel stood," is added before "I was told" in אᶜ 046, 1854, 2329 al sy Tyc.

1. ". . . and around the throne were four living creatures . . ." (Rev 4:6)

The living creatures may have been *cherubim,* heavenly winged beasts, like this one, who stood guard over what was sacred. Biblical regulations provide for wooden cherubim to be placed over the ark housing the Torah.

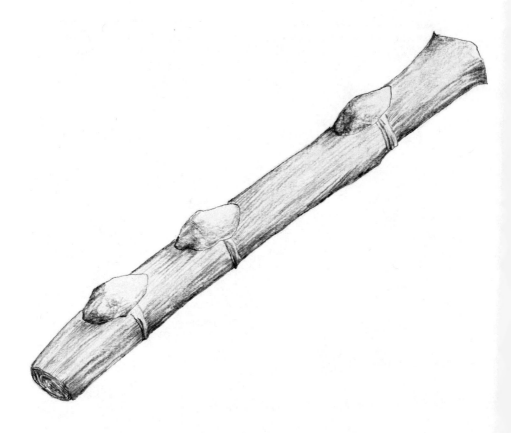

2. "Who is worthy to open the document and break its seals?" (Rev 5:2)

It was customary for documents to be rolled up and fastened with one or more seals. The scroll depicted here is fastened with three seals. The one referred to in Rev 5:2 had seven.

3. "And I saw . . . a little lamb standing as though it had been slain" (Rev 5:6)

At the entrance to the synagogue at Beth Alpha in Israel is this floor mosaic depicting the Sacrifice of Isaac. On the left is Abraham's escort up the mountain —two servants and an ass. On the right is Abraham preparing to cast Isaac onto the burning altar. In the center of all is the unblemished ram, like the lamb a sacrificial animal, which God provided to be sacrificed in Isaac's stead. The hand of God is represented directly above the ram.

4. "Do not hurt the earth . . . until we seal the servants of God on their brows" (Rev 7:3)

A seal was engraved with an identifying mark, like the one above, in such a way that the mark could be imprinted on whatever the owner wished to establish possession over. An object thus imprinted was "sealed."

5. ". . . [the angel] was given abundant incense to add to the prayers of all the holy ones on the golden altar before the throne" (Rev 8:3)

Revelation's original audience probably envisioned the incense as being contained in a bronze shovel of this sort. Such incense shovels were discovered during Yigael Yadin's excavations of the cave occupied by Bar-Kokhba and his band of rebels against Rome.

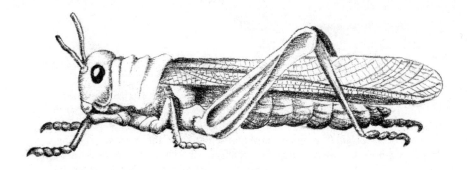

6. "And locusts came out of the smoke onto the earth . . ." (Rev 9:3)
    Hordes of locusts maturing at the same time will devastate every living plant for miles. One of the ten Mosaic plagues on Egypt was an invasion of locusts.

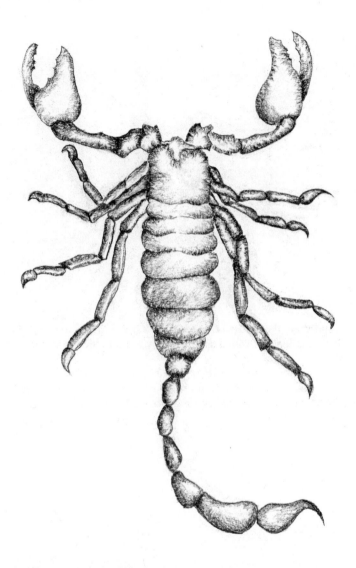

7. ". . . the torture [inflicted by the locusts] was like the torture of a scorpion, when it stings a man" (Rev 9:5)

Like the locust, the scorpion too was a dreaded creature. The sting from a scorpion's tail is excruciatingly painful, but it is not normally fatal to man.

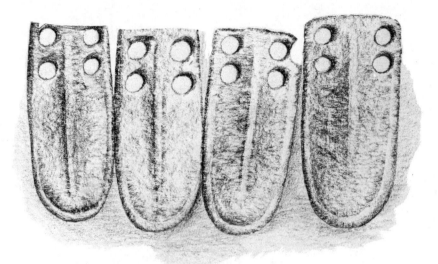

8. ". . . and they [the locusts] had scales like iron breastplates, and the sound of their wings was like the sound of chariots with many horses rushing into battle" (Rev 9:9)

John, the author of Revelation, may have had in mind scales similar to these silver-plated ones used by the Zealot warriors who were fighting Roman soldiers. Hundreds of these armor scales were discovered during the Masada excavations led by Professor Yadin.

9. ". . . I saw horses . . . their heads were like lions' heads, and from their mouths came fire and smoke and sulphur" (Rev 9:17)

Composite creatures like the horse and this bird-animal were familiar supernatural symbols in the ancient Near East. Because they were not of the natural order, they were often used in representations or prophecies of doom and disaster.

10. "I was told, 'Rise and measure the sanctuary of God and its worshipers' " (Rev 11:1)

The third, backmost, floor mosaic of the synagogue at Beth Alpha shows the bejewelled shrine of the Torah flanked by various ritual objects and symbols, two birds, two menorahs, two lions, and two open curtains. The curtained and sheltered Torah rested in the sanctuary.

11. "And a great sign appeared in heaven, a woman clothed with the sun, and the moon under her feet, and on her head a crown of twelve stars" (Rev 12:1)

This major design from the second, central, floor mosaic of the synagogue at Beth Alpha depicts the Greek sun god driving his chariot and four horses. On his crown and throughout the center circle are sprinkled twenty-three stars and a crescent moon. The outer circle is divided into the twelve signs of the zodiac.

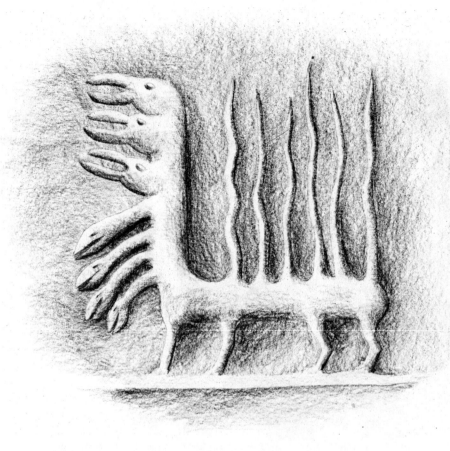

12. "And I saw a monster ascending from the sea; he had ten horns and seven heads, and ten diadems upon his heads . . ." (Rev 13:1)

Drawn from an ancient seal, this is the seven-headed Egyptian dragon of chaos and darkness. At the end of every night the sun god had to vanquish the dragon of chaos. If he failed, day would not dawn.

sanctuary. Gr. *naos.* The *naos* is the sanctuary rather than the temple. In Solomon's temple there were two courts, I Kings 6; cf. Ezek 10:5, 40:17, 20. In Herod's temple the inner court was divided into three. The gates leading to the innermost court had no doors but there was a great arch, rising to the height of seventy cubits (105 feet) and covered with plates of gold, through which one advanced to the *naos* or the dwelling of God. Josephus tells us that there were no doors in order to symbolize the invisible and omnipresent character of the heavens.

The *naos* building was behind the altar. It was made of white marble plated with gold. According to Josephus, *War* 5.222–24, it was "covered on all sides with massive plates of gold, the sun was no sooner up than it radiated so fiery a flash that persons straining to look at it were compelled to avert their eyes, as from the solar rays. To approaching strangers it appeared from a distance like a snow-clad mountain; for all that was not overlaid with gold was of purest white." Earlier, in *War* 5.212, Josephus describes the veil in the *naos* as "of Babylonian tapestry, with embroidery of blue and fine linen, of scarlet also and purple, wrought with marvellous skill . . . it typified the universe." On the door of the *naos* itself was a golden vine and the bunches of grapes were the size of a man. The *naos,* therefore, spells mystery in every way. For the spiritualized cult see I Cor 3:16–17, II Cor 6:16, Eph 2:21. The holy of holies represented the Pentateuch, the holy place the prophets, and the courtyard the writings.

altar . . . worshipers. The altar of burnt offerings was in the court of the priests, the male worshipers congregated in the court of Israel, and the women congregated in their own court. The sacrificial area was complete with rings for tethering animals and marble tables where the carcasses were cut up. However, the killing of the animals was not as important as the libation of the blood and the rise of the smoke from the burnt offering.

2. *outer.* Gr. *exōthen,* lit. "outside." In ℵ 1, 2059, 2329 al Tr the word is *esōthen,* "inside."

outer court. A barrier prevented the Gentiles from passing beyond a certain point; cf. *War* 5.193–94, *Ant.* 15.417, Eph 2:14–15. In the Mishna and Josephus the outer court is called the court of the Gentiles.

exclude. Gr. *ekballō exōthen,* lit. "throw out outside." The same phrase or with *exō* (out) is used in Luke 4:29, reporting Jesus was thrown out of the city; 13:28, Jesus' warning about being thrown out of the kingdom of heaven; 20:15, parable in which tenants throw the heir out of the vineyard; John 6:37, assuring that those who come to Jesus will not be cast out; 9:34–35, where the Jews cast out the man to whom Jesus had given sight; and several times in Acts, e.g. 7:58, 9:40. *Ekballō,* "throw out," is used frequently with reference to casting out devils. At Qumran (see 1QS 6:24–7:25) and among the strict Pharisees there was an elaborate system of excommunication.

P⁴⁷ 046 2059s 2344 al TR read *ekballō exō,* lit. "throw out" instead of *exōthen,* "outside."

Wellhausen thinks that vss. 1–2 may be an independent oracle predicting the preservation of the temple: some of the zealot party, among whom were prophets, believed that Jerusalem would be captured but not destroyed. One zealot oracle suggested that the outer court of the temple would fall but not the temple itself.

will trample. The idea of trampling to destroy, defile, or show contempt is found in Ps 79:1, Isa 63:18, I Macc 4:60, II Macc 8:2. But the texts most influential on this verse are Dan 8:13–14, predicting that the sanctuary will be trampled for 2,300 evenings and mornings but will then be restored to its proper condition, and I Macc 3:45, reporting that "Jerusalem was uninhabited like a wilderness; not one of her children went in or out. The sanctuary was trampled down and the sons of aliens held the citadel; it was the lodging place for the Gentiles. Joy was taken from Jacob; the flute and the harp ceased to play." Cf. Rev 18:22–23. The word also occurs in Psalms of Solomon 2:2, 20, 8:12, where it is used in the sense of profanation rather than destruction. However, perhaps the nearest parallel, i.e. closest in thought, is Luke 21:24, where Jesus predicts Jerusalem will be trampled by the Gentiles. One notes also the future tense "will trample."

In A "will trample" is replaced by "will measure."

holy city. Usually in Revelation "holy city" is used only for the new Jerusalem and the heavenly Jerusalem. In 21:2, 22:19, it is applied to the ideal city of God. The designation probably comes from Dan 9:24 but the phrase is also found in Neh 11:1; Isa 48:2, 52:1; Matt 4:5, 27:53; cf. Neh 11:18, Psalms of Solomon 8:4. In Rev 20:9 the heavenly Jerusalem is called the beloved city in contrast to the earthly Jerusalem. The usage in the present chapter does not seem to be an exception for our author's attitude to the actual city of Jerusalem is revealed in the clause he adds in 11:8 (comparing her to Sodom and Egypt). Thus the phrase "holy city" probably refers to the faithful Jews rather than the actual city.

forty-two months. This and the following chapters introduce even more symbolic numbers than the preceding ones. "Seven" indicates fullness, plenitude, perfection; cf. the seven spirits and the seven-fold terms of the doxologies. Three and one-half, half of seven (Rev 11:9, 11), denotes what is arrested midway in its normal course. The apocalyptic usage of this number goes back to Dan 7:25; cf. 9:27, 12:7; bear in mind that the period from the persecution by Antiochus Epiphanes to the rededication of the Temple was about three and one-half years, i.e. from 168/7 to 165/4. The number six also connotes deficit, a failure to attain the completeness of seven, while eight designates superabundance. Forty-two has two-fold symbolism. It is pejorative, since it is the result of six multiplied by seven, i.e. "perfection missing the mark." It is also messianic, since it is the result of three multiplied by fourteen. The number fourteen is the sum of the letters which in Hebrew stand for four, six, four. *Daledh* is the fourth letter of the Hebrew alphabet, and *waw* is the sixth; thus four-six-four stands for *d-w-d*, i.e. David. Matt 1:1–17 divides the genealogy of Christ from Abraham into three groups of fourteen names each. Christ is the new David.

3. *I will allow*. Note the change from impersonal passive in vs. 1 to first person singular here. The speaker is either God or an angel.

my two witnesses. In the Greek, the definite article is used rather than the personal pronoun substituted here. The definite article is difficult to reconcile because it would suggest that "two witnesses" have been mentioned before. If the hypothesis concerning the small scroll in ch. 10 is tenable, then they may be the two witnesses necessary to confirm *kinnui* and *setirah* in the case of suspected adultery; see COMMENT, Section VII. The adulteress (Jerusalem) pays no heed to them but treats them spitefully. Two witnesses are required by Deut 19:15; cf. John 8:17. The doubling of witnesses here may be due to the reinterpretation of Zech 4:3–14, but in Judaism before and after the Christian era normally only one forerunner of the end-time, the Messiah, was expected. The Apocalypse of Elias, however, mentions sixty precursors of the Messiah.

dressed. This verb is in the nominative, but ℵ* AP **046** 2060, 2329 al have it in the accusative.

sackcloth. This probably refers to the ancient costume of the prophets; II Kings 1:8, Zech 13:4, Isa 20:2, Jonah 3:6.

one thousand two hundred and sixty. This comprises the total of the days in forty-two months, if each month is computed as thirty days. There would be thirty days in each solar month. The Qumran sect and other Jewish sects, e.g. the Samaritans, used the solar calendar. Forty-two months equals three and a half years which equals one thousand two hundred and sixty days.

4. *lampstands.* Josephus, in *War* 6.387–91, records that a certain priest named Joshua ben Thebuthi, delivering up sacred treasury to Rome, "handed over from the wall of the sanctuary two lampstands similar to those deposited in the sanctuary." Carrington, p. 188, thinks the passage suggests that the two lampstands in question stood on the wall which separated the *naos*, "sanctuary," and the altar from the Court of Women, and that there would, therefore, have been a basis in the temple itself for such symbolism. On the Feast of Tabernacles four such lamps were lighted in the court.

stand before the Lord. It is said of prophets that they "stand before the Lord." The phrase is often used with reference to Elijah and Elisha in the sense of "serve."

5. *harm them . . . die.* The verse expresses the *lex talionis,* "law of retaliation." It is possible that the author had in mind the law of the malicious witness (Deut 9:16–21) who was obliged to suffer the penalty which he had caused.

fire. This reflects II Kings 1:10–14 where Elijah calls down fire on the messengers of the King of Samaria. Compare the dramatic passage about Elijah and Elisha in Sir 48:1–14, in which Elijah and his teachings are likened to fire, it is told that by command of God he brought down fire three times, and his ascension is described in terms of fire.

In contrast, Luke 9:54–56 records Jesus' rebuke to the disciples James and John for wishing to call down fire upon the Samaritans who will not accept him. Some ancient authorities added these words to vs. 55: ". . . and he said, 'you do not know what manner of spirit you are; for the son of man came not to destroy men's lives but to save them.'"

mouth. Note the singular (collective) although there are two witnesses. Probably this indicates that their message is identical.

6. *strike the earth.* Cf. I Sam 4:8, which concerns the arrival of the ark of the covenant, and the consequent loud cheering in the Israelite camp. The Philistines became afraid and bewailed the strength of what they construed to be the Hebrew gods: "These are the gods who smote the Egyptians with every sort of plague in the wilderness," RSV.

7. *the wild beast.* P⁴⁷ sa ℵ* read "then the wild beast." This phrase is substituted by "the fourth beast" in A.

beast . . . kill them. This image draws on, and uses phrases from, Dan 7:3 (four great beasts from the sea), 7:7 (a fourth destructive beast), 7:19 (repeats 7:7 but uses definite article).

and will kill them. This phrase is omitted in 1, 2059s al.

8. *corpse.* Gr. *ptōma.* The word is pluralized in P⁴⁷ P 1, 1611, 2059s, 2329 pm lat sy TR. See Judg 14:8, Ezek 6:5 (A). Cf. the indignity to corpses mentioned in Ps 79:2–3, Tobit 1:18, 2:3–9.

will lie. This verb is omitted in the Greek TI.

great city. After this, 2036 pc read "unburied."

Sodom. The name Sodom was given to Judah in her worst days; cf. Isa 1:9–10, Ezek 16:46–55. The name "Egypt" is not applied to Jerusalem in the OT.

crucified. For a discussion, see Introduction, "Lordship of Christ."

9. *three and a half days.* The bodies of the witnesses lie unburied in the middle of a symbolic week; cf. Dan 9:27. Since the ancients considered nonburial as acute shame, the days appear to symbolize years of grief. See last NOTE on vs. 2 for the significance of the number.

tomb. 209 pc vg syᵖʰ sa Prim TR read "tombs."

11. *after the three and a half days.* The definite article is omitted in ℵ P 1, 2059s pm.

breath of life. Cf. Gen 2:7, 6:17, 7:15, 22, II Kings 13:21, Ezek 37:10, Luke 8:55.

12. *"Come up here."* Jewish tradition lists several saints who died by the kiss of the Lord, i.e. an easy death, some being assumed into heaven without corruption. The OT witnesses to the assumption of Elijah and Enoch. The Assumption of Moses is a nonbiblical book dated somewhere between 7–29 A.D. which bears witness to that event. Others privileged in this way were Abraham, Isaac, Jacob, Aaron, Miriam; *Baba Bathra* 17a, *Deut R* 11; cf. *Berakoth* 8a.

watched. P⁴⁷ reads "measured."

15. This verse ends with "Amen" in ℵ 94, 181 pc it vgˢ, ᶜˡ.

17. *Who is and was.* Note that the phrase "who is to come" (*ho erchomenos*) is omitted. It is not found in Rev 12–22. This may imply that the "Messiah" has already come.

18. *nations raged.* This reflects the messianic Psalm 2.

19. *ark.* The ark may have been burned with the temple; II Kings 25:9. It does not appear in Ezekiel's temple. The legend concerning the burying of the ark and the altar of incense occurs not only in II Macc 2:5–8 but also in *Yoma* 53b–54a. Cf. also II Baruch 6:5–9, where an angel rescues the veil, the ark, the mercy seat, the tablets, the priestly vestments, the altar of incense,

and forty-eight precious stones. A comparison between the treacherous behavior of Joshua, the son of Thebuthi, referred to in the first NOTE on vs. 4
and this passage from II Baruch shows how these articles would be esteemed
before the fall of Jerusalem. Tacitus (*Histories* 5:9) scoffs at the ark.

COMMENT

The previous chapters have presented the court of heaven and actions
emanating directly from heaven or from heavenly beings. Ch. 10 bridges the
gap between heaven and earth by the angelic messenger who places his feet
on the sea and the earth, 10:2, and delivers an earthly commission to the
prophet, 10:9, 11. The eating of the bitter scroll spells judgment, which is
expressed in ch. 11 in three ways: the measuring of the temple, the two witnesses, and the seventh trumpet which announces the triumph of the kingdom
of God. In a certain sense the chapter is the epitome and proleptic vision of
the events which will occur in the second part (chs. 12–22) of this apocalypse.
It closes the first part, in which the visionary sees the corruption of and
disciplinary measures against the old order, but looks forward to the second,
in which he sees the obliteration of the old order and the introduction of the
new, symbolized by the new city, heaven and earth, etc.

Some understanding of the theology of the "holy city" or the "temple" (the
concepts are almost interchangeable, cf. II Baruch 6:2–4) is necessary in order
to appreciate the second part of Revelation, which portrays the judgment of
the harlot (faithless Jerusalem) and the establishment of the New Jerusalem.
Originally the temple was both the religious and civil (military) center of the
nation. The idea of building a temple was held to come from God Himself
who gave the divine model. It represented His presence among His people;
its destruction meant the loss of this presence; II Kings 24:1 – 25:21, Ezek 9:3,
10:4–5, 11:23; cf. I Sam 4:21–22.

After the fall of the temple in 587 B.C. there emerged the concept of a
new temple to replace it. The most famous description occurs in Ezek 40–48.
The original temple had been part of the royal complex; the new temple was
revolutionary in that it was to be set apart from the city. It was to be four
cubits square and to have both an inner and an outer court to be the symbol
of the new people of God. Its symmetry represented unity and cohesion among
these people. There is some evidence that Gentiles would have their place in
the new temple. Haggai and Zechariah also speak of the new temple to which
they expect numbers of exiles to return; however, in contrast to Ezekiel's
temple, the royalty is not separated from the one they envision. Zech 3:1 –
4:14, for example, shows both Joshua, the high priest representing the common people, and Zerubbabel, governor of Jerusalem representing the royal
line of David which it was hoped would be restored, being announced together
as anointed of the Lord. The sect at Qumran held a similar belief. The task
of rebuilding the temple was assigned to a particular individual, namely a
descendant of David. In the Targum on Zech 6:15 this is Zerubbabel. The
Messiah, in most traditions, was also to be of the line of David. Thus the

ingathering and reunion of Israel and the temple were seen as tasks of the Messiah.

That the Messiah is to build the new temple points to its eschatological aspect, with which is linked the concept of universalism. The notion originates from the concept of Yahweh as creator and the new temple as the symbol of the unity of all mankind. The new temple will be the place of worship for the exiles and also for the Gentiles; see Sir 36:11–14. This reunion of the people will take place at the temple and at that time the ark of the tabernacle and the altar of incense which were missing since the destruction of the old temple, will be revealed; II Macc 2:4–8.

The Psalms of Solomon elaborate these concepts and show the Messiah throwing off the Roman yoke (17:24) and gathering the tribes together. It will be his duty to cleanse Jerusalem (17:32–33), for it is here that the nations of the earth will come. This messianic office is seen as the fulfillment of the prophecy contained in II Sam 7. Indeed, in spite of the rededication of the temple by Judas Maccabeus, there was still a feeling that the temple was polluted (cf. I Enoch 89:73), and that even the second temple would disappear in the eschatological age to be replaced by a new one; cf. II Baruch 32:2–6 *Yoma* 9b, cf. *Pesachim* 57a. For the second temple not only lacked the ark of the covenant, the altar of incense and some other furniture but some even inferred that the divine presence had not returned; Targum on *Haggai* 1:8; *Taanit* 65a, cf. *Yoma* 53b.

Tobit 14:5 says that the new temple will not be like the former, and I Enoch 90:29 proclaims that the new house will be greater and loftier than the first. Similarly Testament of Benjamin 9:2 declares that the last temple shall be more glorious than the first; cf. II Bar 4:2–4. Sibylline Oracles 5:414–433 shows the new temple erected by the Messiah. It takes the form of a tower reaching to the clouds (cf. Sibylline Oracles 3:98–104) and this represents the unity of mankind. A tower is probably chosen because of the narrative of the Tower of Babel; there unity was lost, here it will be recovered in the new age (see McKelvey, pp. 1–24).

One can trace an evolution of thought. Ezekiel looks forward to a new temple not directly associated with the Davidic king or Messiah. Haggai and Zechariah do make this link and further sources elaborate upon the theme. Eventually the temple becomes more eschatological and a center for unified mankind. The Qumran community took the thought a step further.

The attitude of the members of the Qumran community towards the Jerusalem temple and sacrifice is extremely complex, but they shared with the apocalyptic writers the idea that the temple needed to be cleansed. They regarded both the priests and the altar as unclean (1QpHab 8:8–13, 9:4–5, CDC 4:17–18, 5:6–7; cf. 6:11–16, 12:1–2) and they may have offered their own sacrifices locally. Thus it is probably true to say that at Qumran there was opposition not to the sacrificial cult but rather to the Jerusalem temple and the rejection of sacrifices offered there. The Qumran members thought of themselves as men from the house of Peleg who "went out of the Holy City and leaned upon God at the time of the unfaithfulness of Israel. They declared the sanctuary to be impure and turned to God"; CDC 20:22–24 (D-S), see Gaston, pp. 123–24. The same document says that God hid His face from Israel and from His sanctuary (CDC 1:3) because it had been profaned (4:18, 5:6). 1QpHab reports that the wicked priest did abominable things and profaned the sanctuary (12:7–8) and that the temple had been defiled by violence (10:10), robbery (9:4–5; cf. CDC 6:16) and uncleanness (CDC 12:1–2). Jerusalem is viewed as a place of impurity (CDC 12:2), "a city of vanity, built with blood." Further, Joshua is reported as cursing the man who will rebuild Jerusalem (4QTestimonia, Gaston, p. 125):

> And see, a cursed man, one of Belial's, arises to become a fowler's trap to his people and a ruin to all his neighbors . . . both become vessels of violence, and they have rebuilt (Jerusalem) and set up within it a wall and towers to make it a fortress of wickedness . . . like water on the rampart of the daughter of Zion and in the district of Jerusalem.

However, although the members of the Qumran community appear to have offered sacrifices locally, within the texts there is no mention of the new Jerusalem; normally sacrifice was not offered outside Jerusalem. The fragments which bear the title "Description of the New Jerusalem" do not mention Jerusalem but they do mention a temple which is to be measured; cf. Ezek 40–48. For the members of Qumran the Jerusalem temple was a "house of judgment"; and the "doers of the law" will be rescued from her in the time of favor; 1QpHab 8:2. 1QpHab 9:12–10:5 reads as follows:

> It is the house of judgment whose judgment God will hold in the midst of many peoples, and from there He will lead it out to judgment and in their midst He will declare it guilty and judge it with sulphurous fire.

God will choose as the agent of His judgment "the head of the kings of Javan" (CDC 8:11) and "the army of the Kittim" (1QpHab 9:7), and, even more relevant to Rev 11, 4QpNah 1:11–12 says that Jerusalem "will be trampled underfoot by the Kittim" and "be delivered into the hands of the army of the Kittim." The Qumran members expected the temple to be cleansed by destruction, but they did anticipate a new temple, as seen from the unpublished Temple Scroll.

The final text for consideration is 4QFlorilegium 1:1–13, which speaks of the raising up of the tabernacle of David. As Professor D. Flusser has pointed out, the text involves a contrast between the temple at Jerusalem and the house promised in II Sam 7. The temple is to be desolate, but the "sanctuary of the Lord," "the tabernacle of David" will remain, and this will be a sanctuary of men where the sacrifices are not physical offerings but the deeds of the Torah. See Gaston for further details. Thus Qumran also developed the concept of a new temple built of living, faithful men and women which would replace the Jerusalem temple.

The tradition of measuring the temple occurs in both the OT and nonbiblical Jewish literature. In Ezek 40–48 the prophet sees the new temple in a vision and the man whose appearance was like bronze takes minute measurements of it. He measures the wall outside the temple, the threshold, the side rooms, the various vestibules and gateways. He takes the prophet into the outer

court and then into the inner court, then into the nave until the whole temple
was thoroughly measured. Perhaps, the most important portion of this text
occurs in ch. 43 where the glory of the Lord comes from the east and shines
on the earth. Ezekiel describes this vision as similar to the one "which I had
seen when he came to destroy the city, and like the vision which I had seen
by the river Chebar"; 43:3, RSV, cf. the angel in Rev 10.

Ezekiel saw the glory of God enter the gate facing the east and fill the temple. Then he heard a voice saying:

> Son of man, this is the place of my throne and the place of the soles of
> my feet, where I will dwell in the midst of the people of Israel forever.
> And the house of Israel shall no more defile my holy name, neither they,
> or their kings, by their harlotry, and by the dead bodies of their kings,
> by setting their threshold by my threshold and their doorposts beside my
> doorposts . . .

This section appears to have influenced Rev 10, 11: the angel as a manifestation of the glory of God, the measuring, the destruction of the city, the
"place of the soles of my feet," the harlotry, and the dead bodies.

The next passage about measuring in the OT is found in Zech 2:1–2, 5–6,
where once again it is an angel who performs the measuring, the object of
which is to ensure the safety of Jerusalem: "For I will be to her a wall of fire
round about, says the Lord, and I will be the glory within her," RSV. In the
previous chapter (1:16) Zechariah spoke of saving Israel and of the measuring
line which would be stretched out over her. Further, in Zech 12:2–3 the
prophet refers to the siege of Jerusalem, but announces that Jerusalem will be
"a heavy stone for all the people." I Enoch 61:1–5 mentions the measuring
of the righteous. This is done by angels with cords, and the purpose is to preserve the elect. With regard to these texts it is important to notice that they
all refer to Jerusalem, whether with reference to her safety or her destruction
or to both. None of them refers to the measuring of a non-Jewish city. Thus,
there may be four explanations of the measuring in Rev 11:1–2: for rebuilding
or restoring (Ezek 40:2 – 43:12, esp. 41:13, 47; Zech 2:2–8, Jer 30:11), for destruction (II Kings 21:13, Isa 34:11, Amos 7:7–9, Lam 2:8, II Sam 8:2a),
for preservation from physical harm (II Sam 8:2b), and for preservation from
spiritual harm (Rev 7:4–17, I Enoch 41:1–2). However, one of these explanations clearly applies best.

The inner court is measured for protection. Feuillet concurs. He thinks that
the passage refers to the earthly temple of Jerusalem and signifies her preservation from woe, not her destruction, although he acknowledges also that it
might be a figure of speech for a group of people. He avers that if one applies
the words *ekballō exōthen,* "throw out, outside" (translated in vs. 2 as "exclude that"), to the material temple, they are not intelligible. One does not
throw the construction outside and the expression is even more puzzling because the court is already outside. In the NT the expression "throw out, outside" almost always applies to excommunication or exclusion; cf. third NOTE
on 11:2; Luke 4:29, 20:15; Acts 7:58; see especially John 9:34–35, 12:31, 15:
6; Rev 22:14–15. At Qumran exclusion of unfaithful covenanters from the

community was a prominent feature. It is likely, therefore, that Rev 11:2 is to be interpreted as keeping out the Gentiles and unfaithful Jews.

The Qumran community moved towards a spiritualization of the cult and saw the community itself as a sanctuary and the house of truth (1QS 5:5-6), as a "house of holiness for Israel" and as the "company of infinite holiness for Aaron", as "the dwelling of infinite holiness for Aaron"; as the "house of perfection and truth in Israel" (1QS 8:4-10). They expected to be "set apart as a holy place for Aaron, in order to be united as the holy of holies and the house of community for Israel"; 1QS 9:3-6 (D-S). Gärtner, pp. 26-30, commenting on 1QS 8:4-5, suggests that the two groups in the community, Israel and Aaron, represent the two important rooms in the temple, the holy place and the holy of holies. If we apply this to Revelation, the holy of holies probably represents a community akin to Qumran, which is to be measured and preserved. Those not of the community are to be thrown outside; they are represented by the outer court. In Revelation reference has already been made to the remnant of Israel, and here their preservation is formally expressed. Measuring the holy and excluding the outsiders precedes the seventh trumpet just as the sealing of the elect preceded the seventh seal. The outer court or the apostate Jews are trampled by the heathen for forty-two months.

Revelation mentions three periods of time: forty-two months, 11:2; one thousand two hundred and sixty days, 11:3, 12:6, and three and one half days 13:5 (cf. 12:14, a time and times and half a time); see last NOTE on 11:2. They are equal periods if one understands "day" in the sense of "year" in the phrase "three and a half days." This interpretation is consonant with Dan 7:25, 12:7 which appear to describe the duration of the sufferings of the Jews under Antiochus from June, 168 B.C. to December, 165 B.C., or from December, 168 B.C. to May, 164 B.C. The computation of the epoch in Daniel seems to be an interpretation of Hosea 6:2. Hosea speaks of physical and moral rebirth, i.e. a religious conversion of the Jews. Later the text was understood in an eschatological sense, e.g. in *Sanhedrin* 97a (Epstein):

> R. Kattinaz: six thousand years shall the world exist, and one [thousand, the seventh], it shall be desolate, as it is written, *and the Lord* alone *shall be exalted in that day*. Abaye said: It will be desolate two [thousand], as it is written, *After two days will he revive us: in the third day, he will raise us up, and we shall live in his sight*.

In Revelation, the duration of the triumph of the Gentiles (11:2) is equal to the duration of the prophesying of the two witnesses (11:3) which in its turn is equal to the duration of the woman's sojourn in the wilderness (12:6). However, on a historical level, there may be an allusion to the time when the temple was held by the Zealots during the siege of Titus, which lasted three and one half months.

A number of candidates have been offered for the two witnesses in vss. 3-12. Hippolytus and Tertullian see in them Enoch and Elijah. I Enoch 90:31 represents Enoch and Elijah as witnesses of the end of days; see APCh, II, 259-60. In his commentary on Revelation, Victorinus names Jeremiah and Elijah; cf. 11:5 with Jer 5:14. Bacon (see Feuillet, p. 241) thinks of James the

Bishop of Jerusalem and John the Apostle. Gelin (ibid.) suggests two Christian prophets martyred by Titus. Zahn (ibid.) and others think of eschatological figures who appear in the world (ibid.). Munck, Boismard, and others turn to the possibility of Peter and Paul martyred by Nero, who is the beast; in this case the city (vs. 8) would be Rome. Some see the one thousand two hundred and sixty days to cover the period of the burning of Rome in July, A.D. 64.

The influence of Zech 4:1–3, 11–14, suggests another explanation. In Zechariah the high priest, Jesus (in Hebrew, Joshua) and Zerubbabel are symbolized by two olive trees. They are the two anointed ones, the priest and prince; cf. the two Messiahs spoken of in la règle annexe 2:11–22 at Qumran. Similarly the author of Revelation may think of the two witnesses as type symbols whose role corresponds to that of Joshua and Zerubbabel in the restoration and preservation of the postexilic Jewish state, i.e. priesthood and laity. The two witnesses could represent the house of Israel (the laity) and the house of Aaron (the priesthood) into which the Qumran Community was divided. In 1QS 8:4–10 these are said to be *"the witnesses of truth unto Judgment* and the chosen of loving kindness appointed to offer expiation for the earth and *to bring down punishment upon the wicked"* (italics mine). As individuals these witnesses might be the Messiah of Israel (Davidic king) and the Messiah of Aaron (priestly Messiah) who represent the civil and religious authorities as in Zechariah.

It has already been suggested that a "house of holiness" akin to the notion at Qumran, that is, a metaphor for the faithful, is represented in Rev 11:1–2 by the sanctuary or *naos*. Further, the Qumran community is described as an everlasting plant; 1QS 8:4–10; cf. 1QS 11:8, CDC 1:7, 1QH 4:15. Thus there is a similar imagery to that which is used of the witnesses who are regarded as olive trees. The fusion of architectural and plant images is not unfamiliar in the NT, e.g. in I Cor 3:5–16 where Paul passes from an agricultural to a building metaphor. Cf. Eph 2:19–22. Gärtner, pp. 28–29, thinks that the combination of the building and plant metaphors in the Qumran texts may go back to Jewish speculations on the rock of the temple and paradise.

One notes, however, that at this time the community would still be in Jerusalem. It has not as yet gone into the desert; cf. Rev 12:14. This would concur with Murphy-O'Connor's thesis pp. 528–49, that part of 1QS should be assigned to a time before the retreat to Qumran.

In Rev 11:5–6 the witnesses are described in terms of Elijah and Moses. Rev 11:5 echoes Elijah's calling down fire on Ahaziah's messengers; II Kings 1:10–14; cf. Luke 9:54, II Ezra 13, Jer 5:14, Sir 47:1. Vs. 6 reflects I Kings 17:1, Elijah's prophecy that there would be no rain; Josephus, citing Menander in *Ant.* 8.324, says that this was for one full year, but a tradition of three and a half years is found in Luke 4:25, James 5:17. Vs. 6 may also allude to an actual occurrence, for Josephus *War* 5.410, says that the fountain of Siloam was almost wholly dried up before the coming of Titus to Jerusalem. The same sign occurred in the days of Zedekiah.

Authority over the water in vs. 6 reflects the Moses tradition in Exod 7:20 (cf. Ps 104:29), and the idea of striking the land may come from I Sam 4:8 where the Philistines refer to the "gods" striking Egypt. The two witnesses have these powers as long as they desire, so their authority is greater than that of Elijah and Moses. These characteristics need not conflict with the suggestion that the two witnesses represent the religious and civil leaders, for they are leaders endowed with the charismatic gifts of Elijah and Moses. They succeed to the rod of Moses and the mantle of Elijah. The return of a Moses-like figure is suggested in Deut 18:18 (cf. John 16:14), and that of Elijah in Mal 4:5 (cf. Sir 48:10, Mark 9:11, *Exod R* 18:12). Elijah's duty was to spread repentance *Pirke, Rabbi Eliezer,* 43, 47). His "messianic" activity would begin three days before the coming of the Messiah; *Elijahu Rabba* 25 ff.

In vs. 7 the wild beast from the abyss is mentioned for the first time, yet the definite article suggests that he is a familiar figure. He seems to be different from the sea beast in 13:1. We have associated "the men of the pit" in the Dead Sea scrolls with the angel of the abyss and his forces in 9:3–11. However, the enemies of Qumran are also symbolized by wild animals. 4 QpNah 2:11b (D-S) reads:

[*Where is the den of the lions, the pasture of the young lions?*] The [explanation of this concerns Jerusalem . . . which has become] a dwelling-place for the wicked of the nations.

For a lion went to enter in, a lion cub, [*with none to frighten* (it).] [The explanation of this concerns Deme]trius king of Yāwān who sought to enter Jerusalem on the counsel of those who seek smooth things. [But he did not enter, for] from Antiochus until the rising of the commanders of the Kittim [God did not deliver it] into the hand of the kings of Yāwān. But afterwards it will be trampled under foot [by the Kittim . . .].

This Demetrius may be Demetrius I who came to the throne two years after the death of Antiochus IV. However, it is more likely to be Demetrius III Eukairos, who invaded Palestine and defeated Alexander Jannaeus at Shechem. This seems to be reflected further on in the same text 2:13b:

[*It filled*] *its den* [*with prey*] *and its lair with torn flesh.* The explanation of this concerns the furious Young Lion [who . . . took ven]geance on those who seek smooth things—he who hanged living men [on wood . . . which was not] formerly [done] in Israel; but he who was hanged alive upon [the] wood [. . .].

Josephus, in *War* 1.92–97, *Ant.* 13.376–83, reports that after Demetrius had returned to his land, Alexander crucified eight hundred Pharisees. While this awful deed was being perpetrated Alexander "looked on, drinking, with his concubines reclining beside him," *War* 1.97. Yadin questions the rendering of the Qumran text quoted above. He argues for an old Israelite law under which certain offenders were actually crucified.

From an examination of both texts Yadin concludes that the "Lion of wrath" (D-S "furious Young Lion") could be regarded as an instrument in the hands of God (cf. Hosea 5:13–15 where Yahweh is likened to a young Lion rending and carrying away his prey) to punish those who had been guilty of political crime and therefore liable to the old Israelite penalty of "hanging alive."

Yadin's discoveries may also elucidate the phrase "where also their Lord was crucified" in Rev 11:8. It need not be an expression of sympathy but, rather, on the part of our author an acknowledgment of a just penalty suffered by those whom the faithful Jews regarded as traitors and who would be in coalition with the "beast" of vs. 7. "Their" (Lord) would refer to the enemy.

We cannot use these Qumran texts to precisely identify the historical situation, if there is one, reflected in Rev 11, but the figures of speech in the Dead Sea scrolls can throw light on the meaning of those in Revelation. The beast from the abyss can be a political (domestic or foreign) enemy who attacks the civil and religious leaders of the faithful. This enemy prevails over the witnesses and kills them. Their bodies lie exposed. Giet finds here a historical allusion possibly to the two high priests, Ananus and Joshua, who were martyred by the Idumeans just before the campaign of A.D. 68.

Josephus reports this incident and describes how the Idumeans slew the chief priests and, standing over their dead bodies, scoffed at Ananus because of his patronage of the people and at Joshua because of the address which he delivered from the wall, *War* 4.238–70, 316. They cast their bodies out without burial although, says Josephus, the Jews were extremely careful about funeral rites, and even buried before sunset those who were crucified. Josephus thinks "that the overthrow of the walls and the downfall of the Jewish state dated from the day on which the Jews beheld their high priest, the captain of their salvation, butchered in the heart of Jerusalem," *War* 4.318. Josephus follows this statement with a eulogy on both Ananus and Jesus (Joshua) which he ends thus (*War* 4.324–25):

So they who but lately had worn the sacred vestments, led those ceremonies of world-wide significance and been reverenced by visitors to the city from every quarter of the earth, were now seen cast out naked, to be devoured by dogs and beasts of prey. Virtue herself, I think, groaned for these men's fate, bewailing such utter defeat at the hands of vice. Such, however, was the end of Ananus and Jesus.

Josephus' account records an atmosphere similar to that which is recorded in Rev 11:10, the people keeping holiday, *euphainesthai*, and sending portions, probably presents of food, to their friends or neighbors; cf. II Ezra 18:10, 11–12, Esther 9:22.

The great city in vs. 8 cannot be other than Jerusalem. This designation is used in Sibylline Oracles 5:154, 226, 413; Josephus *Against Apion* i.197; cf. "most strongly fortified," 209, Pliny *Natural History* 5.14.70. Further, in 11:13 the numbers suit Jerusalem and not Rome, and in vs. 10 the dwellers on the earth appear to denote dwellers in a single country, namely, Palestine. Jerusalem is traditionally the killer of the prophets; cf. e.g. Matt 23:37–39. The city is allegorically called Sodom, as the exemplar of wickedness; cf. Ezek 16:46, 48, 48; Wisd Sol 19:14, 15. Egypt is also a symbol of idolatry and slavery. This is quite in keeping with the attitude prevailing at Qumran.

The bodies remain unburied for the three and one-half days, i.e. a long and fiendish time of triumph, if a day represents a year. Then the breath of life enters the bodies of the witnesses and they stand upon their feet. The text is obviously influenced by Ezek 37, especially 37:10. Here the prophet receives a vision of dead bones on a battlefield and he is bidden to command breath to enter them. They rise, a mighty army. This text is an allegory symbolizing the expected restoration of the state of Israel. It would support the argument that the two witnesses in our text are collective figures. Their death and resurrection would be that of the community as in Ezek 37:10. Indeed, the singular "corpse" (*ptōma* in vss. 8, 9, plural, *ptōmata*, in 9b) and mouth (vs. 5) seem to be collective. Further, as Gry remarks, it would be strange for the beast to war against two isolated individuals, especially if the beast represents the Roman empire, as it appears to in Rev 13. Moreover, how could so many people (vs. 9) know about the death of two individuals?

In the sight of their enemies the witnesses go up to heaven "in the cloud." God rewards them as he did Elijah (II Kings 2:11) and, according to non-biblical Jewish tradition, Moses; cf. Clement of Alexandria *Stromateis* 6.15, *Ant.* 4.326, where Josephus described how when Moses was alone with Eleazar and Joshua a cloud descended and he disappeared into a ravine.

In vs. 15 at last the seventh trumpet is sounded. Just as the sixth seal was broken at the end of ch. 6 but the seventh was not broken until the beginning of ch. 8, so the seventh trumpet was not sounded until a considerable breathing space, ch. 10 and two-thirds of ch. 11, had accumulated after the sounding of the sixth. There is, however, a marked contrast between the seventh seal and the seventh trumpet. The former brought silence; the latter brought voices (probably from the living creatures) rejoicing in the kingship of God. The world empire is now pronounced to be in the hands of the true owner but the vision or songs in vss. 16–19 are probably proleptic, foretelling the future victory realized at the end of this apocalypse. However, they form a fitting conclusion to the Baptist part (chs. 4–11).

God in vs. 15 appears to be identified with God the Father, and the Lord's Anointed introduces a technical name for the messianic king which is first found in I Enoch 48:10, 52:4, and subsequently in Psalms of Solomon 17:36; 18:6, 8; cf. also Luke 2:11, 26; 9:20. The singular "he will reign" is curious; it may either mean the Anointed will reign or indicate that "and his Anointed" is interpolated. However, the idea that God will establish an imperishable kingdom, found in Dan 2:44; 7:14, 27; cf. Luke 1:33, argues that the phrase was indeed part of the original.

Vss. 17–18 form a hymn concerning the establishment of God's sovereignty and the outbreak of the nations, which probably foreshadows the reference to Gog and Magog in 20:8, and corresponds somewhat with the two hymns in ch. 19 celebrating and rejoicing in God; 19:1–3, 6b–8. This hymn shows progressive movement from God's assuming power, to the nations' raging, to God's wrath, to His judgment of the dead, to His recompense to the holy, and finally to His destruction of "the destroyers of the earth." The order of events presented in vss. 17–18 violates chronology; destruction should follow the raging of the nations so that God's recompense to the holy would appear in the climactic position at the end of vs. 18.

The hymn shows universal judgment. The wicked who are condemned are the nations; cf. Ps 2:1. There are three groups of servants who are recompensed—the prophets, the saints or "holy ones," and those who fear the Lord's name. "Those who fear Your name" may denote proselytes or pious Pharisees; cf. Psalms of Solomon 2:37. The phrase "small and great" appears not only in vs. 18 but also in 13:16; 19:5, 8; 20:12; cf. Gen 19:11, Wisd Sol 6:7. It includes all conditions of men. The "destroying of the destroyers of the earth" may be a phrase borrowed from Jer 51 MT[28 LXX]:25, and may be used in the double sense of both destroy and corrupt; cf. Rev 19:2. The remaining chapters of this apocalypse, excluding chs. 1–3, will describe these "destroyers of the earth"; see Caird. In vs. 19 the sanctuary in heaven is opened and the ark of the covenant or testimony is seen. The first earthly ark of the covenant was a chest made of acacia wood, in which were placed the two stone tablets with the ten commandments; Exod 25:10–22, 26:33–34; Deut 10:1–5. Aaron's rod and the pot of manna were placed before it, according to Exod 16:33–34, Num 17:10–11, although Heb 9:4 records that these objects were within the ark. The ark was the war palladium of Yahweh, the God of hosts (cf. I Sam 4:1–9), but was later regarded as the holy place where Yahweh revealed himself. In the historical books the ark appears for the first time at the crossing of the Jordan (Josh 3–4) and then at the conquest of Jericho (Josh 6:6–14). When the temple was completed the ark was placed in the innermost room of the sanctuary; I Kings 6:19, 8:1–9; II Chron 5:5–10. But then it seems to disappear from Israelite tradition. Jer 3:16 intimates that in messianic days the Israelites will not feel the lack of the ark and will not make a new one. However, according to the later tradition of II Macc 2:4–8 Jeremiah hid the ark in a cave on Mount Nebo at the time of the destruction of the temple by the Babylonians. It was to remain there until the Lord restored the glory of Israel. Its revelation here intimates the beginning of the restoration of that glory which will be associated with the creation of a city of living stones, i.e. people, who, like the witnesses, died and rose. Rev 11 stands parallel to the millennium and the white throne of judgment in 20:10–15.

There is, however, another aspect of the ark. Originally it was a war palladium which was carried into battle and which threw Israel's enemies into panic; cf. the warrior's chant in Num 10:35–36 and Pss 68:2. The accompanying noises, lightning and thunder, earthquake and hail, may be seen as the instruments of war of the god of war and/or even angels fighting alongside the earthly hosts of Yahweh; cf. Exod 19:16–19, Ps 29:3–9, Rev 16:21. The manifestation of the ark at this stage implies that God has pledged himself to fulfill all the great deeds celebrated in the heavenly song sung in vss. 17–18, i.e. to win the victory and reign.

With 11:15–19 the first segment (chs. 4–11) of Revelation ends in an epiphany, a vision of the heavenly order. Such an ending is appropriate, since the second segment (chs. 12–22) will be terrestrially oriented. The heavenly war-ark of 11:19 is a fitting prelude to the Holy War against the fleshly beast which will be portrayed in the second segment. The tent of witness will appear again, and the seven angels, each carrying a bowl of God's wrath that causes a plague when it is poured on the earth, will come out of the sanctuary; chs.

15–16. So far the messianic figure of the Lamb has been seen only in heaven. He will appear on earth, albeit in another guise, in the second segment of this apocalypse. The seventh trumpet sounded in vs. 15 announces the epiphany in vss. 16–19 which clears the way for a new circle of prophecies beginning with ch. 12.

BIBLIOGRAPHY

Caird, G. B. *The Revelation of St. John the Divine.*

Carrington, P. *The Meaning of Revelation.*

Feuillet, A. "Interpretation of Chapter XI of the Apocalypse," in *Johannine Studies.*

Flusser, D. "Two Notes on the Midrash on 2 Sam 7 (4QFlorilegium): I. The Temple 'not made with hands' in the Qumran Doctrine . . . II. 'The Shoot of David who will stand with the Interpreter of the Law,'" *Israel Exploration Journal* 9 (1959), 99–109.

Gärtner, B. *The Temple and the Community in Qumran and the New Testament.* Cambridge University Press, 1965.

Gaston, Lloyd. *No Stone on Another: Studies in the Significance of the Fall of Jerusalem in the Synoptic Gospels.* Leiden: Brill, 1970.

Giet, S. RevueSR 38 (1964), 71–92, 255–64.

Gry, L. RB 31 (1922), 203–14.

McKelvey, R. J. *The New Temple.*

Murphy-O'Connor, J. "La Genèse Littéraire de la Règle de la Communauté," RB 76 (1969), 528–49.

de Vaux, R. *Ancient Israel, Its Life and Institutions.*

Yadin, Y. "Pesher Nahum (4QpNahum) Reconsidered," *Israel Exploration Journal* 21 (1971), 1–12.

Part Two: Revelation to a Baptist Disciple Concerning the Punishment of Jerusalem

12 1 And a great sign appeared in heaven, a woman clothed with
the sun, and the moon under her feet, and on her head a crown of
twelve stars, 2 and she is with child, and cries out in her pangs of
birth, and is in anguish to bring forth. 3 And there appeared another
sign in heaven, and behold a great red dragon having seven heads
and ten horns and seven diadems on his heads, 4 and his tail sweeps
down a third of the stars of heaven and he hurled them to the earth.
And the dragon stood before the woman who was about to give birth,
waiting to devour her baby when it was born. 5 And she gave birth
to a son, a man, who is destined to rule all the nations with a rod of
iron; and her child was caught up to God and his throne. . . .

14 And the two wings of the great eagle were given to the woman,
that she might fly to the desert to her place, where she might be supported for a time and times and half a time because of the serpent.
15 And the serpent spat water like a river from his mouth behind the
woman, that she might be overwhelmed. 16 And the earth came to
the assistance of the woman, and the earth opened its mouth and
swallowed up the river which the dragon spat from his mouth. 17 And
the dragon was furious with the woman, and he went off to fight
against the rest of her children, who observe the commandments of
God and have the testimony of Jesus: 18 And the dragon took up his
stand on the sand of the sea.

6 And the woman fled to the desert, for there she has a place prepared by God, that there she might be nourished for one thousand
two hundred and sixty days. 7 And there was a war in heaven, the
Michael and his angels fighting with the dragon. And the dragon and
his angels fought, 8 and he did not prevail, neither was there found
a place anymore for him in heaven. 9 And the great dragon, the ancient serpent, who is called Devil and Satan, was cast out, he who deceives the whole world, was cast out onto the earth, and his angels
were cast out with him. 10 And I heard a loud voice in heaven, saying,

"Now is the salvation and the power and the kingship of our God
and the authority of His Anointed, for the accuser of our brothers

has been cast out, he who accused them day and night before our God. 11 And they overcame him through the word of their testimony, and they loved not their life unto death. 12 On account of this rejoice, heavens and you who dwell there; woe to the earth and the sea, for the devil has descended to you with great fury, knowing that his time is short."

13 And when the dragon saw that he was cast down onto earth, he pursued the woman who had given birth to the man-child.

NOTES

12:1. *sign.* The word "sign" is often accompanied by "wonder," Gr. *teras,* and "power," Gr. *dunamis;* cf. John 4:48, Acts 2:22. It is so used in Revelation, but only of evil powers; cf. 13:13–17, 15:1, 19:20. The Gospels speak of a sign from heaven (Mark 8:11, Matt 16:1, 24:3, 30) but this attends the parousia. Carrington, p. 204, remarks that the felicitous sign of the woman occurs in the highest region, i.e. heaven, just as sin occurs in the lowest, namely the abyss. He also observes that the woman appears to be the counterpart of the strong angel in ch. 10. See COMMENT.

woman. In Revelation "woman" or "women" occurs nineteen times: 12:1, 4, 6, 14, 15, 16, 17, 17:3, 4, 6, 7, 9 f., 18 and elsewhere in 9:8, 14:4, 19:7, 21:9. It might be said therefore, that the woman symbol is almost as important as the Lamb. This woman and the new Jerusalem are the antithesis of the harlot.

clothed. Gr. *periballomai.* Codex A gives a variant *periblepomenē,* "looking at," which produces the picture of the woman "looking at" the sun instead of being "clothed with" it. The greater authorities support "clothed" nevertheless. Further, *periballomai* occurs twelve times in Revelation and examination of these other texts (7:9, 10:1, 11:3, 17:4, 18:16, 19:8, 13) shows that there is no doubt that the woman is wearing the sun as her garment. Further, the secondary meaning of *periballō* is "to throw up a rampart around" (cf. Luke 19:43), which would be consonant with the idea of the "army with banners" in Song of Songs 6:10, which may have affected our text. The sun, perhaps representing God, is a rampart or protection around the woman-community.

sun. Some scholars have found here an allusion to the sun goddess. The sun deity myth was a popular cult in the first century A.D. and coins depicting the emperor's head show his radiant crown like the rays of the sun. Christ's crown of thorns may be a deliberate caricature of this; see Hart, pp. 66 ff. The goddess Roma, who was worshiped in Asia, was akin to a mother goddess. A coin from Pergamum shows the head of Augustus and a female figure, while another coin from the reign of Tiberius shows Augustus and Livia as a sun and moon. However, it seems unlikely that a book like this apocalypse, devoted to a polemic against idolatry, should utilize pagan symbols of the faithful community.

crown. Gr. *stephanos*. See COMMENT.

twelve stars. Some compare the stars or zodiac with the twelve stones on the breastplate of Aaron, cf. Philo *De Vita Mosis* 3.24, and Josephus *Ant.* 3.186. Le Frois, p. 116, note 2, also refers to Wisd Sol 13:2 where the author speaks of a circle of stars which may refer to the zodiac. See illustration 11.

2. *is with child.* The same phrase is used of Mary in Matt 1:18, 23.

and. Omitted in **P 046 051**, 1, 82, 1611, 2329, pl vg[s,cl] bo TR.

cries out. Gr. *krazō*. In Hellenistic literature this has either the significance of demonic shouting, with magic incantations, or solemn proclaiming. In Luke 23:46 a similar expression is used of Christ commending his spirit to the Father. In this apocalypse it occurs with reference to the fall of Babylon in Rev 18:18–19, proclaiming the saving power of God and the lamb in 7:10, the accomplishment of God's decrees in 7:2, 10:3; cf. 15:18. It appears to be confined to proclaiming by persons on the side of God, not Satan.

in her pangs of birth. Gr. *ōdinō*. Philo uses this word in the literal sense and also in the sense of the soul bringing forth thoughts, e.g. three times with reference to persons (Leah, Tamar, and Balak). Leah and Tamar are in spiritual travail and bring forth virtue (e.g. *De Cherubim* 42), and Balak is in distress and anguish.

in anguish. Gr. *basanizomenē*. In IV Maccabees the verb appears nineteen times and the noun forty-one, associating the word with martyrdom. The pains seem to be in sharp contrast with the wonderful description of the woman in vs. 1. Feuillet and others think that John 16:19–22 casts light upon this allegorical interpretation of the woman in travail and John's text itself is influenced by Isa 66:7 (see NOTE below). The birth is something more than physical childbirth.

to bring forth. Otto Betz, NTS 3 (1956/57), 314–26, sees the woman as the Teacher of Righteousness and the child as the members of the community. If this is so, there might be an allusion to Num 11:12 and the Teacher would appear as a second Moses. In this way the passage would be close to I Thess 2:7 ff. or Gal 4:19. However, this interpretation is debatable in the light of "the rest of her children" in vs. 17. For woman as community see Isa 54:5; Jer 3:6–10; Ezek 16:8b; Hosea 2:19–20; IV Ezra 9:38 – 10:59. These texts depict mainly distress and destruction. In 1QH 3 the womb of the woman in travail is compared to Sheol, to the pit, perhaps also to a furnace. One might translate vss. 9–10 "from the bonds of Sheol, from the furnace of her who is pregnant, has leapt the wonderful counselor with his strength." The author apparently plays on the Hebrew words *bkwr*, "firstborn," and *kwr*, "furnace," as he also plays upon *mšbrym*, "waves," and *mšbrym*, "orifice of womb."

Our apocalyptic text, however, may be influenced by passages which suggest creative suffering, a suffering which in the end brings joy. One finds such a text in Isa 66:7, again referring to Zion, but the metaphor is one of a very easy childbirth, either a precipitate birth, i.e. without labor pains (vs. 7), or at least immediate birth and an exceedingly short labor (vs. 8). The oracle in Isa 66 is one of great joy and consolation for Jerusalem and, incidentally, is one specially marked in 1QIsa beside vs. 5. IV Ezra 9:43–45, 10:43–45 speak of Zion bearing a male child after thirty years of barrenness, but it is difficult to identify this child.

The early church regarded the resurrection as a kind of birth and thus they could use Ps 2:7 "thou art my son; this day have I begotten you" in this light; cf. Acts 13:33 and perhaps Rom 1:4; Heb 1:5, 5:5. For other texts which express the passion and resurrection in the images of childbirth, see Gal 4:18; cf. Rev 1:5, John 12:24 (cf. I Cor 15:36, Acts 2:24, "having loosed the sorrows of hell," an expression taken from Ps 38:6; cf. also Ps 96:8, II Sam 22:6). The NT speaks of the bonds of death but with the change of the pointing in the Hebrew equivalent this could mean the pains of childbirth.

3. *red*. Gr. *purros*, lit. "fiery red." There is a variant reading in C **046** 1, 82, 1006, 1611, 2059*, 2329 al sy: *puros*, "of fire." The stronger reading is *purros*, which agrees with Rev 6:4, the red horse, but not with the beast described in 17:3, which is scarlet, Gr. *kokkinon*, rather than fiery red. The red color could denote the murderous work of the dragon; cf. John 8:44, I John 3:12.

dragon. Gr. *drakōn*. "Dragon" translates the Hebrew word *tannīn* (e.g. Exod 7:9, 12, Aaron's rod which became a serpent; Deut 32:33, the wine of Yahweh's enemies compared to the poison of serpents; Gen 1:21, the great sea monsters, cf. Pss 91:13, 148:7). For further references to Rahab, the monster, compare Isa 30:7, 51:9, Job 9:13, Ps 87:4. The Mishnah (*Abodah Zarah* 3.3, tr. Blackman) deems the dragon as an emblem of idolatry: "If one find objects, and on them is a figure of the sun, [or] a figure of the moon, [or] a figure of a dragon, he must cast them, into the Salt Sea." Blackman, IV, 462, observes that the Roman cohorts used the figure of the dragon as a military ensign. The Salt Sea appears to mean the Dead Sea. In Song of Songs 6:4 the beloved is compared to Tirzah, the capital of the northern kingdom before the time of Omri, and in the same verse she is also compared to Jerusalem, the capital of the southern kingdom. This would suggest that the woman, Israel, unites in herself the once-divided kingdom (cf. Ezek 37:15–28, Jer 23:6, Isa 11:11–12, 27:13, 28:5–6, 46:12–23, Zech 3:9–10; see Feuillet, p. 275). The monster who opposes her may be the personification of the ocean or the dweller of the Nile which in some sources prevents the rising of the sun.

seven heads. For many-headed monsters, one may compare Ps 74:13–15 which speaks both about the heads of the dragons and of the Leviathan. *Kiddushim* 29b refers to a demon in the guise of a seven-headed dragon. The Ras Shamra tablets also mention a seven-headed monster and the hydra of Lerna had seven heads. Ten horns are found on the fourth beast in Dan 7:7.

diadems. For the concept of a diademed serpent compare Pliny *Natural History* 8.21, 33. The Persian diadem was a blue band with white edging on the turban characteristic of royal dignity; cf. Esther 1:11, etc. "Diadem" is used of a royal crown in Sir 11:5, 47:6, and frequently in I and II Maccabees. In Wisd Sol 5:16 it is a symbol of heavenly reward, and in 18:24 it refers to the high priestly headdress.

4. *a third of the stars*. A hyperbole to suggest the colossal size and strength of the monster. For "sweep" or "drag," Gr. *surei*, compare John 21:8; Acts 14:19, 17:6.

hurled them to the earth. Frequently understood as a reference to the angels' fall; cf. Jude 6. The tense changes from present to past.

the dragon stood before the woman. "Stood" is strange for the dragon but one may compare the serpent in Gen 3:14. The two sides now confront each other. Feuillet, p. 261, observes that the dragon standing before the woman cannot parallel Herod's plot to kill Jesus since the slaughter of the innocents was not accompanied by Jesus' ascension into heaven. Further, the innocents do not play a part in the Johannine tradition; also the devil does not appear at the beginning of the Savior's earthly life but at the beginning of his public ministry. In the fourth Gospel Satan comes to the fore as Christ approaches his passion; cf. the enmity of the devil towards Jesus in Luke 22:3–6; John 13:27.

Waiting. TI.

5. *gave birth.* There is no reference to virginity or to the son being the firstborn.

son, a man. The peculiar phrase "son, a male," is found in Tobit 6:11(S), Jer 20:15. The neuter *arsen,* "male," is peculiar but it is found in the LXX of Isa 67:7, Jer 37(30):6. The Targum of Isa 66:7 (Stenning) refers to a king: "Before distress shall come upon her she shall be delivered, and before trembling shall come upon her, as pangs upon a woman with child, her king shall be revealed." Alhertz (see Feuillet, p. 259, n. 6) thinks that the newborn child is an allusion to the son of Domitian who died when he was six years old and appears on coins as climbing up the heavenly throne and playing with seven stars.

rod of iron. Cf. 2:27.

caught up. Gr. *harpasthē.* In the secular sense this can be used of soldiers taking people by force (e.g. Acts 23:10), people being saved from fire (Jude 23), snatching sheep (John 10:12), the evil one snatching the seed (Matt 13:19). The words used for the ascension of Jesus are *analambanō,* "received up," and *anapherō,* "carried up." But the idea of being "caught up" like Paul in II Cor 12:2 is at variance with what is known of Jesus' life: he is not represented as a visionary or ecstatic. However, it is possible that there may be an allusion here to the hidden Messiah. In the Targum to Micah 4:8 it is said that the Messiah is concealed on account of the sins of the people. Trypho, the Jew, discoursing with Justin Martyr, says, "But Christ—if He has indeed been born, and exists anywhere—is unknown, and does not even know Himself, and has no power until Elias come to anoint Him, and make Him manifest to all . . ." (Justin, *Dialogue with Trypho* 8). A similar idea may underline John 7:27. Charles thinks that "the birth of the Messiah, therefore, followed by his sudden disappearance, was an idea familiar to Judaism, but impossible as a purely Christian concept. Whether he remained on earth or was carried off to heaven as in our text is a subordinate question" (Charles, *Revelation,* p. 308, note 1). However, II Baruch 29:3; IV Ezra 7:28, 13:32, which he cites, do not seem entirely germane.

14. *the two wings.* The definite article is omitted in P⁴⁷ 046 82, 2060 pm TR.

the great eagle. For the wide wing span, see p. 140. In Isa 40:31 the symbol of the eagle's wings given to the Israelites is associated with the return from exile.

be supported. The verb "support," Gr. *trephein,* is employed in Deut 32:18 (the Song of Moses, God supporting His people). It can mean "nourish" or "bring up" (children). The verse recalls God's providing quails and manna to feed the Israelites in the desert.

a time and times and half a time. Le Frois, pp. 185–86, refers to the forty-two months mentioned in 12:6 (see NOTE) and suggests that forty-two is three times fourteen. Fourteen is a messianic number, also the numerical value of the name of David. Three is also a sacred number, probably because the ancients divided the universe into three—heaven, earth, and water—which in turn were represented by the three Babylonian deities—Anu, Bel, and Ea. Cf. also I Kings 17:21, I Chron 21:12, Dan 6:10, and see *Jewish Encyclopedia* under "numbers." There were reputed to be forty-two generations before the coming of Christ and it was believed that a similar number of generations would precede the second coming.

Allo, *Saint Jean,* p. 164, also thinks that this time is symbolic of the messianic era. However, Rev 11:2, 13:5–6 show a different symbolism, of corruption and upheaval, and in the OT where forty-two occurs there is always an association with violent death. In II Kings 2:23–24 two bears tear up forty-two boys because they mocked Elijah; in II Kings 10:14 Jehu killed forty-two people. Therefore, forty-two may symbolize violent, useless killing.

However, it is not certain that forty-two is meant in this verse. "A time and times and half a time" may represent three and one-half years; if so, it has its prototype in the woe which Elijah called upon the land (cf. Luke 4:25, James 5:17). Le Frois opines that the phrase three and one-half years is a technical symbol which does not express so much a period of time as a period of tribulation and woe. Three and one-half years may be a type of a final woe. In Dan 7:25 the three and one-half years is associated with the reign of a godless king, and in Rev 12:14 it may well be associated with the reign of the beast (13:5–6) which coincides with the third woe (8:13).

15. *water like a river.* There are no real parallels to this verse in Jewish tradition but the dragon is considered a water monster in Ezek 29:3, 32:2–3; Ps 74:13. However, spitting of water is more characteristic of an elephant. In the Hellenistic period the elephant was used as a military animal. Lysias included thirty-two in the forces sent against the Jews in 163 B.C. (I Macc 6:30). There is also an interesting parallel to our verse in Testament of Asher 7:3 (APCh, II, 345) but it contains obviously Christian additions: "And ye shall be set at nought in the dispersion *vanishing away* as water. Until the Most High shall visit the earth, coming Himself [as man, with men eating and drinking], breaking the head of the dragon in the water."

The flood of waters may have been suggested by the Red Sea engulfing the Egyptians, or the Jordan, or even the Palestinian wadis; cf. Matt 7:27. Further, one might find here another creation motif, the water resembling the powers of chaos against which Yahweh fights.

Dubarle, p. 518, taking a different view, thinks there may be an allusion to Song of Songs 7:7. The love of the woman is not able to be diminished by any temptation. In the same way, the love of the martyrs is as strong as death (12:11). Roberts, emphasizes the similarity between Song of Songs 7:6–7 and Isa 43:2 where Yahweh promises that He will be with the people when they pass through water.

16. *earth opened its mouth.* The author may also have had OT themes in mind; the earth drank the blood of Abel shed by Cain (Gen 4:11). But a more pertinent text is Num 16:32 where "the earth opened its mouth and swallowed" Korah, etc.; cf. also Num 26:10, Deut 11:6, Ps 106:16–18, where the same incident is recorded.

17. *the rest of her children.* If this verse means that the dragon went away from the desert, this phrase could signify the faithful Jews elsewhere in Palestine against whom persecutions are now directed. But the "son" (vs. 5) could be an individual similar to the Teacher of Righteousness and the rest of the children the remaining community in the desert. With reference to the word "children," lit. "seed," Le Frois draws attention to Isa 1:9, Wisd Sol 16:6, Rom 4:13, 9:27–29. He rightly observes that no text other than Rev 12 and Gen 3:15 places such an emphasis on the seed of the woman. The rest of the children are described as keeping the commandments of God and having the testimony of Jesus. This is considered as an addition by Wellhausen and Weiss, but "who keep the commandments of God" would seem to be perfectly in accord with a community such as that found at Qumran.

18. *took up his stand on the sand of the sea.* Unlike the angel in 10:2, the dragon does not stand on both sea and land but rather between the two, as if he were watching the whole world from a vantage point at the center. See also COMMENT.

6–13. Most scholars would see this segment as composite in character. Many argue that vss. 7–12 are an interpolation and they point out the similarity to 20:1–4, which may form a doublet. Others think that vss. 1–6 and 7–14 are parallel accounts. Boismard places 20:1–3 in Text One together with 12:1–6a, 13b–17, and 12:7–12 in Text Two. See COMMENT. Many scholars argue that the text was not originally Christian. It omits all reference to the earthly life, work, death, and resurrection of Christ, and attributes a passive and subordinate role to the Messiah: Satan is overcome by Michael, not by the Messiah. In this work it has therefore been placed as an appendix to ch. 12. See COMMENT.

6. *desert.* In Heb 3–4 the crossing of the desert seems to be a symbol of earthly existence. In our text the desert is not necessarily the same as "a place prepared," although this is likely.

place prepared. This phrase is also found in John 14:2–3. It might, however, suggest the Garden of Eden, which symbolism would be consonant with the reference to the serpent (vs. 14 and Gen 2:8–23) and to the seed of the woman. Le Frois, pp. 181–82, remarks ". . . the symbolism of the 'place prepared' may have to do with the state of integrity which the woman enjoys in paradise." There is nothing inconsistent in blending wilderness symbolism with Eden symbolism.

7. *the Michael.* The definite article preceeds the name "Michael." He seems to be captain of the host and bears the title "archangel" (Jude 9). It has been

remarked that it is strange for it to be Michael, rather than the Messiah, who overcomes the dragon, identified with the devil or Satan in vs. 9.

8. *he did not prevail.* P⁴⁷ P 1, 1006, 1611, 2059s, 2329 pm vg sy sa TR; R read "they did not prevail." Cf. Dan 7:21, the horn which made war with the saints and prevailed over them. Cf. also Ps 13:4 and perhaps, too, Gen 30:8, Rachel prevailing over her sister and therefore calling her son Naphtali, and Gen 32:28, Jacob prevailing over "God" (cf. the reference to the same incident in Hosea 12:4).

place. Cf. Zech 10:10, "room."

anymore. Gr. *eti.* This seems to imply that up to this point Satan's claim to a place in heaven had not been wholly disallowed; cf. Job 1:6, Zech 3:1–2).

9. *cast out . . . cast out . . . cast out.* Note the three-fold use of *ballō* (cast out, or cast down) in this one verse. *Ekballō* is a technical word for excommunication. Cf. John 9:34–35. A similar vision, Satan falling from heaven, is recorded in Luke 10:18. In 1QH 3 the enemies of the sect are pregnant with the viper. "The persecution (birthpangs) which cause this viper to be born correspond perfectly to the crushing which causes the viper's egg to hatch in Isa (lix 5)" (Chamberlain).

10. *voice.* Cf. I Enoch 40:7 (APCh, II, 211): "I heard the fourth voice sending off the Satans and forbidding them to come before the Lord of Spirits to accuse them who dwell on the earth."

11. *loved not their life unto death.* Cf. Mark 8:35–36; Matt 10:39, 16:26; Luke 9:24, 17:33; John 12:25.

12. *rejoice.* Perhaps there is a deliberate comparison with 11:10, where the earth-dwellers rejoice over the two witnesses.

heavens. Cf. Isa 44:23, 49:13. Only here in Revelation is heaven found in the plural. A 1, 1006, 1611, 2059 pm TR read "the heavens."

you. The text reads the definite article, Gr. *hoi.*

dwell. Gr. *skenein.* This word applies to God in 7:15, 21:3, and to heavenly beings in 13:6. It may have a deeper meaning in the sense of "pitching their tabernacle."

woe to the earth and the sea. In 1, 2026 pc TR, the reading is "woe to those inhabiting the earth and the sea."

13. *he pursued.* P⁴⁷ reads "he went away to pursue."

COMMENT

Ch. 11 introduced the reader to the separation between the faithful (the sanctuary) and the unfaithful (the outer court), and to the collective figures (probably the House of Israel and House of Aaron) who would suffer persecution but, like the Suffering Servant in Isaiah, would receive their recompense. Ch. 12 reveals the whole community of the faithful under the traditional figure of a woman and shows her adversary the dragon, who may or may not be identical with the beast from the abyss in 11:7. The conflict which has been directed mainly from heaven will now take on a terrestrial dimension.

Ch. 12 begins a new division of our work, one which might be called the "book of signs." The word "sign" does not occur in chs. 4–11, but appears seven times in chs. 12–19. Three of the signs are in heaven (12:1, 3, 15:1) and four are on earth (13:13, 14, 16:14, 19:20). But the woman in 12:1 is the only felicitous sign; the others are associated with evil happenings, the beasts and their servants. Thus, the woman is the chief and only sign from God standing in opposition to the six other signs and presaging the new Jerusalem from heaven (ch. 21).

In this second part of Revelation the struggle between good and evil develops into a clear dualism, not wholly unlike that found in Zoroastrianism, but even closer to the struggle between good and evil reflected in the Qumran writings. The covenanters saw that the course of history was in God's hands, and that he would allow battle between the powers of light and darkness "until the appointed time and the new creation" (1QS 4:25) or "until the last time" (1QS 4:16, 1QpHab 7:7). In Rev 12 the woman, surrounded by cosmic symbols, sun, moon, stars, seems to be the earthly complement of the angel in Rev 10. A personification of light, she faces the hostile forces of darkness symbolized by the dragon. The battle will not end until all evil is conquered and the new creation comes to pass. This end will be indicated in 20:1–4 when the themes of the angel descending from heaven (10:1, 20:1), the key of the abyss (9:1, 20:1), and the dragon who is the ancient serpent (12:9, 20:2) are resumed.

The new vision is not introduced by the usual formula, "after this I looked . . ." Rather, there appears a sign, Gr. *sēmeion*. In the LXX *sēmeion* usually translates *'ôt*, i.e. "some event assuring man of a divine intervention. It is a form of revelation" (F. L. Moriarty, in *The Jerome Biblical Commentary,* eds. R. E. Brown et al. [Englewood Cliffs, N.J.: Prentice-Hall, 1968], p. 270), and is used for celestial phenomena, e.g. Gen 1:14, 9:12–17, or tokens of God's presence or purpose, e.g. the miracles in Egypt (Exod 7:3, etc.). A text which is peculiarly pertinent is Isa 7:10–17. Here the Lord asks Ahaz to request a sign, be it "deep as Sheol or high as heaven" (RSV). The sign is a young woman who will conceive, bear a son, name him "God with us," Heb. *Immanuel.* It is a confirmation that the Davidic dynasty will continue; cf. II Sam 7:12–16. Our sign appears to be something similar, especially as the woman brings forth a male child who will rule (vs. 5).

Although the woman may be an individual, a study of the OT background suggests that she is a collective figure, like the two witnesses. In the OT the image of a woman is a classical symbol for Zion, Jerusalem, and Israel, e.g. Zion whose husband is Yahweh (Isa 54:1, 5, 6, Jer 3:20, Ezek 16:8–14, Hosea 2:19–20), who is a mother (Isa 49:21, 50:1, 66:7–11, Hosea 4:5, Bar 4:8–23), and who is in the throes of birth (Micah 4:9–10, cf. Isa 26:16–18, Jer 4:31, 13:21, Sir 48:19[21]).

The woman is "clothed (*peribeblēmenē*) with the sun," just as the angel was "clothed" (*peribeblēmenon*) with a cloud. The psalmist speaks of Yahweh clothing himself with the light as with a garment (Ps 104:2) and other texts use the analogy of the sun in order to illustrate good qualities of men and women. In Ps 89:36 the writer desires David's lineage to last as long as the sun. In Judg 5:31 Deborah and Barak pray that God's friends will be "like the sun as he rises in his might" (RSV). Sir 26:16 compares a good wife to the sun "rising in the heights of the Lord." In contrast to these texts stands the oracle against Jerusalem, in Jer 15:5–9, which describes the mourning of widows and bereaved mothers; vs. 9a reads:

> She who bore seven has languished;
> she has swooned away;
> her *sun went down* while it was yet day;
> she has been shamed and disgraced.

RSV; italics mine.

The sun or light of Jerusalem is the Lord; cf. Isa 60:1. The faithful Jerusalem in our text is surrounded by this light. The harlot in chs. 17–18 is in a situation comparable to those about whom Jeremiah speaks. Later in Revelation God takes the place of the sun in the new Jerusalem (21:22). However, the OT text nearest to ours is the description of the bride in Song of Songs 6:10 (RSV):

> Who is this that looks forth like the dawn,
> fair as the moon, bright as the sun,
> terrible as an army with banners?

Previously (vs. 4) the beloved has been described as "comely as Jerusalem, terrible as an army with banners." The Targum accommodates the whole chapter to those who came from the Babylonian captivity with Ezra, Nehemiah, etc., and built the house of the sanctuary establishing the priests and the Levites. It also refers it to the house of the Hasmoneans and Alexander's attempt against Jerusalem. The Targum on Song of Songs 6:8 describes the assembly of Israel as a perfect dove and speaks of the victory of Mattathias and the Hasmoneans, declaring that their youths were beautiful as the moon and their good deeds as the sun, and describing how terror fell upon the inhabitants of the earth when they walked with their banners through the desert. Although this Targum is later than the NT it does illustrate the kind of symbolism that could arise from the Song of Songs. If this type of text is influential, then the woman would not be a passive figure but rather the responsive remnant.

Over and above the biblical texts one finds quite a remarkable parallel to Rev 12:1 in Testament of Naphtali 5:1–8. The writer reports a vision in which Isaac bids the sons of Jacob to try to seize the sun and moon. Levi procured the sun and Judah the moon, "and they were both of them lifted up with them. And when Levi became as the sun, lo, a certain young man gave to him twelve branches of palm; and Judah, was bright as the moon, and under their feet were twelve rays" (APCh, II, 338). Here the sun is associated with a priestly figure, Levi, and the moon with the house which will give kings to Israel, Judah. In a similar way in Qumran literature the anointed of Aaron (priest-messiah) takes precedence over the anointed of David (1QS adjunct 2:11–15). This superiority may perhaps be indicated in our vision by the fact that the sun is around the woman, the moon under her feet. The sun represented strength, perhaps even the power of God. On the other hand, one Hebrew word for the moon comes from *yerah*, probably akin to *arah*, "wander," designating it "the wanderer." The injurious influence of the moon is suggested in Ps 121:6, although its beauty is mentioned in Song of Songs 6:10 and it is symbolic of eternity in Pss 72:5, 7, 89:37. At least one can say that the moon is the lesser light and, as such, lies in a subordinate position under the woman's feet.

If the woman is the community, the cosmic features surrounding her may suggest a priestly community. Josephus describes at some length the cosmic significance of the high priestly vestments: the tunic is the earth, the blue color heaven, the pomegranates lightning, the bells thunder, the upper garment universal nature, the girdle the ocean, and the two sardonyxes the sun and moon (*Ant.* 3.179–87). In this way the crown of the woman is significant. Josephus calls the headdress of the high priest a crown (*stephanos* as in 12:1). Moreover, he says, "As for the twelve stones (in the breastplate), whether one would prefer to read in them the months or the constellations of like number, which the Greeks call the circle of the zodiac, he will not mistake the lawgiver's intention."

Philo gives a similar, but not identical, interpretation of the priestly vestments. He says the two emerald stones of the ephod represent the sun and moon, but he also associates the complete set of stones with the zodiac (*De Vita Mosis* 2.122–26). This concurs with the suggestion of modern scholars that the woman's crown of twelve stars represents the signs of the zodiac. Many synagogue mosaics and other archaeological data show the popularity of these signs among the Jews. See illustration 11. Qumran also indicates an interest in the zodiac. Further, the twelve constellations represented the twelve tribes (and) their standards corresponded to the zodiacal signs of the constellations (*Yalk* Num 418 reference in *The Jewish Encyclopedia*, under "zodiac"). Thus, if the stars of the crown reflect the zodiac, this does not preclude their also representing the sons of Jacob as in Gen 37:9. There the sun and moon represent Jacob and Rachel. All these features would suggest that our woman is the priestly community (cf. Exod 19:5–6), closely associated with the twelve tribes just as the sealed were in Rev 7.

In sharp contrast to the resplendent appearance of the woman is the description of her painful childbirth. Although the word "and," Gr. *kai*, is used frequently throughout our apocalypse there seems to be a peculiar emphasis on it in this sentence. Le Frois (p. 125) translates as follows:

> And she is with child,
> and cries out in her pangs of birth,
> and is in anguish to bring forth.

The present tenses indicate prolonged suffering, the terminology no ordinary childbirth. Le Frois (p. 127) recalls that the phrase "with child," Gr. *en gastri echein*, does not always refer to physical motherhood. A similar phrase is used of Moses in Num 11:12 where he complains to God concerning his responsibility for the people and the community of Israel (cf. Isa 26:17–18).

Similarly, "cries out," Gr. *krazō*, "to cry out with a loud voice," is not confined to association with ordinary childbirth. In the LXX it is also used for crying out to Yahweh (Pss 22:5, 34:6, 18, 107:6, 13) and for the seraphs calling to Yahweh (Isa 6:3–4). Josephus employs it in his description of

Jeremiah crying aloud his prophetic message (*Ant.* 10.117). In the Gospel of John it occurs four times in the sense of proclaiming in the face of contradiction (1:15, 7:28, 37–38, 12:44–50). In Revelation the verb refers to the cry of the martyrs to God (6:10). In I Enoch 71:11 it denotes crying out with the spirit of might, and in rabbinical literature, "the loud attestation of the Holy Spirit in the prophetic and hagiographic writers . . ." (TWNT III, 900). It would seem, therefore, that the writer meant the reader to understand that the woman's cries were directed to Yahweh.

The community is not only priestly but also prophetic, proclaiming the Spirit in the face of contradiction. "In her pangs of childbirth," Gr. *ōdinō*, connotes intense pain in general, i.e. the physical, mental, and spiritual senses (cf. I Thess 5:3, Mark 13:8, where the noun is employed; the Marcan use is eschatological). The word "in anguish," Gr. *basanizomenē*, "being in torment," is consistent with this interpretation. The verb does not occur with reference to the physical pangs of childbirth in a literal sense anywhere in the LXX, in the NT, Apocryphal books, patristic writings, or papyri. In surviving secular Greek literature there is one passage where it is used as reference to a mother dog. It means "to apply the touchstone," "to test the genuineness of something," and later to apply torture or the rack in order to ascertain the truth. In the LXX it is used of punishment inflicted by God (Wisd Sol 9, II Macc 1:28, etc.) and of punishment inflicted by the impious on the god-fearing (II Macc 7:13, 17, 9:16). In the MT it refers to spiritual and physical affliction.

Taken altogether these phrases depict the birth pangs, that is, the sufferings, which would precede the coming of the Messiah and the new era; cf. *Sanhedrin* 98b. The image of a woman in childbirth is frequently used in OT prophetic literature. In Isa 21:3 the prophet's loins are troubled with pangs like a woman in travail. In Jer 4:31 the daughter of Zion cries in anguish, gasping for breath like a woman in travail (cf. 13:21), and in Jer 30:6 the men of Judah hold their hands on their loins like a woman in labor (cf. also 49:24, of Damascus; 50:43, of the king of Babylon). The same image is used graphically in Micah 4:9–10, and in Sir 48:19–21 of Jerusalem as she faces Sennacherib.

However, the text which may have influenced our passage more directly is Isa 26:17. There are several points of affinity. First, although the woman in childbirth does endure suffering, it is followed by blessing from the Lord and a promise of "resurrection." Second, the suffering of the people is to be for a little time until the wrath is passed and the Lord comes. Third, in the following chapter there is reference to "Leviathan the fleeing serpent, Leviathan the twisting serpent, and he [the Lord] will slay the dragon that is in the sea" (Isa 27:1, RSV). In the same way, Rev 12:2 is followed immediately by reference to the dragon, and Rev 12:9 refers to the ancient serpent.

Thus, the biblical background would suggest 1) that the woman portrays faithful Jerusalem; 2) she suffers, but will receive help from the Lord; 3) her opponent is the dragon, who appears in the next verse.

The dragon is introduced with this phrase: "And there appeared another sign in heaven." Vs. 1 reads, "And a great sign appeared in heaven." In the LXX the word "dragon" translates Heb. *nahas*, "serpent" or "viper," Heb.

tannīn, "serpent," "dragon," "sea-monster," and Leviathan. Three OT figures, very similar to one another, seem to have influenced our author: the dragon, the Leviathan, and Rahab. The dragon is usually a mythical sea monster who is the enemy of Yahweh (Isa 27:1, 51:9; Job 7:12; cf. Amos 9:3; Ps 104:26). Dragons generally are the embodiment of evil, but their appearance varies in the different mythologies. The Babylonian dragon is a sacred beast which guards the god Marduk against opposing powers. It is portrayed as a red snake. Some idea of its appearance can be gained from the remains of the Ishtar Gate at Babylon. Its head is horned and it has a long neck with a scaly body; its front legs are like a lion, the back ones like an eagle, and the tail like a scorpion; cf. Dan 7:23–27. The number of heads varies, e.g. in Greek mythology Hercules slays a seven-headed or nine-headed hydra.

It is impossible to determine precisely which mythologies have influenced Revelation either in this chapter or the following. Yet here it is significant that the color of the dragon is red like the Babylonian snake and the Egyptian typhon. The Leviathan, which will be discussed in COMMENT on Section X, is the monster who comes out of the sea. He also has many heads and Yahweh is said to smash them (Ps 74:13–14) and pierce "the fleeing serpent" (Job 26:13, AB). Rahab means "the restless, stormy one" (Job 26:12, Ps 89:10–11; cf. Sir 43:25).

The monster is the embodiment of chaos, the antithesis of Yahweh who is the source of all order in the world. Thus he is aligned with the hybrid creatures like the locusts in ch. 9 and all the cosmic disturbances, while the woman represents poise and harmony and beauty in the universe. The dragon wears diadems upon his heads. The diadem is a symbol of royalty (Sir 11:5, 47:6), wisdom (Wisd Sol 5:16), and high priesthood (Wisd Sol 18:24). In the NT "diadem" occurs only in Revelation (12:3, 13:1, 19:12); in all instances it is used of royal power. Our dragon is king (and possibly priest) of chaos. Salvation will recapitulate creation, and the cosmological myth of Yahweh's victory over the monster(s) will be realized on an eschatological level. A new heaven and a new earth appear in Rev 21 after the conquering of the dragon; cf. Isa 9:6–8, 65:17, 25, Hosea 2:18–22.

The eschatological aspect need not preclude a historical allusion. Babylon is compared to a devouring dragon in Jer 51:34; Pharaoh to one (perhaps a crocodile) who lives in the Nile in Ezek 29:3, 32:2; Pompey is probably alluded to as a dragon in Psalms of Solomon 2:29. Hence it need cause no *admiratio* if the dragon, who has appeared as a mythological figure in ch. 12, emerges as a historical one later in our text. The dragon performs two actions. First, he sweeps a third of the stars from heaven with his tail. Second, he stands before the woman, who wore the crown of twelve stars, and waits to devour her child. The zodiacal imagery seems to blend the symbols.

Carter, p. 65, suggests that the dragon has an astral significance. He opines that the circle of the zodiac has its pivotal point in the coils of the dragon. According to ancient belief the planets, created by the evil one, were hostile to the fixed stars, and "their variable and serpentine motion gives a significance to their association with Draco in whose convolutions are reproduced their mazy movement." Draco (the Dragon) is "the center of the knotted circle of the intertwined paths taken by the planets in the ecliptic. He is the maker of eclipses, the disturber of regularity and order," p. 66. Doubtless, the stars which his tail sweeps down are the fallen angels who traditionally turned away from God with Satan as their leader. A similar concept is found in Dan 8:9–11, where the little horn casts some of the host of the stars down to the ground and tramples upon them; cf. the star fallen from heaven in Rev 9:1.

The dragon's second action is not wholly dissociated from the first. If the woman is the faithful community, such as one finds at Qumran, it is a community which lives, works, prays, and fights, in the company of the good angels which may even be included in the imagery of the stars round her head. The dragon, seeking to devour her child, makes an attempt upon the friends of the good angels. At this point the woman appears to be on the earth rather than in heaven; cf. vs. 6. The dragon "stood," Gr. hestēken, before the woman. This could be the imperfect of stekō, "he persisted" or "remained in a certain state," or the imperfect of the intransitive of histani, "he came to a halt" or "he stands"; contrast vs. 18 where the passive is used. Le Frois remarks that both meanings are acceptable in vs. 4 but after the sweeping down of the stars the idea of the dragon coming to a halt rather than remaining in a certain stance is more reasonable. He came to a halt or he took up his stand before the woman, like Nebuchadnezzar, the king of Babylon, who tried to swallow up Jerusalem; Jer 51:34. The same metaphor of devouring occurs in 1QpHab 3:11 where the Kittim (Romans) attempt to devour the people, and in 11:5–6 where the wicked priest persecutes the Teacher of Righteousness, "swallowing him up in the anger of his fury in the place of exile." In Hebrew "swallowing up" means to kill or to do away with. Thus our dragon is portrayed as acting in two dimensions, the heavenly and the earthly; supernatural evil mingles with human evil and supernatural good with human good.

The woman gives birth to "a son, a man"; vs. 5. The phrase is a peculiar one and although it may sound redundant it probably stresses the "manliness" of the son, his characteristics as a warrior, which may be confirmed by Ps 2:7. Ps 2 itself refers to birth, even though this is meant in a metaphysical sense: "you [the king] are my son, today have I begotten you" (RSV). The psalm is a messianic hymn; however, the Messiah is not mentioned in this part of our text. The child is caught up to God and to his throne. The verb harpazō, "snatch," is never used of the ascension of Christ, although anabainō, "ascend," used of the two witnesses in 11:12, does have this connotation, and is used in relationship to the ascension of Jesus. But in our present text there seems to be no Christological reference. In the LXX and the NT harpazō means to take away by force, usually with the implication that resistance is impossible. However, there is also a religious use, e.g. Acts 8:39 where Philip is snatched up by the Spirit of the Lord; II Cor 12:2–4 where the man is caught up to paradise; I Thess 4:17 where those who are alive on earth are caught up to meet Christ in the air. The verb occurs in a similar sense in Apocalypse of Moses 37, Apocalypse of Ezra 5:2.

In Rev 12 there is no explicit reference to the death of the child, and in the light of the texts cited above, one might suggest that here we are given another characteristic of the son-warrior, namely, that he enjoys mystical experiences. The last phrase "to his throne" suggests the vision of the chariot or the *merkabah*. According to this interpretation he would have privileges similar to those of Moses, who spoke to God face to face, Elijah, Isaiah (Isa 6), Ezekiel (Ezek 1, 10), and Daniel (Dan 7). This interpretation would also intimate that he, like his community, bears the characteristics of a prophet. Spiritually precocious infants were not unknown in Jewish tradition; cf. the birth of Noah referred to in 1QGen^apoc 6–15. But the possibility of the child being taken from the earth must not be precluded.

Rev 12:6, which expresses some of the thought of 12:14, is suspect because of the sudden changes in tense. The woman fled into the wilderness (aorist) where she has (present tense) a place, and then a new subject seems to be introduced, "that they might feed her" (*trephōsin*, third person plural present subjunctive). It is logical to omit vs. 6 and proceed directly from vs. 5 to vs. 14; vss. 7–13 should also be omitted as coming from a different source (see below, p. 205).

The woman is given the wings of the great eagle in order to fly into the desert—with or without the child, we are not told. "The" (note the definite article) protecting eagle stands in contrast to the one which gave vent to the three-fold woe in 8:13. Our writer is probably resuming the Exodus motif; the eagle is the symbol of God's providence in Exod 19:4, Deut 32:10–12, in which the wings of the eagle are explicitly mentioned. The Palestinian Targum to Deut 32:10–12 enlarges on this metaphor (Etheridge):

> As an eagle stirreth up and careth for his nest, and hovereth over his young, so did His Shekinah stir up the tents of Israel, and the shadow of His Shekinah overspread them; and as an eagle outstretches his wings over his young ones, beareth them and carrieth them upon his wings, so bare He them and carried them, and made them dwell upon the strong places of the land of Israel. The Word of the Lord made them to dwell in His land, nor suffered any among them to be followers of strange worship.

He enables her, like the children of Israel, to reach the desert, which in both the OT and the NT represents a place of provisional safety, of discipline, of waiting for the promises of God. It was thus in the Exodus period for the forty years before the Israelites entered the promised land; cf. Deut 8:2–10. Twice Elijah withdrew to the desert; I Kings 17:2–3, 19:3–4. Yahweh lured his bride into the desert; Hosea 2:14. Isaiah commanded a highway to be made for the Lord there; Isa 40:3. It is possible also that the author is influenced by the Song of Songs; in this work Solomon's litter and the bride are said to come from the desert (3:6–8, 8:5). In Rev 12 the woman flees to the desert.

Nearer the time of Revelation, Mattathias and his followers went out into the desert: "Then many who were seeking righteousness and justice went down to the wilderness to dwell there, they, their sons, their wives, and their cattle, because evils pressed heavily upon them" (I Macc 2:29–30, RSV). The community at Qumran prepared to conduct themselves in the same way (1QS 8:12–16, D-S):

And when these things come to pass for the community in Israel at these appointed times, they shall be separated from the midst of the habitation of the perverse men to go into the desert to prepare the way of 'Him': as it is written, *in the wilderness prepare the way of . . . Make straight in the desert a highway for our God.* This (way) is the study of the Law which He has promulgated by the hand of Moses, that they may act according to all that is revealed, season by season, and according to that which the Prophets have revealed by His holy spirit.

It is in the wilderness that the Baptist prepared himself and the people for the Coming One; Luke 1:80, 3:2. Here God had prepared a place for the woman.

"Prepare," Gr. *hetoimazō* (vs. 6), has a religious significance in the LXX and in the NT. There are four passages in which "prepare" is used with the word "place," Gr. *topos*. David prepared a place for the ark (I Chron 15:1, 3, 12); Solomon built the temple of the Lord in the place which David had prepared (II Chron 3:1); Christ speaks of a place that he will prepare (John 14:2–3); and in our passage (Rev 12:6, 14) "prepare" appears to have an eschatological significance.

"To nourish," Gr. *trephōsin*, also seems to have a religious connotation, similar to God's nourishing Israel with manna in the desert, or his care of Elijah in e.g. I Kings 17:4, 19:5, 7. A similar thought is found in CDC 1:7–9, D-S, which speaks of a remnant in the time of the Babylonian captivity:

> He (God) visited them, and caused a root of planting
> to spring from Israel and Aaron to possess His land
> and to grow fat on the good things of His earth.

The woman is nourished for "a time and times and half a time" (vs. 14) or "one thousand two hundred and sixty days" (vs. 6), perhaps meaning until the end of the persecution (but cf. vs. 14 and fourth NOTE). It is a time of trial which comes before the final commencement of the kingdom of God. It also represents the opposite of eternity. But it may, in addition, be a messianic number. The woman's stay in the desert is characterized both by trials and favors from God, just as the journey of the Israelites was.

When our author says that the woman is nourished "before" (Gr. *apo prosopou,* "in the presence of") the serpent, he may mean either "in the presence of" or "because of"; cf. II Thess 1:9, Rev 6:16, 20:11. The meaning is obscure. The serpent, who seems now to be interchangeable with the dragon, attempts to drown the woman with a flood of water. Moulton and Milligan, *Vocabulary,* point out that the word "swept away" (Gr. *potamophorē-tos,* implying the action of a river or a stream) was not coined by "John" but occurs as early as 110 B.C. The word is a combination of "river," *potamos* and "carry," *pherō,* and, although it is found nowhere else in Scripture, the papyri bear witness to the sense of "swept away by the river" or "flood." A proposal for the lease of land and property which dates from A.D. 78 contains this clause (italics mine): "if any part of the land becomes under water or is *carried away by the river* (*potamophorētos*) or covered by sand . . . ," Grenfell and Hunt, *The Amherst Papyri,* 2, No. 85, London, 1901. Further, in a second century A.D. papyrus, in which is found a land survey list, the word occurs four times with the same meaning (Grenfell and Hunt, "Gebtunis," *Papyri*, 2, No. 610 [1907]). The oldest papyrus is from Egypt and shows the frequent use of the word in that country (see Le Frois, p. 159).

From this literal sense of the word arises the metaphorical meaning; it becomes the symbol of great dangers, of foreign invasion or persecution. Floods of water indicate destruction in Pss 32:6, 69:1–2, 124:2–5, Nahum 1:8. In Isa 8:5–8, the waters of the river is a metaphor for the king of Assyria and all his glory which will overwhelm Judah. Probably the same metaphor occurs in Isa 52:2; at least, it is so interpreted in the Targum of Isaiah (Stenning):

At the first when ye passed through the Red Sea my Memra was your support, Pharaoh and the Egyptians who were as numerous as the waters of the river prevailed not against you; also the second time, when ye shall go among the nations that are as strong as fire, they shall not prevail against you; neither shall the kingdoms which are as powerful as the flame destroy you.

Stanislaus Giet, *L'Apocalypse et l'Histoire*, p. 111, suggests that the river may symbolize either the nations which come to Jerusalem, or the soldiers who besiege it, or those who pass through Perea. But it may also represent falsehood. In CDC 1:14–15 one reads: ". . . when the Man of Mockery arose who by his preaching let flow over Israel the waters of falsehood and led them astray in the roadless desert . . ." (D-S). Revelation uses fire as an agent for destruction from God but not from the evil powers: water is so used. The earth came to the help of the woman and swallowed the water from the dragon. The image may have arisen from purely natural phenomena, e.g. in Asia streams disappear into the earth. Ramsay refers to Herodotus vii 30, who mentions that the Lycus flowed underground near Colossae; Strabo and Pliny confirm this (W. M. Ramsay, *The Cities and Bishoprics of Phrygia*, I, 210–11). The Chrysorrhoas is said to bury itself in the plain between Hierapolis and Laodicea (ibid., II, 82, n. 1). Moreover, during heavy rainfalls the caves in the desert of Judea are filled with water—the water literally swallowed up by the earth. On the other hand, the caves could provide protection from the "flood" of persecution. Archaeological remains witness to habitation of the caves, probably during persecution; cf. Isa 2:19, which mentions men entering the holes of the earth, the caves of the rock. But Rev 12 speaks of the earth swallowing the river, not the woman, and our author may have been influenced by Num 16, which refers to Korah, Dathan, and Abiram, who questioned the authority of Moses and whom the Lord punished by allowing the earth to open and swallow them alive (vss. 30–35). Our dragon may stand in a position similar to that of these men in that he embodies those who questioned the lawful authority of Israel. There seems to be a deliberate play on the idea of the "mouth" of the dragon producing the water and the "mouth" of the earth swallowing it. In Scripture "mouth" is used of the organ of eating and speech, the mouth of God and the opening of a well, cave, abyss, Sheol, and a sack.

More light is thrown on Rev 12 by 1QH 3, which may indicate further that the woman is indeed the faithful remnant (portrayed as the inner court in Jerusalem in ch. 11) now fleeing to the desert in the face of opponents. 1QH 3, portrays suffering, probably of the Qumran community, and uses the image of two women in childbirth. The first woman brings forth her firstborn, who is a man child, a marvelous counselor who will deliver "every man from the billows" (D-S). His birth takes place in the face of death and suffering. Standing in antithesis to this woman is one who was "big with the Asp" and with whom are associated the sufferings of the wise, who are compared to sailors in a storm. She "who is big with the Asp" (D-S) appears to signify the unrighteous community, the sons of perversity or of the pit. The pregnancies are of course metaphorical; the births occurred "amid the throes of death . . . amid pangs of hell . . ." (1QH 3:8–9, D-S, taken from II Sam 22:4–6), expressing the lethal danger brought by persecution. The good woman is a symbol for Zion or Israel or the congregation of the just. When "I" is used it appears to represent the community or, some suggest, the Teacher of Righteousness. As Feuillet points out, 1QH 3 is similar to Rev 12, which speaks of three figures: the woman, the son, and the dragon. The three mentioned in 1QH 3 are the woman with child, the viper or asp, and the child himself. The word for viper occurs thrice in the OT (Isa 30:6, 59:5, Job 20:16), but doubtless the hymn alludes to Gen 3; cf. Rev 12:9, "the ancient serpent, who is called Devil and Satan."

In 1QH 3 the Messiah is born through terrible pain (see esp. 1QH 3:10–12 and Rev 12:2). He is referred to as "man child" or "warrior," Heb. *gbr;* cf. Rev 12:5. Robert G. Boling, in *Judges,* AB, vol. 6A (1975), defines *gbr* as "aristocrat," someone wealthy and influential enough to muster, support, and command an armed force; hence "warrior."

Much discussion has taken place concerning this child. Some see "wonderful counselor" (vs. 10) as a title for God. Thus, the author of 1QH 3 would have changed the text of Isa 9:6, and vs. 10 would refer to God who counsels with His power and saves men from the waves. Others identify the wonderful counselor with the Messiah. He is the firstborn and is designated as a man of distress, which may be an allusion to the Suffering Servant in Isa 53 (Chamberlain, 180–82). He is delivered from the waves of death. Dupont-Sommer supports this idea and asserts that, if this is so, the Jewish sect of Qumran one hundred years before Christianity would have integrated the representation of the mother with the idea of the man overcome with sorrow. In other words, they would have applied to the mother of the Messiah the famous oracles of Second Isaiah on the Suffering Servant, notably Isa 52:13 – 53:12.

Another point of contact between Rev 12 and 1QH 3 is the metaphor of water as trial and tribulation (a metaphor from the Psalms). 1QH 3 describes the suffering of "his" soul "like a ship in the depths of the s[ea]" (vs. 6), and mentions "billows" (vss. 8, 9, 10, 12). The sufferings (of the righteous) are "like them that sail the seas, terrified because of the roaring of the waters" (vss. 14 ff.), etc. The psalmist of 1QH 3 praises God for his redemption from the pit (vs. 19) and "the nets of the wretched upon the face of the waters" (vs. 26). He is brought "to everlasting heights" and "an infinite plain." He enjoys communion with the Sons of Heaven (vs. 22). The male child in Rev 12 is "snatched up to God and His throne" (vs. 5) and his mother rescued from the water issuing from the mouth of the dragon (D-S). If both 1QH 3 and Rev 12 contain an allusion to Gen 3, then the Asp=the dragon=the serpent=Satan and the man child=the seed of the woman (Gen 3:15) and there is enmity between them. Curiously enough the man mentioned in 1QH 3:9–10 is not mentioned again in the hymn, just as in Rev 12 the child does not reappear (unless he is to be identified with the Anointed One in the interpolated passage in 12:7–13).

In the light of the OT texts and 1QH 3 it seems reasonable for the woman to be the faithful priestly and prophetic community, the child a prominent leader, and the dragon Satan. Rev 17–18 mention the harlot, which may be another version of the mother of the asp, the faithless community allied with the fallen angel.

Rev 12 records that the dragon went to attack the rest of the seed of the woman. One may be surprised at the distinction between the woman and the members of the group, if she represents the group. But the same distinction between the ideal Jerusalem or Israel and the Israelites occurs in prophetical texts. Le Frois, pp. 169 ff., observes that the word "seed" devolves around the prophecy in Gen 3:15 and is a word commonly used in the covenant prophecies to Abraham and David (II Sam 7:12–14). Apart from the general meaning it refers to a small group of survivors, i.e. the remnant from which a new generation arises. He points out that "the rest," Gr. *loipoi,* may merely mean the rest or the remnant in a special sense as in IV Ezra 6:25, 7:28, 12:34, 13:24, 25, 48, II Baruch 29:4, 40:2, I Enoch 83:8.

Rev 12 ends by representing the dragon coming to a halt by the seashore. Allo (see *Saint Jean, L'Apocalypse*) says that the dragon was standing on the sea, i.e. the west representing the great pagan forces, but if the verse is to be closely associated with 13:1, it looks as if he is calling upon or waiting for his two colleagues, the sea monster and the earth monster, who will assist him in the persecutions. See NOTE on 12:18.

Vss. 6–13 seem to come from another source and to interrupt the flow of thought between 12:5 and 12:14. They seem, indeed, to form an appendix to ch. 12. Neither the war in heaven or Michael are mentioned elsewhere in our text; in fact in the NT Michael occurs only here and in Jude 9. Nevertheless, Michael's "war-role" is traditional. Dan 10:13, 21, 12:1 present Michael as helping Daniel against the kingdom of Persia and then assisting Israel. He is styled "your prince." In 1QM Michael (Prince of Lights) is Israel's chief helper against Belial (1QM 13:10, 17:6–8, CDC 5:18–19). He is regarded as the angel of truth and justice (1QM 13:10, 1QS 3:20) and has an office which is higher than that of the other angels (1QM 17:7). Pseudepigraphical sources show his being prince of Israel, set over "the best part of mankind" (I Enoch 20:5); his taking vengeance against Israel's enemies; being at the head of the angels and holding the kingdom of heaven; offering sacrifice in the fourth heaven and revealing to Enoch the secrets of mercy and justice; etc. (see Yadin, *Scroll of the War,* p. 236). In *Pirke,* Rabbi Eliezer, 26, when Sammael, the wicked angel was thrown from heaven, he tried to take hold of the wings of Michael and bring him down with him but Michael was saved by God. Other rabbinic sources associate the liberation of Israel from Edom or Rome with Michael.

According to Jewish sources there are two conflicting traditions concerning Satan's residence in heaven. In one he has a place, e.g. Zech 3:1–2, I Enoch 40:7, II Enoch 7:1, Ascension of Isaiah 7:9 ff. In the other he was hurled down from heaven because he tried to place his throne beside God's (II Enoch 29:4–5; Book of Adam and Eve 9:1). The appendix to Rev 12 appears to follow the last tradition. In vs. 9 for the first time the dragon is identified with the ancient serpent, who is called Devil and Satan. In this way the author introduces the theme of Gen 3, but his text shows that, instead of succumbing to the serpent, the woman by the power of God prevails over him. The dragon-serpent was cast down to the earth. Ordinarily "to cast," Gr. *ballō*, means to place or cast down with vigor, but there is also a judicial aspect to the word; it denotes judicial punishment (e.g. Matt 3:10, 5:29, 13:41–42; Rev 2:10) or expulsion from the community (Matt 13:48, John 15:6; cf. the ruler of this world being cast out in John 12:31).

As Le Frois, *Woman Clothed with the Sun*, p. 157, asserts, "in the Apocalypse the judiciary nature of chapters 4–20 leads one to expect the same judiciary meaning for the word. But this is evident in its occurrence in the figure of the vintage (14:19); the figure of the millstone thrown into the sea; Babylon sentenced (18:21); the binding of the dragon who is then thrown into a pit (20:3)." The legal sense is continued in the use of the word "accuser," Gr. *katēgōr*, of "our brothers" in vs. 10; this word is used of one who accuses another before the judgment seat.

Many scholars argue that vss. 10 and 11, but especially vs. 11, did not originally belong to the text. They introduce features such as the Anointed One, the Lamb, and the martyrs, which are alien to our present context. The text should probably proceed directly from vs. 10a, "and I heard a loud voice in heaven, saying, to vs. 12 "On account of this rejoice, heavens. . . ." Vs. 10 may have been introduced because of another tradition concerning Michael: "Michael and Sammael are like the advocate and the accuser who stand before the court . . . Satan accuses but Michael upholds the merits of Israel" (cf. *Exod R* 17:5, *Lev R* 21:4, Deut 11:10). Moreover, vss. 10–11 give the impression that the time of martyrdom is over and the trials of the Anointed One are complete, but this does not happen until later in this apocalypse.

In order to keep the text in its present traditional order we must see vss. 10–11 as proleptic. One of the arguments in favor of this being so may be found in the reported visions or portents of battles in the sky recorded in I and II Maccabees, Josephus, and the Sibylline Oracles. In II Macc 5:1–4 (RSV) one reads:

About this time Antiochus made his second invasion of Egypt. And it happened that over all the city, for almost forty days, there appeared gold-clad horsemen charging through the air, in companies fully armed with lances and drawn swords—troops of horsemen drawn up, attacks and counterattacks made on this side and on that, brandishing of shields, massing of spears, hurling of missiles, the flash of golden trappings, and armor of all sorts. Therefore all men prayed that the apparition might prove to have been a good omen.

In Josephus a similar sign is reported among other portents and visions and omens before the fall of Jerusalem in A.D. 70: "For before sunset throughout all parts of the country chariots were seen in the air and all the battalions hurtling through the clouds and encompassing the cities" (*War* 6.229).

The vision in ch. 12 bears similarities to these two passages. However, the joy of the song is immediately diminished by the expression of woe with regard to the earth and the sea because Satan stands, watching, between them.

Note: the present writer is not convinced about the Marian interpretation of Rev 12, but see Plate D for Mary portrayed in Aaronic high-priestly robes.

BIBLIOGRAPHY

Betz, O. "Das Volk seiner Kraft: zur Auslegung der Qumran-hodajah iii 1–18," NTS 5 (1958/59), 67–75.

———. "Die Geburt der Gemeinde durch den Lehrer," NTS 3 (1956/57), 314–26.

Bissonette, G. "The Twelfth Chapter of the Apocalypse and Our Lady's Assumption," *Marian Studies* 2 (1951), 170–92.

Bonnefoy, J. B. "Les Interpretations Ecclesioliques de Ch. 12 de l'Apocalypse," *Marianum* 9 (1947), 208–22.

Braun, F. M. "La Femme et Le Dragon," *Bible et Vie Chretienne* 7 (1954), 63–72.

———. "La Femme Vetue de Soleil," *Revue Thomiste* 35 (1955), 639–69.

Bruns, J. E. "The Contrasted Women of Apocalypse 12 and 17," CBQ 26 (1964), 459–63.

Carrington, P. *The Meaning of Revelation.*

Carter, F. *The Dragon of Revelation* (London: Harmsworth, 1932), pp. 96 ff.

Cerfaux, L. "La Vision de la Femme et du Dragon de l'Apocalypse en Relation avec le Protevangile," *Ephemerides Theologicae Lovanienses* 31 (1956), 21–33.

Chamberlain, J. V. "Further Elucidation of a Messianic Thanksgiving Psalm from Qumran," *Journal of Near Eastern Studies* 14 (1955), 180 ff.

Crossan, D. M. "Mary's Virginity in John (Apoc. 12): An Exegetical Study," *Marianum* 19 (1957), 115–26.

Dubarle, A. M. "La Femme Couronée d'Etoiles (Apoc. 12)," *Festschrift* for André Robert. Mélanges Biblique (Paris, 1957), pp. 512–18.

Dupont-Sommer, A. "La Mère du Messie et la Mère de l'Aspic dans une Hymne de Qumrân," *Revue de l'Histoire des Religions* 147 (1955), 174–88.

Feuillet, A. "The Mother of the Messiah," in *Johannine Studies.*

Hart, H. St. John. "The Crown of Thorns in John 19, 2–5," *Journal of Theological Studies* 3 (1952), 66–75.

Johnson, S. E. "Notes and Comments: Apoc. 12," *Anglican Theological Review* 21 (1939), 314–15.

Le Frois, B. J. *The Woman Clothed with the Sun.*

———. "The Mary-Church Relationship in the Apocalypse," *Marian Studies* 9 (1958), 79–106.

Michl, J. "Die Deutung der Apokalyptischen frau in der Gegenwart (Apk. 12)," *Biblische Zeitschrift* 3 (1959), 301–10.

Murphy, R. E. "An Allusion to Mary in the Apoc. 12," TS 10 (1949), 565–73.

Ramsay, W. M. *The Cities and Bishoprics of Phrygia,* 1895.

Rigaux, P. "La Femme et Son Lignage dans Genesis 3:14–15," RB 61 (1954), 321–48.

Unger, D. J. "Cardinal Newman and Apocalypse 12," TS 11 (1950), 356–67.

———. "Did St. John See the Virgin Mary in Glory? (Apoc. 12, 1)," CBQ 11 (1949), 249–62, 392–405; 12 (1950), 75–83, 155–61, 292–300, 405–15.

X. THE DRAGON'S ALLIES SEEK TO
DELUDE THE FAITHFUL
(13:1–18)

13 1 And I saw a monster ascending from the sea; he had ten horns and seven heads, and ten diadems upon his heads, also blasphemous names upon his heads. 2 And the monster which I saw was like a leopard, and its feet like a bear, and its mouth like a lion's mouth. And the dragon gave to him his power and his throne and great authority. 3 And one of his heads seemed to have a lethal wound and the lethal wound was healed. And the whole world followed after the monster with admiration, 4 and they worshiped the dragon, because he gave authority to the monster; also they worshiped the monster, saying, "Who is like the monster?" and, "Who can fight against him?"

5 And the monster was given a mouth which spoke haughty and blasphemous words, and authority was given to him to exercise for forty-two months. 6 And he opened his mouth to blaspheme against God, blaspheming His name and His dwelling, those who dwell in heaven. 7 And he was allowed to fight against the holy ones and to conquer them, and he was allowed to have authority over every tribe and people and tongue and nation. 8 And all the earth-dwellers will worship him, those whose name is not written in the book of life of the Lamb which was slain from the beginning of the world. 9 If anyone has an ear, let him hear.

10 If anyone goes to captivity, to captivity he goes; if anyone kills with the sword, he must be killed by the sword. Hence the endurance and faith of the holy ones.

11 And I saw another monster ascending from the land, and he had two horns like a lamb, and he spoke like a dragon. 12 And he exercises all the authority of the first monster on his behalf. And he makes the earth and its inhabitants worship the first monster, whose lethal wound is healed. 13 And he performs great signs, so that he even makes fire from heaven fall on the earth in the sight of men. 14 And he deceives the earth-dwellers through the signs which he is allowed to perform in the presence of the monster; he tells the earth-dwellers to make an image for the monster, who was wounded by the

sword and revived. 15 And he was allowed to put breath into the image of the monster, so that the image of the monster might even speak, and to cause those who would not worship the image of the monster to be killed. 16 And he made everyone, small and great, rich and poor, free and slave, be marked on their right hand or their forehead 17 so that no one could buy or sell if he did not have the mark, the name, of the monster or the number of its name. 18 This requires special insight. Let the person with understanding calculate the number of the monster; for it is the number of a human being. And its number is six hundred and sixty-six.

NOTES

13:1. *monster.* Gunkel, cited by Charles, suggested that Behemoth and Leviathan correspond to Tiamat (the abyss) and Kingu (the serpent) of Babylonian mythology. Cf. the destruction of these animals in Hab 2:15. Both Job 41:18 and rabbinic literature (*Baba Bathra* 74a) mention the great illuminating power of the eyes of the Leviathan but our author is silent on the matter, perhaps because eyes are associated with the living creatures and the Lamb (5:6). The seven eyes of the Lamb are identified with the seven spirits of God sent out into the world.

sea. Ch. 12 left the dragon on the sand of the sea or the sea shore. Did the dragon deliberately summon the monsters to assist him in fighting against the woman and her offspring? Cf. Rom 10:7. The sea can also be the place whence enemies are thrown. Wisdom guided Israel through the Reed Sea but drowned their enemies and cast them up "from the depth of the Sea" (Wisd Sol 10:19). But contrast IV Ezra 13 where one like a son of man comes from the sea.

horns . . . heads. Both the dragon in ch. 12 and the sea beast here have seven heads and ten horns but in the description of the sea beast the order is reversed. The horns are not necessarily on the head but may be on the back as in illustration 12. On the horns are ten diadems, although we would expect these diadems to be on the heads; perhaps room has to be left on the heads for the blasphemous names. The horns are explained in 17:12.

blasphemous names. In II Thess 2:4–12 the Antichrist also has divine pretensions. Minear, p. 94, says, "the dramatic procession of the beasts indicates a progressive delegation of power, and a progressive accentuation of deception and temptation. But in essence each temptation is the same; each is a call for the alertness and endurance of the saints (xiii 10; xiv 12)." Indeed, the dragon and his companions form a kind of satanic trinity. Further the dragon has fallen down from heaven, one dimension; one beast rises from the sea, another dimension, and another comes from the land, a third dimension.

In P47 C P 1, 1006, 2059s, 2329 al TR "names" appears in the singular.

2. Jesus indicated no hostility towards the state (Matt 22:15–22, Mark 12:

13–17, Luke 20:20–26) and Paul not only prided himself on his Roman citizenship (Acts 21:38, 22:25–28) but was also protected by the state (Acts 16; 18; 19; 21; 22). The idea of reverence for authority is found in the Pastoral Epistles (I Tim 2:1), I Peter 2:13–17, and II Thess 2:6–7, which last text may suggest that the Roman empire is the power which restrains the chaos of the end. Quite a different attitude is expressed in Revelation.

lion's mouth. Cf. II Tim 4:17, I Peter 2:3. ℵ 69, 1611 pc read plural possessive, "lions'."

3. *lethal wound.* According to Suetonius, Caligula had a dangerous illness (*Caligula* 14; cf. Dio Cassius 59.8, Philo *Legatio ad Gaium* 14–21) and people wondered at his recovery. However, the favorite candidate for the "healed wound" is Nero. Tacitus tells us that a snake was found in Nero's cradle when he was a baby (*Annals* 11.11).

Nero became very unpopular towards the end of his reign, and in A.D. 67 and 68 there were open revolts against his authority in Gaul and Spain. At length he was repudiated by the Praetorian Guard and by the Senate. The Senate proclaimed him a public enemy and approved Galba as his successor. They cut Nero's throat with a sword on June 9, 68. The rumor spread that he had not died but had escaped to Parthia and would regain his throne. The rumor was especially popular in the eastern provinces, and at one time people expected him to return with an enormous army. Sibylline Oracles 4:119–27 (APCh, II, 395) reads:

And then from Italy a great king, like a fugitive slave, shall flee unseen, unheard of, over the passage of the Euphrates; when he shall dare even the hateful pollution of a mother's murder, and many other things beside, venturing so far with wicked hand. And many for the throne of Rome shall dye the ground with their blood, when he has run away beyond the Parthian land. And a Roman leader (Titus) shall come to Syria, who shall burn down Solyma's temple with fire, and therewith slay many men, and shall waste the great land of the Jews with its broad way.

As early as A.D. 69 a pretender arose who claimed to be Nero (Tacitus *Histories* 2.8, 9). He was either a slave from Pontus or a freedman from Italy, a mad musician like Nero; he gathered a following of doubtful characters and even seduced soldiers. However, he was pursued by Galba's officers and was killed. In 88 another pretender arose and finally still another, this time in Parthia. He nearly launched Parthian armies against Rome (Tacitus *Histories* 2.1, Suetonius *Nero* 51).

If Vespasian's candidacy is considered, one may compare Suetonius' words concerning his banishment by Nero, "*Etiamque extrema metuenti* (fearing even death)" (*Vespasian* 4). For the cessation of anarchy at the accession of Vespasian cf. IV Ezra 12:18, Suetonius *Vespasian* 1, Josephus *War* 4.655, 7.63–74. Caird observes "only with the accession of Vespasian did the monster come to life again" (p. 164).

followed after. Lit. "admired after."

4. *"Who is like . . . ?"* The phrase is reminiscent of Job 41:33–34 saying that the Leviathan has no equal or like on earth, and Ps 35:10 asking rhetorically

who is like the Lord. If Ps 35 is in our author's mind, then there is a deliberate comparison between the power of the Lord and that allegedly bestowed on the beast by the dragon. But the two questions in this verse, "Who is like the monster?" and "Who can fight against him?" may also allude to Michael whose name means "Who is like God" and who is leader of the angelic hosts fighting on behalf of God. The author introduced us to Michael in ch. 12.

5. *was given . . . haughty and blasphemous words, and authority.* Cf. I Macc 1:24. Note the passive "was given" or "allowed," that is, by the dragon with God's tolerance, for nothing can happen outside the divine plan. For the universal empire of the beast, cf. Mark 4:6 where Satan offers to Christ universal domination if he worships the tempter.

P **046, 051** 82, 1824, 2060 pm read the singular for "blasphemous words," and A 2059, 2329 al read *blasphēma.* ℵ 792, 2042 omit "authority."

6. *His dwelling, those who dwell in heaven.* In P **046*** 1, 2059 al lat arm 1r TR "and" appears where this translation has a comma. The omission of "and" identifies the dwelling of God with the people, who dwell in heaven, or a temple of living men as at Qumran (1QS 8:5–9) and in the teaching of Paul, e.g. I Cor 3:9, 16. However, if "and" is to be retained, the first blasphemy would be against the name of God, the second against the temple or heaven, and the third against the angels or martyrs. The Qumran community stressed the evil of blasphemy, by stating e.g. that the spirit of perversity brought in its train numerous vices among which were "a blaspheming tongue, blindness of eye and hardness of ear, stiffness of neck and heaviness of heart causing a man to walk in all the ways of darkness, and malignant cunning" (1QS 4:11, D-S). Those who followed Belial or Satan were said to have defiled their holy spirit and "with a blaspheming tongue have opened their mouths against the precepts of the Covenant of God, saying, They are not true!" (CDC 5:11–12, D-S). The Qumran community believed rebellion caused sacrilegious speech.

In P[47] g "those who dwell" is omitted, rendering this phrase "his dwelling in heaven."

7. *he was allowed to fight against the holy ones and to conquer them.* This phrase is borrowed from Dan 7:21 but is omitted in P[47] A C P 1* 2059s al sa arm[pt] lr; R[m]. Such universal authority mimics that of the Lamb. All those who come to the monster are those who are "not written in the book of life of the Lamb which was slain from the beginning of the world" (vs. 8, see NOTE).

and people. Omitted in P[47] 1, 1006, 2059s al TR.

8. *earth-dwellers.* Note the contrast with "those who dwell in heaven" (vs. 6). "Earth-dwellers" worshiped the monster in the person of the emperors.

those whose name. P[47] * 1006, 1611, 2060, 2329 al read "their name."

whose. Gr. *tou onoma autou,* the genitive singular. In ℵ P **046 051** 182, 1006, 1611, 2059s, 2329 pl lat TR this pronoun appears as *autōn,* the genitive plural.

name. Pluralized in P[47] ℵ P 1, 1006, 2329 al TR.

the book of life of the Lamb which was slain from the beginning of the world. Predestination is forcibly expressed, suggesting perhaps that the Lamb was redeemer from the first just as Moses was said to be mediator from the foundation of the world (Assumption of Moses 1:14). Vs. 8 is cumbersome, and "the Lamb which was slain" might have been a gloss. It does not appear in the parallel verse 17:8, and only approximates 21:27 which mentions the Lamb's book of life.

10. Kiddle, p. 248, sees this verse as the focal point of the whole chapter. The patience and faith of the saints is necessary for the implementation of God's plan through the monsters' maneuvers. Vos, pp. 104–9, after a discussion of the textual difficulties in vs. 10 and its affinity with Matt 26:52b, suggests that the second part of the verse, which unlike the first part is not parallel to Jer 15:2, expresses the idea of the *ius talionis,* "law of retaliation": "if anyone kills with the sword, he must be killed with the sword." He thinks there is an affinity between the saying of Jesus in Matt 26:52 and Rev 13:10, for the thought of both passages is identical even though the wording is not the same. He does, however, find some linguistic affinity between them in that both contain the phrase *en machairēi,* "with a sword"; Jer 15:2 contains a different phrase, *eis machairan,* "to a sword."

If anyone goes to captivity, to captivity he goes. In 172, 424 pc g vg[s,cl] sy sa Ir[lat] Prim, another "he goes" is added; the reading is, "If anyone goes to captivity, he goes to captivity he goes." P[47] א C P **046,** 205, 1006, 1611, 1834 omit the second "captivity"; the reading in these manuscripts is, "If anyone goes to captivity, he goes."

11. *the land.* This could mean Asia in contrast to the west, represented by the sea (Rome came over the sea from the west). However, it is more likely that "the land" means Palestine, since Heb. *aretz,* "land," is synonymous with Israel in Jewish writings.

like a lamb. Note the absence of the definite article, indicating that the second beast is a parody not of the Lamb but of the two witnesses. Cf. Matt 24:24, which predicts the rise of false Christs and false prophets who will try to seduce the populace with great signs and wonders; cf. Rev 13:13.

he spoke. The reading in P[47] is "he speaks."

like a dragon. The phrase is difficult. Perhaps the definite article should be added before "dragon." Then it might indicate the deceitful character of the second beast, like the serpent in Genesis. Charles, *Revelation,* p. 358, suggests it might go back to the Hebrew original "and the beast had two horns like a lamb . . . but he was a destroyer . . . like the dragon." Then one would have the same antithesis as in Matt 7:15 (sheep and ravening wolf).

12. *on his behalf.* Or the phrase could be translated "in his (its) presence."

13. *great signs.* Cf. II Thess 2:9–10 and for sorcery Acts 13:6–12, 16:16, 19:13–20. Didache 16:3–4 predicts these, too:

for in the last days the false prophets and the corrupters shall be multiplied, and the sheep shall be turned into wolves, and love shall change to hate; for as lawlessness increaseth they shall hate one another and persecute and betray, and then shall appear the deceiver of the world as a Son of God, and shall do signs and wonders and the earth shall be given over into his hands and he shall commit iniquities which have never been since the world began.

The second monster might also be the "religious antichrist" including false cults and false philosophers. He is subordinate to and in the service of the first monster, the political antichrist. For the concept of plural antichrists, see I John 2:18 and contrast the two messiahs at Qumran (*La règle annexe* 2:11–22).

14. *the earth-dwellers*. **051** 82 al read "my earth-dwellers."

an image for the monster. The dative is used, not the genitive, "an image for the monster" rather than "of the monster." Emperor worship began as veneration of Roma (Rome) and at first was not imposed upon the people. It was natural for a pagan people who accepted polytheism to desire to worship the Caesars from whom so much peace and security arose under Roman rule. The cult was especially strong in Asia Minor. The first temple to the spirit of Rome was erected in Smyrna in 195 B.C. (Tacitus *Annals* 4.56). Asia had suffered much from avaricious Roman officials, but the emperor Augustus changed this and became something of a savior of the people, indeed of mankind. The first temple actually to be erected to the godhead of Caesar was at Pergamum and dates from 29 B.C. (Tacitus *Annals* 4.37). However, before the end of the first century all the cities mentioned in Revelation possessed such temples.

Augustus forbade emperor worship in Italy, and Tiberius continued this decree. The situation was altered with Caligula (Roman emperor from A.D. 37–41). He was both an epileptic and a madman, and it is significant that Suetonius (*Caligula* 22) in speaking of him says, "So much for Caligula as an emperor; we must now tell of his career as a *monster*" (italics mine). In *Caligula* 22 Suetonius elaborates. He ordered the heads of the statues of the gods from Greece to be removed and replaced with his own. He made the temple of Castor and Pollux a vestibule of his palace, and established a temple to his own godhead with a rich priesthood and a life-size statue of himself in gold. He talked to Jupiter Capitolinus, he invited the moon to his embraces, and he executed those who would not swear by his godhead. He even went so far as to try to place his image in the holy of holies in Jerusalem (*Ant.* 18.261–62). Although he collected an army and sent Petronius to enforce this order, the emperor died before it could be implemented.

Caligula is alone among the earlier emperors who aspired to be worshiped as a god. Nero was more desirous of flattery for his music, his acting, and his chariot racing, and although a temple to him was proposed, it was thought that divine honors should be withheld until after the death of an emperor (Tacitus *Annals* 15.74). The height of emperor worship was reached with Domitian, emperor A.D. 81–96, who invited his wife to the divine couch and allowed people to call him lord and god.

who was wounded. The neuter relative pronoun appears in ℵ 1, 82, 1006, 1611, 2059, 2329 pm TR, rendering this clause "which was wounded."

15. *he was allowed*. The feminine pronoun appears in A C R.

16. *he made everyone*. Here Caesar worship is not only tolerated but demanded. Caesar worship became the means of unifying the empire, but it was not exclusive; as long as one acknowledged Caesar one could also revere other gods. A man paid his respects to the godhead of Caesar and received certification. One document from A.D. 250 runs,

to the commissioners of sacrifices from Aurelia Domos . . . daughter of Helena and wife of Aurelius . . . I have always been one to sacrifice to the gods, and now also in your presence, in accordance with the command, I have made sacrifice and libation and tasted the offering, and I request you to certify my statement. Farewell. Signed I, Aurelia Domos, have presented this declaration. I, Aurelius Irenaeus spoke for her, as she is illiterate. Attested Aurelius Sabinus Prytanis for your sacrificing dated the first year of the Emperor Caesar Gaius Messius Quintus Trajanus Decius Pius Felix Augustus Pauni 20" (P. Ryl. 12); A. and S. Hunt and D. C. Edgar, *Select Papyri*, 2 [Number 0319]; cited from Barclay, p. 262.

For further examples of certificates for sacrificing to the emperor see H. B. Workman, *Persecution in the Early Church,* p. 341 (P. Oxy. 658) and also Hunt and Edgar, *Select Papyri*, 2, pp. 352–55.

be marked. One example of marking persons is found in the defeat of the slaves under Nicias in the Sicily campaign. Some Athenians were captured and branded with the sign of a galloping horse (Plutarch *Nicias* 29). Ambrose says slaves were "inscribed with the seal of their master" (*On the Death of Valentinus* 15.8). Soldiers were also branded, and their marks were usually called stigmata. The mark was often on their hands. Deissmann (*Light from the Ancient East* [Tübingen, 1923], pp. 344–45) says that it was a custom to impress on deeds of sale and similar documents a stamp with the name of the emperor and the year of his reign, and that the stamp was called *charagma.* Such imperial stamps have been found dating back to A.D. 448. In the OT the Jews were forbidden to cut themselves, e.g. in Lev 19:28, 21:5, Deut 14:1. The Babylonian Talmud is even more scrupulous. *Megillah* 24b says "Whoever placed the tephillin on the brow or on their hand followed the practice of the minim (heretics)." In our present passage the marking of those who worshiped the beast is a blasphemous parody of the protective sealing of the faithful in Rev 7:1–3.

17. *buy or sell.* In the reign of Decius (Roman emperor A.D. 249–51) any man who did not possess the certificate of sacrifice to Caesar could not pursue ordinary trades but faced imprisonment, death, or banishment. For a reference similar to Rev 13:17 see I Macc 13:49, but the circumstances differ.

the mark, the name, of the monster. P[47] 1778 pc g vg[s,cl] TR read "the mark of the name of the monster"; "name" in these manuscripts is an alternative to, rather than the appositive of, "mark." Another variation occurs in C 2028 pc (vg[w]) sy lr: "the mark of the name of the monster." Still another is found in ℵ pc: "the mark of the monster or his name."

18. *number of a human being.* This may mean a number which is intelligible from a human point of view, that is, does not require supernatural wisdom to understand it (but cf. 21:17), or it may mean "of a certain individual." For gematria, a cryptogram giving the numerical value of the letters of a name, see *Yoma* 20a, *Nazir* 5a, *Sanhedrin* 22a. H. A. Sanders lists further solutions from patristic sources. Andreas of Caesarea (Migne, *Patrologia Graeca* [Paris, 1844–55], vol. 106) gives seven names: *Lampetis*, daughter of the Sun God; *Teitan*, Titan, one of the pagan gods associated with vengeance; *Palaibaskanos,*

Ancient Sorcerer; *Benedíktos,* Blue Bastard; *Kakos Odēgos,* Wicked Guide; *Alēthēs Blaberos,* Really Harmful; and *Amnos Adikos,* Unjust Lamb. Victorinus gives *Teitan,* Titan; *Diclux,* probably Double-Dealer; *Antenos,* Opponent; and *Genserikos.* The last one is Gothic, Genseric, the vandal king who conquered Rome in A.D. 455. *Diclux* is supposed to be the Latin counterpart of *Titan.* Bede has three names, all of which have been suggested before, and the Spanish monk Beatus has eight names of which *Damnatus* (Damned), *Antichristus* (Antichrist) and *Acxyme* (for *aichime* or *achine,* six hundred sixtysix) have not occurred before.

Sanders studied several manuscripts of Beatus and found one which appeared to be the parent of the Morgan Manuscript. On the basis of this and others he discovered that it was possible to reach a definite conclusion about the biblical text of Beatus. With regard to Rev 13 the text is given twice. Text I omits vss. 17–18, and text II all of vs. 18. Therefore, the number of the beast is missing in both texts. Yet it appears in the commentary, and the commentary closes with the passage very close to vs. 18: "This is wisdom; he who has understanding, let him count the number of the beast. For it is the number of a man, that is, of Christ whose name the beast takes for itself . . ." (Sanders, p. 98).

Similarly the anonymous commentator in Augustine omits the sentence concerning the number. In view of these findings it is probable that the old Latin text of North Africa omitted the number. Incidentally Beatus bears witness to the persistence of a rumor concerning the return of Nero: "Because the Jews crucified Christ and expect Nero, the antichrist, in the place of Christ; therefore will God send this one resurrected as king worthy of those worthy of him and as their christ such as the Jews have deserved" (Sanders, p. 99).

Sanders does not think that 666 can be identified easily with any of the Roman emperors. Marcus Aurelius is the only emperor who satisfies the numerical value 666. He ascended the throne thirty years before Irenaeus began to write so that this might account for the change from 616 to 666. McNeil suggests that the writer of Revelation does not necessarily suggest that the number of the beast conceals a man's name. 616 in Pythagorean language is the number of a triangle. Philo sees the number 10 as the sum of $1+2+3+4$ so that 10 equals 4. Van Der Bergh, "The Gnosis Combatted in the Apoc," ZNW 13 (1912), thinks that this gnostic thought may explain the number of the beast: 616 equals $1+2+3$ . . . $+36$. 36 is the number of a triangle. 36 equals $1+2+3$ . . . $+8$, that is to say, 666 equals 36 equals 8. The beast is the *ogdoas* who is *sophia* in the gnostic system. In Hebrew 8 is represented by *heth,* the initial letter of *Hokmah,* "wisdom." The prototype of the beast is then the heavenly mother goddess of Western Asia. "When, therefore, the seer writes 'here is wisdom necessary,' he cryptically supplies the very solution of the problem."

The number has also been used against the Catholic Church: *Italika Ekklesia* (Italian Church) of which Elliot remarks that "the name of no other national church would give the same result!"; *He Letana Basileia* (the Latin Kingdom) of which Clark observes, he has tried out more than four hundred other kingdoms without again finding the results of 666 which fits Rome; *Papeiskos* which is taken to mean pope. Roman Catholics have tried the same game suggesting: *Loutherana,* that is Luther; *Saxoneios,* which means Saxon, again representing Luther. Others have suggested *Maometis* which refers to Muhammad or *Nabonaparti* which refers to Napoleon or Hitler. Others have attempted solutions in Latin (but not all Latin letters have a numeral equivalent), e.g. the title of the pope *Vicarius Generalis Dei In Terris,* or they have tried *Diocles Augustus.* Deissmann (cited by Barclay) solicited the solution *Kaisar Theos.*

six hundred and sixty-six. C arm^pt, quidam apud lr; R^m read "six hundred and sixteen."

COMMENT

Ch. 12 showed the faithful community in the throes of messianic birth pangs and opposed by the dragon, who is Satan. It intimated that a new creation will begin with the conquering of the monster of chaos by Yahweh as in the first creation. Ch. 13 introduces another Jewish belief associated with the coming of the messianic era, namely, the activity of Leviathan and Behemoth. These creatures also resume the creation myth hinted at in ch. 12.

Leviathan and Behemoth are the names of gigantic beasts or monsters described in Job 40, 41. Pope (*Job,* AB, vol. 15, NOTES on 40:15a, 41:1) gives a fascinating discussion of these two creatures. He suggests that "the monstrous bullock of the Ugaritic myths and Behemoth are both connected with the Sumero-Akkadian 'bull of heaven' slain by Gilgamesh and Enkidu in the Gilgamesh Epic (J. B. Pritchard, *Ancient Near Eastern Texts Relating to the Old Testament,* 2d ed. [Princeton University Press, 1955], pp. 83–85)." Behemoth seems to be a plural of majesty (NOTE on Job 40:15a). The reference to the lotus, reeds, and willows in Job 40:21–22 seems to refer to the marine monster called Lotan in the Ugaritic myths; the goddess Anat slew this monster among others (NOTE on Job 41:1). Pope also draws attention to a Mesopotamian seal cylinder from Tell Asmar which shows a seven-headed dragon being killed by two divine heroes. Four heads are drooping and three are still erect. There is also a small plaque (J. B. Pritchard, *The Ancient Near East in Pictures* [Princeton University Press, 1954], p. 671) which depicts a god before a seven-headed monster from whose back flames arise (NOTE on Job 41:1).

Although these creatures are mythical, the crocodile or the hippopotamus may have provided the details for their description. Leviathan is the king of the water animals, and Behemoth is the king of the land animals. In later rabbinic literature Leviathan is thought to be female, Behemoth male. Both are regarded as unconquerable by man (Job 40:14, 17–26). In the description of Leviathan in Job 41 the text refers to its mighty jaws and tongue, thick skin, breath of fire, "eyelids like dawn," and its "heart hard as stone, hard as the nether millstone" (vs. 24). No human weapons prevail over it, and man "is laid low even at the sight of him" (vs. 9). The targum of Job 36 from Qumran Cave 11 does not make any significant change in the text except in line 26b where the leviathan (crocodile) is said to be "king over all the reptiles" in distinction from "over all the sons of pride" (MT, vs. 34). The description of Behemoth in Job 40:15–24 gives details about his strength, his "tail stiff as a cedar," his "limbs like bars of iron," etc. What the writer wishes to stress with regard to both animals is their invincibility by man. Only God has power over them.

There are not a few non-biblical speculations about these two creatures. I Enoch 60:7–8 says that the two monsters parted and the female monster, Leviathan, was to dwell in the abysses of the ocean, and the male, Behemoth, was to occupy the waste wilderness on the east of the garden where the elect and the righteous were to dwell. But when Enoch enquires further about them he is told that it is a "hidden" matter. John's apocalypse reveals this mystery. IV Ezra 6:49–51 (APCh, II, 579) gives further details:

> Then didst thou preserve two living creatures; the name of the one thou didst call Behemoth and the name of the other thou didst call Leviathan. And thou didst separate the one from the other; for the seventh part, where the water was gathered together, was unable to hold them (both). And thou didst give Behemoth one of the parts which had been dried up on the third day to dwell in, (that namely) where are a thousand hills: but unto Leviathan thou gavest the seventh part, namely the moist: and thou has reserved them to be devoured by whom thou wilt and when.

II Baruch 29:4 predicts that when the Messiah begins to be revealed, Behemoth will come from his seclusion on the land, and Leviathan will come out of the sea, and their flesh will serve as nourishment for the elect who will survive in the days of the Messiah. Rabbinic speculation elaborated the theme, e.g. *Lev R* 13:3, Midrash Rabbah, Soncino Press, London, 1961 (3d impression):

> R. Judan b. R. Simeon said: Behemoth and the Leviathan are to engage in a wild-beast contest before the righteous in the Time to Come, and whoever has not been a spectator at the wild-beast contests of the heathen nations in this world will be accorded the boon of seeing one in the World to Come. How will they be slaughtered? Behemoth will, with its horns, pull Leviathan down and rend it, and Leviathan will, with its fins, pull Behemoth down and pierce it through.

In other traditions Gabriel kills the monster, but he can only do so with the help of God, who will divide it with His sword. Jewish haggadoth also allegorize these two beasts, sometimes seeing them as the destructive powers which are hostile to the Jews.

As our writer now not only draws his scenes on earth but also introduces subtle contrasts with the heavenly realities, his mythological data are accommodated to a historical level. The monsters represent the Roman empire and those who cooperate with her. The inspiration for the first beast comes from the female monster, Leviathan. She, or it (the text uses the neuter gender in keeping with the neuter "monster," Gr. *therion*), rises from the sea like the beasts in Daniel (7:3). On the earthly dimension the sea is probably the Mediterranean and the beast is seen as coming from Rome or the West, i.e. it is an empire born on the Mediterranean. As Ramsay (pp. 103–4) asserts, "whatever comes from the land is a native product." However, the sea also has symbolic meaning. In Revelation it often bears the nuance that is given to the term "abyss" in Gen 1:2.

"Abyss," Heb. *tehom,* is the primitive chaos devoid of the Spirit of Yahweh. Earth is the place of creation and harmony subject to God, but *tehom* is the place of the monsters, of chaos, of opposition to God. The sea, therefore, is a symbol of unregenerate humanity, and "especially of the seething caldron of national and social life, out of which the great historical movements of the world arise," (Swete, *The Apocalypse,* p. 161; cf. Isa 7:12, Rev 17:15).

This reservoir of evil is the antithesis of the heavenly glass sea in Rev 4:6 and of the living creatures who are stationed near it. Their name, *zoē,* means "living" (creature). *Zoē* can also refer to man, but the monsters in Rev 13 are described as *theria,* "wild animals," which include insects and birds and are distinguished from *ktēnos,* a collective noun meaning "domesticated animals." *Therion* has essentially the meaning of beast of prey bent on destruction and attack. All four living creatures are compared to animals but they are not portrayed as monstrosities, i.e. hybrid animals, of mixed species. On the other hand the first monster is a composite figure made up of all the animals in Dan 7, where the first was like a lion, the second like a bear, and the third like a leopard; the fourth beast is not said to be similar to any particular animal, and Daniel only alludes to its teeth and its feet. These are the very two characteristics which are described with reference to the sea monster in Rev 13:2, and our writer may mean to identify it with Daniel's fourth beast; both have ten horns. The sea beast's leopard qualities suggest cat-like agility and vigilance; cf. Sir 28:23[27], Hosea 13:7, Jer 5:6, Hab 1:8. Its bear-like feet show strength with the power to crush; cf. I Kings 17:34, II Kings 2:24, Amos 5:19. Its lion-like mouth suggests the roar of the lion which haunted the Jordan Valley (Jer 27:17) and the Judean hills, a beast dreaded by shepherds; cf. Zeph 3:3, Zech 11:3.

The dragon is the antithesis of God, but the sea beast is the antithesis of the Lamb. The lamb was presented "as though it had been slain" (5:6); the same condition is true of the first monster (vs. 3). The dragon gave to this monster its power and its throne and its great authority, titles which are quasimessianic and quasidivine; the lamb shares similar privileges with God. The beast has authority over every tribe and people and tongue and nation; the lamb, too, is the recipient of this power. Later in Revelation one learns that the beast "was and is not and is to come" (17:9), a blasphemous parody on the name of God; cf. Exod 3:14, Rev 1:8. The beast seeks to be tyrant; the "Lamb" will be King of Kings. Kiddle, p. 224, speaks of "the revelation of its heavenly antithesis." In other words, wishing to indicate the scope and nature of the beast's power the author uses "terms pointedly reminiscent of those proper to Christ or the Anointed One.

Our enquiry into the nature of the Lamb in Section IX, COMMENT, suggested a war-like leader opposing the state, as in Maccabean days. This chapter expresses an attitude toward the state, not found in the rest of the NT but present e.g. in Daniel and I–II Maccabees. The state is seen as diabolically inspired, leading people away from the true God. Here our writer presents himself as a prophet reinterpreting Daniel, whose text is cited in 13:1, 2, 5, 7, 8, 15. He offers a quasimidrash mainly on Dan 7.

In Daniel the beasts represent various pagan kingdoms: Assyria, Babylon, Persia, and Greece, or Babylon, Persia, Greece, and Rome. They are brought into association with one like a son of man (Dan 7:12–13) just as the beasts of Rev 13 are with the Lamb; cf. Rev 14. It has been suggested that the beast from the sea is the fourth one of Daniel, now the Roman empire. This is confirmed by the eagle vision in IV Ezra 12:10–32 which is explicitly identified with the fourth kingdom of Daniel 7. Its symbolism is similar to that in Rev 13. The twelve wings are twelve kings; a voice from the body, rather than the heads (vss. 18–19) means that there will be contentions in the kingdom, it will be in peril of falling but shall be restored; the eight underwings are eight kings who will not last long. The three heads are three kings. The lion speaking to the eagle is the Messiah. Although no complete interpretation of the vision in Revelation is given, we are told in 17:9, 10 that the seven heads are seven hills (probably, the seven hills upon which Rome was built) and at the same time seven kings or emperors. With the help of the eagle vision in IV Ezra one is able to expand the interpretation.

Eagle Vision	*Sea Monster Vision*
12 wings=12 kings	7 heads=7 kings or emperors
voice from body=contention	wound=contention
8 underwings=8 kings	10 horns=10 provinces or their governors
3 heads=3 kings	crowns=imperial majesty
lion=Messiah	lamb (ch. 14)=Messiah.

In the sea monster vision the seven emperors may be Tiberius, Caligula, Claudius, Nero, Titus, Vespasian and Domitian; see COMMENT, Section XIV. The ten provinces may be Italy, Achaea, Asia, Syria, Egypt, Africa, Spain, Gaul, Britain, and Germany. The diadems on the horns are royal crowns, not *stephanoi,* that is victors' wreaths. They suggest governors who shared in the imperial power and those who were subject to Rome, such as Herod, and yet retained the title of "king." However, the blasphemous names are on the heads, not the horns, because it was the emperors who were declared divine, not the provincial governors and kings. The blasphemous names must be the divine titles which the Roman emperors arrogated to themselves, especially *Kurios,* "Lord," *Divus Augustus,* "Divine Augustus," and *Dea Roma,* "Goddess Roma." Julius Caesar, Augustus, Claudius, Vespasian, and Titus were officially declared divine at their death; the latter three used the title *Divus* on coins during their lifetime. The wound on one of the heads is equivalent to the voice from the body, not the heads, in the eagle vision. Many scholars have explained this by reference to the legend of the return of Nero; see NOTE on vs. 3).

Dr. Minear has brought the most challenging argument against this theory. He draws the reader's attention to the fact that the wound of this beast is mentioned three times in this chapter, and points out that the wound, "although first assigned to one of its heads (13:3), is later assigned twice to the beast itself" (13:12, 14; cf. 17:8, 11):

13:3	*13:12*	*13:14*
And one of his heads seemed to have a lethal wound and the lethal wound was healed.	. . . the first monster, whose lethal wound is healed.	. . . the monster who was wounded by the sword and revived.

In all three verses the healed monster is said to be worshiped.

Dr. Minear points out that Nero's wound was a personal one rather than a wound on the Roman empire, which the beast represents. Further, the healing of the wound increases the prestige of the beast and impels men to worship it with greater devotion; the empire did not become more prestigious under Nero. He then offers a Christological interpretation, which is discussed later on in this COMMENT.

Accepting the first part of Dr. Minear's thesis, but omitting for the moment the reference to Christ, we may link it with the interpretation of other scholars. Many have suggested that the wound of the whole beast may refer to the anarchy of A.D. 69 which followed Nero's death, the year of the four emperors (Galba, Otho, Vitellius, Vespasian), and the healing to the accession of Vespasian, who ruled until A.D. 70. In the eagle vision of IV Ezra 12:10–11, 18–32, which appears to have been written around the time of Vespasian, one reads: "In the midst of the time of that kingdom there shall arise no small contentions, and it shall stand in peril of falling; nevertheless it shall not then fall, but shall be restored again to rule" (vs. 18, APCh, II, 613). Cf. Suetonius *Vespasian* 1, *War* 4.655, 7.73–74. Only with the accession of Vespasian did the monster come to life again.

In keeping with the plural symbolism used by our author and the fact that the wound is predicated both of the head and the whole beast, the injury and recovery could apply to Vespasian as well as the empire. Suetonius reports that Vespasian fell into disfavor with Nero because he would either absent himself from Nero's musical performances or fall asleep during them. On this account Nero directed "the sword," i.e. the power residing in the Roman empire, against Vespasian and he was exiled. He fled and was even in fear of death (*etiamque extrema metuenti, Vespasian* 4; cf. 14, reporting that one of the ushers told him to "go to Morbovia," a word derived from *morbus* "illness"). He was restored again because he was needed in Judaea. Suetonius also refers to many portents which led Vespasian to look for imperial dignity and which marked his life even from his very birth. It might seem, therefore, that the beast is the Roman empire, the wounded head is Vespasian, and the healed wound represents Vespasian's being brought back into favor and thus able to restore the empire. However, it is Vespasian and his son, Titus, who conquered Jerusalem. The Jews cannot rejoice at the healing of that mortal wound.

The whole world "wondered at" or "gaped after" the beast and they worshiped both it and the dragon. Certainly Josephus draws a graphic picture of the enthusiasm with which the people received Vespasian after the restoration of peace to the empire (*War* 7.63–74). While he was still some distance away, "all the Italians were paying respect to him in their hearts . . . and exhibiting an affection for him wholly free from constraint" (7.64). The people could not wait patiently for his arrival but poured out in throngs to meet him (7:69). The city was like a temple, filled with garlands and incense (7.72). When he came they hailed him: "benefactor," "saviour," "only worthy emperor of Rome" (7.71). However, our writer places more provocative words in the mouths of the people. They ask "Who is like the beast?" and "Who is able to fight against him?" These questions are a deliberate parody on Exod 15:11, the Song of Moses, after the Egyptians had been overwhelmed in the Sea of Reeds. Implicitly the people compare their hero to God and his victory to the triumph over the Egyptians. In this way the author has reintroduced his Exodus motif which runs throughout Revelation. The questions are the very heart of the book; they epitomize the struggle between the worship of the beast, or the imperial cult, and the worship of God, the true cult. John's apocalypse does not leave the questions unanswered.

In vss. 5–8 the writer resumes his use of the impersonal passive "it was given" or "allowed," Gr. *edothē,* and the agent is the same as the one in the previous part of this apocalypse. The text implies that it is God who permits the monster four (temporary) "privileges" which the four-fold use of *edothē* (vss. 5a, b; 7a, b) spell out: 1) a mouth which blasphemes; 2) authority for forty-two months; 3) conquest of the holy ones; 4) power over all people.

The first privilege is expressed in phraseology from Dan 7:8, 11, 20, 25, where the horn speaks haughty words against the Most High and harasses the saints. Daniel's text appears to refer to Antiochus Epiphanes who went up to Jerusalem, arrogantly entered the sanctuary, and took the golden altar, the lampstand, all the utensils together with the table for the bread of the Presence, the cups, the bowls, the censers, the curtain, the crowns, and the golden decoration on the front of the temple; cf. I Macc 1:20–28. The text declares specifically that he also spoke with "great arrogance" (*huperēphaneian megalēn,* I Macc 1:24).

The second privilege, forty-two months of authority, is influenced by Dan 7:25, which speaks of the time of great terror for the Jews, namely, the same persecution under Antiochus Epiphanes. During this persecution it was not permissible to possess a copy of the Torah or to circumcise a male child. The temple was desecrated, the priests' rooms were turned into brothels, the altar was made into an altar of Zeus, and the temple courts were defiled with swine's blood and flesh. The desecration of the temple lasted from 168 B.C. to 165, i.e., for three and one-half years. Thus forty-two months became symbolic of a period of terror and demonic evil before the final victory of God. The author appears to anticipate a similar sacrilege when he says that the beast "opened his mouth" (a phrase used frequently, though not exclusively, of the beginning of divinely inspired speech; cf. Sir 15:5) "to blaspheme against God . . . His name and His dwelling, [and] those who dwell in heaven" (13:6). The blasphemy against God's name may refer to the assumption of the divine names by the emperors in public documents and in inscriptions. The one against His dwelling may be against the temple, e.g. when Caligula (whose real name was Gaius, sometimes spelled Caius) attempted to set up his statue there (*Ant.* 18. 261, *War* 2.184–87, Philo *Legatio Ad Gaium* 29, 43) or when Titus entered the Holy of Holies at the end of the siege of Jerusalem. Blasphemy against the dwellers in heaven may refer to the angels or martyrs or, if used metaphorically (contrasted with earth-dwellers), to the sacred ministers. One may compare Assumption of Moses 8:5, APCh, II, 419:

> And they shall likewise be forced by those who torture them to enter their inmost sanctuary, and they shall be forced by goads to blaspheme with insolence the word, finally after these things the laws and what they had above the altar.

The third privilege, conquest of the holy ones, is modeled on Dan 7:21. The fourth power over all people, reflects Dan 3:5–6, where peoples, nations, and languages are commanded to worship the golden image set up by Nebuchadnezzar. In Rev 13:8 the beast is contrasted with the Lamb, just as the kings of the pagan nations stand against the figure of the Son of Man in Daniel. The reason these four privileges are granted to the monster is to test the endurance and faith of the saints. The writer is saying, "What Daniel foretold and was fulfilled will be repeated; therefore, keep your faith." Thus this chapter is brought to a climax by an exhortation to hear what seems to be a prophetic word. Vs. 10 bears affinity to Jer 15 1–3, 43:11; Matt 26:52; all four passages deal with death and captivity, and exhibit similar kinds of parallel construction. The affinity with the two texts from Jeremiah suggests the dire and inevitable fate of those who persist in their rebellion against God. Barclay suggests it means that during the time of terror human resistance is of no avail; one can only wait upon God.

The appearance of the land-monster is very subtle. Inspired by the concept of Behemoth and conscious of the fact that that which is from the land is a "home product," the author shows the merging of the two forces, the Roman empire and the apostate Jews. The alliance will appear all the more dramatically in the picture of the harlot. The land-monster is a "wolf in sheep's clothing" (cf. Rev 13:11, Matt 7:15), the false prophet who since the earliest days of prophecy has urged unwise political moves (cf. I Kings 22) and countenanced idolatry. The Deuteronomic law provides for him (Deut 13:1–3, RSV):

> If a prophet arises among you, or a dreamer of dreams, and gives you a sign or a wonder, and the sign or wonder which he tells you comes to pass, and if he says, "Let us go after other gods," which you have not known, "and let us serve them," you shall not listen to the words of that prophet or to that dreamer of dreams; for the Lord your God is testing you, to know whether you love the Lord your God with all your heart and with all your soul.

His punishment is death for he is essentially a false witness. Our author has portrayed him as the land beast and contrasts him with the two witnesses in ch. 11. God has His chosen and particular servants, the Lamb and the two prophets (ch. 11); so has the dragon, in the two monsters.

Kiddle, pp. 253–261, spells out some of the points of comparison:

Two Prophets (Ch. 11)	*The Land Beast (13:11 ff.)*
The witnesses are two prophets, leading men with stern admonition to the true God.	The land beast elsewhere is called the "false prophet" (14:13, 19:20, 20:10), leading men to the worship of false gods, the dragon and the first beast.
The two prophets were enabled to perform extraordinary miracles.	The beast performs great wonders.
They "stand before the Lord of the earth" (11:4).	He exercises the full authority of the first beast in his presence (13:12).
They have special power over fire (11:5).	He makes fire come from heaven (13:13).
The final stage of the martyrs' testimony after their death is when the "breath of life from God" revives them.	The beast animates the image with the "breath of life," thereby mimicking the power of the creator God.
This convinces mankind of God's supreme power (11:11).	He kills all who do not worship the image (13:15, contrast Deut 13:5).
They are the two lampstands and the two olive trees (11:4).	He has two horns like a lamb (13:12).

This contrast animates the idea of conflict between good and evil, between God and Satan, which recurs throughout Revelation. The second monster co-operates with the first. Barclay, ET 70 (1958/59), thinks that, as the Caesar worship was organized into dioceses with priests and officials who had powerful status, so the beast from the land represents provincial organization which enforces the Caesar cult. Swete, p. 170, states that "the pagan priesthood wrought their *semeia* (signs) before these representatives of the empire; their jugglery addressed itself to persons in authority and not only to the ignorant populace"; cf. Simon Magus in Acts 8:9–24. Tiberius surrounded himself with astrologers in Capri; Apelles of Ascalon was welcome at the court of Caligula; Apollonius of Tyana was a friend of Nero, Vespasian, and Titus. The Pythagorean philosophers practiced an amalgam of magic, mysticism, and mathematics, and Simon Magus is reported to have brought statues to life (Clement *Recognationes* 3. 47; cf. Justin *Apologia* 1.26, Irenaeus *Haereses* 1.23, Eusebius *Ecclesiastical History* 2.13.1–8). The pagan world apparently expected miracles at the time of the Neronic antichrist. The monster succumbs to the charlatanry of the pagan gods.

The actual making of an image for the monster is a direct infringement of Exod 20:3–4 and possibly recalls the golden calf in Exod 32. But the danger was ever present. The mad Caligula issued a decree commanding his statue to be adored. Tacitus (*Annals* 15.29) records obeisance to the Roman emperor Nero after the defeat of Tiridades by Corbulo. The Parthian and Roman armies were gathered together with their standards and the images of their gods and between the two armies was a tribunal supporting a curule chair upon which was an effigy of Nero. The sacrifices were offered until Tiridades took the diadem off his head and laid it at the feet of the effigy. The present text may suggest something comparable. There were also numerous representations of the emperor on shields, coins, and standards, which were offensive to Jews. Vs. 15 reports that breath was put into the image of the beast. The superstition of talking and moving statues was widespread at this time; cf. Clement *Recognationes* 3.47, Lucian *De Syria Dea* 10. Ventriloquism or a hidden operator explains the phenomenon. The penalty for not worshiping the beast is death, as in Dan 3:5–6, when those who did not fall down and worship the golden statue of Nebuchadnezzar at the sound of the orchestra were thrown into the fiery furnace.

The monster from the land also compels people of every social class to receive the mark of the beast on their right hands and foreheads. Those without it cannot engage in commerce or marketing. It is significant that the sign of the beast (mentioned also in 14:9, 11, 16:2, 19:20) contrasts with the sign of God with which the true worshipers are marked, as in 7:3, 9:4. Two entirely different words are used; for the faithful, the "seal," Gr. *sphragis*, of God, and for the unfaithful, "mark," Gr. *charagma*. *Charagma* may be used to indicate a work of art, such as a graven image (Acts 17:29), or an impress made by a stamp, or branding. III Macc 2:29 reports that Ptolemy Philopator I (219 B.C.) ordered the Jews, who submitted to registration, to be branded with the badge of Dionysiac worship.

Stauffer, p. 179, conjectures that the High Priest and the false prophet wore the imperial image on the golden circlet on their brow and signet ring, but he gives no reference. The mark may have a more subtle meaning. *Charagma* can describe a serpent's sting (Henry George Liddell & Robert Scott, *Greek-English Lexicon* [Oxford: Clarendon Press, reprinted 1953]; *sphragis* is not so used. The "mark" could, therefore, be the scar or abrasion from the bite of the wild monster. Ironically, the mark is on the right hand and the brow, an obvious travesty of the practice of orthodox Judaism which required the faithful to wear phylacteries on the left hand and the head; Deut 6:8.

The mark of the monster is either identified with or closely associated with his number. Here our author uses the method of gematria (from Heb. *gīmatrīyā*), that is, the process of adding up the numerical value of the letters that make up a proper name, e.g. a=1; b=2; d=4, etc. (It was called *isopsephia* in Greek.) It is a cryptogram and special insight is necessary to decipher it. Barclay gives several examples of other uses of gematria. There is a very simple one on the walls of Pompeii: "I love her whose number is 545" (A. Deissmann, in Barclay, p. 276). The lover conceals the name of his loved one by giving the numerical value of the letters of her name. An example from the Hebrew would be the numerical value of the word for serpent, *nhsh*, which has the same numerical value as the Hebrew for messiah. Thus it was argued that the title of serpent was the title of the messiah. This might explain why Moses lifted up the serpent in the wilderness; John 3:14. Pagan gods were known by the numerical value of their names, e.g. Jupiter, or Zeus, was known as 717. One of the most interesting examples of gematria found is one contemporary with Nero. People apparently wrote on the walls what they were afraid to say concerning him. One such graffito is reported by Suetonius *Nero* 30: "A calculation new. Nero his mother slew." The numerical value of the letters in the name Nero is equal to that of the letters in the rest of the sentence.

Many and various have been the attempts to decipher the cryptogram 666. Barclay's comprehensive article gathers up most of the suggestions prior to the date of his writing. Three names for 666 were suggested by Irenaeus: Euantas, but this is meaningless; Teitian, which could be a reference either to the Titans who rebelled against the gods or to the emperor Titus although he was not a persecutor; and Lateinos, which would stand for the Roman (Latin) empire and for the Roman church. Primasius suggested *Arnoune* which could be connected with the Greek verb *arneisthai*, "to deny" or "apostatize." Barclay himself suggests that we use Hebrew letters to represent Neron Caesar; if the final n in Neron is dropped, the word is brought into line with its Latin form and the result is 616. The writer of Revelation saw emperor worship as satanic power, and he saw the power culminating in the return of Nero, the antichrist.

Hillers, commenting on the identification of Nero with 666 if it is spelled *Nrwn Qsr*, says: "It may now be pointed out that in an Aramaic document from Murabba'at (DJD, II, 18, plate 29), dated to the 'second year of the Emperor Nero,' the name is spelled Nrwn Qsr, as required by the theory. The last two consonants of Qsr are damaged, but enough is preserved to show that no vowel letter was written between the Q and the s." Thus there would be no need to use the variant reading 616.

Another variant is 606, which would be the sum of Gaios Kaisar, known as Caligula. Christian readers would have noticed the contrast between the number of the beast, 666, and the number of Jesus, 888 (the sum of the Greek letters Jesus). In 888 could be seen superabundant perfection, the three-fold 7+1. On the other hand 666 indicates the three-fold failure to reach perfection, 7−1. This showed how precarious and how doomed to failure the reign of the beast must be.

*Examples of Gematria**

Hebrew	Greek		
Q=100	I= 10	K= 20	
S= 60	E= 8	A= 1	
R=200	S=200	I= 10	
N= 50	O= 70	S=200	
R=200	U=400	A= 1	
W= 6	S=200	R=100	
N= 50	888	Th= 9	
666		E= 5	
		O= 70	
		S=200	
		616	

* Fr. Edward Siegman's notes.

Perhaps the most interesting suggestion has been made by Bruston. He believes that one needs to search not for a Roman name but rather for a Babylonian one. The founder of the empire of Babylon was Nimrod, who according to Gen 10:8 was the son of Kush. The true name of the Roman emperor is Nimrod, which means "rebellious." Bruston observes that it is a question of the Roman emperor past and present, not the future Roman emperor or the Antichrist. In depicting the beast as an animal with ten horns (as the fourth beast in Daniel), like a bear (as the second in Daniel), and like a lion (as the first in Daniel) which represents the Babylonian empire, the emperor clearly indicates the origin of the Roman empire. Its true founder is the founder of the first empire described by Daniel, namely Babylon. There is only one human name which can designate this, and the significance of this name in Hebrew agrees perfectly with the emperor in the abstract who is the enemy of God and His church. It is only in Rev 17 that the future Roman empire is spoken about, after the seventh emperor who has still not come at the time of the composition of the book. This theory fits admirably with the use of Daniel and mythology throughout the whole chapter.

The Roman emperor is identified with Nimrod. If the name were derived from Hebrew (but it is more likely to be Mesopotamian) the root would be *mrd*, "to rebel." The original form may have been "Ninurta," the name of a Babylonian war god, and the name of the first Assyrian king to reign over Babylonia; cf. Gen 10:10. In the OT Nimrod occurs in Gen 10:8–12, I Chron 1:10, Micah 5:6. Therefore if the cryptogram 666 does mean Nimrod, it is understandable why Babylon plays such an important part in the second section of Revelation (*Interpreter's Dictionary of the Bible*). In rabbinic literature Nimrod threw Abraham into a fiery furnace because he would not worship idols; Gen R 38:13.

Why should "John" have spoken so cryptically. It would seem that in time of persecution or war the faithful should be warned. However, the warning had to be given in such a way as to obscure its meaning for the pagans into whose hands the Book of Revelation might fall. If it violated the sacrosanct majesty of Rome, the faithful might be charged with treason. Hence the gematria was a measure of prudence.

A tentative suggestion concerning the second beast is offered here. It is usually identified with the local priesthood, which cooperated with Rome, but why is this beast from the land specifically described as a false prophet? Could our writer have had any historical priestly person in mind who influenced his choice of a second beast even if he did not wholly identify him with it? If we are to understand "land" in the sense of "Palestine," and if we are to see the land beast as a caricature of a prophet who looks like a lamb but speaks like a dragon (or like the dragon), i.e. Satan, then one may ask who at the time of the Jewish war would be most aptly associated with this second beast, the prophet from Palestine. It must be a prophet who served Rome, i.e. the first beast. If the first beast is identified with Vespasian, the most obvious choice for the second beast is Flavius Josephus.

For information about Josephus we are dependent on his autobiography, *Vita* (Life), and some notes in his *Jewish War*. The autobiography itself is an apologia, probably published in order to answer the criticisms of a rival historian, Justus of Tiberias, who blamed the war, or at least its results in the city of Tiberias, on Josephus; Thackeray, p. 5. Josephus came from a priestly family and had royal blood on his mother's side. He was born in the year of the accession of Caligula, A.D. 37–38. His life, therefore, would seem to have comprised about thirty-three years of tension spent in Palestine as a priest, a general, and a prisoner, and then a period of comparative peace as a Roman citizen and a writer in Rome.

In his twenty-sixth or twenty-seventh year (A.D. 64), he went to Rome in the interests of certain priests who had been charged by Felix, the procurator of Judaea, and were to be tried by Nero. Although he was successful in the case, he made some disreputable acquaintances, notably the Jewish actor, Aliturus, and the notorious Poppaea, who was once mistress and then wife of the emperor, and who was exceedingly powerful at court. This woman dabbled in Judaism, and Josephus even gave her the epithet, *theosebēs*, "God-fearing," a technical word for proselyte (*Ant.* 20.195).

Josephus' visit to Rome may have had some connection with the war threatening Palestine. His importance in the war increased at the time of the arrival of Vespasian in the spring of 67. He was in control of Galilee, but he was not only suspected but also severely censured by the Jewish leaders and especially by his rival, John of Gischala. John accused Josephus of aiming at tyranny and tried to induce his friends to deprive him of his command. Josephus appeared to be playing a double game. It was certainly strange to find a young priest known to be a pacifist and also with pro-Roman tendencies being appointed to such an important post in Galilee. When Vespasian approached from Antioch in the spring of 67, Josephus was deserted by most of his army, and went to the fortified city of Jotapata. The town was besieged for forty-seven days and fell in July 67. In *War* 3.340–98 Josephus left a dramatic description of his capture by the Romans. He tricked his companions in hiding. After trying to dissuade them from suicide, lots were cast and—*mirabile dictu*—he was left the sole survivor. Thus, Josephus could, without doubt, be regarded as a traitor to his countrymen.

Josephus also let it be known that he possessed spiritual powers, as in passages like this one from *War* 3.351–54.

But as Nicanor [the Roman who came to persuade Josephus that the Romans meant to save him] was urgently pressing his proposals and Josephus overheard the threats of the hostile crowd, suddenly there came back into his mind those nightly dreams, in which God had foretold to him the impending fate of the Jews and the destinies of the Roman sovereigns. He was an interpreter of dreams and skilled in divining the meaning of ambiguous utterances of the Deity [cf. also Josephus *Life* 208 ff.]; a priest himself and of priestly descent, he was not ignorant of the prophecies in the sacred books. At that hour he was inspired to read their meaning, and recalling the dreadful images of his recent dreams, he offered up a silent prayer to God. "Since it pleases Thee," so it ran, "who didst create the Jewish nation, to break Thy work, since fortune has wholly passed to the Romans, and since Thou has made choice of my spirit to announce the things that are to come, I willingly surrender to the Romans and consent to live; but I take thee to witness that I go, not as a traitor, but as thy minister."

It is against the background of such sentiments that one can understand Josephus' prediction of Vespasian's rise to imperial power. Vespasian had intended to send his prisoner to Nero for trial, but Josephus requested a private interview with his conqueror. Vespasian asked all to withdraw and only his son, Titus, and two friends remained. Then Josephus addressed him, as recorded in *War* 3.400–2:

"You imagine, Vespasian, that in the person of Josephus you have taken a mere captive; but I come to you as a messenger of greater destinies. Had I not been sent on this errand by God, I knew the law of the Jews and how it becomes a general to die. To Nero do you send me? Why then? Think you that [Nero and] those who before your accession succeed him will continue? You will be Caesar, Vespasian, you will be emperor, you and your son here. Bind me then yet more securely in chains and keep me for yourself; for you, Caesar, are master not of me only, but of land and sea and the whole human race. For myself, I ask to be punished by stricter custody, if I have dared to trifle with the words of God."

At first Vespasian was disinclined to believe him, but Josephus' message gradually gained credence, for the general had received other portents of his future power; cf. Tacitus *History* 1.10, 2.1, 5.13, Suetonius *Vespasian* 5. Vespasian discovered that Josephus had also foretold that Jotapata would fall after forty-seven days of siege and that he would be taken alive by the Romans. Vespasian questioned the prisoners on these statements and found that they were true. Although he did not release Josephus, he presented him with clothes and precious gifts and treated him with kindness. Titus also was extremely courteous to him. Josephus' prediction that Vespasian would be emperor is also confirmed by Suetonius in *Vespasian* 5, and by Dio Cassius in *Epitome* 66.1.

When Vespasian did become emperor one of his first acts was to release his Jewish prisoner whose prophecy had proved true. Josephus accompanied Vespasian to Alexandria, then returned to Jerusalem with Titus and saw the end of the city. During the siege he acted as a mediator and went around persuading submission to the Romans. After the fall of Jerusalem Titus presented him with land outside Jerusalem and some "sacred books." He obtained the freedom of a number of his friends and then went to Rome with the conqueror. He spent about thirty years in Rome and was commissioned to write the history of Rome's triumph over the Jews. He was given Roman citizenship, a dwelling in the former palace of Vespasian and a pension (*Vita* 423; cf. Suetonius *Vespasian* 18).

He was present for the triumph of Vespasian and Titus, but, although he enjoyed peace with his Roman friends in the time of Vespasian, he was constantly accused and slandered by his countrymen, including those of his own family. After the death of Titus in 79 his position was less advantageous, and he became the apologist of his nation in his later writings. However, he could never again recapture the affection or appreciation of his countrymen. It was Rome that perpetuated his memory, and Eusebius tells us his statue was erected in Rome and his works placed in a public library (Thackeray, p. 16).

Although one may not take Rev 13:11–18 literally, it might be that, with poetic license, the author of Revelation has depicted the monstrous behavior of Josephus and others like him who led his countrymen to submit to and honor Rome. It might not be without significance that Josephus adopted Vespasian's family name, Flavius, probably out of gratitude (cf. *War* 4:622–29), something which could indeed be regarded as equal to taking the mark or name of the beast. It might also be remarked that neither Vespasian (*Vita* 424–25, *War* 7.447–50) nor Domitian would accept any slander against Josephus, and that Josephus was in favor not only with Poppaea in the first instance but also with the empress Domitia.

BIBLIOGRAPHY

Barclay, W. "Revelation 13, Great Themes of the N.T." ET 70 (1958/59), 260–64, 292–96.

————. *Letters to the Seven Churches.*

Bobichon, M. "666 Le Chiffre de la Bête," BTS 59 (1963), 3–4.

Bruston, C. "La Tete Egorgée et le Chiffre 666," ZNW 5 (1904), 258–61.

Hillers, D. R. *Bulletin of the American Schools of Oriental Research* 170 (1963), 65.

Interpreter's Dictionary of the Bible, III, under "Nimrod."

Kiddle, M. and Ross, M. K. *The Revelation of St. John.*

Minear, P. S. JBL 72 (1953), 93–101.

Pope, M. H. *Job,* AB, vol. 15, 1965; 3d ed., 1973.

Sanders, H. A. "The Number of the Beast in Revelation 13, 18," JBL 37 (1918), 95–99.

Stauffer, E. *Christ and the Caesars.*

————. "666 (Apoc. 13, 18)," *Coniectanea neotestamentica* 11 (1947), 237–41.

Thackeray, H. St. J. *Josephus, The Man and the Historian.*

Vos, L. A. *The Synoptic Traditions in the Apocalypse.*

14 1 And I looked, and behold the Lamb standing on Mount Zion, and with him one hundred and forty-four thousand who had his name and the name of his Father written upon their foreheads. 2 And I heard a voice from heaven like the sound of many waters, like the sound of mighty thunder, and the voice which I heard was like the harpers playing on their lyres. 3 And they sang a new song before the throne and before the four living creatures and the elders; and no one could learn the song except the one hundred and forty-four thousand, who were redeemed from the earth. 4 These are they who have not defiled themselves with women; for they are virgins. These follow the Lamb wherever he goes. These were redeemed from men, the first fruit to God and to the Lamb, 5 and in their mouth was found no falsehood: they are unblemished.

6 And I saw another angel flying in mid-heaven, who had an eternal gospel to preach to those who are enthroned on the earth and to every nation and tribe and tongue and people. 7 He said in a loud voice, "Fear God and give Him glory, for the hour of his judgment has come, and worship the creator of heaven and earth and sea and the springs of water." 8 And another angel, a second one, followed saying, "Fallen, fallen is Babylon the great, who gave every nation to drink of the wine of the lust of her harlotry." 9 And another angel, a third one, followed them saying in a loud voice, "If anyone worships the monster and his image, and receives a mark on his forehead or on his hand, 10 that man will drink also of the wine of the wrath of God poured undiluted into the cup of His anger, and he will be tormented with fire and brimstone in the presence of the holy angels and in the presence of the Lamb. 11 And the smoke of their torment will go up for ever and ever, and they will have no rest day and night, those who worship the monster and his image, and anyone who receives the mark of his name." 12 Hence the endurance of the saints, who keep the commandments of God and the faith of Jesus. 13 And I heard a voice from heaven saying, "Write: Blessed are the dead who die in the Lord

from now on. Yes, says the Spirit, that they may rest from their labors; for their works follow them."

14 And I looked, and behold a white cloud, and on the cloud one like a son of man was enthroned; he had a golden crown on his head and in his hand a sharp sickle. 15 And another angel came out of the sanctuary, calling with a loud voice to the one who was enthroned upon the cloud, "Put in your sickle and reap, for the hour to reap has come, for the harvest of the earth is fully ready." 16 And the one who was enthroned upon the cloud cast his sickle upon the earth, and the earth was reaped. 17 And another angel came out of the sanctuary which is in heaven; he also had a sharp sickle. 18 And another angel came out of the altar; he had authority over fire, and cried with a loud voice to the one who had the sharp sickle, saying, "Put forth your sharp sickle, and gather the clusters of the vine of the earth, for its grapes are ripe." 19 And the angel swung his sickle onto the earth, and gathered the vine of the earth and threw it into the great winepress of the wrath of God. 20 And the winepress was trodden outside the city, and blood poured out of the winepress up to the horses' bridles for one thousand six hundred stadia.

Notes

14:1–5. E. Power finds that this segment falls into six parts. Parts 1–4 are descriptive and parts 5–6 explanatory. The words "one hundred and forty-four thousand" are included in the first and the last stanzas of the description. Power divided vss. 1–5 thus:

Part 1. a) ¹And I looked, and behold the Lamb standing on Mount Zion, and
     b) with him one hundred and forty-four thousand
     c) who had his name and the name of his Father written upon their foreheads.
Part 2. a) ²And I heard a voice from heaven
     b) like the sound of many waters,
     c) like the sound of mighty thunder,
Part 3. a) and the voice which I heard was like the harpers
     b) playing on their lyres. ³And they sang a new song
     c) before the throne and before the four living creatures and the elders;
Part 4. a) and no one could learn the song
     b) except the one hundred and forty-four thousand,
     c) who were redeemed from the earth.

Part 5. a) ⁴These are they who have not defiled themselves with women;
         b) for they are virgins.
         c) These follow the Lamb
         d) wherever he goes.
Part 6. a) These were redeemed from men,
         b) the first fruit to God and to the Lamb,
         c) ⁵and in their mouth was found no falsehood:
         d) they are unblemished.

Power observes the correspondence between "not being defiled" and "virgin" and also between "not false" and "blameless." He notes also that the fifth and sixth parts (vss. 4–5) are in the qina meter.

1. *the Lamb*. In P⁴⁷ 1, 2059s pm TR the definite article is omitted. Charles, APCh, II, 5–6, thinks that the article may have been removed by one who interpolated vss 4–5. Compare the anarthrous lamb of 13:11.

Gr. *hestākos*. That the Lamb is standing forms a contrast with the beasts who are rising, Gr. *anabainō*, in ch. 13. "being established," "standing firm," "holding one's ground," as opposed to "falling" (Gr. *piptō;* cf. 9:1).

Mount Zion. This is the only time Zion is mentioned in this apocalypse. It appears only seven times in the NT, five of which occur in OT quotations. Mythical traditions surrounded Zion/Jerusalem. One suggested that it was the highest mountain in the world (Isa 2:2, Micah 4:1, Ezek 17:22, 50:2, Zech 14:10, Ps 48:1–2, and others associated it with the water of life (cf. "the springs of water" in vs. 7). In the NT Mount Zion is a symbol of rejoicing and security; Heb 12:22. As the abyss is the place of evil, so the mountain is the place of revelation (cf. Mount Sinai) and security.

one hundred and forty-four thousand. 144,000 is $12,000 \times 12$, i.e. the number of those sealed from the twelve tribes as in Rev 7:4–8. This number is symbolic of perfection and appears to be in obvious contrast to 666, the number of the second monster in ch. 13, the figure of imperfection in all three digits.

the name. Cf. Joel 2:32, Zeph 3:12, Acts 9:14, 21, Rom 10:13, I Cor 1:2. There is no mention of a name on the hand as in 13:16 which says that the mark of the monster was either on the right hand or the forehead.

his Father. In Christian eyes this could be seen as a reference to the unique sonship of Christ, but in Hebrew thought it refers to the concept of the king as the adopted son of Yahweh; cf. e.g. Ps 2:7, II Sam 7:14. It is significant that Jesus used Heb. *abba*, "Daddy," as well as *ab*, "Father" when referring to God.

2. *voice*. the author accumulates similes in order to describe it. A voice sounding like many waters is predicated of one like a son of man in 1:15; the thunder is linked with the sound of Yahweh's voice, but the lyres with that of angels or the elders. Thus the voice is a blending of divine, human, and angelic sounds.

3. *new song*. To commemorate their deliverance from Egypt, Moses and the Israelites sang a triumphal song on the shores of the Reed Sea; Exod 15:1–18. A new song is mentioned in Pss 33:3, 40:3, 96:1, 98:1, 99.9; Isa 42:10. But this new song may be mystical songs unable to be learned by those

who are not advanced in prayer; cf. the Testament of Job where the three daughters of Job receive the ability to know angels' songs. A C 1, 1006, 2059s al vg TR read, "as it were, a new song."

redeemed from the earth. "Redeemed" translates Gr. *agorazō*, lit. "buy" or "purchase," but also is used of the emancipation of slaves. In the context of vs. 3 it may denote liberation from the tyranny of the earth-dwellers and the beast.

4. Some commentators take the expression "defiled themselves with women" literally: the one hundred and forty-four thousand would then refer to virgins specifically, or at least to those who observed the counsels in the clerical or religious state, "ascetics" as Allo, pp. 196–97, calls them. They would "follow the Lamb" as Israel followed Yahweh in the desert, which time was regarded as one of espousals; cf. Jer 2:2–3, Hosea 2:14–15. They would be "first fruit" in the sense of their distinct relationship compared to that of other Christians; the term includes the idea of consecration to God.

Cambier sees this verse as an indirect reference to virginity. The one hundred and forty-four thousand refer to all Christians as in ch. 7. However, just as in ch. 7 Christians are described as martyrs because they were the typical saints of that time, so in 14:4 Christians are described as virgins because virginity represented an ideal, a kind of anticipation of their life in heaven; cf. Matt 22:30.

Kiddle takes the phrase "have not defiled themselves with women . . . virgins" quite literally. He thinks that John felt that complete celibacy alone would give the strength to be a faithful witness unto martyrdom. However, he suggests that in the Greek word translated as "first fruit," Gr. *aparchē*, there is an implication that martyrdom equals sacrifice, that their being "undefiled" means, primarily, sacrificial purity.

Charles, II, 8, finds a difficulty because the redeemed must comprise both men and women. If so, he asks why the author did not use the word *porneia*, "unchastity," instead of "defiled with women." The noun *porneia* is used metaphorically in 14:8; 17:2, 4; 18:3; 19:2, and the verb *porneuō* is used in 17:2; 18:3, 9, in the sense of idolatry. Charles, II, 9, thinks that vss. 4–5 were inserted by a monkist interpolator who thought of male celibates as the first fruits of the church.

Caird, pp. 179–81, gives the most compelling explanation. He observes that the military setting helps us to understand what would otherwise be John's most puzzling sentence. The background for Caird is the regulations for the holy war found in Deut 20, 23:9–10; cf. I Sam 21:5, II Sam 11:11. The technical term "to consecrate war" is found in Jer 6:4, Micah 3:5, Joel 3:9. These "virgins" are the ritually pure soldiers around the military Lamb-Lion.

However, if this is the origin of the phrase, it does not preclude an additional nuance. Carrington, pp. 337–40, thinks that these verses may refer to men who have not polluted themselves with women in the sexual rites practiced in the heathen temples such as those at Ephesus, or that vs. 4a may be a metaphor referring to apostasy.

Swete, p. 179, refers to Exod 19:15 and I Sam 21:4, which would make the context one of abstinence for liturgical purposes. A priest abstained from his wife before offering sacrifice. Zahn, however, suggests that the one hundred and forty-four thousand are the Israelites who have abstained from all unchastity and are part of the eschatological kingdom. The Essenes were apparently celibate and engaged in the Holy War.

follow. The word indicates discipleship; cf. Mark 2:14, 10:21, Luke 9:59, John 1:43, 21:19; also I Peter 2:21 for the oriental concept of the shepherd with the sheep following, and John 8:21, 22, 13:33, 36.

redeemed from men. 046 051 82, 1611 al read "redeemed by Jesus."

first fruit. Gr. *aparchē.* Cf. Rom 16:5, I Cor 16:15, where Paul uses this term in referring to the first converts of the church. Charles, II, 6, estimates that in forty-seven occurrences out of sixty-six in the LXX *aparchē* means "tithes" rather than "first fruit"; of the four references in ben Sirach, only one means first fruit. Nevertheless, the symbolism of first fruit appears to suit our context. The Hebrew is usually from the Hebrew root *bkr* "to be the first born, first ripe." Until the first fruit of harvest or flock were offered to God the rest of the crop could not be put to profane or secular use. Rituals for the offering are given in Deut 26:1–11, Lev 23:9–21. Israel is regarded as the first fruit of God's harvest (Jer 2:3 although, as often, *re'šīt* not *bkr* is used). In ℵ pc t Prim, "first fruit" is replaced by "from the beginning"; this would translate *re'šīt*, further evidence for "first fruit."

5. *no falsehood.* Cf. Isa 53:9, which refers to the servant of Yahweh who has done no violence and "there was no deceit in his mouth," RSV. In both this text and Rev 14:5 there is probably a prophetic ring in the phrase, i.e. they uttered no false prophecies; cf. Isa 9:15, Jer 14:14, 20:6, 23:25, 26, 32, 27:10, 14, 15, 16, 29:21, Zech 13:3. See COMMENT. Gärtner, pp. 49–50, discusses the "idols of the heart" in 1QS 2:11, etc. "Idol" does not refer to "image" but to unfaithfulness to the Law.

they are unblemished. P[47] 046 1, 2329 al vg[s,cl] co TR read, "for they are unblemished," implying a causative relationship between blemish and falsehood, i.e. no falsehood is in their mouths because they are unblemished.

unblemished. Gr. *amōmoi.* This is a Levitical sacrificial term meaning not spoiled by any flaw, equivalent to Heb. *tāmīm,* "perfect." The translation should be "unblemished" rather than "blameless." If "unblemished" continues the metaphor of the "first fruit" it would refer to "flock," rather than "crop," and Lamb.

6–20. The arrangement of this segment is a septet which is constructed in three parts. The first part, vss. 6–12, recounts the deeds of the three angels, forming the first three units of the septet. The second part, vss. 13–14, deals with "a voice from heaven" and "one like a son of man," forming the fourth, central, unit. The third part, vss. 14–20, reverts to the angel motif by recounting the deeds of three more angels, forming the last three units of the septet. Gaechter, pp. 551–52, calls attention to the similarity between this arrangement and that of Ps 20, which comprises three stanzas—God is addressed (vss. 2–7, the first three parts); the king confides in God (vs. 8, the fourth, central, part); God is again addressed (vss. 8–14, the last three parts)—seven parts in all. He also compares Zech 3:6–7 and John 5:9–30. Kiddle, pp. 211–77, also suggests that this seventh oracle is itself septiform:

1) The Woman, the Messiah, and the Dragon, 12:1–6; 2) Atonement, 12:7–12; 3) Church Flees from Vanity Fair, 12:13–17; 4) Emergence and Character of Antichrist, 13:1–4; 5) Antichrist's Brief Reign, 13:5–10; 6) The Risen Martyrs, 14:1–5; 7) Day of Wrath, 14:6–13. The seven angels portend the fulfillment of God's final decrees. See COMMENT, pp. 248 ff.

6. *another angel.* It is not clear from the text whether the seer saw "another, an angel," or "another angel" flying in the mid-heaven; cf. 8:13. "Another" is omitted in $\mathbb{P}^{47}$ $\aleph$* 046 1, 82 pm sa.

an eternal gospel. Gr. *evaggelion aiōnion.* This phrase should not be translated as if the Gospel were meant. The gospel referred to here is the proclamation of the impending end of the world, bringing good tidings to the faithful and bad to the nations. In 10:7 the announcement is to the prophets, but here it is to the whole world. However, Caird, pp. 181–82, thinks that the proclamation means martyrdom. The "great martyrdom, then, is the earthly reality which corresponds to the flight of the angel." He compares John 12:31–32, where Jesus announces another judgment of the world, which is to liberate all men from Satan's accusation and draw them into unity with himself. Caird finds the words of the angel in vss. 6–7 so reminiscent not only of this passage in John but also of other Johannine passages, where the phrase "the hour has come" occurs, that this phrase, in his view, is like the "strokes of a great bell" (John 12:23, 13:1, 16:21, 32, 17:1). It would be surprising if there were no relationship between them.

One might ask whether the gospel has influenced Revelation or *vice versa.* The contents of the NT Gospel are almost entirely different from that which one finds here. Contrast also the wording of this phrase with Mark 13:10 and Matt 24:14, where the epithet "eternal" may either be retrospective or prospective. "Eternal" is found only once in Revelation but is frequent in the Gospel and the first epistle of John, e.g. John 3:15–16, 36, 4:14, 36, I John 1:2, 2:25.

7. *God.* 046 82 al g vg[s,cl] read "Lord."

the creator. The angel speaks of the creator in terms which recall the plagues of the first four trumpets.

springs of water. Gr. *pēgas hudatōn.* Some scholars find it strange that the author added "springs of water" to heaven and earth and sea, the traditional three parts of the universe. The addition of "springs of water" makes a fourth member. Why should the springs be mentioned rather than trees or animals or even men?

Masson, p. 65, finds the answer in the role of the fountains of water in the Bible in general and Revelation in particular. In the Bible they reflect the conditions of existence in Palestine, a country, surrounded by desert, where life depends upon the presence of water. In the desert the oasis signifies living water. In Revelation the fountains of water are smitten twice (8:10, 16:4), and men die en masse. But in other passages the fountains serve as symbols of eternal life, the gift of God to those who have accepted death rather than disobey His commandments; cf. 14:7. The Lamb leads people to the fountains of water (7:17; cf. 21:6, 22:17). It is difficult to believe that in adding "springs of water" to the reference to heaven, earth, and sea, the angel had not a special intention in mind, namely, to remind men that they owe the preservation of their life to the creator; Masson, p. 66.

"Springs of water" stands in bold contrast to "desert" (cf. 12:6, 14; 17:3, the harlot in the desert) and to the dragon's stream of water intended to drown the woman (12:16). The phrase is also extremely appropriate for the Zion-Jerusalem theme; cf. Ezek 47.

8. *"Fallen, fallen is Babylon the great."* The words are strongly influenced by Isa 21:9b, which tells of the fall of Babylon and the shattering of the images of her gods; cf. Rev 13:14. The epithet "great" is probably inspired by Dan 4:30, where Nebuchadnezzar surveys the city from the roof of his palace and says, "Is not this great Babylon, which I have built by my mighty power as a royal residence and for the glory of my majesty?" (RSV). Note his self-reliance.

wine. This indicates the intoxicating influence of Babylon's vices. The same concept appears in Jer 51:7, 8, which refers to Babylon as "a golden cup in the Lord's hand" that has intoxicated the earth and driven the nations mad.

9. *followed them.* A arm^pt Prim read "followed him."

10. *man will drink also.* Lit. "man, also he will drink." The "also," Gr. *kai,* precedes "he," Gr. *autos,* indicating that the pronoun is there to emphasize "man," not to indicate another person. Hence the present translation. The author probably means that one cannot drink one cup and not the other for both are linked; the consequence of drinking Babylon's cup is the inescapable necessity to receive the Lord's; cf. 16:19. For other references to the cup of anger see Isa 60:17, 22; Jer 25:15; Rev 18:6. Cf. also Ps 75:8, Psalms of Solomon 8:15 (in the last reference the wine is undiluted).

tormented. The torments are before the holy angels but not before God's people. These could be angels of vengeance but the allusion to the Lamb is embarrassing for the Christian. For a similar idea see I Enoch 48:9, APCh, II, 217:

> And I will give them over into the hands of Mine elect:
> As straw in the fire, so shall they burn before the face of the holy:
> As lead in water so shall they sink before the face of the righteous.
> And no trace of them shall any more be found.

In I Enoch 63:11 the wicked are driven from the presence of the Son of Man. Cf. also 90:26, 27. In Luke 12:9 the wicked are to be disowned by Christ in the presence of the angels, but there is no reference to punishment.

11. *day and night.* Cf. I Enoch 63:6, dealing with the ceaseless torment of kings. There is a clear parallel to the living creatures in Rev 9:8 who have no rest from their worship.

12–13. Some (see Allo, p. 219) argue that these verses are either interpolated or misplaced. The present writer believes they were added by a later hand as they break the sequence of the chapter, they contain one of the scant references to "Jesus," and they introduce the Spirit, who appears in Rev 2–3 and Rev 22:17, both of which are probably also from a later hand.

13. *in the Lord.* Contrast I Cor 15:18, "those who sleep in Christ," and I

Thess 4:16, "the dead in Christ." Revelation refers to "Lord" but Corinthians and Thessalonians make a clear allusion to Christ.

from now on. Gr. *aparti,* lit. "henceforth." The presence of this word is interesting in that it is found written *ap'arti* in Matt 23:39, 26:29, 64; John 13:19, 14:7. In Matthew it means "soon, in a short time," that is, it is used with reference to the beginning of a state or condition which is to be pro-longed, rather than simply, "henceforth." In the Johannine writings cited it means "from now on." Authors differ as to the construction: does *aparti* go with what precedes as suggested by Charles, Lohmeyer, Bousset, Allo, etc., or is it connected with what follows as Boismard believes?

Yes. Omitted in P⁴⁷ ℵ* bo.

Spirit. This word is found primarily in what have been described in the Introduction as additions, i.e. chs. 1–3 and some verses in chs. 20–22.

works. Gr. *erga.* Cf. Psalms of Solomon 9:9, which speaks of "laying up life" for oneself with the Lord. Cf. also Rev 2:2, 19, 3:2, 15; also 2:23, 22:12, and note that in Revelation this word occurs mainly in those passages which may be additions to the text.

14–17. The angels seem to associate closely with the "son of man" in the messianic judgment. In vss. 14–16 one angel appears to discharge the duties assigned to the Messiah, but in vs. 17 "another angel" distinguishes the being from "one like a son of man" in vs. 14. However, although Charles, II, 21, observes that "nowhere throughout our author is the Son of Man conceived as an angel," in I Enoch 46:2–4 the Son of Man has a face "full of graciousness, like one of the holy angels."

14. *on the cloud one like a son of man.* This and Rev 1:7 are the only references in John's apocalypse to Dan 7:13, where one like a son of man came down with the clouds.

was enthroned. Gr. *kathēmenon.* Note the similarities with the Gospels, Mark 14:62, Matt 26:64, Luke 22:69.

golden crown. This is perhaps a reminder of the sovereignty which the victors will share; see 20:4, 6; 22:5. Cf. the association between one like a son of man and the prophecies in Rev 1–3, esp. 3:21. See COMMENT.

15. *the hour to reap.* ℵ pc read, "the hour of the harvest."

the harvest of the earth. The harvest seems to be the faithful souls. The three angels coming out of the temple and from the altar continue the sacrificial element (first fruit, unblemished) already noted in vss. 4, 5. Caird, p. 190, observes that Gr. *therismos,* "harvest," and *therizō,* "to harvest," are used for in-gathering, not for mowing down, as enemies. The idea of judgment as a harvest is found in both the OT (cf. Joel 4:13) and the Gospels (cf. Matt 12:30). However, it does not occur in Revelation except in this passage.

17. *another angel.* Charles, II, 19, observes that this phrase shows the inter-polater "failed to recognize the one like the son of man in verse 14 as Christ, and took him to be simply an angel, and hence assigned a mightier role to the second and unnamed angel. But to place beside the son of man a second figure, and that merely an angelic one as a judge of the earth, is hardly in-telligible from any point of view." This difficulty, however, is partly explained

if the son of man gathers in the good harvest (as in the Gospels) and the angels destroy the bad, therefore vs. 17 must be original.

18. *came out.* Omitted in P⁴⁷ A 1611, 2060 pc g vgʷ.

authority over fire. Compare I Enoch 60:11–21 and Jubilees 2:2 where angels of various other elements are mentioned. This verse seems to be a paraphrase of Joel 4:13.

voice. P⁴⁷ CP 182, 1611, 2059s, 2329 pm TR read, "cry."

19. *the vine.* Caird, p. 192, observes that the gory vintage may be the death of the martyrs. He remarks, too, that 13:15 threatens death for the enemies of the beast, ch. 14 describes the battle, and ch. 15 describes the victory. There is no note of triumph in this harvest.

20. *outside the city.* The neighborhood of Jerusalem was thought of as a judgment place for Gentiles; cf. Joel 4:2, 12; Zech 14:2–12; I Enoch 53:1.

blood poured. The rivers of blood outside the city may be contrasted with the water from the temple in Ezek 47:1–12.

one thousand six hundred stadia. About two hundred miles. Caird, p. 195, observes that because this is a square number (40×40) it may provide some slight confirmation that the vintage is to be interpreted as the great martyrdom. The only other square numbers in the book are the 144,000, i.e. twelve contingents of one thousand from each of the twelve tribes, of the army of the Lord and the dimensions of the city. The number could also connote that the destruction is as complete as the preservation. 2036 pc read, "one thousand six hundred six," and ℵ* pc syᵖʰ read, "one thousand two hundred."

COMMENT

After the description of the emergence of the two monsters one expects to meet one who has power to oppose them, namely, God or his Anointed, perhaps "the Son of Man" who in Dan 7 stands over against and superior to the beasts and to whom is given dominion. Peoples, nations, and languages serve him, and his kingdom will not be destroyed (vs. 14). II Baruch 29:1–4 also indicates that the appearance of the beasts and the Anointed One will coincide. Further, Caird, p. 178, is probably right in suggesting that the writer is still expounding Ps 2 (cf. Rev 11:18, 12:5), in seeing God's Anointed as suppressing the nations and in associating this with Mount Zion: "I have set my king on Zion, my holy hill," Ps 2:6, RSV (cf. also Ps 110:2). The psalm ends with an appeal to the rulers to do homage to God.

The conqueror appears in the guise of the Lamb. He is shown standing firm (vs. 1), in contrast to the beasts in ch. 13 who are rising, i.e. in motion; see second NOTE on 14:1. The mountain on which he stands is in contrast to the sea and the land from which the monsters rise (13:1, 11). Since Mount Zion is the holy mountain, the dwelling of God (cf. Pss 9:12, 74:2, Isa 8:18), the sea and land would be symbolic of idolatry; indeed, the first monster is specifically said to blaspheme in 13:6.

It is with 14:1 that the author introduces a theme of overriding importance,

Zion/Jerusalem. Part Two of his book begins here; it is devoted to the destruction of the old Jerusalem and the building of the new. Hence it is significant that the Lamb and his followers appear on Mount Zion.

"Zion" and "Jerusalem" are practically interchangeable, although Jerusalem is more commonly used, 660 times as compared with 154 times for Zion; TWNT, VII, 295. Zion is the "city of Yahweh" (Isa 60:14; cf. Ps 48:2), His sanctuary (Ps 20:2), His holy mountain (Joel 2:1). It is used especially for "the city of the eschatological age of salvation (Is 1–39, Jer, Dt, 3rd Is, Joel, Mic 4 and Zech 1–9) . . . the seat and city of God . . . for the royal residence and capital, the symbol of the people or community (esp. Dt Is, Ps and Lam)," (TWNT, VII, 300), and the cultic site and temple city (esp. Pss, e.g. 77:68–72, and Lam). It is from Zion that God as a warrior roaring from heaven comes to judge (Jer 25:30) and to Zion that he will return (Ezek 43:1–9). Here he will inaugurate his eschatological reign; Isa 24:23; 52:7; Obad 21; Micah 4:7; Zeph 3:16; Zech 14:9; Pss 146:10, 149:2. It is here that the Anointed One is established (Ps 2:6) and receives the scepter as an investiture of power (Ps 90: 2). On this mountain God swears to preserve the dynasty of David; Ps 132:11–12. God chooses it for his resting place; Ps 132:13–18. From here will come material blessings (vs. 15), blessings for the righteous (vs. 16), permanence for the monarchy (vs. 17). This will be the place of entry for the messianic ruler (Zech 9:9) and the rallying point of the remnant—the nucleus of the messianic restoration—cf. II Kings 19:30–31, Obad 17, 21.

A pseudepigraphical text showing some affinity with Rev 14 is II Baruch 40, which follows the prophet's vision of the forest (symbolizing the four kingdoms which will be destroyed, the vine, and the fountain which are the principate of "My Messiah"). The vision concludes by predicting that the leader of the hostility will be taken alive to Mount Zion, where the Messiah will convict him of his impieties, put him to death, " 'and protect the rest of My people which shall be found in the place which I have chosen. And his principate will stand for ever, until the world of corruption is at an end, and until the times aforesaid are fulfilled' "; APCh, II, 501.

IV Ezra 13:25–40, which may contain Christian interpolation, is even nearer to Rev 14. It is an interpretation of the preceding vision of the Man from the sea who flies with the clouds of heaven (APCh, II, 618; words in italics are interpolations):

[26]. . . this is he whom the Most High is keeping many ages . . . [27]and the same shall order the survivors . . . [34]and an innumerable multitude shall be gathered together . . . to fight against him. [35]But he shall stand upon the summit of Mount Sion. [36]*And Sion shall come and shall be made manifest to all men, prepared and builded* . . . [37]But he, my Son, shall reprove the nations . . . [38]and shall reproach them to their face with their evil thoughts and with the tortures . . . [39]and then shall he destroy them without labour by the Law which is compared unto fire. And whereas thou didst see that he summoned and gathered to himself another multitude which was peaceable—[40]These are the ten tribes . . .

13. "And I saw another monster ascending from the land, and he had two horns like a lamb, and he spoke like a dragon" (Rev 13:11)

Perhaps the author had in mind a supernatural creature like this winged and horned Assyrian demon.

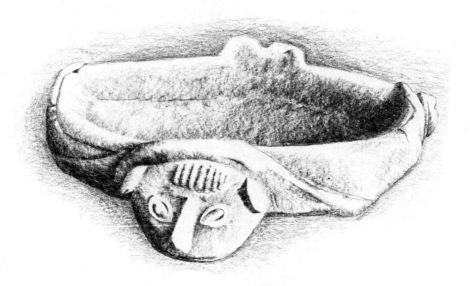

14. "And one of the four living creatures gave to the seven angels seven golden bowls filled with the wrath of God who lives forever and ever" (Rev 15:7)

Libation bowls like this one decorated with a lion's head from the twelfth century B.C. held sacrificial animal blood, considered in the early Hebrew religion to be God's due.

15. "And I heard a voice from the altar saying, 'Yes, Lord God Almighty, Your judgments are true and just" (Rev 16:7)

When the ancient Hebrews spoke of an altar they meant one constructed of stone with four horns according to biblical regulation, like this tenth-century B.C. altar discovered at Megiddo.

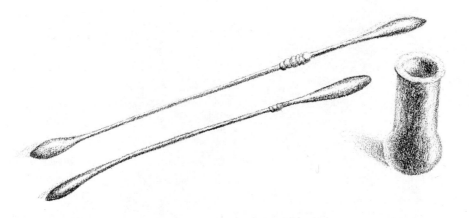

16. "And the woman [the harlot Babylon] was clothed in purple and scarlet, and bedecked with gold and precious stones and pearls; she had in her hand a golden cup filled with abominations . . ." (Rev 17:4)

Cosmetics and scents were common feminine accoutrements, although at times they were held in some disrepute. A harlot would certainly have outlined her eyes with colored salves, perhaps with the help of a bronze applicator like the ones drawn here. She would also have daubed herself with essences, perhaps from clay perfume vials like this one. These objects were found during Professor Yadin's Masada excavations.

17. "And the ten horns which you see are ten kings, who have not yet received their sovereignty . . ." (Rev 17:12)

One of the kings referred to here was undoubtedly the Roman emperor Titus, whose stone statue is pictured here.

18. ". . . and on his head were many diadems" (Rev 19:12)

The figure so described is Faithful and True, the Word of God. His head may have been crowned somewhat like this one, which bears a diadem adorned with twelve small heads.

19. ". . . and when I turned I saw seven golden lampstands, and in the middle of the lampstands one like a son of man . . ." (Rev 1:12-13)

The seven lampstands were menorahs, seven-branched candelabra like this one, a Jewish ceremonial object. This menorah is adapted from the one looted by the Romans from the Second Jerusalem Temple in A.D. 70 and depicted on the Arch of Titus.

20. ". . . yes, I hold the keys of death and of Sheol" (Rev 1:18)

This is what most keys looked like around the first century A.D. Probably used to open a large door, this particular key was discovered during the Bar-Kokhba excavations led by Professor Yadin.

A. "the ark of the covenant was seen" (Rev 11:19)

"Mater Misericordiae" (The Madonna in Childbirth), painted by the fifteenth-century Italian artist Piero della Francesca. By permission of Hawthorn Books, Inc., from *All the Paintings of Piero della Francesca*, text by Piero Bianconi, translated by Paul Colacicchi. Copyright © 1962 by Rizzoli, Editore, s.p.a. All rights reserved.

B. "And I saw a monster ascending from the sea; he had ten horns and seven heads . . ." (Rev 13:1)

From a Rhenish manuscript, 1310-1315, of The Apocalypse. The Metropolitan Museum of Art, The Cloisters Collection, 1968

C. "These make war with the Lamb and the Lamb will conquer them, because he is Lord of Lords and King of Kings . . ." (Rev 17:14)

From a Rhenish manuscript, 1310-1315, of The Apocalypse. The Metropolitan Museum of Art, The Cloisters Collection, 1968

D. "And I saw the holy city, the new Jerusalem, descending out of heaven from God, prepared as a bride adorned for her husband" (Rev 21:2)

The Virgin Mary represents the Christian priestly people par excellence.

"Le sacerdos de la Vierge" (The Priest of the Virgin), painted by an unknown artist of the School of Amiens, 1437. By permission of Phaidon Press, Ltd., London, from *A Century of French Painting, 1400–1500,* edited by Grete Ring. Copyright © 1949 by Phaidon Press, Ltd. All rights reserved.

Cf. Rev 14:10–11 concerning the torment before the saints and the Lamb.

This reflects the climate in which Rev 14 was written; the Anointed One was thought of as a military Messiah with "soldiers." Caird, p. 178, correctly suggests that the "one hundred and forty-four thousand" of vs. 3 are numerated by tribes and that the scene is reminiscent of the military roll call, a census as in I Chron 4–7. The song mentioned in vs. 3 is a paean of victory. The multitude appears to be the same as the one depicted in ch. 7, but the situation is different; the people here are deliberately contrasted with the beast worshipers.

The followers of the beast bear his mark, the Lamb's soldiers his name and that of his Father on their foreheads; cf. Ezek 9:4. The text, though worded differently, bears the same concept as Joel 3:5 (cf. Zeph 3:12), but instead of simply calling upon the name, that is, accepting the deity, the remnant have actually the name upon their forehead, just as the Deuteronomic law provided that the phylactery containing the *Shema‘* (Deut 6:4–5) should be "as frontlets between your eyes" (Deut 6:8, RSV).

There is another deliberate contrast between the beast and the Lamb in the variations on the theme of mouth and voice in Rev 14:2. In Rev 12:15 the serpent spits water from his mouth in an attempt to drown the woman. In 13:5–6 the blasphemous mouth of the beast speaks arrogant words against God, His name, and His dwelling. But in Rev 14:2 there issues forth a heavenly voice from the one hundred and forty-four thousand, for which the author gives a three-fold description. It is "like the sound of many waters," a welcome sound in a land which often suffered from drought, like thunder, reminiscent of the voice of Yahweh (see NOTE on vs. 2) and like the music of harpers, suggesting temple worship. It utters, not three-fold blasphemy, but a new song, not against God but before the throne, the living creatures and the elders, i.e. the dwellers in heaven; cf. 13:6.

We have heard a new song twice before, once for the Lamb (5:9) and once for the conquerors (7:14–17). All three new songs are associated with triumph, with victory. The beast can make an image speak (13:15) but no one can learn the new song except those redeemed from earth; it is probably like a secret password used in war or the names of angels only revealed to mystics. The phrase "redeemed from the earth" is probably meant in the sense of "released from slavery or bondage to the beasts."

According to vss. 4–5, the characteristics of the people who can learn the new song are: 1) that they are not defiled with women, they are virgin; 2) that they follow the Lamb; 3) that they are as first fruits; 4) that no lie is found in their mouth, they are blameless; 5) that they are male. The Greek for "virgin" in this text is masculine, for the demonstrative pronoun *outoi* is masculine. For the various interpretations see the NOTES on vss. 4–5.

In order to understand these verses it is appropriate to keep them within the context of Zion. Zion is the city of the servants of Yahweh. Her inhabitants are variously called "daughter" (II Kings 19:21, Micah 4:8, etc.), "sons" (cf. Joel 1:12); "daughters" only in Song of Songs: "prophets" (Jer 23:14–15); "virgins" (Lam 2:10). It is the title "virgin" which is most pertinent for our text. "Virgin" is a frequent epithet for Zion herself in the OT (II Kings 19:21;

Isa 23:12; 37:22; Jer 14:17, 18:13; 31:4, 21; Lam 1:15, 2:13; Amos 5:2) but this is rendered differently in the *targumim*. The Targum of Isa 23:12 reads "the people that were in Zidon," on 37:22, "congregation of Zion." The Targum of Jer 14:17 has "congregation" as do those on Jer 18:13, 31:4, 21. The Targum of Lam 1:15 has "virgins of Israel," and of 2:13, "virgin of the congregation of Sion." Lam 2:10 keeps "virgins of Jerusalem" and it is this text which may have influenced our own (AB):

> In silence they sit on the ground, the elders of Zion.
> They put dirt on their heads; they wear sackcloth.
> The virgins of Jerusalem bow their heads to the ground.

Lam 2:10 is in the context of the absence of true prophetic vision (vs. 9) and the presence of false prophecy (vs. 14). One may have a poetic parallel in the phrases "elders of Zion" and "virgins of Jerusalem."

That "virgin" is masculine is not unheard of, and probably indicates a metaphoric meaning. The LXX version of Lam 2:10 contains the phrase "chief virgins of Jerusalem," Gr. *archēgous parthenous;* the adjective shows that the virgins are masculine. The Hebrew for "virgin," *bethulah,* can be used in several senses: of a human being (virgin), of soil (unbroken), and of sycamore trees (untrimmed). It bears also the sense of "retired" or "ascetic," i.e. a maid who has retired from social pleasures, a prayerful maid (Jastrow, under *bethulah*).

Philo uses the feminine form of "virgin," *parthenos,* in a figurative sense; e.g. in *De Cherubim* 49–50 he calls Sarah "virgin," meaning that her passions were perfectly controlled, and in *De Posteritate Caini* 134 he calls Rebecca "ever virgin." In *De Cherubim* 50 he says that God makes the soul turn from being a woman to become a virgin again, "for He takes away the degenerate and emasculate passions which unmanned it and plants instead the native growth of unpolluted virtues." In *Questions and Answers on Genesis* 4.95 Philo says that the sign of a virgin is "a pure and sincere intention which honours the sincere and incorruptible nature without passion." He speaks in 4:99 about two virginities, one with respect to the body and one with respect to the incorruptible soul. In the same treatise, 132 on Gen 24:57 LXX, he expounds, somewhat curiously, on the phrase "question her mouth," saying that one does not question thoughts for only God can hear these, but one examines "their servant, (namely) the speech that is uttered." In *Questions and Answers on Exodus* 2.3 Philo says that "when souls become divinely inspired, from (being) women they become virgins, throwing off the womanly corruptions which are (found) in sense-perception and passion. Moreover, they follow after and pursue the genuine and unmated virgin, the veritable wisdom of God"; note the similarity to Rev 14:4. In *on Exodus* 2.46 he speaks of the "ever-virginal nature of the hebdomad," the earth-born first molded man coming into being on the sixth day and the heavenly one on the seventh.

In the light of the metaphorical meaning of virgin it would seem that Rev 14:4 refers to faithful elders of Jerusalem or all the faithful who have not defiled themselves with idolatry, the lust (Gr. *thumos*) of Babylon's harlotry, as in vs. 8. Not being defiled with women may look back to the female monster in ch. 13, but much more probably it looks forward to the harlot in Rev 17, 18.

Instead of "followed after . . . with admiration" the beast, as does "the whole world" in 13:3, the "virgins" follow the Lamb. Instead of the blasphemous words in the mouth of the beast (13:5), in their mouth is no lie. Thus one has a fairly clear parallelism:

God	dragon
first beast	Roman empire
Lamb	second beast
immaculate followers	apostate followers.

What distinguishes the followers is their possession of truth or, as the author expresses it in vs. 5, the absence of falsehood. His statement is influenced by Zeph 3:9, 12–14, where the prophet speaks the words of the Lord:

"Yea, at that time I will change the speech of the peoples
    to a pure speech,
that all of them may call on the name of the Lord
    and serve Him with one accord . . .
For I will leave in the midst of you
    a people humble and lowly . . .
they shall do no wrong
    and utter no lies,
nor shall there be found in their mouth
    a deceitful tongue.
For they shall pasture and lie down
    and none shall make them afraid."
Sing aloud, O daughter of Zion;
    shout, O Israel!
Rejoice and exult with all your heart,
    O daughter of Jerusalem!

There are also nonbiblical texts on the same theme. We have already referred to the blaspheming tongue mentioned in 1QS 4:11 and CDC 5:11–12 in the NOTE on 13:6, but it might be profitable to recall here that the antithesis to the Teacher of Righteousness or, indeed, to the Qumran Community as a whole, is the Man of the Lie. In 1QpHab 2:1–2 certain people are said to follow the Man of the Lie, Heb. *iš hak-kazab*. They do not heed the words of the Teacher of Righteousness, neither do they believe his interpretation of the prophets concerning the events of the eschatological era; 1QpHab 2:6 ff., cf. 7:4–5. Further, in 1QpHab 5:9 ff. there is a reference to those who remained silent when the Teacher of Righteousness was chastised and did not aid him against the Man of the Lie, who rejected the law. The Man or Preacher of the Lie is further mentioned in 10:9 ff., where it is said that he "enticed many to build a city of falsehood through bloodshed and to establish a congregation (*'edah*) in lies (*šeqer*) . . . that he made many grow weary in the service of falsehood." Ringgren, p. 33, n. 87, observes that in the phrase "preacher of the lie" the word *maṭṭip* is a word used of ecstatic prophetic preaching. In Rev 14:5 one cannot tell whether "falsehood" is equivalent to *kazab* (falsehood, false prophecies), *šeqer* (deceit) or *maṭṭip* (ecstatic prophetic preaching), but the context is such that one might surmise that the "virgins" might not only be faithful elders but also true prophets standing opposed to the second beast who is the false prophet. It would seem that our text has nothing to do with unmarried persons but that the symbol of "virgin" is used to express fidelity to Yahweh.

This interpretation is not inconsistent with the thorough examination of Boismard, although he takes a Christian view of the text. He observes that in vss. 4–5 John explains the identity of those faithful to the Lamb in three parallel phrases, each commencing with an emphatic "these," *Gr. outoi*. Boismard agrees with scholars who identify the virgins with those who remain faithful and refuse to adore the beast. However, he takes the interpretation further, (1) by analyzing the context in which the vision of the one hundred and forty-four thousand virgins is found, (2) by comparing this vision to those which present some analogy with it in the rest of Revelation, and (3) by clarifying the sense of this vision in the light of the prophetic oracles which influenced John.

1) The two visions in chs. 13 and 14:1–5, respectively, form two facets of a contrasting picture, and the contrast continues in the vision of 14:6–11, where John sees three angels who caution the followers of the beast that the hour of judgment is near. The time of their conversion is near and thus the vision of the virgins is inserted between the two complementary visions and forms an antithesis to them (Boismard, p. 164). Now, if the followers of the beast represent all those who adore the beast from every tribe, etc., (as in 13:7; cf. 14:6), i.e. all those whose names are not written in the book of life of the Lamb (13:8), the virgins would represent all those who are faithful to the Lamb, all those who have refused to adore the beast, and by extension all those whose names are written in the book of life of the Lamb. That this equation is remarked by "John" himself is evident in that the virgins carry the name of the Lamb and this is the symbol of all the faithful without distinction; cf. 22:4.

The contrast between the visions in chs. 13, 14, indicates in what sense one should interpret the expressions in ch. 14. The prophets of the OT (especially Jeremiah, Ezekiel, and Hosea; cf. Hosea 2:14–21; Jer 2:2–3, etc.) represent the covenant of Sinai under the image of espousals between God and his people. Consequently, all idolatry was considered as adultery or fornication. "John" himself uses these images: the faithful community is the spouse of the Lamb (19:7, 21:2–9); Babylon is its antithesis and is represented as a prostitute (17:4–6), as is the faithless Jerusalem of Ezek 16, 23. If, then, the one hundred and forty-four thousand are contrasted with the followers of the beast, precisely because they do not adore him, it would be reasonable to interpret fornication and virginity in a metaphorical sense (Boismard, p. 164). That one hundred and forty-four thousand are not defiled with women harlots means they have not given themselves to the worship of the beast. There is no question of Christian ascetics.

2) One is persuaded to adopt this interpretation also if one compares 14:1–5 with the other visions in 7:3–8, 5:6–11. John has already used the number of one hundred and forty-four thousand in 7:4 to indicate the number

of the servants of God who are marked on the forehead by the angel and spared the plagues. It would be surprising if John had a different symbolic meaning for the same number in ch. 14 (Boismard, p. 165). The people concerned both bear the "seal" or "name" of God on their foreheads. In ch. 7 the symbolism is evidently in relationship to the number of tribes of Israel. 144,000=12,000×12, and 1,000 is the symbol of the great multitude. Thus in ch. 14 the number 144,000 is chosen only to represent the multitude of the faithful forming the new Israel, the new and perfect Israel (Boismard, 166). This idea occurs also in other authors in the NT, e.g. Gal 6:16; cf. Rom 9:6, Phil 3:3. Thus, in view of Rev 7, the virgins around the Lamb must represent all, not only a fraction, of the faithful, who are redeemed. This conclusion is confirmed by the parallels between 14:1–5 and 5:6–11.

Rev 14:1–5	*Rev 5:6–11*
1 And I looked, and behold the Lamb standing . . .	6 And I saw . . . a little Lamb standing.
3 . . . before the throne and before the four living creatures and the elders.	between the throne and the four living creatures and among the elders.
2 . . . the voice which I heard was like harpers playing on their lyres.	8 . . . elders . . . each held a harp.
3 And they sang a new song . . .	9a And they chanted a new song . . .
4 These were redeemed from men, the first fruit to God and to the Lamb.	9b You are worthy . . . because you were slain and you purchased for God by your blood men from every tribe and tongue and people and nation.

The relationship between these texts becomes even more striking when one considers that of the expressions outlined above, the new song and the redeemed occur nowhere else in Revelation, and the harp occurs only here and in 15:2. In addition, a hymn sung by the elders to the glory of the lamb in ch. 5 corresponds to the hymn which is sung by the heavenly voices in ch. 14.

3) The vision of the one hundred and forty-four thousand virgins contains a number of allusions to the oracles of the OT. All the allusions converge toward the same idea, namely, that of the remnant, those who have escaped and are regenerated when God comes to reestablish Israel and deliver her from her enemies on the great day of his wrath. Among the OT prophets, Mount Zion was traditionally conceived as a place where the survivors would reassemble on the day of restoration.

We have already cited some texts, but it is worth giving special reference to the prophet Obadiah to whom Boismard refers. The prophet announces the great day of the wrath of God who strikes Edom and all the nations who have persecuted Israel. In vs. 17 he says, "But in Mt. Zion there will be those that escape, and it shall be holy." In the preceding verse Obadiah announces the chastisement of the persecutors and uses the metaphor of the cup or quaffing bowl. Similarly in Rev 14:9–11 an angel announces that the followers of the monster will drink "the wine of the wrath of God . . . the cup of His anger." We find the same contrast in Revelation and in the prophet Obadiah, namely, the faithful of God are assembled on Mount Zion where their persecutors drink the wine of the wrath of God. Boismard (p. 168) makes a similar comparison with Joel 3–4 and observes that here the prophecy is followed by a series of prophecies about the extermination of the pagan nations who persecute Israel (Joel 4:13). With this, one may compare Revelation where John takes the symbol of the harvest (14:14–21), and announces the gathering of the pagan nations with a view to their extermination (14:14–16, 19:19–21).

Boismard also deduces, from the text of Zeph 3:12–13 and Jer 23 that "the lie" is equivalent to religious infidelity or idolatry. Jer 2:2–3 shows that the youthfulness and the espousals of Israel imply the idea of her virginity; cf. vs. 32. Notice the similarity between the expressions in Jer 2:2–3 and the triple characteristic of the redeemed one hundred and forty-four thousand. Jeremiah says Israel, in the time of her youth and espousals, followed God in the desert, and God considered Israel as the first fruit of his harvest. In Rev 14, the same is true of the virgins of the Lamb; they are not defiled with women, they follow the Lamb, and they are redeemed as the first fruit of God.

The similarity of the texts cannot be fortuitous. First fruit is the peculiar property of God, that which he has reserved, and which he has forbidden others to touch under pain of death. The number redeemed in Rev 14:3 is the first fruit of the total harvest which God will bring in. The prophets of the OT foretold an era of great tribulation for Israel because of her infidelities to Yahweh. Normally this took the form of invasion by foreign peoples, but because of the covenant God can never let his people be entirely destroyed. He will purify them by trial, and those who are redeemed will form the nucleus of the new people.

Such are the broad outlines of the theology of the remnant of Israel among the prophets, and John has reproduced the same scheme in the second part of Revelation. After having described the great persecution of the beast against the faithful which causes a number of apostasies (ch. 13), he sees the remnant of those who remain faithful to God grouped on Mount Zion. The day of God's wrath approaches. The destruction of the prosecutors is predicted first in 14:6–21 and then realized by the fall of Babylon in ch. 16 and the destruction of the beast and his allies in 19:11–21. After this will appear the celestial Jerusalem (21:1–8), and God will reign in the midst of his people (22:3–5).

In vss. 5–20, as Gaechter and others have shown, our author has a sevenfold structure, three angels, then the Son of Man and, then, three more angels. See NOTE on 14:6–20. The form is so arranged that the climax comes in the fourth part, describing the Son of Man, around which the rest are grouped.

The first angel (vs. 6) flies in mid-heaven, i.e. to the zenith, to the point of heaven where he was able to see men spread out on the whole face of the earth. His position is symbolic of the universality of his message (Masson, p. 64). He has an eternal gospel to preach to those who reside upon the earth and to nations and tribes and tongues and peoples.

There have been many interpretations of the words "eternal gospel." Swete, p. 182, suggests "a gospel which has had an age-long history," with which he compares Rom 16:25, or "a gospel belonging to, stretching forward to, the eternal order"; cf. Mark 3:29, "eternal sin." He observes that this gospel may be the antithesis to the promise of brief indulgence which excited the hopes of

Roman subjects. Masson gives a fuller explanation. He remarks, with other commentators, that this text is the only Johannine one which contains the word "gospel." It is called "eternal" in order to distinguish it from all the other divine messages. The angel does not announce the gospel of Jesus Christ but an eternal gospel whose contents are clearly defined in vs. 7, and which differ significantly from the Christian message. It has two imperatives, "Fear God and give Him glory," and it appears to be addressed to a humanity which is idolatrous and superstitious (9:20, 21), seduced by the beast and the false prophet (13:3–8, 11–17). The call to adore the creator takes on a new meaning if we compare it with a negative commandment in vs. 9, the prohibition of beast-worship. The designation of God as creator, as Bousset remarks, is used very often in Jewish apocalyptic writings but is rare in the NT; cf. Masson, pp. 63–65. Indeed Masson is right; the content of the gospel is not specifically Christian. However, it is very close to the solemn summons of John the Baptist.

There is another aspect of the "eternal gospel" which deserves attention. One cannot overlook the correspondence between the eagle flying in mid-heaven (8:13) and perhaps symbolizing Rome, who calls "woe" three times, and this angel who proclaims an eternal gospel or, indeed, the first three angels in ch. 14, two of whom proclaim woeful messages. Indeed, "gospel" itself may have a significance different from the NT concept. In secular Greek *euaggelion*, "good news" or "gospel," is a technical word for the "news of victory" (TWNT, II, 722) but of special interest is its use in association with the imperial cult.

The emperor was regarded as divine either after death or (with Caligula and Domitian) during his lifetime. His power was thought to extend over nature including the animals, earth, and sea; even healing and miracles were attributed to him. Vespasian, e.g., is reputed to have cured a blind man and a lame man (Suetonius *Vespasian* 2) and at the same time "by the direction of certain soothsayers, some vases of antique workmanship were dug up in a consecrated spot at Tegea in Arcadia and on them was an image very like Vespasian" (ibid.). The emperor was a Savior who redeemed men from their troubles and brought the *Pax Romana*, "Roman peace." He proclaimed the *euaggelia*, "gospel," through his appearance, at his birth, his coming of age and his accession; see TWNT, II, under *euaggelion*. We have submitted that the mortal wound of the beast was healed by the accession of Vespasian and it is of interest that the word "gospel," Gr. *euaggelion*, is used in association with him. Josephus uses both the verb and the noun when recording how Marsyas, the freedman of Agrippa, announced the "good news" of the death of Tiberius to Agrippa, saying "The lion is dead"; *Ant.* 18.228–29. He uses it again with reference to the revolt at the time of Florus where the strange phrase "dire news was a godsend," Gr. *deinon euaggelion*, is employed. *Euaggelia* is used with reference to the accession of Vespasian in *War* 4.656.

The author of Revelation creates extreme irony in his use of *euaggelion*, for he proclaims not the accession of Vespasian, but the sovereignty of God, an "eternal gospel." He thereby implies a contrast between the everlasting nature of God's sovereignty and the transitory nature of the emperor's rule, placed in the context of a proclamation of the downfall of the idolatrous state (vs. 8) and the ceaseless or eternal punishment of its citizens (vss. 9–11). The tidings are directed not toward those "living," Gr. *katoikousin,* on the earth, the author's usual phrase, but toward those "enthroned," Gr. *kathē-menous,* on the earth. There seems to be a reference back to the One seated, Gr. *kathēmenos,* on the throne (ch. 4) and those who sat upon the horses (ch. 6). The angel is likened to the heralds who announced the imperial good news. According to TWNT, II, under *euaggelion,* they came, raised their right hand (cf. 10:5), and proclaimed with a loud voice (14:7). The herald angel in 14:6–7 announces the reaffirmation of the decalogue and the worship of one God, in opposition to the worship of the image (13:15) which violated the commandments. The reference to God as creator is understandable in the light of the reference to heaven, earth, and the water under the earth in Exod 20:4. Further the reference to the hour of judgment (vs. 7) bears affinity to Exod 20:5, God's declaration of jealousy and vengeance on those who hate Him.

The second angel predicts the fall of Babylon, i.e. the pagan state. Her destruction is mentioned seven times in John's Revelation: 16:17–21, 17:16, 18:1–3, 4–8, 9–20, 21–24. In the OT Babylon was the empire that best epitomized hostility to God, and many oracles predict her destruction. Isa 21:9 has an exclamation almost identical with Rev 14:8, "Fallen, fallen is Babylon," but the second part of the verse is different: "and all the images of her gods he has shattered to the ground" (RSV). An even closer text is Jer 51:7–8a (AB):

> 7 A golden cup was Babylon
>   In Yahweh's hand,
>   To make all the earth drunk.
>   Of its wine the nations drank,
>   Thereupon went mad
> 8 Suddenly Babylon fell and was broken;
>   Wail over her!

The third angel warns those who adore the beast and receive his mark of the consequences of such an action. If they have drunk Babylon's wine of harlotry, lusted after other gods, then they must drink God's wine of wrath unmitigated, and they will be tormented night and day before the Lamb and his angels. The cup or wine of God's wrath is a familiar OT symbol found e.g. in Isa 51:17, Jer 25:15. It indicates the fearful punishments which God will visit upon evildoers; cf. Rev 18:6, Ps 75:9. The cup itself is probably the wide wine bowl without handles; cf. Prov 23:31, Ezek 23:32, Amos 6:6, and see illustration 14. Hartman and van den Born, *Encyclopaedic Dictionary of the Bible,* under "cup," suggest that the custom that the head of the family fills the cups of all those at table gave rise to the metaphorical use of "cup" in the sense of "lot in life which God has destined for each one." In this case the contents of the cup, wrath, may be associated with poison, for one Hebrew equivalent for "poison" is *ḥemāh,* meaning also heat or wrath. The verb implies mixing the wine with the elements that will render it more poisonous, whereas the adjective states that it is unmixed, that is, neat. One might translate with Charles, II, 16, "the wine of the wrath of God which is mingled sheer in the cup." This emphasizes the unmitigated severity of the punishments.

The description of the punishment with fire and sulphur or brimstone suggests the influence of the narrative concerning the destruction of Sodom and Gomorrah (Gen 19:24–26) and the text of Isa 34:8, predicting the punishment of Edom and the other heathen nations (cf. Rev 19:20, 20:10, 21:8). Why the punishment should be "in the sight of the holy angels and the lamb" is difficult to say. "Before the angels" may be a Jewish periphrasis for "before God"; cf. Luke 15:10. Alternately, Caird, p. 187, suggests that this concept arose from a mistranslation of Isa 66:24 "the words 'they shall be repulsive to all of mankind' were read . . . as if they were 'they shall be a spectacle to all mankind.'" A relic of punishment by fire before witnesses remains in I Thess 4:16–17, II Thess 1:7–10, where the wicked are overcome in flames of fire before the saints. The torment is shown to be continuous. A text which shows affinity to this and which contrasts vividly with the saints resting from their labors in vs. 7 is I Enoch 63:1–2, 6, which says that the mighty and the king will pray for some rest from their eternal torment so they may confess their sins, but rest is not granted them.

Vss. 12–13 contain the second of the seven beatitudes which occur in Revelation, and here, for the first time, the faithful are called blessed. (The first beatitude, according to the traditional order, occurs in 1:3.) There seems to be no middle way; one either adores the beast and is doomed or one accepts with patient endurance the persecution of the beast, obeys the commandments of God, dies in Him, and receives reward for one's good works (vs. 13).

The meaning of "works" is ambiguous. I Enoch 41:1 refers to the actions of men weighed in the balance; cf. Job 31:6, Prov 16:2, 21:2. I Enoch 38:2 mentions the righteous "whose elect works hang upon the Lord of Spirits" (APCh, II, 209). II Baruch 14:12 speaks of the righteous having with God "a store of works preserved in treasuries" (APCh, II, 491); cf. II Baruch 24:1. A similar idea occurs in IV Ezra 7:77: "For thou hast a treasure of works laid up with the Most High, but it shall not be showed thee until the last times" (APCh, II, 587), and in Pirke Aboth 6:10: "in the hour of a man's death it is not silver or gold or precious stones or pearls which accompany him, but Torah and good works" (APCh, II, 713). Because the Law is not specifically discussed in Revelation and this would lead one to surmise that works entail more than ritual observance or supererogatory works or good deeds, Charles is probably right in saying that the author simply points to "the manifestation of the inner life and character" of the saints.

The first three angels have proclaimed the sovereignty of God, predicted the fall of Babylon, and described the future torment of idolaters. The fourth and central vision is of one like a son of man to whom is committed the task of the grain harvest. The figure and the harvest imagery recall the preaching of John the Baptist who prophesied that He Who Cometh would be an agent of judgment and would separate the wheat from the chaff and administer punishments and rewards; Matt 3:12; Luke 3:17. Scobie, p. 66, observes: "It is worth noting that in Rev xiv 14, a passage which very probably reproduces an earlier Jewish Apocalypse, the Son of Man is pictured as holding a sickle and reaping the earth"; cf. M. Goguel, *Au Seuil De L'Évangile; Jean Baptiste* (Payot, 1928), p. 41. This harvest, therefore, is one of protection rather than of destruction and therefore follows naturally after the exhortation to the saints (vss. 12–13).

Rev 14:14 is similar to Mark 13:26–27: "And then shall they see the Son of Man coming in the clouds . . . And then shall he send his angels, and shall gather together his elect" (KJ). But in Rev 14:14 the figure is "sitting," Gr. *kathēmenos*, not "coming," Gr. *erchomenos*. This recalls the "One seated on the throne" in ch. 4 and the riders on the horses in ch. 6. The verb "sit" implies ruling or judging, e.g. to sit in judgment; cf. Dan 7:13, Mark 14:62 and its parallels Mark 9:1, 13:26: the synoptics use the word *kathēmenos*. The "golden crown" (see NOTE on vs. 14) also distinguishes the one like a son of man from the six angels. When the angel gives the time signal, the son of man gathers in the harvest but there is no indication of the destruction of any part of it.

Carrington, pp. 251–61, observes that it is an angel (vs. 17), not the son of man, who implements the vintage of the wrath of God, and he is sent on his mission by the angel who has power over fire. This may be Uriel (fire of God), one of whose duties was to preside over Hades. Our author uses the same Greek word, *drepanon,* for the sickle held by the Son of Man and the instrument used by the destroying angel. However, *drepanon* may mean either a sickle or a vine dresser's tool: the latter is appropriate here. Charles, II, 19, associates the "vintage angel" with the souls of the dead who cried out for vengeance (16:10); he comes in answer to their prayer, cuts down the vine, and casts it into the winepress.

The vine can be a figure for Israel, as in Isa 5, Ps 80, but this does not preclude other meanings. However, there are two striking points in vs. 20 which suggest that the author did have Israel in mind. First, the trampling of the winepress is performed outside the city. The author will reach the destruction of the city in chs. 17, 18, but now he is concerned only about those "outside the city." Second, the amount of bloodshed is enormous. The measurement of one thousand six hundred stadia is approximately the distance from Tyre to El Arish, two hundred miles. On a historical level one might suggest that the author predicted, or his work reflected, conditions in Palestine. In A.D. 66 Vespasian (with Titus), after strengthening his forces, captured nearly all the cities in Galilee which were held by the Zealots. Then he marched to Caesarea and Jerusalem. It was at this time that the whole of Palestine suffered bloodshed, with the exception of the Holy City. It may be this kind of situation to which the vision of the vintaging of the land addressed itself.

The vine as a symbol of Israel is well known; the most popular passage is Isa 5, but a text more pertinent to Rev 14 is Ps 80, which describes the devastation of the land by the enemy through the image of a vineyard being cut down. A similar thought is found in an oracle in Ezek 15:6: "As the vine tree among the trees of the forest, which I have given to the fire for fuel, so will I give the inhabitants of Jerusalem" (KJ), and Isa 63, where the trampling figure is used with reference to Edom.

Rev 14 is a prelude to the victory to be completed by the figure on the white horse in Rev 19 and to the total destruction of the enemies' force in chs. 19–20 but more fuel must be added to the fire. The next chapter resumes the theme of the wrath of God intimated in 14:10 and brings it to a climax.

BIBLIOGRAPHY

Allo, E. B. *Saint Jean, L'Apocalypse.*

Boismard, M.-E. RB 59 (1952), 161–81.

Bousset, W. *Der Antichrist in der Überlieferung des Judentums des Neuen Testament und der alten Kirche, Ein Beitrag zur Auslegung der Apokalypse.* Gottingen: Vandenhoeck & Ruprecht, 1906.

Caird, G. B. *The Revelation of St. John the Divine.*

Cambier, J. "Les Images de l'Ancien Testament dans l'Apocalypse de Saint Jean," *Nouvelle Revue Theologique* 77 (1955), 113–22.

Carrington, P. *The Meaning of Revelation.*

Cerfaux, L. "L'Evangile Eternel (Apoc. 14, 6)," *Ephemerides Theologicae Lovanienses* 39 (1963), 672–81.

Charles, R. H. *Revelation,* ICC, I, II.

Devine, R. *Scripture* 16 (1964), 1–5.

Ford, J. M. "The Meaning of Virgin," NTS 12 (1965/66), 293–99.

Gaechter, P. TS 8 (1947), 547–73.

Gärtner, B. *The Temple and the Community in Qumran and the New Testament.* Cambridge University Press, 1965.

Grillmeier, A. "Ihre Werke Folgen Ihnen Nach," *Geist und Leben* 37 (1964), 321–24.

Kiddle, M. *The Revelation of St. John.*

Jastrow, Marcus. *Dictionary of Talmud Babli, Yerushalmi, Midrashic Literature and Targumim,* I & II. New York: Pardes, 1950.

Masson, C. "L'Evangile eternel de Apocalypse 14:6," in *Hommage et Reconnaissance,* ed. K. Barth (Neuchatel: Delachaux & Niestlé, 1946), pp. 63–67.

Power, E. *Biblica* 4 (1923), 108–12.

Ringgren, H. *The Faith of Qumran.* Philadelphia: Fortress, 1963.

Sandmel, S. "Son of Man (Apoc. 14, 14) in the Time of the Harvest," in *Essays in Honor of Abba Hillel Silver on the Occasion of His Seventieth Birthday* (New York, 1963), pp. 355–67.

Scobie, C. H. H. *John the Baptist.* Philadelphia: Fortress, 1964.

Skrinjar, A. "Virgines Enim Sunt (Apoc 14, 6)," *Verbum Domini* 15 (1935), 136–52.

Swete, H. B. *The Apocalypse of St. John.*

Zahn, T. *Die Offenbarung des Johannes,* I, II.

XII. THE CLIMAX OF THE WRATH OF GOD
(15:1–8)

15 1 And I saw another sign in heaven, great and wonderful, seven angels who had the seven last plagues, for in them is the wrath of God brought to completion. 2 And I saw, as it were, a crystal sea mingled with fire, and those who prevail over the beast and over his image and over the number of his name standing by the crystal sea; they held harps of God. 3 And they sang the song of Moses, the servant of God, and the song of the Lamb; they said:

> "Great and marvelous are Your works,
> Lord God Almighty;
> just and true are Your ways,
> King of Nations.
> 4 Who indeed will not fear You, Lord,
> and glorify Your name;
> because You alone are holy,
> because all the nations will come
> and worship in Your presence,
> because Your righteous acts have been revealed."

5 And after this I looked, and the sanctuary of the heavenly tent of witness was opened, 6 and the seven angels who had the seven plagues came out of the sanctuary; they were dressed in pure shining linen and wore golden girdles about their breasts. 7 And one of the four living creatures gave to the seven angels seven golden bowls filled with the wrath of God Who lives forever and ever. 8 And the sanctuary was filled with the smoke of the glory of God and of His might, and no one was able to enter into the sanctuary until the seven plagues of the seven angels were completed.

NOTES

15. Charles observes that this chapter is heavily Hebraic and full of OT phrases.

1. *plagues.* The same word, in the singular, is used for the last wonder worked against Egypt (Exod 11:1–9, LXX, the death of all their firstborn), and

occurs in the rest of the OT to designate various other catastrophies which befall men. It is used by Josephus in *War* 1.373 for visitations from heaven, and in the same sense in *Ant.* 6.94 in the context of Samuel warning the people that thunder, lightning, etc. was a witness to the people's sin. It is used with reference to the Suffering Servant in Isa 53:3, 4, 10 and in I Clement 16.3.4. In the NT, except for Revelation, the word is mentioned only seven times and never in an eschatological sense but rather in its other meaning of blows and persecution, e.g. blows dealt to the man on the road to Jericho (Luke 10:30). In Revelation it occurs fifteen times, all in an eschatological sense (9:18, 20, 11:3, 12, 14, 15:1, 6, 8, 16:9, 21, 18:4, 8, 21:9, 22:18).

wrath. Here and in ch. 16 we are introduced to a graphic description of the wrath of God. The word used is *thumos,* rather than *orgē,* although sometimes both occur together as in 19:15. All the occurrences of *thumos* in the Gospels, save Luke 21:23, Mark 3:5, are in the passages about John the Baptist. The same word is used in the phrase "wrath of the Lamb" in Rev 6:16.

2. *a crystal sea mingled with fire.* As this sea was seen in heaven, the fire would be heavenly fire, perhaps associated with the throne vision; cf. Ezek 1:4, 13, 27.

crystal. Gr. *hualinēn.* In the NT this word is used only in Rev 4:6 and here. See NOTE on 4:6, "glass sea."

over his image and over the number. **051** 1, 2059ˢ pm TR read "over his image (and) over his mark and over the number."

harps. Or "lyres." Torrey assumes an Aramaic origin and suggests "harps of aloes wood," *'lh',* instead of "God," *elohe.*

3. *song of Moses.* Cf. Philo *De Vita Contemplativa* 11, "Therapeutae," and *De Agricultura* 17.

song of the Lamb. This phrase does not appear in some manuscripts.

King of Nations. P⁴⁷ ℵ* C 1006, 1611 pc vg sy sa(2); Rᵗ read, "King of Ages." 296, TR read, "King of Saints."

4. *will not fear You.* Only in P⁴⁷ ℵ 1006, 2329; **051** 82 pm vg TR does "you" appear.

righteous acts. Gr. *dikaiōmata,* lit. "judgments." See COMMENT, p. 257.

5. *I looked, and the sanctuary.* . . . In 2344 lat bo Prim TR the reading is, "I looked, and behold the sanctuary . . ."

tent of witness. The only occurrence in the NT is Acts 7:44. Philo, *Legum Allegoriane* 2.54–55, calls the tabernacle the Tent of Witness (*skene marturiou*) on the basis of Exod 33:7; cf. *De Ebrietate* 127, 138–39. Josephus describes the tabernacle in *Ant.* 4.100, 102–3; he calls it the dwelling of God, *Ant.* 4.22, 79; 5.343; 6.66; 7.156.

6. *the seven angels.* In P⁴⁷ ℵ P 046 1, 006, 2036, al TR the definite article is omitted.

linen. Gr. *linon.* AC 2053 pc vgʷ, Rᵗ read "stone," Gr. *lithon.* If *lithon* were correct there might be an indirect reference to the high priest's breastplate with the oracular stones foretelling either good or evil. Cf. Ezek 28:12–13 describing the king of Tyre with "every precious stone" as his covering. However, the reading "linen" is better attested than "stone."

girdles. The high priest wore a special golden sash. See Rev 1:13.

7. *one of the four living creatures.* Although the throne of God is not mentioned it seems to be implied by the presence of the four living creatures who give seven golden bowls filled with the wrath of God to the seven angels. Once again the directives for action come from the throne room. P^{47} $\aleph^*$ 1, 2059s al omit "one."

golden bowls. Gr. *phialas.* The representation of the ark on the Arch of Titus shows two cups resting on the table. Josephus, *Ant.* 3.150, says, "Over against the altar were set wine-cans and cups (Gr. *phialai*), along with censers and bowls; these were (of gold), and whatsoever other objects were made for the sacred services were all of gold." The LXX has "cups" (*phialai*) in common with Josephus; see *Ant.* 3, p. 386, fn. *a.* The stress on "gold" by the author of Revelation might be explained by the association of the angels with the liturgy; see the beginning of the COMMENT on ch. 16. The Targum to Isa 51:17–23 speaks of Jerusalem's having received the cup of the Lord's fury, draining the bowl of the cup of cursing, and being beset by six afflictions; she is drunk with affliction, not wine (vs. 21). The chapter ends (vss. 22b–23) with the dramatic words:

> Behold, I have received from thy hand the cup of cursing, the bowl of the cup of my fury; thou shalt no more drink it. And I will put it into the hand of them that were oppressing thee; that wcrc saying to thy soul, Bow down, that we may pass over; and thou didst bow down thy glory as the earth, and wast as a street to them that passed over (Stenning).

8. *filled with the smoke.* In the prayer recorded in I Kings 8:22b–53 Solomon speaks about the intercessory power of prayer offered in the temple of God in averting catastrophe arising from the people's sins. Incense rose up to God, mercy descended upon the people; cf. Ps 141:2.

COMMENT

The preceding chapter introduced a theme characteristic of the preaching of the Baptist, the harvest as judgment. This chapter and the next elaborate another element, the wrath of God; cf. Matt 3:7, Luke 3:7, John 3:36. It is represented in vs. 1 as seven plague-bearing angels and announced as a sign or portent, Gr. *semeion,* which groups it with the signs of the woman (who represents the faithful community) and the dragon (Satan) in ch. 12. Thus the three signs are human, diabolic, and divine respectively. All occur "in the heaven."

The sign in this chapter is distinguished from the others by the adjective "wonderful," Gr. *thaumaston.* In the NT and early patristic literature "wonderful" is not normally applied to human persons and matters. The word occurs in Dan 9:4 (Theodotion) where the seer prays about the mystery of the words of the prophecy of Jeremiah concerning the seventy years before the end of the desolation of Jerusalem. In Ps 92:4b (LXX) it describes the character of God. I Clement 60:1 speaks of God as being "wonderful in strength and majesty." *Thaumaston* is also used for things related to God—His name, His light, His course of action. Through this word, therefore, the author strikes a note of divine awe, and probably resumes the theme of the warrior-God with his attendant angels.

The angels hold the seven last "plagues." It is difficult to find an adequate translation for *plēgē* for it means plague, blow, stroke, wound, or misfortune; see first NOTE on 15:1. Here the author is probably influenced by the Holiness Code in Lev 17–26; cf. Deut 28, Exod 23:20–33. "Plague" occurs in both the Leviticus and the Deuteronomic texts, but Lev 26 seems the most relevant here because it contains the prohibition against idolatry (vss. 1–2). Also, in the promise of blessings and curses consequent upon obedience or disobedience, the text mentions seven-fold punishment four times (vss. 18, 21, 24, 28) but the last three stand out because they are prefaced with similar phrases "if you walk contrary" (vss. 21, 23–24, 27–28; bowls are punishment for walking contrary) and the last mentioned includes a reference to wrath or fury: "And if in spite of this you will not hearken to me, but walk contrary to me, then I will walk contrary to you in fury, and chastise you myself sevenfold for your sins" (vss. 27–28).

In Rev 15:1 the author(s) announces that these are the "last plagues." He has already recorded two seven-fold chastisements in the seven seals and the seven trumpets, and he has made it clear in chs. 13, 14, that the sin is idolatry. There are two more to come, the seven bowls of wrath introduced here, and the fall of the seven kings of Babylon associated with the harlot; cf. Rev 17:10. The editor of Revelation may have patterned the four seven-fold punishments on Lev 26 and then elaborated the concept of fury in Lev 26:28. If we enumerate the punishments in Lev 26:18–34 there are seven: famine, wild beasts, pestilence, divine abandonment, desolation of the land, invasion of enemies, and diaspora. See chart on pp. 267 ff.

The word which he selects for "wrath" is *thumos* as in Lev 26:28 (LXX), not *orgē;* see second NOTE on 15:1. *Thumos* occurs only in the second part of Revelation. In 12:12 it is used for the "fury" of the devil and in 14:8 the "lust" of the harlotry of the nations, but in 14:10, 19; 15:1, 7; 16:1, 19; 19:15 it is used for the wrath of God; ch. 16 will show the form this kind of wrath takes. The *thumos,* "wrath," of God is almost wholly absent from the rest of the NT although it may be implied in Rom 2:8. Only once does Paul qualify the word "wrath" with "of God," in Rom 1:18, which differs from Revelation in that the noun *theos,* "God," is anarthrous. The full phrase, "wrath of God," is found only in John 3:3b; Col 3:6 but in Rev 6:16, 17; 14:10, 19; 15:1, 7; 16:1, 19; 19:15. However, the idea of the wrath of the Lord is frequent in the OT.

According to Hanson, pp. 11–12, in the preexilic period God's wrath was directed mainly against Israel and was of a personal nature because Yahweh was the personal God of Israel. In the postexilic era two new characteristics of God's wrath arise. The Chronicler sees wrath as an inevitable process in history, something remote, awesome, automatic, and very impersonal (Hanson, p. 37). A similar view is found in some of the later Psalms, Proverbs, and Daniel. The postexilic prophets still speak of wrath as God's personal reaction to sin, but it is directed just as much against the Gentiles as against the faithless Jews and takes on an eschatological aspect. Ezekiel, by whom the author of Revelation is greatly influenced, emphasizes the wrath of God more than any other OT writer (Hanson, p. 39).

In the intertestamental period two new facets of divine wrath are shown: the idea that the death of the innocent appeases divine wrath, and the concept that it can be disciplinary (Hanson, p. 66). The theme of wrath also appears in the Qumran scrolls. CDC 2:5, D-S, for one, deals with God's treatment of the wicked (through the agency of angels as in Rev 15):

> but (He wields) Might and Power and towering Fury
> in the midst of flames of fire
> by [the hand of] all the angels of destruction
> against them that have departed from the way
> and loathed the Precept
> with no remnant remaining of them nor survivor.

Similar ideas occur in 1QS in the section concerning the ceremony of entry into the covenant. In 2:6–15, D-S (cf. 4:12–13), the Levites curse the men of the lot of Belial with the words

> May God make of thee an object of dread
> by the hand of all the Avengers of vengeance!
> May He hurl extermination after thee
> by the hand of all the Executioners of punishment!
> . . .
> Be thou damned
> in the night of eternal fire!
> . . .
> May He lift His angry face to revenge Himself upon thee,
> and may there be for thee no (word) of peace . . .
> (And then the priests and the levites say)
> May the Wrath of God and the Zeal of His judgment
> burn him in eternal destruction.

1QH 3:28–30 associates the images of fire and water in the context of the "destiny of wrath." 1QpHab 10:13 also speaks about the judgment of fire upon the preacher of lies because of his insult to the elect. The angels in ch. 15, with their bowls of wrath, may well be the avengers of vengeance, the executioners of punishment, analogous on a celestial level to the Levites in the Qumran scrolls: one notes their dress in vs. 6, of linen belted with gold, which may be ministerial garb. Also pertinent to Rev 15 is the fact that 1QM associates the destruction of the wicked with a theme pertinent to Rev. 15–16, the Exodus motif: 1QM 11:9–10, D-S:

> Thou wilt deal with them as with Pharaoh
> and as with the commanders of his chariots
> in the Sea of Re[eds].
> And those whose spirit is broken
> Thou wilt cause to pass
> like a flaming torch in the straw,
> devouring the wicked and returning not
> until the destruction of the ungodly.

The Exodus motif is touched again in 1QM 14:1 but there is a break in the manuscript: "Like the fire of His Wrath against the idols of Egypt" (D-S).

In the light of this it is not surprising that the author of Revelation himself reintroduces the Exodus theme through the "sea" and the "song." The crystal sea stands in contrast to the one from which the sea monster emerged, and the singing conquerors stand in a position comparable to the Israelites after their escape through the Reed Sea from idolatrous Egypt; one recalls that the city in Rev 11:8 was allegorically called "Sodom" and "Egypt." The righteous will be saved but the "Egyptian plagues" will visit the faithless (Rev 16).

In Rev 15:2 the author sees those who win a three-fold victory, over the beast, his image, and the number of his name. The tense of "prevail" is present, not perfect; these people *are triumphing at the present* over the beast, etc. They appear to be the same people as the redeemed remnant portrayed in 14:1–5. They are standing either on or by a sea, which is probably the counterpart of the heavenly one in 4:6, and they hold harps of God, probably harps used in the worship of God.

Although their song is called the song of Moses, it is not one of triumph such as is found in Exod 15; it is more like Deut 32, also called Song of Moses. The hymn is not christological. It is addressed only to God and is woven out of OT reminiscences. The first line, "Great and marvelous are Your works," recalls Pss 92:5, 111:2, 139:14. It is also reminiscent of the ceremony of entry into the covenant at Qumran when the priests recount the "deeds of God in His mighty works" (1QS 1:21, D-S). Line 3, "just and true are Your ways," recalls Deut 32:4, Ps 145:17. Vs. 4 is influenced by Jer 10:6–7, Ps 86:9, Mal 1:6. One notes the element of fear, rather than love, of God. The verse contains an element of hope for the conversion of the nations and "righteous acts," Gr. *dikaiōmata*, lit. "judgments," in the last line, takes up the Exodus motif, for *dikaiōmata* appears to refer to divine judgments or condemnation as in Exod 6:6, 7:4, 12:12, etc. The song seems to be more influenced by Deut 32 than Exod 15, but this is understandable in the light of the stress on wrath and justice in the Deuteronomic writings; cf. Hanson, pp. 5, 37. Rev 15:4a is akin to Deut 32:3, Rev 15:3b to Deut 32:4, and Rev 15:4b to Deut 32:4b. Further, the theme of the fire of God's anger is found in Deut 32:22. Some of the plagues—hunger, burning heat, pestilence, wild beasts, vermin, the sword—are reflected in Deut 32:23–27. Moreover, Deut 32:32 refers to the vine of Sodom and the fields of Gomorrah and describes their wine as the poison of serpents; cf. Rev 14:8, 10; 17:1–6.

In vs. 5 the seer receives another vision, that of the sanctuary or shrine of the tent of witness in heaven. This must be distinguished from the vision in 11:19 where the ark of the covenant was seen. The tent was the shelter for the ark and it was here that Moses went to find God and to receive orders and revelations. It was believed that when Moses constructed it in the desert he did so on a model of the tent in heaven; cf. Heb 8:5, 9:11, 13:10. Its appearance does not seem fortuitous here, for the manifestation of the ark and the tent and the altar of incense had eschatological significance. In II Macc 2:4–8 the appearance of the tent and the manifestation of the glory of God (cf. Rev 15:8), as at the time of Moses (Exod 40:34–35) and

Solomon (I Kings 8:10), were expected to mark the advent of messianic times and the restoration to dominance of the chosen people. II Macc 2 records that the prophet Jeremiah found the tent, the ark, and the altar of incense, and sealed them up in a cave. Some people followed him and tried to find the way but were not successful and Jeremiah rebuked them, saying: "The place shall be unknown until God gathers His people together again and shows His mercy. And then the Lord will disclose these things, and the glory of the Lord and a cloud will appear, as they were shown in the case of Moses, and as Solomon asked that the place should be consecrated" (II Macc 2:7b–8, RSV). In Revelation the people have been gathered near Mount Zion with the Lamb in ch. 14.

The appearance of the seven angels may suggest either priestly, levitical, or kingly figures. They are dressed in either "linen" or "stone" (see second NOTE on 15:6) bound with golden girdles, and are given bowls. In the NT "bowl," Gr. *phialē*, occurs only in Revelation, but it is used in the OT, e.g. for the altar utensils in Exod 27:3, Num 7, I Kings 8:3. *Phialē* is a broad, flat bowl often used for drinking or pouring libations; sometimes it means a bowl filled with ointments. But the bowls in ch. 15 could also be incense bowls. Josephus, *Ant.* 3.143, speaks of two cups (*phialai*), made of gold and filled with incense, which were placed above the loaves, the shewbread, on the table.

The shrine is filled with the smoke of the glory and might of God and no one is able to enter. This is an obvious allusion to Exod 40:35, where Moses cannot enter the tent because the cloud covered it and the glory of God filled it; to I Kings 8:10–14, where the priests are unable to enter the temple because of the cloud and the glory of God filling the house; II Chron 7:2–3, where the priests again cannot enter the house and where the children of Israel see the fire and the glory of God coming upon the temple. Cf. also Isa 6:4, where the temple again is filled with smoke, and Ezek 10:3–4, where the house of God was filled with a cloud. This phenomenon occurs at strategic points in Israel's history; all instances of it are associated with the dwelling place of God and the destiny of his people. It also has eschatological import, as in II Macc 2; see p. 257. The present incident seems to look forward to the fall of the harlot and the establishment of the true city or dwelling place of God.

BIBLIOGRAPHY

Hanson, A. T. *The Wrath of the Lamb*. London: SPCK, 1957.
Torrey, C. C. *Zeitschrift für die alttestamentliche Wissenschaft* 65 (1953), 230.

XIII. EGYPTIAN PLAGUES VISITED UPON THE FAITHLESS
(16:1–21)

16 ¹ And I heard a loud voice from the sanctuary saying to the seven angels, "Go and pour out the seven bowls of the wrath of God onto the earth." ² And the first one went out and poured out his bowl upon the earth; and pernicious and evil sores came upon the men who had the mark of the beast and on those who worshiped his image. ³ And the second angel poured out his bowl upon the sea; and it became like the blood of a dead man, and every soul of life in the sea died. ⁴ And the third angel poured out his bowl upon the rivers and the springs of water; and it became blood. ⁵ And I heard the angel of the waters saying, "You are just, You Who are and were, the Holy One, because You have made these judgments, ⁶ for they poured out the blood of the saints and prophets, and You have given them blood to drink. It is their desert." ⁷ And I heard a voice from the altar saying, "Yes, Lord God Almighty, Your judgments are true and just." ⁸ And the fourth (angel) poured out his bowl upon the sun; and it was allowed to scorch men with fire. ⁹ And men were scorched with a scorching heat, and they blasphemed the name of God who had power over these plagues, and they did not repent and give Him glory. ¹⁰ And the fifth angel poured out his bowl upon the throne of the beast; and his kingdom was plunged in darkness, and men gnawed their tongues in anguish, and ¹¹ they blasphemed the God of heaven because of their anguish and sores, and they did not repent of their works. ¹² And the sixth angel poured out his bowl upon the great river, Euphrates; and its water was dried up, a road was prepared for the kings of the east. ¹³ And I saw from the mouth of the dragon and from the mouth of the beast and from the mouth of the false prophet three unclean spirits like frogs; ¹⁴ for they are the spirits of demons who perform signs, who go out to the kings of the whole universe, to gather them for the battle of the great day of the Lord, the Almighty. ¹⁵ Behold, I come as a thief; blessed is he who maintains vigil and keeps his garments, so that he does not walk naked and they see his shame. ¹⁶ And they gathered them to the place which is called in Hebrew Armagedon. ¹⁷ And the seventh (angel) poured out his bowl upon the air; and a loud voice came out of the sanctuary from the throne saying, "It is done." 18 And there were lightnings, and voices and thunders, and there was a great earthquake, such as had not been since man was on the earth, so great was the earthquake. 19 And the great city was split in three parts, and the cities of the nations fell. And Babylon the great was remembered before the Lord to receive the cup of the wine of the fury of his wrath. 20 And every island fled away, and no mountains were found. 21 And heavy hail like hundredweights fell from heaven upon men; and men blasphemed God because of the plague of hail, because that plague was very great.

Notes

16:1. *loud voice.* Cf. *Hullin* 59b for the strength of God's voice. The Palestinian Targum on Deut 28 speaks of a *bath-qol,* "mystical voice," coming from the high heavens when Moses began to pronounce the words of threatening.

from the sanctuary. Omitted in P⁴⁷Vid **046** 82 al. In 42 pc c vg (2) sa the phrase reads "from heaven."

seven angels. If one were to name the seven angels of punishment, they would probably be as follows: 1) Kushiel, "rigid one of God"; 2) Lahatiel, "flaming one of God"; 3) Shoftiel, "judge of God"; 4) Makatiel, "plague of God"; 5) Hutriel, "rod of God"; 6) Pusiel or Puriel, "fire of God"; 7) Rogziel, "wrath of God" (Davidson, also *Testament of Solomon*).

pour out. Gr. *ekcheō.* This word occurs repeatedly in this chapter but not elsewhere in Revelation. It is used in Leviticus, LXX, directing the priest to "pour out" the rest of the blood of sacrifice at the base of the altar after he has touched the horns with it; Lev 4:7, 18, 25, 30, 34, etc. Carrington comments on the drink offering which was poured at every major sacrifice. The pouring completed the ceremony and it had a special appropriateness for the Feast of Dedication. Hence our author is using a cultic term although it also has a secular usage. In the rest of the NT this word appears in Matt 9:17; John 2:15; Rom 3:15; Acts 2:17, 18, 33; Titus 3:6. The last two references are to the pouring out of the Spirit.

bowls. See illustration 14.

wrath. In Jer 42:18 the prophet warns the people that the anger and wrath of God will be upon them when they go out to Egypt. Cf. Dan 9:11–12, which refers to the curse and the oath in the law of Moses which have come upon the Israelites because of their sin.

earth. Charles, II, 45, observes that the bowls affect more than one class of people. They are all-embracing with the exception of the fifth bowl which is confined to the kingdom of the beast, just as the fifth seal affected only the faithful.

2. *pernicious and evil sores*. "Evil," Gr. *ponēros*, sometimes qualifies the noun "sore" in OT texts besides Exodus. Here the Exodus motif is qualified by the addition of *kakos*, "pernicious."

sores. In Exod 9:10–11 the ashes from the kiln, which Moses threw toward heaven, became boils. We are probably to suppose that the ashes from the incense shovels or the contents of the libation bowls became sores. If this disease were leprosy it would entail segregation. Contrast 13:16–17 where the mark of the beast enables one to engage in business and consequently amass wealth (a blessing promised to those who obey the commandments of God, see table below p. 266–69).

upon the men. Gr. *epi tous anthropous*. For this construction see Luke 1:65, 3:2; cf. Rev 16:8, 21.

who had the mark. Some scholars think this might be a gloss. However, if it is an authentic part of the text, then it means only the adherents of the Roman empire, not all people, are affected by the plague. This would be correct according to the law of retribution. Swete, p. 201, observes that the Egyptians' sores attacked even the magicians, and asks "Is the Seer mindful of this when he represents the first of the last plagues as breaking out in sores on the Caesar-worshippers who were controlled by the magicians of the temples of Rome and the Augusti" (cf. Rev 13:13–18 and NOTES).

3. *angel*. TI.

blood. Consumption of blood in meat was forbidden for the Hebrew; Gen 9:4.

dead man. Contact with the dead also produced uncleanness; Num 5:2. Note the parallelism in this verse:

blood of a *dead* man
soul of *life*.

For the Hebrews, blood equalled life; Gen 9:4.

soul of life. This phrase is "living soul" in P⁴⁷ ℵ P 046 051 1, 2059s pm lat TR and "soul of living creatures" in 2329, armᵖᵗ. In 82 al, no reference is made to "life."

4. *angel*. TI.

it became. P⁴⁷ A 1006, 1611, 2329 pc; Rᵐ read "they became."

5. *angel of the waters*. In Jewish thought every element, every form of created life had an angel "guardian." The spirit of the water may be compared with the spirits of angels in I Enoch 66:1–3. Enoch saw angels of punishment who possessed ability to loose all the powers of the water which were under the earth to bring destruction upon the dwellers of the earth.

you who are and were. "You" is TI. The angel addresses God with a name akin to that which was revealed to Moses in the burning bush (Exod 3:14) before he vindicated his firstborn son, Israel, according to the principle of the *lex talionis*. Note the omission of "Who is to come" as in Rev 1:4, etc. The spirit of water does not resent the judgment. Indeed, his words are a kind of "antiphon" to the canticle of 15:3–4, for they illustrate the divine holiness and righteousness proclaimed in that song.

the Holy One. The definite article does not appear in P⁴⁷ A C 046 82, 1611, 2329 al.

6. *poured out the blood.* Cf. Gen 4:10, 11, 9:6; here again is the principle of retribution.

In ℵ pc, this (first) occurrence of "blood" in vs. 6 is plural.

their desert. Cf. 3:4, where those who have not soiled their garments are said to have their reward or desert; literally, they "are worthy" to "walk with" God.

7a. *a voice.* TI.

from the altar. Mention of the altar calls to mind the liturgical service. It also evokes the altar from which the martyrs cried out for retribution; cf. 6:9, 8:3–4. "Cried out" is a legal term meaning "appealed for the execution of justice."

7b. A voice from the altar confirms the words of the angel in vs. 5 with this couplet taken almost verbatim from the Song of Moses and of the Lamb in 15:3.

true and just. This phrase is repeated with reference to the fall of Babylon in 19:2.

8. *angel.* TI.

it. Presumably the antecedent is "the sun," but because the verb following is "was allowed" the antecedent might be "the fourth angel."

to scorch men with fire. "Scorch" here translates *kaumatizō kauma*, respectively verb and cognate noun. Note the relentless stress on the scorching by the use of both the verb and the noun in addition to the phrase "with fire." This stress is continued in vs. 9, with the verb "were scorched" and the adjective "scorching." Swete, pp. 203–4, compares the fiery furnace in Dan 3:6; the phrase there is *tēn kaminon tou puros tēn kaiomenēn*.

9. *scorched . . . scorching.* See preceding NOTE and NOTE on 7:16.

blasphemed. The theme of blasphemy is carried throughout this chapter, both here and in vss. 11, 21. It is present also in 13:1, 5–6.

did not repent. This phrase is repeated like a refrain; cf. 9:20–21, 16:11.

10. *darkness.* Charles, II, 45, suggests that, if the cause of the darkness is the smoke arising from the pit (cf. 9:2), then the cause of the torments may be the demonic locusts, with their scorpion stings, that came out of the smoke (cf. 9:10). Caird, p. 204, thinks that this may be the "total eclipse of the monster's imperial power." Allo believes this darkness to be suggestive of the political, economic, and social future of Rome, which is dark and hopeless. Cf. also Amos 5:20, warning those who desire the day of the Lord that it will be darkness and not light.

gnawed. Gr. *masaomai.* This word occurs only in Revelation, and in Job 30:3, LXX; cf. Sir 19:9a. Job refers to men among whom he sat like a king but who now make sport of him. To emphasize how lowly they are, he says they are in such material want that they gnaw the ground for sustenance.

12–14. Allo and others think the effect of this sixth bowl represents the various forces that cause the social and political machinery of the Empire to crumble and thus render it defenseless before the barbarian invasion. Cambier adopts an eschatological interpretation; he sees the demons gathering "the kings of the universe" for the battle with the Lord (vs. 14) as symbolic of the end of the world.

12. *water was dried up.* Cf. Isa 44:27, Jer 50:38. Cyrus is said to have walked across the drained bed of the Euphrates as he went to conquer Babylon; Herodotus i 191.

kings of the east. This may foreshadow 17:12–13, 16–17, the conflict with the Lamb.

13. *frogs.* The frog was classified as an unclean animal, an abomination; Lev 11:10, 41. For animals issuing from the mouth, cf. Shepherd of Hermas, Visions 4.1.6, where locusts are seen proceeding from the mouth of a great monster.

Here "frogs" is in the nominative case, but P⁴⁷ ℵ* 94 pc have it in the accusative.

14. *kings of the whole universe.* Cf. Ps 2:2–3, where the kings of the earth set themselves against the Lord and His anointed. For "universe," Gr. *oikoumenē;* cf. Luke 2:1, Acts 16:6, 19:27, 24:5.

for the battle. This is one of the seven references to war or attacking in Revelation; cf. 6:4, 9:13–21, 14:19–20, 17:16, 19:17–21, 20:7, 9. Note the definite article; the battle is *the* eschatological war, not an ordinary battle.

15. This may be an interpolation, for it seriously interrupts the sequence of thought between vss. 14 and 16. It is the third of the seven beatitudes in Revelation (in traditional order). If it does have any relation to the surrounding verses, it could refer to the first coming of the Anointed One; cf. 4:8, 11:17. The thought could be "the kings are coming together, but, do not fear, *I* am coming, too."

I come. ℵ* pc read "he comes."

maintains vigil and keeps his garments. The explanation of John Lightfoot (see Carrington, p. 265) appears to be the most sensible. The officer on duty at the temple was to see that the guards kept awake. If they were asleep he was to beat them; if they were asleep a second time he was to burn their clothes. Carrington thinks that this is the only explanation of the passage and that it means "now is the time for those who are guarding the temple to keep awake."

16. *Armagedon.* Charles, II, 50, remarks that the gathering of the kings to Armagedon is an echo of the forces of Gog referred to in Ezek 38–39. This theme reappears in Rev 20:7–10. The present context shows an earlier form of the expectation as in 14:14, 18–20, 19:11–21. In these three passages one finds that the nations rebel before the messianic kingdom. The forces of evil are destroyed by the messiah, the beast and the false prophet fall into the pit. In the final insurrection at the close of the messianic kingdom the nations rise at the instigation of Satan. The nations are then annihilated by fire from heaven, and Satan is cast into the lake. The final conflict (Ezek 39:1–2, 6, 11) involves Gog and Magog near the mountains of Israel. Gog is to have a burial place in Israel, the valley of the travelers east of the sea. This is to be called the valley of Hamon-gog; cf. also Ezek 38:8, 21. Joel 4:2 mentions the gathering of the nations in the valley of Jehoshaphat where God will judge them.

Lohmeyer suggests the translation "the Megiddo range" and thinks it refers to Mount Carmel. The only prophet to mention Megiddo is Zechariah (12:11).

He expected hostile armies to besiege Jerusalem (14:2), and speaks of her destruction, vengeance on her inhabitants, and a new Jerusalem under the house of David with Gentiles coming to worship God (Carrington, p. 271). Zechariah has greatly influenced the author of Revelation. Cf. also Heb 12:18–22 for heavenly and earthly mountains.

82 al c vg (4) 60 (3) read "Magēdon," and **046** 1611, 2053 pc Prim read "Mageddōn."

17. *loud*. Omitted in A 1, 205 pc.

sanctuary. In 051* 1, 2059s al g, "heaven"; in **046** 82 pm TR, "sanctuary of heaven."

throne. א reads "God," and 2027 pc reads "throne of God."

It is done. Farrer observes that the tenth and greatest of the Egyptian plagues, the slaying of the firstborn, finds no place in the bowls, and suggests that this stroke must be reserved for the rider on the white horse. The blow must be from the hand of the Lord. Indeed there is a gathering momentum from ch. 16 to ch. 19, for the sixth bowl gathers the people at Armagedon and they wait for the rider on the white horse (but see COMMENT on section XIV).

18. *lightnings . . . thunders*. For the fear of thunderstorms see Josephus' observation after describing the Idumaeans encamped before Jerusalem. A storm broke out during the night. After recounting the incident in detail Josephus adds, "Such a convulsion of the very fabric of the universe clearly foretokened destruction for mankind, and the conjecture was natural that these were portents of no trifling calamity" (*War* 4.287).

such as had not been since man was on the earth. Cf. Dan 12:1, which refers to a time of trouble "such as never has been since there was a nation till that time . . ."

man was. This phrase is "men were" in א **046 051** 1006, 2059s 2329 al; R^t.

19. *great city was split in three*. Zech 14 speaks in a similar vein of a day when all the nations will be gathered against Jerusalem and the city will be taken. But the Lord will fight against those nations, as predicted in 14:4–5, which says that the Mount of Olives will be split in two on the day the Lord comes. In the very catastrophe itself is the seed of hope, for as the cosmic calamities occur the spiritual realities dawn. It is, however, important to notice that Zechariah is speaking of Jerusalem, not of Rome, just as our text directs attention to Jerusalem.

great city. The juxtaposition of this phrase with the "cities of the nations" suggests that it is not a Gentile location, such as Rome. The same phrase occurs in 11:8. Both appear to refer to Jerusalem.

20. The disappearance of the islands and mountains is a typical apocalyptic feature. In I Enoch 1:5–8 the author predicts that the high mountains shall be made low and melt like wax; there will be an earthquake and all men will be judged, but the elect will be protected. In Assumption of Moses 10:1–2, 4–7, the same thought occurs together with the failure of the light of the sun and the moon, the disturbance of the stars, the retirement of the sea into the abyss, and the failure of the fountains and rivers before God comes to punish the Gentiles.

21. *hail like hundredweights*. This recalls the seventh plague in Exod 9:

23–24 and the first trumpet in Rev 7:7. The talent, translated here as hundredweight, weighs about a hundred and eight to a hundred and thirty pounds. One might conjecture that the author had in mind not so much hail from heaven as the stones sent by catapults and other army equipment; see Yadin, *Masada*, pl. 15B. Josephus, in describing certain Roman artillery used in Titus' attack on Jerusalem writes in *War* 5.270–71:

. . . The rocks which they (the stone-projectors) hurled weighed a talent (three quarters of a hundred weight) and had a range of two furlongs or more; and their impact not only to those who first met it but even to those considerably in rear was irresistible. The Jews, however, at the first were on their guard against the stone, for, being white, its approach was intimated not only to the ear by the whiz, but also to the eye by its brilliance. . . .

The Romans eventually blackened the stone. However, white stone might have reminded our author of hail.

COMMENT

Ch. 15 brought into prominence once again the Exodus theme through the song of Moses (vs. 3), the tent of witness (vs. 5), and the glory of God in the sanctuary (vs. 8). Within this context it portrayed seven priest-like angelic figures, who have come from the sanctuary (vs. 6). In ch. 16 these "priests" pour a libation, not of wine, but of the fury of God, which will take a form similar to the Egyptian plagues from which the Israelites in the time of Moses were delivered. Whereas the original song of Moses commemorated especially the crossing of the Reed Sea and the drowning of the enemies, the "Exodus memorial" especially in the Passover celebration would encompass all the miracles in the whole Exodus event. The victors in 15:2–4 give God premature thanks for delivery from the plagues in ch. 16 and the subsequent events described in the last part of Revelation.

Carrington, pp. 261 ff., sets the seven bowls of wrath within a liturgical background, but also suggests that they may represent the Day of Atonement. On this occasion some of the blood was sprinkled seven times towards the veil of the Holy of Holies, some was smeared on the four horns of the altar, and the remainder was poured at the foot of the altar; see fourth NOTE on 16:1 for the levitical use of "pour out." Carrington thinks that the seven bowls are based on this ritual, but the effect is both simplified and magnified; indeed, the whole symbolism is reversed. Instead of the high priest with the blood of reconciliation, there are seven angels with the "blood" of retribution (blood is mentioned four times in this chapter). Instead of seven sprinklings towards the veil, there are seven pourings upon the land. Instead of atonement or reconciliation there is rejection, retribution, and just judgment. The "liturgy" is the answer to the prayer of the souls under the alter (6:9). This is made clearer by a certain parallelism between the Song of Moses and of the Lamb in 15:3–4 and the words of the angel of the waters and the voice from the altar in 16:5–7. The singers of the Song of Moses use harps, Gr. *kithara,* of God; these may be equivalent to the harp or lyre, Gr. *nebel,* which seems to have been used exclusively for religious purposes (Amos 5:23, Ps 144:9; see *The Jewish Encyclopedia,* under "harp and lyre"). Both 15:3–4 and 16:5–7 may be based on the song sung by the priests and levites during the interval between the preparation and the offering of the sacrifice. One need not be surprised at the boldness with which our author parodies the sacrificial system, for his invective is no stronger than that of many OT prophets (e.g. Isa 1).

For the form of the pericope, the author takes one similar to that which he has used before, the repetitive phrases, in this chapter "the . . . (angel) poured his bowl upon . . . ," which build up with monotonous foreboding to the seventh bowl. He has his usual break (vss. 5–7) between the third and fourth parts of the septet.

The whole chapter must be understood against the background of the Exodus. The Exodus was the deliverance *par excellence* which Yahweh performed for his people; all thought of future redemption was colored with features from the first Exodus; cf. Isa 40–55. Rev 16 offers a complete antithesis to this; instead of "Exodus redemption" there will descend upon God's own people "Exodus retribution." The idea is not new; Yahweh had been known to threaten such plagues as a consequence of disobedience, especially of idolatry. The Deuteronomist is explicit: "And he will bring upon you again, all the diseases of Egypt, which you were afraid of; and they shall cleave to you" (Deut 38:60, RSV).

The following tabulation may indicate that our author is simply reinterpreting Scripture when he portrays increasing catastrophes in the seals, the trumpets, and finally the bowls as the result of apostasy.

Blessings for Observance of the Law

Exod 23:22–31	Lev 26:4–13	Deut 28:1–14
1. victory over enemies (vss. 22–24, 27–28)	5. victory over enemies (vss. 7–8)	7. victory over enemies (vs. 7)
2. blessing of bread and water (vs. 25)	8. abundance of food (vss. 5, 10) 1. rainfall (vs. 4)	6. blessing of bread (vs. 5) 10. rainfall (vs. 12)
3. removal of sickness (vs. 25)		
4. fertility of women (vs. 26)	6. fertility of people (vs. 9)	3. fertility of people (vss. 4, 11)
5. long life (vs. 26)		
6. productivity of land (vs. 29)	2. fertility of crops and trees (vss. 4–5)	4. fertility of land (vss. 4, 8, 11)
7. preservation from wild beasts (vs. 29)	4. removal of evil beasts (vs. 6)	
8. possession of Palestine (vss. 30–31)	3. secure possession of the land (vss. 5–6)	8. possession of land (vs. 8)

Lev 26:4–13	Deut 28:1–13
7. confirmation of covenant (vs. 9)	9. confirmation of covenant (vs. 9)
9. presence of God among His chosen (vss. 11–13)	
	1. elevation above other nations (vss. 1, 10, 12, 13)
	2. blessing of city-folk and farmers (vs. 3)
	5. fertility of flocks and herds (vss. 4, 8, 11)

Afflictions in Exodus, Leviticus, and Deuteronomy

Exod 7:17 – 12:32
Egyptian Plagues

1. water into blood; 7:17–21
2. frogs; 8:2–4
3. gnats; 8:16–19
4. flies; 8:21–24, 29–31
5. pestilence; 9:3–7
6. boils; 9:8–12
7. hail; 9:18–26
8. locusts; 10:4–20
9. darkness; 10:21–17
10. killing of first born; 11:4–9, 12:29–32

Lev 26:16–45
Covenantal Curses

1. sudden terror, wasting fever; vs. 16
2. consumption of crops by enemy; vs. 16
3. defeat by enemies; vs. 17
4. government in hands of enemies; vs. 17

IF NO IMPROVEMENT; vs. 18

1. humiliation; vs. 19
2. heavens like iron and earth like brass; vs. 19
3. infertility of land; vs. 20
4. trees will not bear; vs. 20

IF NO IMPROVEMENT; vs. 21

1. more plagues; vs. 21
2. wild beasts destroy cattle; vs. 22
3. wild beasts destroy children; vs. 22
4. cultural bankrupty; vs. 22

IF NO IMPROVEMENT; vss. 23–24

1. sword; vs. 25
2. pestilence; vs. 25
3. deliverance into hands of enemies; vs. 25
4. famine, "bread by weight"; vs. 26

Lev 26:16–45
Covenantal Curses

IF NO IMPROVEMENT; vs. 27

1. cannibalism, eating of sons and daughters; vs. 29
2. destruction of high places and placing of corpses on idols; vs. 30
3. desolation of cities; vs. 31
4. desolation of sanctuaries; vs. 31
5. refusal of sacrifices; vs. 31
6. devastation of land; vs. 32
7. exile among the nations; vs. 33
8. desolation of land; vs. 33
9. anxieties of exiles, "the sound of a driven leaf shall put them to flight"; vss. 36–37
10. pining away in enemy lands; vss. 38–39

IF THEY REPENT, then Yahweh will remember His covenant; vss. 40–45

Deut 28:16–57
Covenantal Curses

1. curses in city and field; vs. 16
2. lack of fertility of body, ground, cattle, flock; vs. 18
3. confusion, frustration, destruction; vs. 20
4. pestilence; vs. 21
5. consumption, fever, inflammation, fiery heat, drought; vs. 22
6. blasting, mildew; vs. 22
7. heavens as brass; vs. 23
8. earth as iron; vs. 23
9. rain as powder and dust coming down from heaven; vs. 24
10. defeat by enemies; vs. 25
11. Israel will be horror to all kingdoms of the earth; vs. 25
12. dead bodies given as food for birds and beasts; vs. 26
13. boils of Egypt; vs. 27
14. ulcers, scurvy, the itch which cannot be healed; vs. 27
15. madness, blindness, confusion of mind; vss. 28–29
16. oppression, robbery; vs. 29
17. loss of spouse, home, vineyard; vs. 30
18. removal of ox, ass, sheep; vs. 31
19. enslavement of sons and daughters; vs. 32
20. consumption of crops, etc., by foreign nations; vs. 33
21. grievous boils; vs. 35
22. Israel will be a horror, a proverb, a byword among the peoples; vs. 37
23. locusts; vs. 38
24. worms eating vines; vs. 39
25. poor olive crops; vs. 40
26. capture of sons and daughters; vs. 41
27. resident alien shall rise in power; vs. 43
28. conquest by foreign nations; vs. 49
29. besieging of towns; vs. 52
30. cannibalism and refusal to share food; vss. 53–54
31. women will consume placenta and children; vss. 56–57

Curses Against the Unfaithful in Revelation

Seven Seals Rev 6, 8:1–6	Seven Trumpets Rev 8:7–12, 9:1–11, 13–19, 11:15–19	Seven Bowls Rev 16:1–12, 17–21
1. white horse pre-Messianic woes (6:1–2)	1. hail and fire mixed with blood burning trees and grass (8:7)	1. on the earth causing sores (vs. 2)
2. red horse civil war (6:3–4)	2. fiery mountain turning sea to blood (8:8–9)	2. on the sea turning it to blood (vs. 3)
3. black horse famine (6:5–6, 8)	3. burning star turning drinking water bitter (8:10–11)	3. on the rivers and springs turning drinking water to blood (vss. 4–7)
4. yellowish-green horse murder famine plague wild beasts (6:7–8)	4. solar bodies darkened causing diminishment of light (8:12)	4. on the sun causing it to scorch (vss. 8–9)
5. martyrs just judgment (6:9–11)	5. hellish locusts torturing men (9:1–11)	5. on the beast's throne causing darkness (vss. 10–11)
6. earthquake destruction of land destruction of people (6:12–17)	6. hellish cavalry killing ⅓ of mankind (9:13–19)	6. on the Euphrates causing it to dry up as pathway for eastern invaders (vs. 12)
7. silence; thunder and lightning call for new plagues (8:1–6)	7. kingdom of God announced causing storm, earthquake, hail (11:15–19)	7. on the air causing storm, earthquake, and hail (vss. 17–21)

Thus the chapter is but a graphic elaboration of the statement in 11:8 that the city is allegorically called Sodom and Egypt, Egypt because of the plagues and Sodom because of the destruction. But, as in the plagues of Egypt, the description throws into high relief the element of the hardening of hearts. Although the actual phrase is not used, the idea is abundantly clear from 16:9, 11, 21b in the references to blasphemy and refusal to repent.

The great voice (vs. 1) which is heard from the sanctuary, or heaven, must be the voice of God, for no one else is able to enter the sanctuary (15:8), this also reminds the reader that the events emanate not from human, but divine sources. The mystical voice, Heb. *bat qol,* sometimes fell from heaven when a judgment was about to occur; e.g. Nebuchadnezzar is purported to have heard a voice announcing that his kingdom was to depart from him (cf. Dan 4:28) and this voice sounded like a shout of a nation (*Exod R* 30:20). However, perhaps more pertinent is the report of Josephus in *War* 6.299–300: "Moreover, at that feast which we call Pentecost, as the priests were going by night into the inner [court of the] temple, as their custom was, to perform their sacred ministrations, they said that in the first place they felt a quaking, and heard a voice, and after that they heard a sound as of a great multitude, saying 'Let us remove hence.'" Cf. Rev 19:1, 6. Josephus reports this among other portents concerning the destruction of the temple. This is not the first loud voice from heaven which has occurred in Revelation; cf. 10:4, 8, 9:12, 15; etc.

The first plague recalls the sixth in Egypt; Exod 9:9–11. The word "sore" (Gr. *helkos,* also meaning abscess, ulcer) occurs in Deut 28:27, II Kings 20:7 (Hezekiah's illness), Job 2:7, and elsewhere in the OT only in Lev 13 in reference to leprosy. It is employed only once elsewhere in the NT; Luke 16:21, the sores of Lazarus. In the light of the repeated use of the word *helkos* in Lev 13, and the statement in Rev 16 that the sores affect only men, not beasts too as in Exod 9, our author may indeed have meant his readers to think of leprosy. In the first five plagues in Egypt described in Exodus, and in the first four trumpets sounded in Rev 8:7–12, there is no personal suffering for man, but in this cycle of plagues man is personally attacked at the very outset (Swete, p. 200).

That the sores were both "pernicious," Gr. *kakos,* and "evil," Gr. *ponēros,* might denote the incurable form of leprosy in distinction from the curable one, which would be described by *ponēros* alone, for which the expiatory sacrifices are prescribed in Lev 14, but the word *kakos* could also describe the hideous disfigurement, sometimes covering the whole body. In the LXX "evil" sometimes qualifies "sore" but "pernicious" seldom does. More significant is the fact that the sores come only upon those who have the mark of the beast and worship his image. In Biblical times leprosy, Heb. *zāra'at,* was seen as an affliction sent by God for evil thoughts or deeds. Many lepers mentioned in the OT have committed some transgression, e.g. Miriam in Num 12:9–15, Gehazi in II Kings 5:27, King Azariah in II Kings 15:5. The association of the disease with idolatry would call to mind the curses in Deut 27 and especially vs. 35: "The Lord will smite you on the knees and on the legs with grievous boils of which you cannot be healed, from the sole of your foot to the crown of your head," RSV. The sin towards which the curses in Deuteronomy are directed is apostasy. Further, the Egyptian sores attacked even the magicians, and Swete, p. 201, asks whether the seer was mindful of this in his representation of the first and the last plagues breaking out upon the Caesar-worshipers who were controlled by the magicians of the temple of Rome; cf. 13:13–18. The first plague, therefore, shows the recipients as religiously unacceptable; in the OT lepers, those with a discharge, and those defiled with the dead were removed from the camp and could only be readmitted if they were purified; Num 5:2.

The second and third plagues, the sea and all drinking water turning to blood, recall the first plague in Egypt (Exod 7:17–21) and the second and the third trumpets in Rev 8:8–12, but they are more frightful. In the Exodus narrative the Nile, the rivers, the canals, and the pools of water are turned to blood, but not the sea itself, and the Egyptians are able to dig around the Nile for water; Exod 7:24. With the second and third trumpets, only one third of the sea and rivers are contaminated. With the third and fourth bowls in Rev 16, however, the whole sea and every living thing in it are injured, and so are all the rivers and springs. The "sea" need not refer only to great seas such as the Mediterranean, but may be used of smaller areas of water such as lakes. Lake Gennesareth is called the "Sea" (Gr. *thalassa*) of Galilee or the "Sea" of Tiberias. The arresting point about the second bowl of wrath is that it turns the water not to ordinary blood but to blood like that of a dead man, stagnant and defiled.

The author may have been influenced by the amount of bloodshed in Palestine during the Roman War. Consider Josephus' description of the naval battle on Lake Gennesareth between Vespasian and the Jewish fleets in *War* 3.522–31. After mentioning the desperate plight of his countrymen and the ensuing battle he records in 530–31 the condition of the lake or sea afterwards:

> One could see the whole lake red with blood and covered with corpses, for not a man escaped. During the following days the district reeked with a dreadful stench and presented a spectacle equally horrible. The beaches were strewn with wrecks and swollen carcases: these corpses, scorched and clammy in decay, so polluted the atmosphere that the catastrophe which plunged the Jews in mourning inspired even its authors with disgust.

This is thrown into higher relief by the fact that before the description Josephus in 506–8 supplies geographical data concerning Lake Gennesareth with special reference to the excellency of its drinking water; he describes it as perfectly pure:

> Notwithstanding its extent, its water is sweet to the taste and excellent to drink: clearer than marsh water with its thick sediment, it is perfectly pure . . . Moreover, when drawn it has an agreeable temperature, more pleasant than that of river or spring water, yet invariably cooler than the great expanse of the lake would lead one to expect . . .

One cannot assert that the author has this particular incident in mind, but one can suggest that such and similar catastrophes influenced his vision.

Turning the seas to blood causes not only the death of fish, as in the Egyptian plague, but of "every soul of life." "Soul," Gr. *psychē*, is more generally, but not always, used for human beings. "Every soul," Gr. *pasa psychē*, can mean "everyone" or, in the plural, "persons"; Lev 7:27, 23:29, etc. Corpses strewn on the Sea of Galilee could lead to the supposition that most of the drinking water was unsafe, hence the death of "every living soul," through drinking bloody water.

This would be confirmed by the words of the angel of the waters and the voice from the altar (vss. 5–7) who introduce the theme of the *lex talionis,* "law of retaliation." The shedding of the blood of the saints and the prophets must be compensated for by making the culprits drink blood. God used the same principle of retribution in the Exodus event (Exod 4:22–23); if Pharaoh would not release God's firstborn son, Israel, then his firstborn would be

slain. The same principle is implicit in the Holiness Code and the Deuteronomic blessings and curses "if you walk contrary, I will walk contrary"; Lev
26:21, 23–24, 27–28. This was mitigated in the Pharisaic and Christian traditions. The awful deed of drinking blood finds a parallel in the prediction of
Isa 49:26 that all will recognize God after He causes oppressors to become
drunk on their own blood. But this is directed towards Israel's enemies.

The fourth plague (vss. 8–9) finds no actual parallel in the Egyptian
catastrophes but the theme is within the Exodus event. This bowl causes
scorching heat from the sun; in Exod 13:21 God provided a cloud to protect
the Israelites by day. The Palestinian Targum on Exod 13 says the Israelites
were covered by seven clouds of glory to protect them from hail, rain, burning
by the heat of the sun, etc. Cf. Isa 49:10.

The plague of scorching is the exact opposite of the condition of the sealed
in 7:16. It also reverses the promise proclaimed in favor of the pilgrims going
up to Jerusalem in Ps 121:5–6, AB:

> Yahweh is your guardian,
>> Yahweh is your shade,
>> the Most High is your right hand.
> By day the sun
>> will not strike you
> Nor the moon at night.

These verses from Ps 121 are particularly arresting in view of the
liturgical context of this chapter and the burning of the harlot Jerusalem in
ch. 17. Such a punishment was anticipated for the impious. *Gen R* 78:5 says
that just as the sun healed Jacob and burned up Esau, so will it heal Jacob's
descendants (Israel) and burn up the heathen, that the sun will heal the
righteous and burn up idolators. This scorching by the sun may be one aspect
of baptism by fire. Note that the sun will scorch "with fire" in vs. 8. Allo
sees in this plague a prediction of extreme pessimism which leads only to
further blasphemy, not repentance. The verse forms a distinct contrast to
Rev 11:13 where after the great earthquake, which kills seven thousand men,
the rest of the population feared God and gave glory to Him.

The fifth bowl (vss. 10–11) causes a plague reminiscent of the ninth Egyptian
plague (Exod 10:21–23). Here the kingdom of the beast is "plunged in
darkness"; there Moses stretched his hand to heaven and thick darkness fell
upon the land of Egypt for three days (contrast the pillar of fire by night for
the Israelites in Exod 13:21). However, the fact that men "gnawed their
tongues in anguish" suggests something even more terrible than the ninth Egyptian plague. A citation from the Midrash on the Exodus in Wisd Sol 17:2–6
probably represents the image in our author's mind. It says, in effect, that
evil-doers are in truth captives within their own dark deeds. They convince
themselves they have not been observed, but are always haunted by the fear
of discovery. No light can penetrate the darkness of the "hateful night" of
dread and terror that they create for themselves. The whole text should be read.

The Homily on the Passover by Melito of Sardis (ca. A.D. 160) also elaborates this theme. Charles, II, 45, is probably right in linking this plague

with the fifth seal when the sun is darkened by smoke from the pit (9:2). The same smoke may not only darken the kingdom of the beast, but produce something similar to the locusts (9:3–12). Blindness, madness, confusion of the mind, and groping about at noon (the brightest part of the day) is mentioned in Deut 28:28–29. The Palestinian Targum on these verses reads: "The Word of the Lord will smite you with fearfulness which bewildereth the brain, and with blindness and stupor of heart. And you will seek good counsel for enlargement from your adversities, but there will be none among you to show the truth, so that you will grope in darkness like the blind. . . ." Our author is probably thinking of mental and spiritual lack of light as well as physical. In Isa 8:19–22 this type of darkness is especially associated with consulting mediums and wizards, the very practice which seems to be implied in Rev 13:15 (the talking image probably produced by ventriloquism). The text from Isaiah also mentions both the sinners cursing their king and God and the "gloom of anguish."

The sixth bowl (vss. 12–16) precipitates a disaster that has some affinity to the plague in Exod 8:2–3, in which the Nile is overrun by frogs, and to the sixth trumpet, the second woe in Rev 9:13–21, where the demonic horsemen come from the Euphrates. It marks the transition from the plagues affecting elements to those dealing with war. War appears as one of the "curses" in both the Levitical and Deuteronomic lists. However, the irony of the sixth bowl lies in the fact that on at least two occasions waters "stood still" so that the Israelites could pass over safely; in Exod 14:21 it was the Reed Sea and in Josh 3 it was the Jordan.

Similar miracles were predicted for the future. Isa 11:15–16 prophesies that the Lord will dry up the sea of Egypt by the scorching heat so that it would form a highway on which the remnant of the people could return home. Zech 10:10–12 foretells that the Nile will be dried up so that people may return from the land of Egypt. This expectation continued in nonbiblical literature. IV Ezra 13:39–47, speaking of the ten tribes captured in the days of King Josiah, says that they went to a distant land where they could keep their statutes and that the Most High stayed the springs of the river, i.e. the Euphrates, until they passed over. He predicts that the same phenomenon will occur when they wish to return to their land.

All these incidents profit Israel and bring disaster to their enemies, but the author of Revelation predicts the exact opposite. The Euphrates is dried up so that the way will be clear for an invasion from the east. The reader might expect the Parthians, the terror of the Roman world in the first century A.D. or, as happened in the Jewish War, recruiting from the Euphrates. When Titus began to besiege Jerusalem he gathered together reinforcements, "among them were three thousand men from the legions on the Euphrates frontier" according to Carrington, p. 265. But the enemy is more demonic than these.

With a careful threefold stress once again on the word "mouth" (Gr. *stoma*; cf. 9:17, 18, 19, 11:5, 12:15, 16, 13:5, 6), probably in the sense of "command," the author presents the emergence of the hostile forces, "unclean spirits like frogs," from the dragon and the two monsters. These can be conquered only by the one from whose mouth issues a sharp two-edged sword (19:15, 21). The

Seer views three unclean spirits like frogs coming from these mouths. The simile serves as a link with the Exodus narrative. "Frogs," Gr. *batrachoi,* occurs only here in the NT, and in Exod 8:2–13, Wisd Sol 19:10, and Josephus, *Ant.* 2.296, who gives a graphic description of the plague. Thus all mentions of frogs refer to the Egyptian plague. The association gains in significance because the frog may be connected with the Egyptian goddess Heqt (she assisted women in childbirth). There may be another association particularly relevant to this apocalypse. The tongues of frogs formed one of the ingredients of a fourth century A.D. magic charm (M-M, P Lond 46 294); this belief may be much earlier, thus the frog may be symbolic of sorcery and magic. Caird, p. 206, suggests that they may represent seductive propaganda (cf. 13:12–15) and blasphemous pretensions to deity (13:6). Through magic and other means these evil spirits, like the lying prophets of old (cf. I Kings 22:22), seduce the kings and lead them to assemble together for the battle on the great day of the Lord.

Rev 16:16 records that the forces meet in a place called either Armagedon or Harmagedon. Jeremias has summarized the research which attempts to give a satisfactory explanation of the name. It may refer to the city of Megiddo; cf. Zech 12:11, RSV: "On that day the mourning in Jerusalem will be as great as the mourning for Hadadrimmon in the plain of Megiddo." Megiddo was the scene of the defeat of the Canaanite kings (Judg 5:19) and the tragic death of King Josiah, who was slain by the Pharaoh (II Chron 35:22–25; cf. II Kings 23:29). Thus the Megiddo pass, which commanded control of northern Palestine, became a symbol of disaster. However, F. Hommel cited by Jeremias (TWNT, I) proposes that Armagedon was the Greek rendering of Heb. *Har Mo-ed,* "the mountain of meeting." This is mentioned in Isa 14:13 with reference to the mountain on which the deities assemble and which the arrogant king of Babylon attempts to mount with his blasphemous pride. Thus Armagedon would be the demonic counterpart of the Mount of God (cf. 14:1, Mount Zion). Here the final battle will take place.

The seventh bowl (vss. 17–21) resembles the third woe (11:14–19). The air, which all men breathe (cf. Wisd Sol 7:3) is affected and this has a wider significance than any other plague. A heavenly voice declares "it is done," i.e. the consummation is reached; cf. the cry after the seventh trumpet 11:15 and the voice announcing the kingdom of God in 21:6. Further, whereas in Rev 11:13 a tenth part of the city fell into ruins, here an unprecedented earthquake splits it into three. Carrington, p. 266, proposes that this may refer to the three factions in Jerusalem after the return of Titus. Josephus in *War* 5.1–4 suggests that these three factions fighting against each other might be considered "the work of divine justice." Carrington finds some linguistic affinity with Revelation and this passage, and points out that the three leaders of the factions were Simon, Eleazar, and John.

The earthquake may not be a sign of complete hopelessness but rather a sign of hope. Hag 2:6–7 predicts cosmic upheaval before the Lord of hosts "will fill this house with splendor," RSV. The same thought is found in Heb 12:27–29, which reflects on Hag 2:6. The passage in Hebrews points out that what Haggai predicted indicates the unshakeable quality of God's kingdom. The earthquake affecting the city, therefore, may be a preparation for the new Jerusalem. The old must be destroyed before the new comes.

The climax of the chapter is reached in vs. 19, where Babylon is "remembered before the Lord," a cultic term. The phrase suits the liturgical setting of the text. The libations have been poured, but instead of the memorial being a turning of God towards his people with grace and mercy, it is for judgment. God's "remembering" is always an efficacious and creative act, not a mere intellectual activity; he remembers in the acts of blessing (transmitting vitality or life) and cursing (destroying). The irony of vs. 19 lies in the exhortation to Israel to "remember" God's covenant and kindness in general. She was especially admonished, as in Deut 6, to keep a perpetual remembrance of the Exodus and Sinai events, to recall them day and night, and never to forget God who brought them to pass. The text of Deut 6 was often printed on parchment in the phylacteries worn on the hand and brow. Cf. Rev 13:16. Remembrance should encourage them to faithfulness.

In this chapter the author intimates that because Israel forgot and became arrogant, the Egyptian plagues were turned back on her. Even then she did not repent but blasphemed (cf. Job 1:22, 2:10), and God remembered her for judgment. The next chapter will concentrate on the city.

BIBLIOGRAPHY

Allo, E. B. *Saint Jean, L'Apocalypse.*

Caird, G. B. *The Revelation of St. John the Divine.*

Carrington, P. *The Meaning of Revelation.*

Charles, R. H. *Revelation.* ICC, I, II.

Conybeare, F. C. "Testament of Solomon," *Jewish Quarterly Review* 11 (1898/99), 1–45.

Daube, D. *The Exodus Pattern in the Bible.* London: Faber & Faber, 1963.

A Dictionary of Angels, ed. G. Davidson. New York: Free Press, 1967.

Farrer, A. *A Rebirth of Images.*

Jeremias, J. ZNW 31 (1932), 73–77.

Lohmeyer, E. *Die offenbarung des Johannes.* Tübingen: J. C. B. Mohr, 1953.

"Melito of Sardis, 'Homily on the passion,'" tr. C. Bonner, in *Studies and Documents,* eds. K. Lake and S. Lake. University of Pennsylvania Press, 1940.

Swete, H. B. *The Apocalypse of St. John.*

Testament of Solomon (Pseudepigraphal work on demons), Migne, *Patrologia Graeca,* vol. 122, appendix to treatise of Psellus.

Yadin, Y. *The Excavation of Masada.*

XIV. THE BEGINNING OF THE LAST PLAGUE
(17:1–18)

17 1 And one of the seven angels who held the seven bowls came, and spoke with me, saying, "Come, I will reveal to you the verdict upon the great harlot who is established upon many waters, 2 with whom the kings of the earth have committed adultery, and the earth-dwellers have been intoxicated with the passion of her impurity." 3 And in spirit he carried me away into a wilderness: and I saw a woman enthroned on a scarlet monster, which was full of blasphemous names; it had seven heads and ten horns. 4 And the woman was clothed in purple and scarlet, and bedecked with gold and precious stones and pearls; she had in her hand a golden cup filled with abominations and the impurities of her adultery, 5 and on her forehead was written a mysterious name, Babylon the great, the mother of harlots and of the abominations of the land. 6 And I saw the woman drunk with the blood of the saints and with the blood of the martyrs of Jesus. And I wondered with great wonder when I saw her. 7 And the angel said to me, "Why do you wonder? I myself will tell you the mystery of the woman and of the beast who bears her, who has seven heads and ten horns. 8 The beast which you saw was and is not, and will rise from the abyss and goes his way to perdition; and the earth-dwellers, whose name is not written in the book of life from the foundation of the world, will marvel when they see the beast that was and is not and is to come. 9 Here one needs a mind with wisdom. The seven heads are seven mountains, upon which the woman is established, and they are seven kings; 10 five have fallen, one is in existence, the other has yet to come and when he comes it is his destiny to remain for a short time. 11 And the beast which was and is not, indeed he is the eighth, and belongs to the seventh and goes to perdition. 12 And the ten horns which you see are ten kings, who have not yet received their sovereignty, but for one hour receive authority as kings with the beast. 13 These have one mind, and they give their power and authority to the beast. 14 These make war with the Lamb and the Lamb will conquer them, because he is Lord of Lords and King of Kings, and his companions are called and elect and faithful." 15 And he said to me, "The waters which you see, on which the woman is seated, they are people and multitudes and nations and tongues. 16 And the ten horns which you see and the beast, these will hate the harlot, and will make her desolate and naked and they will eat her flesh, and they will burn her with fire; 17 for God has put it into their minds to implement His decree and to be of one mind and to give over their royal power to the beast, until the words of God are fulfilled. 18 And the woman whom you saw is the great city who has dominion over the kings of the earth."

Notes

17:1. *reveal.* Gr. *deiknumi.* This verb is used to mean uncovering divine revelation. John 5:20; I Tim 6:15 of the parousia. I Clement 35:12 and Epistle of Barnabas 5:9 also contain this word.

verdict. Gr. *krima.* This may mean lawsuit, judgment, judicial verdict, or sentence of condemnation.

harlot. In prophetic language prostitution or adultery equals idolatry.

established. Gr. *kathēmenēs.* This would appear to indicate more than "sitting upon"; it could, as elsewhere in this apocalypse e.g. 6:2, 14:14–16, imply the notion of acquiring sovereignty.

many waters. The picture is well known from ancient iconography: a city represented as a goddess, enthroned on the shore of the river which suggests its richness and power. Cf. II Baruch 67:1, 6–8, which refers to the black eleventh waters representing the calamity which befalls Zion when the king of Babylon arises and destroys her. They may also be reminiscent of the primeval watery chaos; Carrington, p. 281. Here the woman sits upon the water in contrast to the woman in Rev 12 who escapes the water spewed out by the dragon.

2. *kings.* These need not be confined to contemporary kings. The author may, like Ezekiel, look back to "prostitution" with Assyria, Babylon, etc.

committed adultery. This is the picture which is given in Ezek 16. The adultery would probably include trade relationships and treaties and refer not only to the city of Jerusalem herself but to the several millions of Jews scattered throughout the empire by whose trade with the kings of the earth Jerusalem had grown powerful, rich, and luxurious; cf. Carrington, p. 277. Josephus, *Ant.* 14.110–11, refers to the riches in the temple during the time of Hyrcanus II; these fell into the hands of Pompey and Crassus.

3. *wilderness . . . scarlet monster.* Carrington observes that the mention of the desert and the scarlet here may suggest the scapegoat which was sent out into the desert; cf. 18:5. To his remarks one might add that a strip of crimson wool was tied half to the rock from which the scapegoat was to be hurled and half to his horns (*Yoma* 6.6) and a similar strip was tied to the door of the sanctuary (*Yoma* 6.8). The double stress on scarlet, for the beast and for the woman (vs. 4), might remind the reader of the symbolism of atonement or purification in Lev 14:4, 6, 49, 51, 52; cf. Num 19:6 *Yoma* 6.6, 8. The author may find irony in the use of Gr. *kokkinos,* "scarlet," for both harlots, for adornment, and priests, for atonement. A different word, *purros,* is used for the fiery red of the horse that carries out one part of God's judgment. The voluptuous scarlet of the monster and the woman's robes may be in contrast to the chaste white of the Lamb and the robes worn by the twenty-four elders (4:4) and the 144,000 redeemed (7:9). Scarlet was a blended color, another contrast to the purity of the Lord's fury represented by the fiery red of the horse.

seven heads and ten horns. This must describe the same blasphemous sea monster in ch. 13, where the description is "ten horns and seven heads and ten diadems" (13:1). In ch. 17 the heads and horns are explained. The ten diadems in 13:1 might refer to the ten evil kings in 17:1. It might also be a variation on the Lamb with seven horns and seven eyes in Rev 5:6.

4. *bedecked with gold and precious stones.* Carrington observes that the precious stones may recall the stones of the temple which gleamed like snow. In Rev 4:3–4 precious stones are used to describe the heavenly throne room. Carrington also suggests that the gold may be reminiscent of Herod's temple, which was regarded with suspicion by orthodox Jews of that day. In *War* 5.212 Josephus remarks that the sanctuary of Herod's temple contained "Babylonian tapestry in which blue, purple, scarlet and linen were mingled with such skill that one could not look upon it without admiration." In Isa 3:18–23 the prophet criticizes the extravagant dress of the daughters of Zion and in Jer 4:30 we find a similar approach with regard to Jerusalem.

That the harlot is bedecked with gold and precious stones also sounds like a perversion of the high priest's breastplate. In the first half of Revelation (chs. 4–11), gold especially is associated with heaven; 4:3–4, 5:8, 8:3, 9:13. Even the gold-wreathed locusts in 9:7 were commanded from heaven. Only in 9:20 is gold associated with a nonheavenly thing, the worship of "idols of gold and silver and bronze and stone and wood." Notice how markedly unprecious is the progression of these other materials, in contrast to the precious stones that appear with the gold in heavenly objects.

pearls. Like scarlet, pearls had an ironic double significance. On the one hand they could be compared to good things like wisdom and truth as in Job 28:18, Matt 7:6, 13:46, and on the other hand they could signify feminine voluptuousness, as in I Tim 2:9. Cf. Rev 21:21, which says that the twelve gates of the new Jerusalem are each made of a single pearl.

golden cup. Gr. *potērion,* "cup." Cf. Jer 61:7 which speaks of Babylon being a golden cup in the Lord's hand and making all the earth drunk: the nations drank of her wine and became insane. The symbolism of the cup in the hand of the harlot gains in significance when one recalls the golden vines portrayed on the gate opening to the temple (*War* 5.210).

5. *forehead.* Jews' obstinacy in continuing improper practices is a fault commonly denounced in the OT by God. A metaphor frequently used for this fault is hard or brazen forehead. Cf. Isa 48:4, Ezek 3:7. On the other hand, God's

servants were sealed on their foreheads (Rev 7:3, 22:4), and the monster's worshipers were marked either there or on their right hand (14:16).

name. There does not seem to be sufficient evidence that ordinary harlots wore their names on their foreheads. Charles, II, 65, cites two texts, one of which the present writer has been unable to procure (Seneca *Controversies* 1.2). The other is from Juvenal *Satires* 6.122. This passage concerns the wife of Claudius but merely appears to mean that she dissembled the name of Lycisca, rather than that she wore a label on her forehead. The word "forehead" does not occur in that text.

There was placed on the forehead of the high priest a golden plate engraved with a consecrating word. Aaron in his priestly vestments is described in Exodus and in the works of Josephus. Also in Sir 45:12, RSV, there is a full description of Aaron wearing the engraved plate:

> with a gold crown upon his turban,
>> inscribed like a signet with "Holiness,"
> a distinction to be prized, the work of an expert,
>> the delight of the eyes, richly adorned.

mother of harlots. Cf. Tacitus *Annals* 15.44.

6. *the blood of the martyrs of Jesus.* One suspects that this phrase may be an interpolation. First, *martus,* in the sense of one who dies, occurs here only; the usual way martyr is expressed in Revelation is "those slain for the word of God" (6:9). In the rest of the NT *martus* indicates a witness rather than one who dies in order to witness. In the Christian part of this apocalypse *martus* refers to Christ (1:5, 3:14) and to Antipas (2:13). At the end of the first part, 11:3, it refers to the two witnesses which we have suggested are the house of Israel and the house of Aaron. Second, this phrase differs from that in Rev 16:6, "the blood of the saints and prophets," and from that in 18:24, "the blood of prophets and of saints, and of all who have been slain on earth." In 19:2 it is said that God "vindicated the blood of His servants shed by her hand." In no case is there another reference to the blood of the martyrs of Jesus. Charles, II, 66, remarks that this verse gives a Christian character to the originally Jewish source and transforms an oracle of Vespasian's date into a prophecy of the destruction of Rome in the last days; the reference to the martyrs of Jesus is regarded as an addition to the Jewish source and the saints may refer to those who fell in the war of A.D. 66–70.

I wondered with great wonder. The Greek uses the verb in past tense, *ethaumasa,* with its cognate noun, *thauma,* and the adjective, *mega,* for emphasis.

7. *angel.* Cf. IV Ezra 12:10–30, where the angel explains the meaning of the eagle which is symbolic of Rome.

bears. Gr. *bastazō.* This word also has the connotation of "bearing a burden" (e.g. a cross, Luke 14:27), "bearing patiently," "bearing one's judgment" (Gal 5:10), and "carrying away" or "removing." Perhaps the author meant to contrast "is established," Gr. *kathēmenē,* vs. 1.

8. *abyss.* This seems to be the exact antithesis to heaven. One recalls that

the pit, Heb. *šḥt*, is frequently mentioned in 1QH 3, which describes the woman who brought forth the man child and the woman who was pregnant with the asp. The harlot may represent the woman who is big with the asp. In the LXX "abyss" translates Heb. *tehom,* the original floods of water, but in later Judaism *tehom* came to signify the original flood, the interior of the earth which corpses defile, and the place of rebellious spirits (Jubilees 5:6–11, I Enoch 10:4–6, 11–14, 18:11–16, etc., Jude 6, II Peter 2:4). In Rev 17:8 the word is used for the prison of the spirits, and the inmates of the abyss are the beast, the angel who is king of the underworld, the demons, and the scorpion centaurs; cf. 9:3–12. God has power over this abode. The word *šḥt* which has a different meaning from *tehom.* The root of the former means "to go to ruin," "be corrupted," e.g. it is used of moral perversion or corruption in Gen 6:12, Prov 6:32; cf. Zeph 3:7, and esp. Ezek 23:11. The noun is used figuratively of Babylon as destroyer in Jer 51:25; cf. II Kings 23:13.

perdition. Just as the abyss is the antithesis to heaven, so is perdition the antithesis of life and salvation.

goes. ℵ P **046** 1, 82, 1006, 2059s, 2329 pm vg TR; R^t have this verb in the infinitive.

book of life from the foundation of the world. Rev 13:8, 20:12, 15, 21:27. Ringgren, pp. 52 ff., discusses some texts from Qumran which seem to suggest that God not only knows men's deeds but predestines them. On p. 54 he draws attention to the following phrases from 1QH 16:10: "everything is engraved ("ḥāqûq") before God with the stylus of remembrance (1QH 1:24) or that God has recorded ("rāšam") the spirit for the righteous ones."

is to come. Gr. *pareimi.* This verb is from the same root as *parousia,* which can be used in the technical sense of the arrival of an emperor, etc. Cf. 4:8 (of God) and 1:8 (also of God).

9. *wisdom.* At Qumran a whole series of synonyms for "wisdom" and "insight" are used; see Ringgren, pp. 114–20. The object of the knowledge or insight or wisdom is usually God's truth, His mysteries, His plan of salvation. A typical dictum is found in 1QH 7:26–27 (Ringgren, p. 115):

> I thank thee, O Lord
> that Thou has given me insight
> into Thy truth
> and given me knowledge of Thy
> wonderful mysteries.

heads. Charles suggests that 9b may be an addition. It appears to interpret the heads as if they belonged to the woman rather than the beast. According to Boismard there were two versions of Revelation and the editor grouped passages from Text 1 and Text 2 in presenting the symbolism of the beast, his heads, and horns (the angel speaks only of the beast, not of the harlot); vs. 11 is the editor's, Text 1 equals vss. 8–9, 15–18; Text 2 equals vss. 10, 12–14.

is established . . . seven kings. Favors bestowed upon those ruling in Palestine would be seen as association with the foreign powers; cf. CDC 12:6–9, on association with Gentiles.

10. *have fallen.* Gr. *epesan.* Swete, p. 220, observes this does not imply merely that they have died, but that they have fallen from an exalted position.

it is his destiny. Gr. *dei,* "destiny." Note the statement of predestination as in vs. 8.

short time. Some think this applies to Domitian who was assassinated in A.D. 96 after a struggle with his murderers. Even pagans saw some similarity between Domitian and Nero; cf. Juvenal *Satires* 4.37–38, and Pliny *Panegyricus* 53 (Swete, p. 220).

11. *he.* Lit. "himself." ℵ 046 82, 1006 al read "this."

eighth. It is possible that this may not refer to an actual Roman emperor, but to a supernatural monster from the abyss which is to play the part of the Nero Redivivus. Some would identify the emperor who "is" as Vespasian and the one who "has yet to come . . . to remain for a short time" as Titus (A.D. 79–81). The prediction may be influenced by knowledge of the criticial condition of Titus' "health"; cf. Suetonius *Titus* 7, Dio Cassius 66.26.2.

On the other hand, there is the traditional view that the empire would have seven emperors before its destruction. See chart on p. 289. For Column *II,* see Cambier, Gelin, Martindale and others who begin with Augustus. According to this theory Revelation would have been written under Vespasian, or, in harmony with the standard device of apocalyptic, been artificially placed in this time. By disregarding the successors of Nero, who reigned less than a year each, the emperor that "is" would be Vespasian, with Titus his successor, "the other (who) has not yet come." The eighth, then (under whom Revelation was written), is Domitian, who is one of the first seven because he is a kind of reincarnation of Nero, "one of the seven, and on his way to destruction."

Columns *III* and *IV* both begin with Nero (Allo and Bonsirven). Allo commences with the tradition that Revelation was written under Domitian: hence he is the sixth head. Nerva would be the emperor "who must remain only a short time," while Nero "who was, but is not, is moreover eighth" will reopen the persecutions in the person of Trajan and his persecuting successors.

Lohse finds that the difficulties of identity lead one to the conclusion that the meaning of the seven heads of the beast is not purely *zeitgeschichtlich.* Rather, underlining it is a very ancient viewpoint, developed in Babylon, according to which the world time is divided into seven periods, each of which is under one of the seven planets, and under a ruler. The resulting number seven finds in our pericope a point of reference to the Roman emperors that follow one another. But the seer does not trouble to adjust the number seven to the past course of history. His interpretation is directed rather to the eighth king, who will be present in a short time, who will break through every measure, who actually is no longer present and will come as one of the seven past kings. He will be a contrast to God and the Messiah, a parody of the death and resurrection of the Lamb, and will snatch all rulership to himself.

Lohse's remarks are important because whatever be the particular historical allusions which one sees in this description, one must not make the mistake of stopping here as if our author's interest were only or primarily centered on the particular event. A particular event is the point of departure, and so we must start with it and take into consideration the universal application. Here, beyond the specific emperors to whom John refers, he sees the whole force of evil in all ages led by individuals whom the world follows and admires. One might say the same, e.g. when one considers the biblical commentaries at Qumran where the wicked priest keeps recurring: he need not be one particular individual.

perdition. The verse is associated with or is a doublet of vs. 8; see NOTE on vs. 8, "perdition."

12. *yet.* Omitted in A vg(2).

14. *Lamb . . . Lord of Lords and King of Kings.* Just as there are Christian additions in Testament of Joseph 19:8, where a virgin is said to bring forth a lamb, and 19:11, which mentions the Lamb of God who takes away the sin of the world, so in Rev 17:14 there may be a Christian addition, in this case, the title "Lord of Lords and King of Kings." In 19:16 the title is predicated of the rider on the white horse who is the Word of God, but there "Lord" and "King" are in the reverse order. Cf. Deut 10:17, Dan 2:47, III Macc 2:20. The title would be especially appropriate in the time of Domitian; cf. Suetonius *Domitian* 13.

16. *and naked.* Omitted in **046*** 1, 2059s al.

burn her with fire. In the OT this appears as a punishment for incest (Lev 20:14), harlotry (Lev 21:9), keeping forbidden articles (Josh 7:15), and generally for not obeying the word of God, as in Jer 38:18, 23, where there is a threat that Jerusalem would be burned if (in complete contrast to Revelation) the king would not surrender to Babylon.

17. *words of God are fulfilled.* This may mean oracles, but cf. the similar phrase in Luke 18:31, 22:37; Acts 13:29 (all with reference to Jesus' suffering and death). Cf. also Rev 10:7.

COMMENT

Commentators have observed that the last of the Egyptian plagues, the death of the firstborn, does not feature in our apocalypse. Yet the author has followed carefully, albeit with ingenuity, the Levitical and Deuteronomic warnings, even to the point of portraying three seven-fold punishments as in Lev 26:18, 21, 24, and taking very literally the text of Deut 28:60–61, that if the Israelites do not obey "the words of this law" (cf. Rev 17:17b, "the words of God"), then Yahweh would turn all the plagues of Egypt back on them, and add even those not mentioned in the book of the law. In the light of this, has the author omitted the last plague or has he concealed it under his powerful imagery by bringing together inspiration from the Pentateuch and the prophetical writings?

In Lev 26 there are four references to seven-fold punishment (vss. 18, 21, 24, 27). The author appears to have modeled the seals, the trumpets, and the bowls upon the first three and one may suggest that the fall of the harlot comprises the last: it is a seven-fold (in the metaphorical sense of "complete," "perfect") punishment inflicted with "fury" (vs. 28; cf. Rev 16:1). In Revelation the fury is brought to a climax in chs. 17, 18, 19. Seven figures suffer loss: the harlot (18:1–8), the kings of the earth (18:9–10), the merchants (18:11–

17a), the sailors (18:17b–19), the seven or nine classes of men (19:17–18), the first and second beasts (19:19–20), and Satan (20:1–3, 7–10). The Levitical text (26:27–33) suggests that one should look for cannibalism (cf. Rev 17:16, "and devour her flesh and burn her up with fire" and Rev 19:17–21), for desolation (cf. Rev 17:16b, 18:17), and for a devastation of the land which will astonish the enemies (cf. Rev 18:10, the kings of the earth in fear of the harlot's torment; 18:15, the merchants; 18:18, the sailors crying out). These are creatively displayed in the remaining chapters.

The author has blended the prophetic theme of "harlot" (cf. Hosea, Isaiah, Jeremiah, Ezekiel) with the Levitical text. A study of the metaphorical use of "harlot" in the OT shows a marked tendency to depict faithless Israel thus. There are five principal texts which refer to Jerusalem or Israel as a harlot and only two which refer to non-Israelite cities with the same image.

Hosea 2:5, 3:3, 4:15 speak of the harlotry of Israel; there is no suggestion that her Canaanite neighbors are so designated. The whole book of Hosea seeks to bring the adulteress back to her true husband, Yahweh. In Isaiah 1:4 the prophet addresses Israel as "a people laden with iniquity" (RSV) and in 1:9 calls her by the names of Sodom and Gomorrah (cf. Rev 8). Then in 1:21 he exclaims: "how the faithful city has become a harlot, she that was full of injustice" (RSV). In Jer 2:20 (cf. 3:1, 6, 8–10) once again Israel is called a harlot and in 5:7 Jerusalem is accused of harlotry and adultery. Micah 1:7 makes the same complaint against Samaria and Jerusalem. This theme is resumed in Ezek 23, where Jerusalem is seen as the worse of the two. In Ezek 23:31–34 the metaphor of the cup occurs; cf. Rev 17:4.

The text that influences the author of Revelation most is Ezek 16, which is a prophetical attack on Jerusalem. The prophet finds no kind word for her. His description is as graphic as in Rev 17–18, for he describes how God has seen Israel in her poverty, had compassion for her and caused her to live and grow to full maidenhood. When she reached the age of love He spread His skirt over her and plighted His troth to her and entered into a covenant with her. She became his. He washed her, clothed her, decked her with ornaments (cf. Rev 17:4) and placed a crown upon her head (cf. the reference to "queen" in Rev 18:7). She reached a regal estate and her renown went forth among the nations (cf. Rev 17:18) because of her beauty. However, she trusted in her beauty and played the harlot with Egypt, Assyria, and Babylon. Unlike other harlots, she gave gifts rather than received them. On account of her sins, Ezekiel says that God threatens to gather her lovers against her and uncover her nakedness to them; cf. Rev 17:16. He will judge her as an adulteress or a murderer would be judged. He says that she is more sinful than Sodom and Samaria. Yet Ezek 16 ends with a promise of forgiveness and establishment of an everlasting covenant.

The two texts which apply the epithet "harlot" to non-Israelite cities are Isa 23:15–18 and Nahum 3:4. In Isa 23:17 it is predicted that Tyre "will play the harlot with all the kingdoms of the world upon the face of the earth . . ." (RSV); cf. Rev 17:2, etc. However, Tyre may be different from other pagan cities because, although she was a non-Israelite city, she had contracted a covenant with Israel and was closely associated with the building of the first temple. King Hiram of Tyre was a close friend of both David and Solomon. The second non-Israelite harlot is Nineveh, in Nahum 3:4. However, the Qumran scroll 4QpNah has accommodated the whole text to Jerusalem so that the prophetical attack on Nineveh becomes one upon the Holy City. It is Jerusalem that has become a den of lions, the lions being the wicked of the nations; Nahum 2:12a. In 4QpNah Demetrius, the king of Greece who sought to enter Jerusalem, is called "the lion," and the priests in Jerusalem who will be slain are called young lions; as in Revelation animal symbolism is used for political leaders. Further, Ephraim is graphically described as the harlot (4QpNah 2; DJD, V, 40):

". . . The multitude of the whoredoms of the well-favored harlot, the mistress of witchcrafts, that sellest nations through her whoredom and families through her witchcraft" [its] interpretation [con]cerns those who lead Ephraim astray, who by their false teaching and their lying tongue and lip of deceit, (cf. Rev 16:13) will lead many astray . . . they say "Behold, I am against thee, says Yahweh of hosts, and thou shalt lift up [thy] skirts over thy face and show nations thy nakedness and kingdoms thy shame."

If Ephraim was seen in such a light and such metaphors were used of her at the time when the Qumran commentaries were written, the same accommodation might well have been made years later with reference to Jerusalem under the Romans. Similar evidence is given in another Qumran text, the lamentation over Jerusalem (4QLam 179). This speaks of her breaking her covenant and of her desolation (cf. Rev 17:16) and compares her to a hated wife. It refers to the children who were brought up in purple and pure gold (cf. Rev 17:4). The end of the fragment describes Jerusalem, who was a princess of all nations (cf. Rev 18:7), as a lonely city. Her children weep and mourn; cf. Rev 18:7, 10. Further, from Qumran Cave 5 we have a substantial portion on the harlot who utters vanities (5Q 184). The harlot is given no name but she is portrayed as a woman who has no inheritance among those who gird themselves with light; her garments are shades of twilight. There is some similarity with the picture of Mistress Folly, the harlot, in Prov 7:10–27, but it is mingled with Qumran motifs, e.g. light and darkness, the waves of the pit, etc. These texts from Qumran suggest, therefore, that there is a line of continuity with the classical prophets in the portrayal of Jerusalem as a harlot and the prediction that she will be attacked by her enemies as a consequence of her sin. Perhaps the most important text for interpreting Rev 17 is 1QpHab. This speaks against Jerusalem; 9:2–6 (D-S) reads:

And as for that which He said, *Because thou hast plundered many nations all the remnant of the peoples will plunder you,* the explanation of this concerns the last Priests of Jerusalem who heap up riches and gain by plundering the peoples. But at the end of days, their riches, together with the fruit of their plundering, will be delivered into the hands of the army of the Kittim; for it is they (the Kittim) who are *the remnant of the peoples.*

Cf. also 12:5–9 concerning the wicked priest:

For God will condemn him to destruction even as he himself planned to destroy the Poor. And as for that which He said, *Because of the murders committed in the city and the violence done to the land,* the explanation of this is (that) *the city* is Jerusalem, where the Wicked Priest committed abominable deeds and defiled the Sanctuary of God; *and the violence done to the land,* these are the towns of Judah where he stole the goods of the Poor.

These texts together with the OT ones indicate that the harlot in Rev 17 is Jerusalem, not Rome. Indeed, if it is the covenant relationship with Yahweh which makes Israel his special people, his bride, how could a non-Israelite nation be called "harlot" except in a much less precise sense? It is the covenant which makes the bride, the breaking of it which makes the adulteress.

It might be objected that the great city in Revelation appears too important among the nations to be identified with Jerusalem rather than Rome. However, Jerusalem was thought to be the "navel" or center of the earth (*Gen R* 59:5), "destined to become the metropolis of all countries" (*Exod R* 23:10), and the Psalms (e.g. 48:2–3, 50:2); Lamentations (e.g. 1:1, 2:15) and Prophets (e.g. Zech 14:16–21, Isa 2:2–4, Micah 4:1–3) speak in the loftiest terms of Jerusalem's place among the nations. Rev 17:18 is probably a similar hyperbole; cf. 4QLam which describes her as "princess of all nations."

Moreover, the author does use dual symbolism, so even if it is correct to identify the harlot with the faithless Jerusalem, this does not preclude her identification also with one particular character or office within the city. The liturgical setting of much of Revelation, especially ch. 16, together with the stress on the priesthood in Jerusalem and the wicked priest in the Qumran scrolls, might lead one to suppose that the harlot depicts particularly the condition of the high priesthood. Many Jews were not satisfied with the choice of high priest in the days preceding the capture of Jerusalem. Josephus, in *War* 6.151–92, cites a notable and scandalous example on the occasion when the Zealots occupied the temple and selected in the primitive way a high priest by lot instead of following the hereditary succession. He was a fool who could be used as a puppet by the Zealots, who joked about the whole affair, to the infinite horror of the pious. After this sacrilegious action Ananus spoke to the general assembly, his eyes filled with tears and constantly directed toward the temple. He spoke of the house of God "laden with such abominations" (cf. Rev 17:4) and the "hallowed places crowded with the feet of murderers" (cf. Rev 17:6), of his own high priestly vestments and the fact that he bore "that most honoured of venerated names" (cf. Rev 17:5.), and upbraided the people for their apathy in the face of these atrocities and such domestic tyrants. It would seem that Rev 17, 18 were perhaps written in a climate similar to the one described above.

There are several further reasons for arguing that the harlot is Jerusalem rather than Rome. First, if one identifies the first beast (13:1; see third NOTE on 17:3) with the Roman empire one must argue for a different identity for the harlot: Rome cannot be seated upon Rome. Some have argued that the beast is the Roman empire and the harlot the city of Rome, but this appears to be contradicted by the text. In 17:9 the woman is said to be seated on the seven hills (equal the seven heads) and these surely symbolize the city of Rome. Secondly, Rome is never mentioned in our text, but the new Jerusalem does occur and there is great emphasis on Jewish temple imagery, etc. Further, the phrase "the great city" first found in 11:8 appears to refer to Jerusalem, not Rome, and one would expect the same identity when the phrase recurs in Rev 18:16. Thirdly, the blood of the martyrs and the saints is found in our city (18:24) but it was Jerusalem, not Rome, who slew the prophets. Fourthly, if the beast imagery is taken from Daniel then it would seem to depict a foreign power against the Jewish nation. Lastly, the symmetry of the apocalypse might urge us to inquire whether the true counterpart of the new Jerusalem (ch. 21) is not rather the old, defiled Jerusalem, rather than Rome. This would be in keeping with the theology of Qumran.

The opening verses of ch. 17 show it is closely associated with ch. 16; one of the angels with the bowls comes to the seer and offers to show him the judgment of the great harlot. The harlot "is established upon many waters"; in vs. 15 these are identified as "peoples and multitudes and nations and tongues." The text may be influenced by Jer 51:11–13, which is an oracle directed against Babylon who will be destroyed "for that is the vengeance of the Lord, the vengeance for his temple" (vs. 11, RSV). Jeremiah proclaims, "O you who dwell by many waters, rich in treasures, your end has come, the thread of your life is cut" (vs. 13, RSV). But the interpretation of the metaphor is closer to 1QpNah. Here the "sea" and "waters" have several meanings. In 1QpNah 1:3–4 in the commentary on "he rebukes the sea and dries it up" the following explanation is given: ". . . 'the sea' is all the *Ki[ttim* . . .] to exe[cute] against them judgment and to exterminate them from the face of [*the earth*] with their [rul]ers whose dominion will be brought to an end" (DJD, V, 37). But in 3:8 one reads: ". . . 'Art thou better than Am[on that dwelt by] the rivers?' Its interpretation: 'Amon' is Manasseh, and 'the rivers' are the nobles of Manasseh, the honoured ones of thee [. . .] 'Waters are around her, whose rampart is the sea and waters her walls.' Its [inter]pretation: they are her warriors, mighty men of [w]ar. . . . (DJD, V, 40).

The harlot, therefore, is probably in political alliance with the Romans, with nobles and warriors. Associated with these seem to be the kings of the earth (17:2) who have committed adultery with her. Adultery may mean pagan practices arising through trade. Ezek 16:28–29 utters a similar sentiment: "You played the harlot also with the Assyrians, because you were insatiable . . . You multiplied your harlotry also with the trading land of Chaldea . . ." (RSV). Through commerce the Jews could be involved in idolatrous practices and customs unacceptable to their brethren; hence the separation of communities like Qumran from mainline Judaism. Both 4QpNah 1:11 and 1QpHab 9:3–7 mention the wealth amassed by the priests in Jerusalem, and the latter text predicts that the fruit of their plundering will be handed over to the army of the Kittim; cf. Rev 18, which elaborates the trading and riches.

Along with the kings of the earth are mentioned the earth-dwellers who are said to be drunk with the passion of the harlot's impurity. It is difficult to tell whether the earth-dwellers are to be identified with the kings of the earth or whether the kings belong to the "class" of earth-dwellers. However, if the earth-dwellers are intoxicated, this vice may be predicated also of the kings of the earth. The idea of drinking the harlot's cup is found in Ezek 23:33–34. Speaking to Jerusalem, the Lord says: "A cup of horror and desolation, is the cup of your sister Samaria; you shall drink it and drain it out, and pluck out your hair, and tear your breasts" (RSV). The Qumran scrolls use this metaphor of drunkenness, as in 4QpNah 4:4–6, which refers to the "wicked ones of Ephraim whose cup will come after Manasseh" (DJD), and 1QpHab 11:13–14, which specifies of the priest whose ignominy was greater than his glory and who walked in the ways of drunkenness that the cup of the fury of God either "swallow him up" or "befuddle" him (the text is not clear) and humiliation poured upon him. However, it is not actually said in this text that the nations drink of his cup, but rather that he drinks of the cup of Yahweh.

In order to see the vision, vs. 3 says the seer is carried away to a wilderness. The noun, Gr. *erēmon,* is anarthrous and in this way is contrasted with "the desert" in 12:6, 14, in which *erēmon* does appear with the definite article. In order to keep a distinction we have translated "wilderness" instead of "desert" although the Greek word is the same. A wilderness symbolizes the absence of God, the place of demons and impure spirits; cf. 18:2. *The* wilderness would conjure up the picture of the Exodus when God was present in the desert. The author may have been influenced by Isa 21:1, where the vision of the fall of Jerusalem is entitled "the oracle of the wilderness of the sea." He intends to contrast 1) the true Israel, clothed in heavenly glory, the mother of the male child, who was persecuted by the red dragon, who escapes to the desert as a place of sanctuary prepared by God (12:6) with the harlot, clothed in worldly luxury, upon the scarlet beast, and 2) the new Jerusalem seen from a high and lofty mountain (21:10), with the fallen harlot Babylon. The color of the beast on which the woman is seated matches her own dress (vs. 4); it is scarlet or crimson, Gr. *kokkinon,* in distinction from the dragon in 12:3 who was fiery red, Gr. *purros. Kokkinon* is crimson blended with dark blue (cf. Isa 1:18). It was a color used to attract attention, e.g. the scarlet thread attached to the first twin of Tamar (Gen 38:28) and to the home of Rahab (Josh 2:18); cf. NOTE on 17:3, its use on the scapegoat. Both references are indirectly associated with the theme of harlotry. Whereas the color may denote splendor and distinction, it also indicates ungodly conduct, e.g. Isa 1:18, sin like scarlet; cf Ps 51:7. It stands in sharp contrast to the white robes of the redeemed and the riders on the white horses.

In vs. 4 scarlet again appears, but this time in conjunction with purple. This combination, together with the mention of gold, precious stones, and pearls, might remind the Jewish reader of the offerings for the sanctuary which comprised gold, silver, bronze, blue, purple and scarlet, fine linen, goat's hair, ram's skin, acacia wood, oil, spice, incense, and for the ephod onyx stones (Exod 25:3–7 and the products in Rev 18). Similar materials and colors are mentioned in Exod 26:1 (the tabernacle curtains), 26:31 (the veil for the tabernacle), 26:36 (the screen for the door of the tent), and 27:16 (the gate or screen for the court). The garments for the priests have similar colors gold, blue, purple and scarlet, fine linen; cf. Exod 28:5, 15, 23.

These colors were not associated only with the sanctuary but also with the vestments of the high priest. These required much more gold work as well as jewels for the ephod; Exod 28:31–35, Josephus *Ant.* 3.159–61. In *Ant.* 3.151–78 Josephus describes the apparel of the ordinary priests and the high priest, including the ephod (Exod 28:6) and the turban or crown of gold (Exod 28: 36–39). This account of the headdress in *Ant.* 3.172–78 (there is a similar one in *War* 5.235) is peculiar to Josephus:

> For headdress the high priest had first a cap made in the same fashion as that of all the priests; but over this was stitched a second of blue [or violet] embroidery, which was encircled by a crown of gold wrought in three tiers, and sprouting above this was a golden calyx recalling the plant which with us is called *saccharon,* but which the Greeks expert in the cutting of simples term henbane. [Josephus then describes this] . . . It was, then, on the model of this plant that was wrought the crown extending from the nape of the neck to the two temples; the forehead, however, was not covered by the *ephielis* (for so we may call the calyx), but had a plate of gold [or band or garland of filet], bearing graven in sacred characters the name of God. Such is the apparel of the high priest.

The harlot here has two characteristics. She holds a golden cup (vs. 4) and she has a name of mystery upon her forehead (vs. 5). One recalls that the sacred utensils were made of gold. Simon the high priest is depicted with the cup of libation in Sir 50:14–15; the occasion is probably the Day of Atonement, and the wine is described as "the blood of the grape" (RSV). In the picture of the adulteress what one may have is a parody of the high priest on the Day of Atonement wearing the vestments specially reserved for that occasion and holding the libation offering. However, instead of the sacred name upon his brow the "priest-harlot" bears the name Babylon, mother of harlots and the abominations of the earth, a title illustrating Ezek 16:43–45 (RSV), where Yahweh speaks of the lewdness of Jerusalem.

The irony is heightened because the symbol of the high priestly miter, like the sacrifices, represented the forgiveness of certain sins; e.g. Rabbi Hanina said, "Let the miter on high combat the high spirit of the arrogant" (*Arakhin* 16a). Ch. 17, therefore, brings to a climax the parody in ch. 16. A touch of painful reality is added when it is recalled that the vestments of the high priest were in charge first of Herod and then of the Romans at least until Tiberius (*Ant.* 15.403–9). The bedecked harlot could only have her finery at the whim of the beast. The woman is intoxicated with the blood of the saints (vs. 6). Jerusalem was traditionally the murderer of the prophets; cf. Matt 23:29–39. Josephus, too, in *War* 5.355, referring to the factions within Jerusalem during the Roman siege, speaks of the war party being able to feed upon public miseries and "to drink of the city's life blood."

In vss. 7–18 an interpreting angel explains the vision to the seer. If the name on the forehead of the harlot is a mockery of the sacred name on the high priest's miter, the character of the beast which "was and is not" is a parody of the divine name; cf. Exod 3:14, Rev 1:4, 8, 4:8. There may be some association with the healing of the mortal wound. We have suggested in NOTES on vs. 11 that this refers to Vespasian. Vs. 8 may take the symbolism a step further. The beast "was" (Vespasian was in favor with Nero) and "is not" (he fell from favor) and will come from the abyss (he was restored with the help of the "men of the pit," an epithet for perverse men from Qumran). Vespasian stands parallel to "he who is to come." In a sense the empire passed through the same stages; "it was," from Caesar to Nero, "was not" in the critical year of the four emperors, and came again with Vespasian. Does vs. 8, using the present tense "is not," point to the year A.D. 69 for the date of this apocalypse? Cf. Rev 17:11.

The seven heads are said to be seven mountains upon which the woman is sitting (vs. 9). The "and" (Gr. *kai*) may mean either "and there are seven kings" or, "indeed," or, "namely," seven kings. A parallel is found in the Targum of Isaiah. In Isa 41:15 the prophet predicts that the hills will be blown away like chaff, but in the Targum this is interpreted as "kingdoms as chaff." Vs. 10 informs the reader that five of the kings have fallen, one is present, and the other has yet to come, but when he does come he will only remain a little time.

The identity of these kings has exercised many scholars. Most would identify them with the Roman emperors, but they differ in deciding where the calculation should be begun, with Julius Caesar or Augustus or even Galba. Charles considers the five fallen kings to be Augustus, Tiberius, Caligula, Claudius, and Nero. The one who "is" is Vespasian (A.D. 69–79) and the one who "is not yet come" is Titus (79–81); Titus comes last as the seventh and is the destroyer of Jerusalem, but he dies after a short reign. The writer may have known of the poor physical health of Titus; cf. Suetonius *Titus* 7, Dio Cassius 64.26.2. For the convenience of the reader a list of the emperors and the main lines of interpretation is given in the following table devised by Father Edward Siegman:

EMPERORS		HEADS		
	I	II	III	IV
Caesar (49–44 B.C.)	1			
Augustus (31 B.C.–A.D. 14)	2	1		
Tiberius (A.D. 14–37)	3	2		
Caligula (37–41)	4	3		
Claudius (41–54)	5	4		
Nero (54–68)	6	5	1	1
Galba (68–69)			2	2
Otho (69)			3	3
Vitellius (69)			4	(3)
Vespasian (69–79)		6	5	4
Titus (79–81)		7	6	5
Domitian (81–96)		8	7	6
Nerva (96–98)				7
Trajan (98–117)				8
Hadrian (117–138)				

Column *I* under "Heads": Boismard and Giet reconstruct according to this scheme: a) Although Caesar did not take the title emperor, he was actually the founder of the empire. According to this interpretation the mortal wound in 13:3 could refer to the assassination of Caesar. The empire, which seemed to be destroyed so soon after its birth, took on a new and stronger life in the person of Augustus. b) The wonder of the nations at the vitality of the beast could allude to the fact that Augustus was the first to assume the title of emperor, and he received divine honors during his lifetime. c) This part of Revelation could therefore have been written toward the end of Nero's reign. d) The number 7 is symbolic and could, therefore, be no precise reference to one particular emperor. e) However, to reconcile the two texts from which our apocalypse seems to be derived (Boismard) when they were fused under Domitian, Rev 17:11 was added; it likens Domitian to Nero (because he re-opened the persecution) and alludes to the legend of the Nero redivivus. Giet adds considerable validity to this theory. He notes (p. 449) that it is usual to identify the seven hills with Rome and the beast with the Roman empire and refers one to Pliny *Natural History* 3.9 and to Stauffer, p. 173, who mentions a medallion made in the reign of Vespasian which showed the goddess Roma on the seven hills. He remarks that some do not count Caesar and Augustus in their calculations, but according to Josephus, from the battle of Pharsalus to the reign of Vespasian there were ten emperors and their reigns form the framework for his chronology of the Jewish war. This pattern of counting is not peculiar to Josephus, for it is used by Suetonius as well and by some of the patristic writers. Giet gives a table on p. 54. The only legitimate way of counting for Josephus was to begin with Julius Caesar, even if he were not really counted as "king." But Giet also remarks that Galba, Otho, and Vitellius, although they exercised power, did not belong to the series of Caesars. This distinction is not without interest. Only the Caesars of the Julian and Flavian dynasty had effective power over the territory inhabited by the Jewish people.

My choice would be to start with Caesar, omit the three interim emperors, make Vespasian the seventh and Titus the eighth. If these kings are the "kings of the earth" (vs. 2), one might suggest further that their association with the harlot is reflected in the following historical situations: a) Caesar associated with Antipater and Hyrcanus (*War* 1.187–203). After the death of Pompey, Antipater paid court to Caesar and rendered him assistance with an army of three thousand Jewish infantry together with other services. b) Augustus co-operated with Herod (*War* 1.386–400). After Augustus' defeat of Anthony, Herod "presented himself before him without a diadem, a commoner in dress and demeanor, but with the proud spirit of a king" (*War* 1.387). After a suitable speech Augustus confirmed the kingdom of Herod and replaced his diadem. Later he extended his kingdom. c) Pilate, while not a Jew, sought to implement the command of Tiberius to introduce into Jerusalem the effigies of the Caesar (medallions which are attached to the standards; *War* 2.169–74). However, this was not effected. Later he committed atrocities with regard to the Samaritans. d) Caligula liberated Agrippa and made him king (*War* 2.181). e) Agrippa acted as mediator between the emperor "elect" Claudius and the senate (*War* 2.206–8). On his accession the emperor extended the kingdom of Agrippa by confirming the annexation of the kingdom of Lysanias (*War* 2.214–16). f) Nero extended the kingdom of Agrippa II (*War* 2.252).

Similar alliances occurred with regard to the three successors of Nero. Indeed Josephus dismisses their history quite briefly (*War* 4.494–96). Vespasian and

Titus were conquerors of the Jews. Josephus speaks of Titus "under divine impulse" hurrying to join his father (*War* 4.501). This remark is consonant with the purported promises which Titus received from a priest, Sostratos, in the temple of Venus at Paphos (Tacitus *Histories* 2.4, see n. 4; see also Giet, p. 60, n. 4). Josephus records that the Flavians had put an end to the period of revolution. Vespasian was a man of providence who reestablished order and peace and in a way revived the days of the Julian Dynasty. Besides, all this was exactly what Josephus had predicted (*War* 3.401). We may also compare Vespasian's words when he was elected (*War* 4.626) and what is said about Titus (*War* 4.337). The work above is elaborated from Giet (pp. 49–62).

For Giet, Vespasian becomes the seventh emperor, followed by Titus, who only lasts a short time and does belong to the seventh, i.e. is the son of Vespasian (Rev 17:11). The emperors appear to be represented by the seven heads of the beast while kings in vs. 12 are represented by the ten horns (vss. 12–14). The number ten may be dictated by Dan 7:24. These kings may refer to confederates of the returning emperors, the Parthian satraps, governors of senatorial provinces who held office for one year, and demonic powers. Charles favors the governors, and suggests that the reference to not having received royal power is intelligible if the horns symbolize the Parthian satraps; the unanimity of the Parthian kings is explained in 17:17.

Alternatively the horns might be ten governors in Palestine who supported the Romans or legates of the army (a list is suggested by one of my former students, Rev. R. J. Genovese). This would explain better why they have not yet received kingship and why they have one mind and give their power and authority to the beast. When they make war on the Lamb (vs. 14) we have a picture akin to Testament of Joseph 19:3–9, which probably should read "and I saw that in the midst of the horns a bull calf became a lamb." The beasts and the reptiles rushed against this "lamb" and he overcame and destroyed them, at which the bulls and the other good animals rejoiced together. In this text the lamb is probably representing Judas Maccabeus or Hyrcanus. Cf. also I Enoch 90:38, where there is a lamb who became a great animal with black horns on its head who seemed to be the chief of the animals and over whom the Lord of the sheep rejoices. Thus our Lamb is still the apocalyptic war figure of the non-Christian literature. There is little here which could be predicated of Jesus.

The Lamb's title is one applied to Yahweh in the OT. The appellation is influenced by Deut 10:17: "For the Lord your God is God of Gods and Lord of Lords, the great, the mighty and the terrible God, who is not partial and takes no bribe" (RSV), and Dan 2:47, the words of King Nebuchadnezzar: ". . . truly, your God is God of Gods and Lord of Lords, and a revealer of mysteries, for you have been able to reveal this mystery" (RSV). This title is not used of Jesus in the NT, but by its use our author does appear to attribute divinity to the Lamb. In I Enoch 9:1–4 the four angels, Michael, Uriel, Raphael and Gabriel address the Lord of ages as "Lord of Lords, God of Gods, King of Kings." The title in Rev 17:14 is possibly introduced deliberately as a contrast to the title of the emperors proclaimed as "Lord of Lords and King of Kings." The epithets for the companions of the Lamb are "called and elect and faithful" (vs. 14); this forms an antithesis to the predestination to destruction in 17:8. Thus there is a parallel in ch. 17. The beast bears a parody of the name of Yahweh and the dwellers of the earth are predestined to damnation, the Lamb has the title of Yahweh and his followers are predestined to eternal felicity.

In vss. 15–18 the waters are identified with peoples, multitudes, nations, and tongues. The text seems to be influenced by a passage from Isaiah which is a prophecy against Jerusalem. The prophet predicts in 8:7–8 (RSV) that the Lord will bring against her:

> . . . the waters of the River, mighty and many, the king of Assyria and all his glory; and it will rise over all its channels and go over all its banks; and it will sweep into Judah, it will overflow and pass on, reaching even to the neck; and its spread wings will fill the breadth of your land, O Immanuel.

Jeremiah used a similar image when prophesying about the Philistines before Pharaoh who smote Gaza, saying that waters are rising from the north and will become an overflowing torrent and fill the land and the city; Jer 47:1–2; cf. Rev 12:15. This, however, is not an oracle against Jerusalem. The author of Revelation then predicts that those who have connived with the harlot will turn against her. He may be inspired by Ezek 23:25–27, which describes the primitive punishment of an adulteress: mutilation, death for her accomplices and her sons and daughters, stripping her naked, and taking away her jewels. The daughter of a priest was subject to burning rather than stoning; Lev 21:9, see p. 303. But Lev 26:29–33, threatening severe famine and desolation, may also be in his mind; see the table on p. 268.

A horrendous example of famine is recorded by Josephus in *War* 6.197. He speaks of the famine in Jerusalem during the siege and he tells how the victims stripped off the leather from their bucklers and chewed it. He describes the horrors of the famine which gave rise to internal fighting, panic, and unbelievable brutality even toward relatives. He emphasizes the case of a woman who even cooked and ate her own baby (*War* 6.201–13; cf. II Kings 6:28–29). However, it is God who has put this intention into the minds of the kings represented by the horns (Rev 17:17). This concept, that God uses the pagan nations to punish his people, is common in the OT. This is a permissive decree of God. The word "decree," Gr. *gnomē*, lit. "his purpose" or "his royal decree," is employed frequently in I and II Ezra, and Daniel, LXX, where it refers to the edicts of the Persian kings. The implication is that God who is the supreme King unites the others, making them of one mind to give their allegiance to the beast. When this is done the word of God will be fulfilled. This fulfillment is highly significant; it may refer to the words of the prophets but it may go back to the Holiness Code and the Deuteronomic precepts, as in Deut 28. Deut 28:58 refers to the "words of this law which are written in this book" (although there is no linguistic affinity between the LXX and our text). On the other hand "words," Gr. *logoi*, might simply mean "oracles."

Vs. 18 explains that the woman is "the great city," a phrase already used of Jerusalem, in 11:8, 16:19. The image recalls IV Ezra 9:38 – 10:24. Here the prophet sees a woman mourning; her clothes are torn and there are ashes upon her head. She has lost her son on his wedding night, a son for whom she had waited for thirty years. The prophet reproaches her for mourning in the light of the desolation of Jerusalem, but as he looks at her, her countenance changes and becomes brilliant. Then she is no longer visible to him but instead there is a city built with large foundations. The angel then explains to the prophet that the woman whom he saw was Zion. Now he sees her as a built city (IV Ezra 10:25–49). The angel explains different details in the vision. But what is of interest for our apocalypse is the fact that the son symbolized "the (divine) dwelling in Jerusalem" (vs. 48) and his entry into the marriage chamber and his death represented the fall of Jerusalem. The importance of the IV Ezra vision is that it gives us an example of a vision in the apocalyptic era which symbolizes both the fall and the rise of Jerusalem. In the same way, Rev 17 looks forward to the new Jerusalem in ch. 21. However, the description in IV Ezra 10:21–24 of the fate which befell Jerusalem is akin to that which we shall find in Rev 18; see Jacob M. Myers *I & II Esdras,* AB, vol. 42 (1974), 266, 273–74, 279.

BIBLIOGRAPHY

Allo, E. B. *L'Apocalypse de St. Jean.*

Boismard, M. E. RB 56 (1949), 507–41.

Bonsirven, P. J. *L'Apocalypse de Saint Jean.*

Cambier, J. "Les images de l'A.T. dans l'Apocalypse," *Nouvelle Revue Theologique* 77 (1955), 113–23.

Carrington, P. *The Meaning of Revelation.*

Giet, S. *L'Apocalypse et l'histoire.*

Ringgren, H. *The Faith of Qumran.* Philadelphia: Fortress, 1963.

XV. THE "DEATH" OF THE "FIRSTBORN"
(18:1–24)

18 ¹ After this I saw another angel descending from heaven; he had great authority, and his glory filled the earth with light. ² And he cried out with a powerful voice, saying,
"Fallen, fallen is Babylon the great,
   and she has become the dwelling of demons
   and the watchtower of every unclean spirit
   and the watchtower of every unclean and hateful bird,
³ because all the nations drank of the wine of the lust of her harlotry,
   and the kings of the earth have committed adultery with her,
   and the merchants of the earth have grown rich on the power of her lust."
⁴ And I heard a loud voice from heaven, saying,
   "My people, come out of her,
     so that you do not share in her sins,
     and so that you do not receive her misfortunes,
   ⁵ because her sins have clung to the heaven,
     and God has remembered her unjust deeds.
   ⁶ Render to her as she has rendered,
     and double the punishment for her double crimes;
     in the cup she mixed, mix a double draught.
   ⁷ Just as she clothed herself in splendor and went awhoring,
     so in that measure give her torment and grief.
     Because she says in her heart, 'I am established queen
     and I am not a widow and I experience no grief at all,'
   ⁸ therefore, in one day her plagues will come upon her,
     death and mourning and famine,
     and she will be burned with fire;
     for powerful is the Lord God Who judges."
⁹ And the kings of the earth, who committed fornication with her and went awhoring, will wail and beat their breasts over her when they see the smoke of her burning; ¹⁰ standing at a distance because of her torment, they say,

"Woe, woe, great city,
 powerful city, Babylon,
 because in one hour your judgment has come."

11 And the merchants of the earth will wail and mourn over her, because no one buys their cargo anymore, 12 cargo of gold and silver and precious stone and pearls and linen and purple and silk and crimson and all kinds of scented wood and every type of vessel of ivory, and every type of vessel of precious wood and of bronze and iron and marble, 13 and cinnamon and spice and incense and myrrh and frankincense and wine and oil and fine flour and wheat and cattle and sheep, and horses and chariots and slaves, that is, human souls.

14 The fruit for which your soul longed has gone from you,
 and all your luxuries and splendors have perished never to be
 found again.

15 The merchants of these wares, who grew rich from her, will stand at a distance for fear of her torment, weeping and mourning, 16 saying,

"Woe, woe, great city,
 clothed in fine linen and purple and scarlet,
 and ornate with gold and precious stones and pearls,
 17 in one hour all your wealth is devastated."

All the shipmasters and seafarers and sailors and whosoever works on the sea stood at a distance 18 and seeing the smoke of her burning cried out, saying,

"Who is like the great city?"

19 And they threw dust upon their heads and cried out wailing and mourning, saying,

"Woe, woe, great city,
 by whom all those who had ships on the sea grew wealthy,
 because in one hour there is devastation."

20 "Rejoice over her, heaven and saints and apostles and prophets,
 for God has pronounced judgment against her for you."

21 And one powerful angel lifted a stone like a great millstone, and threw it into the sea, saying,

"Thus will Babylon, the great city, be hurled down with violence,
 and will not be found anymore.

22 And the sound of harpers and musicians and flute players and
 trumpeters
 is not heard within you anymore,

and no craftsman of any art
is found in you anymore,
and the sound of the mill
is not heard in you anymore,
and 23 no light of a lamp
appears in you anymore,
and the voice of the bridegroom and the bride
is not heard in you anymore;
for your merchants were the great men of the earth,
for all nations have been deceived by your sorcery
and 24 in her was found the blood of prophets and of saints,
and of all who have been slain on earth."

NOTES

18:1. *angel.* There is no verbal affinity between Ezek 43:2, LXX, where it is said the glory of the Lord comes from the east, and Rev 18:1. It may describe the Shekinah, which is the revelation of God's glory and was at times confused with an angel. Cf. the Holy Spirit as an angel in the Shepherd of Hermas (see introduction, under "pneumatology," in APCh, II). Cf. also Rev 10:1, 14:4.

great authority. Gr. *exousian megalēn.* This phrase occurs only in Revelation in the NT although Gr. *pasa exousia,* "all authority," is found quite frequently.

2. *powerful voice.* Gr. *en ischupa phōnē.* Notice the departure from "loud voice," which occurs frequently in Revelation, e.g. 5:2, 12, 6:10, 12:10, etc.

Fallen, fallen. Cf. the dirge or lamentation which Amos sang over Israel even before she fell (Amos 5:2, RSV):

> Fallen, no more to rise,
>   is the virgin Israel;
> forsaken on her land,
>   with none to raise her up.

dwelling. Gr. *katoikētērion.* This word occurs only here in the NT, but in the LXX it is used frequently. E.g. in I Kings 8, LXX, the word is used in Solomon's prayer dedicating the Jerusalem temple, as part of the plea that God in His dwelling which is heaven would grant forgiveness (vs. 39), act on the prayers of foreigners to the temple so they might fear Him (vs. 43), and remain favorable to the Israelites (vs. 49). The word is also found in the LXX of II Chron 30:27 and Ps 32:14 signifying God's dwelling in heaven, in Ps 76:2(3), God's dwelling in Zion; Ps 107:4, no city for the Israelites to dwell in; and in Ps 107:7, God's leading them to a city to dwell in. Dan 2:11 refers to the dwelling of the pagan gods. Nahum 2:11(12), 12(13) refers to the dwelling of lions.

demons. Among ancient peoples ruins were thought to be the preferred dwelling place of demons and all kinds of wild animals and birds. Isa 13:21 speaks of the satyrs dancing in the ruins; cf. Zeph 2:14–15. Swete, p. 227, says, "the evil spirits, watching over the fallen Rome like night birds or harpies that wait for their prey, build their eyries in the broken towers which arise from the ashes of the city."

watchtower. In Isa 21:11–12 the targum reads "prophet" instead of "watchman."

unclean spirit. A 2080, 2329 al g read "hated unclean spirit."

and the watchtower of every unclean and hateful bird. This clause is omitted in AP 1, 2059s al, and changed to "and watchtower of every unclean wild beast" in A 1611, 2329 al g (sa).

unclean and hateful bird. Cf. Isa 34:11a, 13b, which mention the hawk, the owl, the raven, and the ostrich together with unclean animals, the porcupine and the jackal. Jer 50:39 speaks of ostriches and hyenas. Most of these are scavengers; cf. Rev 19:17–18.

3. *drank.* P **051** (1) 2059 al TR use the verb *pinō*, "drink"; 94 pc sy[ph] use *potizō*, "give to drink"; A C pc co; R[t]; ℵ 046 82, 1006 al 1854, 2060 pc use *piptō*, "fall."

merchants . . . grown rich. Jeremias, p. 49, cites Jerusalem *Betzah* 2:4, which reports that a contemporary of Herod the Great had three thousand head of livestock brought to the temple to be sold. To the orthodox Jew (e.g. from Qumran or Zealotism) anyone prospering under Rome was suspect.

4. *My people.* Cf. Jer 51:45, where God calls His people to leave Babylon before the catastrophe.

come out. Contrast Isa 48:20, calling Israel to "go forth with joy" from Babylon.

share. Gr. *sunkoinōneō.* This word is used in Eph 5:11, having fellowship with the unfruitful works of darkness, and in Phil 4:14, sharing in Paul's affliction, Gr. *thlipsis.*

5. *her sins have clung to the heaven.* Cf. Luke 10:11, the dust of a town cleaving to one's feet. *IV Ezra* 10:43, 45–46 speaks of the insolence of Rome ascending to the Most High.

unjust deeds. Gr. *adikēma.* The more common word would be *adikia*, "unrighteousness," but the author may have chosen *adikēma* for its linguistic resemblance to *dikaiōma*, "regulations" or "commandments," especially those given by Yahweh. *Adikēma* is found here and in Acts 18:14, 24:20 with reference to crime in the legal sense of the word. It occurs in Josephus *Ant.* 3. 321, where he speaks of the priests who would not consume flour brought in during the feast of unleavened bread even when there was a famine for fear that God should punish them even for "crimes (Gr. *adikēmasin*) which elude detection." See also *Ant.* 5.234, speaking of Abimelech the tyrant in Judg 8:30. God does not remember Jerusalem's observance of the ritual and moral law but her lack of observance.

6. The command, "Render to her," is probably addressed to the ministers of divine justice although the subject of the sentence seems to be "My people." For double recompense see Exod 22:4, 7, 9 where the law goes beyond the *lex talionis.* In this verse, however, there is precise compensation: double punishment for double crimes. It would not seem permissible to trans-

late it "repay her double for her deeds" as in the RSV, particularly in view of the phrase "as she has rendered." The point is that her deeds have been doubly bad and, therefore, the punishment must be doubly bad. The opposite idea is found in Isa 40:2, where Yahweh comforts Israel and informs her that she has suffered double for her sins.

One notes throughout this verse the rhetorical device of repetition. Alliteration is extensively used: the initial alpha occurs in four words out of six in 6a, there are two initial kappas and two initial deltas in 6b, and to culminate the alliteration the last three words of 6c begin respectively with kappa, alpha, delta. There is repetition of roots in "render . . . rendered," Gr. *apodote* . . . *apedōken* "double (verb) . . . double (adjective)," Gr. *diplōsate* . . . *dipla*, and "mixed, mix," Gr. *ekerasen kerasate*. The adjective "double" appears twice. The author also uses the rhetorical device of the balanced sentence.

she has rendered. "To you (plural)" is added to 1, 2059s pm it vg[s,cl] arm TR.

7. *clothed herself.* Cf. 18:16.

went awhoring. Gr. *strenaō*. This is found only here in the NT, but it does occur in Isa 61:6, Symmachus (see Arndt and Gingrich), a text which is the exact antithesis to vs. 7. Cf. also Isa 3:16.

queen. Cf. Jerusalem as "princess of all nations" in 4Q 179.

am established. 82 al read "just as."

widow. Cf. Isa 47:7–8, the address to Babylon, for she is portrayed as saying "I am, and there is no other; I shall never be widowed; I shall not know bereavement" (vs. 8, AB).

8. *in one day.* It is not quite certain why the punishment should come upon her in a single day, but the phrase may merely mean suddenly, like a thief in the night; cf. 3:3, 16:15. Note, however, that whereas this verse speaks of one day, vss. 10, 17 and 19 have "in one hour." In 69 pc m Cypr Prim "hour" replaces "day."

death. Gr. *thanatos*. This may mean pestilence. This, together with mourning and famine, recalls the curse in Exodus, Leviticus, and Deuteronomy.

burned. Death by burning was also perpetuated because the priests kept the older form of capital punishment. This form is also upheld by Jubilees 20:4, which prescribes burning for all cases of adultery.

powerful. Gr. *ischuros*. This word is used by the Baptist to describe He That Cometh (Matt 3:11, cf. 12:29; Mark 1:7; Luke 3:16, cf. 11:21–22).

Lord. Omitted in A 1006 pc vg R[m].

10. *Woe, woe.* Ch. 18 has a threefold expression of woe by the kings (vss. 9–10), merchants (vss. 11–17a), and sailors (vss. 17b–19); cf. the eagle with the triple woe in 8:13.

11. *cargo.* Gr. *gomos*. This is used of a load on the back of a horse, camel, or ass, but may also be used of a ship's cargo, as in Acts 21:3. *Kiddushin* 49b says that ten measures of wealth came into the world and that Rome received nine while all the rest of the world received only one.

12. *linen.* Fabrics also came from India. According to *Yoma* 3:7, in the afternoon of the Day of Atonement, the high priest was clothed in Indian linen.

silk. As well as being a priestly, especially a high priestly, material, silk was used commonly in Rome about A.D. 70. Charles refers to Josephus, *War* 7. 126, who describes Vespasian and Titus dressed in silk robes for their triumphs.

scented wood. Gr. *thuia articulata.* This is a tree which grew in North Africa and was used for making costly tables; cf. Martial 14.87; Juvenal *Satires* 1.137. Swete, p. 233, observes that this type of wood was much valued because of the veining; the best specimens appeared like the eyes of the peacock's tail (Martial 14.85) or the stripes of a tiger or the spots of a panther (Pliny *Natural History* 13.96) or the seeds of parsley. Seneca *Dialogues* 61.10.3, speaks of three hundred tables of citrus wood with ivory feet. A 1006 pc vg read "stone," Gr. *lithos.*

ivory. Ivory was used by the Hebrews for boxes (cf. Song of Songs 5:14), beds (Amos 6:4), and building (I Kings 22:39).

13. *and cinnamon.* Omitted in **046** 1, 82, 1006, 2059s pm dem vg^{cl} TR. Cinnamon came from China. It was much used in Rome, as we know from Propertius, Lucian, and Martial.

spice. Mesopotamia exported spices; cf. *Pesachim* 116a and *Lam R* Proem 5.

incense and myrrh and frankincense. From Arabia.

flour and wheat. Grain came from Egypt. These would be used for temple sacrifice.

horses. Horses were sent from Armenia and beyond.

human souls. Cf. Ezek 27:13.

14. *fruit.* Gr. *opōra,* lit. "late summer fruit." This word is used by Jeremiah in his lamentation over Moab; Jer 31(48):32; cf. 47(40):10, 12.

luxuries. Gr. *lipara,* lit. "oil" or "fat." Josephus, *Against Apion* 2.229, says that the Spartans were "sleek (*liparoi*) of person and cultivating beauty by physical training . . ." Does our writer make an indirect allusion to the Greek athletes to which many Jews objected, especially when the priests left the sanctuary for the arena? Cf. II Macc 4:14–15.

17. *shipmasters.* Gr. *kubernētēs,* probably "shipmasters" in distinction from "ship owners," Gr. *nauklēros;* cf. Acts 27:11. It refers to one who steers, and may also describe one who directs the state.

20. *Rejoice.* In Revelation God appears to establish a correspondence between the chastisement of the persecutors and the recompense of the elect; cf. II Thess 1:5–6. The verse is akin to Jer 51:48, rejoicing over the destruction of Babylon, but a closer parallel is found in Deut 32:43, which speaks of avenging the blood of Yahweh's servants.

apostles. Cf. 21:14, where the names of the twelve apostles are on the twelve foundations of the city wall. Swete, p. 238, remarks that "apostles" here may connote not only the twelve Christian apostles but all those "sent." He remarks the surprising absence of any reference to local ministry in Revelation but says that this "is characteristic of a book which emanates from prophetic circles and is charismatic throughout." His reading looks more probable than 21:14, "the twelve apostles of the Lamb." There is an affinity of thought, but not of word, with Matt 23:37, where Jerusalem is said to kill the prophets and stone those sent, Gr. *apestalmenous,* to her. The idea in this verse is completed in vs. 24.

22. *of any art.* Omitted in ℵ A R^m.

24. *was found the blood of prophets.* A similar statement is made about Jerusalem in Matt 23:35, but the wording is not the same. Rome shed martyrs' blood but not necessarily that of the prophets. **046 051** 82, 1006, 2059s pm R have "blood" in the plural.

COMMENT

In vivid contrast to the scarlet woman established upon the scarlet beast in ch. 17, here an angel with great authority descends from heaven. His glory is so bright that the earth is filled with light. He seems to be no ordinary angel, for in this apocalypse "glory," Gr. *doxa,* is an attribute of only God and the Lamb except in 18:1, where the angel has this special characteristic in common with God and the Lamb. Further, the author is influenced by Ezek 43:2, where the earth is said to shine with the glory of God and where the prophet compares that vision with the one that he saw "when he came to destroy the city" (Ezek 43:3, RSV). The angel in Rev 18 stands in an analogous position; he comes to sing a dirge over the fallen sacred city. His cry, "Fallen, fallen is Babylon . . . ," is the first of four dirges sung over the burning city. The second is sung by the kings (vss. 9–10), the third by the merchants (vss. 11–13, 15–16), and the fourth by the ship owners and sailors of the whole world (vss. 17–19). The chapter ends with another angel's song of doom prefaced (vs. 21) by the symbolic action of throwing a large stone into the sea and saying thus shall Babylon be destroyed.

The first dirge is especially reminiscent of Isa 13:21, the oracle against Babylon, and Isa 47, another oracle against Babylon and one closer to our text. Isa 47 addresses Babylon as a "virgin daughter," bids her sit in the dust on the ground, and tells her she will no longer be delicate but will be stripped of her clothing and suffer shame. She is called mistress of kingdoms and lover of pleasures. She has indulged in sorceries and, by implication, idolatry. Vss. 8c, 10b report that she says in her heart: "I am, and there is no other . . ." (AB). See NOTE on 18:7, "widow." This contrasts sharply with the recurring idea in Second Isaiah (Isa 40–55) as expressed in 43:11–13 (AB):

> I, I am Yahweh, and besides me there is no savior.
> . . . I am God.
> Yes, from eternity I am;
> There is no one delivers from my hands.

We have noted similar usurpations of divine prerogatives in Revelation, e.g. 13:4. Rev 18:7 is also influenced by Isa 21:9b: "Fallen, fallen is Babylon; and all the images of her gods he has shattered to the ground" (RSV). The targum on vs. 10, after "Fallen, fallen is Babylon," adds "kings who are skilful in waging war shall come against her to plunder her"; cf. Rev 17:16–17. The targum to vs. 11, the oracle concerning Dumah, adds "the oracle of the cup of cursing to give to Dumah to drink"; cf. Rev 16:19.

But just as the glory of God in Ezek 43 is associated with the fall of Jerusalem, not that of a pagan nation, so further confirmation that the angel in

Rev 18:2 heralds the same news rather than the fall of Rome is found in the author's selection of the word "dwelling," Gr. *katoikētērion*. See third NOTE on 18:2. To a Jewish reader the use of this term would evoke the memory of the sanctuary of the Temple, "the place (*katoikētērion*), O Lord, which thou hast made for thy abode, the sanctuary, O Lord, which thy hands have established" (Exod 15:17b, RSV). It would also bring to mind Hezekiah's passover; when the priests and the Levites blessed the people, their voice was heard and their prayer ascended to God's holy habitation; II Chron 30:27. Instead of the dwelling of the Presence of Yahweh, Jerusalem "has become the dwelling of demons and the watchtower of every unclean spirit and the watchtower of every unclean and hateful bird" (vs. 2). The word "watchtower," Gr. *phulakē*, could be translated as prison or stronghold as well. Its repetition here suggests that the author is still influenced by Isa 21, the watchman standing on the watchtower watching for the fall of the enemy, and by Hab 2:1, where Habakkuk says he will stand on the *phulakē* and watch for what Yahweh will say to him.

The stronghold used for looking for good news is now abandoned; no human being stands watching, only the demons and the unclean birds. Jeremiah predicted that God would make Jerusalem a heap of ruins and a dwelling place of jackals (9:11; cf. 21:13) but our author paints a more ominous picture. The birds are not only unclean but also "hateful." Deut 14:11–20 lists the unclean birds: the eagle, the vulture, the osprey, the buzzard, the kite, the raven, the ostrich, the night hawk, the seagull, the hawk, the owl, the water hen, the pelican, the carrion vulture, the cormorant, the stork, the heron, the hoopoe and the bat, many of which are scavengers. The smallest offerings one could make to the temple were clean birds (cf. Luke 2:24, where Mary and Joseph bring a pair of turtle doves and two young pigeons); here not even these are found. The stress on "unclean" twice in the one verse contrasts strongly with Rev 21:27 where it is said that nothing unclean will enter the New City. The scene in ch. 18 is one of the most extreme religious defilement.

Commenting on Nahum 2:12a, 4QpNah says that Jerusalem has become a dwelling place for the wicked of the nations. In Rev 18:3 their relationship with the Holy City is described. We have commented already on the cup and the wine and the kings of the earth. It remains to discuss the merchants; cf. also commentary on vss. 15–20, pp. 304–5. The author continues to follow Ezekiel, where the merchants, especially sea traders, are mentioned in the lamentation over Tyre (Ezek 27:3, 8–9). Here, however, the text concerns Jerusalem, to whom commerce was no less important than to Tyre (or Rome), especially with regard to the temple activities. Jeremias, p. 49, cites the evidence of Zech 14:21, which he dates between the fourth and third centuries B.C., with reference to traders in the house of the Lord of hosts, and *Shekalim* 1:3; 174, with reference to money changers in the temple court. There were shops on the aqueduct (*Lam R* 4:7), and the Sanhedrin appears to have been housed there for forty years before the destruction of Jerusalem. Many shops apparently belonged to the high priestly family. Indeed, Josephus called the high priest Ananias (A.D. 47–55) "the great procurer of money" in *Ant.* 20.205. Tosephta, Menahoth 13:22, 534, speaks of the temple going to ruin because of avarice and hatred. Jeremias concludes, pp. 48–49, that the court of the Gentiles appears to have been the scene of a flourishing trade in animal sacrifice, perhaps supported by the high priestly family. In the light of this one can understand both our author's abhorrence of traders (cf. also Jesus' cleansing of the temple, John 2:13–22) and the voice bidding "My people" to come out of her (vs. 4).

"My people" could not be addressed to the Romans, for it is a covenant appellation (cf. Hosea 2:23, etc.) and begins a series of words reminiscent of the covenant and/or the Exodus in the following verses. The voice bids the people "go out" (cf. Exod 4:22–23), an exhortation which is akin to Jer 51: 44–45 when the wall of Babylon fell and God bade his people come out of the midst of her so that their lives may be saved from his anger. In 18:4 the reason given for the departure is that her sins have cleaved to heaven.

In 18:5 the harlot's sins are said to "have clung to the heaven." The Greek word *kollaō achri*, lit. "cleave to," is a powerful expression. It can adhere not only to evil but to the good, as in Hezekiah clinging to the Lord and walking in the way of righteousness (II Kings 18:6), the men of Judah following David rather than the rebel leader (II Sam 20:2), and the people who chose to follow the father of Judas Maccabeus (I Macc 3:2). It can also apply to the intimate union of marriage. The covenant use of *kollaō* occurs in Deut 6:13, cleaving to Yahweh, although the preposition there is *pros*, "to," rather than *achri*, "as far as." This same expression appears in Deut 10:20, cleaving to God. The act of cleaving can also apply to evil or harlotry, as in Deut 28:60, the pain of Egypt which will cling to those who rebel against God, and in Deut 29:20(19), the curses of the covenant clinging to the people who are stubborn and sinful. In Rev 18:5 both senses of this ambivalent word are important; Jerusalem's sins (not her love) have cleaved to God. The concept of sin rising to heaven is present also in the OT, in Jer 51:9, MT (29:9 in LXX): "We would have healed Babylon, but she was not healed. Forsake her, and let us go each to his own country; for her judgment has reached up to heaven and has been lifted up even to the skies" (RSV). However the word *kollaō* is not used in the LXX.

At this point we are reminded that "God has remembered her unjust deeds" (vs. 5). The words "remember" and "unjust deeds," Gr. *emnēmoneusen* and *adikēmata*, are chosen with precision. God "remembered" Israel in her affliction in Egypt (Exod 2:24) and sent His judgments, Gr. *sun ekdikēsei megalē*) on her oppressors; cf. Exod 7:4, etc. Justice is dealt according to the *lex talionis* in Rev 18:6–8, just as it is in Exod 21:24–25, ". . . eye for eye, tooth for tooth, hand for hand, foot for foot, burn for burn, wound for wound, stripe for stripe" (RSV); cf. L. M. Epstein, pp. 228–29. Evidence for a literal interpretation of this text is found as late as Jubilees. In Jubilees 4:31–33 it is surmised that Cain was killed by a stone, which fell from his house, because he had killed Abel with a stone. It was ordained on the heavenly tablets "With the instrument with which a man kills his neighbour with the same shall he be killed; after the manner that he wounded him, in like manner shall they deal with him" (APCh, II, 19). In Jubilees 48:14–15 God is said to cast the Egyptians into the midst of the Jordan because they themselves cast the Israelite children into the Nile. The harlot is to be dealt with in the same way.

Epstein, p. 228, shows how the "rule of justice, the measure for measure" explains one detail after another in the trial by bitter water described in Num 5. We have suggested that the second scroll in Rev 10:8–11 is associated with this ordeal. The present chapter appears to resume the theme. Epstein points out the application of the *lex talionis* with regard to adultery as it is found in the Palestinian Targum, Etheridge, p. 354 (see also *Num R* 11:23 and Rev 12:5):

> . . . because she may have brought delicacies to the adulterer, she ought to bring an appointed oblation of her own, a tenth of three sata of barley flour, that being the food of beasts: (cf. *Num R* 9:13) he (the priest) shall not pour *oil,* (cf. Rev 18:13) nor . . . *frankincense* . . . (cf. Rev 18: 13) . . . the priest shall take holy water . . . and pour it into an earthen vessel (cf. Rev 18:11–12); because she may have brought the adulterer sweet wine to drink in precious vases; and he shall take of the dust that is upon the ground of the tabernacle,—because the end of all flesh is dust, —and put it into the water . . . and bind a cord over her loins . . . because she should have bound her loins with a girdle; and he shall uncover the woman's head, because she tied a fillet upon her hair.

The harlot in Revelation is depicted in a similar way. She is to be naked and desolate (17:16). Her fine clothes are to be removed; cf. 17:4, 18:16. She will lose her ornaments, delicacies, rich possessions 18:11–12. The wine of fornication has been consumed (17:2) and so she drinks a double draft (18:6). Further, just as the ordeal to detect adultery took place publicly (*Sotah* 1:5–6), so the harlot Jerusalem is exposed to the public gaze (Rev 18:10). The people stand afar in fear of her torment (18:15); in the ordeal the woman was removed quickly after the draft of bitter water lest she die and so pollute the temple (*Sotah* 1:5–6; 2:1–6; 3:1–4).

But this harlot is no "commoner"; she appears to be of the priestly class. The form of her punishment is significant; she is to be burnt with fire. Burning was the punishment for adultery or harlotry only if the adulteress was a daughter of a priest. Less severe execution, such as stoning or strangulation, was employed in other cases. The law is expressed in Lev 21:9: "And the daughter of any priest, if she profane herself by playing the harlot . . . shall be burned with fire" (RSV). Such behavior was thought not only to profane the priesthood but also to be a defiance of parental authority. The daughter was treated like the "rebellious son" for whom Deuteronomy prescribes the death penalty (Deut 21:18–23). The burning was correctly carried out by pouring molten lead or a wick down the condemned person's throat (*Sanhedrin* 7:2). This makes the double draught in vs. 6 particularly significant; cf. "the smoke of her burning" in vs. 9. However, in *Sanhedrin* 52b there appears to be an illegitimate case of burning an adulteress by surrounding her with fagots. J. Derenbourg, in *The Babylonian Talmud* (Epstein), p. 353, n. 2, thinks that this burning of the priest's daughter by fagots described by Rabbi Eleazar ben Zadok occurred in the interval between the death of Festus, the Roman Procurator in A.D. 62, and the accession of Albinus in A.D. 63, during the high priesthood of Hanan ben Hanan. If Derenbourg is correct, then the incident might well have influenced our author's choice of imagery. It also shows the strict application of the Levitical law.

The burning of the harlot is followed by three lamentations. First comes the dirge of the kings of the earth, who in this chapter appear to represent all those in authority who have refused to accept the rule of Yahweh and cooperated in the unfaithfulness of Jerusalem. Herod the Great, e.g., and many other rulers of different parts of Palestine, introduced Hellenistic and Roman customs, contrary to orthodox Jewish beliefs. In the dirge of the kings of the earth in vss. 8–10, note the solemn alliteration on the consonant *kappa: krinas,* "the one who judges" (vs. 8); *kalusousin,* "will wail," the professional wailing with great noise found among the non-western people (vs. 9); *kopsonti,* "will mourn greatly" or "beat their breasts" (vs. 9); *kapnon,* "smoke" (vs. 9).

The three dirges all end with the expression, "Woe, woe," e.g. vs. 10. This exclamation would have peculiar significance for the citizens of Jerusalem. Josephus, *War* 6.305, 306, tells the story of the prophet Jesus, the son of Ananias, who prophesied disaster to Jerusalem. The reference is particularly arresting because Josephus reports that those who were annoyed with him chastized him and when this did no good they took him to the Roman governor (*War* 6.303–9):

> . . . there, although flayed to the bone with scourges, he neither sued for mercy nor shed a tear, but, merely introducing the most mournful of variations into his ejaculation, responded to each stroke with "woe to Jerusalem!" . . . During the whole period up to the outbreak of war he neither approached nor was seen talking to any of the citizens, but daily, like a prayer that he had conned, repeated his lament, "Woe to Jerusalem!" . . . His cries were loudest at the festivals. So for seven years and five months he continued his wail, his voice never flagging nor his strength exhausted, until in the siege, having seen the presage verified, he found his rest. For, while going his round and shouting in piercing tones from the wall, "Woe once more to the city and to the people and to the temple," as he added a last word, "and woe to me also," a stone hurled from the *ballista* struck and killed him on the spot. So with those ominous words still upon his lips he passed away.

In Rev 18 it is the kings of the earth, the merchants, and the sailors, who echo the cry of the poor prophet.

The second lament is sung by the merchants. These people were not dissociated from the temple in Jerusalem, for merchants were employed both in the building of Herod's temple and in its maintenance. According to B. Mazar (book on Temple Mount, forthcoming) items of worship were purchased at the shops. Most commentators suggest that the text is influenced by Ezek 27:12–24, the oracle against Tyre. However, while there is some association, the wares cited differ considerably; those cited below appear to be more in keeping with those which would be used for the temple and its services.

Of the items which are listed in Rev 18, gold and silver, precious stones, fine linen, purple, silk (for vestments) scarlet, precious wood, bronze, iron (cf. Deut

8:9), marble, cinnamon (as an ingredient of the sacred anointing oil), spices, incense, ointment, frankincense, wine, oil, fine meal (Gr. *semidalis,* used frequently in Leviticus for fine flour offerings), corn, beasts, sheep are all found in use in the temple. Ivory and probably pearls were found in Herod's temple. Although horses and chariots do seem to be incongruous, the Greek word for chariot is *rhedē,* a four-wheel chariot, a fairly rare word which appears to come from the Latin name. The author may be insinuating that Roman ways were introduced into the sacred city.

The popularity of commerce among all classes in Jerusalem can be judged by the fact that merchants were held in such respect that even priests and scholars joined their ranks. The high priestly family, too, had a flourishing trade; see p. 301. The extent of commerce is indicated by certain statistics. There were camel caravans sometimes composed of about two hundred beasts passing from places like Tyre to Jerusalem. Josephus, *Ant.* 15.390, speaks of a thousand wagons bringing stone to build Herod's temple (Jeremias, pp. 31–51). Wares catalogued in vss. 11–17 are mentioned in a number of ancient texts. Dealers in spices are spoken of in Jerusalem *Pesachim* 10:3.37d.9; cf. Babylonian *Pesachim 116a,* which calls them "dealers in parched corn." When Agrippa II decided to improve the temple, c. A.D. 66, he imported timber from the Lebanon, buying only long, straight beams (*War* 5.36) and cedar wood to roof the arcades (*War* 5.190; cf. Jeremias, p. 35). Tyre exported goods, especially glassware and costly purple dye, to Jerusalem. Jerusalem also bought Babylon's exports of blue, scarlet, and purple materials, and fine white linen, e.g. for the curtain in front of the holy place (*War* 5.212–13; cf. 6.390, which mentions purple and scarlet for the temple veil), for the high priest's miter (*War* 6.235) and for the ceremonies on the Day of Atonement (*Yoma* 3:4). Arabia supplied Jerusalem with precious stones, gold, frankincense, and spices such as cinnamon and cassia (*War* 6.390) used in the temple. Jeremias, p. 36, describes the slave trade: "In Jerusalem there was a stone upon which the slaves were displayed for auction." Josephus frequently refers to male and female slaves, especially in association with the court of Herod the Great. Jeremias concludes that foreign trade had a great influence on the holy city, and the temple drew the largest share. The chief items were food supplies, precious metals, luxury goods, and clothing materials.

There was, of course, local trade, e.g. flour for the temple was obtained from Michmash and Zanoah or Ephraim; *Menahoth* 8:1; Jeremias, p. 40. Olives were suitable for the limestone soil around Jerusalem; Jeremias, p. 41. Trees must have grown in abundance in the area around Jerusalem, for Herod deforested it in 37 B.C. (*War* 1.334), and when the Romans laid siege to Jerusalem in A.D. 70, they turned a district which was once one of trees and ornamental gardens into a wilderness (*War* 5.264, 6.5–6, 151). There were also vineyards (*Ta'anith* 4:8), e.g. the Kidron Valley, which was very suitable for gardens (Jeremias, p. 44). Thus, the merchants in Rev 18:11–17 may well have been those in association with Jerusalem, and the luxury described may have been that enjoyed by the holy city.

This chapter foretells that all these things will disappear; the merchants who have been made rich by the city stand afar and wail and mourn over her because in one hour such great wealth becomes "devastation" (vs. 19). Gr. *erēmoō*, lit. "made desolate," is not a common word, but it does occur in Josephus, *War* 2.279, when he speaks of Gessius Florus (A.D. 64–66). With reference to his extreme cruelty, shamelessness, and contempt for the truth, Josephus remarks, "his avarice brought desolation (Gr. *erēmōthēnai*) upon all the cities"; *War* 2.278–79.

The third lament, that of the seafaring men (vss. 17–20), is influenced by the dirge of the mariners and pilots. Tyre is described as "in the midst of the sea"; Ezek 27:27. In our text the sailors could refer to foreign traders, but it is likely that they would also include sailors from the Sea of Galilee and men employed in the brisk trade involving the salt industry at Qumran in the Dead Sea area. Josephus tells us that there were fifteen cities around the Sea of Galilee. Some of these have been discovered by underwater excavation. Carrington refers to Titus striking a medal with the words "Victoria Navalis." It referred to Jerusalem as a second Carthage; details are in a speech attributed to Titus by Josephus (P. Carrington, *The Meaning of Revelation*, p. 291). The cry of the mariners in vs. 18b, "Who is like the great city?" echoes the cry of the men who worshiped the dragon and the beast, saying "Who is like the beast, and who can fight against it?" (13:4). That the mariners threw dust on their heads is a sign of grief, for dust was a symbol of lowliness or worthlessness. The practice is mentioned throughout the OT, e.g. Josh 7:6, Job 2:12, Lam 2:10, Ezek 27:30.

In vs. 8 the harlot's punishment appears to be in the future but the dirges speak in the past tense (vss. 10, 17, 20). In vs. 21 the angel speaks first in the future and, after the throwing of the stone, in present tenses. His action in throwing the millstone is a prophetic *'ōt*, or dramatic symbolic action, which brings to pass a future event; cf. II Ezra 19:11, Jer 25:10–14, 51:63, Ezek 26:13, Deut 32:43, Matt 18:6. It recalls the Song of Moses in Exod 15:5, which describes Pharaoh's chariots and host going down into the depths like a stone. A millstone was made of two round, flat stones. A small one could be used by hand but a large one was worked by donkeys. It is the latter type, which was introduced in the Greco-Roman period, that the angel hurls into the sea. The fact that our angel uses the large size indicates his strength. Vs. 21 is modeled on Jer 51:63–64, where the prophet is bidden to finish reading the book, bind a stone to it, and throw it into the midst of the Euphrates, saying "Just so shall Babylon sink to rise no more, because of the evil that I am going to bring upon it" (AB).

In Rev 18:22–24 the author then describes the silence and stillness which embrace Jerusalem. Music ceases, not only secular music but religious; the flute was used in the festivals and the trumpet was nearly always limited to religious services. Industry is no more. The familiar sound of women or slaves grinding the corn disappears. There are no lamps to take away the darkness. The joy of marriage is gone. The reason for Jerusalem's punishment is repeated in vss. 23–24. The verses are based on Jer 25:10, which is an oracle against Jerusalem and Judah. "All nations were deceived by thy sorcery" recalls Nahum 3:4, where Nineveh is called "the mistress of witchcraft that selleth nations through her whoredoms and families through her witchcraft" (RSV); cf. also Isa 47:12.

Rev 18 ends with a reference to the blood of the prophets and the saints who have been slain. The writer seems to portray the whole land as an altar on which is poured the blood of the martyrs which is an offering more solemn than the blood of animal sacrifice; the whole victim is burnt and the smoke goes up to God. As Carrington, p. 294, expresses it, "Alas such offering has now been made; Jerusalem herself has gone up to God as a whole burnt offering . . . nothing was left but the trail of smoke which marked the end of the priesthood, law and sacrifice . . ."

BIBLIOGRAPHY

Arndt, W. F., and Gingrich, F. W. *A Greek-English Lexicon of the New Testament*. Cambridge University Press, 1957.

Epstein, L. M. *Sex Laws and Customs in Judaism*.

Jeremias, J. *Jerusalem in the Time of Jesus*.

Swete, H. B. *The Apocalypse of St. John*.

19 1 After this I heard, as it were, a loud sound of a great multitude in heaven, saying,

"Alleluia; salvation and glory and power belong to our God,
2 for true and just are His judgments;
   for He has judged the great harlot who corrupted the earth by her
     adultery,
   and He has vindicated the blood of His servants shed by her hand."
3 And a second voice said,

     "Alleluia; indeed her smoke goes up forever and ever."
4 And the twenty-four elders and the four living creatures prostrated themselves and worshiped God Who sits upon the throne, saying, "Amen, Alleluia," 5 and

    "Praise our God, all His servants,
      those who fear Him, small and great."

6 And I heard, as it were, the sound of a great crowd and, as it were, a sound of many waters and, as it were, a sound of mighty thunder, saying,

"Alleluia, the Lord our God, the Omnipotent, has taken sovereignty.
7 Let us rejoice and be glad and give glory to Him,
  because the marriage of the Lamb has come,
  and his wife has prepared herself,
8 and it is granted to her to be clothed in fine linen, bright and clean."

For fine linen is the just deeds of the saints. 9 And he said to me, "Blessed are those who are called to the marriage feast of the Lamb. And he said to me, 10 "These words of God are true." And I fell at his feet to worship him. And he said to me, "Do not do that; I am a fellow servant with you and your brothers who have the testimony about Jesus; worship God. The testimony about Jesus is the spirit of prophecy.

11 And I saw the heaven opened, and behold a white horse, and he who rode upon it was called Faithful and True, and he judges with justice and makes war. 12 His eyes are a flame of fire, and on his head are many diadems; he has a name inscribed which no one knows ex-

cept himself, 13 and he is clothed in a robe sprinkled with blood, and his name is the Word of God. 14 And the armies of heaven dressed in clean white linen, follow him on white horses. 15 And from his mouth proceeds a sharp sword, with which to smite the nations, and he himself rules them with a rod of iron, and he himself tramples the winepress of the wine of the wrath of God the Omnipotent. 16 And on his cloak and on his thigh (or banner) he has a name written, "King of Kings and Lord of Lords."

17 And I saw one angel standing in the sun, and he cried with a loud voice, saying to all the birds which fly in the mid-heaven, "Come gather for the great supper of God, 18 so that you may eat flesh of kings and flesh of captains and flesh of mighty men and flesh of horses and their riders, and flesh of all men slave and free and small and great." 19 And I saw the beast and the kings of the earth and their armies gathered to make war against the rider of the horse and his army. 20 And the beast was captured and with him the false prophet who performed signs before him, by which he deceived those who received the mark of the beast and worshiped his image; the two were hurled alive into the lake of fire which burns with sulphur. 21 And the rest were killed with the sword of the rider on the horse, which proceeds from his mouth, and all the birds were gorged with their flesh.

NOTES

19:1 *After this.* **051**, 1, 2059s pm TR read "And after this."

as it were. Omitted in 1, 1006, 2059s al g sy sa Prim TR.

Alleluia. The songs (vss. 1–2, 3, 4, 5, 6–8) are liturgical celebrations in heaven where God is praised because of the fall of the harlot and consequently the overcoming of evil and the establishment of His kingdom, i.e. the fulfillment of His plan. In part they are proleptic. The word Alleluia comes from *hallel* (to praise) in combination with the word Yahweh and, therefore, means "praise God."

power. Gr. *dunamis.* See COMMENT, p. 316.

2. *vindicated.* Cf. Rev 6:10, 15:3–4; also II Kings 9:7, which refers to vengeance on Jezebel for "the blood of my servants the prophets, and the blood of all the servants of the Lord" (RSV); cf. Rev 2:20.

3. *second voice.* The Greek reads "second" in the neuter, *deuteron,* without a noun. As "voice" (vs. 1) is feminine and "multitude" (vs. 1) is masculine, it is difficult to ascertain who or what this second (one) is.

indeed. Gr. *kai,* lit. "and." *Kai* has a number of uses. In this sentence it is used to emphasize the clause following it. The closest English equivalent is "indeed."

her smoke goes up forever and ever. This statement may represent the same idea as the unquenchable fire, Gr. *pur asbestos,* found in the Baptist tradition in Matt 3:12, Luke 3:17, also Mark 9:43, although the actual phrase "unquenchable fire" is not found in Revelation. Cf. also Isa 34:9–10, RSV:

> And the streams of Edom shall be turned into pitch,
> and her soil into brimstone;
> her land shall become burning pitch.
> Night and day it shall not be quenched;
> its smoke shall go up for ever.
> From generation to generation it shall lie waste;
> none shall pass through it for ever and ever.

A similar but not identical idea is found in 1QM: ". . . and He shall render their retribution like the burning of wood (?), and they shall be those tested in the crucible" (D-S). Cf. the servants of the Lamb who reign forever; Rev 22:5.

4. *elders . . . living creatures.* This shows that once again the seer is experiencing a throne vision. One notices that "the God," Gr. *ho theos,* is added to "Who sits upon the throne" as in 7:10, "God Who is enthroned"; usually the deity is not mentioned directly.

6. *sound.* See 8:5, "claps of thunder and loud voices," and Notes on 4:1, "first voice"; 8:5, "voices"; 10:1, "the seven thunders."

the Lord our God. "Our" is omitted in A 1, 1006 al t co TR.

taken sovereignty. Gr. *ebasileusen,* lit. "has reigned."

7. *marriage . . . wife.* The reference to the wedding looks forward to chs. 21–22. The figure of marriage denotes the intimate and indissoluble union of the community with the Messiah, which community he has purchased with his blood; cf. 5:6, 9, 7:17, 14:1. The giving of the Law on Mount Sinai was known as the "Day of Espousals," as in *Song of Songs R* 3.11.2:

IT WAS THE DAY OF HIS ESPOUSALS:

this was the day of Sinai, when Israel were like bridegrooms.

AND IN THE DAY OF THE GLADNESS OF HIS HEART:

this refers to [when they received] the Torah, as it says,

. . . Another explanation:

ON THE DAY OF HIS ESPOUSALS:

this refers to [the consecration of] the Tent of Meeting . . .

In the OT, Israel and Jerusalem are frequently called "bride." The Midrash and Targum on the Song of Songs interpret various facets of the bride's beauty as various aspects of the holy community; see e.g. *Song of Songs R* 1.10.2 (the bride's cheeks=rabbis), 1.15.2 (her eyes=the Sanhedrin), 4.11.1 (her ornaments=Scripture). The concept of the bride is accommodated to the Exodus theme in 4.10.1. Her love-sickness=Israel's yearning for deliverance from Egypt (5.8.1). The groom's haste to marry her=God's haste to redeem Israel from Egypt (4.8.1). The queens, concubines, and maidens without number=the infinite number of proselytes (6.9.4). The bride's ravishing the groom's heart=Israel's ravishing God's heart at the Reed Sea (4.9.1). The kisses=Yahweh's acknowledgment of Israel's consent to obey His commandments (1.2.1). The groom's taking off his coat=Israel's sweet sleep while the Law was given (p. 234, n. 6, comments, "Yet Israel awoke to receive the Law"). Yahweh comes down like a bridegroom and meets his bride Israel. The consummation of their union is effected by the setting up of the Tent of Meeting in which Yahweh communes directly with His people and in which His *shekinah*, "throne," rests.

prepared herself. Most probably by keeping the Torah. *Song of Songs R* 4.11.1 interprets the bridal ornaments as parts of Scripture or Torah. Cf. also Qumran's preparation in the desert; 1QS 8:13–16, which has affinity with the Baptist's message.

granted. This infers that it was through God's goodness rather than her own merits that she was clothed in bright and clean (*lampron katharon*) linen which, it is commented later in this verse, is the righteous deeds of the saints. Cf. the four horsemen in ch. 6 to whom were "granted" various powers of destruction. This type of expression is often used when God is the agent; see Section II, COMMENT.

9a. *Blessed*. This is the fourth of the seven beatitudes.

called. Gr. *keklēmenoi*. Charles claims that *kalein* means "to name" in Revelation, but that here and in 17:14 the word may have been chosen because of its association with *ekklesia*, "assembly," "the calling together of the people."

marriage feast. For NT references to the nuptial union, see Rom 7:4, II Cor 11:2, Eph 5:25, 32, Mark 2:19, Matt 22:2–11, 25:1, John 3:29. ℵ* P 1, 2059s al g bo omit "marriage."

9b–10. *And he said to me, "These words of God are true." . . . The testimony about Jesus is the spirit of prophecy*. This passage may be a redactor's interpolation. See NOTES on vs. 10. Many argue that it is a doublet of 22:6, 8–9. Both passages avow the truth of "These words of God." In both, the seer falls down to worship at the feet of the angel messenger. In both, the angel refuses to be worshiped; rather, he declares that like the man he is a servant of God and that God is the One Who is to be worshiped. Both 19:9b-10 and 22:8–9 come after beatitudes.

In discussing 19:9b–10, Vos, pp. 203–9, refers to scholars who claim that the angel identifies himself with Christians in general. He also points out that there are scholars who think the phrase "who have the testimony about Jesus" (cf. 12:17) refers to those who have been slain, and others who think it refers to the prophets. This is said specifically in 22:9: "your brethren the prophets."

From a literary point of view, too, these verses appear misplaced. They break the dramatic continuity apparent when one connects vs. 8 and vs. 11.

10. *These words of God are true*. Charles, II, 128, feels that this clause is not suitable here, for it appears to refer to the triumphant songs of the angels and martyrs. Charles feels it would be appropriate in ch. 22 because it gives a solemn attestation at the close of the book. Further, the one who speaks these words in ch. 19 appears to be an interpreting angel, but there is no indication in the chapter that this is really so. "And he said" is the first, abrupt, indication that anyone was speaking directly to the seer. The context of 19:9b–10

gives no clue as to who "he" is. In ch. 22, however, it is clear from the very first verse that an angel is in direct communication with the prophet. The words "And he said" in 22:6 therefore come as no surprise and lead logically into the avowal of truth.

fellow servant. A number of themes associated with the Baptist occur in vss. 6–10: the sovereignty of God (vs. 6, cf. Matt 3:2); divine nuptials (vs. 7, cf. Matt 9:14–15, John 3:25–30); just deeds (vs. 8, cf. Luke 3:10–14); words or oracles, Gr. *logoi,* which may have a prophetic connotation (vs. 9, cf. Matt 11 although *logoi* does not actually occur there); and testimony about Jesus (vs. 10, cf. Mark 1:7, Matt 3:1, Luke 3:16, John 1:27). "Fellow servant" might therefore suggest a circle of prophets around the Baptist. Hence the pericope of Rev 19:9b–10 would be more appropriate in ch. 22, where it would refer to a major theme of Revelation, the first coming of Jesus.

The testimony about Jesus is the spirit of prophecy. This strange sentence may mean that witness to or about Jesus is confirmed by the return of the gift of prophecy. It may, on the other hand, have arisen from some confusion with the more probable phrase which follows the clause "I am a fellow servant" in 22:9: "with you and your brethren the prophets, and with those who keep the words of this book." It is in question whether the genitive "Jesus" is objective or subjective; it may mean either that the testimony belongs to Jesus or that the testimony concerns Jesus (perhaps what is referred to is the testimony about Jesus given by the prophets). The latter would apply much more properly to the words of 22:8–9.

11. *heaven opened.* The place of origin of the white horse is different from that of the beasts and akin to that of the woman in ch. 12. Cambier calls 19:11 – 22:5 "the consummation"; others describe this section as "extermination of the pagan nations" (Boismard) and regard the beginning of ch. 21 as the starting point of "the consummation."

white horse. This horse does not have a great deal of association with the white horse of the first seal (6:2); the only common feature is the color. The riders are different; the one in 6:2 is an anonymous conqueror, while this one has a name, "Faithful and True," and is leading armies rather than specifically conquering. The weapons are different; the rider in 6:2 carries a bow while this one carries a sword. The sword might indicate more personal and perhaps fiercer combat than a bow. The headgear is different; in 6:2 the rider wears a wreath, Gr. *stephanos,* but this one wears many diadems, Gr. *diadēmata polla;* see NOTE on 6:2, "wreath." The word "conquer" is not mentioned in ch. 19, yet one cannot preclude an elaboration of the first vision in the second. The first may be a kind of prophecy of the second, who certainly comes to win complete victory.

called Faithful and True, and he judges with justice. Cf. 1:5, 3:7, 14, 22:6; III Macc 2:3. The Anointed or Elect One is called righteous in I Enoch 38:2. In I Enoch 53:6 is the phrase "the Elect One of righteousness and faith." Cf. also Ps Sol 17:31, 35–36, 46 (41).

A P **051** 1, 2059s al; R^m do not contain "called," and **046**, 82, 1006, 1611, 2329 pm vg sy lr or TR reverse the order of "called" and "Faithful."

he judges with justice. The seer may be pointedly contrasting true justice with the corrupt practices of the eastern courts and the injustice often found at the proconsul's tribunal. Note the present tense. Cf. Acts 17:31.

makes war. For the "Messiah" as a man of war see Philo *De Praemiis et Poenis* 16.95: "For 'there shall come forth a man' (Num 24:7 LXX), says the oracle, and leading his host to war he will subdue great and populous nations, because God has sent to his aid the reinforcement which befits the godly. . . ."

12. *eyes are a flame of fire.* This may signify that his judgment is incapable of deception or fraud, i.e. it penetrates all things, even the secrets of the heart, and consumes his enemies; cf. 1:14; Heb 4:13. In A 1006 al lat sy sa TR, "as it were" appears before "flame."

name . . . no one knows. Some have argued that this clause is interpolated because it appears to be contradicted by 13b where we learn that the rider's name is the Word of God and because of the title in vs. 16 "King of Kings and Lord of Lords." Perhaps, however, the name can only be known when the apocalypse is fulfilled and the name or character which will then be revealed is "Jesus Christ is Lord"; cf. Phil 2:11.

13. *robe sprinkled with blood.* Some have suggested that the blood on the garment is that of the Parthian kings whose destruction is foretold in 17:14. On the other hand, one could take the reading "sprinkled" in the ritual sense; see COMMENT, pp. 320–21. Just as the people and the altar were sprinkled with the blood of sacrifice at the reading of the covenant from Mount Sinai (Exod 24:3–8), so perhaps this rider also is purified or sprinkled with sacrificial blood. Caird, p. 243–44, with reference to Christ, says that the rider's garments bear the "indelible traces of the death of his followers, just as he bears on his body the indelible marks of his passion" (1:7, cf. John 20:20–27). Readers might be interested in the versions of Isa 63; see COMMENT, p. 321.

Isa 63:1–3 (MT)	*Isa 63:1–3 (LXX)*	*Targum to Isa 6:31–3*
Who is this that comes from Edom, in crimsoned garments from Bozrah, he that is glorious in his apparel, marching in the greatness of his strength? "It is I announcing vindication, mighty to save." Why is thy apparel red, and thy garments like his that treads in the winepress? "I have trodden the winepress alone, and from the peoples no one was with me; I trod them in my anger and trampled	Who is this that comes from Edom, *with* red garments from Bosor? Thus fair in his apparel with mighty strength? I speak of righteousness and saving judgment. Wherefore are thy garments red, and thy raiment as *if fresh* from a trodden winepress? I am full of trodden *grape,* and of the nations there is not a man with me; and I trample them in my fury, and dash	He who hath said these things is about to bring a plague upon Edom, a mighty vengeance upon Bozrah, to execute a just vengeance of his people as he sware unto them by his Memra. He said, behold, I reveal myself as I spake in righteousness; great before me is the power to save. Why then are the mountains red with the blood of the slain, and *why* do the plains flow forth like wine in the press? Behold, as the

Isa 63:1–3 (MT)	Isa 63: 1–3 (LXX)	Targum to Isa 63:1–3
them in my wrath; their lifeblood is sprinkled upon my garments, and I have stained all my raiment.	them to pieces as earth, and brought down their blood to the earth.	treading wherewith *grapes* are trodden in the winepress, so shall the slaughter be great among the armies of the peoples, and they shall have no strength before me; and I will slay them in my anger, and trample them in my wrath, and break the strength of their mighty ones before me, and all their wise ones will I destroy.

Word of God. Philo took an idea similar to the Merkabah with its charioteer, Metatron, and applied it to God or his Logos, i.e. the Word; see e.g. *De Somniis* 1.157–9.

14. *armies.* Gr. *strateuma.* This could mean a small body of soldiers such as Herod's bodyguard (Luke 23:1), or the garrison at Antonia (Acts 23:10, 27), or it could mean a great host or many troops. The troops in this verse are cavalry. For the idea of heavenly armies, see Testament of Levi 3:33, II Enoch 17, IV Ezra 19:6, Matt 26:53.

dressed in clean white linen. This phrase may apply to the horses or to the riders; the position and the gender would suggest the former.

15. *from his mouth proceeds a sharp sword . . . and he himself rules them with a rod of iron.* Cf. Isa 11:4, "the rod of his mouth," and Ps 2:9, "rod of iron"; they are combined in Psalms of Solomon 17:24, 27.

sword. Gr. *rhomphaia.* See NOTES on 6:4, "great sword," and 6:8, "sword," for the difference between *rhomphaia* and *machaira.* In 046 82, 2028, 2329 pm vg[s,cl] sy this sword is described as "two-edged." See COMMENT, p. 322, and NOTE on 2:12.

smite. Gr. *patassō.* Arndt and Gingrich compare Gen 8:21; Exod 9:15, 12:23; Num 14:12; Deut 28:22; II Kings 6:18; II Macc 9:5; etc. In Acts 12:7 there is a good example of *patassō* not meaning strike to hurt; the angel of the Lord strikes Peter to wake him up and deliver him. See NOTE on 2:27.

rules. Gr. *poimainein.* Charles observes that neither here nor in 2:27, 12:5, does this word have a favorable meaning. It may have a second meaning, "devastates"; see NOTE on 2:27.

16. *thigh (or banner).* Charles comments that the writer may be referring to an equestrian statue at Ephesus which is inscribed with its name on its thigh. However, this word may be a mistranslation for "banner," Heb. *dgl,* as this could easily be mistaken for Heb. *rgl,* "leg"; or "foot." In 1QM the word for banner is not *dgl,* but *'ōt.* See COMMENT, p. 323.

King of Kings and Lord of Lords. The same title occurs in I Tim 6:15; cf. Dan 2:47, where the phrase is "God of gods and Lord of kings, and a revealer of mysteries . . . ." Note the different order from Rev 17:14.

17. *one angel.* ℵ pc sy co read "another angel."

birds. In Matt 24:28, Luke 17:37 "eagles" (or "vultures"), not "birds," are mentioned, and the dictum that they will gather where the body is seems to be proverbial and have little or no bearing on our text. T. W. Manson comments that "vulture" did not then have the unpleasant associations it has for us, but that one of its characteristics was "the almost incredible swiftness with which it discovers and makes its way to its prey" (*The Sayings of Jesus* [London: SCM, 1961], p. 147). Vs. 17, therefore, expresses the imminence of the doom.

mid-heaven. This recalls the eagle flying in mid-heaven in 8:13 crying "Woe, woe, woe": "to make good the final threat of the eagle that flew in midheaven"; Caird, p. 248.

great supper. It forms a terrifying contrast to the divine banquet intimated in 3:20 and to the heavenly manna promised in 2:17.

18. *flesh.* Notice the almost monotonous stress on the word, five times.

19. *their armies.* A pc sa read "his armies."

make war. It is difficult to know whether one should identify the battle in this chapter with that in 16:16 and in 20:8–9. In ch. 16 the forces are gathering but the battle has not yet been fought. There seems to be no reason why we should not find the consummation here. It is, however, less easy to correlate our present passage with 20:8–9, for this battle comes after the millennium and is based on the same chapter in Ezekiel.

20. *captured.* Gr. *piazō*, lit. "arrested." See Section XVII, COMMENT.

with him. 051 1, 2059s pc TR read "with this." 1611, 1854 al TR R; **046** 82, 1006 al read "who was with him." A pc bo read "who were with him."

the lake of fire. Cf. I Macc 11:35 (S'al). The use of the definite article with lake denotes that it was a familiar concept to the audience for this apocalypse. It might be identified with Gehenna. The Targum on Isa 30:33 reads "Gehenna" instead of "burning place" (Stenning):

> For from of old is Gehinnam prepared for their transgressions; the king of ages has prepared it making deep and broad the place thereof; fire burneth therein as in much wood, even the Memra (Word) of the Lord like a mighty river; brimstone burneth therein.

The association of the Word of the Lord with fire shows affinity to the text from IV Ezra cited in COMMENT, p. 322.

COMMENT

The dirges in ch. 18 are balanced in ch. 19 by the alleluias and songs of praise which precede the appearance of the rider on the white horse. They are liturgical celebrations in heaven praising God for the fall of the harlot and the consequent triumph over evil and establishment of His kingdom, i.e. the fulfillment of His plan. In part they are proleptic.

The first and second thanksgivings (vss. 1b–2, 3) are related through their singers—"a great multitude in heaven" (vs. 1b) and "a second one" (vs. 3, see NOTE)—as well as through content. The first commemorates the victory over the harlot, and the second celebrates the eternal nature of that victory. The third (vs. 4) is a simple "Amen, Alleluia" from the elders and living creatures.

The fourth (vs. 5) is a voice from the throne bidding all to praise God. The fifth (vss. 6–8a) is a song from a great multitude celebrating the marriage of the Lamb.

The five hymns in vss. 1b–8a have the appearance of OT battle prayers and resemble those found in 1QM. The first, e.g., is typically Jewish. In taking up the theme of Rev 18:24, blood of prophets and saints, it echoes the Song of Moses, Deut 32:43–44, which says that God will avenge His servants. In 1QM 1:5–7 there is a hymn celebrating salvation for the people of God and the annihilation of the people who belong to the lot of Belial. The hymn is preceded by a reference to His (presumably God's) anger which will utterly destroy the horn of Belial. In 1QM 4:6, which describes the words written on the banners or standards, one finds "truth of God," "justice of God," "glory of God," and "judgment of God," four of the attributes mentioned in the first hymn of Rev 19. 1QM 4:7 mentions slaughter through the judgment of God, the might of God (cf. *dunamis* in 19:1b, see NOTE on "power"), and retribution upon the nations of vanity (4:12).

The purpose of the first hymn appears to be the attribution of power, victory, etc. to God rather than to human strength; note the nouns followed by the possessive genitive, "of God." This again finds a parallel in 1QM 11:4–6, which reminds God of how merciful He has been to Israel; through His strength and will alone is she delivered, despite her sinful deeds: "Thine is the battle, and from Thee is the might, not ours." This prayer is part of the high priestly exhortation before the battle and is followed in 1QM 12 by an appeal to God to arise and join the fight with His army. The exhortation is before the fighting as in the OT (Deut 20:8 ff.). It is noticeable that no such prayers precede the attack by the godless in Revelation.

At Qumran seven phases of the war were expected, three successful, three unsuccessful but the seventh was the Day and Battle of Yahweh; 1QM 1:13–14 (D-S):

> For three lots, the sons of light shall be strongest to overthrow ungodliness, and for three (lots) the army of Belial shall make answer to beat into retreat the lot [of God]. [And the batt]alions of infantry shall melt the heart, but the power of God [shall] strengthen the h[eart of the sons of light]. [And in] the seventh lot the mighty Hand of God shall subject [the sons of darkness to al]l the angels of His empire and to all the men [of His lot].

Rev 19 seems to represent this last phase. Rev 19:1–2 is not the only hymn to indicate that battle is led by God. Vs. 4, with the mention of the elders, the living creatures, and the throne, suggests the same pattern as in e.g. 8:6, the angels directing operations for God, but now not angels (as with the trumpets and bowls) but the Word of God Himself will come to lead the battle.

With the last hymn, vss. 6–8, Revelation is brought to a peak. Theocracy triumphs over the kingdoms of the world and the kingdom of Satan. The tone is set in vs. 6b with the word *ebasileusen*, translated as "taken sovereignty"; the Lord God Omnipotent has established His rule (note the aorist tense of completed action). The next verses, 7–8a, may seem to be unconnected to vs.

6b but this is not so if one recalls the pattern of the history of redemption. The second redemption of the Israelites was to be modeled on the first, namely, the escape from Egypt and the destruction of their enemies in the water of the sea, like a stone sinking down; cf. Rev 18:21. After this the theocracy was established on Mount Sinai. In rabbinic tradition this was seen as the espousals of Yahweh and his people, Israel. Moses took the place of the best man; cf. the Baptist's relationship to Jesus. Eventually the theme in the Song of Songs became accommodated to the love relationship, betrothal, and marriage of Yahweh to his people Israel. For some illustrative texts from rabbinic sources see NOTES on vs. 7. Prophetic texts also portray this theme. In Hosea 2:16–17 God says that Israel will call him "My husband." The idea of covenant is implied in the concept of bride because of the binding promise in both cases stating the obligations of each partner. The same passage from Hosea continues by referring to a covenant which God will make with creation (cf. the new creation in Rev 21) and the peace which he will establish. The prophecy ends with a declaration of Israel's betrothal to Him "forever . . . in righteousness and in justice, in steadfast love and in mercy . . . in faithfulness" (Hosea 2:19–20, RSV). In Revelation, however, it is not Yahweh but the Lamb who carries out the covenant relationship.

The bride appears to be the community. The word *kallah* (assembly) can also mean crown, bride, daughter-in-law or general assembly, especially the assembly of Babylonian students in the months of Elul and Adar. The bride would, therefore, be identified with the faithful Torah-abiding Jews, such as those at Qumran. In this passage one can see clearly that the idea of community and bride overlap, but a chapter which portrays this even more graphically is Isa 54, in which God promises numerous children to the desolate woman. She appears to symbolize Israel (and is also a reflection of Sarah). Isa 54:5–6, AB, reads:

For your spouse is he who made you—Yahweh of hosts is his name;
And your avenger is the Holy One of Israel—
he is called the God of all the earth.
For like a forsaken wife, and one grieved of spirit Yahweh, has called you;
Like the rejected wife on one's youth—says your God.

The targum accommodates this passage to Jerusalem. It begins, "Sing praises, O Jerusalem, who wast a barren woman that bear not . . . for more shall be the children of desolate Jerusalem than the children of inhabited Rome, saith the Lord" (Stenning). Other verses which are of interest in the targum are vss. 7–8, in which God declares that although He had abandoned Jerusalem for a short time, He will remember the covenant, be merciful, and redeem her from her enemies.

Another OT passage which speaks dramatically of Jerusalem as the bride of God is Ezek 16:8–10. God says, ". . . yea, I plighted my troth to you and entered into a covenant with you, says the Lord God, and you became mine . . . I swathed you in fine linen and covered you with silk" (RSV). Like the bride in Ezekiel, the bride in Rev 19:8 is dressed in fine linen. So are the martyrs in 6:11 and the angels in 15:6. The two epithets, "bright" and "clean," are in contrast to the clothing of the harlot as is also the simplicity of the bride's clothes compared with the multicolored ones of the harlot. There is no doubt that the bride takes the place of the harlot, and with Carrington we may say, "It is impossible any longer to maintain that the harlot means Rome; the antithesis must lie between the old Israel and the new, the false Israel and the true, the Israel that is to appear so soon as the new Jerusalem." The symbolism of linen as the just deeds of the saints confirms this.

Marriage is a metaphor for the covenant relationship, but it should not cause surprise that the marriage theme is associated with war. Two OT texts show the same alignment, Ps 45 and Wisd Sol 18 (see p. 319). Ps 45 is a royal psalm probably composed on the occasion of the marriage of an Israelite king to a foreign princess (vss. 11–13). The king is praised for his virtue and his military ability. Ps 45:3 mentions the sword upon the thigh (cf. Rev 19:15, 16); 45:4 refers to riding on in victory and majesty; 45:2 speaks of grace upon the king's lips; 45:5 mentions conquest of peoples (cf. Rev 19:15); 45:6 refers to the royal throne and the royal scepter. Ps 45 was converted into messianic prophecy and the bridegroom was portrayed as both king and conqueror; after slaying his enemies he claimed the bride; Carrington, p. 308. This psalm, therefore, presents a "military bridegroom" carrying a sword, riding (either on horse or chariot), a victor conquering people and acquiring a royal throne and scepter. His speech (lips) are gracious. The rider on the white horse also is a military figure. He has royal insignia (diadems and royal title), he conquers and/or rules nations, and his speech is unique.

However, he bears other characteristics which raise him above the bridegroom in Ps 45. Our first clue is the presence of the adjectives, "faithful" and "true." Although these epithets may be used of man, they are also applied to God, e.g., "true" meaning "truly dependable" as in Exod 34:6–7; cf. Num 14:18, I Esdras 18:86, III Macc 2:11, *Ant.* 11.55, Rev 6:10 (cf. true deeds in 1QM 13:9, etc.). One of the synonyms for God was "Truth," Heb. *emeth*, Gr. *alētheia*. For God as *pistos* see Deut 7:9, 32:4, Isa 49:7, Philo *Quis rerum divinarum heres sit* 93, *De Sacrificiis Abelis et Caini* 93, *Legum Allegoriae* 3:204. God's judging in righteousness (19:11) is well known; cf. also 1QM 11:14. These three virtues contrast vividly with the characteristics of Satan and the beasts. However, is the military character consonant with God? The answer may certainly be in the affirmative, particularly as it fits in with the Exodus motif.

Exod 15:3 depicts God as a man of war. Some of the targums alter this, probably because of the bold anthropomorphism, but the Palestinian targum retains the metaphor except that it uses Heb. *gbr'*, "aristocrat" or "warrior," instead of *'iš*, "man." The Mekilta of Rabbi Ishmael expounds on Exod 15:3 (see Section III, COMMENT, p. 102) and ends by mitigating the anthropomorphism with a remark which is pertinent to our present passage with reference to the idea of "name": "With His name does He fight and has no need of any of these measures." However, the next paragraph in the Mekilta resumes the anthropomorphic strain; God appears "as a mighty hero." The same idea is found in Isa 42:13: "Yahweh marches forth like a hero; like a man of war he arouses his ardor. He shouts—yes, raises the war cry; he shows his prowess against his enemies" (AB).

The idea of God as a warrior persists in the deuterocanonical books. E.g. in II Macc 3:22–30, when Heliodorus attempted to confiscate the temple treasury, the high priest and the people prayed in anguish and terror for the sanctity of the temple and all that had been entrusted to it. On Heliodorus' arrival at the treasury, God sent a horse and rider outfitted with golden armor and weapons and two assistants who beat Heliodorus almost to death. (Another appeal for divine intervention on the part of the high priest caused the Lord to spare Heliodorus' life on condition that he reform and report to the world God's might; vss. 31–34.)

It is significant that the writer of II Maccabees describes the apparition as the appearance of the Almighty Lord (vss. 22, 28, 30). The Qumran scrolls also contain allusions to God as a warrior. There are two graphic descriptions in 1QM which are almost identical, although there are a few variants; these are 1QM 12:10b–11 and 1QM 19:2–4. In practically the same words, these texts urge God to crush His enemies and "devour" them with His sword; cf. the sword issuing from the rider's mouth in Rev 19:15.

As has been shown, OT, deuterocanonical, and Qumran sources contain a strong tradition of Yahweh as a warrior who often sends down avenging angels; the rider of the white horse is therefore in the guise of His *Memra* (Word). This is plain from the text because he is given two attributes of God, "Faithful and True," in vs. 11, and is called "the Word of God" in vs. 13. In later Jewish literature and even in the deuterocanonical books the Word "substitutes" for God on earth. In Wisd Sol 18:14–16, e.g., the Word of God leaps down from heaven to rescue the children of Israel from Egypt. Both this passage and Rev 19:11–16 describe the Word as from heaven. Wisd Sol 18:15 adds that he is "from the royal throne," and Rev 19:16 establishes royalty with "King of Kings." Both Words carry "a sharp sword." In Wisd Sol 18:16 he "filled all things with death," and in Rev 19:15 he tramples God's winepress of wrath. Wisdom of Solomon implies the Word of God delivers the faithful from "Egypt"; cf. Rev 11:8.

If the rider is identified with the Word of God, then he also shows affinity to the concept of Messiah. He would therefore bear affinity to the "messianic," but not necessarily military, figure in Isa 11. Isa 11 depicts an individual upon whom the spirit of the Lord will rest, as one who judges with righteousness; cf. Rev 19:11. His mouth shall smite the earth and slay the wicked (Isa 11:4, cf. Rev 19:15). He does not judge, apparently, by outward appearance (vs. 3 "He shall not judge by what His eyes see," RSV). His mission is to bring peace and the knowledge of God. The targum interprets this figure as a king and an anointed one, but the commentary from Qumran is an even more interesting exemplar of Isaiah, Qumran Cave 4 (lines 17–24, DJD, V, 13–15):

. . . *Its interpretation concerns the shoot of* [David who will arise at the e]nd of days . . . . . . [his] ene[mies, and God will sustain him with] . . . *the* [Law] . . . . . . th[rone of glory, a ho]ly [crown, and garments of variegat]ed stuff . . . . . . [in his hand, and over all the

G]entile[s he will rule, and Magog] . . . al[l the peoples shall his sword judge. And as it says, 'Not] . . . or decide by what his ears shall hear': its interpretation is that [. . .] and according to what they teach him so shall he judge, and according to their command [. . .] *with him,* one of the priests of repute shall go out with garments of [. . .] in his hand [. . .

This figure bears some features characteristic of the rider. It is an eschatological figure (at the end of days). He will rule over the Gentiles, and royal elements will probably be associated with him. But the text is corrupt. Moreover, the figure is not associated with divinity, as is ours. Our figure, who appears to be the anointed one of Yahweh, reflects the divine character. One presumes that he is to be identified with the Lamb (cf. Rev 17:14, 19:16), especially as the statement in 17:14 is in the future and the same title is attributed to both figures.

Both the Qumran figure and the rider are regal in character. On the rider's head are many diadems to denote sovereignty. This was not unusual, for it is recorded in I Macc 11:13 that Ptolemy wore two diadems when he entered Antioch, one for Egypt and one for Asia. On the diadems is a name which no one knows except he himself (vs. 12). This would appear to suggest that he is divine, for God Himself being omniscient would know the name; cf., however, the song which only the redeemed can know, Rev 14:3. There does not seem to be a contradiction between this unknown name on the diadems and the revealed one on the thigh or banner. The banner would be for all to see. The unknown name is more "personal" but its position cannot but recall the name of mystery on the head of the harlot (17:5). See below for the importance of the title in vs. 16. Cf. also Ascension of Isaiah 9:5: "This is . . . the Lord Christ, who will be called Jesus in the world, but His name thou canst not hear till thou hast ascended out of thy body." However, if Revelation were a Christian work, then the name of Jesus or the Christ would be known. Cf. John 1:33–34, where John the Baptist avers that he did not know Jesus until his baptism. The name, therefore, may be "Son of God" or even "Son of the Man."

The vesture of the rider is also curious. He is dressed in a cloak sprinkled with blood and this feature may be associated with his name "Word of God." The text of vs. 13 is very uncertain; the main readings are:

bebammenon (*babatō*) to dip; A **046 051** 1 W **S** (ph) **E** sah **A** (vg) Andr. 2/3 Are

errantisnenon (*rhantizō*) to sprinkle or purify in the ritual sense;? al. pauc Hipp. Orig. 1/2 Andr. 1/3

rherantismenon, same definition as *errantisnenon;* 105 Orig. 1/2

errammenon (*rhainō*) to sprinkle (e.g. Ezek 36:25) vg^mss syr^h Orig.

rherommenon, same definition as *errammenon;* 1611 Orig.

perirerammenon (*peri[r]rainō*) to sprinkle around; ℵ*

perirerantismon, same definition as *perirerammenon;* ℵ^c syr^ph? Cypr.

The garment is either dipped or dyed or sprinkled with or in blood; see NOTE on 19:13, "sprinkled." One does not know whether the blood is the rider's own or that of other people, e.g. his enemies; see NOTE on 19:13, "robe sprinkled with blood." Most commentators refer to Isa 63, which speaks of Yahweh coming to save His people, being afflicted with their affliction, and saving them even though they had rebelled and grieved His Holy Spirit. This figure in Isa 63 has his garment stained through treading the winepress and the stain is from the people's blood; cf. Rev 19:15. Further, Isa 63 stresses the individual's own work, "It is I" (vs. 1), "my own arm" (vs. 5), "he himself" (vs. 10). Rev 19 uses the same device by emphasizing he himself, Gr. *autos,* twice in vs. 15. Moreover, to confirm the affinity it is interesting to note that the targum speaks of the action performed by the Word of God, the *Memra;* cf. Rev 19:13. It has been suggested that Isa 63 is a Passover haggadah.

There is one more text which might cast light on Rev 19:13. The association of the garment sprinkled with blood and the Word or Logos may give us a clue to the author's meaning. Philo portrays the Logos of God as the high priest. Have we here the idea of the priestly messiah who is also the Word of God and who has the blood upon his garments owing to the sacrifice which he offers? As mentioned above, the high priest used to sprinkle blood seven times in the Holy of Holies and it would not be unlikely for his garment to be stained with the sacrificial blood; *Yoma* 5:4. If the rider is the priestly messiah he could be mounted on horseback, for the priests and Levites took a full part in the holy war and led the prayers in 1QM, although they are not explicitly said to ride. Their apparel is described in 1QM:

And when they form the battle lines facing the enemy, one line facing the other, then from the middle gate towards the space (between) the lines shall go out seven priests from among the sons of Aaron clothed in garments of fine white linen; in tunics of linen and breeches of linen and girded with girdles of linen, of fine twisted linen in purple, violet, scarlet, and crimson, many-coloured, the work of an artist. And they shall wear on their heads a head-dress in the form of a tiara. These shall be their garments for battle and into the Sanctuary they shall not bring them.

The heavenly armies follow the rider, and either they, or their horses, or both are dressed in white, pure linen. In 1QM 6:12 the war horses are required to be "swift-footed stallions, tender-mouthed, long-winded, and of the required age, trained for battle and able to hear the shouts; *and they shall all look alike*" (italics mine, contrast Rev 9:17–19 and note the simplicity of the description).

The war seems to be a fulfillment of Rev 17:14. The armies are heavenly armies and one is reminded of the role of the angels in the holy war at Qumran, e.g. according to 1QM 12:7–9 (D-S):

And Thou art a ter[rible] God in Thy kingly glory and the congregation of Thy saints is in the midst of us (for) fina[l] [succour]. [Among] us (is) contempt for kings, disdain and mockery for the brave! For Adonai is holy and the King of Glory is with us accompanied by the saints. The pow[ers] of the host of angels are among our numbered men and the Valiant of Battle is in our congregation and the host of his spirits accompany our steps. And o[ur] horsemen are [like] the clouds and like the mists of dew which cover the earth and like the shower of rain which waters in the desired way all its fruits.

Commenting on the passage, Yadin, pp. 237 ff., says that it expresses Qumran's faith that Israel will overcome her enemies because God and his angels fight along with her. This idea is also found in Biblical passages, e.g. Exod 23:20, the angel leading the people; Exod 33:2, the angel driving out the Canaanites; II Kings 19:35, II Chron 32:21, the destruction of Sennacherib's camp; also Pss 34:7, 35:5–6. Yadin also draws attention to the fact that the Maccabees frequently prayed to God to send his angels to help them; I Macc 7:41, 10:29, II Macc 11:6, 15:23, IV Macc 4:10. The pseudepigrapha and the Midrashic literature also show angels helping in the fighting, e.g. I Enoch 56:5 (sic) and *Num R* 16, which Yadin quotes in note 4: "At the Red Sea I descended for your sake at the head of millions of myriads of myriads of angels and appointed for each of you two angels, one to help him in girding on his weapons, the other to place a crown upon his head."

The four towers of the battle formation (1QM 9:14–16) are inscribed with the names of the four angels; Michael, Gabriel, Sariel, and Raphael. Yadin, pp. 241–42, remarks the belief that the "elect of the holy People," i.e. those who formerly dwelt upon earth, but are now in heaven, would fight side by side with the angels. This would mean that the martyrs would join the armies. These might be suggested in Rev 19 by the apparel of the riders, namely, clean white linen.

From the mouth of the rider on the white horse proceeds a sharp sword. The concept is not novel. In Isa 11:4 the descendant of Jesse smites the earth with the rod of his mouth and slays the wicked with the breath of his lips. In Psalms of Solomon 17:26–27, 39, the Messiah destroys the godless and smites the earth with the word of his mouth. See first three NOTES on vs. 15. In I Enoch 62:2, in the context of the judgment of the kings and the mighty when the Lord of spirits has seated the Elect One on the throne of his glory and poured the spirit of righteousness upon him, he (the elect one) slays all sinners by the word of his mouth. These passages might imply that the sword is a figure for forensic or judicial condemnation. One thinks of the *ius gladii*, "right of the sword," i.e. the authority to inflict capital punishment according to Roman law. However, there is another passage which may cast light on the meaning of the sword issuing from the rider's mouth. In IV Ezra 13 the prophet sees the form of a man coming out of the heart of the seas. He flew with the clouds of heaven "and wherever he turned his countenance to look everything seen by him trembled; and whithersoever the voice went out of his mouth, all that heard his voice melted away, as the wax melts when it feels the fire"; IV Ezra 13:3–4, APCh, II, 616. After this the prophet saw an innumerable multitude gathered to make war on the man (13:9–11, APCh, II, 617):

And lo! When he saw the assault of the multitude as they came he neither lifted his hand, nor held spear nor any warlike weapon; but I saw only how he sent out of his mouth as it were a fiery stream, and out of his lips a flaming breath, and out of his tongue he shot forth a storm of sparks. . . .

This fiery stream burned up all the multitude and nothing was left but ashes and the smell of smoke. Then the man gathered a peaceable multitude around him.

In view of the symbolic meaning of "mouth" for our author (see Section XI, COMMENT, p. 241), what proceeds from the rider's mouth is not only judicial condemnation but the prophetic word which is creative and dynamic and brings to pass what it pronounces. The word of a true prophet, such as the rider, transforms word into action; that of the false prophet, such as the second beast, is ineffectual. A good example might be the dispute between the false prophet, Hananiah, and the true prophet, Jeremiah in Jer 28. Jeremiah predicts that Hananiah will die: this occurs without (apparently) any further intervention on the part of the true prophet (vss. 16–17). The rider on the white horse may have similar charisma; he takes on a prophetic as well as regal and priestly character. As God said "Let there be light" and there was light, so the rider could say "Let them fall" and they would fall.

Not only does he smite the nations but, he himself (notice the emphatic *autos*) rules them with a rod of iron; the influence of Ps 2:9 is obvious here and adds a "messianic" note. The rider's "smiting" does not seem to denote destruction; he would not be able to "rule" dead people. Perhaps the explanation lies in the fact that "strike," Gr. *patassō*, is used figuratively of heavenly beings. Arndt and Gingrich observe, under *patassō*, "it cannot be determined whether any actual touching or striking is involved, nor how far it goes." See also NOTES on 19:15. The result may be equivalent to be "slain in the Spirit"; cf. Ezek 1:28 – 2:2, John 18:6. The rider himself treads the winepress of the wrath of God, a statement which is linked with his blood-spattered robe in vs. 13 and may recall Isa 63:3 as mentioned earlier in this COMMENT, p. 313, and NOTES on 19:13. The rider appears to win the victory himself.

There is no completely satisfactory explanation of vs. 16 where the Greek reads that the rider has his name written on his garment and on his thigh. Some think that the title is on the girdle, others that it is on the garment which falls over the thigh, others that the name might be on the hilt of the sword. Still others refer to the branding of horses on the thigh among the Greeks and to names written on the thighs of statues in Rome (Cicero *Verr.* 4:43, Justinius 15:4–5). However, perhaps the most probable explanation is that the words for "banner" and "thigh" have been confused. Banner is *dgl* and foot or leg is *rgl:* the Hebrew letters *daledh* and *resh* look very much alike and could easily be confused. See NOTE on 19:15, "thigh (or banner)." The banners or standards in 1QM are an important aspect of the military equipment. They bear inscriptions, e.g. the large banner at the head of all the people bears the inscription "People of God" and the names of Israel and Aaron and the twelve tribes; see 1QM 3:13 – 4:17.

The banner and the apparel of the rider bear the title attributed to the Lamb in 17:14. See Section XIV, COMMENT, p. 291. P. W. Skehan has developed an important and arresting interpretation of this title. Noting the importance of the number seven to the author, he observes (p. 398) that "leaving out the 'and' by which St. John tells us to add the two titles into one name, the combination 'King of Kings, Lord of Lords,' in Aramaic adds up to 777," the epitome of perfection, in contrast to 666, the number of the beast.

What we have, therefore, in ch. 19 is a proleptic hymn of the sovereignty of God, the introduction of a figure in complete contrast to the first beast and one whose title and number is one of perfection. He is the victor.

This chapter ends with a ghastly paragraph. It describes a battlefield where corpses are strewn and the scavenger birds, e.g. vultures, come to feed. But this is called the great supper of God in vs. 17. The text is strongly influenced by Ezek 39:17–20 where the prophet is bidden to speak to the birds and to say (vss. 17–18, RSV):

Assemble and come, gather from all sides to the sacrificial feast which I am preparing for you, a great sacrificial feast upon the mountains of Israel, and you shall eat flesh and drink blood. You shall eat the flesh of the mighty, and drink the blood of the princes of the earth . . .

It is important to notice the context of the Ezekiel passage; it lies within the prophecy or prophecies against Gog (38:1 – 39:8). In 39:9–20 Gog is slain and the weapons which he used against Israel are burnt. There are corpses lying unburied (vs. 14), but they may belong to another army for Gog has already been buried.

In addition to the comparison with Gog, the author of Revelation may have had a further reason for including the dreadful scene. It is the climax of his portrayal of the desolation of the sanctuary in 18:2. The prophet Ezekiel was told to be a watchman-prophet (Ezek 32) but his vigilance was apparently fruitless; Jerusalem fell. In Revelation the unclean and hateful birds of 18:2 did not watch in vain. They were able to take their fill (19:21) from the people who had suffered from pestilence, sword, famine, and death. Human flesh is consumed (cf. Lev 26:27–33, Deut 28:53, Jer 19:9, Ezek 5:10, II Kings 6:28 ff.) but not by humans yet. It is important to note that in Ezekiel this horrendous picture is followed by the vision of the restored community (40:1 – 48:35) which includes the vision of the new temple (40:1 – 43:27). The author of Revelation, therefore, may have included vss. 17–21 to show the fulfillment of this part of the prophecy of Ezekiel before showing the fulfillment of the vision concerning the restored community and new city. The slaughter seems to include all classes in society and the horror lies in the fact that they will not be buried, a matter of great shame to the ancients and sometimes thought to exclude people from the resurrection. This may also be the climax of the *lex talionis:* because the two witnesses lay unburied and peoples and tribes and nations gazed at their dead bodies (11:9–10), their enemies now lie unburied.

In Rev 19:19–21 the superhuman powers of evil are destroyed. The beast and the false prophet are cast alive into the lake of fire while the rest are killed by the sword of the rider on the white horse and the birds eat their flesh. When the beast was last encountered he was in league with the ten kings against "Babylon" but now that "Babylon" has been destroyed he is allied with the second beast, the false prophet, against the rider on the white horse; vs. 19. The punishment of the beast, who could be identified with the fourth beast or kingdom in Daniel, is akin to the fate of the horn in Daniel. He was slain and burned with fire, the other beasts lost their dominion but their lives were prolonged for a season; Dan 7:11–12. In Rev 19 the kings are slain and the beast and the false prophet are cast alive into the lake of fire. Yet the text of Daniel seems to be influential and this might suggest that while 666, the beast, is burnt, 777, the King of Kings and Lord of Lords, receives universal and everlasting dominion (cf. Dan 7:14) and stands in a position analogous to one like the Son of Man.

BIBLIOGRAPHY

Arndt, W. F., and Gingrich, F. W. *A Greek-English Lexicon of the New Testament,* Cambridge University Press, 1957.

Boismard, M. E. RB 56 (1949), 507–41.

Cambier, J. "Les images de l'A.T. dans l'Apocalypse," *Nouvelle Revue Theologique* 77 (1955), 113–23.

Carrington, P. *The Meaning of Revelation.*

Ford, J. M. "The Epithet Man for God," *Irish Theological Quarterly* 38 (1971), 72–76.

Skehan, P. W. CBQ 10 (1948), 398.

Vos, L. A. *The Synoptic Traditions in the Apocalypse.*

Yadin, Y. *The Scroll of the War of the Sons of Light Against the Sons of Darkness.*

Part Three: The "Resurrection" of the "Firstborn"

XVII. SATAN BOUND
(20:1–3)

20 1 Then I saw an angel descending from heaven, holding in his hand the key of the bottomless pit and a great chain. 2 And he seized the dragon, the ancient serpent, who is the devil and the Satan, and bound him for a thousand years, 3 and threw him into the pit, and shut it and sealed it over him, that he should not deceive the nations anymore, till the thousand years were ended. After that he is destined to be loosed for a little while.

NOTES

20:1. *key.* Notice the contrast between the star fallen from heaven (Rev 9:1), who has the key of the pit of the abyss from which comes smoke, darkness, and locusts, and our present angel. The former fell; the latter descended.

chain. Gr. *halusis.* This can mean chain, handcuffs, or leg irons. Cf. the binding of the demonic in Mark 5:3. Gaechter suggests that the chaining took place a thousand years before the end of the beast; because he (Satan) was chained he sent his agents the beast and the false prophet into the world.

2. *seized.* Gr. *krateō,* implying fast or forcible seizure. See COMMENT.

the devil. ℵ 1611, 2329 al co have the definite article.

the Satan. 1, 2959s pm TR omit the definite article.

bound. Gr. *deō.*

3. *sealed.* Gr. *sphragizō.* This can mean the sealing of a stone to prevent its being moved (Dan 6:17, *Ant.* 10.258; cf. Matt 27:66), and may apply to the closing of a building so that one cannot open it (Bel and the Dragon 11:14, same as Dan 14). It may be used ironically in the light of Rev 7 where the elect are sealed on their foreheads for security. The author may have been influenced by the Book of Daniel.

COMMENT

Just as the first creation appears to have involved a struggle between Yahweh and the water monster of chaos, so the new creation is preceded by similar victories, first a victory which establishes the millennial Jerusalem and its kingdom, and second a "terrestrial" battle which anticipates judgment, a new heaven and earth, and the new holy and eternal city.

The rider on the white horse, bearing the name of perfection (the numbers of the letters equal 777), has triumphed over and captured the beast (whose number is 666) and the false prophet and slain the remainder of the enemy. Now only Satan remains. An angel descends from heaven. He is given no glorious description as is the one in 10:1–3 or in 18:1–2. Yet he did not only capture the dragon (Gr. *piazō*, "arrested,"), as for the beast and false prophet in 19:20, but seized him fast or forcibly, Gr. *krateō*, and used both key and large chain or handcuffs to bind, Gr. *deō*, and secure him.

John's Gospel appears to reflect this idea, for John 12:31 speaks about the prince of this world being cast out. Rev 20:1–3 tells us that Satan was cast out of the physical world and hurled into the abyss. A similar but more soberly expressed idea is found in Isa 24:21–22, which says that God will punish the host of heaven and the kings of the earth and that they will be gathered together, imprisoned in a pit, and punished. A text, however, which is closer to Rev 20:1–3 is I Enoch 10:4–6, where the Lord tells Raphael to bind Azazel (an evil spirit who lives in the desert; cf. Lev 16:8, 10, 26) hand and foot, to cast him into darkness, in an opening in the desert, and to place over him rocks so that he will remain there. However, Enoch also foretells that Azazel or Satan will be cast into the fire on the day of the great judgment. In I Enoch 18:12–16, 19:1–2, 21:1–6, Enoch sees an abyss of fire where the angels who have transgressed are punished for ten thousand years until the great day of judgment. In these texts, there is less sharp a contrast between the abyss and the lake of fire, while in Revelation the abyss appears to be a securely fastened prison.

As in 12:9, the dragon is called the ancient serpent, the devil, Satan. Satan's destruction is so important that it has two themes to describe it instead of one, namely his chaining and his downfall. The angel chains him for a thousand years and locks and seals the abyss into which he places him. The angel's purpose is to prevent him from deceiving the nations; cf. 12:9. One may recall Gen 3, where Satan deceived Adam and Eve. Rev 20 provides a reversal of Satan's fortune for a long period represented by a thousand years.

Satan's imprisonment differs from that of the two beasts in that a short respite will be allowed him after the millennium. Gaechter suggests that chronologically Satan's capture, 20:1–3, should precede that of the beasts, 19:19–21, but that the author chose to put the undoing of Satan last to emphasize his character as the ultimate enemy of God and man. He comes first and last "in the great chiastic symmetry of chapters xii-xx." In ch. 12 he lost his place in heaven, and in ch. 20 he is sent even below the earth. He must be secured before the new Jerusalem, the faithful Jews (and Christians) symbolized by the woman, is established by their union with God's mediator, the Lamb, rather than with the harlot established by the beast. Ch. 12 is but a prelude to the remainder of this apocalypse.

XVIII. THE MILLENNIAL JERUSALEM
(21:9–27, 8; 22:1–2)

21 ⁹ Then came one of the seven angels who had the seven bowls full of the seven last plagues, and spoke to me, saying, "Come, I will reveal to you the bride, the woman who is the wife of the Lamb."

10 And in spirit he carried me away to a great, high mountain, and revealed to me the holy city Jerusalem descending out of heaven from God, 11 possessing the glory of God, her radiance like a most rare jewel, like jasper, clear as crystal; 12 she had a great, high wall, with twelve gates, and at the gates twelve angels, and on the gates the names of the twelve tribes of the sons of Israel were inscribed, 13 on the east three gates, on the north three gates, on the south three gates, and on the west three gates. 14 And the wall of the city had twelve foundations, and on them the twelve names of the twelve apostles of the Lamb.

15 And he who spoke with me had a golden measuring rod to measure the city and her gates and wall. 16 And the city was four-square, its length the same as its breadth; and he measured the city with his rod, twelve thousand stadia; her length and breadth and height was equal. 17 He also measured her wall, a hundred and forty-four cubits by man's measure, that is, an angel's.

18 And the structure of the wall was jasper, while the city was pure gold, clear as crystal. 19 The foundations of the wall of the city were adorned with every jewel; the first foundation was jasper, the second sapphire, the third agate, the fourth emerald, 20 the fifth onyx, the sixth carnelian, the seventh chrysolite, the eighth beryl, the ninth topaz, the tenth chyrsoprase, the eleventh jacinth, the twelfth amethyst. 21 And the twelve gates were twelve pearls, each of the gates made of a single pearl. And the highway of the city was pure gold, clear as crystal. 22 And I saw no temple in her; for its temple is the Lord God, the Omnipotent, and the Lamb.

23 And the city had no need of sun or moon to shine upon it, for the glory of God was its light, and its lamp was the Lamb. 24 By her light shall the nations walk; and the kings of the earth shall bring their magnificence into her; 25 and its gates shall never be shut by day; there shall be no night there; 26 they shall bring into her the

glory and the honor of the nations. 27 But nothing unclean shall enter it, nor any who practice abomination or falsehood, but only those who are written in the Lamb's book of life.

8 But as for the cowardly, the faithless, the polluted, as for murderers, fornicators, sorcerers, idolaters, and all liars, their lot shall be in the lake that burns with fire and brimstone, which is the second death.

22 1 Then he revealed to me the river of the water of life, clear as crystal, flowing from the throne of God and of the Lamb, 2 through the middle of the highway of the city; and on either side of the river, there was a tree of life with its twelve kinds of fruit, yielding its fruit each month; and the leaves of the tree were for the healing of the nations.

NOTES

21:9. *bride, the woman who is the wife.* The phrase seems to be tautological. Some scholars think that "the bride" should be excised, for it may be a marginal gloss based on 19:7. On the other hand, "bride" may have been introduced deliberately to contrast this woman with the harlot, called "harlot" in 17:1 and "woman" in 17:3.

who is. TI.

10. *great, high mountain.* cf. the high mountain in Ezek 40:2. Jubilees 4:26 states that the Lord has four places on earth: the Garden of Eden, the mount of the east, Mount Sinai, and Mount Zion "(which) will be sanctified in the new creation for a sanctification of the earth; through it will the earth be sanctified from all (its) guilt and its uncleanness throughout the generations of the world" (APCh, II, 19).

holy city Jerusalem. The same phrase is found in 21:2 but there the adjective "new" is added. **051**, 1, 1854, 2059s pm TR reads "the great, the holy city, Jerusalem."

11. *radiance.* Gr. *phōstēr.* For saints described as "light-giving bodies" see Dan 12:3, Phil 2:15.

12. *great, high wall, with twelve gates.* The walls and gates of the city were a matter of great importance in the ancient world, for protection especially in war, and for committees (councils) held in rooms in the walls, as one sees e.g. in the conduct of Nehemiah in his night ride around the walls (Neh 2:13–16) and the alacrity with which the priests built and consecrated the gates (Neh 3). Contrast Zech 2:1–5, where the prophet sees an angel who is to measure Jerusalem but is informed that the city shall be inhabited as villages without walls because the multitude of people will be so great. This part of the prophecy concludes (vs. 5), "'For I will be to her a wall of fire round about,' says the Lord, 'and I will be the glory within her,'" RSV. In II Enoch 65, the

seer instructs his sons about the end of time, the great judgment, and the great eon when the righteous will live eternally and there will be no sickness, humiliation, anxiety, need, etc. In 65:10 it is said that the righteous "shall have a great indestructible wall, and a paradise bright and incorruptible, for all corruptible things shall pass away, and there will be eternal life" (APCh, II, 468).

gates. Gr. *pulōnas.* In classical Greek *pulōn* means gatehouse, porch, gate tower, as distinguished from *pulē,* gate (although Ezek 48, LXX, uses *pulē* as gatehouse). *Pulōn* can also mean the vestibule of a great house through which visitors pass from the street into the courtyard; cf. Gen 43:19, Luke 16:20, Acts 12:13.

angels. Cf. Isa 62:6: "On your walls, Jerusalem, I have posted watchmen" (AB). The presence of the angels at the gates indicates special protection from God, probably comparable to the cherubim at the Garden of Eden (Gen 3: 24).

twelve tribes. Each of the twelve tribes of Israel was represented by a gem on his high priest's breastplate; see NOTES on vss. 19–20.

13. The position of the gates lies towards the four points of the compass but the order, east, north, south, west, is different from Ezekiel's.

14. *foundations.* Each foundation probably was a stout oblong block like the stones which may still be seen in the lower rows of the Herodian masonry at Jerusalem. Bousset thinks the description is based on Jewish apocalyptic works written after the destruction of Jerusalem. He compares II Enoch 55:2, IV Ezra 7:26, 8:52, 10:54–59, 13:36, II Baruch 4:2–6, and Gal 4:26, Heb 12:22. The same idea is intimated in I Enoch 53:6.

apostles of the Lamb. This phrase looks suspiciously like an interpolation. The word "apostle" occurs only in 2:2, 18:20, 21:14; in other words, the apostles have not the prominent place which is enjoyed by the tribes of Israel in this apocalypse. Further, there seems to be some lack of continuity. "Wall" and "gates" depend on "having," Gr. *echousa,* agreeing with Jerusalem, but vs. 14 seems to begin another structure without a main verb and takes the appearance of something which has been added.

Cf. Shepherd of Hermas, Similitudes 9.2–9.16.7, where he receives a vision of the building of a tower. The rock and the door belonging to the tower represent the Son of God (9.12.1) and the tower is the church (9.13.1). There seems to be no direct reference to Rev 21:14. The foundation consists of ten stones (9.4.2), then twenty more, then thirty-five more, and after these forty (9.4.3). "So there became four tiers in the foundations of the tower." No explanation seems to be given of the ten, twenty, and thirty-five stones, but the shepherd does ask about the forty stones (9.16.5), and is told that these represent the apostles and teachers who preached not only to those living on the earth but also to those who had died before them. It can be seen, therefore, that the text differs considerably from Revelation.

This phrase is most likely to be found among the followers of John the Baptist, who alone alludes to Jesus directly as the Lamb (I Peter 1:19 has "a lamb"), than in the main stream of the church.

The most surprising feature of this phrase, if it came from the main Christian tradition consonant with the other "building" metaphors in the New

Testament, is the omission of any reference to Jesus. Gaston, p. 213, comments, "with the exception of II Cor 6:14 – 7:7, all of the temple texts in the epistles have also a Christological orientation." Some scholars have argued that II Cor 6:14 – 7:1 is an interpolation or a Christian reworking of a Qumran text which has been introduced into the Pauline epistle; see Fitzmyer, "Qumran and the Interpolated Paragraph in II Cor vi.14–vii.1," CBQ 23 (1961), 271 ff.

15. *golden measuring rod.* Cf. the bronze man with the measuring rod who measures the holy city and temple in Ezek 40:3.

16. *four-square.* Cf. the Holy of Holies in I Kings 6:19–20. The author seems to be influenced most of all by the legislation in Exod 27:1 where the altar must be a square of five cubits, Exod 28:16 where the breastplate is square, and Exod 39:9 again with reference to the breastplate; cf. too Exod 30:1–2, the altar of incense which is also square. According to Herodotus i 178, Babylon was a square, and according to Strabo, *Geography* 12.4.7, so was Nicaea.

twelve thousand stadia. Fifteen hundred miles. Such a vast extent is, of course, symbolic. Cf. Sibylline Oracles 5:251 and *Song of Songs R* 7:5 which say that Jerusalem will be enlarged until it reaches the gates of Damascus and exalted until it reaches the throne of God. *Baba Bathra* 75 a-b contains many interesting speculations about the future Jerusalem's measurements.

and height. Omitted in 2329.

17. *man's measure, that is, an angel's.* This may mean that the measures used by angels are those which are also used among mankind; this would be understandable since the covenanters of Qumran believed they had a close association with angels (cf. Rev 19:10, 22:9). But the text might also be influenced by that of Ezek 40:3, where the one who measures the holy city looks as though he were made of bronze. Cf. also Dan 10:5–6, where the prophet sees a man "clothed in linen, whose loins were girded with gold of Uphaz. His body was like beryl, his face like the appearance of lightning, his eyes like flaming torches, his arms and legs like the gleam of burnished bronze, and the sound of his words like the noise of a multitude" (RSV). It would seem that the personage is an angel rather than a man although he is described with the word "man," Gr. *anthrōpos.*

18. *structure.* Gr. *endomēsis.* This word is found only here, in *Ant.* 15.335, and in a pre-Christian inscription quoted by Moffatt. Josephus describes the great mole at Caesarea, two feet in width.

was. This verb is included in ℵ* **046,** 1, 82, 1006 pl vg TR.

19. This verse begins with "and" in ℵ* **051** 1, 2059s pm vg[s,cl] sy TR.

every jewel. There seems to be no standard order for the list of stones. Farrer (p. 219), however, observes that

It is reasonable to suppose that he ("John") did not trouble to do more than give a euphonious list of some general correspondence with the Exodus catalogue. He has so arranged the Greek names, as to emphasize the division by threes. All but three of them end with s sounds, and the three exceptions with n sounds. He has placed the n endings at the points of division, thus: jaspis, sapphiros, chalcedon; smaragdos, sardonyx, sardion; chrysolithos, beryllos, topazion; chrysoprasos, hiacinthos, amethystos.

See second NOTE on 4:3 for the order of the stones in the high priest's breastplate.

jasper. Gr. *iaspis.* Jasper is a variety of quartz found in various colors, commonly red, brown, green, and yellow, more rarely blue and black, and seldom white. In antiquity the name *iaspis* could denote any opaque precious stone; cf. Isa 54:12. Arndt and Gingrich suggest that the opal is meant here, but according to some it is the diamond, which is not opaque. According to Ginzberg, III, 170 ff., jasper is Benjamin's stone: "This stone changes color even as Benjamin's feelings towards his brothers changed." Max Bauer, *Precious Stones,* tr. L. J. Spencer ([1904] New York: Dover, 1968), pp. 499–502, says, "Jasper is too abundant to be worth very much, and the value of all but exceptionally fine and uniformly coloured specimens is small." However, he says that white jasper occurs as a great rarity in the Levant. The jasper here is probably the white Levantine variety which is precious.

sapphire. Gr. *sapphiros.* This is a blue, transparent, precious stone. In the ancient world, however, it seems to have been identified with the lapis lazuli; cf. Isa 64:11, Tobit 13:16. Precious lapis lazuli is deep blue like the sapphire but lacks the sapphire's luster. Says Ginzberg, III, 170 ff., "Issachar's stone was sapphire because this tribe devoted themselves to the study of the Torah and the two tables of the law were made out of sapphire. The stone increased the strength of vision and healed many diseases."

agate. Gr. *chalkēdōn.* Arndt and Gingrich suggest that the stones designated by this term in modern times (agate, onyx, carnelian, etc.) were known by other names in the ancient writers. Pliny, *Natural History* 37.7.92 ff., calls a kind of emerald or jasper "chalcedonian," but it is uncertain what is meant by the name. Ginzberg does not list this stone.

emerald. Gr. *smaragdos.* This is a bright green transparent precious stone, the most valued variety of beryl. Ginzberg, III, 170 ff., says, "Simeon's stone was smaragd which protected against unchastity. Judah's stone was emerald and had the power of making its owner victorious in battle." Perhaps Ginzberg took "beryl" to mean "emerald."

20. *onyx.* Gr. *sardonux.* This is a variety of agate (which is a type of chalcedony). It is a deep brown, practically opaque stone banded with white. "Joseph's stone was onyx and endowed the wearer with grace" (Ginzberg, III, 170 ff.).

carnelian. Gr. *sardion.* A reddish or brown jewel, this too is a variety of chalcedony. Perhaps this is the carbuncle of which Ginzberg (III, 170 ff.) speaks: "Levi's stone was carbuncle and had the property of making one who wore it wise." Ginzberg mentions another red stone, the ruby: "Reuben's stone was ruby which promoted pregnancy."

chrysolite. Gr. *chrusolithos.* The ancients seem to have used this term for the yellow topaz; cf. Pliny *Natural History* 37.42. According to Ginzberg,

III, 170 ff., "Asher's stone was chrysolite which aided digestion and made the owner sturdy."

beryl. Gr. *bērullos.* A precious stone ranging from transparent sea green to opaque blue; cf. Tobit 13:17, Pliny *Natural History* 37:20, 38:5. See NOTE on "emerald."

topaz. Gr. *topazion.* This is a bright yellow to pale brown, more or less transparent stone. In ancient times it was often used in the making of seals and gems. However, it may denote the more valuable golden yellow chrysolite. Says Ginzberg, III, 170 ff., "Dan's stone was topaz and the inverted face of a man was visible in it, this symbolized that the Danites were sinful."

chrysoprase. Gr. *chrusoprasos.* This is an apple green, finely grained horn stone, a variety of quartz, highly translucent; cf. Pliny *Natural History* 37.113. Ginzberg does not list it, but says (III, 170 ff.), "God's stone was crystal which gave the owner courage in battle."

jacinth. Gr. *huakinthos,* a gem perhaps blue in color (Arndt and Gingrich) something like sapphire or yellowish-red (Bauer). Ginzberg does not list it, but does say (III, 170 ff.), "Naphtali's stone was turquoise which gave speed in riding."

amethyst. Gr. *amethustos,* a variety of quartz in color clear transparent purple or bluish violet. Ginzberg does not list it.

21. *twelve gates.* Cf. vs. 12, where the gates are associated with the tribes of Israel.

pearl. In the Greco-Roman world a perfect pearl was worth more than its weight in gold. *Baba Bathra* 146a mentions a pearl which was valued at thousands of *zuzim* and Jerusalem *Berakoth* 9:12d mentions a pearl that has no price. The beauty of pearls was proverbial; cf. Matt 13:45–46. But see note on Rev 17:4 for the double significance. Ginzberg, III, 170 ff., says, "Zebulon's stone was white pearl and the pearl had the property of bringing the owner sleep. Moreover the pearl was round and therefore reminded the tribe of Zebulon of the fickleness of fortune."

clear. Gr. *diaugēs.* This is a rare word not known in the LXX (although cf. Prov 16:4, Codex Alexandrinus) and used only here in the NT. It is employed by Josephus (*Ant.* 3.37) of the water which gushed out of the rock struck by Moses. He refers to this as "a copious stream of most pellucid (Gr. *diaugēstaton*) water."

22. *temple.* Gr. *naos.* This may mean "temple" e.g. Matt 23:17 or sanctuary e.g. Acts 17:24. The city is regarded as a temple, Gr. *hieron,* and God as the Holy of Holies, Gr. *naos,* "shrine." Here God and the Lamb are said to be the temple or sanctuary, but in the Qumran texts discussed below (p. 343) it is the community, and especially the leaders of the community, who are regarded as the holy place. Prayers for the restoration of the dispersed at a new temple are found in the *Shemoneh 'Esrēh,* especially in the tenth, fourteenth, and seventeenth benedictions. The fourteenth appears to date before the fall of Jerusalem in A.D. 70; cf. McKelvey, pp. 20 ff. II Baruch 6:1–7 describes how an angel descended from heaven into the Holy of Holies and took the veil, the holy ark, the mercy seat, the two tables, the raiment of the priests, the altar

of incense, and the forty-eight precious stones together with the holy vessels, presumably to preserve them for future time.

22–23. *Lamb*. The two references to the Lamb in vss. 22–23, like the one in vs. 14, appear to be added to the text. In vs. 22 one would expect ". . . the Lord God and the Lamb are its temple," rather than the Lord God almighty is its temple and the Lamb. Equally, in vs. 23 reference to the lamp, Gr. *luchnos*, seems tautological. If the glory of God enlightens the city then there is no further need of another lamp, even if this is the Lamb. Further, the text might suggest that the Lamb does not share in the glory of God.

There is division of opinion upon the part to be played by the Messiah (whom the Lamb appears to symbolize) with reference to the new Jerusalem. Gaston asserts that the only passage which speaks clearly of the Messiah building the temple is the Targum to Zech 6:12–13, which he renders on p. 149 as follows:

Thus said Yahweh of hosts: this man, Messiah is his name, will be revealed and grow and build the temple of Yahweh. He will build the temple of Yahweh and he will exalt its splendor and he will sit and rule on his throne, and there will be the high priest by his throne, and the kingdom of peace will be between them.

Gaston recognizes a different situation in Samaritan eschatology. The *Taheb* ("Messiah") will restore the tabernacle and the ark; see Gaston, pp. 147–54.

McKelvey, p. 14, takes a different view. He refers to the Targum to Zech 6:12, but also to the Sibylline Oracles. In the fifth oracle it is said that the new temple will be erected by the Messiah and that it will have a tower which reaches to the clouds. The nations will gather together around it (p. 19). He thinks the idea of the tower looks back to the Tower of Babel; the unity which was lost at Babel will be restored when the Messiah erects the new temple (p. 190).

Betz, pp. 87–92, discussing the Nathan prophecy (II Sam 8:13) and the question about the temple brought up at the trial of Jesus, sees a development of thought from the offspring of David, who is to build the temple in II Sam 7:13, to Zech 6:12–13 where David's descendant, Zerubbabel, is to build the temple and then this develops into the eschatological interpretation of Nathan's prophecy, which suggests that the building of the temple of the house of God is a messianic duty. Therefore, anyone who claimed to be a builder of the temple claimed also to be Messiah. However, despite these references the association between the appearance of the new Jerusalem and the Messiah is absent in Revelation.

23. *no need of sun or moon*. Isa 60:19–20 intimates that the splendor of the sun and moon are put to shame by the glory of God.

24. *nations*. Cf. Zech 2:11, 8:23, Isa 65–66, Dan 7:14, Tobit 13:12, 14:6, I Enoch 90:32 ff.; Testament of Judah 25:5; Testament of Naphtali 8:4; IV Ezra 11:46. There seem to be two contradictory traditions concerning the Gentiles and the new Jerusalem. One speaks of the great battle of the nations against the holy city (Ps 46, Ezek 38–39, Isa 17:12 ff., 29:8, Micah 4:11,

Zech 12, Sibylline Oracles 3:663, Jubilees 23:22 ff., I Enoch 26, IV Ezra 13).
The other suggests a pilgrimage of the Gentiles to Mount Zion which is regarded
as the center of God's redemptive activity for the whole world (Isa 2:1 ff.,
Micah 4:1 ff., Isa 45:14, 61:7, 60, 65:18 ff., Jer 3:17, Zeph 3:10, Zech 8:20 ff.;
14 Tobit 13:9 ff., Sibylline Oracles 3:772 ff.). In Zion God reigns as king
and, as His presence was transferred from the ark to the temple in the time of
Solomon, so now it is transferred from the temple to the city; see Gaston,
p. 106. Both traditions seem to be present in Revelation. To Gaston's texts on
the conversion of the Gentiles, may be added I Enoch 10:21–22, where it is
said that the children of men will become righteous and all nations adore
God and the earth will be cleansed from defilement; Testament of Levi 18:
8–14, which speaks of the Gentiles being enlightened through the priesthood of
Levi and sin coming to an end, and the Testament of Asher 7:3–4, which
avers that God will save Israel and the Gentiles when He Himself comes as
man, with man eating and drinking. This, however, appears to be a Christian
addition. In the text speaking of the Gentiles coming to the holy city, this
place becomes a symbol not only of the unity of Israel but also of all mankind.

magnificence. In **046** 82, 1854 al vg sy TR the kings bring into the city
"magnificence and honor."

25. *be shut.* The gates would be closed for security at night. However,
this verse seems to be incongruous with the concept of the high protective
wall in vs. 12.

27. *enter.* Cf. *Baba Bathra* 75b:

> Rabbi said in the name of R. Johanan: Jerusalem of the world to come will
> not be like Jerusalem of the present world. [To] Jerusalem of the present
> world, anyone who wishes goes up, but to that of the world to come only
> those invited will go up.

21:8. The present writer has placed this verse after 21:27. See NOTE on
2:11 below, p. 393.

22:1. *river.* The adjective "pure" is added in **051** 2059s pm 1 TR.

water of life. Cf. Zech 14:8: "On that day living water shall flow out from
Jerusalem" (RSV). There may also be an association between the Spirit and
the living water as in Ezek 36:25–26, 1QS 4:21, John 3:5, 4:10, I John 5:6–8.
I Enoch 26:1–2 mentions a stream coming from the east side of the holy
mountain and flowing towards the south. Ps 46:4 speaks about the river which
gladdens the city of God. II Enoch 7:5 refers to two springs which send forth
honey and milk and either the same or different springs which send forth oil
and wine. God Himself seems to be identified with the fountain of living
waters in Jer 2:13, and a similar thought is expressed in I Enoch 96:6.

2. *highway.* Note the singular. Probably one is meant to think of one main
broad street in contrast to the narrow streets in eastern cities.

tree of life. I Enoch gives us further information about this tree. It was one
which had "a fragrance beyond all fragrance; and its leaves and blooms and
wood wither not for ever: and its fruit is beautiful, and its fruit resembles the
dates of a palm" (I Enoch 24:4, APCh, II, 204). We also learn that no
mortal was permitted to touch it till the great judgment. After that time

it will be given to the righteous and its fruit will be for the elect. It will be transplanted to the holy place, to the temple of the Lord "and its fragrance shall be in their (the elect's) bones, and they shall live a long life on earth, such as thy father lived: and in their days shall no sorrow or plague or torment or calamity touch them" (I Enoch 25:4–6, APCh, II, 204–5). This seems to suggest that the fruit gave immortality but our text is sparing in its detail concerning this tree.

leaves . . . healing. Cf. Ezek 47:12. The nations must be those who have survived the visitations of ch. 19 and perhaps are to be evangelized by the inhabitants of the heavenly city.

COMMENT

The old Jerusalem (the harlot) is destroyed only so that the new one might take her place. As McKelvey, pp. 9 ff., asserts, Israel was able to survive the crisis of faith suffered at the destruction of the Jerusalem temple and the dispersion of the nation because the prophets had prepared the people in advance. The chief tenets of the prophetic message were that a remnant would be preserved and the nation would grow from this (Isa 4:2–4, Jer 23: 5–6), the outcasts of Israel would return home (Isa 11:11 ff., 27:13, Jer 31: 6 ff., Ezek 34:11 ff.), and the city and/or temple would be restored and become not only the center for Israel but also for the nations (Isa 2:2–4, Micah 4:1–3, Jer 3:17–18). The glory of Yahweh would dwell once again in the city and community; Ezek 43:1 ff. This is also the message of Revelation.

It is, therefore, significant that it should be one of the angels associated with the seven last plagues, which preceded the fall of the harlot city, the faithless Jerusalem, who has the responsibility of revealing the bride, the new city, to the seer. The lament over the destruction must be followed by the kindling of new hope. The author makes this clear by using an almost identical introduction for the two acts. As Swete, p. 283, observes, "Its repetition here serves to place the *numphē* (bride) in marked contrast with the *pornē* (harlot)":

Rev 17:1: And one of the seven angels who held the seven bowls came, and spoke with me, saying, "Come, I will reveal to you the verdict upon the great harlot who is established upon many waters."	Rev 21:9: Then came one of the seven angels who had the seven bowls full of the seven last plagues, and spoke to me, saying, "Come, I will reveal to you the bride, the woman who is the wife of the Lamb."

The contrast is continued in 21:10. Whereas in 17:3 the seer was taken to a wilderness to see the harlot, in 21:10 he is taken to a high mountain. We are probably meant to conclude that the holy city, Jerusalem, comes down upon this mountain. The text is influenced by Ezek 40:2, where the prophet is brought in visions into the land of Israel and set upon a mountain "on which was a structure like a city opposite me" (RSV). In a similar way Isa 2:2 speaks of "the mountain of the house of the Lord" being established "as the highest of the mountains," and "raised above the hills, to this all the nations shall come" (RSV); cf. Micah 4:1–2.

The expectation of a new Jerusalem seems to have taken two forms, one of a transformed Jerusalem upon this earth and the other of a heavenly Jerusalem; see Section XXIII on 21:1–4c. The first tradition is represented by Second Isaiah (Isa 40–55) who expects not only a reelection of God's people and a new exodus but also a new Zion. However, this does not necessarily include the concept of a new temple, in distinction from "city." Postexilic eschatology (Isa 24–27, 34–35, Joel 3, Zech 12–14, Ezek 38–39) remains in this Zion tradition. God's dwelling on earth will be in the glorified city, whose description becomes increasingly elaborate. It is Ezek 40–43 which includes the expectation of a new temple. This thought is taken up in Tobit 13:9–18, 14:5, which speak of the holy city in terms similar to those found in Isa 40 but say also, "the house of God will be rebuilt there with a glorious building for all generations forever" (Tobit 14:5, RSV). Jubilees 1:17 also speaks of the restoration of the sanctuary, and I Enoch 90:28–29 sees the Lord of the sheep bringing "a new house greater and loftier than that first . . . all its pillars were new and its ornaments were new and larger than those of the first, the old one which He had taken away, and all the sheep were within it," (see Gaston, pp. 103–14). In the light of these traditions, it is not surprising that Revelation contains no direct reference to the rebuilding of the temple, only to the arrival of the new Jerusalem.

The holy city, Jerusalem, which comes down from heaven is endowed with the glory of God (vs. 11, cf. Ezek 43:4 which sees the glory of God return from the east before he receives plans for the future temple). In Rev 21:11 glory is described as "radiance," Gr. *phōstēr,* which denotes a light-giving-body: it recalls Gen 1:14, 16, Wisd Sol 13:2, Sir 43:7. This light-giving body is similar to a most precious jewel "like jasper, clear as crystal." This comparison immediately recalls the throne vision in ch. 4 where the one who sits upon the throne is compared to jasper and sardis. The holy city, therefore, appears to resemble the throne of the deity.

The city has a high wall (vs. 12). Gaechter finds this one of its most striking features, as a protective wall would not be necessary if all the enemies were destroyed. Later (vs. 17) one learns that the wall is one hundred and forty-four cubits, which seems singularly out of proportion when compared to the size of the city. However, the walls of the historical city of Jerusalem were of tremendous importance. Tacitus, *Histories* 5.8–12, mentions that, with their towers, they were 120 feet high. Josephus reports in *War* 7.3–4 that when the Romans razed the city they left only the loftiest of the towers and a portion of the west wall:

All the rest of the wall encompassing the city was so completely levelled to the ground as to leave future visitors to the spot no ground for believing that it had ever been inhabited. Such was the end to which the frenzy of revolutionaries brought Jerusalem, that splendid city of worldwide renown.

If this part of our apocalypse were written just before or after the fall of the city, the emphasis on the wall would be understandable in the light of Tacitus' and Josephus' information.

The author's vision of the wall and the gates were doubtless influenced by Ezek 48:30–35. Although this text does not mention the word "wall," Gr. *teichos,* there had to be one, for the gates about which the prophet speaks are the gatehouses, porches or gate towers which constitute a city wall. Ezekiel predicts that the gates will be named after the tribes of Israel: on the north side the gates of Reuben, Judah, and Levi; on the east the gates of Joseph, Benjamin, and Dan; on the south the gates of Simeon, Issachar, and Zebulon; and on the west the gates of Gad, Asher and Naphtali. In a similar way the Temple Scroll states that the middle and outer courts of the temple have twelve gates named after the twelve tribes of Israel (Yadin, *Biblical Archaeologist* 30 (1967), 139). Whereas the ordinary guardians of walls (cf. Isa 62:6) are watchmen, in 21:12 an angel is placed at each gate. This might recall the cherub who guarded the entrance to Paradise, but it could also suggest the close association between human and supernatural beings such as one finds at Qumran, especially if the angels have a military function. In Jewish tradition angels fight even on horseback (e.g. II Macc 5:1–4.)

Just as in the opening of this vision there was a clear contrast with the vision of the harlot, so into vs. 15 our author introduced a feature which corresponds to the measuring in Rev 11. There the measuring was for judgment (cf. Amos 7:7–9), but here it is a seal on the perfection of the city. Vs. 15 is akin to Ezek 40:3–5, where the man who appeared to the prophet measures the wall around the outside of the temple area. The city in Rev 21 is four-square, the symbol of perfection. The temple in Ezekiel's vision was situated at the center of a series of concentric squares and the temple itself was four-square (42:15–20). The holy place and the Holy of Holies lay in the inner court and each was perfect in length and breadth (41:3–4, 13–15). McKelvey, p. 10, comments, "The meaning of the plan is not difficult to discern. The new temple is the symbol of the new people of God. The symmetry and the unity of its plan represent the unity and cohesion of the twelve-fold Israel."

The new city (in distinction from the temple) which Ezekiel sees has the same symmetrical design, for it is a square (48:15 ff.) and has twelve gates, three on each side. In Rev 21:17 the city wall is one hundred and forty-four cubits, symbolically a perfect number. The city itself is made of pure gold like clear crystal. The writer may have recalled the gold of the Herodian temple referred to in Josephus *War* 5.222–24. Cf. Mark 13:1–2:

> The exterior of the building wanted nothing that could astound either mind or eye. For, being covered on all sides with massive plates of gold, the sun was no sooner up than it radiated so fiery a flash that persons straining to look at it were compelled to avert their eyes, as from the solar rays. To approaching strangers it appeared from a distance like a snow-clad mountain; for all that was not overlaid with gold was of purest white. From its summit protruded sharp golden spikes to prevent

birds from settling upon and polluting the roof. Some of the stones in the building were forty-five cubits in length, five in height and six in breadth.

If this is so, then the writer of vs. 17 has condensed the description drastically and has not differentiated between the gold and the white according to Josephus. Over and above this, however, the author appears to be influenced by the rabbinic tradition of the temple built by God as a house of jewels and pearls through which shone the overwhelming radiance of the Shekinah. This was believed to have been seen in a vision by Moses, according to Ginzberg, III, 446.

Ginzberg further states (III, 447) that Jacob is purported to have seen the two Jerusalems, the heavenly one and the earthly one. On this occasion he exclaimed that it will not be the earthly Jerusalem that will last forever, but the heavenly Jerusalem that God Himself builds. Jacob further refers to the Messiah: ". . . know then that with his hands also He will build the Temple upon earth."

The author pays special attention to the foundations which could be said to be the most crucial part or the key structure in city building in ancient times because they supported the wall, which formed the main fortification. He describes the foundations of the wall in detail; one of the details is that they are adorned with every precious stone. He seems to be influenced by three traditions: the jewels on Aaron's breastplate (Exod 28:17–20), the jewels on the dress of the king of Tyre (Ezek 28:13, see p. 253), and the association between jewels and the signs of the zodiac. See the following table.

Rev 21:19–20	Exod 28:17–20	Exod 39:10–13	Ezek 28:13
jasper	carnelian	carnelian	carnelian
sapphire	topaz	topaz	topaz
agate	carbuncle	carbuncle	jasper
emerald	emerald	emerald	chrysolite
onyx	sapphire	sapphire	beryl
carnelian	diamond	diamond	onyx
chrysolite	jacinth	jacinth	sapphire
beryl	agate	agate	carbuncle
topaz	amethyst	amethyst	emerald
chrysoprase	beryl	beryl	
jacinth	onyx	onyx	
amethyst	jasper	jasper	

If, as is most likely, the author is influenced by the breastplate of the high priest, then he would have portrayed the city as the corporate personality of Aaron or the high priest, that is, the exact antithesis to the bad priest who is personified by the harlot (see NOTES on 17:3, 4, 5). The jewels in the breastplate of Aaron represented the different tribes. Tribal unity is the foundation of the new city; cf. Rev 7:4–8. A similar, though not wholly corresponding, concept occurs in the Midrash on Isaiah 54:11–12 from Qumran where important personages, especially leaders, are represented as precious stones; DJD, V, 28.

. . .] all Israel sought thee according to thy word. 'And I shall lay your foundations in lapis [lazuli.' . . . *its interpretation* is th]at they have founded the Council of the community, [the] priests and the peo[ple . . .] a congregation of his elect, like a stone of lapis lazuli among the stones [. . . 'And I will make as agate] all thy pinnacles.' Its interpretation concerns the twelve [. . .] giving light in accordance with the Urim and the Thummim [. . .] that are lacking from them, like the sun in all its light. And ['. . .]' Its interpretation concerns the heads of the tribes of Israel at the [*end of days* . . .] his lot, the offices of [. . .]

From this text it appears that the community of the elect are the stones and among these the priests are either lapis lazuli or sapphires.

This Qumran text is only an extension of others which refer to the foundation of the community as the building of the house. Gärtner, p. 74, refers to 4QpPs 37:2, 16, which reads, "(God) established him (the Teacher of Righteousness) to build him the community (of elect?) . . ." and CDC 3:19, where God Himself is said to build the community like a house: "And He built for them in Israel a firmly established house . . ." The Hebrew term *kīn*, which means to found or establish, occurs in some important "temple" texts which describe the founding of the community (1QS 8:5, 10, 1QH 7:18; see Gärtner, p. 74). Thus, although the author of Revelation states that the names of the tribes are on the gates (vs. 12), this does not preclude the rest of the building representing other members of the community.

Farrer, pp. 216–44, associates the jewels with the signs of the zodiac. This is probably because according to *Berakoth* 32b the twelve constellations represent the twelve tribes. The standards of the tribes corresponded to the zodiacal signs of the constellations. In the east were the standards of Judah, constellation Aries, stone sard; Benjamin, constellation Taurus, stone sardonyx; Joseph, constellation Gemini, stone emerald. In the south were those of Zebulon, constellation Cancer, stone chalcedon; Issachar, constellation Leo, stone sapphire; Levi, constellation Virgo, stone jasper. In the west were those of Simeon, constellation Libra, stone amethyst; Manasseh, constellation Scorpio, stone jacinth; Naphtali, constellation Sagittarius, stone chrysoprase. In the north were those of Asher, constellation Capricorn, stone topaz; Gad, constellation Aquarius, stone beryl; Reuben, constellation Pisces, stone chrysolith. The signs of the zodiac are depicted in mosaics in synagogues in Palestine, indicating the Jews felt no incongruity in adopting these pagan signs and linking them with Jewish ideas. See illustration 11.

Vs. 21 says the twelve gates were made of pearl. Once again the author may be influenced by Jewish haggadah. In *Sanhedrin* 100a Rabbi Johanan says, ". . . the Holy One, blessed be He, will bring jewels and precious stones, each thirty cubits long, and thirty cubits high, and make an engraving in them, ten by twenty cubits, and set them up as the gates of Jerusalem, for it is written, And *I will make thy windows of agates, and thy gates of carbuncles*." A certain disciple derided Rabbi Johanan, saying, " 'We do not find a jewel even as large as a dove's egg, yet such huge ones are to exist!' Sometime later he took a sea journey and saw the ministering angels cutting precious stones and pearls. He said unto them: 'For what are these?' They replied: 'The Holy One, blessed be He, will set them up as the gates of Jerusalem.' "

The fact that each of the gates of the new Jerusalem is made of only one pearl emphasizes the size of the pearls and, therefore, their greater value. However, the author may not be speaking about the white pearls known to us. The Hebrew "pearl" (*peninim;* cf. Prov 3:15, 8:11, 20:15, 31:10, Job 28:18; Lam 4:7) may mean coral. In the Reed Sea was found a kind of oyster, red on the outside with bright red mother of pearl on the inside. Also in vs. 21 is a description of the highway of the city. In contrast to the narrow lanes of eastern towns, the new Jerusalem will have a wide road, Gr. *plateia,* of pure gold clear as crystal.

Thus the city is exotic but not more so than the descriptions of the future Jerusalem in Jewish literature. Tobit's prayer (13:16–18, RSV) ends with this expectation:

For Jerusalem will be built with sapphires and emeralds,
her walls with precious stones,
and her towers and battlements with pure gold.
The streets of Jerusalem will be paved with beryl and ruby and stones of
Ophir;
all her lanes will cry 'Hallelujah!' and will give praise,
saying, 'Blessed is God, who has exalted you forever.'

The description of the new earthly Jerusalem concludes with several succinct ideas. First, there is no temple (vs. 22); second, there is no need for sun and moon (vs. 23); third, Gentiles will enter (vss. 24–26); fourth, anyone or anything defiled is excluded (vs. 27); and fifth, a Paradise motif (22:1–2).

The absence of the temple is not a new motif. It is suggested in Jer 3:15–17. After God says that He will give the people shepherds who will teach them knowledge and understanding, He predicts (in 3:16–17, AB) they will have no need to say:

"The Ark of the Covenant of Yahweh." It will not enter their minds; they will neither remember it nor miss it, nor will another one ever be made. At that time Jerusalem will be called Yahweh's throne; and all nations will gather to it, and will no longer follow their own stubbornly wicked inclinations.

Gaston finds that although the expectation of a new temple could find its place in the hope for a new Jerusalem it can also be specifically excluded. To support this he quotes the oracle from Jeremiah cited above and Isa 40, 46:1–6, where there is a glorious description of the new Jerusalem but also a fierce denunciation of the temple and sacrificial worship and no reference to the rebuilding of the temple. That our author follows the tradition of the Isaiah texts is verified by his further use of Isa 40:19 in vs. 23b and Isa 40:3–5, 11 in vss. 24, 25. Isaiah predicts that the sun and moon will not give Jerusalem light by day and night but that everlasting light and glory will came from God, that the nations will walk by that light, that kings will bring their wealth or glory into her, and that her gates shall not be closed for there will be no night.

The exclusion of unclean things (vs. 27) confirms that this city must be the millennial Jerusalem existing before all wickedness in the earth is destroyed. Rev 21:27, 8, are probably closely associated with 22:15. Vss. 27, 8 exclude those who are not ritually clean (the word used is "common," Gr. *koinon*), those who practice idolatry (*bdelugma*, i.e. anything which would incur God's wrath if brought before him), and those who practice deceit. Rev 22:15 appears to refer mainly to unethical conduct: the "dogs" mean sodomists; the "sorcerers," Gr. *pharmakoi*, refer to poisonous magicians or abortionists; then follow the prostitutes (probably both male and female are meant), murderers, and idolaters. The last three were regarded as the most hideous sins both in Judaism and in the early Church, as attested in 4QFlorilegium 1:16–17. The text continues by discussing David's rest from his enemies (II Sam 7:11b) and interpreting this to mean that they will have rest from the sons of Belial.

The paradisal character of the pericope 22:1–2 is indicated by the presence of the river of the water of life and the tree of life. Jewish eschatology included the hope of a future paradise, e.g. Isa 11:6–9. Further, in Ezek 36:35 and Isa 51:3 the hope is expressed that Palestine will become another Eden; cf. Isa 65:17–25, which refers to the longevity of people in that age. In the pseudepigraphical and rabbinic writings one finds the expectation of a paradise in which the righteous will live, either in the days of the Messiah or in the coming age. However, what had the greatest influence on this pericope is that I Enoch 25:4 locates this paradise in Jerusalem and predicts the tree of life will grow again; cf. I Enoch 24:4 – 25:7(8); Testament of Levi 18:11; IV Ezra 7:123–24, 8:52. In the Testament of Levi the high priest of the messianic age is to open the gates of paradise and remove the sword which is held by the cherub. I Enoch 32:2–3, Jubilees 8:16 locate paradise on earth in the far east, while I Enoch 77:7, II Enoch 61:1–4 see it in the north, and Josephus, *War* 2.155–56, finds it a place refreshed by the west wind.

The angel in 22:1 reveals to the seer a river of living water (or water of life), as bright as crystal (contrast the water polluted with blood), which proceeds from the throne of God and of the Lamb. The idea of the Lamb sharing the throne of God is not surprising when we recall the texts of I Enoch which refer to the Elect One and/or the Son of Man seated on his throne of glory; I Enoch 45:3, 51:3, 61:8, 62:3, 5, 69:27, 29. Rev 22:1 shows affinity to Ezek 47:8–11, which speaks of water issuing from the threshold of the temple; cf. Ezek 47:1. Although in Ezekiel this water is not actually called "the water of life," the idea is implied in that wherever the water goes it brings life to creatures and plants and makes the stale waters fresh. This idea, which is associated with Ezekiel's new temple, is adapted in Revelation to the new Jerusalem. The author has also indicated that the city is the seat of God by referring to the throne of God from which the water flows. A kindred idea is found in Zech 14:8–9, which speaks of living waters flowing from Jerusalem, half to the eastern sea and half to the western, in both summer and winter. The prophecy is followed by the announcement that "the Lord will become king over all the earth . . ." (RSV).

In addition to the river is another paradisal feature, the tree of life; the picture is probably one of the river running down the middle of the great highway, flanked on each side by the trees of life. Rev 22:2 reads "tree of life" in the singular, but this is most probably to be taken in the collective sense. The author probably recalls Ezek 47:12, which speaks of all kinds of trees on either side of the river; their leaves do not wither and they bear fresh fruit every month because they are watered by the stream from the sanctuary. Their leaves are for healing; our author adds "of the nations." This is a final detail which suggests that "redemption" is not complete and confirms the temporal nature of the new Jerusalem.

XIX. THE FINAL BLESSING
(22:14–15)

22 ¹⁴ Blessed are those who wash their robes, that they may have the privilege of the tree of life and that they may enter the city by the gates. ¹⁵ Outside are the dogs and sorcerers and fornicators and murderers and idolaters and all who delight in and practice falsehood.

NOTES

14. *Blessed.* This would be the seventh of the seven beatitudes according to the present order of our text but the sixth according to Gaechter's order.

wash their robes. Gr. *plūno*, "wash"; *stolas*, "robes." An important variant, "perform his commandments," occurs in **046** 1, 82, 1611, 2059s 2329 pl g sy bo Tert Cypr TR. However, the action of washing robes could be the fulfillment of a commandment, e.g. purification before meals. Thus Philo in *De Vita Contemplativa* 9.69 ff. describes the preparation for the cultic meal of the Therapeutae which recalls the offering of the bread of the presence in the temple. Cf. also Rev 7:14 and NOTE on "bathed their robes."

tree of life. Presumably the blessed will partake of its fruit. When the Qumran community took their own sacred meal they may have done so in anticipation of the perfected ritual in the heavenly temple; see Black, pp. 110–11.

15. *dogs.* Deut 23:18 forbids the bringing of a harlot or a dog (sodomite) into the house of God; both are abominations. Cf. 21:8 and COMMENT, p. 345.

COMMENT

Gaechter adds vss. 14–15 to the description of the millennial Jerusalem; this would appear to be correct.

Like 7:14, 22:14 is a beatitude. However, it does differ from 7:14, as a comparison will show:

7:14	22:14
And he said to me, "these are the people who have come from the great tribulation, and have bathed their robes and made them bright in the blood of the Lamb."	Blessed are those who wash their robes, that they may have the privilege of the tree of life and that they may enter the city by the gates.

The absence in 22:14 of an allusion to the tribulation and the blood of the Lamb permits one to interpret this text differently from the earlier one. The word *plunō,* "wash," is used in Philo (*Legum Allegoriae* 3.144.147) when citing Lev 1:9, 9:14 (LXX), the washing of burnt offerings. Further the word *stolē,* a long, flowing robe, can describe the garments of Aaron and his sons, as in Lev 8:30 (LXX). These words, therefore, might suggests a levitical washing of robes in preparation for a sacred meal, as in the temple or at Qumran or among the Essenes. The levitical washing must be done before entering the holy city and partaking of the tree of life. In this way 22:14 can be linked with the millennium text, 20:6, where those who reign with the Anointed One are said to be priests.

A priest officiating in the temple was obliged to wear the appropriate garments which must be free from defilement. However, at Qumran many of these rules which ordinarily governed only priestly conduct were implemented by the whole community, i.e. they lived up to the priestly ideal of sanctification. Many of the Pharisees did likewise. The priests' garments in 1QM 7:10–11 correspond to those worn by the priests in the temple, but this document also states specifically, "These shall be their garments for battle and into the Sanctuary they shall not bring them." In the light of this there may be a link with 7:14. The faithful fight the Holy War with the "Lamb" but they must change their apparel before they enter the holy area and perhaps partake of the eschatological banquet. Gärtner, p. 11, refers to the Qumran Aramaic fragment which probably describes the sacred meal in the heavenly temple; see Baillet, pp. 228, 243–44. This interpretation is confirmed by vs. 15. All those who are not pure are excluded from this new Jerusalem; see Rev 21:8.

XX. THE MILLENNIAL KINGDOM
(20:4-6)

20 4 Then I saw thrones, and seated on them were those to whom judgment was given; also I saw the souls of those who had been beheaded for their testimony about Jesus and for the Word of God, and whosoever had not worshiped the beast nor its image and had not received its mark on their foreheads or on their hands; and they came to life, and reigned with the Anointed One for a thousand years. 5 The rest of the dead did not come to life until the thousand years were completed. This is the first resurrection. 6 Blessed and holy is he who shares in the first resurrection; over such the second death has no power, but they will be priests of God and of the Anointed One and they shall reign with him for the thousand years.

NOTES

20:4. *thrones.* Gaechter asserts that wherever thrones are mentioned in Revelation they are always in heaven, that judgment always proceeds from the throne of God, and that "throne" refers either to the throne of God or the thrones of the elders. However, neither God nor elders are mentioned here. Nor is there any elaborate description to suggest a "throne vision."

seated on them. In the Greek there appears to be no subject of this clause. In ch. 4 it is the elders who sit upon the thrones.

given. Gr. *edothē,* "it was given" or "it was granted," impersonal passive denoting an action by God. This word has appeared frequently before. Cf. e.g. the four horsemen in ch. 6. See Section III, COMMENT.

beheaded. Gr. *pelekizomai.* This occurs only here in the NT. The martyrs are described in 6:9 as "slain"; cf. 7:14.

about Jesus and for the Word of God. See Introduction, "The Christology." The phrase seems tautological if one identifies Jesus with the Word of God unless one reads "and," Gr. *kai,* in the exegetical sense of "namely."

whosoever had not worshiped the beast. One notes that the phrase "the souls of those who had been beheaded" is in the accusative and naturally follows "I saw," but "whosoever had not worshiped the beast . . ." is in the nominative and seems to fit badly into the text. It is probably an interpolation. Although it is not said that they have died, one might surmise this because the next sentence reads "and they came to life."

and they came to life . . . This follows more naturally in connection with the phrase "for the Word of God."

a thousand years. In 046 82 al TR the definite article is used.

5. This verse is omitted in ℵ 82 al sy.

rest of the dead. This also follows more smoothly if the clause concerning those who abstained from worshiping the beast were omitted. There is no reference to the resurrection of the wicked.

6. *first resurrection* . . . *second death.* There appears to be no evidence for the belief in a first resurrection in Christian literature. The idea and terminology may have been introduced to balance the idea of a first and second death. If there is a first death, then there must be a first resurrection and, if there is a second death, there must be a second resurrection. However, it is probably better to understand it in the sense of "the first group to enjoy resurrection"; cf. I Cor 15:23. For the significance of the second death, see NOTE on 2:11.

6. *priests.* Cf. 1:6, the priestly kingdom. In that text kingdom comes before priests and the priests are said to be priests to God and Christ's father, whereas here they are priests of God and of the Anointed One. Cf. also I Peter 2:9–10.

the thousand years. For the concept of a messianic period, not necessarily the millennium, cf. Jubilees 1:29, I Enoch 10, 11, 21:6. The definite article is omitted in A 051 1, 82, 1006, 2059s pm TR; Rᵗ.

COMMENT

Resurrection of the righteous, the reign of the Anointed One, and frequent mention (once in each of the three verses) of a "thousand years" indicate that Rev 20:4–6 is a vision of the millennial kingdom. At this period the concept of the millennium (or an interregnum) was generally accepted, but in later years it was the occasion for some controversy.

Several Christian writers in the early period thought Christ would reign a thousand years at Jerusalem before the last judgment. The Epistle of Barnabas 15:4–9 is fervently millenarist. Papias is a naive, extravagant millenarist; see Eusebius *Ecclesiastical History* 39.11–13. Justin Martyr, *Dialogue* 80–81, thinks that millenarism is orthodox. Irenaeus, *Against Heresies* 5.28.3, followed by Tertullian, *Against Marcion* 3.24, accepts the belief. At Rome Hippolytus was its champion against the priest Caius who denied the authenticity of Revelation precisely to combat millenarism more readily. In Egypt the controversy was even livelier. Near Alexandria a number of small towns became schismatic because the inhabitants were millenarists. Bishop Dionysius tells about an argument that lasted for three days (Eusebius *Ecclesiastical History* 7.24). There are hints of millenarism in Apollinaris of Laodicea, Lactantius, Victorinus of Petau, Sulpicius Severus, Saint Ambrose. Jerome, ordinarily caustic against those with whom he disagreed, was somewhat indulgent towards these writers.

In the fourth century the Donatist (a schismatic body in the African Church in the fourth century), Tyconius, launched the spiritual interpretation of the millennium (which was given its classic form by Augustine) although he had in his early sermons favored millenarism. In A.D. 431 the Council at Ephesus spoke of chiliasm, the belief in the earthly reign of Christ incarnate which willl usher in the millennium, as a deviation and fable. It practically died out in the church, although it enjoyed occasional revival; e.g. Joachim of Flora in the twelfth century taught that the millennium would begin in 1260. Traces of it are found in the followers of John Hus, the Anabaptists, the Mormons, the Adventists, Jehovah's Witnesses, and the modern Pentecostal movements. There was a mitigated form of millenarism in certain Catholic circles in South America, but this was repudiated by the Holy See in 1941; see "Responsum de millenarismo" in *Biblica* 23 (1942), 385. The Holy See issued a decree concerning this on July 21, 1944; see *Acta Apostolicae Sedis* 36 (Rome, 1944), 212.

Concerning the spiritual interpretation of the millennium, according to Saint Augustine John adapted the imagery of the Jewish intermediate reign and eschatological combat to Christian realities. The millennium is the whole phase of the reign of Christ on earth from the incarnation to the parousia. During this time the influence of the devil is in abeyance. It is the church militant, Augustine continues, that reigns with Christ until the end of the world; the first resurrection is to be understood spiritually as birth into the life of grace (Col 3:1–2, Phil 3:20; cf. John 5:25). The thrones of Rev 20:4 are those of the Catholic hierarchy which has the power of binding and loosing. (Evidently, John did not intend to be that precise.) The image intends to show the greatness of the Christian, already beginning to reign with Christ (Matt 19: 28, Luke 22:30, I Cor 6:3, Eph 1:20, 2:6, Rev 1:6, 5:9–10).

Augustine tends to emphasize the church militant but he does not forget the church triumphant: in the thousand-year reign John has included the souls of the martyrs and the confessors, all those souls of the blessed still living on earth who have not worshiped the beast. Boismard suggests another interpretation of the first resurrection: it may indicate the renewal of the church after the persecutions by Rome, like the resurrection of the dry bones (Ezek 37) which symbolize the restoration of Israel after the dispersion of the exiles. (The above pages of this COMMENT are taken mainly from the notes of the late Father Siegman.)

The context of the millennium suggests that the thrones the seer witnesses are of the earthly dimension, although this is not made clear. The pericope appears to give further information about the earthly kingdom. The occupants are the judges, the martyrs, and the faithful who did not indulge in idolatry and who presumably died naturally or in a way different from beheading; those who were beheaded are mentioned separately. The judgment appears to affect the saints for good; the first resurrection is the prerogative of these righteous. Those who take part in the first resurrection are not injured by the second death which is defined in 20:14 as the lake of fire. They have a sacerdotal and regal role with the Anointed One for a thousand years. Swete, p. 264, points out that the "inclusion of Christ with God in the Object of Divine Worship is peculiar to this passage, but it agrees with what has been said in c.v. 8 ff. as to the joint worship of God and of the Lamb by heavenly beings, and with the general tendency of the book to regard Christ as Equivalent of God."

Only here (and 20:2–3) in the NT is there a reference to the millennium. Indeed, it seems to be a Jewish concept adopted by our author and then used by some (usually deviant) Christians in later periods, as was noted above. In earlier writings Israel contemplated a new historical and national era, but eventually developed a more transcendental hope which included the concept of new heavens and a new earth. These would be preceded by a universal judgment and the introduction of the eternal reign of God. It was, perhaps, in order to harmonize these divergent views that the belief in an interim messianic period arose. This temporary messianic reign would be followed by the heavenly kingdom.

During the period prior to the writing of Revelation there was lively discussion about the duration of this temporary messianic kingdom. In I Enoch 91–103 it was said that the present age lasts seven weeks and the messianic kingdom is established in the eighth. In the eighth week the house of the great king is built and the wicked are subject to the righteous (91:12–13), in the ninth week there is a final judgment upon the wicked (91:14), and in the tenth the angels are judged (91:15). After this the first heaven and the first earth pass away and new heavens appear (91:16). It is then that the eternal age begins; this is described as "many weeks without number forever." Thus for Enoch the messianic age lasts from the eighth to the tenth week. The order of events is similar to those in Revelation. In Jubilees 23:26–31 there is a description of the messianic time when man "will draw nigh to one thousand years" and "no satan or evil destroyer will be in the land." The Book of Adam and Eve 42:2–5 states that the world will endure five thousand five hundred years until the Messiah comes.

Bailey includes Sibylline Oracles 3:46–62, 741–61, 767–84 among "millennial" texts, and observes that these sections and the book as a whole seem to suggest that the golden age is a temporary period preceding the end, but the author or authors of these fragments does not seem to have a definite belief in this regard. Bailey also discusses Samaritan beliefs and draws attention to the work of Cowley, Montgomery, Gaster, and Bousset (we should now add the work of John McDonald). The Samaritans entertained the belief in a temporary reign of the *Taheb* (their name for the Messiah) who would restore the nation to God's favor for a thousand years and then would die until the time of the general resurrection. Josephus (*Ant.* 18.85–86) bears witness to the first century presence of a similar belief. Bailey declares, "If this phase of Samaritan thought can be dated as early as suggested it gives the earliest known use of the thousand years for the duration of the messianic era. But if the Samaritans are leaning on old Jewish thinking at this point the idea must be still older. The concepts reflected in Jubilees then come to a new significance" (JBL 53 [1934], 179–80).

An examination of the Jewish sources before the Christian era suggests the idea of a temporary messianic era but (except for I Enoch 91:93) gives no clear indication as to the duration of this. However, in the literature of the first century A.D. this point is clarified. In II Enoch (ca. A.D. 50) the thought comes very close to that in Revelation. From an examination of chapters 25–33 Bailey considers that the day equals a thousand years, the seventh day is a rest day "apparently the messianic age of a thousand years," and the eighth is the "time where there is to be no computation and no end, neither years, nor weeks, nor days, nor hours." He concludes that this is the oldest passage in the literature of Judaism which mentions an intermediate period of a thousand years between the end of creation and the eternal age. It does not appear, however, to mention an individual Messiah. In II Enoch 65:3–8 the great judgment at the end of creation and before the eternal period is mentioned.

G. F. Moore, in *Judaism in the First Centuries of the Christian Era,* II, 375–76, draws attention to three apocalypses, normally assigned to the period A.D. 70, which indicate a definite limitation to the messianic age. The Apocalypse of Baruch predicts that the Messiah will be revealed in glory (30:1), the earth will be extraordinarily fertile and the righteous will rise from the dead (30:2–4), but the souls of the wicked will perish (30:5). In 39:3–8 and 40:1–4 it is said that the kingdom of the Messiah will be revealed at the time of the fourth kingdom (Rome). The Messiah will kill the leader of that kingdom near Mount Zion and his own reign will last until the end of the world. In chs. 72–74 the Messiah gathers the nations, spares some, and the age of incorruptibility begins. In summation we have three details of particular importance: the messianic kingdom will last only until the end of the world of corruption; the end is near; and the consummation will be associated with the fall of Rome.

IV Ezra 7:26–30 is a passage which might cast most light on Revelation. We are told that a city which is now invisible will appear, and land now concealed will be seen. The Messiah will be revealed with those who did not taste death, and the survivors will rejoice for four hundred years. At the end of these years "my son, the Messiah" shall die, along with all other human beings. The world will return to primeval silence for seven days. There will be a general judgment, the resurrection of the good and the wicked, and the final end. That time is near.

The early rabbis gave a good deal of attention to calculating the duration of the messianic age; see Strack and Billerbeck, *Kommentar zum Neuen Testament,* III, 823–27; IV, 799–1015. There was no settled tradition except that it would be a limited intermediate period between the present age and the age to come. The following list comes from Strack and Billerbeck, III, 826:

Eliezer ben Hyrcanus (A.D. 90) suggested a thousand years;
Joshua (A.D. 90), two thousand years;
Eleazar ben Azariah (A.D. 100), seventy years;
Akiba (A.D. 135), forty years;
Jose of Galilee (A.D. 110), sixty years;
Dasa (A.D. 180), six hundred years;
Eliezer ben Jose of Galilee (A.D. 150), four hundred years;
A number of rabbis about A.D. 90 said two thousand years.

Eliezer is the oldest rabbinic authority to name the extent of a thousand years for the messianic period.

Bailey concludes with the observation of Strack (III, 827) "that the possibility that the Apocalypse depends for its thousand-year period upon Jewish tradition cannot be denied upon chronological grounds." Bailey's concluding remark is as follows: "The evidence in Apocalypse of Baruch, 4 Ezra, Secrets of Enoch, and rabbinical sources abundantly justifies the statement that both this particular concept, and the general framework of the eschatology of the Apocalypse of John, are accepted views of time and community and are the background of his thinking and his description of the millennial period" (p. 187). The present writer would concur. In keeping with the rest of Revelation 4–22, the verses 20:4–6 are primarily of Jewish origin not Christian.

XXI. SATAN UNCHAINED
(20:7–10)

20 7 And when the thousand years are completed, Satan will be released from his prison, 8 and will come out to deceive the nations which are at the four corners of the earth, that is, Gog and Magog, to gather them for battle; and their number will be like the sand of the sea. 9 And they marched up over the broad earth and surrounded the camp of the saints and the beloved city; but fire came down from heaven and consumed them; 10 and the devil who had deceived them was thrown into the lake of fire and brimstone where the beast and the false prophet were, and they will be tormented day and night forever and ever.

NOTES

20:8. *to deceive the nations . . . to gather them*. This reading implies that Satan will deceive the nations in order to gather them for battle. The implication is lost in ℵ 051 2059s al g vg by the addition of "and": "to deceive . . . and to gather."

nations. According to the accusative in apposition, "Gog and Magog," the nations appear to be identified with these mythical characters.

Gog and Magog. The land of Gog is mentioned in Jubilees 8:25; cf. 7:19, 9:8. Sibylline Oracles 3:319 ff., 512 proclaim woe against both Gog and Magog. The origin of Gog as the personification of evil is unknown. In the OT, Magog is the land from which Gog will lead his forces against the Lord (see COMMENT). Here Magog is transformed into a personage.

sand of the sea. This text may be influenced by Josh 11:4 (the Canaanites, Hittites, Perizzites, etc., gathered against Israel) and Judg 7:12 (the camels of the Midianites, and the Amalekites, and all the people of the east fighting against Gideon) where the enemy is described as "as numerous as grains of sand on the seashore" (AB).

9. *they marched up*. The change from the future tense in vss. 7–8 to past tense from here through vs. 10a is curious. One presumes the subject of the verb is Gog, Magog, and Satan, but it may also include the nations which are at the four corners of the earth, especially if these are identified with mythical figures; see NOTE on vs. 8.

camp. Gr. *parembolē*. This is a military term found in both secular and religious literature. It is used of the Israelite camp in Exod 29:14. Heb 13:11

takes "camp" in the literal sense, but 13:13, "let us go out to him (Jesus) 'outside the camp'" uses it metaphorically in the context of repudiating transitory and impermanent things (H. W. Montefiore, *Epistle to the Hebrews*, p. 246). It is associated with aspiring towards the city which is to come, "for we do not have here a continuing city, but we are looking for the [city] which is to come" (Heb 13:14, AB).

beloved city. In our apocalypse, as it stands, we appear to have the wrong order, but if we change the text according to Gaechter's suggestion (see Introduction, "The Last Two Chapters"), the reference to an encampment of the saints in 20:9 and to the city here is understandable. The corrupt earthly Jerusalem is destroyed and replaced by the millennial Jerusalem, "the beloved city," a term not used of the earthly Jerusalem in Revelation, and then this millennial Jerusalem is transformed into the heavenly Jerusalem. Some find the assault on the beloved city inconceivable, but there is a close parallel in IV Ezra 13:5, 30–38. Sibylline Oracles 3:652–706 speaks of the advent of a king who will give relief from war and at whose coming the people of God will enjoy excellent wealth. However, the kings of the nations shall come against the land and seek to ravish the shrine of God and the noblest men. They will form a ring around the city (vs. 667). But then, fiery swords shall fall from heaven and God shall win the victory. There will be lamenting throughout the breadth of the land; after this the sons of God shall live quietly round the temple and He will protect them, "encircling them, as it were, with a wall of flaming fire" (vs. 706, APCh, II, 391). In Revelation, however, the coming of the Messiah or king is merely presumed or implicit.

from heaven. In 046 82, 2329 al g sy^ph, also P (1) 1006, 1611 (2059s) pm vg sy^h TR; R^m the phrase reads "from God from heaven."

COMMENT

The immunity from Satanic attacks is removed at the end of the thousand years and the enemy rallies his earthly allies to fight against the beloved city, presumably the millennial Jerusalem (vs. 9). The earthly allies are epitomized in Gog and Magog. They symbolize the climax of evil and are overcome by the direct action of God. As Caird, p. 257, observes "the myth of Gog enshrines a deep insight into the resilience of evil. The powers of evil have a defence in the depth, which enables them constantly to summon reinforcements from beyond the frontiers of men's knowledge and control." The mention of Gog and Magog is clearly a reflection of Ezek 38–39. In Ezek 38:1–3 the prophet is told to prophesy against Gog of the land of Magog, and in 39:1, 6 the same admonition is given but God also says that He will send fire on Magog and those who dwell in the coastlands.

Gog and Magog appear also in nonbiblical literature. In the Palestinian Targum to Exod 40 the laver is to be anointed on account of Joshua, the chief of the Sanhedrin, and of the Messiah of Ephraim "by whose hand the house of Israel is to vanquish Gog and his confederates at the end of days." In the Jerusalem Targum Eldad and Medad prophesy that at the end of days

Gog and Magog and armies will rise against Jerusalem and will be vanquished by the Messiah. Gog is also mentioned in the Palestinian Targum to Num 24: 17, where it is said that all the carcasses of the armies of Gog who battle against Israel will fall before the Messiah; cf. Jerusalem Targum to Deut 32:39. *Eduyoth* 2:10 states that the judgment of Gog and Magog will last for twelve months. They are associated with the rebellious nations referred to in Ps 2, *Abodah Zarah* 3b, *Berakoth* 7b, etc. In Josephus (*Ant.* 1.123) Gog is identified with the Scythians. From these references (see also NOTE on vs. 8, "Gog and Magog") one can see that the concept of Gog and Magog was well established by the first century A.D.

The forces of Gog and Magog are said to be as numerous as the sand of the sea. There is a certain irony in this, for in Gen 22:17 God promises Abraham that his descendants will be as "the sands on the seashore" (AB). Further, the drama is heightened because the Jewish reader would know that thrice Ezekiel predicts Gog will come when Israel is living in security (Ezek 38:8, 11, 14). It is said the forces "marched up" (*anabainō*). This may be used with reference to the hill country of central Palestine and the situation of Jerusalem. They proceed through "the broad earth" which may refer to either a widespread invasion as in Hab 1:6 or their goal, namely, Jerusalem; in Ezek 38:12 Jerusalem is called the center or the navel of the earth.

The evil forces encircle the camp of the saints. This recalls not only the Israelite camp in the wilderness but also of the camps mentioned in 1QM. In Numbers the tribes are divided into camps as follows:

Camp of Judah	Camp of Reuben	Camp of Ephraim	Camp of Dan
Judah	Reuben	Ephraim	Dan
Issachar	Simeon	Manesseh	Asher
Zebulun	Gad	Benjamin	Naphtali

(Yadin, p. 46). In 1QM "camp" denotes both a military grouping and a place of encampment in the field (Yadin, p. 47).

The saints are rescued by fire descending from heaven and consuming their enemies. The picture is less graphic than Ezek 38:22 where God rains upon the hordes of Gog "torrential rains and hailstones, fire and brimstone. So I will show my greatness and my holiness and make myself known in the eyes of many nations. Then they will know that I am the Lord" (RSV); cf. Ezek 39:6.

Finally the devil is thrown into the lake of fire with his colleagues. Unlike the sources cited above the Anointed One does not conquer Gog and Magog. If he is to be identified with the rider on the white horse, then his work is accomplished by crushing the terrestrial forces. God (the Father) Himself conquers the supernatural.

XXII. THE LAST JUDGMENT
(20:11–15)

20 11 Then I saw a great white throne and Him Who sat upon it from Whose presence earth and sky fled away, and no place was found for them. 12 And I saw the dead, great and small, standing before the throne, and books were opened; also another book was opened, which is the book of life; and the dead were judged by what was written in the books according to their deeds. 13 And the sea gave up the dead in it, and Death and Hades gave up the dead in them, and all were judged according to their deeds. 14 And Death and Hades were thrown into the lake of fire. This is the second death, the lake of fire. 15 And if anyone's name was not found written in the book of life, he was thrown into the lake of fire.

NOTES

20:11. *white throne.* In I Enoch 18:8 the visionary sees seven mountains of magnificent stones and "the middle one reached to heaven like the throne of God, of alabaster, and the summit of the throne was of sapphire" (APCh, II, 200). The color white is mentioned many times in Revelation and always with a good connotation.

Him Who sat. The same phrase is used in the throne vision in the first part of the apocalypse (Rev 4), for the riders on the four horses (Rev 6), and for the rider on the white horse (Rev 19).

earth and sky fled away. Cf. the wrenching apart of the heavens rolled up like a scroll in 6:14. Apocalyptic events are usually heralded by the fleeing of the immovable, e.g. mountains, rivers.

12. *of life.* TI.

14. *Death and Hades.* For a similar thought cf. II Baruch 21:23, "Bring to an end therefore henceforth mortality. And reprove accordingly the angel of death, and let Thy glory appear, and let the might of Thy beauty be known, and let Sheol be sealed so that from this time forward it may not receive the dead, and let the treasuries of souls restore those which are enclosed in them" (APCh, II, 494–95); cf. II Baruch 30:2. See NOTE on 2:11.

This is the second death, the lake of fire. Completely omitted in 051 1, 2059s al bo, but vg^{s,cl} sy^{ph} TR omit only "lake of fire." Cf. 21:28. For the significance of the second death, see NOTE on 2:11.

COMMENT

This section appears to depict the universal judgment of the dead. In Rev 14:14–20, 19:11–21, the Christ appears to judge the living, but here the final judgment seems to be given to God the Father. In assigning the final judgment to the Father, the author differs, as Charles observes, from John 5:22; Matt 7: 22–23, 25:31–46; Acts 17:31; II Cor 5:10; i.e. he differs from NT teaching. In other places, too, he shows judgment as the prerogative of God; cf. Rev 6: 10, 16:7, 19:2. On the other hand I Enoch 45:3 shows the Elect One sitting on the throne of glory and judging the works of men, and in I Enoch 69:27 the sum of judgment is given to the Son of Man (although this may suggest the judgment of the living rather than the dead since the Son of Man causes sinners to be destroyed "from off the face of the earth").

There is evidence here of influence by Dan 7:9–14, where the Ancient of Days (God) takes his seat, the court sits in judgment, and books are opened. However, it does not seem to be as transcendent as Daniel. Indeed, it may be closer to I Enoch 90:20 where a throne is erected in the pleasant land and the Lord of the sheep takes his seat and sealed books are brought to him; cf. I Enoch 47:3, IV Ezra 6:17–20, II Baruch 24:1. As Caird, p. 258, remarks, "the judgment itself is described with stark economy."

In vs. 12 the "books" seem to be distinguished from the "other book" in that the books appear to record works and the single book of life to have the names inscribed. Charles, in his note on I Enoch 47:3 (APCh, II, 216), remarks that there appear to be references to books recording good and evil deeds in Mal 3:16, Jubilees 30:22, Dan 7:10 (cf. also Ascension of Isaiah 9:22) but that in I Enoch these books seem to record evil deeds only (as in Isa 65:6, I Enoch 81:4, 89:61–77, 90:17, 20, 98:7, 8, 104:7–10, II Baruch 24:1). The book of the living was probably equivalent to the register of Israelite citizens in the OT; cf. Exod 32:32, etc., Ps 69:28, Isa 4:3, Jubilees 30:20, 22; cf. also I Enoch 103:4 for the memorial of the righteous.

Specific mention of those who died at sea occurs in vs. 13 probably because there was a tradition that only those who died on dry land would rise from the dead. It is unclear why Death should give up the dead, but the reference to Hades is more explicable. It suggests that there will be a resurrection of the wicked. Hades was the abode of the wicked souls, and according to some traditions only the souls of the righteous would be resurrected. Finally, Death and Hades are cast into the lake of fire, signaling the end of the mortal era or the first age. This creates a natural transition to the new heaven and the new earth discussed in the next chapter, Rev 21.

XXIII. THE ETERNAL JERUSALEM
(21:1–4c 22:3–5 21:5a, 4d, 5b, 6, 7 22:6–7a, 8–13, 7b, 17b, 18–19)

21 ¹ And I saw a new heaven and a new earth; for the first heaven and the first earth had passed away, and the sea was no more. ² And I saw the holy city, the new Jerusalem, descending out of heaven from God, prepared as a bride adorned for her husband. ³ And I heard a great voice from the throne, saying, "Behold, the dwelling of God is with mankind. He will dwell with them, and they shall be His people, and God Himself will be with them, ⁴ᵃ and He will wipe away every tear from their eyes, ⁴ᵇ and death shall be no more, ⁴ᶜ neither mourning nor crying nor pain anymore."

22 ³ There shall no more be anything cursed. Indeed, the throne of God and of the Lamb will be in her, and His servants shall worship Him ⁴ and they will see His face, and His name shall be on their foreheads. ⁵ᵃ And night will be no more; ⁵ᵇ and they need no light of lamp or light of sun, for the Lord God will shed His light upon them, and they will reign forever and ever.

21 ⁵ᵃ And He Who sat upon the throne said, "Behold, I make all things new." ⁴ᵈ For the former things have passed away. ⁵ᵇ Also He said, "Write this, for these words are trustworthy and true." ⁶ And He said to me, "It is done! I am the Alpha and the Omega, the Beginning and the End. To the thirsty I will give water without price from the fountain of the water of life.

Clausula

⁷ He who conquered shall have this heritage, and I will be his God and he shall be My son.

Conclusion of the Visions

22 ⁶ And he said to me, "These words are trustworthy and true. And the Lord, the God of the spirits of the prophets, has sent His angel to show His servants what must soon take place. ⁷ᵃ And behold, I am coming soon."

⁸ I John am he who heard and saw these things. And when I heard and saw them, I fell down to worship at the feet of the angel who showed them to me; ⁹ but he said to me, "You must not do that! I

am a fellow servant with you and your brethren the prophets, and with those who keep the words of this book. Worship God."

10 And he said to me, "Do not seal up the words of the prophecy of this book; for the critical time is near. 11 Let the evildoer still be evil, and the filthy still be filthy, and the righteous still do right, and the holy still be holy." 12 "Behold, I am coming soon, bringing My recompense, to repay everyone according to his deeds. 13 I am the Alpha and the Omega, the First and the Last, the Beginning and the End."

7b Blessed is he who keeps the words of the prophecy of this book.

17b Indeed, let him who is thirsty come, let him who desires take the water of life without price.

Conclusion of the Book

18 I warn everyone who hears the words of the prophecy of this book; if anyone adds to these words, God will add to him the plagues described in this book; 19 and if anyone takes away from the words of the book of this prophecy, God will take away his share in the tree of life and in this holy city, which are described in this book.

Notes

21:1. *a new heaven and a new earth.* Gr. *kainos,* "new." Cf. Isa 65:17, 66:22. Note the repetition of "new." The newness might imply ritual purity or greater power.

the sea was no more. The author may be thinking of the sea as a symbol of evil, danger, and distress. In Ugaritic literature Baal conquers Yamm, the sea god. But he may also be introducing an Exodus theme, for in a certain sense, one could say the sea was no more when the Israelites walked on dry land through the Reed Sea. Cf. also Sibylline Oracles 5:158 ff., Assumption of Moses 10:6.

2. *new Jerusalem.* For more details concerning the heavenly Jerusalem in later rabbinic texts, see Volz, pp. 371–78. For the idea of the heavenly temple in Philo, see McKelvey, pp. 38–41. The concept of the heavenly tabernacle/temple sometimes overlaps with that of the heavenly Jerusalem; cf. I Enoch 14:16–20, 25:3, 71:5–7, 85–90, Testament of Levi 3:4–9 (cf. 5:1–2).

descending out of heaven. For the heavenly Jerusalem see Gal 4:26, Heb 12:22.

bride. The idea of the city of Jerusalem as a bride occurs also in the Targum to Ps 48. The Targum on the Song of Songs sees the bride as the assembly of Israel.

adorned. The adjective may suggest that the bride was bedecked with jewels.

For the symbolism of jewels, see the present author's article. "Orthodox Judaism and the Heavenly Jerusalem," in the forthcoming festschrift in honor of Professor David Daube. The adornment of the bride may be contrasted with the simple dress of linen mentioned before in 19:7–8. For the ethical significance of the bride's "ornaments," see Isa 49:18, 61:10, III Macc 6:1, I Peter 3:3, I Tim 2:9–10, II Cor 11:2, Eph 5:26–27.

3. *from the throne.* P **046 051** 82, 1006, 1611, 2059s, 2329 pl g sy TR read instead, "from heaven."

dwelling. Gr. *Skēnē,* from the same root as *Shekinah,* "God's presence."

people. Gr. *laos.* A 1, 2059s, 2329 pm 1r TR read *laoi,* "peoples." P **046 051** 82, 1006, 1611 al lat sy keep the singular. See COMMENT, p. 368.

4a. *He will wipe away.* A 1, 2059s pm vg Tert TR read "God will wipe away."

4b–c. Notice that the exact opposite is said of Babylon in 17:5; there will be death, mourning, and pain for her.

22:3. *more.* This is replaced by "there" in **051,** 1, 2059, 2329 al.

cursed. Gr. *katathema.* This word is found only here in the NT and nowhere in the LXX. There are several possible renderings: curse; cursed person; or Heb. *ḥerem,* the highest form of excommunication in Judaism. This last meaning would fit well into the context of 21:3, 7, God dwelling in the midst of the elect, and the explicit exclusion of the defiled and immoral in 21:8, 27, 22:15. If this is the meaning then the word catches up the idea of mourning and death found in 21:4, for these features would accompany excommunication which involved ostracism from both the religious and the social community. However, in the light of the prominence in Revelation of the concept of the Holy War, another meaning might be suggested. The *ḥerem* associated with the Holy War was the anathema perpetrated on the vanquished and their goods. It meant that the fruits of victory were given over to God; see Deut 7:2, 20:17, Josh 8:2, I Sam 15:3, and Boling's COMMENT on Judg 8:22–29 in AB, vol. 6A (1975). In theory everyone and everything was destroyed save the metal objects which were dedicated to Yahweh (Joshua 6:18–24). See de Vaux, pp. 260–61.

and of the Lamb. This phrase is suspect and some critics see it as an insertion. Certainly it is awkward in the context, for the last part of the verse reads "and *His* servants will worship *Him*" (third person singular), vs. 4 reads *"His* face, and *His* name," and vs. 5 refers to God but not to the Lamb (in contrast to 21:23, which mentions that the Lamb is the light of the city). One would expect the third person plural instead of singular if the Lamb was originally part of the text. Rev 22:3–4, therefore, should probably read, "and the throne of God will be in her (the city) and His servants will worship Him . . ."

4. *see His face.* McKelvey, pp. 37–38, draws attention to the Qumran text which portrays the priest "like an angel of the Presence in the holy dwelling (to serve) the glory of the Lord of hosts (forever. And thou) shalt be a faithful servant in the temple of the kingdom, sharing the lot of the angels of the Presence, and in the counsel of the community (with the holy ones) forever and forever and for all eternity" (exemplar b of 1QS 4:25 ff.; see DJD, I, 126).

foreheads. Gr. *metōpon.* In the NT this word is found only in Revelation, where it occurs in three different connections, the foreheads of those who are sealed for God, the foreheads of those who bear the mark of the beast, and the harlot's forehead which bears "a mysterious name, Babylon the great, the mother of harlots and of the abominations of the land" (17:5).

5a. *night.* In ancient times night was given over to evil and magic, for then the demons had special power. Hence this apocalypse states that in the time of judgment even the night stars will be darkened (8:12). Job 7:1–8 complains of the length of the night. In the Hellenistic world night was personified as a goddess who was feared and respected even by Zeus. In Hesiod she is born of Chaos, associating the darkness of night with Chaos and Tartarus, the infernal region of Hades. In the place of the celestial bodies such as the sun to give light, or artificial lighting such as lamps, the blessed have the light of God, the *Shekinah;* cf. Isa 60:19. Philo expresses this belief in *De Josepho* 24.145–46:

> . . . while earthly things are brim full of disorder and confusion and in the fullest sense of the word discordant and inharmonious, because in them deep darkness reigns while in heaven all moves in most radiant light, or rather heaven is light itself most pure and unalloyed. And indeed if one be willing to look into the inner realities he will find that heaven is an eternal day, wherein there is no night or any shadow, because around it shine without ceasing unquenchable and undefiled beams of light.

Paul uses night with reference to the time before the consummation of God's rule (Rom 13:12). The Gospel of John also speaks of lack of faith as darkness, e.g. John 3:19. G. Vos, in *Pauline Eschatology* (Eerdmans, 1972), pp. 82–83, calls the Day of Yahweh "the light-reign (day) of Jehovah."

more. As in 22:3, this word is replaced by "there" in 1, 2059s al TR.

21:5b. *He said.* ℵ P 051 1, 1006, 2059s pm vg[s,c1] co TR read, "He said to me."

6. *am.* This verb appears in A 1006 al lat TR.

the Alpha and the Omega. For a discussion of this title see NOTE on 1:8.

the Beginning and the End. This declaration is found in Isa 48:12b, where it is followed by a reference to God's creative power.

water. There is no mention as such in the Isaiah text 48:12 (see previous NOTE) of the "water of life." In the Qumran texts one finds references to the garden of paradise, and water and trees of life. All these are associated with the foundation and future of the community. Gärtner, p. 28, thinks that the idea of plantation and water is associated with Jewish speculations about the rock of the temple and paradise. Cf. also exemplar b of 1QS 1:3–4 (DJD, I): "May He open for thee from the heights of heaven the everlasting spring which shall n[ever run d]ry! . . ." 22:6–9. They are a repetition of 21:5b, 19:9b–10c.

22:10. *Do not seal up.* The opposite command is given to Enoch (cf. I Enoch 1:2); he is to "seal up" his message until the time for disclosure comes. However, some of the instructions received by Enoch and written down by him appear to have been used by the human race; cf. I Enoch 104:10 – 105:2; II Enoch 33:5–6, 8–10, 35:1–3.

11. This is a couplet made of parallel clauses, with "evil" balanced by "righteous," "holy" balanced by "holy."

filthy. Cf. Zech 3:3–4; in this context Joshua the high priest is accused by Satan before God, but the Lord describes him as "a brand plucked from the fire." Joshua's filthy garments were removed at the command of an angel and after this it was announced to him "Behold, I have taken your iniquity away from you, and I will clothe you with rich apparel." And then they put a clean turban on his head and clothed him with the garments.

Filthiness, Gr. *rhuparos,* may be used in either a ritual or a moral sense, and is often used, as in Zech 3:3–4, to describe clothes (cf. vs. 14).

do right. In 2060 pc vg[s,cl] Epist Lugd apud Eus TR the phrase is "be righteous."

12. *coming.* This is used in the eschatological sense (see Comment, pp. 368–69).

according to his deeds. Translator has pluralized "deeds." Cf. Jer 17:10, Ps 61:12, Prov 24:12b, Rom 2:6, I Clement 34:3.

18. *God will add to him.* A different word order appears in א 051 2059s pm. A omits "to him."

plagues. See above, p. 339.

19. *takes away.* Cf. the remark of Rabbi Meir (*Sotah* 20a) "My son, be careful; for it is a divine work: if thou writest, were it but a word more or less, it is as if you were destroying the word."

COMMENT

The chief portion of Part Four of this apocalypse presents some of the most exquisite and hopeful eschatology in the NT. Four themes are interwoven, the new creation (21:1, 4d); the new Exodus or Sinai tradition (21:2, 3); the new city (21:2–3); the state of unmitigated bliss (21:4abc, 22:3).

First of all one notices the stress on *kainos,* "new." The seer witnesses not only a new heaven and a new earth, but also a new Jerusalem (21:2), and the novelty reaches its climax in the words of 21:5a "Behold, I make all things new." This idea of newness is not found in the description of the millennial Jerusalem in 21:9 – 22:2; that Jerusalem, which comes down from heaven (21:10), is merely described as the "beloved city." Newness is emphasized by the author's stress on the first heaven and the first earth disappearing. The concept of a new heaven and a new earth is not unbiblical, for it is bound up with the exodus and creation motifs in the Book of Isaiah, e.g. Isa 65:17: "For look! I create a new heaven and a new earth. The past will not be remembered, it will not enter your mind" (AB). Further, Wisd Sol 19:6, which appears to be a Midrash on Exodus, sees the miracles which occurred at the time of the exodus as a new fashioning of nature, almost a new creation.

The idea of the renewal of creation is elaborated in the pseudepigraphical literature, e.g. in Jubilees 1:29 where, importantly for our text, it is associated with the idea of the sanctuary of the Lord in Jerusalem, on Mount Zion; cf.

I Enoch 72:1; II Baruch 32:6, 57:2. In I Enoch 45:4–5 the transformation of heaven and earth and their becoming a blessing (contrast the cursing of the earth at the time of Adam's transgression) follows the judgment by the Elect One. II Baruch 51–52 is more graphic and refers to the transformation of human bodies into the splendor of angels.

The theme of the new Jerusalem is also elaborated in the pseudepigrapha. II Baruch 4:2–7 speaks specifically of this belief, saying that the present city "is not that which is revealed with Me." This passage also reflects the paradise and Exodus themes: "that which was prepared beforehand here from the time when I took counsel to make Paradise, and showed it to Adam before he sinned," and "also I showed it to Moses on Mount Sinai" (APCh, II, 482). IV Ezra 10:54 distinguishes the new city from its predecessor, as "the City of the Most High" where "no building-work of man could endure" (APCh, II, 607); cf. 9:24. Later we are told that, although the city is invisible at present, it will be revealed to men (13:36; cf. 7:26). Strack and Billerbeck give a number of late *midrashim* which speak of the heavenly Jerusalem, e.g. *Bet Ha-Midrash* 1.55.23: "When Moses saw the love which God had for Israel he said to Him: Lord of the universe, bring her (Israel) and plant her there in the holy land and let it be a plantation which shall never be uprooted. Let Jerusalem come down from heaven and never destroy it. Gather there the dispersed of Israel that they may live there in safety" (McKelvey, p. 35); cf. *Baba Bathra* 75b.

In our text the new Jerusalem comes down from heaven from God arrayed like a bride for her husband. Rev 21:2 resumes the thought of 19:7, which refers to the marriage of the Lamb. However, while the bride in 21:1–2 is on earth, the scene in 19:1–10 takes place wholly in heaven and is the prelude to what occurs in this section. There are two important points made here about the new Jerusalem. First, the city comes down from heaven, thus fusing the celestial and the terrestrial; the new Jerusalem is probably to be the center of the new creation. Second, and more important, the city, unlike the millennial city, is not made of inanimate material but is personified as a bride, bringing a personal and active aspect to the picture. The concept is a biblical one, an elaboration of the theme of Israel as bride. It is founded in Isa 61:10 which speaks of God clothing Israel with the garments of salvation as a bride adorns herself with her jewels, and in Isa 62:4–5 (AB) which is even more pertinent:

> You will no longer be called Abandoned, nor will
>   your land be called Desolate; (Cf. Rev 18:19)
> You will be called "She is my Delight," and your
>   land will be called Married;
> For Yahweh delights in you, and your land will be married.
> For as a young man marries a virgin, so your builder
>   will marry you;
> Like the joy of the groom in his bride is the joy
>   of your God in you. (Cf. Hosea 2:14–23)

The symbol of Jerusalem as a bride is also dramatically portrayed in IV Ezra 10:25–28 in his vision of the woman who becomes a city; see J. M. Myers, *I & II Esdras*, AB, vol. 42 (1974), pp. 263–72, 279–80: when she was transformed she became the heavenly Jerusalem (the son, who dies, is the earthly counterpart). The bride appears to be the corporate personality, the true theocratic community. The voice from heaven (21:3) says "Behold, the dwelling (*skēnē*) of God is with mankind," and it seems to be identifying this "tabernacle" with the bride. The terminology used is that of the covenant. What we appear to have, therefore, is that to which we alluded in ch. 19, the Exodus concept of Israel married to God on the occasion of the giving of the Law on Mount Sinai and the descent of the cloud on the tabernacle. This is now repeated in a superior way. God dwells not in a tent but among His people; His real presence is there. In later texts God's presence is called the *Shekinah*, who was called the bride; cf. Rev 22:17.

The concept is in advance of the Qumran one discussed above which saw the covenanters' community as the new temple and described it with such expressions as "a foundation of truth," "a sanctuary in Aaron," and "a house of truth." As Gärtner, p. 23, asserts, the "community occupied the same position in the eyes of its members as did Jerusalem and the temple in the eyes of Judaism as a whole." The community is the true Jerusalem which replaces the holy city which would probably be restored at the end of days. In Revelation the action is on the part of God; the people may have prepared themselves but the more important feature is that His presence descends among them and the covenant is sealed again. If ideas similar to those found at Qumran have influenced our text, then the meaningfulness of 21:4 is increased. In 21:4 the author speaks in terms similar to those of Isa 25:8; God will swallow up death, wipe away tears and take away mourning. Considering the wars, persecutions, deaths, and calamities which raged in first-century A.D. Palestine, very often against such communities as Qumran, the importance of that promise cannot be exaggerated. This is exactly opposite to the experience of the harlot, Babylon.

Having described the felicity of the new era, the author predicts that there will be no "curse," Gr. *katathema*, anymore (22:3). Rev 22:3 is influenced by Zech 14:11, which speaks of Jerusalem as inhabited and secure; the prophet mentions that there will be no more curse and there will be continual day (vs. 7; cf. Rev 22:5). The reader of Revelation may have been relieved by this statement if he did actually consider that the curses or punishments predicted in Deut 28 and the Holiness Code (see p. 292) to have been fulfilled, according to our text, in the seals, trumpets, bowls, and the destruction of the city. This verse would then confirm immunity from the seven-fold plagues. The immunity would be assured by the presence of the throne of God in the city; cf. I Kings 8:23–53, the prayer of Solomon. Thus, one moves towards the climax of the theocracy which has been in the process of establishment throughout our apocalypse.

We have pointed out that Revelation is a struggle between theocracy and the rule of satanic powers, and this section now shows us the victory of God. The Kingship is established; His throne, not that of an alien, is in the city. Not only is the Kingship of God established forever but the beatific vision will be granted to his servants (22:4). To see the face (or enter the presence) of an earthly monarch was a great honor, but to see God was unprecedented save in such modalities as Ezek 1 describes. The vision of God was even withheld from

Moses (Exod 33:11–23), for the Jews did not believe that it was possible to look upon the face of God and live. However, this privilege appears to have been promised to the faithful in messianic times, as attested in some of the pseudepigraphical literature, e.g. Testament of Zebulun 9:8, IV Ezra 7:97–99.

Associated in 22:4 with worshiping God and seeing his face is the notion, which the reader has encountered before, that God's name will be on the foreheads of the redeemed; cf. 7:3, 9:4, 14:1. The present context may indicate the writer has in mind the name of God on the forehead of the high priest, thus implying that now all the righteous are priests (cf. 20:6). They bear the name of Yahweh and stand in His presence, a privilege denied to all save the high priest on the Day of Atonement.

The transition from priestly worship to the absence of night (22:5) seems a little awkward but may be explained in the light of the Targum to Num 6 quoted below. The writer probably meant to recall the Aaronic blessing (Num 6:25–26) which follows the passage concerning the Nazirites consecrated to God. The prayer asks that God's face shine upon His people and give them peace. The Palestinian Targum to this passage in Numbers further illuminates Rev 22:5, in that it shows the blessing of the Lord as a special protection against night (Etheridge):

> . . . The Lord lift up His countenance upon thee, and grant thee peace. The Lord bless thee in all thy business, and keep thee from demons (liliths, that is, female demons) of the night, and things that cause terror, and from demons of the noon and of the morning, and from malignant spirits and phantoms. The Lord make His face to shine upon thee, when occupied in the law, and reveal to thee its secrets, and be merciful unto thee. . . .

The end of Rev 22:5 introduces the subject of the theocracy again, but we note that the righteous reign not only for the thousand years as in 20:6 but for eternity.

If we adopt Gaechter's order, the words of God from the throne (21:5ab, 4d, 5c–6, 7a) follow smoothly after the reference to the throne in 22:3. The words bring to a close the description of the new creation, summarizing as it were the main features. The title "The Alpha and the Omega" (see pp. 379–80) for God echoes Isa 44:6b (cf. 41:4, 48:12) where God makes a similar statement but adds that there is no God besides Him. The title is a succinct proclamation of the theocracy, the sovereignty of God. It is followed by another proclamation (that the thirsty will be given water from the fountain of life) also influenced by Isaiah (40:1, 3, 11), where God promises nourishment free of charge, an everlasting covenant, and that His word will not return to him without accomplishing the object for which it was sent. This is the only chapter in Deutero-Isaiah which mentions the everlasting dynasty promised to David, and it opens with an invitation to the thirsty. If the reader of our text were meant to recall all of Isa 40, which is possible, then he or she might see the clause in 21:5c, "these words (or oracles) are trustworthy and true," in the light of the assurance of the successful mission of Word promised in Isa 40, the oracle concerning the Davidic dynasty. In this way the clausula (21:7) is understandable for it is a quotation from II Sam 7:4–29, the oracle of Nathan promising the everlasting dynasty to David. The same promise is made to all those who are victorious. II Sam 7:14 was important to the Qumran covenanters. In the 4QFlorilegium (D-S), which is a midrash on the oracle and on Pss 1–2, the following points are made:

> no son of wickedness shall afflict Israel; no foreigner shall enter the sanctuary; the sanctuary will not be desecrated again; a sanctuary of people will be established; they will have rest from their enemies; the Branch of David will arise with the Interpreter of the Law; the tent of David will be restored.

Nearly all these have been predicted in this apocalypse. However, a more pertinent point is that the florilegium speaks of the "seed" of David who will be the "son" of God; cf. Rev 21:7b. This need not refer merely to an individual Messiah; both the OT and the Qumran texts vacillate between the individual and the collective. In the midrash it appears that the seed of David, who is the son of God, is to be linked with the idea of the "house" as the temple or community. Gärtner, pp. 35–42, thinks that "root," "house," and "tabernacle" of David might well refer to the community rather than the individual Messiah. Gaston, pp. 163–76, argues in a similar way, and observes that "son of God" may refer to the community which "along with the interpreter arises then not a Davidic messiah but a community which can be called son of God" (p. 166). In the same way Rev 21:7 may refer not to an individual but to the community mentioned already in 21:3, where the author, according to many manuscripts, has changed "people" to "peoples" in his OT quotation (see NOTE on 21:3, *people*). The community who overcomes inherits God's promises and beatitudes and becomes the son of God. However, this is not to preclude One who will be Son of God in a unique way.

If one follows Gaechter's order, the concluding words of Revelation (22:10–13) are spoken by the One who sits upon the Throne rather than by the interpreting angel; cf. 22:8–10. The words are both surprising and important. The seer is bidden not to seal up the words of the prophecy, and is told that the time is near. This is in direct contradiction to the instructions received by Daniel: "seal up the vision, for it pertains to many days hence" (Dan 8:26, RSV), and "But you, Daniel, shut up the words, and seal the book, until the time of the end" (Dan 12:4, RSV). It also differs from I Enoch 1:2 which speaks of Enoch understanding what he saw "but not for this generation, but for a remote one which is to come." In contrast the time of our apocalypse is the time for breaking seals (chs. 5–6). The words in our present text bring a sense of urgency and imminence. The news is to be broadcast for the time of crisis (Gr. *kairos,* "critical time") is near. During this time judgment (by mankind) is to be suspended. This seems to be the import of the *laissez-faire* message in vs. 11. The message is strange. It appears to mean that the time for repentance is no longer available; it seems to contrast with Dan 12:10 which speaks of many being "refined, purified and tested." A statement with such an implication does not seem to be consonant with the preaching of John the Baptist or Jesus but might have been the sentiment of many orthodox Jews as the fall of Jerusalem approached. Vs. 12 tends to confirm this interpretation. It echoes Isa 40:10; Pss 28:4, 62:12; Jer 17:10, all of which refer to God as the One who brings recompense for good or bad. Such retribution could be seen in the fall of the Holy City. Vs. 13 proves that the preceding statements do come from the mouth of God.

If vss. 7b, 17b follow next, we have a final beatitude promising felicity to those who keep the words of the prophecy of this book and another allusion to the logion from Isa 55:1 which uses the symbols of thirst and water to represent drinking in the Word of God. The Targum to Isa 56:1, 3, reads that all who wish may learn the Word, without payment, and God will make an everlasting covenant with them: it takes bread and water in a spiritual sense.

Revelation ends (22:18–19) with a solemn curse upon those who will alter its message. This curse is in true Deuteronomic style. A similar warning is found in Deut 4:2 (cf. Deut 12:32). Such admonitions are also found in non-biblical literature, e.g. I Enoch 104:10–13, which expresses both the fear that sinners will alter the word and the hope that it will be a joy and source of wisdom to the righteous: the righteous may have the books. Cf. Rev 20:12. Perhaps an even closer parallel is found in the Letter of Aristeas, which contains a legend describing how the LXX was miraculously written. It is dated somewhere between 200 B.C. and A.D. 33. Lines 310–311 refer to a curse on anyone who should alter the words and end with the statement, "This was a very wise precaution to insure that the book might be preserved for all the future time unchanged."

Revelation, therefore, ends in a way similar to some of the canonical and the noncanonical Jewish literature. Yet, if my thesis is correct, Dr. Freedman points out to me the irony in the notion that a Christian writer took the Jewish apocalypse and violated the admonition by adding to and altering the original. I should answer that in the strength of Jesus' power he did not fear the curse. There is no parallel to this threat in the NT. It is, however, consonant with the austerity of such "anti-Jerusalem" communities as Qumran (cf. 1QS 2:11–18) and with the woeful cry of the prophet Jesus son of Ananias before the fall of the Beloved City. It is perhaps significant that the son of Ananias cried: ". . . a voice against Jerusalem and the sanctuary, a voice against the bridegroom and the bride, a voice against all the people" (*War* 6.301). The bridegroom (the Lamb) in our apocalypse rejects the old Jerusalem and espouses the new Jerusalem. This will be a central theme in Luke's two volumes.

On the whole the concept of the heavenly Jerusalem and the heavenly temple is present throughout Rev 4–22 and is far more prominent than the concept of the millennial Jerusalem which occurs only in 21:9 – 22:2. Thus, e.g. ch. 4 is a vision of heavenly worship around the throne of God; ch. 5 introduces a lamb as though slain, and liturgical features such as harps, bowls of incense, and the prayers of the saints. Ch. 7 presents the great multitude, the scene which may recall the Feast of Tabernacles or the Feast of Pentecost; ch. 8 mentions more liturgical equipment, such as trumpets, a golden censer, the golden altar, and the fire from the altar. Rev 14:19 refers directly to God's temple in heaven and the ark of His covenant within the temple. Ch. 14 seems to fuse the heavenly worship with the earthly, for the Lamb is standing on

Mount Zion but the one hundred and forty-four thousand who are with him sing a new song "before the throne and before the four living creatures and before the elders." In 14:15 one angel comes out of the temple, in 14:17 another, and in 14:18 a third comes from the altar. In ch. 15 the seer witnesses another portent in heaven, seven angels with seven plagues; then (vs. 5) he sees the sanctuary of the tent of witness in heaven.

Thus, Revelation clearly accepts the principle of a temple together with its liturgical equipment in heaven, and therefore ch. 22 comes as a climax. Perhaps the heavenly temple and the heavenly city are synonymous with each other and thus they come down from heaven as a dwelling of God with men.

BIBLIOGRAPHY

Bailey, J. W. JBL 53 (1934), 170–87.

Baillet, M. "Fragments araméens de Qumrân 2," RB 62 (1955), 228, 243.

Betz, O. *What Do We Know About Jesus?*

Black, M. *The Dead Sea Scrolls and Christian Origins.*

Boismard, M. E. RB 56 (1949), 507–41.

Bousset, W. *Die Offenbarung Johannis.*

Charles, R. H. *Revelation.*

Farrer, A. *A Rebirth of Images.*

Flusser, D. "Two Notes on the Midrash on 2 Sam. 7 (4QFlorilegium)," *Israel Exploration Journal* 9 (1959), 99–109.

Ford, J. M. "The Heavenly Jerusalem and Orthodox Judaism," forthcoming in Festschrift in honor of David Daube.

Gaechter, P. TS 10 (1949), 483–521.

Gärtner, B. *The Temple and the Community in Qumran and the New Testament.* Cambridge University Press, 1965.

Gaston, L. *No Stone on Another.* Leiden: Brill, 1970.

Gaster, M. *The Samaritans.*

Ginzberg, L. *The Legends of the Jews,* I–VIII.

Macdonald, J. *The Theology of the Samaritans.*

McKelvey, R. J. *The New Temple.*

Moffatt, J. *The Revelation of St. John the Divine.* London, 1910.

Montefiore, H. W. *Epistle to the Hebrews.* London: Black, 1964.

Montgomery, J. A. *The Samaritans.*

Strack, H., and Billerbeck, P. *Kommentar zum Neuen Testament aus Talmud und Midrasch.*

de Vaux, R. *Ancient Israel.*

Volz, P. *Die Eschatologie der Jüdischen Gemeinde.*

Yadin, Y., ed. *The Scroll of the War of the Sons of Light Against the Sons of Darkness.*

Part Four: The Prophecies
to the Seven Churches

XXIV. FIRST INTRODUCTION AND
SALUTATION
(1:1–3)

1 ¹ A revelation concerning Jesus Christ, which God entrusted to
him, to disclose to His servants the events which are destined to happen soon; indeed, by sending it through His angel He has given a sign
of this beforehand to His servant John ² who was borne witness to
the Word of God, namely, the witness concerning Jesus Christ, all
that he saw. ³ Blessed is he who reads and those who listen to the
words of the prophecy and observe what is written in it; for the
critical time is near.

NOTES

1:1. *A revelation concerning Jesus Christ.* An alternative title, "an apocalypse of John of the divine word," appears in **046** 2329 al TR; R.

concerning Jesus Christ. Gr. *lēsou Christou.* The genitive may be objective,
i.e. a revelation about Jesus Christ, or subjective, i.e. given by Jesus to John.
The present writer prefers the former because Rev 4–11 predicts Jesus as the
Lamb but the Baptist does not seem to have identified him until his baptism
(John 1:33).

servants. The prophets may be meant. The phrase "His servants the prophets"
is found frequently in the Qumran scrolls, e.g. 1QpHab 2:9, 7:5, 4QpHosᵇ
2:5.

events which are destined to happen soon. A similar concept occurs in Dan
2:28–29 with reference to the revelation which God gave to King Nebuchadnezzar about the latter days; Daniel interpreted this for him.

are destined. Gr. *dei.* Predestination is a feature of apocalyptic literature and
is also found in Luke's Gospel. It denotes divine destiny and decree; cf. also
4:1, 22:6.

soon. This is also characteristic of our apocalyptic genre since it is crisis
literature and presupposes urgency; cf. II Thess 2:2 ff. The crisis appears more
urgent in Revelation than in earlier apocalyptic literature.

by sending. Gr. *apostellō,* lit. "he was sent." The same word is used of the
Baptist in John 1:6; John "was sent" by God. Here it was an angel who "was
sent" to John.

His angel. In apocalyptic literature an angel usually accompanies the seer on
his visionary journeys, e.g. Daniel, Enoch, and the Shepherd of Hermas. His
duty normally is to explain the meaning of the visions but he does not always

play this role in this apocalypse. The angelic companion may be a literary device, characteristic of later biblical and Judaic literature, e.g. Dan 9:21–22, to keep God at a distance by introducing an intermediary. This would be an adaptation of the OT "angel of Yahweh."

given a sign. Gr. *esēmanen.* In secular Greek this word can mean simply to inform or indicate beforehand. In the NT it is used, especially by John (12:33, 18:32, 21:19), in association with the manner of Jesus' death. The Gospel of John begins with seven signs; Revelation from ch. 12 onward is also a book of signs.

2. Boismard suggests a hendiadys (two words or phrases expressing one idea): "the Word of God as witnessed by Jesus Christ."

has borne witness. The tense here is epistolary aorist; one would be permitted to translate it as present tense. "Bear witness," Gr. *martureō,* is a favorite Johannine word. It occurs thirty-three times in the Gospel, ten times in the Johannine Epistles, and four times in Revelation (1:2, 22:16, 18, 20, twice in vss. 16, 18). It is significant that it occurs only at the beginning and the end of Revelation. This might provide one more argument in favor of the prologue and epilogue being regarded as later Christian additions. It would appear that the word "martyr" or "witness" does not approach the technical meaning which it bore later, i.e. bearing supreme witness to the faith by shedding one's blood.

Word. Gr. *Logos.* John bears witness to the *Logos.*

3. *Blessed.* This is the first of seven beatitudes in our apocalypse as it appears in the traditional order; cf. 14:13, 16:15, 19:9, 20:6, 22:7, 14. They may be contrasted with those found in Matt 5:3–12, Luke 6:20–21.

he who reads and those who listen. This suggests that the prophecies are to be related in a liturgical setting such as described in I Cor 14:26–33. Tertullian tells of a woman visionary who related her experiences after the service (*De Anima* 9).

the words. The singular appears in ℵ 046 1854 pc.

the critical time. The Greek, *kairos,* means "decisive moment." In Scripture *kairos* became an established term in salvation history, conveying the idea of the "time of judgment" and the "last time," which God brings. In the NT *kairos* is often the "fateful and decisive point" (cf. Mark 1:15), e.g. Jerusalem did not recognize the *kairos* when Jesus came (Luke 19:44); cf. Mark 12:56, Matt 16:3–4. Jesus' *kairos* is the hour of his death (Matt 26:18). The word is used with reference to the commencement of messianic power over demons (Matt 8:29), the persecution of believers (I Peter 4:17), the removal of the power of the restrainer, Gr. *katechon* (II Thess 2:6), final judgment of believers (I Cor 4:5), and general judgment of dead (Rev 11:18). On hearing this word, readers of John's Apocalypse would direct their thoughts to such themes.

COMMENT

The title ("A revelation concerning Jesus Christ") and three opening verses of this apocalypse seem to form an introduction either to Part One (chs. 4–11) or perhaps to Parts One, Two, and Three (chs. 4–11, 12–19, 20–22). To some extent the language resembles the portion of the Prologue to the Gospel of John which concerns the Baptist. There is a man called John (Rev 1:1, John 1:6). He was sent by God in John 1:6; in Rev 1:1 God sent through His angel a sign to His servant John. See NOTE on 1:1, "by sending." John's mission is to bear witness to the light which is the Word; cf. John 1:4, 8:12. In Rev 1:2 John bears witness to the Word; see NOTES on 1:2. The Baptist appears to have received a revelation concerning Jesus (John 1:15, 26–27, esp. 29–34). Further, the Baptist preached that the time was near; cf. Matt 3:2. This prologue, there-fore, may have been written by a disciple of the Baptist who recorded the visions of his master, especially those concerning the Lamb (cf. John 1:37) and the superiority of Jesus (cf. John 1:27, 34). The "critical time," (see NOTE, vs. 3) referred to is the first coming of Jesus, the Lamb, and his public ministry, death, and resurrection (cf. John 7:6–8), which culminates in his "hour" (Gr. *hōra;* cf. John 17:1, etc.).

1   4 John to the seven communities in Asia; grace to you and peace from He Who is and was and is to come and from the seven spirits which are before His throne 5 and from Jesus Christ, the faithful witness, the firstborn from the dead and the ruler of the kings of the earth. To him who loved us and freed us from our sins by his blood 6 and has established us as a priestly kingdom for God even his Father, to him be glory and power forever and ever, Amen. 7 See, he comes with the clouds and every eye will see him, even those who killed him, and all the tribes of the earth will beat their breasts in mourning over him, yes, may that happen. 8 I am the Alpha and the Omega, proclaims the Lord God, Who is and was and is to come, the Omnipotent.

Notes

1:4. *seven*. The number is chosen intentionally because it designates completeness, perfection, totality. In Judaism its sacredness was enhanced because the Sabbath was the seventh day, the sabbatical year was the seventh year, and the seventh sabbatical was the Jubilee, the year of release. In the temple were seven altars, seven lamps, etc.; cf. I Enoch 21:3–6, 61:11.

communities. Gr. *ekklesia*. The word does not appear in the Gospel of John.

Asia. Asia was coterminous with, i.e. had the same boundaries as, the empire of the Seleucids, the Greek dynasty that flourished in the last three centuries B.C. By Roman times it was identified with the Pergamene Kingdom when in 129 the possessions of Attalus III passed into Roman hands.

from He Who is and was and is to come. Gr. *apo hō ōn kai hō ēn kai hō erchomenos*. The preposition *apo*, "from," is followed by three nominative phrases joined by the connective *kai*. They are probably intended to be one word, an indeclinable noun, a paraphrase of the tetragrammaton, Y-H-W-H, "He who is."

McNamara, pp. 101–2, discusses the origin of the Divine Name in Revelation and concludes that the author did not borrow from non-Jewish Hellenism. The LXX has *hō ōn* referring to God in Jer 1:6, 14:13, 39(32):17; Wisd Sol 13:1; cf. Philo *De Abrahamo* 121, *Quod Deus sit Immutabilis* 69, Josephus *Ant.* 8.350. In rabbinic Judaism the Name in Exod 3:14 expresses the providence of God. McNamara cites *Mekilta,* tr., ed. Lauterbach, II, 31–32:

> Scripture, therefore, would not let the nations have an excuse for saying there are two powers, but declares: Adonai is a man of war (Ex 15, 3). He it is who was in Egypt, and he who was at the sea. It is he who was in the past and he who will be in the future. It is he who is in this world, and he who will be in the world to come, as it is said: "See now, it is I, even I, am He" (Dt 32, 39). And it also says: "Who hath wrought and done it? He that called the generations from the beginning. I, the Lord, who am the first, and with the last am the same" (Is 41, 4).

The Alphabet of Rabbi Akiba also explains the Divine Name as past, present, and future: before creation, after creation, and in the world to come. *Exod R* 3:14, which is attributed to Rabbi Isaac (ca. A.D. 300), has it that the Holy One said something similar to Moses: "I am he who was and I am he (who is) now, and I am he (who will be) forever" (McNamara, p. 105). McNamara also cites the Palestinian Targum to Exod 3:14 and, closest parallel of all, the Jerusalem Targum to Deut 32:39: "I am he who is and who was and I am he who will be . . ."

When referring to God in the future, all of these Jewish texts use the phrase "he who will be." Revelation uses the phrase "he who is to come."

the seven spirits. There has been much speculation about this phrase. There are, in the main, two different interpretations.

Many Greek writers and modern scholars think that the seven mighty throne angels of Jewish tradition are meant. These are mentioned in both the OT Apocrypha and the Pseudepigrapha, e.g. Tobit 2:15, and I Enoch 20:1–8 which even give their names: Uriel, Raphael, Raguel, Michael, Saraqael, Gabriel, and Remiel. Although the term "spirits" for angels is rare in both the OT and the NT (except I Kings 22:21–23 and Heb 1:7, 14), Justin, *Apologia* 1.6, mentions "good angels who follow and are made like to" the Son and come from the Father. Also, the seven spirits seem to be correlated with the seven churches (1:4) and it is implied that each church is under the tutelage of a guardian angel (1:20).

Second, in the early days of Christianity before the development of a Trinitarian theology angels might have been confused with the Holy Spirit. The Latin Church and many modern scholars regard the expression as referring to the Holy Spirit, called seven because of his seven gifts (cf. Isa 11:2–3 LXX; MT lists six gifts). This interpretation fits better with the seven spirits in the throne visions of Rev 4:5, 5:6 (collated with Zech 3:9, 4:10). Thus, Swete opts for diversity of ministries of the Spirit and quotes the old Latin commentators and Heb 2:4, I Cor 12:10, 14:32, Rev 22:6.

There is a third possible interpretation. A fragment of the Qumran scrolls, 4QSerek concerns the "Chief Princes" of the angelic hierarchy who offer seven words of blessing. There were apparently eight stanzas of which the first three and part of the eighth are lost. These may be throne angels. See Strugnell.

5. *from Jesus Christ.* The order is strange for Jesus is not normally men-

tioned after the Holy Spirit. In 4:5, 5:6, Jesus Christ is not mentioned with the seven spirits; in his place stands the Lamb.

who loved us. This is the first of many doxologies; cf. 4:11, 5:9, 12–13, 7:10, etc. Some variants have the present participle, probably indicating the time-lessness of his love. The verb "to love" occurs only in 3:9 (I have loved you) and 12:11 (they loved not their life unto death), the noun only in 2:4, 19, and the adjective only in 20:9 (the beloved city). "Love," therefore, is not a domi-nant theme in this apocalypse.

and freed us. Gr. *lusanti ēmas.* The ancient manuscripts and versions are divided between "washed" and "freed"; P **046** 82, 2059 al g vg TR; R^m read "washed." Modern scholars generally favor "freed" as the *lectio difficilior* (more difficult reading), but some, e.g. Boismard, opt for "washed." The term "washed" (*louein*) would allude more directly to baptism or immersion, as distinct from *plunein* for washing clothes and *nizein* or *niptein* for washing the face: *louein* is employed for washing the whole body. In NT the noun *loutron* (Eph 5:26, Titus 3:5) is a baptismal term. This would be the only verse in our text where *louein* is used and also the clearest allusion to baptism.

by his blood. Gr. *en,* "by," is instrumental. To the Hebrews blood was synonymous with life. The baptized person is spiritually immersed in the blood of Christ by which he is cleansed or freed from sin and given supernatural life. Probably there is an allusion to the blood of the covenant. Blood was used to effect purification and atonement (reconciliation). It denoted self-offering and obedience to God which restored the covenant relationship. For the atoning power of blood in the OT see Lev 17:4; the cleansing power, Lev 14:1–9, 14, the sanctifying power, Exod 19:20–21 (dedication of priests); apo-tropaic power, that is, power to turn away evil, Exod 12:22–23. Both the sprinkling of the blood on the altar and the ascent of the flesh in smoke symbolized union or reunion with Yahweh, since the offerer had previously placed his hand on the victim to symbolize oneness with it.

6. *has established us as a priestly kingdom.* The dative "to (or for) us" occurs in P^18 A 325 al, and the genitive plural occurs in C 3239 b vg^w. Most manuscripts have the accusative, as here.

priestly kingdom. "Kingdom" is abstract for the concrete "kings," but "kings" does appear in P 1, 2059s al TR. "Priesthood" appears in 42, 69 al. Exod 19:6 MT has "kingdom of priests," i.e. "royal priesthood." Throughout the NT the Christian Church is conscious that it is the new Israel and succeeds to the prerogatives of the historic Israel, but with this qualification: what those pre-rogatives signified and forecast is now fulfilled and perfected in Christ. Hence Exod 19:4–6, saying that the Hebrew nation, by virtue of the covenant, is a "kingdom of priests," i.e. possessing the sacerdotal dignity and duty of in-termediary between the other nations (who knew not the one true God) and Yahweh, is interpreted by the Church as preparation for the far sublimer truth that the new Israel, in virtue of its incorporation by baptism into Christ, priest and king (cf. Exod 19:6, Isa 61:6, I Peter 2:9) became also mediators of the new covenant.

to him be glory and power. This is the first doxology of two members but it differs from the longer doxologies (usually seven members) found elsewhere in Revelation (see second NOTE on vs. 5). The word "power," Gr. *kratos,* may be significant. In secular Greek, *kratos* is used especially of political power. In Revelation it is employed only here and in 5:13 ("might"). Christ, not the Roman emperor, has *imperium* (authority or power).

Amen. Amen is acknowledgment of that which is valid. In the synagogue it is the response of the community to the prayers uttered by the leader. It was also the response to the three parts into which the priests divided the Aaronic blessing in Num 6:24–26.

7. *See, he comes with the clouds.* Quotation from OT: Dan 7:13. See COM-MENT, p. 380, and NOTE on 4:14.

every eye. The original of this text stands in the great mourning scene of Zech 12. Rev 1:7 is a combination of Dan 7:13 and Zech 12:10 which agrees with the form in John 19:37 against the LXX. Cf. also Didache 16:6–8, which says that the world will see the Lord at the time of truth.

will see. Quotation from OT.

killed. Gr. *ekkenteō.* Quotation from OT: Zech 12:10. *Ekkenteō* means to pierce, kill, severely wound, or smite (e.g. Judg 9:54, 1 Chron 10:4). In the NT it occurs only here and in John 19:37. John does not seem to be verbally dependent on the Greek versions. Cf. also Epistle of Barnabas 7:9, Justin *Apologia* 52.12, *Dialogos* 32.2, 118.1.

8. *the Alpha and the Omega.* The Hebrew would be *aleph* and *taw,* probably standing respectively for *Urim* and *Thummim,* the sacred lots of the high priest used to determine the will of God, and also meaning "all encompassing."

the Omnipotent. Gr. *pantokratōr.* This occurs nine times in Revelation: 4:8, 11:17, 15:3, 16:7, 14, 19:6, 15, 21:22, and here in 1:8. Probably it is in con-trast to the Roman Emperor's self-designation as *autokratōr.* In ℵ* 2036 pc 1 al q vg sa TR this phrase is followed by "Beginning and End."

COMMENT

This second introduction or prologue is quite different from the first. The language does not appear to be so Johannine and the epistolary greeting is quite disconsonant with the apocalyptic genre. *Ekklesia* does not appear in the Gospel of John, and the "seven spirits" does not suit the advanced pneuma-tology of the Gospel as we now have it. However, the quotation from Zech 12:10 is used in John 19:37. One might say that the theology is Johannine, but not the language. The writer probably purports to be John the evangelist, the same John who appears in 1:9, but the pneumatology and the apocalyptic tone of 1:8–20 might suggest other disciples of the Baptist; cf. Acts 19:1–7.

"John" writes to the seven churches of Asia, but these are not all churches of Pauline foundation. Perhaps they were founded from Ephesus by the disciples of John the Baptist. The churches seem to be Jewish Christian, if one may judge from the Jewish populations in those cities, the references to those who called themselves Jews but are not (2:9, 3:9), and to the precept to abstain from meat offered to idols (2:14, 20; contrast I Cor 8).

The Christology here is richer than in the rest of this apocalypse. The author links Jesus Christ with the name of God (1:4–5). He calls him "faithful witness" (cf. I Tim 6:13), probably because he was influenced by Isa 55:4 which refers to the descendant of David as a witness. Davidic descent was a prerequisite for messiahship and was therefore claimed for Jesus. The author therefore sees Jesus as a faithful witness to God's sure covenant with David. In 1:5 he calls him "the firstborn from the dead and ruler of the kings of the earth." The phrase is nearly the same as Col 1:18, "the first-born from the dead, that in everything he might be preeminent" (RSV; cf. I Cor 15:20). The ruler of the kings of the earth probably suggests a contrast to the pretensions of the Roman emperors, but it also recalls Ps 89:27(28), a messianic prophecy containing this promise: "I will make him my first-born, the highest of earthly kings" (AB).

Here the author writes of Jesus' love (1:5, 3:9), a theme absent in the main corpus of the work (see second NOTE on 1:5), and implicitly of his expiatory death (1:6; cf. Heb 9:14). He knows of the Christian election in Christ (cf. I Peter 2:5, 9) and can give Christ equal honor with the Father (vs. 6). He anticipates the second coming, and with reference to this cites Zech 12:10, 12, 14, which are also alluded to in John 19:37, Luke 23:27, 28. He thinks of this parousia in terms of the coming of one like a son of man from Dan 7:13, a text used by Jesus in his trial before the high priest (Mark 14:62, Matt 26:64). The only other reference to Dan 7:13 in Revelation is in 14:14 but there "cloud" is in the singular.

Scott observes that Driver, Dalman, and Charles remark the influence of Dan 7:13a and refer to the "supernatural majesty and state" of the figure of the Son of Man, and Hitzig speaks of him coming "on the clouds like God himself." However, Stott, although noting the association of clouds with the verb "coming," also notices the altered order when the text is compared to Dan 7:13a. In Daniel the clouds of heaven seem to be introductory to the whole scene rather than the description of the manner of the man-like being's approach to the throne. But in the NT this is changed. When the Son of Man is thought of as a supernatural being, as in Enoch, it is easy to connect him with "coming," like Yahweh's "coming" in the OT theophanies. Perhaps our author also added vs. 8 as an affirmation that Christ, as well as the Father, is Alpha and Omega and Lord. One notes the "Johannine" *Egō eimi* (I am) in vs. 8, in contrast to 21:6 which reads merely "*egō* (I) the Alpha and the Omega . . ." The author may have known the *Egō eimi* (I am) sayings now recorded in John's Gospel.

Thus, this second prologue may have been written by a Jewish-Christian who knew about the death and resurrection of Jesus and, like the very early Church (cf. I Thess 4:13–18), expects a second coming soon. It is in this vein that he writes to the seven communities or churches.

XXVI. THE VISION OF THE ONE LIKE A
SON OF MAN
(1:9–20)

1 ⁹ I John, your brother and comrade in the tribulation and kingdom and patient endurance in Jesus, was on the island which is called
Patmos on account of the Word of God and the testimony of Jesus.
¹⁰ I was in the Spirit on the Lord's Day, and I heard behind me a
voice loud like a trumpet, ¹¹ saying, "Write what you see in a book
and send it to the seven communities, to Ephesus and to Smyrna and
to Pergamum, and to Thyatira and to Sardis and to Philadelphia and
to Laodicea." ¹² And I turned to see the voice which spoke to me; and
when I turned I saw seven golden lampstands, ¹³ and in the middle
of the lampstands one like a son of man, clothed in an ankle-length
garment tied above the waist with a golden girdle; ¹⁴ the hair of his
head was snow-white, like white wool; his eyes were like flaming fire;
¹⁵ his feet glowed like bronze that had been fired in an oven; and his
voice sounded like the roar of rushing waters. ¹⁶ In his right hand he
held seven stars and a sharp, two-edged sword issued from his mouth
and his face shone like the sun in its strength.

¹⁷ At the sight of him I fell at his feet like one struck dead; and he
touched me with his right hand, and said, "There is nothing to fear!
I am the First and the Last, ¹⁸ the Living One; indeed I was dead,
but, behold, I live for all eternity; yes, I hold the keys of death and of
Sheol. ¹⁹ Now you are to write down whatever you see in vision, both
present things and things that are to take place in the future. ²⁰ The
symbolism of the seven stars that you see in my right hand, and of the
seven gold lampstands, is this: the seven stars represent the seven
angels of the communities, while the lampstands represent the seven
communities."

NOTES

1:9. *brother.* The usual designation of Christians.

in the tribulation and kingship and patient endurance in Jesus. This is a
literal translation. That there is only one article indicates the close connection
among the three nouns and shows that the phrase "in Jesus" modifies each.
The Christian suffers in union with Christ, by virtue of the patient endurance

that Jesus gives, and thus attains the full participation in Jesus' kingship; cf. Rom 5:3, II Tim 2:12, I Peter 5:1.

in Jesus. This phrase appears as "in Christ" in **046** 82 al vg^{s,cl}, and "in Jesus Christ" in 1, 2329 al TR.

10. *was in the Spirit.* The Greek has simply "in Spirit," which some exegetes take to mean in an ecstasy. Ecstasy need not imply loss of consciousness. John is able to inform the reader that he knew full well what was happening. In any case, he wishes to recount a supernatural experience, one due to the special intervention of the Spirit, as in Ezek 3:12.

the Lord's Day. Gr. *en tē kuriakē hēmera.* Although I Cor 16:2 and Acts 20:7 may show that Christians began to assemble for the Lord's Supper on Sunday, and thus gradually substitute it for the Sabbath, this would be the first time in the NT that it is called Lord's Day. Like many other expressions in Rev, "the Lord's Day" implies a protest against the emperor's feast, also called *hēmera kuriakē.* Given the many liturgical allusions in Revelation, O. Cullmann's surmise that John may have had this vision during the liturgical service has great merit; see I Cor 14:26–29.

behind me. See Ezek 3:12; perhaps the point is introduced to give the effect of surprise.

like a trumpet. The particle *hōs,* "as," or "like," occurs some fifty-six times in Revelation. Its frequent use is necessitated by the apocalyptic genre which attempts to express by symbols and approximate terms heavenly realities for which earthly speech is inadequate.

Trumpets, as we have seen, e.g. in NOTE on 8:6, are very important liturgically and theologically in the OT, in 1QM (eschatological warfare), and in apocalyptic literature. They herald the glory of God (Exod 19:16, 19), and victory (Josh 6:6, Judg 7:18), and are used in the liturgy (Lev 25:9; cf. Ps 98:6). In the NT, the trumpet heralds the parousia; Matt 24:31, I Cor 15:52, I Thess 4:16.

11. *saying.* After "saying," (P) 1, 2059s pm TR have " 'I am the Alpha and the Omega, the first and the last,' and," before "Write . . ."

Write what you see. Kenyon has computed that Revelation made up a monobiblion or single papyrus roll about fifteen feet long.

seven communities. These were seven tribunal cities and postal districts situated on a great circular road that bound together the most important part of the Roman province of Asia Minor. If one begins at Ephesus, and goes on to Smyrna, and thence in turn to the nearest of the other cities, the average distance between them is from thirty to forty-five miles.

12. *lampstands.* Solomon arranged ten lamps in his temple (I Kings 7:49); the priestly tradition does not specify the number (Exod 27:20–21, Lev 24: 3–4). The seven-branched lampstand made by Herod the Great, a representation of which was placed on Titus' arch, goes back, it seems, to the postexilic temple; cf. Zech 4:1 ff., I Macc 1:21, 4:49. John fuses the two, since he is anxious to keep the sacred number and yet make it possible to visualize Jesus walking among the lamps; see 2:1.

14. *snow-white.* Cf. the description of the "Head of Days" in I Enoch 46:1, 71:10: "His head white as wool. . . ."

his eyes were like flaming fire. This probably refers to his omniscience, penetrating into all hidden and mysterious things (cf. Dan 10:6, II Enoch 1:5) and qualifying him to judge absolutely.

15. *his feet glowed like bronze.* This signifies the Son's strength and stability, which overcomes all opposition and tramples and melts like hot metal anything that stands in the way; cf. the contrast with the feet of clay of the statue in Dan 2:33, 44. The Greek word here rendered bronze is *chalkolibanos,* a hapax legomenon, that is, it occurs only here. Its exact meaning is uncertain, though it must be a metal or alloy like gold ore or fine brass or bronze. Ezek 1:27 (LXX) translates with *electron* the Hebrew *ḥašmal,* which according to Pliny, *Natural History* 33.4, is a natural alloy of gold and silver. Cf. the Blessing of the Prince of the Congregation from Qumran, 1QS, adjunct b, 5:24–26 (D-S):

> . . . and by the breath of thy lips
> shalt thou slay the ungodly.
>
> . . .
>
> And righteousness shall be the girdle
> [of thy loins]
> [and faith] the girdle of thy haunches.
> May He make thy horns of iron
> and thy shoes of bronze!

his voice sounded like the roar of rushing waters. A favorite biblical simile suggesting that all else is drowned out and his judgment alone prevails; cf. Ezek 1:24, 43:2.

16. *seven stars.* Just as the OT frequently pictures the stars wholly in God's hand or power, so here Christ holds seven stars which represent the seven angels or heavenly counterparts of the churches.

sharp, two-edged sword. Gr. *rhomphaia,* denoting pain and anguish; see NOTES on 6:6, "great sword," and 6:8, "sword." This is an image of Christ's word, found frequently in varying forms, all of which intend to suggest the irresistible power and unfailing force of his judgment, punitive or otherwise. See Isa 11:4, 49:2, Wisd Sol 18:15, Eph 6:17, Heb 4:12, II Thess 2:8, Psalms of Solomon 17:39, I Enoch 62:2, II Esdras (IV Ezra) 13:10.

shone like the sun. A similar comparison is found of the transfigured Jesus in Matt 17:2: the divinity, as it were, shone through the countenance of Jesus.

17. *fell at his feet.* See e.g. Isa 6:5, Ezek 1:28, Dan 8:17–18, 10:8–10, I Enoch 14:24.

nothing to fear. Cf. Dan 10:12, 19, Matt 14:27, Mark 6:45–52, John 6:20.

the First and the Last. Cf. Rev 22:13: a divine title from Isa 44:6, 48:12.

18. *the Living One . . . I hold the keys of death and of Sheol.* Life is the essential property of Yahweh, who calls himself or is called the "living God" in both OT and NT; cf. Rev 4:9, 10:6, 15:7, John 5:26, 11:25, 14:6. Because he is the Living One, Christ has full power over the resurrection. He passed through death at a definite moment of history, but he lives forever. Hence he has the keys of death and Sheol (cf. Matt 16:19), and can accordingly guarantee the faithful a sharing in his resurrection (contrast Rev 9). G vg (2) omit these words.

eternity. After this word, **046,** 1006, 2060, 2329 pm sy TR read "Amen."

20. The Greek *mustērion,* "symbolism," like the Hebrew *raz* in Dan 2:28 ff., means a hidden symbol the interpretation of which must be given by revelation. The explanation that follows is somewhat involved, since we are to take into consideration a two-fold level of symbolism, on earth and in heaven. On earth the seven lampstands signify the communities in which Christ is always present and active. In heaven the stars in Christ's hand also represent the communities, but in their heavenly realities: like the stars created by Yahweh. The angels of the communities are said to be the stars and the spirits. In the thinking of the ancients, the connection between stars and angels was quite close; see e.g. Job 38:7.

COMMENT

The writer appears to be suffering persecution and/or exile in Patmos, a rocky island about ten miles long, five wide, made up of volcanic hills. It was one of the Sporades Islands in the Icarian Sea lying about thirty-seven miles west and southwest of Miletus. According to Tacitus (*Annals* 3.68, 4.30, 15.71) and Pliny (*Natural History* 12:4–13, 23) it was a place of banishment for political offenders. Thither John was banished, probably for preaching the word of God and being thus an apostolic witness to Jesus; like Jesus, he was called upon to suffer for his faith. Perhaps he was exiled as an agitator, for disloyalty to the emperor for refusing to take part in civic affairs that implied worship and even for encouraging others to abstain from such practices. Whether he was sentenced to hard labor, for example in the quarries, is not stated, but this may well have been the case.

He was "in the Spirit," probably prophetically inspired or even in ecstasy (cf. II Cor 12:1–6 where a certain person, probably Paul, was rapt "to the paradise," but John does not speak of being out of the body; cf. II Cor 12:2–3) on the Lord's Day. This would mean either Sunday, or the seventh day of the week (Strand), or Easter Day or the Day of the Lord (Judgment Day). However, it is very difficult to determine which is meant. Most probably the Christian would still be keeping the Sabbath, the seventh day. As, however, the vision is that of the Risen Christ, Easter Day would be very appropriate. It would be the Lord's Day, the first day of creation and of consummation.

He heard a voice commanding him to write what he sees to the seven communities (or churches) but the command does not clearly indicate that what he sees embraces anything beyond Rev 2–3, that is, Rev 1–3 may not have had any connection, originally, with Rev 4–22. Certainly, although features of the prophecies are found in the seven letters of chs. 2–3, especially the characteristics of the one like the Son of Man, their contents do not reveal a clear knowledge of the rest of the book.

The voice of command John heard was behind him. When he turned to identify it, he saw seven golden lampstands, such as stood in the sanctuary or holy place of the Jerusalem temple. The *menorah,* the seven-branched candlestick, was a symbol of the unity of God. The position, therefore, of the figure whom he sees is significant; it indicates association with the deity. Moreover, the vision is a combination of Ezek 1:26, 9:2, 11 (the vision of God on His throne), and Dan 7:13 (the vision of one like a son of man who comes into the presence of the Ancient of Days and receives "dominion and glory and kingdom"). Indeed some of the features of God in Dan 7, "the hair of his head like pure wool" (vs. 9) and fire (vs. 10) have been transferred to our figure (the eyes in Rev 1:14).

In addition to the attributes of divinity, the one like a son of man bears signs of priesthood and royalty in his dress (1:13). The garment worn by him was that of the high priest; see the description in Josephus *Ant.* 3.7. The golden belt or sash indicates royalty; see I Macc 10:89, 14:44. His lordship of the churches also is indicated by a scepter made up of seven stars, symbolic of the churches, and his divine word is like a sword that infallibly attains its mark (vs. 16). But over and above this, our author, as if struggling to describe the figure adequately, ascribes to him the characteristics of the angel seen by Daniel in Dan 10:5–6. Both were girded in gold, both had flaming eyes and limbs like shining bronze, both spoke with awesome strength.

What one notices especially in the whole description of Rev 1:13–16 are the cosmic features, some of which could not obtain together on an earthly level, e.g. snow, fire, and water. The writer has introduced human features—head, hair, and eyes; inanimate materials—wool, snow, fire, bronze, water; celestial objects—stars and the sun; and finally, a spiritual symbol, the two-edged sword, i.e. the Word of God (Heb 4:12).

This vision appears to be of the resurrected Christ; cf. Acts 7:56, one of the two texts other than the Gospels which uses the Son of Man title for Jesus. Cf. John 12:34. That the celestial personage is the resurrected Christ is clear from the words which he speaks to the prostrate seer. He identifies himself as the "Living One"; cf. Acts 3:15, Jesus as the Prince or author of life, and John 1:4, "in him was life," etc. He cannot be God or an angel, for he affirms that he was dead (vs. 18) but now lives eternally; cf. John 3:16, 36, etc. He has power over death and Sheol or Hades; cf. John 11:25, I Cor 15, etc. There is nothing clearly comparable to this vision or these words in the rest of the text. The figure is far more majestic than one like a son of man in Rev 14:14. The explanation of this unique vision may be ascribed to Jewish-Christian meditation on Jesus' apocalyptic sayings concerning the Son of Man which are now in the Gospels and their association of the Son of Man with the vision of the Risen Christ. The Gospels themselves, unlike II Peter, do not describe the appearance of Christ when he rises from the dead. The present vision, however, may grant us a glimpse into the imagination of some of the early Christians, e.g. converted disciples of the Baptist, in their eschatological thinking.

In the next seven sections the figure in this vision will address the seven communities in a manner not unlike that of Amos delivering his seven oracles (Rife).

2 ¹ Write to the angel of the community in Ephesus: This is the prophecy of the one who governs the seven stars with his right hand, who walks among the seven golden candlesticks. ² I discern your works and your toil and your steadfastness, also that you cannot tolerate evil people, indeed, you have tested those who called themselves apostles and who are not, and you have discovered that they are false; ³ certainly, you do possess steadfastness and you endure on account of my name and have not grown weary. ⁴ Yet I have this against you, that you have forsaken your first love. ⁵ Remember the height from which you have fallen and repent and perform what you did at first. If not I will come to you and snatch your lampstand from its position, if you do not repent. ⁶ But you have this to your credit, that you hate the works of the Nikolaitans which I also hate. ⁷ Let the one who has spiritual hearing heed what the Spirit says to the communities. To the one who prevails I will grant that he may partake of the tree of life, which is in the paradise of God.

NOTES

2:1. *angel.* Gr. *aggelos.* The Greek word may be translated "angel," i.e. a supernatural being or "messenger." Scholars find it difficult to decide exactly what is meant by the angels of the communities. The main suggestions are angel guardians, bishops, and heavenly counterparts of the respective kingdoms. The "angel guardians" interpretation is consonant with the ideas of the Qumran community that good and bad angels were intimately involved in the affairs of the world. In favor of this suggestion, scholars cite passages like Dan 10:13, 20, 21, 11:1, 12:1, where angels are identified with certain nations in a way that suggests the contemporary concept of guardian angels. That the seven angels are bishops is an interpretation favored by the Latin fathers. Against this it may be observed that in Revelation the term "angel" is used only of superterrestrial beings, and that nowhere in the NT is it used of bishops. Moreover, church officials are not mentioned in the text. A clue to the proper understanding of "angel" may be found in the careful reading of the passages in Daniel mentioned above, where the angels of the various kingdoms are a kind of heavenly counterpart of the respective kingdoms. There is a gradual evolution from angels as guardians first of nations, then of cities, and finally of individuals. This may be a refinement of the Hellenistic tradition of guardian deities of city-states.

community. Gr. *ekklesia.* Although the term may have the technical sense of "church," it could refer to the regular legal assembly; cf. Acts 19:32–39. This meaning occurs very frequently in Ephesian inscriptions which refer to the meeting of the assembly.

in Ephesus. When the rabbis speak of Ephesus, they appear to mean the whole of Asia Minor. The Dialogue between Justin and Trypho, the Jew, is reputed to have taken place in this location.

In 1, 2028 al the phrase reads "of the Ephesians."

governs. Gr. *kratōn.* The verb means "to take possession of," "grasp," "hold fast" or "hold in one's power." See second NOTE on 1:8.

walks among. Gr. *peripatōn.* This verb may be taken literally but the symbolic meaning is more likely; the figure walks in the light in contrast to those who walk (*peripateō*) in the dark; cf. John 8:12, 12:35, I John 2:11). The idea of "walking" is associated with the "walk of life" implying "live" or "conduct oneself." Cf. the sons of light as a name for the covenanters at Qumran.

3. *you endure.* In 1, 2059 pc this appears as "you have baptised."

4. *first love.* Feuillet finds here and in 3:20 an allusion to the Song of Solomon.

5. *come to you.* In 046 82, 1006 pl vg⁸ this is modified by "quickly."

snatch. Gr. *kineō.* The Greek can imply simply "remove" but may have a stronger or hostile sense when applied e.g. to rousing a city or exciting a revolt.

repent. Cf. 1QS 3:1–11.

6. *hate.* This seems to strike a harsh note to the modern reader, but as Sutcliffe explains, this does not involve personal animosity. Rather, an examination of the OT, Dead Sea scrolls, and NT material proves that what is meant here is akin to the wrath of God Who hates sin and sinners insofar as they are attached to sin but does desire their repentance and long to forgive them. In the same way, people may speak about hating sin but not the sinner.

In CDC 8:6 one of the characteristics of the faithless is that they hate their neighbors; 1QH 15:18–19 shows further that they take no pleasure in what God has commanded but choose rather what He hates. On the contrary the faithful brethren "are to love all that (God) has chosen and to hate all that He has rejected" (1QS 1:3–4, D-S). However, this does not involve any private hatred or revenge; rather, the members of Qumran were taught to repay their enemies with good.

Nikolaitans. There is no reason to link the Nikolaitans with the proselyte Nicolaus (Acts 6:5) as Irenaeus (*Adv. Haereses* 1.26.3, 3.11.1) and other Church Fathers have done. According to Hippolytus (*Haereses* 7.24) and Epiphanius (*Haereses* 1.2.25), the Nikolaitans were a Gnostic sect which practiced immoral habits. The "heresy," however, may have been associated with the figure of Balaam. In Hellenistic and Haggadic literature, Balaam is the great sorcerer; Philo *De Vita Mosis* 1.48. Josephus calls him "greatest of the prophets at that time" in *Ant.* 4.102–30, and brings him into connection with the story of Moses' war with the Ethiopians in *Ant.* 2.10; cf. *Sanhedrin* 106a, *Sotah* 11a). The two sons of Balaam, Jannes and Jambres, are mentioned in Jude.

7. *tree of life.* Perhaps the symbol was suggested because the sacred tree associated with the worship of the nature goddess appears on Ephesian coins. The sacred tree has also been found on chests unearthed in excavations on the site of Ephesus. However, our text suggests a greater supernatural reality by qualifying "tree" with life. There may be some connection with Gen 2:9, "the tree of life in the middle of the garden" (AB), suggested not only by the words "tree of life" but also by the variant reading "in the paradise in the center."

in the paradise. (P) 1, 2036 pm (g) TR add "in the center." According to Jewish thought, paradise and the tree of life were to reappear at the end of time. Some rabbis imagined three paradises: that of Adam, the interim reward of the just in heaven, and the eschatological one on earth near Jerusalem. In the Targum of Jonathan God is said to have prepared the Garden of Eden for the righteous, that they might eat the fruit of the tree as a reward for having practiced the doctrine of the Law in this world. From I Enoch 24:3–5 we learn of a tree of special fragrance and peculiar beauty whose fruit resembled the dates of a palm, and from 25:4–5 that no mortal could touch it until the judgment, after which it would be for the elect and would be transplanted to the temple of the eternal king (cf. the end of Revelation). According to Testament of Levi 18:9–12, the priest of Levi was expected to remove the threatening sword and allow the saints to eat of the tree of life. Perhaps the speaker to Ephesus is to be identified with this priest.

of God. In 046 1611, 2023 al latt sy[h] co, the phrase is "of my God."

COMMENT

The first of the seven prophecies is directed to Ephesus, the city where some disciples of the Baptist dwelt; Acts 19:1–7. Ephesus had a long history. It was founded by Ionian colonists and in the Roman era (133 B.C.) it was rivaled in the east only by Alexandria in Egypt and Antioch in Syria. It became the residence of the proconsul of the province of Asia, but was not the capital of the province. Its importance may have been due to its very favorable location at the mouth of the river Cayster. It therefore became a concourse of trade routes for the cities of Greece and Asia Minor.

Its temple to Artemis was world renowned; cf. Acts 19:35. Indeed, it brought both prestige to the city in that it was one of the seven wonders of the world and revenue in that money was deposited in it for safekeeping as in a modern bank. See Parvis, pp. 67–68, for the archaeological remains and a conjectural reconstruction. There was also in Ephesus a great theater approximately 495 feet in diameter which could accommodate 24,500 people. It was here that a riot was directed against Paul; Acts 19:34. This is important for those scholars who argue that the theater and drama influenced the writer of Revelation.

Vss. 4–5 of this prophecy contains a warning against abandoning the faith. Five factors in particular suggest the reason for this warning.

First, there was a history of hostility between Jew and Gentile. The large Jewish population in Ephesus during the Hellenistic period was granted citizenship and the right to practice their own customs; cf. Josephus *Against Apion* 2.39, but contrast *Ant.* 12.125–28. In Roman times, it appears that the Ephesian Jews not only were granted citizenship but also were exempt from certain military service (*Ant.* 15.228–30). Another decree issued by Augustus Caesar assured the Sabbath observance and other privileges with regard to Jewish law (16.262–64). These decrees did not result in an entirely amicable coexistence between Jew and Gentile. The Gentile Ephesians demanded that the Jews should worship Roman gods if they were allowed to have equal citizen rights, and the intervention of several Roman governors, e.g. Agrippa, Gaius, Norbanus, Flaccus, and Julius Antonius, was necessary to persuade the Ephesians that the Jews should be permitted this freedom (*Ant.* 16:167, 172–73; cf. Philo *Legatio ad Gaium* 315). Perhaps it is under this stress that some of the Jews of Ephesus succumbed to pagan practices.

Second, Ephesus was associated with emperor-worship. In the mid-first century a temple was dedicated to the emperor. Later the city gained the distinction of being thrice named temple-keeper. Filson observes that at the close of the century, as Revelation and other evidence shows, emperor-worship had become widespread. Indeed, Acts 19:31 mentions "Asiarchs"; these appear to have come from families of position and to have had leadership over the rites of the imperial cult (see Filson, pp. 77–88).

Third, even the emperor cult was overshadowed by the worship of Artemis in the middle of the first century. This constituted further pagan influence brought to bear on Ephesian Jews and Jewish Christians.

Fourth, Ephesus was notorious for its association with magic. In Acts 19: 13, 14, one meets itinerant exorcists, the sons of Sceva, a Jew who was a chief priest. There seems to have been abundant use of incantations, magical formulae, and such, which were so prevalent that all books or scrolls of such formulae came to be referred to by ancient Greek and Roman writers as "Ephesian writings." Cf. the exorcism and burning of magical formulae referred to in Acts 19:13, 19. Indeed, Filson (pp. 78–79) believes the "deeds" referred to in Acts 19:18 may more accurately be described as "spells."

Fifth, from Paul's farewell speech to the elders of the church at Ephesus (Acts 20:17–38) one learns that the apostle predicted "savage wolves" would come among the flock, and members of the community would distort the true doctrine. Further heterodoxical teachings occur in I and II Timothy, which appear to have been written for the Ephesians. A note of vigilance appears in the NT epistle probably (see the variant to Eph 1:1) written to the same city (Eph 4:17–32, 5:10–20).

This information about Ephesus enables us to understand the import of the prophecy given to that city. As we have observed, the *vox mystica* which gives the message to each community is characterized by an attribute of the "one like a son of man" in the preceding vision. The symbol of control over the cosmic forces (stars) and the close association with the *menorah*, the seven-branched candlestick, is probably brought into relationship with Ephesus because she embodied in herself a replica of the province of Asia. Also, Ephesus was at the head (as one comes from Patmos) of the circular road which connected the seven cities mentioned in Rev 1–3. The "corporate personality" of the Son of Man faces, as it were, the "corporate personality" of Ephesus/ Asia, but the former towers over the latter.

The content of this and other prophecies shows an affinity with Qumran theology, a feature which is not surprising if it emanates from a circle of Christian disciples of the Baptist.

All seven prophecies begin with "I discern (or know) . . ." At Qumran, the practice of discernment of spirits was of the utmost importance, with regard not only to those entering the covenant but also to those who might be weakening in their first fervor. The spirits of covenanters were examined year by year (1QS 5:23–24). The duty of examination fell especially to the instructor, who was obliged to "separate and weigh the sons of righteousness according to their spirits"; 1QS 9:14; cf. 3:14, where the candidates for entry into the covenant undergo a scrutiny of their "works."

In the exhortation to Ephesus, the *vox mystica* remarks the toil or service and the perseverance of the Ephesians, together with their intolerance of wicked men and their discernment of false apostles. These virtues are akin to those prescribed for the sectarians in 1QS, e.g. 8:1–10 where it is emphasized that one must "guard faith upon the earth with firm inclination . . . and undergo distress of affliction . . . to bring down punishment upon the wicked . . ." (D-S). Further, Rev 2:5b appears to speak of expulsion or excommunication in metaphorical language, i.e. removing the candlestick from its place. Cf. the far more elaborate system of punishment and excommunication (unparalleled in the NT) found in 1QS 6:24 – 8:25. No very serious crime is imputed to Ephesus, and rather something like *acedia*, Latin for "spiritual apathy," is predicated of her. The light metaphor recalls 1QH 8:20 where the psalmist declares that God will make him "a father to the sons of Grace" and that he (or his horn) "will shine with a seven-fold light in the Eden which Thou hast made for Thy glory"; 1QH 8:24–25, D-S; cf. "paradise" in Rev 2:7.

However, this resemblance to Qumran writings would not preclude the suggestion that the warning is reminiscent of former catastrophes which befell Ephesus. On several occasions she was obliged to change her site because of the continual silting up of the harbor. The warning would refer to some punishment like loss of preeminence or even destruction on the earthly dimension.

Like the covenanters of Qumran (cf. e.g. 1QS 1:3–4), the Ephesus community is to "hate" those who do not hold orthodox doctrine, namely the Nikolaitans. The Nikolaitans have been a matter of much perplexity to scholars. The author praises the community at Ephesus for detesting their works (2:6); he reprimands the church of Pergamum for harboring "those who cling to the teaching of the Nikolaitans," (2:15) and describes them as adherents of the teaching of Balaam (2:14; see Num 25, 31:16, II Peter 2:15, Jude 11). The same heresy may be referred to in 2:20–24 where the church of Thyatira is blamed for tolerating a self-styled prophetess whom the author calls Jezebel (II Kings 9:22) because she led people astray with her teaching about fornication and the eating of idol-offerings (see Acts 15:20, 29, recording that these are two of the prohibitions which James prescribed for Gentile Christians; cf. also I Cor 8:8–10). The Nikolaitans seem, accordingly, to represent an excessively liberal or even antinomian outlook with regard to Jewish Christianity. The best explanation of the Nikolaitans is cited by Charles (*Revelation*, I, 52), who says that the name appears to come from a translation into Greek of the name Balaam, in Hebrew two separate words, *bala am*, "he hath consumed the people" (a derivation found in *Sanhedrin* 105a, where *balah am* is an alternative reading). Nikolaus could be *nika laon*, "he overcame the people." This play on words is thoroughly Semitic.

The Balaam narrative is found in Num 22–24. Balaam was reputed to be a Mesopotamian prophet who was requested by Balak, king of Moab, to curse Israel. On his way to perform this mission, the angel of the Lord retarded his progress by standing with drawn sword before his ass. Balaam gave four oracles concerning Israel: the people would multiply, Num 23:9; the Lord was with Israel and Israel's strength would be like that of a wild animal, a lion, Num 23:21–24; Israel, its valleys, gardens, rivers, cedar trees, and tents and tabernacles would be blessed and fertile, Num 24:5–6; and from Israel would arise a tribe which would conquer Moab and Edom, Num 24:17–18. The narrative of Num 22–24 is comprised primarily of the Yahwist and Elohist strands, but the priestly tradition is also incorporated in that Balaam is described as a Midianite attempting to seduce Israel through immoral rites; Num 31:16. Thus, although not originally a villain, Balaam gradually came to be regarded as the father of syncretism and mercenary business, a symbol of opposition to Yahweh.

In rabbinic literature Balaam is represented as one of the seven heathen prophets standing in antithesis to Moses. He was regarded as the interpreter of dreams, a magician, and one able to ascertain the exact moment of God's wrath. He was often called *Bala'am rāšā'*, "Balaam, the wicked one." His disciples were depicted as men with an evil eye, haughty bearing, and avaricious spirit. The rabbis held Balaam responsible for the unchastity which led to apostasy in Shittim, when twenty-four thousand people became infected with a pestilence, Num 25:1–9.

In light of this, the impact of including in this apocalypse a reference to Balaam, associated with Nikolaitan, becomes clear. Balaam is the epitome of the false prophet who seduces men to lewdness and obscene idolatry; cf. Rev 2:4, II Peter 2:15, Jude 11, Pirke Aboth 5:22). It is interesting to note, also, that these legends entered Kabbalistic literature, the later Jewish mystical writings.

To the faithful Ephesians is promised the reward of partaking of the tree of life in the paradise of God. The tree of life is mentioned in Gen 2:9, Ezek 31:8, and many pseudepigraphical texts; see second NOTE on 2:7. It need not be understood in an exclusively or even predominantly eschatological sense. In Prov 3:18 wisdom is called the tree of life; in Prov 11:30 the fruit of virtue is said to be a tree of life which could be destroyed by violence. Further, the Jewish mystics were especially interested in the creation accounts of Genesis and made this the object of their prayer and contemplation. They strove to enter paradise. Thus, the symbol of eating from the tree of life and/or knowledge may be equivalent to imbibing supernatural wisdom, distinguishing between good and evil and, possibly, acquiring immortality.

2 ⁸ Write to the angel of the community in Smyrna: This is the prophecy of the First and the Last, who was dead and became alive. ⁹ I discern your tribulation and your poverty, but you are rich and I perceive the blasphemy of those who call themselves Jews and are not but are of the assembly of Satan. ¹⁰ Do not fear the things which you are about to suffer. Behold, the accuser is about to throw some of you into prison that you may be tried, and you will have tribulation for ten days. Be faithful unto death and I will give you the crown of life. ¹¹ Let the one who has spiritual hearing heed what the Spirit says to the communities. The one who prevails will not be harmed by the second death.

NOTES

2:9. *tribulation.* Gr. *thlipsis.* This word is used frequently in LXX for several Hebrew terms. It denotes both internal and external oppression. Although it can be a secular term, it acquires theological significance when it is applied to Israel or to the righteous under oppression, e.g. the oppression in Egypt (Exod 4:31; cf. 3:9) and the exile (Deut 4:29; cf. 28:47 ff.). In II Kings 19:3–4 repeated verbatim in Isa 37:3–4, Obad 13, Isa 33:2, Nahum 1:7 God visits His people on days of affliction. According to Dan 12:1, these days of affliction are preliminary to the future day of tribulation when Michael will come, the people will be delivered and those whose names are written in the book of life will rise from the dust, some to contempt and others to shine like the brightness of the firmament. People expected God's judgment to be totally revealed in the eschatological tribulation; cf. Hab 3:16, Zeph 1:15). ℵ 046 1, 82, 2059s pl TR read "works and tribulation."

poverty. Gr. *ptōcheia.* This term may apply to material poverty but it is also used in a spiritual sense, both good and bad; cf. Luke 6:20, Matt 5:3. It refers to a religious poverty of spirit, an inner quality found in the righteous or the pious, especially when they are confronted with adversaries in Psalms of Solomon 5:2, 11, 10:6, 15:1, 18:2. The community of Qumran identified itself with the poor who would be preserved through persecution; CDC 19:9.

assembly of Satan. Gr. *sunagōgē,* "assembly." This phrase is used here and in 3:9 but nowhere else in biblical or nonbiblical writings. However, there may be a parallel in the community or assembly of Belial mentioned in 1QH 2:22 (cf. the community of God in 1QM 4:9), although some scholars have questioned whether Belial here is to be taken as a personal name. These scholars prefer the translation "assembly of destruction" or "assembly of uselessness." Tarn (p. 225), however, refers to the fact that Jewish synagogues in Mysia and at Delos did actually worship Zeus. He suggests that the synagogues of Satan at Smyrna and Philadelphia, who claim that they are Jews but are not genuine Jews, may indicate some syncretistic worship of that kind. This is especially possible as the altar of Zeus at Pergamum is referred to in our apocalypse as "Satan's seat." There are also Palestinian synagogues which depict the sun god in the center of a zodiac mosaic. Oesterley and Robinson, p. 424, agree with this interpretation and give illustrations of the Jewish diaspora's adoption of the Graeco-Oriental cults. Helfgott, p. 42, further asserts that throughout the empire the victory of Jupiter over the God of Israel was celebrated with "fanatical hatred and violence against the Jewish inhabitants." There may be a contrast with the synagogue of the Lord; Num 20:4, 26:7; cf. Psalms of Solomon 17:18, synagogues of the pious. Charles observes that the word *ekklesia* was chosen by the church as a self-designation; *sunagōgē* was used only once in the NT for the Christian assembly (James 2:2).

10. *Do not fear the things.* ℵ P 1, 82, 2344 pm latt sy TR read "Fear nothing."

accuser. Gr. *diabolos.* Basically the verb *diaballō* means to separate, accuse, or slander, but the LXX uses the noun *diabolos* for Satan in the sense of one who separates, accuses, slanders, seduces; cf. Zech 3:1 ff.

11. *second death.* This phrase occurs four times in Revelation but does not appear elsewhere in the NT. The first reference is this one; it seems to differentiate this death from martyrdom or physical death. The second reference occurs in 20:6 in the context of the millennium; those who reign with the Christ for the thousand years will not be overcome by the second death. The third occurs in Rev 20:14 and the fourth 21:8, when the second death is identified with being cast into the lake of fire whence the devil, the beast, the false prophet, Death, and Hades are thrown. Strack and Billerbeck give two instances of the phrase in nonbiblical literature. In the Targum on Jer 51:39, 57, concerning an oracle against Babylon, it is said that they shall die the second death and not live in the world to come. The MT of Jer 51:39, 57 reads "sleep of the age," perhaps meaning eternal sleep, which is interpreted in the Targum as second death. McNamara, pp. 117 ff., cites also the Targums of Deut 33:6, Isa 22:14, 65:6, 15: (a) Targum Deut 33:6 reads, "Let Reuben live in eternal life and die not the second death" (MT "Let Reuben live and not die . . ."). McNamara observes that from *Sanhedrin* 92a one realizes that this was the *locus theologicus* from which the resurrection or "vivification" of the dead was proved. (b) The second targum on that verse reads "Let Reuben live in this world and die not in the second death in which death the wicked die in the world to come." (c) McNamara also cites Targum Isa 22:14 which is an oracle against Epicurean-minded Jews: "The prophet said: 'With my ears was I hearkening when this was decreed before the Lord of Hosts: "This sin shall not be forgiven you till you die the second death says

the Lord of hosts"'" (MT "Surely this iniquity will not be forgiven you till you die"). (d) McNamara also finds the phrase "second death" used in Targum Isa 65:6. In this context God complains that His people have become faithless and have turned to immoral conduct and to idols. However, the remnant shall prosper and there shall be a new age for the holy city. The text is very close to Rev 20:14 and 21:8; it reads, "Their *punishment shall be in Gehenna* where the fire burns all the day. Behold, it is written before me: 'I will not *give them respite during* (their) *life* but will render them the punishment of their transgressions and *will deliver their body to the second death'*" (McNamara, p. 123, MT ". . . I will repay, yea, I will repay into their bosom"). (e) Targum Isa 65:15 reads, "And you shall leave your name for a curse to my chosen and the Lord God will slay you with the second death but his servants, *the righteous,* he shall call by a different name" (MT ". . . the Lord God will slay you . . ."). All these are Jewish, not Christian, texts.

COMMENT

Smyrna was originally an Aeolian colony on the mouth of the Hermos river, forty miles north of Ephesus and fifty miles south of Pergamum. It was founded before 1200 B.C., destroyed in the sixth century B.C., and rebuilt by King Lysimachus, according to plans made by Alexander the Great, in 300 B.C. This brought about Hellenization of the city.

In the first century A.D. Smyrna was a large and beautiful city proud of its riches and splendor; it was a most important seaport of Asia Minor because of its location at the terminus of the trade route that went east to the hinterland. The city was crowned with temples and other buildings, forming an ideal acropolis, hence the epithet "the crown of Smyrna," which often designated this cluster of buildings (see p. 395). From the very beginning of Rome's intervention in eastern affairs, Smyrna proved to be a faithful ally and supported Rome against Mithridates, Carthage, and the Seleucid kings. As early as 195 B.C. it dedicated a temple to the goddess of Rome, and in A.D. 26 it alone secured the privilege of erecting a temple to Tiberius, Livia, and the Senate. The coins at Smyrna depict the Smyrnian goddesses, the two sphinxes. They also depict merchant ships, indicating Smyrna's importance as a seaport, which brought that city into close relationship with Rome.

In this prophecy to Smyrna one notices the artistic arrangement of the constant contrasting of extremes:

first	and	last
became dead	but	came to life
poverty	but	in abundance
say they are Jews	but	are not
unto death	and	crown of life

The figures of speech in the prophecy are closely related to the history of the city. The speaker is the Son of Man. The epithet for the speaker is "the First and the Last" and "who was dead and became alive." The former contains a subtle allusion to the fact that Smyrna vied with Ephesus and Pergamum for the title *protē Asias* ("first of Asia," according to Ramsay);

the speaker insists that he is First. The latter may allude to the destruction of Smyrna by the Lydians: for three to four hundred years there was no city. The words of the ancients are, literally, that Smyrna was dead and yet lived (Ramsay, p. 270). Our speaker may indicate that the losses which Smyrna has sustained on the earthly level are compensated for by spiritual "success."

Of all the seven prophecies this one is the most complimentary. This may be the intention behind the assertion that the speaker knows her tribulation and poverty and yet can declare Smyrna is rich. Like the *'anāwīm of Yahweh* (the poor in spirit who relied on Yahweh), she suffers persecution . . . lives in humility, but she is in the midst of spiritual wealth. This idea may also underlie the reference to the blasphemy of those who say they are Jews but are not for they are of the "synagogue" of Satan. After the destruction of Jerusalem in A.D. 70 Smyrna was a favorite settlement for Jews, who became powerful in the city.

The use of the word "synagogue" is significant for it stands out in sharp contrast to "church" (or community, *ekklesia*) employed elsewhere in these prophecies. The statement may indicate either that the speaker is a Jew who, like the covenanters at Qumran, regarded those not following his rigid way of life as the "assembly of Satan." In confirmation of this, we may refer to Ramsay, p. 272, who cites an inscription of the second century A.D. in which the *quondam* Jews are mentioned as contributing ten thousand denarii to the city. Bockh understood this enigmatic phrase to refer to persons who had forsworn their faith and placed themselves on the same level as the ordinary pagan Smyrnians. On the other hand, if the speaker were a Jewish Christian he would have seen the "genuine" Jew as one who found the messianic expectation fulfilled in Christ and the "pseudo-Jew" as one who persecuted those of the Christian way. According to tradition, in Smyrna the Jews joined the heathens in inciting the people towards the martyrdom of Polycarp. See Martyrdom of Polycarp 12. Thus the warning about accusation and imprisonment in vs. 10 may be linked with the Jews mentioned in the previous verse.

The imprisonment is to last for ten days. This may simply imply "a short period," but it may have an indirect reference to such texts as Dan 1:12–14 where Daniel and his companions are "tested" with a vegetarian diet for ten days and Gen 24:55 where Rebekah's family ask that she remain with them ten days. The number ten, however, is the basic unit in the round numbers for the measurements of the ark, the tabernacle and the temple and possibly served to measure about a week: it is symbolic of completion like seven. Smyrna is bidden to be faithful unto death. Perhaps here again there is an allusion to her history, for Cicero calls her "the most faithful of our allies." She is bidden to show the same loyalty on the spiritual level as she did on the political.

For her reward she is promised the "crown of life." Once again there is a local touch. As observed at the beginning of the COMMENT, Smyrna's buildings were like a crown on her hill. Apollonius of Tyana speaks of the "crown of porticoes and pictures and gold beyond the standard of mankind." The phrase "crown of Smyrna" arose from the appearance of the hill Pagos with its stately public buildings on the rounded top. Aelius Aristides compares the city to the crown of Ariadne, shining in the ideal heavenly constellation. The crown was probably a garland or circlet of flowers like those worn in honor of the pagan gods. The goddess Cybele is shown with a necklace on Smyrnian coins; her necklace possibly symbolizes the street of gold which was supposed to be found in Smyrna. Rev 2:10 means "the crown which is (eternal) life." Similarly, 1QS 4:6–8 mentions "the glorious crown" worn by the faithful. The text (D-S) reads:

> And as for the Visitation of all who walk in this (Spirit), it consists of healing and abundance of bliss, with length of days and fruitfulness, and all blessings without end, and eternal joy in perpetual life, and the glorious crown and the garment of honor in everlasting light.

Such will be the state of those who are not hurt by the second death (vs. 11). The contrast is obviously with the first or physical death which some Smyrnians were soon to suffer.

XXIX. PROPHECY TO PERGAMUM
(2:12–17)

2 ¹² Write to the angel of the community at Pergamum: This is the prophecy of the one who has the sharp two-edged sword. ¹³ I discern where you dwell; where is the throne of Satan. Indeed, you hold fast to my name, and you did not deny faith in me even in the days of Antipas, my faithful witness, who was killed among you where Satan dwells. ¹⁴ But I hold a few things against you, because you have there those who hold tenaciously to the teaching of Balaam, who taught Balak to throw a stumbling block before the children of Israel, by eating meats offered to idols and by fornication. ¹⁵ So, similarly, you have, too, those who cling to the teaching of the Nikolaitans, therefore, repent. ¹⁶ If you do not, I shall come quickly against you and shall wage war against them with the sword of my mouth. ¹⁷ Let the one who has spiritual understanding heed what the Spirit says to the communities. To the one who prevails, I will give him the hidden manna; also, I shall give him a white stone; and upon the stone is written a new name, which no one knows except the recipient.

NOTES

2:12. *two-edged sword.* Gr. *rhomphaia.* This word occurs over 230 times in the LXX, but the most germane references are Gen 3:24, the weapon held by the cherubim who guarded the gate of paradise, and I Sam 17:45, 47, 51, 21:10, 22:10, the sword used by Goliath. "Sword" is also used in I Enoch 99:16, which depicts God's judgment on sinners, and in Sibylline Oracles 3:673 which again occurs in the context of God's judgment on undisciplined and empty-minded people who will perish at the hand of the eternal. 1QM 6:3 mentions "Flaming sword which devours the wicked slain by the Judgment of God." In the NT the word occurs only seven times, six in this apocalypse and once in Luke 2:34–35 where Simeon prophesies that the sword will pierce Mary's heart. The apocalyptic symbol of the sword is influenced by Amos 9:4, Hosea 6:5, Isa 11:4, Psalms of Solomon 17:24, 25, all of which see the Logos or Word as an instrument of destruction, although all do not plainly call this a weapon or sword. The idea may well have originated in the metaphor of the tongue as a sword, e.g. Pss 56:5, 58:8; cf. Prov 18:21. However, these passages do not actually say that the sword proceeds from the lips; this concept seems peculiar to our author and influences 2:12, 16, 19:15, 21. Doubtless, the speaker is seen as the eschatological judge of nations. To the Roman the sword was the symbol of the highest authority; cf. the phrase *ius gladii* given to an officer, such as the proconsul of the province who wielded power over life and death. Here, therefore, we have the Christ depicted as a warrior king in language derived from Isa 11:4, 49:2; cf. II Thess 2:8. The implication is that the power of life and death belongs to the Messiah, not the emperor.

13. *I discern where you dwell.* In 046 1, 82, 2059s pl TR this clause is amplified: "I discern your works and where you dwell."

throne of Satan. The city of Pergamum was a natural fortress standing on a sharply protruding hill which dominated the plains below. Perhaps Ramsay's description (pp. 281–315) is the most eloquent:

The rock rules over and as it were plants its foot upon a great valley; and its summit looks over the southern mountains which bound the valley, until the distant lofty peaks south of the Gulf of Smyrna, and especially the beautiful twin peaks now called the two brothers, close in the outlook. Far beneath lies the sea, quite fifteen miles away, and beyond it the foreign soil of Lesbos: the view of other lands, the presence of hostile powers, the need of constant care and watchfulness, all the duties of kingship are forced upon the attention of him who sits enthroned on that huge rock. There is here nothing to suggest evanescence, mutability, and uncertainty, as at Sardis or Ephesus; the inevitable impression is of permanence, strength, sure authority and great size. Something of the personal and the subjective element must be mixed up with such impressions; but in none of these seven cities does the impression seem more universal and unavoidable than in Pergamum.

Upon this rock was situated the Augustan temple, which is often represented on the coins of Pergamum of that time and also appears on coins of many other emperors from the time of Trajan onward. To the writer of Revelation, this heathen temple placed on the loftiest site in the city appeared like the "throne of Satan."

name. To the Hebrew and to the ancient world at large the name of an object or person was no mere label but an essential part of its personality or essence. Pergamum and Philadelphia are both praised because they held fast to the name of Christ, i.e. to the characteristics of Christ.

14. *Balaam.* See NOTE on 2:6, "Nikolaitans."

who taught Balak to throw a stumbling block before the children of Israel. This indicates the eating of forbidden foods and indulgence in licentious behavior.

fornication. This may refer to forbidden degrees in marriage (incest) as in I Cor 5:1 and perhaps Matt 5:32; cf. II Macc 6:3 ff.

15. *Nikolaitans.* See second NOTE on 2:6.

16. *sword.* Gr. *rhomphaia.* See NOTES on 6:4, "great sword," and 6:8, "Sword." See also COMMENT, p. 399.

17. *give him the hidden manna.* P 1, 2059s pm g t sy^h TR read "give him to eat the hidden manna," and P adds the adjectival phrase, "from the tree."

manna. There does not seem to be a reference here to the Eucharist. It is John 6:31 that probably links manna with the Eucharist.

white stone. The stone mentioned here is probably the *tessera* of ancient times, which was used variously as a voting ballot or a ticket to public functions. It was also used when drawing lots in a criminal case; the white stone was a favorable verdict, i.e. life. Ramsay sees a play on words since Pergamum is the name from which is derived the word "parchment," which is quite perishable, wheras the stone is not. Another interpretation may be that this stone is an entrance ticket into the promised land or paradise.

new name. A change of name was often given in the case of serious illness. If the patient survived, the new name bore a reference to life or to some OT saint whose life was especially long. A new name, therefore, denoted a new person: it was often theophoric, i.e. compounded with a name of God.

COMMENT

Pergamum was a city of Mysia (northeast Asia Minor) and lay fifteen miles from the sea, eighty-five miles north of Ephesus, forty-five miles north of Smyrna. It overlooked the valley of the Kaikus. The early city was built on a thousand-foot hill which became the site of the acropolis and many of the chief buildings of the later city. Pergamum was famous for its great religious monuments, e.g. in honor of Zeus Soter, Athena Nikephoros whose temple crowned the acropolis, Dionysos Kathegemon, and especially Asklepios Soter whose cult was the most distinctive and celebrated and accounted for Pergamum's famous school of medicine. Already in 29 B.C. a temple was dedicated in Pergamum to Augustus and Rome, and was recognized by the Roman Senate three years later. Thus, the imperial cult of Asia had its center at Pergamum. This fact may account for its designation here as "the throne of Satan," "throne" being suggested also by the conical hill covered with heathen temples and altars which lay behind the city. The reference makes a grim contrast with the mountain of God of the OT; cf. Isa 4:1–6, Ezek 28:14, 16: this is called the "throne of God" in I Enoch 25:3. The city, therefore, was associated with pagan worship.

Pergamum was also the capital of the Roman province of Asia. Therefore the attribute of the sword to the speaker of the prophecy is significant because he is addressing the seat of authority in the Roman administration. Ramsay observes that to none of the other seven cities would this exordium have applied so appropriately. The sword of the Divine Word (vs. 16) overawes the power of the Roman sword, and the faith of the Christians at Pergamum overcomes the fear of an execution like that of Antipas (vs. 13). Antipas was probably put to death precisely for refusing to acknowledge the power of Caesar.

Despite their faith in face of martyrdom the citizens of Pergamum have succumbed to heterodoxy. Vs. 14 complains that there are people who cling to the teaching of Balaam (see second NOTE on 2:6). Two characteristics of this "heresy" are named, eating meat offered to idols and committing fornication. They are two of the four practices forbidden at the first council of Jerusalem which decided upon the precepts to be observed by the Gentile converts; Acts 15:20. The Nikolaitan heresy (vs. 15) may be partially identified with the teaching of Balaam.

The members of Pergamum (vs. 16) are bidden to repent. Otherwise the speaker will come against them with the sword of his mouth. The threat shows affinity with the Prince of the Congregation at Qumran to whom it is promised in 1QS adjunct b 5:24–25 (cf. Isa 11:4): "And [thou shalt strike the peoples] by the might of thy [mouth]; Thou shalt devastate the earth by the scepter, and by the breath of thy lips shalt thou slay the ungodly." The figure implied here is that of the warrior-Messiah, which is familiar in the Pseudepigrapha and can be traced back to the Song of Miriam (Exod 15:21).

To the victors at Pergamum a three-fold reward is promised, the hidden manna, a white stone, and a new name. With regard to the first, there was a Jewish legend that the manna was laid up before the testimony in the ark and hidden away in a cave on Mount Sinai to be revealed when the Messiah came. There is a possible reference to this in II Macc 2:5, II Baruch 29:8. The blessed were supposed to eat of this manna in the messianic kingdom. Perhaps this reward is promised as a contrast to eating food offered to idols (vs. 14).

The second reward is a white stone or pebble. This seems to be a little cube or rectangular block of stone, ivory, or other substance with words or symbols engraved on one or more facets, which was used as a coupon or ticket. It bore a name and was given to successful gladiators. It was also used as a voting ballot by jurors or political voters. But Ramsay, p. 304, thinks that John may have a new concept. John's stones differ in that they are imperishable and white. They may be intended as a contrast to the pieces of lead (regarded as an ill-omened metal in Greece) upon which were written curses and imprecations. John's stones would bear a blessing. The color white would symbolize victory and joy. The pebble itself may be a gem or precious stone. The Talmud mentions precious stones falling with the manna in the desert.

On the stone is engraved a new name. See NOTES: on 2:13, "name," and 2:17, "new name," for the importance attached to the new name in the OT and the fact that in ancient times much was made of the power of secret names. Here, the name may be the name of an angel or a new name for the person, but we also know that the name of the Messiah was supposed to be engraved on a stone in the temple. Therefore, this part of Pergamum's reward may be linked with the reward promised to Philadelphia (3:7–13) concerning the temple of God. The Qumran community were known as men of the name or men of renown, e.g. 1QM 2:6, 3:4. This may be equivalent to renowned men, but it also may refer to men who bore the name of God. Cf. Isa 44:5 where the prophet says people will write upon their hands "The Lord's" and surname themselves by the name of Israel; cf. also Isa 62:2, 65:15. It was generally thought that the pronouncing or writing of the new name upon a person or thing implied that these were the property of the person named. This particular promise looks back to the apocalyptic in 7:4 references to those who are marked or sealed as belonging to Yahweh. Ramsay thinks that there is an implied opposition to the Senate, who gave Octavian the new name of Augustus. He observes:

The readers of this letter, who possess the key to its comprehension, hidden from the common world, could not fail to be struck with the analogy between this new name and the imperial title Augustus. That also had been a new name, deliberately devised by the Senate to designate the founder, and to mark the foundation of the new Empire: it was an old sacred word, used previously only in the language of the priests, and not applied to any human being: hence Ovid says: "Sancta vocant augusta patres" (Fasti i 609, "the fathers call holy things 'worthy of honour' ").

XXX. PROPHECY TO THYATIRA
(2:18–29)

2 ¹⁸ Write to the angel of the community at Thyatira: This is the prophecy of the Son of God, whose eyes are like a flame of fire and whose feet are like fine bronze. ¹⁹ I discern your works and your love and your faith and your service and your patience, and your recent works are even better than the first ones. ²⁰ But I hold this against you, that you tolerate the woman Jezebel, who calls herself a prophetess and teaches my servants to practice immorality and to eat things offered to idols. ²¹ I have given her time that she might repent but she does not wish to turn from her immorality. ²² Behold, I will throw her on a sickbed and those who commit adultery with her into great affliction if they do not repent of her works. ²³ And her children I will slay by disease. All the communities will know that I am he who searches minds and hearts and I will give to each of you according to your works. ²⁴ But to the rest of you in Thyatira, who do not follow this teaching, who do not know the deep things of Satan, as they call them, I place no further burden upon you. ²⁵ Only what you do have cling to until I come. ²⁶ And to the one who prevails and keeps my works to the end, I will give him authority over the nations, ²⁷ and he will rule over and shatter them with an iron scepter, as the potter's earthenware is broken into pieces, ²⁸ as even I have received from my Father; also I will give to him the morning star. ²⁹ Let the one who has spiritual understanding heed what the Spirit says to the communities.

NOTES

2:18. *Son of God.* The title is unique in this apocalypse. In the OT angels are sometimes designated "sons of God" but in that phrase "God" is without the definite article and the meaning is probably "supernatural beings." In the synoptic Gospels Jesus is only called "the Son of the God" by Satan and unclean spirits in the temptation and exorcism narratives and in the Matthean version of the Caesarean confession (Matt 16:16) and Jesus' trial before the high priest according to Matthew and Luke. The Jews did not foresee a divine Messiah or Anointed, but an anointed, human king of Israel as the adopted son of Yahweh; cf. Ps 2. The phrase "Son of God" was not found in the

Aramaic language until a fragment was discovered at Qumran which apparently reads roughly as follows: "He will be called great and will be hailed by his name, and he will be called the Son of God and the son of the Most High." This may refer to a Messiah, either priestly or political, but on the other hand it may refer to some angelic figure, such as Michael or Melchizedek.

In this verse the title has a much more profound significance than the description "one like a son of man" in 1:13; it indicates a unique relationship to God.

fine bronze. Further information about metal work, especially making weapons, is indicated in 1QM 5:11–12, e.g. the swords are to be: "Purified iron refined in the crucible and made white as a mirror, the work of an ar[t]ist goldsmith; and (they shall be adorned) with an encrusted (?) figure in pure gold." See the ornate shield found at Dura (Yadin, *Scroll of the War,* pp. 118–19).

20. *I hold this against you.* ℵ 2026 al g sy^ph read "I hold this much against you," pc t Cypr Tyc read "I hold many [things] against you," and 2049 pc vg^s,cl TR read "I hold a few things against you."

the woman Jezebel. Jezebel's name does not apparently occur in later Jewish writings and there appears to be no trace of any symbolic use. A 046 82, 1006 al sy Prim; R^m read "your woman Jezebel," connoting "your wife." Jezebel is probably a nickname because the woman supported false prophets as did Queen Jezebel in Elijah's day.

22. *sickbed.* The Greek word here can mean a bed or sickbed. Ramsay, however (p. 352), prefers the first interpretation and would like to translate the verse: "I set her on a dining couch (of the club dinners) and her vile associates with her, and they shall have opportunity to enjoy great tribulation: unless *they* repent, for *she* has shown that she cannot repent."

adultery with her. A 1, 2059s pm vg^s,cl, sy^ph TR read "adultery with them."

23. *children.* In this text they are probably disciples or perverts who follow this woman.

disease. Gr. *thanatos.* The Greek may mean "plague" or "death."

minds. Gr. *nephros,* "kidneys," which were regarded as the seat of the emotions, just as the heart was the seat of the intelligence or the will. Hence, the speaker with divine omniscience will prove that no deceit or sophistry of any kind can escape him.

your works. 046 2329 pc vg^s,cl co read "his works."

24. *who do not know the deep things of Satan.* Probably this suggests the doctrines or practices of the Nikolaitans. Cerfaux refers to later related Gnostic sects who claimed that it was licit to sacrifice to the idols in order to escape martyrdom, since true confession was that of the heart, not of the lips. Consistent with this line of thought, they also taught that fornication was of no import. Only the spirit mattered; what you did with the body was insignificant. I Cor 2:10 mentions the "deep things of God" revealed by the Spirit. Just the opposite obtains here; the depths of Satan are revealed through illicit practices. Charles points out that this term would be quite natural to any group which claims special esoteric knowledge. However, one might find a touch of sarcasm. They claim to know the deep things of

God but, in reality, exactly the opposite is true. In 2329 this reads "who do not know the deep things of God but of Satan."

no further burden. The rabbis, basing their opinions on Gen 2:16, declared that the following six commandments were imposed upon Adam: (1) not to worship idols; (2) not to blaspheme against the name of God; (3) to establish courts of justice; (4) not to kill; (5) not to commit adultery; (6) not to steal. A seventh commandment was apparently added after the deluge, namely, not to eat flesh that had been cut from a living animal. These, known as the Noachic commandments, were regarded as obligatory upon all mankind in distinction from those that were binding upon Israelites only. Most Christians believed Gentiles did not have to follow the whole Torah, especially the law of circumcision, in order to be admitted to the kingdom of God that Jesus heralded, but Jews were privileged with the responsibility of following the Torah so they could serve the world as a nation of priests. The whole Torah would have seemed a "further burden" to the Gentile Christians, so here it is affirmed that this burden is removed.

27. *rule over and shatter them.* In the Greek this appears as one verb, *poimanei,* which is generally translated "rule." However, the verse as a whole makes no sense unless we adopt Charles's suggestion that *poimanei* has two meanings, "to shepherd" and "to devastate." Supporting Charles's suggestion is that both here and in 19:15, where Ps 2 (the coronation psalm) is cited, *poimanei* (*n*) is in parallel construction with *suntribetai,* "broken into pieces," and *patassō,* "smite," respectively. The author must therefore have intended a *double entendre.* Since no one English verb will translate both meanings at once, two English verbs had to be used.

scepter. The omission of the "sword" in these verses shows accuracy in the choice of the details in this prophecy. The sword was the symbol of the highest Roman authority and could therefore be used in reference to Pergamum, the official capital, but it is avoided in the case of Thyatira. In its place is mentioned the rod of iron, which signifies force but not authority. For the apocalyptic significance of the scepter see NOTE on 2:28 below.

28. *morning star.* Cf. the military savior of Israel described in Num 24:27 as a star coming out of Jacob and a scepter rising out of Israel. As Farrer, *Revelation,* p. 76, avers, "morning star" is probably associated with the privilege of ruling or sovereignty. He says, "Stars rise and 'reign' in the heavens: kings reign on earth by the influence of their stars."

COMMENT

Thyatira was situated in Lydia on the road from Pergamum to Sardis. It was originally a Macedonian military colony and served as a useful garrison for soldiers to hold the road, first in the interest of the Seleucid kings and afterwards for the Pergamene kings. The power of Pergamum depended to a great extent on the status of Thyatira. The city itself had no proper acropolis. Its situation gave an impression of weakness, subjection, and dependence. It could never be taken for a ruling city or the capital of a province and at all times it had to face the possibility of warfare. Indeed, its coins show a horseman with a battle ax over his shoulder going to conquer and to dash his enemies to pieces; cf. vss. 26, 28.

We infer both from Josephus (cf. *Ant.* 3.119) and from Acts 16:14 that there must have been a Jewish community at Thyatira. Schürer, p. 337, suggests that there may have been a sanctuary of Sambethe, the Oriental Sibyl (prophetess) in the Chaldean precinct of Thyatira. This might have been formed under Hebrew influence and, if so, the sanctuary would have arisen in an attempt to blend Jewish and pagan religious ideas. Thyatira may well have been a city in which the Jews were not entirely faithful to their ancestral beliefs. The same may be said of the early Christians who lived here. Epiphanius reports that the whole city became Montanist, a schismatic apocalyptic movement in the primitive church. The tendency to syncretism may have increased because of the number of trade guilds in the city. First-century coins attest to the industries of weaving, leather, pottery, and bronze melting. The religious importance of the trade guilds lies in the fact that it would be very difficult for the members to abstain from imperial worship, for this was regarded as a proof of the workers' loyalty to the emperor.

There is a certain resemblance between the prophecy to Thyatira and to Pergamum. Both cities were affected by the Nikolaitan teaching, both lay a little apart from the rest, away in the north, and they were the two Mysian cities of the seven (Mysia is a district in Asia Minor).

The description of the speaker to Thyatira is pertinent to the character of the city for it reflects the metal industry. The feet of the speaker are said to be like a fine bronze, a very hard alloyed metal, used for weapons, which under proper treatment assumed a brilliant polished gleam and looked like gold. In fact, the glitter of the weapons and shields in the battle was used to intimidate the enemy. In 1QM 5:5–6 the infantry shields are described as follows:

And they shall all hold shields of bronze polished like a mirror. And the shield should be surrounded with a braided border in the form of a coupling in interwoven (?) gold and silver and bronze, the work of an artist; and (it shall be adorned) with many-coloured (?) precious stones, the work of an artist goldsmith. The length of the shield should be two and a half cubits and its width one and a half cubits.

A more closely related text comes from 1QS adjunct b, the blessing of the Prince of the Congregation "May He make thy horns of iron and thy shoes of bronze!" This is probably based on Deut 33:25.

The prophecy begins with praise of Thyatira; indeed, the speaker seems to emphasize the very characteristics which are lacking in other communities. He commends Thyatira for making progress, her last works being better than the first, whereas Ephesus is reproved for having lost her first love. However, even Thyatira is not without fault; she tolerates the false prophetess Jezebel.

The historical Jezebel was the daughter of the king of Sidon. She married Ahab, the second king of the fourth dynasty of Israel founded by Omri;

I Kings 16:31. Her aggressive character is seen in her ambition to exterminate Yahwism, her association with the guilds of prophets, her violence, bloodshed, and idolatry; I Kings 21:21–24. In Rev 2:20 Jezebel appears to be a real person, although her name may be symbolic. Like Ahab's queen, the Jezebel mentioned here leads the servants of God into immorality and the eating of meats sacrificed to idols. It is uncertain whether immorality is to be taken literally (cf. II Kings 9:22 where harlotries and sorceries are mentioned) or in a spiritual sense with reference to an attack on the worship of Yahweh (cf. Hosea 4:12). However, both meanings might obtain if sacred prostitution were involved.

The misconduct of Jezebel in leading people astray is described in precisely the same words as the teaching of the Nikolaitans at Pergamum; Rev 2:14, 15. But the situation in Thyatira appears to be worse than that in Pergamum. There, only a certain number of the community held Nikolaitan teachings, but here in Thyatira the majority of the community seem to be tolerating the presence of this leader who assumes authority under the guise of a prophetess. Many scholars concur with Charles's judgment (I, 69–70) that the church in Thyatira tolerated this Nicolaitan teaching because it justified their membership in the city guilds and their sharing in the common meals. Martin Kiddle in *Revelation of St. John* draws attention to the powerful social role which such organizations played. In any small town no citizen is a stranger and the penalties of ostracism can easily be inflicted if one does not fall in with the general trend of ideas. One's livelihood might be jeopardized if one refrained from joining a trade guild.

Nevertheless the speaker of the prophecy will not tolerate any apostasy. The threat in vs. 22 portrays a clear parallelism: "Behold, I will throw her on a sickbed, and those who commit adultery with her into great affliction . . ." A similar idiom occurs in Exod 21:18 (". . . the man does not die but keeps his bed . . .") and I Macc 1:5 (" . . . he fell sick and perceived that he was dying . . ."): both suggest critical (lethal) illness. This is confirmed in vs. 23. In the ancient world sickness was seen as the result of sin. The punishment of the children, with the prophetess, may suggest the Jewish belief that the sins of parents are visited upon their children (cf. Exod 34:7) or that the whole family is punished for the iniquity of one member (cf. Achan in Josh 7, Dan 6:24). The punishment will make the citizens of Thyatira acutely aware of the fact that the Son of God (cf. vs. 18) cannot be deceived, for He searches the minds and the heart (vs. 23; cf. Jer 11:20, Ps 64:6–7, etc., in reference to Yahweh's omniscience). Omniscience is suggested also by the description of His eyes in vs. 18.

After this admonition against Jezebel the speaker addresses encouraging words to the faithful, telling them he will impose no other burden upon them. This is reminiscent of the Jerusalem decree in Acts 15:28–29: "For the Holy Spirit and we have decided not to lay upon you any burden [*baros*] other than the following, which is necessary: to abstain from meat that has been offered to idols, from blood, from what has been strangled, and from sexual impurity" (AB). Perhaps the citizens of Thyatira are bidden to observe merely the Noachic precepts; see second NOTE on 2:24.

The reward promised to those who prevail is a share in the messianic authority; cf. 20:6. They will not only rule the nations but crush them. The former attribute, but not the latter, is predicted of the male child in 12:5. The promise is more akin to 19:15–16, the warrior-savior smiting the nations with a sword and ruling (and/or shattering) them with a rod. The reward is significant in the light of Thyatira's political position as the weakest of the seven cities. One notes that a certain irresistible power is promised to the weakest city of the seven, for with Thyatira's disadvantageous position we may contrast the high acropolis of Sardis, the huge hill of Pergamum, the mountain walls of Ephesus, the castled hill of Smyrna (each with their harbors), the long sloping hillside of Philadelphia which rises above the plain, and the plateau of Laodicea with its long walls; cf. Ramsay, p. 175.

In vs. 28 we reach one of the most curious passages in this apocalypse. Here a second promise is given to the faithful, namely, the reception of the "morning star." The interpretation of Farrer, pp. 75–76, seems the most feasible. In Ps 2, which is alluded to in this verse and the preceding one, the Messiah or king of Israel is equipped with the scepter of rule. This text is complementary to the Balaam text from Num 24:17, which comprises the prophecies concerning the Davidic kingdom and uses the symbols of a star coming out of Jacob and a scepter out of Israel. In vs. 27 the rod or scepter has been mentioned indirectly by the allusion to Ps 2, and now the concept of star is added. The word "morning" may qualify "star" because in Jer 23:5, 33:15, Zech 3:8, 6:12, which refer to the shoot out of Jesse, a word is employed which may mean either "shoot" or "dayspring." The reward, then, is the Son of God Himself under the symbol of the morning star.

XXXI. PROPHECY TO SARDIS
(3:1–6)

3 1 And write to the angel of the community at Sardis: This is the prophecy of the one who has the seven spirits of God and the seven stars. 2 I discern your works, that you have a reputation for being alive, but you are dead. Arouse yourself and strengthen what remains which is about to die. For I have not found your works perfect before my God. 3 Therefore remember what you received and heard, and keep it and repent. However, if you do not arouse yourself, I will come like a thief and you will not know the hour I will come upon you. 4 But you have a few people in Sardis who have not soiled their clothes, and they will walk with me clothed in white because they are worthy. 5 The one who prevails will be clothed thus in white vestments and I will not blot his name out of the book of life, and I will publicly acknowledge his name before my Father and in the presence of His angels. 6 Let the one who has spiritual understanding heed what the Spirit says to the churches.

Notes

3:2. *reputation.* Gr. *onoma.* This may mean reputation or name; in vs. 4 it is a synonym for "person."

alive . . . dead. Notice the antithesis between "life" and "death." The word "dead" has metaphorical senses: without truth, as the dead words of a false philosopher or teacher and those who are taught by him; without soul, as things which belong to the sensual world of inanimate objects, especially images of pagan gods (cf. Wisd Sol 15:5). Figuratively, it is used by the rabbis to denote the ungodly; Strack and Billerbeck, *Kommentar zum Neuen Testament*, I, 489 on Matt 8:22; III, 652 on I Tim 5:6. Perhaps the finest example of this antithesis in the NT is Luke 15:24, 32, where the Prodigal Son is said to be dead and become alive again. Cf. also James 2:17, 26, where faith without works is said to be dead, Ignatius *Ad Philippians* 6:1, Shepherd of Hermas Similitudes 9.21.2; cf. 9.26.3–4. In Col 2:13 sinful men are regarded as dead before their baptism.

strengthen. 325, 1611 al syh read "keep."

perfect. Gr. *peplērōmena.* This noun is used of works which are completed. In the Johannine writings it is related to grace "directly brought by the actuality of eschatological salvations; this is 'perfected,' 'brought to full measure'" (TWNT, VI). Thus, the joy of the bridegroom is said to be fulfilled in John 3:29. Johannine writings do not use *teleioun* but *plēroun* as in our text.

Arouse yourself. ℵ* Prim read "repent."

3. *thief.* One recalls the continual insistence on repentance and conversion in the Dead Sea scrolls and the fact that the members of Qumran studied and prayed throughout the night, there being a rota so that people took one-third of the night to watch in prayer and study; 1QS 6:6–8. The messianic hour of judgment could not be known in advance.

4. *soiled their clothes.* The language recalls the inscriptions found in Asia Minor which announced that soiled garments disqualified the worshiper and dishonored the god. But possibly we are meant to see garment here as a synonym for personality. In *Shabbath* 152b, 153a there are several stories concerning foolish men who wore their good garments for working while their wives stored theirs and were prepared to answer the unexpected call of the king with clean clothes. Cf. John 21:7, where Peter dons his coat when the risen Christ waits on the shore. In this context the rabbis recalled Sir 9:8: "Let thy garment be always white; and let not thy head lack ointment." *Shabbath* 14a says that nakedness means "without good deeds." 1QS 3:1–12 stresses the necessity of spiritual purity and the uselessness of physical ceremonial washing unless one has this spiritual purity.

5. *clothed thus in white vestments.* P 046 1, 1611, 2059s pm TR read "this one will be clothed in white vestments." The members of Qumran, the Essenes, and the Therapeutae were clothed in white garments, probably as a symbol of their inner purity.

I will not blot his name out of the book of life. This can be traced back to the OT official lists of citizens and registrars, as in Exod 32:32 ff., Ps 69:28; those inscribed in the lists had the privilege of sharing in the goods of the community. If one's name were blotted out (and this probably means that the parchment was immersed in water so that the name would actually be blotted out; cf. Section VII, COMMENT), one would be denied this privilege and, practically, it meant that one was condemned to death.

While the OT emphasized the book of life as the list of the citizens in the kingdom of God on earth, the term gradually came to be applied to the next life. The book of life then meant the list of those destined for everlasting life. In Dan 7:10 and I Enoch 47:3, the Ancient of Days on his throne of glory has "the book" or "the books of life" open before him. The book or books may be identical with the book of remembrance in which were recorded the deeds of those who feared the Lord; Mal 3:16; cf. II Cor 3:3, Luke 10:20, Heb 12:23; also Rev 4:4, 6:11. In the Pseudepigrapha the names of the friends of God are inscribed on the heavenly tablets (Jubilees 19:9; cf. 30:20–22, I Enoch 47:3, Jerusalem Targum on Exod 32:32–33). I Enoch 104:1 speaks of heretics being removed from the Book of the Living and 108:3 refers to names which are blotted out. The concept of the book of life occurs also in Patristic literature; cf. Shepherd of Hermas Visions 1.3, Mandates 8, Similitudes 2.

In summary, one may say that the book of life is a register of the citizens of the theocracy. Dan 2:1 declares those so inscribed will escape troubles which will precede the establishment of the messianic kingdom.

COMMENT

Sardis lay about thirty miles southeast of Thyatira and was built on the northern confines of Mount Tmolus, a spur of which supported her acropolis. She dominated the Hermas Valley. One of the most ancient cities of Asia Minor, she dated back to 1200 B.C. She was the capital of the ancient Lydian kingdom, which reached its acme under the ill-fated Croesus about 560 B.C. Under the Persian hegemony she was the seat of a satrapy, but then she fell into obscurity. With the Roman rule she recovered some of her former importance, but no city in Asia presented a more melancholy contrast between past splendor and steady decline.

In A.D. 17 she was destroyed by an earthquake but was rebuilt through the generosity of Tiberius, to whom she erected an unauthorized temple. Sardinian coins show the gratitude of the city. They are imprinted with the genius of Sardis kneeling before the emperor, and with the name Caesarean Sardis. The city took this epithet in honor of the imperial benefactor and retained it on coins for some time after Tiberius' death. The reverse of the coin shows the deified Empress Livia sitting like a goddess after the fashion of Demeter. Sardis built a temple in honor of Tiberius and Livia. Sardis worshiped also Lydian Zeus, but was better known for the orgiastic cult of Cybele, the great nature goddess of Anatolia, whose eunuch priests were called Galli.

In the sphere of industry Sardis claimed to be the first community to discover the art of dyeing wool. The manufacture of woolen goods was of commercial importance.

Important archaeological excavations have taken place at Sardis from 1958 onward. The chief finds of interest for Revelation are the synagogue (although it is of a later date), a winged horse, a picture of the evangelist John (see Hanfmann, *Bulletin of the American Schools of Oriental Research* 182 [1966], 52–53, esp. fig. 11 on p. 15), and a portrait of the head of a priest (157 [1959], 5–43, esp. fig. 4 on p. 16) which probably belongs to the second half of the third century A.D. but is similar in style to the portraits at the time of the tetrarchs. "Twelve little heads, themselves diademed, are attached to his diadem; according to one view these heads symbolize the emperors and identify the personage as a priest of the imperial cult; according to others, these are the Twelve Great Gods" (see illustration 18; cf. Rev 17:7, 19:12). Like the busts found in Ephesus, the Sardian diadem bearer may portray a Chief Priest of Asia.

Johnson (*Bulletin of the American Schools of Oriental Research* [1958], 8) discusses some evidence which shows that the city of the Sardians took a prominent part in the imperial cult and cities among others this inscription: "The city of the Sardians, twice temple-warden, [honoured?] the Imperator Caesar Aurelius Antoninus Verus Augustus. Claudius Antonius Lepidus dedicated [this], [being] high priest of Asia, first treasurer, who by virtue of his office took charge of the arrangements for the gymnasium." Several other inscriptions refer to the other high priests of Roma and the emperor. Moreover, by the late first century B.C. Sardis probably had two gymnasia.

The importance of the gymnasia cannot be underestimated, for their presence would mean that the city was exposed to practices which many orthodox Jews could not accept. The athletes played naked, so many Jewish men who wished to take part in the games tried to disguise their circumcision. This was a matter of great offense to their fellow Jews; cf. I Macc 1:15.

The synagogue possessed rich mosaics and other ornate decorations which suggest that it was an important public building. Fallen on its face on the mosaic floor lay a marble slab incised with the stylized menorah, the seven-branched lampstand (cf. Rev 1:12, 2:1), flanked on the left by a palm (Heb. *lulav*) used for the Feast of Tabernacles (cf. Rev 7:9) and some other feasts and a trumpet (Heb. *shofar*) on the right (cf. Rev 8:2). These three symbols are very common, together with the incense shovel (cf. Rev 15:7) and the *ethrog,* another plant used for festival occasions. The design of a lion was found between sprays of acanthus leaves. The lion was the most commonly represented animal in the decorations of the Palestinian synagogues, especially at Capernaum and Chorazin (cf. Rev 5:5). Of special interest for Revelation is the discovery of a seal. It is a small oval stone of yellow carnelian which depicts a "fantastic creature combining bird, animal, and human features; such composite beings are often associated with the amuletic 'Gnostic' gems in which pagan and Jewish symbols occur side by side"; cf. a similar monster in Goodenough, *Jewish Symbols in the Greco-Roman Period,* III, 1086). Although this figure may be much later than the date of Revelation, it probably shows the origin of some of the fantastic symbolism which one meets in this apocalypse; cf. 9:7–11, 17–19, etc. (see illustrations.)

Although this synagogue was probably constructed in the first half of the third century A.D., it does suggest that there was a large community of Jews here. These, of course, might have come to Sardis after the destruction of Jerusalem in A.D. 70. However, there seems to be some evidence for an earlier settlement. For example, some almost life-sized figures of lions have been discovered. These bear some features of the sixth century B.C., although they may be of later date. Hanfmann states: "The occurrence of the 'Leontioi' (the 'tribe of Judah') in inscriptions from the synagogue and the use of the lion as a decorative feature on pilasters and elsewhere explains the presence of the lions, which are taken from an earlier construction; cf. Rev 5:5." One must note, however, that the dedicant's name was Leontios.

Of further interest to us is the fact that the synagogue was very close to the gymnasium, and in a pit nearby which was probably a cooking area have been found remains of nonkosher animals, horse and pig. This would mean either that the ruins did not belong to the synagogue or that the dietary prohibitions obtaining among the Jews were not so strictly observed by the Jews in Sardis. The matter, however, is very puzzling, as a decree of the city of Sardis (*Ant.* 14.259–261) passed some two hundred years earlier states expressly that the market officials are to see that the Jews get the kind of food that they want, implying that there was a need for kosher food. The discovery is of some interest to us in view of the dietary laws which seem to have been violated according to the prophecy to Pergamum (Rev 2:14) and Thyatira (Rev 2:20).

Josephus indicates that there was a wealthy and influential Jewish community at Sardis (*Ant.* 16.171) and the research of L. Robert and J. H. Kroll shows that a high official in imperial financial administration and a number of city councillors were members of the congregation. A decree of the city (*Ant.* 14.259–261) states that the city gave to the Jews "a place in which they may gather . . . and offer their ancestral prayers and sacrifices to God." The numerous marble menorahs and mosaics seem to suggest that there were Jewish marbleworkers and Jewish craftsmen.

There is some analogy between the prophecy to Ephesus and the one to Sardis in the admonitions which they receive and there is a contrast between, Smyrna, who was called dead and yet alive, and Sardis, who is depicted as living and yet dead (vs. 1). Usually, the speaker finds something to praise in each community but here there is only censure. Despite its appearance of life, Sardis is in reality dead. The word "name" occurs four times in this letter, doubtless to emphasize the contrast between Sardis' name or reputation, her past renown, and the present pitiable reality. "Dead" to a Hebrew would denote loss of spiritual vitality. Sardis is, therefore, bidden to waken to new life and to be watchful.

In this admonition there is a biting allusion to two tragic past instances when the city was taken by surprise: by Croesus in 549 B.C. and by a night attack from the Syrians under Antiochus the Great in 195 B.C. This may also allude to the Jewish idea that judgment would come without warning. The Sardians are bidden to undergo conversion, i.e. a genuine return to commitment to God which they had received and heard. Otherwise, they will be surprised by a third (night) attack. L. A. Vos, *The Synoptic Traditions in the Apocalypse*, p. 77, had found a reference to the Gospels in the metaphor of the speaker coming like a thief unexpectedly, and he compares Matt 24:43 ff., Luke 12:39, Mark 13:35, I Thess 5:2, 4.

There are a few people (lit. "names") in Sardis who have kept intact their faith and have not defiled their garments. Here "clothes" seems to signify reputation or personality as in Zech 3:3–5 where Joshua's filthy and clean garments symbolize his sin and innocence respectively.

If garment is a metaphor for wisdom here as in some nonbiblical Jewish texts (see L. Ginzberg, *Legends of the Jews*, VI, 170), those Sardians who are clothed with wisdom are also "aroused." According to Pseudo-Philo 20.20 d: "God spoke to Joshua after the death of Moses, saying: 'take the garments of his wisdom (those worn by Moses?) and put them on thee, and gird thy loins with the girdle of his knowledge; then shalt thou be changed and become another man.' And it came to pass when he put them on, that his mind was kindled, and his spirit was stirred up." Further, a famous teacher mentioned in the Mishnah is said to have ascribed his learning to his use of a staff which belonged to the great master Rabbi Meir; see Jerusalem *Nedarim* 9:41b. Cf. also the mantle of Elijah falling on Elisha; II Kings 2:9–14.

In 1QS, in the section concerning the two spirits, we learn that the visitation of all those who walk in the good spirit consists, among other things, in eternal joy in perpetual life and the glorious crown and the garment of honor in everlasting light (4:7–8). Charles thinks that these garments are symbols of heavenly bodies of the faithful, and refers to II Cor 5:1, 4 and Ascension of Isaiah 4:16 (written ca. A.D. 88–100), which says the saints' garments are now with the Lord in storage until the time they will wear them when the Lord is present, and they with Him, in the world; cf. 19:17. In the Shepherd of Hermas, the faithful are given white garments as a reward (Similitudes 8.2.3) and in the Odes of Solomon 25:8, one reads: "And I was clothed with the covering of thy spirit, and thou didst remove from me my raiment of skin." It seems most of these references are to the resurrected body, which is thought of as the body of light or glory; cf. also I Enoch 62:15–16, II Enoch 22:8, Apocalypse of Peter 13. The symbol is probably chosen also in light of the woolen industry at Sardis.

The garments of the worthy are white (3:4). White was the color used especially on the day of the triumph of a Roman emperor, so that when the speaker says that he who prevails will walk in white vestments with Him, he is probably thinking of a triumphal (perhaps messianic) procession in the Roman style. The phrase "clothed in white" also recalls those who followed the rider on the white horse and, like him, were clothed in white (Rev 19:14).

The reward of the Sardians who repent is three-fold (vs. 5); white vestments, their names in the book of life, and public acknowledgment before the Father. The registration in the book of life is a familiar phrase in Revelation (13:8, 17:8, 20:12, 15, 21:27) and occurs elsewhere in the NT (Luke 10:20, Heb 12:23, Phil 4:3). The readers of this section would recall Moses' plea that he should be blotted out of the book of life if the sins of the Israelites, who made the golden calf, were not forgiven (Exod 32:32–33). It would also remind them of Ezek 13:9, which speaks against prophets who see delusive visions and give lying divinations. They will be excommunicated from the council of the people. Inscription in the book of life would assure the nominees of salvation and removal from it would be associated with death; cf. the references to death in vs. 2. The promise that the speaker will confess the name of the faithful one before his Father and before the angels is strongly reminiscent of Jesus' words in Matt 10:32, Luke 12:8, declaring that he would acknowledge to "my Father" all who acknowledge him and deny those who deny him.

XXXII. PROPHECY TO PHILADELPHIA
(3:7–13)

3 ⁷ And write to the angel of the community in Philadelphia: This is the prophecy of the Holy One, the True One, who has the key of David, the one who opens and no one shall close and who closes and no one opens. ⁸ I discern your works — see, I have placed before you an open door which no one is able to close — that you have little power and yet you have kept my word and you have not denied my name. ⁹ See, I will make those of the assembly of Satan, who call themselves Jews, and are not but are liars, behold, I will make them come and bow down before your feet and they will know that I have loved you. ¹⁰ Because you have kept the word of my endurance, I will keep you in the hour of trial which is to come upon the whole world to test the dwellers upon the earth. ¹¹ I am coming soon. Hold what you have so that no one may seize your crown. ¹² To the one who prevails, I will make him a pillar in the temple of my God, and he will not go out again, and I will write on him the name of my God and the name of the city of my God, the new Jerusalem which comes down from heaven from my God, and my new name. ¹³ Let the one who has spiritual understanding heed what the Spirit says to the churches.

Notes

3:7. *the Holy One, the True One.* Holiness, Heb. *qodesh,* and truthfulness, Heb. *emēth,* are essential attributes of God in the OT, where He is designated the Holy One (Isa 1:4, 5:9, etc.) or the God of Truth (cf. Exod 34:6, Isa 65:16; etc.). These titles are used for God in Rev 6:10, but are applied here to the speaker of the prophecies.

key. In the time of Ezra, four Levites and the chief porters were in charge of the key of the temple; I Chron 9:27. In Rev 9:1, 20:1, the key to the shaft of the bottomless pit gives its possessors power to harass the impious (9:1) or to overpower and bind the dragon (20:1). See illustration 20.

8. *see . . . close.* This may be a parenthesis breaking up the verse which without it would read "I discern your works, that you have little power . . ."

open door. This may refer to the advantageous position of Philadelphia, which was an avenue for Greek culture to the other Asian centers or to missionary work or to entering into a mystic state. Cf. Rev 4:1, which refers to a door in heaven, i.e. entry into the sight of the heavenly court.

and yet. Gr. *kai,* generally "and." Here it has adversative force and so is translated "and yet."

10. *dwellers upon the earth.* Bonsirven, in *L'Apocalypse de Saint Jean,* points out that the phrase "who dwell upon the earth" in 6:19, 11:10, 13:8, 14, 17:8, consistently refers to non-Christians. See also Minear, *I Saw a New Earth,* pp. 261–69.

11. *crown.* Gr. *stephanos.* In the NT *diadem* (Heb. *atarah* or *nezer*) signifies the mark of royalty and *stephanos* (Heb. *kether*) the badge of merit or victory, although the Hebrew does not seem to be so distinct. The latter term is used for the wreath given to the winner of an athletic contest (I Cor 9:25) and is thus used figuratively of any prize, as in II Tim 2:5. An athlete is not crowned unless he competes according to the rules. So, religious people must be watchful lest they forfeit their crown through misconduct. Various Hebrew words are used in the OT to signify different types of crowns or wreaths. The crown set on the forehead of the high priest (Exod 29:6) with the engraving "holy to Yahweh" (cf. 39:30, Lev 8:9) is designated differently from the crown worn by kings. The term is also used in the figurative sense, e.g. a virtuous woman is called her husband's crown (Prov 12:4); the Lord of Hosts is called the crown of his people (Isa 28:5).

In rabbinic tradition, *Shabbath* 88a states that when the Israelites accepted the covenant (Exod 24:7) they were each crowned with two crowns by 600,000 angels — the first when they said, "We will do" and the second at the words, "We will be obedient." However, when they were told to remove their ornaments (Exod 33:6), these crowns were snatched away by 1,200,000 devils. In the messianic age, God will restore the crowns; cf. Isa 35:10.

12. *name of my God.* This designates them as God's own possession. *Baba Bathra* 75b states: "The righteous will in time to come be called by the name of the Holy One, blessed be He; for it is said: *Every one that is called by My name, and whom I have created for My glory, I have formed him, yea, I have made him.* R. Samuel b. Naḥmani said in the name of R. Johanan: Three were called by the name of the Holy One, blessed be He, and they are the following: The righteous, the Messiah and Jerusalem." The statement about the righteous is supported by Isa 43:7, to the Messiah by Jer 23:6, and to Jerusalem by Ezek 48:35.

the new Jerusalem. The Montanists expected a new Jerusalem from heaven and they apparently used this text from Revelation. Calder has argued that the whole of Philadelphia became Montanist.

COMMENT

Twenty-eight miles southeast of Sardis lay Philadelphia. She was founded on the southern side of the Cogamis Valley by Attalus II Philadelphus (159–138 B.C.). Called "little Athens," she became a center of Greek culture and played a part in consolidating, regulating, and educating the central regions of Asia when subject to the Pergamene sovereignty. She continued to be an important place on the imperial post road in the first century. The route coming from Rome by Troas, Pergamum and Sardis passed through Philadelphia and went on to the east. Thus, Philadelphia was a stage on the mainline of the imperial communication (cf. "the open door" in vs. 8).

Philadelphia suffered from the great earthquake of A.D. 17, and was helped in rebuilding her city by the emperor. She took the name Neocaesarea in honor of Tiberius but her former name was restored during the reign of Nero. During the reign of Vespasian (70–79) Philadelphia assumed another title, Flavia. Under Caracalla, she received the title "Temple Warden" of the imperial cult. One sees, therefore, her involvement in pagan worship.

The speaker to Philadelphia is described as "holy" and "true." He holds the key of David. This text is influenced by Isa 22:22: "And I will place on his shoulder the key of the house of David; he shall open and none shall shut; and he shall shut and none shall open" (RSV). Both in biblical and rabbinic literature, handing over a key is a metaphorical expression signifying not an appointment as a porter but the authorization to exercise complete power in a house. The Targum to Isa 22:22 renders the key of the house of David as a "key to the sanctuary and dominion of the house of David." *Sanhedrin* 44b, alluding to this same text, says of the archangel Gabriel or of the Spirit of Shame that ". . . when he closes (the gates of grace) none can open them." Thus the speaker appears to have unlimited sovereignty over the city of David, the new Jerusalem, and can grant or deny entrance to it in the last age; cf. vs. 12.

Although the community in Philadelphia is weak (vs. 8), the speaker will supply her lack and reward her fidelity by causing a door to be opened. The open door may represent missionary work. It may also be associated with conquering the assembly of Satan (vs. 9), which is depicted in terms that recall the OT prophetic descriptions of the conversion of the Gentiles; cf. Isa 45:14, 49:23, 60:14. Isa 60:14, in reference to the new Jerusalem, reads: "The sons of your oppressor shall come to you bowed down; bending low all those who insulted you shall prostrate themselves at your feet; they shall call you the city of Yahweh, the Zion of the Holy One of Israel" (AB). It is here that one can see a link between the conquered assembly of Satan in vs. 9 and the community as a pillar in the temple of God in association with the new Jerusalem in vs. 12. In Isa 60:14 the city is a community of people, not a material building; cf. Matt 16:13 ff.

The speaker promises Philadelphia that because she has kept the word of his endurance (cf. 1QS 8:3) he will keep her in the hour of trial which is to come upon the whole world. The speaker promises to come quickly, a warning which in Revelation occurs only in 2:16, 3:11, 22:7, 12, 20 (although cf. 11: 14), i.e. not in the main corpus of the work. It probably refers to the second coming after the millennium, i.e. after the period of the church, when the final Jerusalem will come; cf. 21:1–7. This explains why our speaker turns next to the sanctuary of God and the new Jerusalem.

The second Jerusalem is not a material one but a community of people, as in Isa 60:14. Hence, the speaker can promise that the victorious Philadelphians will be a pillar in the sanctuary, the position of which will be immovable (vs. 12) in contrast to the earth tremors which the city had experienced so often. The victor will never go out of the temple because he will always be a part of it. Then the speaker promises that he will inscribe on the faithful three names: the name of Yahweh, the name of the city, and the name of the speaker. Inscriptions on pillars were a common feature of ancient oriental architecture. Writing one's own name on a temple wall was thought to keep one in continual unity with the deity of the temple. It was also customary for the provincial priest of the imperial cult to erect a statue in the confines of the temple dedicated to the emperor and to inscribe on it his own name, that of his father, the place of his birth, and his year of office. Thus, the writer is spiritualizing a secular concept, but cf. Jer 23:6, Ezek 48:35. To bear the name of the city is a sign of citizenship of the heavenly city of God, the new Jerusalem. In the Christian dispensation the new name of Jesus is "Lord" (cf. Philip 2:9–10); the victor shares in this name or character of Jesus.

XXXIII. PROPHECY TO LAODICEA
(3:14-22)

3 ¹⁴ Write to the angel of the community of Laodicea: This is the prophecy of the Amen, the faithful and true witness, the beginning of the creation of God. ¹⁵ I discern your deeds, that you are neither hot nor cold. I wish that you were hot or cold. ¹⁶ Thus, because you are lukewarm, and neither hot nor cold, I will spit you out of my mouth. ¹⁷ Because you said: "I am rich and I have grown opulent and I am not in need"; indeed you do not realize that you are wretched, pitiful and poverty-stricken and blind and naked. ¹⁸ I counsel you to purchase from me gold refined by fire so that you may be rich, and white garments so that you may clothe yourself and not reveal the shame of your nakedness, and eye salve to anoint your eyes so that you may see. ¹⁹ Those whom I love I reprove and chasten, therefore stir up your energy and repent. ²⁰ Behold, I stand before the door and knock. If anyone hears my voice and opens the door, I will come in to him and will dine with him and he with me. ²¹ To the one who prevails, I will grant that he may sit with me on my throne, as I have conquered and taken my seat with my Father on His throne. ²² He who has spiritual understanding let him heed what the Spirit speaks to the churches.

NOTES

3:14. *the Amen, the faithful and true witness.* The speaker identifies himself as "the Amen." The meaning of "amen" from the root *āmēn* meaning "trustworthy" would have been common knowledge to a Hebrew-speaking audience, but Revelation was written or translated into Greek for a non-Hebrew-speaking audience. Therefore, "the faithful and true witness" may have been added in order to define "the Amen."

16. *lukewarm.* Gr. *chliaros.* This word is used by Arethas to describe a man who has received the Holy Spirit in baptism but has quenched the grace. Gregory applies it to a man grown cold after conversion. Origen, *De Principiis* 3.4.3, applies it to unregenerate persons.

The metaphor takes on further significance when one considers the effect of the geographical and economic situation of Laodicea on her water supply. Laodicea had no natural water supply and depended on water piped from the hot springs of Hierapolis down a cliff through the Lycus. By the end of its journey the water was tepid and nausea-provoking. Wood, pp. 263–64, refers to the double row of stone pipes forming an aqueduct which transported the hot spring water across the hill and into the city.

I will spit you out of my mouth. 2329 reads "convict" or "condemn" instead, but 2020 pc includes both.

17. *rich.* That Laodicea must have been reasonably wealthy is indicated by her spurning of Roman aid when she was demolished by earthquake; see Tacitus *Annals* 14.27. When earthquake toppled Sardis, that city not only accepted Roman aid but also built a temple to Tiberius in gratitude; see Section XXXI, COMMENT.

18. *white garments.* These may be contrasted with the black wool for which Laodicea was celebrated. Perhaps they are the *penulae* mentioned in II Tim 4:13, seamless garments popular in Rome.

to anoint your eyes. Laodicea had a famous medical school near Men-Karou, where Phrygian powdered stone was used for eye salve; cf. mascara now used to paint the eyes. The manuscripts 046 82, 1006 al read "that you may anoint your eyes."

COMMENT

Laodicea was named after Laodice, the wife of the founder, Antiochus II Seleucid, who established the new city to replace the village. Formerly, Laodicea bore the names Dispolis and Rhoas. Antiochus placed the city under the patronage of his wife, Laodicea, but he divorced her in 240, which proves Laodicea was founded before that date. The city was situated near the boundaries of Phrygia at the center of the rich plain of Lykos, six miles south of Hierapolis, ten miles west of Colossae, and on the south bank of the river Lycus.

Primarily, she was an agricultural and marketing center. Her favorable situation on the imperial system of roads made her the point at which three highways met. This added to her reputation as a great commercial and administrative city, a banking center, and a large manufacturing center of clothing and carpets of native black wool. She was also the seat of a flourishing medical school from which came the well-known eye salve; cf. vs. 18 and NOTE.

Archaeological discoveries have revealed the Statue of Isis, reliefs of Ganymede and the victory of Theseus over the minotaur. Perhaps this is symbolic of the painful triumph of the Spirit over the bestial. So far, two theaters have been discovered, some baths and a stadium probably dating from A.D. 79. Imperial worship began early in Laodicea but there is no evidence that the city received the honor of *neokoros* or was appointed as temple keeper of the imperial cult like Ephesus.

Laodicea seems to have gained greater prosperity in the second century B.C. when she became a meeting place for philosophers as well as farmers and the city grew in great proportions. In 190 Laodicea passed under the authority of the kings of Pergamum and, then, in 133, at the death of Attalus III, she became a Roman possession. When the city was destroyed by earthquakes in A.D. 60–100, she could proudly refuse imperial subsidies and rebuild herself (see NOTE on vs. 17); hence the references in this prophecy to wealth (vs. 17) and gold (vs. 18). Her wealth may be estimated from the fact that Flaccus took more than 22.5 pounds of gold (ca. $92,400 in 1971) collected for the temple at Jerusalem in 62–61 B.C.

The quantity of gold that Flaccus seized indicates there was a large population of Jews in Laodicea. Flaccus also seized one hundred pounds of gold at Apameia, showing the wealth of the Jewish population in the area of Asia Minor. Reinach (cited in Ramsay) calculated that there would have been about 7,500 adult male Jews in Laodicea. We also know that there were many Jews in Hierapolis, especially those belonging to the trade guilds. Inscriptions mentioning the feast of unleavened bread and Pentecost have been discovered. Josephus, *Ant.* 14.241–243, tells of a letter sent by the Laodiceans a few years later than 62 B.C. to Gaius Rabirius, proconsul of Asia, informing him that in obedience to his command they will permit the Jews to keep the Sabbath and the sacred rites, "although the citizens of Tralles," a neighboring city, were opposed to the decree. Coins witness, however, to several treaties of friendship between Laodicea and the other cities of the province, among them Smyrna, Pergamum, and Ephesus. The council of Laodicea, Canon 19, says: "Christians shall not Judaize and be idle on Saturday but shall work on that day." Again, a proof that the Jewish community was still influential.

The church at Laodicea is mentioned four times in the Epistle to the Colossians (2:1, 4:13, 15, 16). Some scholars believe that Paul's Epistle to the Ephesians was originally addressed to Laodicea, but if so his ministry seems to have been rather ineffectual. Paul says to Archippus, in Col 4:17 (RSV): "See that you fulfill the ministry which you have received in the Lord," and in the same epistle he seems to hint that the Laodiceans were blind 2:1). Philemon may have been a Laodicean and it may not be a mere coincidence that at Laodicea an inscription was discovered written by a freed slave to a master called Marcus Sestius Philemon. The name Epaphras (Col 1:7, 4:12, Philem 23) has also been discovered on a marble block at Laodicea. Paul may have passed through Laodicea, but he does not seem to have been personally acquainted with the Christians there; see Col 4:15. It would appear, therefore, that the Jewish population was far more influential at Laodicea than was the Christian Church, although the latter does appear to have been founded early.

The opening verse of this prophecy contains a puzzling designation, "the Amen." Some scholars refer to a Greek version of Isa 65:16 which reads "Amen of God," and others have tried to explain this title by a reference to the divine Yah; cf. II Cor 1:20. Silberman suggests there may be an analogy between the usage here and that found in *Gen R* using Prov 8:20, where the Torah is said to be God's tool. In this Midrash, the *amon*, "master worker," of vs. 30 and the *rēšît*, "beginning," of vs. 22 are related in that they are both titles for the Torah. Silberman sees Rev 14, designating the Amen also as "the faithful and true witness" and "the Beginning," as containing three titles in one, all applied to Christ and all drawn from Proverbs. Two are from the Midrash referred to above. The first is *amon,* Christ as God's advisor in creation (cf. Shepherd of Hermas, Similitudes 9.12.1, "the son of God is older than all his creation, so that he was the counsellor of his creation to the Father . . ."), and the second is faithful and true witness. The third is *arche,* the Greek equivalent of Heb. *rēšît,* "beginning."

Silberman feels "the Amen" refers not to Ps 89:38 (LXX 88:38), but a literal rendering of Prov 14:5, 25. He notes (p. 215, note 13) that the LXX has "faithful witness" in both cases. Therefore, in this particular address, there is a play on the word *amon* and *amen.* Thus, Silberman will translate: "Thus says the master worker, the faithful and true witness, the foremost of his creation." This seems to be a compelling thesis in the light of the Wisdom motif occurring throughout this prophecy.

Although vss. 15–16 are not written with Wisdom terminology, the idea of total commitment and disdain of lukewarmness is a typically Wisdom motif. Wisd Sol speaks of preferring wisdom to political prestige, wealth, or even health (cf. Wisd Sol 7:8–12) and a constant theme in Proverbs, the Book of Wisdom, and Sirach is the eagerness, diligence, and perseverance with which one must seek wisdom; cf. Sir 6:18–37; Prov 4:1–9; Wisd Sol 6:12–20. Vs. 17 continues the Wisdom theme by setting the material wealth of Laodicea at naught. Wisdom is worth more than riches (Wisd Sol 7:9) and light (7:10), and clothes one with glory and honor (Sir 6:30–31). Vs. 19 employs an indirect quotation from Prov 3:12. Vs. 20 introduces the metaphor of the door which is well known in Wisdom literature. Cf. e.g. Wisd Sol 6:14 in which Wisdom is sitting at the gates of the one who rises early to seek her will, 8:3 in which Wisdom calls from the gates and entrance of the town, and 8:34 in which the man who heeds Wisdom, who watches at her gates and doors, is declared happy. Vs. 20 also shows Wisdom coming to the recipient and entering to dine with him. The Wisdom banquet is well known from Prov 9. The prophecy ends on a Wisdom note by reference to the throne of God from whence Wisdom is deemed to have come. Cf. Wisd Sol 9:10, where Solomon prays that God send Wisdom from the holy heavens and from the throne of His glory, that he may learn what is pleasing to God and that she may guide him.

This last of the seven prophecies, therefore, is closely associated with the figure of "one like a son of man" in the vision of Rev 1, especially if this son of man is the epitome of Wisdom. But as Wisdom is traditionally thought of as a woman, it may also form a contrast with the harlot in ch. 17. The Wisdom theology was fulfilled in Christ; cf. Col 1:16–17, Heb 1:2. In Col 1:18 Christ is called the beginning and in Col 1:15 he is named "the firstborn of every creature," i.e. the firstborn in relation to mankind. The wording is similar but not precisely the same as in this apocalypse, but the reference is interesting because Paul probably wished his Epistle to the Colossians to be exchanged with the Laodiceans; cf. Col 2:1.

The community at Laodicea is not accused of any specific disorder, but its condition appears to be worse than that of the other communities because the evil is more insidious. The community members seem to be self-satisfied and indifferent; there seems to be no outstanding evil or persecution to make them aware of the condition of their religion. The speaker of the prophecy expresses repulsion against the community's apathy, and emphasizes its danger of rejection by a most forceful and homely figure of speech, "I will spit you out," vs. 16. This may have come to the author's mind when he recalled that lukewarm water was useful only as an emetic, especially when the waters contained salt, as formed in a ravine when the great cascade petrifies.

Wealthy in material possessions, the community at Laodicea felt self-sufficient and complacent regarding its spiritual condition. The speaker of this prophecy warns that they are utterly poor and wretched spiritually and the terms that he uses—poverty-stricken, blind, naked—designate the extremes of conscious and unconscious wretchedness. Cf. the material poverty but spiritual richness of Smyrna (2:9). True riches may only be purchased from him, not from their own resources. The garments of glossy black wool on which Laodicea prided herself would not cover spiritual nakedness, nor would its famous eye salve or medicines or powders help spiritual blindness—only God can remedy these ills. What Laodicea must purchase is gold refined by fire, white garments, and eye salve. The gold is a symbol of tested faith and love or a new and disciplined spirit and participation in the holiness of God. The white garments will cover their nakedness; nakedness is a figure used to describe the confusion of the damned on the last day (cf. II Cor 5:2–3).

Severe as the speaker has been, he cannot conceal his love and tender solicitude for the community. His severity is only a proof of his love. In vs. 20 he asks admittance and promises indescribable joys to those who receive him. Feuillet finds a parallel in Song of Songs 5:2 where the lover invites his bride into the garden to dine with him, and in the synoptic texts where the Lord is said to be near, e.g. Mark 13:29, Matt 24:23, Luke 12:36. Charles (I, 101) says, "Participation in the common meal was for the Oriental a proof of confidence and affection. The intimate fellowship of the faithful with God and the Messiah in the coming age was frequently symbolized by such a metaphor." The figure also strikes a note of reality because Laodicea was "set four-square on one of the most important road junctions in Asia Minor, and each of the four city gates opened on a busy trade route." The inhabitants must have been very familiar with the belated traveller who "stood at the door and knocked" for admission and, in the east, the supper (*deipnon*) is, of course, the symbol of enduring friendship," (Rudwick, p. 178, note 1). A parallel to this last prophecy is found in I Enoch 62:14–16, which not only says the righteous will eat, lie down, and rise up with the Son of Man, but also mentions they will wear "garments of glory."

Vs. 21 refers to sharing the throne of glory. Cf. Sir 47:11, referring to David in these terms: "The Lord took away his sins, and exalted his power forever; he gave him the covenant of kings and a throne of glory in Israel" (RSV). Rabbi Akiva even thought that the throne of David would be beside the throne of the Holy One. When chs. 1–3 were added to our apocalypse the reference to the sharing of the throne was meant to lead smoothly into ch. 4, the throne vision.

XXXIV. EPILOGUE
(22:16–17a, 20–21)

22 ¹⁶ "I, Jesus, have sent my angel to you with this testimony for the churches. I am the root and the offspring of David, the bright morning star." ^{17a} The Spirit and the Bride say, "Come." And let him who hears say, "Come." . . . ²⁰ He who testifies to these things says, "Yes, I am coming soon." Amen, come, Lord Jesus. ²¹ May the grace of the Lord Jesus be with everyone.

NOTES

22:16–17a. These verses are not placed in sequence before 17b, as Gaechter would (see Introduction, "The Last Two Chapters"), but as an Epilogue.

16. *Jesus.* This is the only occasion in this apocalypse when Jesus speaks in the first person.

with this testimony. Gr. *marturēsai.* This word occurs only in the specifically Christian portions of Revelation; cf. vs. 20. It is frequently associated with the Baptist and appears often in John's Gospel and in Acts.

churches. Gr. *ekklesiai.* This word appears only in the Christian parts of the text.

the root and the offspring of David. See NOTE on 5:5, "Root of David."

bright morning star. Cf. Luke 1:78 and the seven stars in Rev 1:16, 20. See also NOTE on 2:28, "morning star."

17a. *The Spirit.* Contrast the "seven spirits" in 1:4, 4:5, 5:6. The definite article is omitted in ℵ.

the Bride. Here, too, the definite article is omitted in ℵ. The Bride represents the church; cf. Eph 5:25–27.

"Come." This is the appropriate invitation to "He that cometh"; see Introduction, "He that cometh." Here the coming may be the "return" of Jesus, his *parousia,* which the early Church saw as the completion of this first advent (G. Vos, pp. 75–77).

20. *He who testifies.* The phrase could describe the function of the Baptist, but he would hardly promise to "come soon."

Amen. Omitted in ℵ 2028, 2329 pc g sy^{ph} co.

come, Lord. Gr. *erchou,* "come," having an eschatological, theophanic sense. *Maran atha* (Our Lord, come! in Aramaic) is found in I Cor 16:22, probably as a liturgical acclamation. Cf. Didache 10:6 which is in the context of the Eucharist.

Jesus. ℵ^c 1611, 2059s 2329 al read "Jesus Christ."

21. This forms the last verse of the Epilogue, a further departure from Gaechter, who would place it after 17b.

the grace. . . . Cf. I Cor 16:23, II Cor 13:14, Gal 6:18, etc.

the Lord Jesus. 205 pc TR read "our Lord Jesus," and **046** 82, 1006, 2059s pl vg sy TR; R^m read "the Lord Jesus Christ."

everyone. In vg^{s,cl} TR this reads "all of you (plural)." A vg^w; R^m read "all the saints." ℵ **046** 82, 1611, 2329 pl vg sy sa TR; R add "Amen."

COMMENT

These verses appear to come from the hand of the redactor who added chs. 1–3. Vs. 16 completes the prophecies to the seven churches, which are addressed to their angels (2:1, 8, 12, 18, 3:1, 7, 14) by the one like a son of man (1:12–20), who now identifies himself as "Jesus." He further describes himself as "the root and the offspring of David" (see NOTE; cf. the star as "the seeker of the Law" in CDC 7:18–19 which is influenced by Num 24: 17). Luke also appears to point towards Jesus in the Benedictus when he speaks of the "dayspring" dawning (Luke 2:78).

In vs. 17a the Spirit and the church invite Jesus to come, and they bid the hearer of prophecies, who is probably a part of a worshiping community, to join their plea. The invitation to come arises naturally after the last prophecy to Laodicea which depicts the speaker as knocking at the door (3:20).

In vs. 20 Jesus, who bears testimony to the Father's message (cf. John 3:11) and has the Bride (John 3:29) replies that he is coming soon. To this the liturgical assembly answers "Amen, come Lord Jesus"; cf. I Cor 16:22.

Finally, our redactor closes the text (22:21), to which he has added an epistolary structure in chs. 1–3, with an ending suitable for a Christian letter; "May the grace of the Lord Jesus be with everyone."

BIBLIOGRAPHY

Barrett, C. K. "Things Sacrificed to Idols," NTS 11 (1964/65), 138–53.

Bauer, J. B. "Salvator nihil medium amat," *Verbum Domini* 34 (1956), 352–55.

Boismard, M. E. RB 56 (1949), 507–41.

Boyd, W. J. P. *Studia Evangelica* 2 (1964), 526–31.

Brown, S. JBL 85 (1966), 308–14.

———. "Deliverance from the Crucible: Some Further Reflexions on 1QH III, 1–18," NTS 14 (1967/68), 247–59.

Burrows, E. "The Pearl in the Apocalypse," *Journal of Theological Studies* 43 (1942), 177–79.

Calder, W. M. "Philadelphia and Montanism," *Bulletin of the John Rylands Library* 9 (1922), 309–54.

Charles, R. H. *Revelation*, I, II.

Dugmore, C. W. "Lord's Day and Easter," in *Neotestamentica et Patristica*, ed. O. Cullmann (Leiden: Brill, 1962), pp. 272–81.

Fabré, A. "L'Ange et le Chandelier de l'Eglise d'Ephese," RB 19 (1910), 161–78, 344–67.

———. "The Dawn Star," RB 15 (1908), 227–40.

Farrer, A. *The Revelation of St. John the Divine.*

Fenasse, J. M. "Le Jour du Seigneur, Apoc 1, 10," *Bible et Vie Chrétienne* 16 (1957), 29–43.

Feuillet, A. *Recherches des Sciences Religieuses* 49 (1961), 321–53.

Filson, F. V. "Temple, Synagogue and Church," *Biblical Archaeologist* 7 (1944), 77–88.

Foster, J. "The Harp at Ephesus," ET 74 (1962/63), 156.

Fransen, I. "Cahier de Bible: Jesus, le Temoin Fidele (Apocalypse)," *Bible et Vie Chretienne* 16 (1957), 66–79.

George, A. "Un Appel a la Fidelité," *Bible et Vie Chrétienne* 15 (1959), 80–86.

Hanfmann, G. M. A. "Excavations at Sardis," *Bulletin of the American Schools of Oriental Research* 154 (1958/59), 1–35.

Harrison, W. "The Time of Rapture . . . (in Revelation)," *Bibliotheca Sacra* 115 (1958), 201–11.

Helfgott, B. W. *The Doctrine of Election in Tannaitic Literature.* Columbia University Press, 1954.

Holm-Nielson, S. *Hodayot Psalms from Qumran.* Acta Theologica Danica II. Aarhus, 1960.

Hubert, M. "L'Architecture des Lettres aux Sept Églises (Apoc 2–3)," RB 67 (1960), 349–53.

Johnson, S. E. "Early Christianity and its Anatolian Background," in *Theologica Oecumenich,* Festschrift W. E. Kan (Tokyo, 1958), 34–44.

———. "Early Christianity in Asia Minor," JBL 77 (1958), 1–17.

———. "Preliminary Epigraphic Report on the Inscriptions Found at Sardis," *Bulletin of the American Schools of Oriental Research* (1958), 6–11.

Leconte, R. "Laodicée, Porte de la Syrie (Now Hierapolis)," BTS 81 (1966), 12–16.

———. "Les Sept Églises de L'Apocalypse," BTS 46 (1962), 6–14.

Ling, T. "Satan Enthroned," *Southeast Asia Journal of Theology* 3 (1961), 41–53.

McNamara, M. *The New Testament and the Palestinian Targum to the Pentateuch.*

Magie, D. *Roman Rule in Asia Minor (to the End of the Third Century after Christ),* I, II. Princeton University Press, 1950.

Maigret, J. "A l'Ange de l'Église de Laodicée Écris . . . ," BTS 81 (1966), 2–3.

———. "Saint Paul, le Discours aux Anciens d'Ephese," BTS 43 (1962).

Michael, J. H. "A Slight Misplacement in Revelation 1, 13–14," ET 42 (1930/31), 380–81.

Mitten, D. G. "A New Look at Ancient Sardis," *Biblical Archaeologist* 29 (1966), 36–68.

North, R. "Thronus Satanae Pergamenus," *Verbum Domini* 28 (1950), 65–76.

Oesterly, W. O. E., and Robinson, T. H. *History of Israel.* Oxford University Press, 1932.

Oke, C. C. "The Misplacement in Revelation 1, 13–14," ET 43 (1931/32), 237.

von der Osten Sacken, P. "Christologie, Taufe, Homologie—Ein Beitrag zu Apc. John 1, 5f.," ZNW 58 (1967), 255–66.

Parker, P. "The Meaning of 'Son of Man,'" JBL 60–61 (1941–42), 151–57.

Parvis, M. M. "Archaeology and St. Paul's Journeys in Greek Lands," *Biblical Archaeologist* 8, 3 (1945), 62–73.

Poirier, L. *Les Sept Eglises.*

Ramsay, W. M. *The Letters to the Seven Churches of Asia.*

Repp, A. "Ministry and Life in the Seven Churches," *Concordia Theological Monthly* 35 (1964), 133–47.

Rife, J. M. "The Literary Background of Revelation II–III," JBL 60 (1941), 179–82.

Robb, J. D. *"Ho Erchomenos* Apoc 1, 4," ET 73 (1961/62), 338–39.

Roth, C. "Messianic Symbols in Palestinian Archaeology," *Palestine Exploration Quarterly* 87 (1955), 151–64.

Rudwick, M. J. S. "The Laodicean Lukewarmness," ET 69 (1957/58), 176–78.

Sanders, J. N. "St. John on Patmos," NTS 9 (1962/63), 75–85.

Saunders, F. B. "The Seven Churches of the Apocalypse," Thesis, Southern Baptist Theological Seminary, July 1949.

Schürer, E. "Die Prophetin Isabel in Thyatira," in *Abhandl.* Arolsen: Weizacker, 1892.

Scott, R. B. Y. "Behold He Cometh with Clouds," NTS 5 (1958/59), 127–32.

Silberman, L. H. "Farewell to O AMHN," JBL 82 (1963), 213–15.

Skrinjar, A. "Antiquitas Christiana de Angelis Septem Ecclesiarum (Apoc. 1–3)," *Verbum Domini* 22 (1942), 18–24, 51–56.

———. "Praemia in Apoc 2 et 3 Victoriae Proposita," *Verbum Domini* 13 (1933), 182–86, 232–39, 277–80, 295–301, 333–40.

———. "Les Sept Esprits (Apoc. 1, 4; 3, 1; 4, 5; 5, 6)," *Biblica* 16 (1935), 1–24, 113–40.

Stendahl, K. *The Scrolls and the New Testament.*

Stott, W. NTS 12 (1965/66), 70–75.

Strack, H., and Billerbeck, P. *Kommentar zum Neuen Testament.*

Strand, K. A. NTS 13 (1966/67), 174–81.

Strugnell, John. *The Angelic Liturgy at Qumran, 4Q Serek 'Olat Hassabat.* Vetus Testamentum Supplement VII (Leiden: Brill, 1960), pp. 318–45.

Sutcliffe, E. F. "Hatred at Qumran," *Revue de Qumrân* 7 (1960), 345–56.

Swete, H. B. *The Apocalypse of St. John.*

Tarn, W. W., and Griffith, G. *Hellenistic Civilization.* 3d ed. London: E. Arnold, 1959.

Thomas, R. L. "The Glorified Christ on Patmos," *Bibliotheca Sacra* 122 (1965), 241–47.

————. "John's Apocalyptic Outline," *Bibliotheca Sacra* 123 (1966), 334–41.

Tonneau, R. "Ephesus au Temps de St. Paul," RB 38 (1929), 5–54.

Vos, G. *Pauline Eschatology*. Grand Rapids, Michigan: Eerdmans, 1973.

Wirgin, W. "The Menorah as Symbol of After-Life," *Israel Exploration Journal* 14 (1964), 102–4.

Wood, P. "Local Knowledge in the Letters of the Apocalypse," ET 73 (1961/62), 263–64.

INDEX OF AUTHORS

INDEX OF SUBJECTS

INDEX OF SCRIPTURAL AND OTHER REFERENCES

Rabbinic Materials

QUMRAN

KEY TO THE TEXT

Chapter	Verses	Section
1	1–3	XXIV
1	4–8	XXV
1	9–20	XXVI
2	1–7	XXVII
2	8–11	XXVIII
2	12–17	XXIX
2	18–29	XXX
3	1–6	XXXI
3	7–13	XXXII
3	14–22	XXXIII
4	1–11	I
5	1–14	II
6	1–17	III
7	1–17	IV
8	1–13	V
9	1–21	VI
10	1–11	VII
11	1–19	VIII
12	1–18	IX
13	1–18	X
14	1–20	XI
15	1–8	XII
16	1–21	XIII
17	1–18	XIV
18	1–24	XV
19	1–21	XVI
20	1–3	XVII
20	4–6	XX
20	7–10	XXI
20	11–15	XXII
21	1–7	XXIII
21	8–27	XVIII
22	1–2	XVIII
22	3–13	XXIII
22	14–15	XIX
22	16–17a	XXXIV
22	17b–19	XXIII
22	20–21	XXXIV